Pedagogical Innovations in Computer Science Education

Manuel B. Garcia
https://orcid.org/0000-0003-2615-422X
FEU Institute of Technology, Philippines

IGI Global Scientific Publishing
Publishing Tomorrow's Research Today

Vice President of Editorial Melissa Wagner
Director of Acquisitions Mikaela Felty
Director of Book Development Jocelynn Hessler
Production Manager Mike Brehm
Cover Design Jose Rosado

Published in the United States of America by
IGI Global Scientific Publishing
701 East Chocolate Avenue
Hershey, PA, 17033, USA
Tel: 717-533-8845 | Fax: 717-533-7115
Website: https://www.igi-global.com E-mail: cust@igi-global.com

Library of Congress Cataloging-in-Publication Data

LCCN: 2025042349 (CIP Data Pending)
ISBN13: 9798337365466
Isbn13Softcover: 9798337365473
EISBN13: 9798337365480
British Cataloguing in Publication Data
A Cataloguing in Publication record for this book is available from the British Library.

This book is for those who refuse to treat computer science education as neutral, mechanical, or one-size-fits-all. It is for the educators and innovators who understand that what we teach, and how we teach it, shapes not only technical skills but also the values, identities, and futures of learners.

To the teachers building inclusive classrooms where every student can belong, to the researchers strengthening pedagogy through evidence and insight, and to the academic and policy leaders who invest in meaningful innovation without compromising integrity, this work is for you. Your dedication ensures that the next generation does more than master tools; they learn to think critically, create confidently, and apply technology for the good of their communities and the world.

In a time when technology evolves rapidly, may this book serve as a source of inspiration and direction. May it remind us that the most powerful innovation in computer science education is not the technology itself, but the teaching that gives it purpose. And may every page encourage deeper creativity, stronger equity, and a shared commitment to educating learners who will build a better digital future.

Editorial Advisory Board

Table of Contents

Detailed Table of Contents

This chapter proposes a pedagogy first architecture for computing assessment that couples formative routines with minimalist analytics and equity by design. It argues for alignment to disciplinary big ideas, visible success criteria, short revision cycles, and multimodal evidence including code histories, test rationales, diagrams, and oral defenses. Peer and self-judgment are cultivated as disciplined practices, supported by universal design and culturally sustaining tasks. Analytics remain small, interpretable, and privacy preserving, answering concrete instructional questions within hours. Capacity is built through coaching, lesson study, micro credentials, and calibrated observation, with change managed through protected schedules and toolkits. Comparative cases from K to 8, secondary, undergraduate, and reskilling contexts show feasibility and impact. An improvement science agenda links logic models to measurable gains in competence, fairness, and credible external signaling.

Computer science education is undergoing a profound transformation at the intersection of inclusivity, ethics, and rapidly evolving technologies. This chapter explores how innovative pedagogical approaches can effectively address the diverse needs of contemporary learners while simultaneously addressing the ethical, social, and societal challenges posed by technological advancements. Interdisciplinary models such as STEAM (Science, Technology, Engineering, Arts, and Mathematics), along with open-source tools and collaborative platforms, enhance experiential learning, creativity, and critical thinking skills. Central to this vision is the integration of ethical reasoning and responsible computing practices, equipping students to make principled, informed decisions in an increasingly automated and AI-driven world. The chapter concludes with actionable recommendations for educators, administrators, and policymakers, emphasizing the importance of professional development for computer science education.

Despite growing demand for computing professionals, women remain significantly underrepresented in computer science education and technology careers. This chapter presents a narrative review of literature on gender-inclusive pedagogies, examining classroom practices, curriculum design, assessment strategies, mentorship, and institutional initiatives that support female learners' engagement, persistence, and sense of belonging. Drawing on international and regional studies, the review identifies effective approaches such as collaborative learning, identity-affirming and real-world curricula, formative assessment, and structured support systems, while highlighting persistent gaps including Western-centric perspectives, limited intersectional analyses, and misalignment between policy rhetoric and classroom practice. Grounded in technofeminist theory, the chapter discusses implications for educators, institutions, policymakers, and future research aimed at advancing equity in computing education.

Computer science (CS) inclusive teaching provides an opportunity for everyone to learn in a way that is fair and accessible. Through the traditional approaches, neurodiverse and disadvantaged learners are often cut off due to the strictness of the instruction and the surrounding limitations on support. UDL (Universal Design for Learning) and CRP (Culturally Responsive Pedagogy) are the two major strategies for inclusive teaching that facilitate flexible, engaging, and relevant learning. UDL allows you to choose different ways to learn and to express your understanding, and CRP connects the content with the students' cultural backgrounds. Gallaudet University and AccessCSforAll are some of the initiatives that have been proving that learners are more engaged when using assistive tools and through the application of adaptive methods. Supported by educating CS for all, U.N. SDG 4, inclusivity

beyond surveillance-based models and adopt approaches that emphasize uniquely human cognitive capacities. These pedagogical strategies advance the field by shifting the discourse from reactive prevention to proactive, pedagogically aligned assessment design. In doing so, the chapter affirms that the future of programming assessment is not about resisting AI but about designing systems that assess human thinking over code output.

GenAI systems such as ChatGPT are increasingly discussed in programming education, but the ways in which the research literature conceptualizes and frames their role remain unclear. This chapter applies text mining to publications indexed in a leading academic database to map scholarly discourse on ChatGPT in programming education. Term frequency analysis, phrase pattern extraction, and topic modeling reveal four dominant themes: pedagogical implementation, student-centered learning and engagement, AI infrastructure and human–AI collaboration, and assessment, prompting, and model evaluation. The literature prioritizes classroom practice and learner interaction, with comparatively limited attention to assessment design and institutional governance. Across studies, ChatGPT is positioned both as a learning aid that supports explanation, feedback, and efficiency and as a pedagogical risk linked to overreliance, unreliable outputs, and academic integrity concerns. These findings support responsible integration and highlight the need for stronger assessment and governance mechanisms.

diversity of learners, and provides flexible information on transferring this PBL model to other STEM fields involving creativity, technical skill and teamwork.

Advances in Learning Technology are promoting education in Computer Science from models of education utilizing predominantly lectures as forms of education, to innovations in pedagogy and into emerging models of student centered pedagogies. Distance and hybrid education in knowledge delivery and the concepts of the flipped learning environment are changing the learning output in Computer Science, providing more flexible, accessible, and participatory models of education which are synchronous with the evolving demands of the society for skills formation. Challenges to the pedagogical basis, strengths, and weaknesses of these forms of education and how they cope with problem solving and interdisciplinary learning are discussed in the light of the canons of equitable access to education. It examines how distance delivery is increasing access to greater diversity of learner, how hybrid models can help provide a degree of collaborative learning while also affording flexibility, and how flipped learning can enhance levels of active learning and levels of cognitive comprehension.

This chapter provides a bibliometric review of research on Generative Artificial Intelligence (GAI) in Computer Science (CS) education over the past decade. A

Foreword

Computer science education sits at a defining moment. Across schools and universities worldwide, computing is no longer a niche discipline reserved for a select few. It is a foundational literacy that shapes how learners understand the world, participate in society, and imagine their futures. At the same time, the rapid pace of technological change, particularly in artificial intelligence, data systems, and intelligent tools, has placed unprecedented pressure on educators to rethink not only what we teach, but why and how we teach it. This book arrives precisely when such reflection is most needed.

What distinguishes this book is its clear commitment to pedagogy first. Too often, conversations about computer science education are driven by tools, programming languages, or the latest technological trend. While these elements matter, they are secondary to the deeper questions that define meaningful learning. How dos students construct understanding in computational contexts? How do educators design learning environments that are inclusive, ethical, and responsive to diverse learners? How do we assess learning in ways that value process, creativity, and critical thinking, rather than simple correctness? The chapters in this book take these questions seriously and respond with scholarship that is both rigorous and grounded in practice.

The structure of the book reflects a thoughtful progression. The opening section on pedagogical foundations and instructional design sets the tone by emphasizing teaching strategies, interdisciplinary approaches, and sociotechnical perspectives. These chapters remind us that effective computer science education is not neutral or purely technical. It is shaped by epistemology, culture, and values. The contributors highlight constructive alignment, metacognition, and pedagogical innovation as essential components of learning design, offering concrete strategies that educators can adapt across contexts.

The focus on inclusivity, ethics, and social responsibility is especially timely. As computing systems increasingly influence decision making, access to resources, and representations of identity, educators have a responsibility to address issues of equity and justice directly. The chapters in this section move beyond aspirational language and provide frameworks for gender inclusive pedagogy, critical access, and ethical reasoning within computer science classrooms. Importantly, these contributions recognize that inclusion is not an add on. It is a core design principle that must be embedded into curriculum, assessment, and classroom culture.

The section devoted to artificial intelligence and intelligent systems captures one of the most pressing challenges facing educators today. Generative AI has disrupted long held assumptions about assessment, authorship, and academic integrity Rather than positioning artificial intelligence as a threat to education, research increasingly frames AI as a catalyst for rethinking learning goals and pedagogical practice. The chapters in this section reflect this orientation, demonstrating how thoughtful engagement with AI can support pedagogical clarity, transparency, and the development of student agency. Through analyses of assessment strategies, text mining of research discourse, and intelligent system based instructional frameworks, these chapters provide educators with ways to respond thoughtfully and proactively. The emphasis is not on prohibition, but on pedagogical clarity, transparency, and the development of student agency.

Equally compelling is the attention given to innovative learning environments and engagement strategies. Remote, hybrid, and flipped classrooms are no longer exceptions, but they are integral to contemporary education. The chapters in this final section address how computer science education can thrive across modalities through game-based learning, project-based approaches, and thoughtful use of media and learning design. The inclusion of a bibliometric review on generative AI further situates the book within the broader research landscape, offering readers a clear view of emerging trends and future directions.

What makes this collection particularly strong is the diversity of voices represented. The contributors bring perspectives from different countries, institutional contexts, and research traditions. This global orientation is not incidental. It reflects the reality that computer science education is a shared international endeavor, shaped by local needs and global challenges. Readers will find both common threads and productive tensions across chapters, encouraging reflection rather than simple adoption of any single approach. This breadth is the result of careful editorial leadership, and I would like to congratulate Manuel Garcia for bringing together this collection with such clarity and purpose. The volume includes contributions from 50 authors representing 19 different countries, underscoring the truly global nature of contemporary computer science education research.

As someone who has worked at the intersection of educational technology, instructional design, and policy, I appreciate how this book balances theory, research, and practice. The chapters do not shy away from complexity, yet they remain accessible to educators who are navigating real constraints of time, curriculum, and institutional expectations. This is a book that can inform research, support faculty development, and guide classroom practice.

Ultimately, this volume invites us to think more carefully about the kind of computer science education we want to create. One that prioritizes learning over novelty. One that recognizes students as whole people situated within social, cultural, and ethical systems. One that prepares learners not only to code, but to question, design, and lead responsibly in a digitally mediated world. It is my hope that readers will engage with these chapters not as a checklist of solutions, but as a conversation that continues within their own teaching, research, and communities.

This book makes a meaningful contribution to that conversation. It challenges us to be intentional, reflective, and courageous in how we approach computer science education. For that reason, it is both timely and necessary.

Helen Crompton
Old Dominion University, USA

Preface

Long before cloud platforms, version control pipelines, and ubiquitous wireless networks, many of us encountered computing in rooms that smelled faintly of warm circuitry and chalk dust, where time was rationed by lab schedules and programs were carried in on magnetic tape or carefully guarded diskettes. We learned to respect the machine by understanding its limits, memory measured in kilobytes, processors that demanded efficiency, and compilers that offered little mercy for imprecision. Instruction often began with hand-drawn flowcharts and pseudocode on overhead transparencies, followed by patient hours translating logic into FORTRAN, Pascal, or early C. Debugging meant tracing execution line by line, sometimes with nothing more than print statements and perseverance. These formative experiences instilled habits that remain central to the discipline today, algorithmic rigor, disciplined abstraction, and the intellectual humility required to learn from failure. Such practices anticipated what would later be formalized as computational thinking (Tang et al., 2020), a conceptual framework emphasizing decomposition, pattern recognition, abstraction, and algorithmic design as fundamental intellectual skills. Over decades, classrooms evolved alongside the technology itself, yet the enduring challenge has remained constant, how to cultivate deep understanding while inspiring curiosity, resilience, and creativity in successive generations of learners.

In the contemporary era, computer science has become a cornerstone of economic vitality and societal progress. It underwrites advances in artificial intelligence, cybersecurity, data science, and distributed systems while simultaneously reshaping medicine, transportation, governance, and communication. For students, computational competence now directly influences employability, professional mobility, and entrepreneurial opportunity, with digital skills consistently associated with improved labor market outcomes and employment prospects (Đorđević et al., 2025). Organizations increasingly demand graduates who can reason formally, design scalable architectures, interpret complex data, and collaborate across disciplines with technical fluency and ethical awareness (Garcia, 2024). Beyond workforce preparation, computer science education equips individuals with transferable capacities such as systems thinking, evidence-based decision making, and the ability to model and solve ill-structured problems, which are recognized as essential for navigating complexity in modern workplaces. As automation accelerates and digital infrastructures permeate every sector, the responsibility of educators extends far beyond teaching syntax or tools. It encompasses preparing learners to navigate ambiguity, adapt to rapid technological change, and contribute thoughtfully to a world in which computation functions both as a powerful instrument and a profound societal force.

CHALLENGES AND RESEARCH GAPS

Despite sustained advances in curriculum design, instructional technologies, and learning analytics, computer science education continues to face systemic and deeply rooted challenges that extend well beyond the limitations of traditional pedagogy. Contemporary classrooms are marked by extreme heterogeneity in learners' prior preparation, cognitive readiness, cultural context, and access to digital resources (Childs et al., 2024). At the same time, the disciplinary core of computer science is expanding rapidly, encompassing artificial intelligence, data-intensive computing, cybersecurity, and human-centered systems, often at a pace that exceeds institutional curriculum renewal cycles. Educators are thus confronted with a persistent tension between teaching enduring foundational principles and responding to emergent technological paradigms. This misalignment frequently results in fragmented curricula, surface-level coverage of complex topics, and assessment practices that privilege syntactic correctness over conceptual mastery, transfer, and creative problem solving (Weißenrieder et al., 2025).

These challenges are further amplified in the modern era by the widespread availability of generative artificial intelligence systems. While AI offers unprecedented opportunities for personalized learning, automated feedback, and instructional augmentation, it simultaneously introduces profound pedagogical disruptions (Gaitantzi & Kazanidis, 2025; Garcia, 2025). Students now have immediate access to tools capable of generating code, explanations, and complete solutions, raising fundamental questions about authorship, academic integrity, and the nature of learning itself. More critically, reliance on AI-generated outputs risks weakening essential cognitive processes such as algorithmic reasoning, abstraction, and debugging unless instructional designs explicitly foreground these competencies. The educational objective is no longer merely to teach students how to program, but to cultivate their capacity to critically evaluate machine-generated artifacts, reason about system behavior, and exercise informed judgment in human–AI collaboration. Yet empirical guidance on how best to integrate AI into computing classrooms in ways that preserve deep learning remains limited.

From a research perspective, significant gaps persist between educational theory and classroom practice. Much of the existing literature concentrates on isolated interventions or short-term learning gains, offering insufficient insight into longitudinal development, institutional scalability, and cross-contextual transfer. Systematic reviews of active and learner-centered methodologies in computing education confirm both their potential and the difficulty of sustaining them across varied educational contexts (Córdova-Esparza et al., 2024). There is a notable scarcity of studies examining how integrated pedagogical ecosystems, combining curriculum, assessment, faculty development, and learning technologies, influence student trajectories over time. Furthermore, while technical proficiency is frequently emphasized, comparatively less attention is devoted to affective and developmental dimensions, including learner identity, self-efficacy, ethical reasoning, and professional formation. These factors play a decisive role in retention and success, particularly among historically underrepresented populations, yet remain under-theorized and under-measured in computing education research.

Collectively, these unresolved issues point to a broader imperative for evidence-informed innovation. Advancing computer science education now requires more than incremental instructional refinement. It demands systematic inquiry into how pedagogy interacts with rapidly evolving technologies, institutional structures, and societal expectations. It calls for interdisciplinary approaches that bridge computing, learning sciences, and social contexts, alongside rigorous evaluation frameworks that assess sustained impact rather than novelty effects. Articulating these challenges and research gaps establishes a critical foundation for examining contemporary pedagogical responses, preparing the ground for a focused exploration of emerging approaches that seek to reimagine teaching and learning in an era increasingly shaped by artificial intelligence (Bozkurt et al., 2024; Xiao et al., 2025).

ABOUT THIS BOOK

The *Pedagogical Innovations in Computer Science Education* book emerges in response to enduring pedagogical challenges and widening research gaps across computing education. It represents a deliberate shift away from incremental reform and toward a more principled reexamination of how computer science is taught, learned, and institutionalized in an era defined by rapid technological acceleration. While much contemporary discourse emphasizes tools, platforms, and automation, this volume centers pedagogy itself as the primary site of transformation. It advances the position that meaningful innovation does not originate in technology alone, but in the careful alignment of learning theory, instructional design, and educational purpose. Through contributions from an international community of scholars and practitioners, the book foregrounds reflective practice, empirical inquiry, and contextual sensitivity as foundations for sustainable educational change.

Rather than promoting a singular vision of progress, this work recognizes that effective computer science education must respond to diverse learners, institutional realities, and societal expectations. It advocates for pedagogical approaches grounded in intentionality, inclusivity, and intellectual rigor, while remaining attentive to the implications of emerging technologies, including artificial intelligence, for learning, assessment, and professional formation. The volume does not advance nostalgia for earlier instructional models, nor does it subscribe to uncritical techno-optimism. Instead, it argues for a discerning, evidence-informed orientation to innovation, one that prioritizes conceptual understanding, human agency, and ethical responsibility. By situating pedagogy at the center of computing education's future, this book invites educators and researchers alike to engage in sustained dialogue about what it means to prepare learners not merely to operate digital systems, but to think critically, act responsibly, and contribute meaningfully within an increasingly computational world. Written by over 50 authors representing more than 19 countries, this volume reflects a truly global perspective on computer science education. The book unfolds across 15 chapters distributed into four thematic sections:

1. *Pedagogical Foundations and Instructional Design*
2. *Inclusivity, Ethics, and Social Responsibility in CS Education*
3. *Teaching, Learning, and Assessment in the Age of Artificial Intelligence*
4. *Emerging Learning Environments and Educational Media*

Section 1: Pedagogical Foundations and Instructional Design

This section establishes the conceptual and instructional foundations that underpin effective computer science education. It foregrounds pedagogical design as a deliberate and evidence-informed practice, emphasizing curriculum coherence, problem-centered learning, interdisciplinary integration, and metacognitive development. The chapters in this section examine how instructional frameworks can be aligned with learning objectives to foster deeper conceptual understanding, transferable problem-solving skills, and inclusive participation. Together, they articulate core principles for structuring computing curricula in ways that support both intellectual rigor and learner engagement, providing a foundation upon which subsequent discussions of equity, ethics, and emerging technologies are built.

Chapter 1: Pedagogical Innovations for the Modern Computer Science Classroom: 50 Teaching Tips and Practical Strategies for Computing Education

Chapter 2: Interdisciplinary Approaches in Computer Science Teaching: Foundations, Integration, and Transformation of Education

Chapter 3: Recentering Computer Science Education on Problem-Solving: Pedagogical Foundations and Curriculum Design

Chapter 4: Formative Epistemics and Inclusive Design Approach Using Constructive Alignment and Metacognition: Sociotechnical Pedagogy for Computer Education

Section 2: Inclusivity, Ethics, and Social Responsibility in CS Education

This section addresses the human dimensions of computing education, focusing on access, equity, ethical reasoning, and social accountability. It situates computer science within broader societal contexts, highlighting the responsibility of educators to cultivate inclusive learning environments and to prepare students for the ethical complexities of professional practice. The contributions in this section explore pedagogical approaches that promote diversity, gender inclusion, and computational access, while also embedding responsible computing as a core educational objective. Collectively, these chapters emphasize that technical competence must be accompanied by ethical awareness and social consciousness.

Chapter 5: Transforming Computer Science Education: Inclusivity, Ethics, and Emerging Technologies

Chapter 6: Gender-Inclusive Pedagogies in Computer Science Education: Insights, Implications, and Future Directions

Chapter 7: Inclusive Pedagogy in Computer Science Education: A Critical Pedagogical Framework for Computational Access

Chapter 8: Ethics and Responsible Computing in the Classroom: Embedding Ethical Reasoning in Computer Science Education

Section 3: Teaching, Learning, and Assessment in the Age of Artificial Intelligence

This section examines the growing influence of artificial intelligence and intelligent systems on teaching, learning, and assessment in computer science. It considers both the pedagogical opportunities and the methodological challenges introduced by generative technologies and automated instructional tools. The chapters engage with questions of assessment validity, learner development, and instructional design in AI-mediated environments, offering scholarly perspectives on how intelligent systems are reshaping programming education. This section positions AI not merely as a technical artifact, but as a pedagogical force that demands careful integration and critical reflection.

Chapter 9: Assessment of Coding Skills and Programming Knowledge in the Age of Generative AI: Best Practices and Effective Strategies for Computer Science Education

Chapter 10: Pedagogical Promise and Peril of AI: A Text Mining Analysis of ChatGPT Research Discussions in Programming Education

Chapter 11: Pedagogical Framework for Developing Students' Python Programming Competencies Using Intelligent Systems

Section 4: Emerging Learning Environments and Educational Media

The final section explores how evolving learning environments and educational media are transforming student engagement in computer science. It addresses pedagogical innovation across project-based learning, game development, and flexible instructional modalities. The chapters in this section highlight how learning spaces, digital media, and instructional formats can be designed to support active participation, creativity, and future-ready competencies. The section concludes by reflecting on broader trends and research directions, situating these innovations within the continuing evolution of computer science education.

Chapter 12: Game Development as a Pedagogical Innovation for Project-Based Learning in Computer Graphics and Gaming

Chapter 13: Reimagining Computer Science Education in Remote, Hybrid, and Flipped Classrooms for Future-Ready Learners

Chapter 14: A Bibliometric Review of Pedagogical Innovations and Future Directions for Generative Artificial Intelligence in Computer Science Education

REIMAGINING THE FUTURE OF COMPUTING EDUCATION

As computer science education continues to evolve within increasingly automated and data-driven societies, pedagogy itself must assume a more deliberate and reflective role. The accelerating integration of artificial intelligence, intelligent systems, and digital infrastructures into educational environments has fundamentally altered what it means to teach and learn computing. Yet technological advancement alone does not constitute educational progress. What matters, ultimately, is how these tools are situated within coherent instructional designs, inclusive learning cultures, and ethically grounded educational frameworks. Across diverse institutional contexts and global perspectives, a shared imperative emerges to move beyond instrumental views of computing toward pedagogies that cultivate conceptual depth, critical inquiry, and human agency (Everson et al., 2025; Vartiainen & Tedre, 2025).

This moment calls for educators to reassert their professional judgment in shaping learning experiences that emphasize understanding over automation, reflection over efficiency, and responsibility over convenience. Preparing students for contemporary computing careers is no longer sufficient if such preparation neglects the development of systems thinking, ethical reasoning, and adaptive expertise. As generative technologies increasingly mediate problem solving, creativity, and assessment, the educator's role expands from instructor to curator of learning, steward of intellectual rigor, and guardian of academic integrity (Garcia et al., 2025). Teaching computer science in this context requires not only technical fluency, but also a sustained commitment to equity, transparency, and learner empowerment. It demands pedagogical practices that invite students to interrogate algorithms, question assumptions, and recognize their own agency within sociotechnical systems.

At its core, this volume advances the conviction that the future of computer science education will be shaped less by the sophistication of machines than by the intentionality of pedagogical choices. Innovation must be guided by evidence, informed by interdisciplinary scholarship, and grounded in respect for learners as whole persons. By foregrounding reflective practice, inclusive design, and critical engagement with emerging technologies, this work contributes to a broader reimagining of computing education as both a technical and moral enterprise. It is our hope that the perspectives assembled here will inspire sustained scholarly dialogue and purposeful action, encouraging educators and researchers alike to approach innovation not as an end in itself, but as a means toward cultivating thoughtful practitioners, responsible citizens, and lifelong learners in an increasingly computational world.

Manuel B. Garcia
FEU Institute of Technology, Philippines

REFERENCES

Bozkurt, A., Xiao, J., Farrow, R., Bai, J. Y. H., Nerantzi, C., Moore, S., & Asino, T. I. (2024). The Manifesto for Teaching and Learning in a Time of Generative AI: A Critical Collective Stance to Better Navigate the Future. *Open Praxis*, *16*(4), 487–513. DOI: 10.55982/openpraxis.16.4.777

Childs, J., Zarch, R., Dunton, S., Madkins, T. c., Trautmann, K., Taylor, Z. W., & Ottenbreit-Leftwich, A. (2024). Advancing Equity and Access: Addressing the Side Effects of Broadening Participation in Computer Science K–12 Education. *Review of Research in Education*, *48*(1), 121–153. DOI: 10.3102/0091732x241286475

Córdova-Esparza, D.-M., Romero-González, J.-A., Córdova-Esparza, K.-E., Terven, J., & López-Martínez, R.-E. (2024). Active Learning Strategies in Computer Science Education: A Systematic Review. *Multimodal Technologies and Interaction*, *8*(6), 1–20. DOI: 10.3390/mti8060050

Đorđević, B., Milanović Zbiljić, S., & Radosavljević, M. (2025). Impact of the Digital Skills on Employability: Cross-Sectional Analysis. *Economies*, *13*(7), 1–16. DOI: 10.3390/economies13070196

Everson, J., Landesman, R., Kivuva, F. M., & Ko, A. J. (2025). Dreaming of Difference: Imagining the Future of CS Education Pedagogy with Secondary Students. *Proceedings of the 2025 ACM Conference on International Computing Education Research* V.1. https://doi.org/DOI: 10.1145/3702652.3744203

Gaitantzi, A., & Kazanidis, I. (2025). The Role of Artificial Intelligence in Computer Science Education: A Systematic Review with a Focus on Database Instruction. *Applied Sciences (Basel, Switzerland)*, *15*(7), 3960. DOI: 10.3390/app15073960

Garcia, M. B. (2024). Profiling the Skill Mastery of Introductory Programming Students: A Cognitive Diagnostic Modeling Approach. *Education and Information Technologies*, *30*(5), 6455–6481. DOI: 10.1007/s10639-024-13039-6

Garcia, M. B. (2025). Teaching and Learning Computer Programming Using ChatGPT: A Rapid Review of Literature Amid the Rise of Generative AI Technologies. *Education and Information Technologies*, *30*, 16721–16745. DOI: 10.1007/s10639-025-13452-5

Garcia, M. B., Rosak-Szyrocka, J., & Bozkurt, A. (2025). *Pitfalls of AI Integration in Education: Skill Obsolescence, Misuse, and Bias*. IGI Global., DOI: 10.4018/979-8-3373-0122-8

Tang, X., Yin, Y., Lin, Q., Hadad, R., & Zhai, X. (2020). Assessing Computational Thinking: A Systematic Review of Empirical Studies. *Computers & Education*, *148*, 1–22. DOI: 10.1016/j.compedu.2019.103798

Vartiainen, H., & Tedre, M. (2025). The CEDE Model: A Learning-Sciences Based Approach for Critical and Transformative K–12 AI Education. *Proceedings of the 25th Koli Calling International Conference on Computing Education Research*. https://doi.org/DOI: 10.1145/3769994.3770026

Weißenrieder, F., Lenzer, S., & Mühling, A. (2025). Assessing Computer Science Pedagogical Content Knowledge: A Systematic Literature Review. *Computer Science Education*, •••, 1–42. DOI: 10.1080/08993408.2025.2586872

Xiao, J., Bozkurt, A., Nichols, M., Pazurek, A., Stracke, C. M., Bai, J. Y. H., & Themeli, C. (2025). Venturing into the Unknown: Critical Insights into Grey Areas and Pioneering Future Directions in Educational Generative AI Research. *TechTrends*, *69*, 582–597. DOI: 10.1007/s11528-025-01060-6

Acknowledgment

The completion of *Pedagogical Innovations in Computer Science Education* represents a collective effort shaped by the contributions, insights, and encouragement of many individuals. This volume emerged from a shared commitment to advancing teaching and learning in computer science, and I am sincerely grateful to everyone who played a role in bringing this work to fruition.

I extend my heartfelt appreciation to the Editorial Advisory Board members and peer reviewers, whose careful evaluations and constructive feedback strengthened each chapter and elevated the scholarly rigor of this book. Their dedication to academic quality and relevance has been instrumental in refining the ideas presented here.

My deepest thanks go to the chapter authors, whose innovative practices, research perspectives, and thoughtful analyses form the foundation of this volume. Their willingness to share experiences and explore emerging pedagogical approaches has enriched this collection and provides valuable guidance for educators striving to create meaningful learning environments in computer science education.

I also extend my sincere appreciation to Helen Crompton of Old Dominion University (USA) and Yekaterina Kovaleva of LUT University (Finland) for their insightful foreword and afterword, respectively. Their thoughtful reflections provide valuable context for this volume, bridging theory and practice while offering both grounding perspectives and forward-looking insights that enrich the overall contribution of this book.

I am also grateful to the publisher, IGI Global, for their professionalism and continued support throughout the development of this book. Their guidance and collaboration made the publication process both smooth and rewarding, and I appreciate the opportunity to work together in disseminating impactful educational research.

On a personal note, I express my profound gratitude to my family and loved ones for their patience, understanding, and constant encouragement. Their support sustained me through the demanding stages of writing, editing, and revision, and their belief in this work made all the difference.

Finally, I thank all colleagues, students, and members of the broader academic community who inspired this project through dialogue, collaboration, and shared passion for teaching and learning. It is my hope that this book contributes meaningfully to ongoing conversations about pedagogical innovation and supports educators in preparing learners for an ever-evolving technological future.

Manuel B. Garcia
FEU Institute of Technology, Philippines

Section 1
Pedagogical Foundations and Instructional Design in Computer Science

Chapter 1
Pedagogical Innovations for the Modern Computer Science Classroom:
50 Teaching Tips and Practical Strategies for Computing Education

Manuel B. Garcia
https://orcid.org/0000-0003-2615-422X
FEU Institute of Technology, Philippines

Ari Happonen
https://orcid.org/0000-0003-0744-1776
LUT University, Finland & Taylor's University, Malaysia

Friday Joseph Agbo
https://orcid.org/0000-0002-9171-7175
Willamette University, USA

Michael Agyemang Adarkwah
Friedrich Schiller University, Germany

Ioannis Kazanidis
Democritus University of Thrace, Greece

Thomas K. F. Chiu
The Chinese University of Hong Kong, Hong Kong

Robertas Damaševičius
https://orcid.org/0000-0001-9990-1084
Vytautas Magnus University, Lithuania

Serhiy O. Semerikov
https://orcid.org/0000-0003-0789-0272
Kryvyi Rih State Pedagogical University, Ukraine

ABSTRACT

Computer science education is undergoing a global transformation as digital technologies continue to redefine how knowledge is created, shared, and applied. Despite this evolution, many teaching practices in computing remain rooted in

DOI: 10.4018/979-8-3373-6546-6.ch001

instructor-centered models that prioritize syntax and correctness over creativity, collaboration, and reflection. This chapter addresses this gap by presenting pedagogical innovations for the modern computer science classroom. Drawing on contemporary research in computing education and learning theories, it identifies ten interrelated themes and fifty practical strategies for effective instruction. Each theme is grounded in theory, contextualized through classroom examples, and supported by current literature. Collectively, these strategies advocate a shift from transmission-based teaching toward inquiry-driven learning that cultivates computational thinkers, creative problem solvers, and socially responsible innovators. The chapter concludes by discussing the implications of these pedagogical approaches for the future of computer science education.

INTRODUCTION

Computer science is the study of how information can be represented, processed, and transformed using algorithms and computational systems. Its principles underpin the development of intelligent systems that augment human decision-making and expand the frontiers of knowledge (Bozkurt et al., 2024; Gantalao et al., 2025). It holds profound significance in modern society because it shapes the infrastructure of communication, commerce, governance, and innovation (Gill et al., 2024; Tegegn, 2024). As societies become increasingly dependent on data and automation, mastery of computational principles ensures that learners remain competent, ethical, and reflective users of technology. Within educational contexts, computer science functions as both a discipline and a catalyst for interdisciplinary integration that connects mathematical reasoning, scientific inquiry, and humanistic understanding through computational logic (Tariq et al., 2025; Yeni et al., 2024). The study of algorithms and programming enhances precision of thought, persistence in experimentation, and innovation through design. With computer science education developing digital literacy comparable in importance to reading, writing, and numeracy, there is a need to strengthen pedagogies that promote conceptual understanding, creativity, and inclusivity (Liu et al., 2024; Srinivasan et al., 2025).

Computer science education has evolved through a dynamic interplay of pedagogical paradigms that reflect shifting views on how learners acquire computational knowledge and problem-solving skills. Early instruction emphasized procedural fluency and syntax mastery, often framed through behaviorist or transmission-based models. Over time, research in cognitive and constructivist learning prompted a transition toward inquiry-driven and project-based pedagogies that highlight the learner's role in constructing understanding through authentic tasks and collaboration (Garcia, 2023; Tubino et al., 2020). Contemporary frameworks increasingly draw upon sociocultural and humanistic theories, positioning computer science not only as a technical discipline but also as a context for developing creativity, ethical awareness, and social responsibility (Zhou & Zhang, 2024). This pedagogical diversification has produced approaches such as computational thinking integration, pair programming, problem-based learning, and design-based projects that cultivate both technical proficiency and reflective practice. The emergence of artificial intelligence (AI) and immersive technologies further expands these frameworks by introducing adaptive, personalized, and multimodal learning environments (Córdova-Esparza et al., 2024; Holly et al., 2025). Collectively, these evolving pedagogies demonstrate that effective computer science instruction is rooted not in a single method, but in a balanced ecosystem of strategies that adapt to learners' cognitive, social, and ethical dimensions.

MAIN FOCUS OF THE CHAPTER

The primary purpose of this chapter is to bridge the gap between educational theory and classroom practice in computer science instruction. Although substantial evidence supports active, reflective, and inclusive pedagogies (Córdova-Esparza et al., 2024; Pournaghshband & Medel, 2020; Sunday et al., 2025), many instructors still seek practical ways to operationalize these approaches across diverse teaching contexts and learner populations. To address this need, the chapter translates theory into research-informed teaching strategies that can be flexibly adapted for multiple modalities (face-to-face, hybrid, and fully online) and educational levels (K–12, undergraduate, and graduate). This work is significant for its synthesis of established and emerging approaches into a coherent pedagogical framework that supports both instructional effectiveness and inclusivity. It invites educators to reconsider how they design, deliver, and assess computing instruction by reframing teaching as a process of cultivating computational thinkers and socially responsible innovators prepared to navigate the intellectual and ethical complexities of the modern digital era. The ten themes summarized in Table 1 provide a conceptual roadmap for the remainder of the chapter, outlining the major pedagogical domains that underpin the fifty strategies discussed in subsequent sections.

Table 1. Overview of Pedagogical Themes for the Modern Computer Science Classroom

Theme	Pedagogical Focus & Intended Outcome	Reflection Prompt	Theoretical Foundation
Active Learning and Student Engagement	Engagement through participation leads to immediate application and sustained attention.	Where in your current teaching could you pause to let students predict, discuss, or decide before you explain or demonstrate?	**Constructivism**: Knowledge is actively constructed through interaction and experience.
Metacognition and Reflective Practice	Reflection on thinking to promote self-regulation and transfer of learning.	How do you encourage students to reflect not only on what they learned but how they approached learning it?	**Metacognitive Theory**: Awareness and regulation of one's own cognitive processes enhance learning.
Problem-Based and Project-Based Learning	Real-world, authentic learning experiences that foster problem-solving, creativity, and learner ownership.	Do your assignments resemble real-world challenges that require inquiry, creativity, and iteration?	**Experiential Learning Theory**: Learning occurs through concrete experience, reflection, and active experimentation.
Collaborative and Peer Learning	Social construction of knowledge that develops communication and teamwork skills.	How can you structure peer interaction so that every student contributes and learns from others' reasoning?	**Social Constructivism**: Knowledge develops through social interaction and shared problem-solving.
Inclusive and Equitable Teaching Practices	Promoting belonging and access to ensure equity, representation, and participation for all learners.	Do all students in your classroom see themselves represented and supported in the examples, materials, and expectations you provide?	**Universal Design for Learning**: Flexible learning design accommodates variability and promotes equitable access.
Assessment and Feedback for Learning	Using feedback as a tool for learning to foster growth mindset and effective feedback use.	When assessment becomes a conversation instead of a conclusion, how can students view feedback as a roadmap for growth rather than a verdict?	**Formative Assessment Theory**: Feedback should inform and guide learning, not merely evaluate it.
Integrating AI and Intelligent Tools in the Classroom	Encouraging responsible and ethical use of AI tools to build AI literacy and critical reflection.	How can AI tools become learning partners that support exploration and reflection without replacing original thinking?	**Connectivism**: Learning occurs through networks of human and technological connections.
Ethics, Responsibility, and Societal Impact	Cultivating accountability and moral reasoning through reflection on the social impact of computing.	When teaching technical concepts, how do you invite students to consider who benefits, who might be harmed, and what values are embedded in their designs?	**Ethical Reasoning Framework**: Moral understanding develops through awareness, judgment, and reflective action.

continued on following page

Table 1. Continued

Theme	Pedagogical Focus & Intended Outcome	Reflection Prompt	Theoretical Foundation
Blended, Remote, and Hybrid Learning Innovations	Designing flexible and accessible learning environments that sustain engagement across modalities.	How can you design learning activities that connect students meaningfully across physical and digital spaces?	**Community of Inquiry Framework**: Effective online learning emerges through cognitive, social, and teaching presence.
Creativity, Computational Thinking, and Interdisciplinary Learning	Fostering imagination and interdisciplinary fluency through creative applications of computing.	In what ways can your students use programming to express, design, or create—not only to solve problems?	**Constructionism**: Learners build knowledge most effectively when actively creating meaningful artifacts.

METHODOLOGY

The themes of the chapter emerged from a collaborative, design-based synthesis that integrated the expertise of computer science educators, learning scientists, and educational researchers. Through an iterative process of literature review, reflective practice, and research alignment, the authors developed and refined pedagogical strategies addressing engagement, inclusion, and instructional design in computing education. A comprehensive review of scholarship in both computing education and the learning sciences informed the identification of these themes. Foundational frameworks (see Table 1) provided the conceptual grounding, while recent empirical findings contributed additional evidence-based validation. Consistent with principles of practitioner inquiry and collaborative autoethnography (Chang et al., 2013; Cochran-Smith & Lytle, 2009), each strategy was iteratively refined through reflective practitioner dialogue drawing on the authors' collective teaching experience across secondary, undergraduate, and graduate levels. In this process, the authors functioned as practitioner-informants who contributed reflective accounts and experiential insights that served as a form of qualitative data. The framework was further validated through comparison with empirical studies and peer feedback to ensure clarity, adaptability, and alignment with current research (e.g., Huang & Looi, 2021). Insights were drawn from authentic instructional environments representing diverse institutional settings, educational levels, and delivery modalities. This methodological synthesis reflects a reflective, evidence-informed, and practitioner-driven approach that integrates theory, research, and practice to advance a holistic framework for improving engagement, equity, and learning outcomes in the modern computer science classroom.

PEDAGOGICAL THEMES

Theme 1: Active Learning and Student Engagement

"Students learn programming by programming and not by watching someone else do it."

Active learning transforms the computer science classroom from a passive environment into one of active participation and exploration. In traditional lectures, students often copy syntax without internalizing underlying logic. Research in computing education (Córdova-Esparza et al., 2024) consistently shows that interactive learning enhances both engagement and retention. As computer science involves procedural and conceptual knowledge, students learn best when they do something with code (e.g., predict outputs, debug collaboratively, or reason through algorithmic trade-offs). The following teaching practices illustrate simple but powerful approaches to cultivating active engagement in both face-to-face and hybrid courses.

Teaching Tip 1: Live-Coding with Prediction Pauses

Challenge: Students often copy syntax during demonstrations without understanding the underlying logic or anticipating what the program will do next.

Try This: During live-coding sessions, pause before executing each code block and ask, "*What output do you expect?*" Collect responses using *Slido*, *PollEverywhere*, *Mentimeter*, or simple hand-raises. Run the code, reveal the actual output, and discuss any discrepancies. Ask students to explain why their predictions differed, highlighting logical reasoning and debugging thought processes. This activity can work in any coding or data-processing context (e.g., predicting algorithm output, data visualization results, or SQL query behavior).

Why It Works: Prediction activates prior knowledge and promotes mental simulation of code execution, transforming students from passive observers into engaged participants. Research in computing education shows that incorporating prediction tasks lead to more positive emotional experiences, increased motivation, and better learning outcomes (Tucker et al., 2024).

Teaching Tip 2: Pair and Mob Programming for Collaboration

Challenge: Students often default to solitary trial-and-error problem-solving, which limits opportunities to articulate reasoning, learn from peers, and develop collaborative skills.

Try This: Design lab activities using structured collaboration formats. In pair programming, assign one student as the "driver" (typing and implementing code) and another as the "navigator" (reviewing and suggesting improvements). Rotate roles every 10–15 minutes. For mob programming, assign a single "driver" while the rest of the group collaboratively discusses each next step. Use tools such as *VS Code Live Share* or *Replit Teams* for virtual settings.

Why It Works: Collaborative programming practices develop communication, critical thinking, and metacognitive awareness. Explaining code to others strengthens understanding, while structured role-switching promotes equity and accountability. Empirical studies show that group programming increases learning outcomes and mirrors industry practices (Garcia, 2023).

Teaching Tip 3: Code Races and Micro-Challenges

Challenge: Traditional assessments can feel overly punitive, which consequently reduces motivation and engagement throughout formative learning.

Try This: Transform short coding exercises into five-minute "code races." Provide a focused task (e.g., "*Write a loop that prints all even numbers between 1 and 20*"). Students work individually or in pairs to produce working solutions quickly. Emphasize creativity and clarity, not just speed. Afterward, showcase different solutions, discuss trade-offs, and highlight unique approaches.

Why It Works: Low-stakes, game-like challenges create intrinsic motivation and sustained attention. Immediate feedback reinforces fluency and recall, while competitive elements maintain engagement. Gamified learning environments have been shown to improve persistence, engagement, and enjoyment in computing education (Acut, 2026; Garcia & Revano Jr, 2021).

Teaching Tip 4: The "Whiteboard-First" Exercise

Challenge: Jumping directly into a code editor often leads students to focus narrowly on syntax rather than problem-solving logic or algorithmic reasoning.

Try This: Before coding, give students 5–10 minutes to sketch the logic of their approach using flowcharts, pseudocode, or data-structure diagrams on paper, a classroom whiteboard, or online collaborative tools like *Miro* or *Jamboard*. Encourage groups to visualize control flow, data transformations, or memory use before translating ideas into code. This activity can be used for problems in algorithms, database schema design, or system architecture planning.

Why It Works: Externalizing logic encourages deliberate planning and reinforces algorithmic thinking before implementation. By separating design reasoning from code syntax, students reduce cognitive load and strengthen their understanding of program structure. Research indicates that focusing on conceptual structuring before coding enhances comprehension and minimizes syntax-related barriers for novice programmers (Öqvist & Nouri, 2018).

Teaching Tip 5: Real-Time Concept Checks

Challenge: Instructors often move through material assuming comprehension, but many students remain unsure or silently confused.

Try This: Embed frequent, low-stakes concept checks during lectures or laboratory activities. After explaining a new concept (e.g., recursion or database normalization), pose a quick poll or question such as, "*What happens if the base case is never reached?*" or "*Which SQL constraint prevents duplicate entries?*" Use clickers, LMS quizzes, or chat polls to collect responses. Discuss results immediately and clarify reasoning before moving on.

Why It Works: Frequent formative assessment provides immediate insight into student understanding and fosters active engagement with content. Students reflect on their own comprehension while instructors adapt pacing in real time. Active recall and immediate feedback improve retention and conceptual transfer (Thangaraj et al., 2023).

Theme 2: Metacognition and Reflective Practice

"When students learn to debug their thinking, they learn to debug their code."

Metacognition, or the awareness and regulation of one's own thinking, is a hallmark of expert computer scientists who monitor progress, evaluate strategies, and adjust approaches in real time. Yet many novices focus solely on producing working code rather than understanding their reasoning process. Studies in computing education demonstrate that explicit reflection activities (e.g., debugging journals or think-aloud protocols) strengthen problem-solving persistence and transfer of learning (Zarestky et al., 2022). Encouraging students to articulate how they reason, plan, and revise develops self-regulation skills essential for independent learning. The following practices show how reflection can be woven naturally into the rhythm of computer science instruction without disrupting momentum.

Teaching Tip 6: The Debugging Journal

Challenge: Many students fix code errors through trial and error but fail to internalize what caused the issue or how they resolved it, resulting in repeated mistakes.

Try This: Ask students to maintain a brief "debugging journal" throughout the semester. After each lab, assignment, or project, they record: (a) the problem encountered, (b) the debugging process or strategy used, and (c) what they learned from the experience. Entries can be informal and concise like simple text logs submitted weekly or kept privately. In large courses, students can select one representative entry per module for instructor feedback or peer discussion.

Why It Works: Writing about debugging consolidates both procedural and conceptual understanding, transforming troubleshooting into a reflective act. Over time, students recognize recurring error patterns and develop more systematic problem-solving habits. Reflective journaling has been shown to enhance metacognitive awareness, foster self-regulated learning, and improve critical thinking in computational science education (Zarestky et al., 2022).

Teaching Tip 7: Predict–Test–Reflect Coding Cycle

Challenge: Students often rely on the compiler or console for feedback instead of mentally reasoning through code execution, which limits their ability to anticipate or explain behavior.

Try This: Introduce a structured "Predict–Test–Reflect" routine. Before running code, students briefly predict the expected output or behavior. They then execute the code and observe the result, followed by a short reflection: "*What surprised me? What caused the difference between my prediction and the outcome?*" This can be done verbally in pairs, through brief written prompts, or integrated into *Jupyter* notebooks with automated reflection cells.

Why It Works: The cycle reinforces causal reasoning and mental simulation, which are key components of expert programming cognition. By explicitly comparing expected and actual outcomes, students refine their internal models of program behavior and improve debugging accuracy. Research on metacognitive strategies confirms that structured reflection activities (e.g., predicting, monitoring, and evaluating code outcomes) deepen conceptual understanding and enhance problem-solving effectiveness in programming (Çakiroğlu & Er, 2023).

Teaching Tip 8: Think-Aloud Protocols for Self-Explanation

Challenge: Students often produce correct code but cannot articulate why it works or how they reached the solution, which hinders conceptual generalization.

Try This: Incorporate periodic "think-aloud" activities in which students explain their reasoning while solving a problem. This activity can be recorded as short (1–2 minute) audio or video clips or done live in pairs or small groups. The focus is on articulating thought processes, not grading performance. Prompts such as "*Explain what your loop does step by step*" or "*Why did you choose this data structure over other possible alternatives?*" can guide responses.

Why It Works: Verbalizing reasoning activates self-monitoring and exposes gaps in understanding. Think-alouds replicate expert behaviors where self-explanation enhances comprehension and transfer. Research in computational thinking shows that think-aloud protocols effectively externalize learners' cognitive processes, improve metacognitive awareness, and support conceptual retention during problem solving (Pan et al., 2023).

Teaching Tip 9: Learning Checkpoints Through Self-Diagnosis

Challenge: Students frequently overestimate their domain understanding and only recognize knowledge gaps after formal assessments reveal weaknesses.

Try This: At the end of each topic or module, provide students with a brief "self-diagnosis checklist." For each key concept (e.g., recursion, pointers, database normalization), students rate their confidence on a scale of 1–5 and identify one question or uncertainty they still have. Instructors can review aggregate results to adjust upcoming instruction or group review sessions. Use tools like Google Forms or LMS quizzes with short-answer fields for scalability.

Why It Works: Self-assessment fosters metacognitive calibration—the alignment between perceived and actual understanding. It helps students identify learning needs early and enables instructors to target misconceptions before they compound. Research shows that self-diagnosis and other self-regulated learning interventions enhance students' self-regulation and academic achievement in both K–12 and higher education settings (Xu et al., 2023).

Teaching Tip 10: Metacognitive Scaffolding Through Instructor Modeling

Challenge: Students rarely observe how experts manage uncertainty, plan, or recover from mistakes during coding, which reinforces the myth that "*good programmers never get stuck.*".

Try This: During live coding or problem-solving demonstrations, verbalize your own reasoning and decision-making. Explicitly point out uncertainties ("*I'm not sure if this loop will terminate. Let's trace it step by step*") and show how you check, test, and revise your own code. Model strategies like hypothesis testing, use of print statements, or version control checkpoints. Record short "thought process" screencasts for students to review independently.

Why It Works: Instructor modeling makes invisible expert strategies visible and normalizes uncertainty and iterative problem-solving as part of authentic computing practice. Students internalize reflective habits by observing and emulating expert behavior. Loksa et al. (2022) observes that such metacognitive scaffolding supports students in developing self-regulation, resilience, and adaptive problem-solving skills in programming tasks.

Theme 3: Problem-Based and Project-Based Learning

"Real learning happens when students stop solving exercises and start solving problems."

Authentic problem contexts give computing concepts meaning. Rather than practicing isolated algorithms, students who engage in problem-based and project-based learning tackle open-ended challenges that mirror real-world design, data, or ethical constraints. Research in computing education shows that this approach fosters interdisciplinary thinking, motivation, persistence, and (Suleiman et al., 2025). In computer science, it encourages students to connect theory with application, collaboration, and iteration. Designing tasks that require exploration (e.g., building a simulation, developing a data visualization, or creating a socially relevant app) helps learners see computing as purposeful and creative. The strategies below demonstrate how to structure projects for meaningful inquiry while maintaining clear scaffolding and feedback.

Teaching Tip 11: Real-World Scenario Challenges

Challenge: Students often struggle to see how abstract computing concepts (e.g., data structures, AI models, or network algorithms) apply to real-world issues.

Try This: Integrate weekly mini-challenges grounded in realistic scenarios. For instance, ask students to design an algorithm to optimize emergency room scheduling, simulate misinformation spread on a social network, or visualize carbon footprint data from open datasets. Provide open-ended prompts rather than step-by-step instructions to allow multiple valid approaches. Encourage students to document assumptions, decisions, and limitations of their models.

Why It Works: Authentic problems activate intrinsic motivation and situate learning within meaningful frameworks. Students learn to frame and scope problems while transferring abstract knowledge to applied contexts. Practical guidance from Gupta and Nguyen-Duc (2021) stresses that engaging students in real-world software projects helps bridge the gap between theory and professional practice and prepares them for the complexities of industry-based problem-solving.

Teaching Tip 12: Progressive Project Scaffolding

Challenge: Open-ended projects can easily overwhelm novices who lack experience in planning, managing complexity, and approaching tasks incrementally.

Try This: Structure projects through a series of progressive milestones that guide students from conception to completion. Begin with a requirements analysis phase where learners define the project scope and constraints, followed by the development of a prototype or minimum viable solution. Subsequent stages should include testing and evaluation, where students assess performance or usability, and a final reflection stage in which they document lessons learned and proposed improvements. Each milestone should receive formative feedback to encourage iteration and growth. In hybrid or online courses, progress can be tracked collaboratively using shared Kanban boards in tools such as *Trello* or *GitHub* Projects.

Why It Works: This approach reduces cognitive overload by distributing the project into digestible stages that emphasize process over product. It mirrors professional agile development cycles, allowing students to experience iterative refinement and continuous feedback. Scaffolding supports learners' self-regulation by fostering goal setting, planning, and reflection, which are vital skills that enhance effective learning in computing contexts (Tsai et al., 2025).

Teaching Tip 13: The "One Big Problem" Course Model

Challenge: Fragmented assignments often lead to shallow learning, as students approach each topic as a discrete exercise rather than part of a cohesive discipline.

Try This: Organize the course around one multifaceted problem that unfolds throughout the semester. For instance, students might develop a cybersecurity awareness campaign, analyze open civic data to identify policy trends, or design an AI-powered educational tool. Each instructional module introduces new theoretical or technical concepts that enable progress toward the final solution. Teams can work on different sub-problems within the same overarching challenge, such as user research, model design, or data visualization.

Why It Works: Centering the course on an evolving problem helps students connect concepts across modules. Sustained engagement promotes ownership, persistence, and deeper understanding of both technical and contextual dimensions. Research on curricular coherence highlights its role in fostering motivation, conceptual integration, and meaningful knowledge transfer in STEM and computing education (Roehrig et al., 2021).

explanations also diversify voices in the classroom and normalize collaborative reasoning. A recent empirical study on peer instruction in computer science education confirmed significant gains in conceptual mastery, confidence, and engagement through structured peer teaching (Mansour et al., 2023).

Teaching Tip 18: Consensus-Building Tasks

Challenge: Unstructured group discussions can devolve into off-topic conversations or allow dominant voices to steer outcomes without genuine collaboration.

Try This: Design consensus-based tasks that require teams to justify collective decisions. For example, in a cybersecurity course, teams might debate the most ethical response to a data breach scenario. Require a written or recorded consensus statement outlining the rationale behind their choice that must be supported by evidence or reasoning.

Why It Works: Consensus-building cultivates negotiation, argumentation, and justification skills, which are core components of professional collaboration. It encourages balanced participation and accountability, as each team member must contribute to the shared decision. Research on open-source collaboration demonstrates that structured consensus processes enhance reasoning quality, participation equity, and collective decision outcomes (Moghaddam et al., 2012).

Teaching Tip 19: Peer Mentoring Networks

Challenge: Novices often hesitate to seek help from instructors or teaching assistants but feel more comfortable learning from peers with shared experiences.

Try This: Establish structured peer mentoring networks where advanced students or teaching assistants support beginners through labs, discussion sessions, or reflective check-ins. Mentors might facilitate code reviews, guide data analysis practices, or discuss conceptual topics such as system design or ethics. In online environments, sustain the network through communication spaces like *Discord* or *Slack*, where mentors and mentees can interact asynchronously.

Why It Works: Peer mentoring builds belonging, reduces intimidation, and provides authentic opportunities for leadership and collaboration. Mentors consolidate their knowledge through teaching, while mentees gain accessible support and confidence. Anthraper et al. (2024) observe that peer-mentoring systems with structured networks strengthen belonging, self-efficacy, and engagement among underrepresented and transfer students.

Teaching Tip 20: Structured Peer Code Review

Challenge: Students rarely analyze or critically critique others' work, which limits their ability to evaluate design quality, efficiency, and readability.

Try This: Integrate a guided peer review process for code, system design diagrams, or data models. Provide clear rubrics covering readability, logic, documentation, usability, or ethical considerations, depending on the course context. Train students to give specific, constructive feedback using examples such as "*This function could be simplified by...*" rather than generic praise or criticism. Conclude with a short reflection: "*What did I learn from my peer's approach?*"

Why It Works: Evaluating peer work develops critical thinking, professional judgment, and awareness of alternative solutions. It helps students internalize quality standards and design principles in collaborative learning contexts. Kubincová et al. (2016) found that structured peer review in computer science courses enhances communication skills, critical analysis, and engagement, helping students learn from both giving and receiving feedback.

Theme 5: Inclusive and Equitable Teaching Practices

"Equity is the ultimate open-source principle in education."

Equity and inclusion are essential for expanding participation and success in computing. Despite progress, underrepresentation by gender, race, and disability persists in computer science education. Inclusive pedagogy draws from Universal Design for Learning and culturally responsive teaching to create environments where all learners feel respected, supported, and challenged (Moore & Urness, 2024). Inclusive teaching in computer science means designing materials, examples, and assessments that reflect diverse identities and ways of thinking. It also involves addressing implicit bias and ensuring accessibility in both physical and digital learning spaces. The strategies that follow highlight practical ways to embed inclusion intentionally into everyday instructional design rather than treating it as an afterthought.

Teaching Tip 21: Contextualizing Examples to Reflect Diverse Interests

Challenge: Many programming examples focus narrowly on domains such as finance, gaming, or physics, leaving some students disengaged or unable to see the social relevance of computing.

Try This: Incorporate examples and projects from a broad range of domains, such as healthcare analytics, environmental modeling, accessibility technology, social justice data visualization, or creative digital media. Offer assignment variations so students can select the context that resonates most with their background or interests. For instance, in a data science course, one dataset might focus on climate trends, another on local community health, and another on film diversity statistics. Encourage students to propose their own contexts when possible.

Why It Works: Representation in content increases relevance, belonging, and motivation. When students see computing applied to issues they care about, they are more likely to persist and develop identity alignment with the field. According to Detmer et al. (2010), real-world and socially relevant computing projects demonstrates that contextualized learning enhances motivation, engagement, and deeper understanding of computing concepts.

Teaching Tip 22: Using Inclusive Language and Course Materials

Challenge: Technical instruction sometimes perpetuates exclusion through biased examples, non-inclusive pronouns, or culturally narrow references.

Try This: Review all instructional materials for gendered language, stereotypes, or culturally limited examples. Replace "he" or "guys" with gender-neutral terms such as "they" or "team." Use inclusive names and personas in examples (e.g., "*Aisha and Luis are designing an algorithm to match students to mentors*"). Avoid analogies or humor that rely on cultural assumptions. Invite students to participate in identifying inclusive phrasing and provide feedback on course materials.

Why It Works: Language signals belonging. Using inclusive language and examples communicates respect and helps create a classroom culture where all learners feel represented. von Briesen et al. (2025) emphasize that culturally responsive teaching and inclusive materials foster positive learning outcomes and strengthen students' sense of belonging and inclusion. These practices, in turn, support the retention of students from underrepresented groups.

Teaching Tip 23: Representation Through Role Models and Guest Speakers

Challenge: Students from underrepresented groups may struggle to envision themselves as part of the computing community or profession.

Try This: Integrate representation throughout the course. Invite guest speakers from diverse backgrounds and roles (e.g., accessibility engineers, community technologists, or AI ethicists) to share their experiences. Highlight contributions of historically underrecognized computer scientists in readings or brief "spotlight" slides (e.g., Clarence "Skip" Ellis, Margaret Hamilton, Timnit Gebru). Frame these examples as integral to the discipline, not add-ons.

Why It Works: Representation normalizes diversity in computing and broadens students' vision of who belongs in the field. Seeing role models who share aspects of one's identity enhances self-concept and career aspiration. Exposure to diverse professionals improves motivation and identification with computing. According to Garcia (2023), incorporating practitioner-assisted learning strengthens students' confidence, motivation, and belonging in computing. Such experiences promote long-term engagement and retention in the discipline.

Teaching Tip 24: Equity-Oriented Assessment Practices

Challenge: Traditional grading systems often reward prior experience, test-taking ability, or speed, which can disadvantage students from diverse educational or cultural backgrounds.

Try This: Adopt assessment approaches that emphasize growth, reflection, and process. Incorporate low-stakes formative assessments, allow revision opportunities, and provide transparent rubrics that clarify expectations. Evaluate reflection statements, design documentation, or peer feedback contributions. For example, in a database course, include marks for schema design reasoning and iteration logs alongside final query accuracy.

Why It Works: Equitable assessment recognizes multiple ways of demonstrating learning and values progress over perfection. Transparency and flexibility reduce anxiety, particularly for students from nontraditional or underrepresented backgrounds. Tubino et al. (2020) emphasize that authentic assessment frameworks with formative feedback and transparent rubrics promote equitable evaluation of student learning and foster self-efficacy and engagement in diverse teams.

Teaching Tip 25: Building Psychological Safety in the Classroom

Challenge: Fear of judgment or failure often prevents students from asking questions, admitting confusion, or sharing partially formed ideas.

Try This: Normalize uncertainty and error as integral parts of computer science learning. Model vulnerability by narrating your own mistakes during demonstrations ("*I expected this output but got something else—let's debug why*"). Incorporate non-evaluative "warm-up" questions such as "*What's one thing you're still wondering about?*" or "*What was confusing in today's example?*" Use anonymous polls or discussion boards to let students voice uncertainty without fear. Reinforce that intellectual risk-taking and curiosity are valued behaviors.

Why It Works: Psychological safety fosters trust, openness, and persistence. When students feel safe to express confusion, they engage more deeply and recover faster from setbacks. A safe climate particularly benefits students from marginalized groups who may experience stereotype threat or impostor feelings. This is particularly important in computer science, where a sense of non-belonging can inhibit asking questions or exposing confusion (Kumar, 2012).

Theme 6: Assessment and Feedback for Learning

"Feedback is the compiler that turns student errors into understanding."

Assessment in computing courses often emphasizes correctness over growth, reducing learning to test cases and grades. A shift toward formative assessment reframes evaluation as feedback for improvement. Research on assessment for learning demonstrates that actionable feedback promotes reflection, motivation, and self-efficacy. In programming contexts, iterative feedback on process is as valuable as the final output (Thangaraj et al., 2023). Effective feedback loops also make invisible thinking visible, helping instructors identify misconceptions early. The following approaches show how assessment can become a continuous conversation that supports deeper understanding rather than a one-time measurement.

Teaching Tip 26: Low-Stakes Formative Assessments

Challenge: Students often treat every quiz or assignment as high stakes, which leads to anxiety, memorization, and disengagement from authentic learning.

Try This: Integrate low-stakes checkpoints designed purely for feedback. Examples include short quizzes on conceptual understanding (e.g., "*Which algorithmic strategy applies here?*"), five-minute data interpretation tasks, or "predict the output" code snippets. Use automated tools such as *Gradescope* or *Codio* to deliver immediate formative feedback. Emphasize that these activities inform both students and instructors about learning progress rather than affecting grades.

Why It Works: Low-stakes assessment normalizes error as a learning opportunity, promotes consistent practice, and provides diagnostic insight without punitive pressure. Frequent formative feedback supports self-regulation and helps instructors adapt instruction based on real-time data. Grover (2021) argues that embedding low-stakes assessments in programming classes supports timely feedback cycles and helps instructors adapt tasks before misconceptions take hold.

Teaching Tip 27: Code Commentaries for Process-Oriented Evaluation

Challenge: Traditional grading practices often prioritize whether the program runs correctly, not how or why students thoughtfully arrived at their solution.

Try This: Ask students to submit short commentaries explaining reasoning behind key decisions whether in code, system architecture, data model design, or security configuration. Prompts can include: "*Why did you choose this algorithm?*" and "*What was the hardest design challenge, and how did you address it?*" Evaluate both clarity of explanation and evidence of reflective thinking. Use short templates (e.g., "*My main challenge was... / I solved it by...*") for efficiency in large classes.

Why It Works: Commentary assignments shift focus from product to process, making reasoning explicit and assessable. Reflective articulation strengthens meta-cognitive skills and helps instructors understand thought patterns behind student choices. Choi et al. (2023) found that integrating structured reflection prompts into programming assignments enhances students' ability to monitor and evaluate their own code-development process.

Teaching Tip 28: Rapid Feedback Loops During Labs

Challenge: Students may complete entire lab sessions or projects incorrectly before receiving any formative input, resulting in frustration and wasted effort.

Try This: Introduce micro-feedback checkpoints during labs every 20–30 minutes. Use brief oral check-ins ("*Show me your current output*" or "*Explain your data validation step*") or lightweight digital submissions. For instance, in a data science lab, students might share an interim plot or output for instructor verification before proceeding. In online settings, replicate real-time feedback with live chat channels, quick screenshots, or short video walk-throughs.

Why It Works: Incremental feedback prevents errors from compounding and reinforces the feedback–action loop essential for mastery. Immediate input sustains momentum, boosts confidence, and allows timely correction before misconceptions solidify. Chevalier et al. (2022) shows that strategically timed feedback loops promote meaningful engagement by preventing error accumulation and reinforcing reflective practice. This balance between action and reflection strengthens students' problem-solving and confidence over time

Teaching Tip 29: Peer Feedback for Perspective and Accountability

Challenge: Students often misunderstand instructor feedback or fail to see alternative ways of approaching a problem, limiting their evaluative judgment.

Try This: Integrate structured peer feedback into design, data analysis, or systems assignments. Use guided rubrics that focus on specific criteria rather than subjective opinions. For example, in a human-computer interaction project, peers can review wireframes for accessibility and flow; in an algorithms course, they can assess clarity of pseudocode. Encourage students to reflect afterward on one idea they learned from their peer's work. Tools such as *Peergrade*, *Moodle Workshop*, or *GitHub* pull requests can facilitate anonymous reviews at scale.

Why It Works: Providing feedback enhances evaluative judgment and deepens understanding of quality criteria. Receiving peer feedback exposes students to varied strategies and perspectives. Structured peer assessment cultivates accountability and collaboration while improving self-assessment accuracy. Matejić and Milenković (2025) found that students who analyzed peer work, provided qualitative feedback, and then revised their own output produced higher-quality projects.

Teaching Tip 30: Revision and Resubmission Opportunities

Challenge: Conventional assessment often rewards one-time performance, which discourages meaningful iteration and thoughtful reflection after feedback.

Try This: Allow students to revise and resubmit selected assignments or projects after receiving feedback. Require a short reflective statement ("*What I changed and why*") to ensure engagement with the feedback. Offer partial credit recovery for substantive improvement. For example, in a software engineering or data analytics project, students can refine code readability, documentation, or visualization design based on earlier critique. Limit the number of resubmissions or scope (e.g., two major assignments per term) to manage workload.

Why It Works: Revision emphasizes learning as an iterative process that reinforces a growth mindset and mirrors authentic computing practice, where refinement is expected. Students develop persistence and ownership when improvement is recognized. Kopcha and Ocak (2023) support this principle by showing that learners' computational thinking develops through cycles of testing, reflection, and revision, where each iteration builds on prior experience.

Theme 7: Integrating AI and Intelligent Tools in the Classroom

"Teach students to prompt their minds before they prompt the machine."

Generative AI and intelligent tutoring systems are reshaping how students learn to code and how instructors facilitate learning (Garcia, 2025). Tools such as *ChatGPT*, *Copilot*, or automated graders can enhance feedback, creativity, and accessibility when used responsibly. Current discourse in computing education emphasizes the need for critical AI literacy to help students understand both the affordances and limitations of these generative AI tools (Agbo et al., 2025). Instead of substitution or plagiarism, educators must guide learners to use AI for exploration and reflection. The strategies below illustrate balanced ways to incorporate AI that preserve academic integrity while fostering curiosity and responsible innovation.

Teaching Tip 31: Prompt-Based Learning as Computational Thinking

Challenge: Students often struggle to transform open-ended or ambiguous problem statements into computationally precise formulations.

Try This: Treat prompt design as a form of computational thinking. Have students create, test, and refine prompts to elicit accurate, useful, or creative responses from an AI system. For example, in a software design class, students might iteratively prompt an AI to explain or generate pseudocode for an algorithm. In a cybersecurity class, they might craft prompts to simulate threat scenarios responsibly. Require students to analyze how prompt modifications affect the AI's output and to document their reasoning process.

Why It Works: Prompt engineering mirrors the logic of programming. It teaches students how to communicate computational intent clearly and evaluate responses critically. Nathaniel et al. (2025) observe that when students iteratively refine prompts, they develop deeper critical thinking, creativity, and computational precision. This cycle of testing, revising, and interpreting AI outputs reinforces the same analytical skills essential for effective algorithmic problem-solving.

Teaching Tip 32: AI as a Code Critic and Not a Code Writer

Challenge: Students may depend on generative AI tools to produce solutions without engaging in the reasoning needed to understand or evaluate the code.

Try This: Position generative AI tools as reviewers rather than authors. Ask students to use AI to critique or debug their own code, design software documentation, or database schema. Students then annotate the AI's feedback, comparing it to their intentions: "*What did the AI improve?*" or "*What did it miss or misinterpret?*" For advanced computing courses, AI can critique model choices, query efficiency, or interface design rather than generate them. Discuss one AI-generated critique collectively to highlight its strengths and weaknesses.

Why It Works: This approach promotes critical consumption rather than passive reliance. Students strengthen analytical and debugging skills by evaluating both their own work and the AI's reasoning. It reinforces human oversight as essential to responsible technology use. Garcia (2025) emphasizes that balanced AI integration helps maintain critical thinking and learning authenticity by preventing overreliance and fostering reflective engagement with AI feedback.

Teaching Tip 33: AI-Integrated Pair Programming

Challenge: Students either avoid emerging AI-driven tools entirely out of uncertainty or use them privately and inconsistently without pedagogical guidance.

Try This: Implement AI-assisted pair programming where two students collaborate with an AI system as a "third teammate." One student acts as the AI interlocutor (crafting prompts, clarifying requests, and interpreting responses) while the other acts as the analyst (checking accuracy, style, and logic). Roles switch midway. In non-programming contexts, the "AI partner" might assist in brainstorming design ideas or reviewing user interface text.

Why It Works: This structured integration promotes transparency, shared responsibility, and reflective use of AI. Students learn to question, verify, and refine AI outputs collaboratively rather than treat them as authoritative. It models ethical, team-based AI interaction aligned with professional computing practices. Fan et al. (2025) found that AI-assisted pair programming enhances motivation, reduces programming anxiety, and supports collaborative learning, which underscores the value of guided human–AI teamwork in computing education.

Teaching Tip 34: AI Literacy and Transparency Exercises

Challenge: Students often view AI systems as neutral or omniscient, without deeply understanding how data bias, model training, or hallucination shape results.

Try This: Dedicate one class session or module to AI literacy and transparency. Introduce how large language models are trained, what data they rely on, and where bias or inaccuracy can emerge. Use practical demonstrations: show an AI's inconsistent answers to the same query, biased dataset examples, or fabricated citations. Discuss how to verify AI-generated information. Assign short reflections or simulations (e.g., using Google's *Teachable Machine* or *AI Explainability 360*) where students explore bias firsthand.

Why It Works: Understanding how AI systems operate fosters critical AI literacy. Students learn to approach intelligent tools with curiosity and skepticism, recognizing both creative potential and ethical risk. Transparent exploration helps demystify AI and supports responsible, informed use According to Bozkurt et al.

(2024), generative AI is not ideologically or culturally neutral because it reflects the biases and values embedded in its design and data. Engaging students in critical examination of these systems promotes responsible use of AI in learning and society.

Teaching Tip 35: Responsible Use Policies and Reflection

Challenge: Unclear expectations about AI use can lead to ethical dilemmas, plagiarism concerns, or inequitable practices among students.

Try This: Co-create a Responsible AI Use Policy with your students and faculty members at the start of the course. Discuss what types of AI assistance are acceptable (e.g., brainstorming ideas, code critique, debugging) versus prohibited (e.g., submitting AI-written code or essays). Require brief AI usage statements with each major assignment describing if and how AI was used (e.g., "*Used ChatGPT to explain recursion concept; did not use for code generation*"). Revisit the policy mid-term to adapt to evolving technologies or class experiences.

Why It Works: Shared policy design fosters transparency, trust, and ethical reasoning. Students learn to self-regulate their use of AI, developing integrity as a professional competency rather than a compliance rule. Explicit reflection also helps instructors detect misuse while modeling open dialogue about responsible innovation. Research by Xiao et al. (2025) similarly concludes that integrating ethical reflection and shared decision-making about generative AI fosters students' autonomy and professional integrity. This process helps learners internalize ethical reasoning as part of their learning journey rather than treating it as a compliance requirement.

Theme 8: Ethics, Responsibility, and Societal Impact

"Code without conscience is just a well-written bug."

Every computational decision has human consequences. Integrating ethics into computer science education ensures that students consider fairness, accountability, and social impact as inherent to technical practice. Scholarship on responsible computing calls for embedding ethical reflection throughout curricula rather than isolating it in stand-alone modules (Goetze, 2023). Discussing real cases (e.g., privacy breaches, biased algorithms, environmental effects) helps learners connect abstract principles to tangible outcomes. Ethical reasoning in programming also strengthens critical thinking and empathy. The following teaching ideas demonstrate how to make ethical awareness a regular feature of assignments, discussions, and design projects.

Teaching Tip 36: Micro-Ethics Integration in Every Module

Challenge: Ethics is often taught as a one-time discussion or as part of a standalone course rather than as a recurring component of technical learning.

Try This: Integrate micro-ethics reflections directly into each technical topic. When teaching database courses, include a short discussion or poll on data privacy and consent. During an algorithms lecture, ask, "*What could go wrong if this recommendation system were biased?*" In computer systems or networking, discuss energy efficiency and environmental impact. Keep prompts brief (1–3 minutes) but frequent to normalize ethical inquiry.

Why It Works: Embedding ethics within context reinforces that social responsibility is inseparable from computing practice. Regular exposure develops ethical fluency alongside technical competence. Jarzemsky et al. (2023) found that embedding short, reflective ethics components within coding assignments increased students' engagement and sense of social responsibility. Students reported that integrating ethical reasoning directly into programming work helped them see computing decisions as inherently connected to real-world consequences.

Teaching Tip 37: Case-Based Ethical Reasoning

Challenge: Students often struggle to apply broad ethical principles to the complex and context-dependent decisions faced by practitioners.

Try This: Use case-based learning grounded in real or fictional computing scenarios, such as biased hiring algorithms, privacy violations in mobile apps, or data misuse in AI systems. In small groups, have students identify stakeholders, competing values (e.g., accuracy vs. fairness), and possible courses of action. Ask each group to justify its decision and reflect on trade-offs. Follow with a class-wide synthesis comparing approaches.

Why It Works: Analyzing realistic cases develops ethical sensitivity and practical reasoning skills. Students learn that ethical dilemmas rarely have simple solutions. Case-based instruction has been shown to enhance ethical decision-making and engagement in computing education. For example, Hedayati-Mehdiabadi (2022) found that presenting students with computing-specific dilemmas (rather than abstract ethics questions) sharpened their stakeholder-analysis and helped them more accurately predict downstream consequences of design choices

Teaching Tip 38: Algorithmic Fairness Labs

Challenge: Many students perceive algorithms as objective or neutral and overlook how human bias can shape data and outcomes.

Try This: Create hands-on labs where students explore bias in machine learning models or data-driven systems. For example, analyze the *COMPAS* dataset for racial bias in risk prediction, or examine gender representation in image recognition outputs. Ask students to measure bias quantitatively and discuss mitigation strategies such as balanced sampling or fairness metrics. Frame the lab as investigation and reflection, not accusation.

Why It Works: Practical engagement turns abstract ethical ideas into experiential learning. Students witness how technical design decisions directly affect fairness and social justice. Empirical exercises make bias visible and actionable. Research shows that hands-on exploration of algorithmic systems enhances students' ethical understanding and technical competence by linking conceptual learning to real-world data and outcomes (Archambault et al., 2024).

Teaching Tip 39: Ethical Code Review

Challenge: Code reviews and design critiques typically evaluate technical quality (e.g., efficiency, readability) but ignore potential ethical or social consequences.

Try This: Incorporate an "ethics lens" into code or design reviews. Alongside conventional rubrics, include prompts such as "*Could this design inadvertently exclude users?*" or "*Does this code introduce privacy or security risks?*" Students evaluate peers' work for both technical and ethical dimensions. This approach works equally well for software or data visualization projects.

Why It Works: Ethical review integrates moral reasoning into standard quality assurance practices. Students learn that responsible computing involves evaluating potential impacts alongside performance metrics. Embedding ethics in peer review enhances awareness of social responsibility as a professional norm. Research in computer science education emphasizes that integrating critical thinking and reflective evaluation deepens students' ability to connect technical decisions with ethical and societal consequences (Maesschalck, 2024).

Teaching Tip 40: Civic Computing and Social Good Projects

Challenge: Students may view computing as a purely technical or commercial field that is disconnected from community needs or social challenges.

Try This: Incorporate community-oriented projects that address real human issues. Examples include developing accessibility tools for users with disabilities, building educational technology for underserved schools, or visualizing data for advocacy groups. If direct partnerships are not feasible, use open data to simulate authentic problem-solving contexts. Require students to articulate the societal benefit, potential harms, and ethical considerations of their design.

Why It Works: Civic computing projects connect abstract computer science concepts to empathy, service, and civic engagement. Students see computing as a means for positive impact and learn to balance innovation with responsibility. Ellis et al. (2024) asserted that when computing students engaged with socially-oriented computing tasks, they reported greater sense of purpose and willingness to apply their technical skills for community-benefit.

Theme 9: Blended, Remote, and Hybrid Learning Innovations

"Learning has no bandwidth limit when connection is human."

Digital transformation has expanded where and how computer science is taught. Blended and hybrid models combine in-person collaboration with online flexibility, enabling personalized pacing and broader access. Post-pandemic research on technology-enhanced learning highlights that effective hybrid teaching depends less on tools and more on intentional design. Such design builds social presence, clear structure, and equitable participation across modalities. For computer science educators, this means reimagining lectures, labs, and assessments to function seamlessly in mixed environments. Recent research in computer science education underscores that well-designed hybrid frameworks can sustain engagement, foster community, and enhance collaboration among students across physical and virtual settings (Holly et al., 2025).

Teaching Tip 41: Modular and Self-Paced Learning Units

Challenge: Students in hybrid courses often progress at different speeds and arrive with varying levels of prior experience in computing concepts.

Try This: Organize the course into modular learning units, each focused on a discrete skill or concept (e.g., recursion, database normalization, or cybersecurity principles). Each unit includes (a) a concise video or reading overview, (b) a self-check quiz for immediate feedback, (c) a core applied task (coding, modeling, or analysis), and (d) enrichment extensions for deeper exploration. Allow students to progress flexibly within defined timelines.

Why It Works: Modularization and self-pacing respect diverse learning rhythms while maintaining structure and accountability. These approaches promote mastery-based learning, where students focus on understanding before moving forward. Alvarez et al. (2023) found that modular mastery-based units in a CS1 course allowed students to advance when ready, yielded higher completion rates, and supported learners who arrived with varying prior experience.

Teaching Tip 42: Virtual Code Clinics

Challenge: Remote and asynchronous students often lack immediate access to mentoring and collaborative troubleshooting common in in-person labs.

Try This: Host weekly virtual code clinics live, drop-in sessions where students can share screens and discuss challenges with instructors. Clinics can focus on debugging, logic reasoning, system configuration, or project design. Offer structured time slots by topic or difficulty level (e.g., "*Intro to Python*," "*Database Queries*," "*Version Control*"). Encourage peer-to-peer learning within sessions by allowing students to observe or contribute to others' problem-solving processes.

Why It Works: Virtual clinics replicate the spontaneity and human connection of physical labs, providing just-in-time support that reduces frustration and dropout rates. They create a space for informal learning and mentorship, both critical for persistence in computing. Related computing studies on online collaboration spaces (e.g., Gather.Town vs. Zoom) and forum help (Piazza) report meaningful differences in engagement across modalities, which underscores the value of synchronous drop-in support alongside asynchronous channels (Latulipe & Jaeger, 2022).

Teaching Tip 43: Synchronous–Asynchronous Blending

Challenge: Hybrid courses risk creating inequities between students who attend in person and those joining remotely, leading to uneven learning experiences.

Try This: Design every class activity with parallel participation paths. Mirror in-class polls with online survey tools, pair live discussions with asynchronous forums, and ensure that shared documents or digital whiteboards (e.g., *Miro*, *Jamboard*, or *Google Docs*) are used collaboratively by both groups. Form mixed-modality breakout groups where remote and in-person students collaborate on the same design or data analysis tasks, ensuring interaction across modalities.

Why It Works: Parallel design ensures all learners have equitable access to interaction and participation, regardless of location or time zone. Research in the educational technology setting shows that balancing synchronous and asynchronous participation paths improves access and engagement, as live paths boost interaction while asynchronous paths provide flexibility and help equalize participation across modalities (Han et al., 2022).

Teaching Tip 44: Community-Building in Distributed Learning

Challenge: Online and hybrid environments can feel impersonal and that ultimately reduces social presence and leads to disengagement.

Try This: Begin each week with a brief connection ritual: a discussion prompt, a short "tech news spotlight," or a show-and-tell of ongoing projects. Recognize student contributions publicly in announcements or discussion boards. Create informal online spaces (e.g., *Discord* or *Piazza*) for peer collaboration and social exchange, moderated by teaching assistants to maintain respect. Periodically host "coffee chats" or networking sessions to sustain interpersonal connection.

Why It Works: Social presence is a key predictor of persistence and satisfaction in remote learning. Structured opportunities for recognition and informal interaction foster community identity and belonging. For example, Xia et al. (2024) demonstrated that when courses intentionally embed social-presence cues and peer interaction opportunities, students report higher belonging and engage more deeply in online learning

Teaching Tip 45: Instructor Presence in Hybrid Spaces

Challenge: Students frequently perceive online instructors as distant or less responsive, which can diminish motivation and perceived support.

Try This: Cultivate strong instructor presence through consistent, visible communication. Post weekly announcements summarizing progress ("*This week we dive deeper into recursion…*"), provide short video updates or mini-reflections, and respond promptly to forum discussions. Use conversational tone and reference class trends ("*Several of you mentioned confusion about Big-O notation. Let's unpack that!*"). In multi-section or team-taught courses, rotate facilitators for weekly check-ins to sustain responsiveness while managing workload.

Why It Works: Instructor presence conveys care, immediacy, and structure. Students who perceive instructors as present and responsive show greater participation and achievement. Presence bridges the psychological gap between teacher and learner across modalities. For example, Conklin et al. (2024) show that when students perceive instructors as accessible and engaged in online courses, their anxiety decreases and motivation rises

Theme 10: Creativity, Computational Thinking, and Interdisciplinary Learning

"Creativity is the missing semicolon that makes code come alive."

Creativity is central to computing but often overlooked in favor of precision and efficiency. Emerging literature on computational creativity and interdisciplinary learning shows that when students use code to design, tell stories, or model systems, they develop deeper conceptual understanding and motivation (Zhou & Zhang, 2024). Creative computing links logic with imagination and connects computer science to art, science, and social inquiry. Encouraging students to explore open-ended problems, aesthetic design, or cross-disciplinary projects positions programming as a medium for expression and innovation. The following practices illustrate how to cultivate creativity and interdisciplinarity within a rigorous technical curriculum.

Teaching Tip 46: Creative Coding for Expression

Challenge: Students often perceive programming as rigid, rule-bound, and detached from personal meaning or creativity.

Try This: Incorporate creative coding environments (e.g., *Processing*, *p5.js*, or *Turtle Graphics*) into core assignments. Ask students to produce small projects that merge computation with self-expression: generative art that represents an emotion, algorithmic music composition, or interactive visualizations of personal data. Encourage students to document both their aesthetic intent and the computational techniques used.

Why It Works: Creative computing engages both affective and cognitive domains. By linking abstract constructs (loops, conditionals, randomness) to aesthetic outcomes, students experience computation as a tool for expression, not just correctness. Graél et al. (2025) observe that when students engage in creative-coding tasks, they shift their perceptions of programming (attitudes, stereotypes, comprehension) and thus deepen both interest and learning.

Teaching Tip 47: Computational Thinking Through Unplugged Activities

Challenge: Novice programmers often struggle to develop algorithmic reasoning skills when cognitive load is dominated by syntax and debugging.

Try This: Use unplugged activities to teach computational concepts through collaborative experiences. Examples include (a) acting out sorting algorithms as a class, (b) drawing graph traversals on paper, and (c) solving pattern puzzles or binary encoding challenges These activities help students understand sequencing, abstraction, and pattern recognition before transitioning to code. Record short demonstrations or provide printable activity sheets for asynchronous learners.

Why It Works: Separating logic from syntax reduces anxiety and cognitive overload. Unplugged methods make computational thinking accessible across ages and disciplines while reinforcing transferable reasoning skills. A critical review of unplugged pedagogies found these approaches effectively support computational thinking development by helping learners engage with algorithmic and abstraction-based tasks without the burden of code syntax (Huang & Looi, 2021).

Teaching Tip 48: Data Visualization and Computational Storytelling

Challenge: Students may be proficient in data manipulation and visualization but struggle to communicate insights meaningfully or persuasively.

Try This: Assign data storytelling projects that blend technical analysis with creative narrative. Students select a dataset (e.g., climate change indicators, public health statistics, or media trends) and design a narrative infographic using tools like *Tableau* or *D3.js*. Require a written or spoken explanation of design choices and the story the visualization tells about the data.

Why It Works: Data storytelling develops synthesis across analytical, visual, and communicative domains. It transforms computation into a medium for understanding and advocacy, showing how data shapes discourse. This practice integrates computational literacy with civic and narrative competence. Chen et al. (2023) demonstrate that when students build data-stories, they develop both technical competence and communicative agency that is aligned with the goal of transforming computation into meaningful story-based insights

Teaching Tip 49: Creative Constraints as Catalysts for Innovation

Challenge: Total creative freedom can overwhelm students, while overly prescriptive assignments limit exploration.

Try This: Frame tasks with purposeful creative constraints to focus innovation. Examples include: "*Create a visualization without text labels*" and "*Solve a problem using only recursion*." After completion, facilitate discussion on how constraints shaped design and problem-solving strategies.

Why It Works: Constraints encourage divergent thinking within structured boundaries that successfully mirrors real-world innovation where limitations inspire inventive solutions. Students learn to explore computational flexibility and elegance under design restrictions. Tromp and Baer (2022) found that constraints serve both as exclusionary boundaries and focusing mechanisms, helping learners explore and exploit design spaces more effectively.

Teaching Tip 50: Showcasing Interdisciplinary Projects Publicly

Challenge: Creative or cross-disciplinary computing projects often remain unseen, which can diminish students' sense of purpose and pride in their work.

Try This: Conclude the course with a "Demo Day" featuring interdisciplinary student projects. Encourage multimodal formats (e.g., live demos, posters, short lightning talks, or online exhibitions) where projects are presented to peers, faculty, or community partners. Examples include (a) a simulation for ecological systems modeling, (b) a generative art installation exploring algorithmic beauty, and (c) a data-driven story highlighting social justice issues Provide peer feedback rubrics that value originality, impact, and reflection as much as technical quality.

Why It Works: Public presentation validates creativity, promotes communication skills, and strengthens community identity. Sharing interdisciplinary work connects computing to broader human contexts and reinforces that technical rigor and artistic imagination coexist. Authentic audiences deepen engagement by shifting learners' focus from simply demonstrating understanding to meaningfully communicating ideas, fostering reflection, ownership, and professional connection beyond the classroom (Lynch et al., 2021).

CONCLUSION

The ongoing evolution of computer science education requires more than periodic curriculum updates, as it requires a paradigmatic shift in how knowledge, creativity, and human agency are cultivated through computation. This chapter has outlined a pedagogical framework that synthesizes theory, empirical evidence, and reflective practice to support transformative learning in computer science classrooms. The ten themes and fifty strategies presented herein underscore that pedagogical excellence emerges when intellectual rigor converges with authenticity and inclusivity. When learners engage in design-oriented inquiry, collaborate to address complex problems, and interrogate the ethical implications of their work, they acquire a form of literacy that extends beyond coding into critical and creative citizenship. Sustaining this transformation demands a culture of continuous inquiry among educators. As AI, immersive environments, and data-rich ecosystems redefine the contours of education, instructors must remain deliberate in aligning innovation with purpose. Thus, future research should examine how these pedagogical approaches can be contextualized across diverse educational systems and disciplinary intersections where computing informs art, ethics, and environmental sustainability. In essence, the evolution of computer science education must remain guided by the principle

REFERENCES

Acut, D. P. (2026). Gamification in Computer Science Education: A Systematic Review of Pedagogical Strategies and Learning Outcomes. In *Pedagogical Innovations in Computer Science Education.*

Agbo, F. J., Olivia, C., Oguibe, G., Sanusi, I. T., & Sani, G. (2025). Computing Education Using Generative Artificial Intelligence Tools: A Systematic Literature Review. *Computers and Education Open*, *9*, 1–13. DOI: 10.1016/j.caeo.2025.100266

Alvarez, C., Samary, M. M., & Wise, A. F. (2023). Modularization for Mastery Learning in Cs1: A 4-Year Action Research Study. *Journal of Computing in Higher Education*, •••, 1–44. DOI: 10.1007/s12528-023-09366-1 PMID: 37359038

Anthraper, N., Javiya, P., Iluru, S., Chen, L. K., & Kleinsmith, A. (2024). PeerConnect: Co-Designing a Peer-Mentoring Support System with Computing Transfer Students. *Extended Abstracts of the CHI Conference on Human Factors in Computing Systems*. https://doi.org/DOI: 10.1145/3613905.3650936

Archambault, S. G., Ramachandran, S., Acosta, E., & Fu, S. (2024). Ethical Dimensions of Algorithmic Literacy for College Students: Case Studies and Cross-Disciplinary Connections. *Journal of Academic Librarianship*, *50*(3), 1–20. DOI: 10.1016/j.acalib.2024.102865

Belland, B. R., Walker, A. E., Kim, N. J., & Lefler, M. (2017). Synthesizing Results From Empirical Research on Computer-Based Scaffolding in STEM Education: A Meta-Analysis. *Review of Educational Research*, *87*(2), 309–344. DOI: 10.3102/0034654316670999 PMID: 28344365

Bozkurt, A., Xiao, J., Farrow, R., Bai, J. Y. H., Nerantzi, C., Moore, S., & Asino, T. I. (2024). The Manifesto for Teaching and Learning in a Time of Generative AI: A Critical Collective Stance to Better Navigate the Future. *Open Praxis*, *16*(4), 487–513. DOI: 10.55982/openpraxis.16.4.777

Çakiroğlu, Ü., & Er, B. (2023). A Model to Develop Activities for Teaching Programming Through Metacognitive Strategies. *Thinking Skills and Creativity*, *48*, 1–11. DOI: 10.1016/j.tsc.2023.101279

Chang, H., Ngunjiri, F., & Hernandez, K. A. C. (2013). *Collaborative Autoethnography*. Left Coast Press. https://books.google.com.ph/books?id=-yLHAGZ3VeAC

Chen, L., Gillan, J., Decker, M., Eteffa, E., Marzan, A., Thai, J., & Jewett, S. (2023). Embedding Digital Data Storytelling in Introductory Data Science Course: An Inter-Institutional Transdisciplinary Pilot Study. *Journal of Problem Based Learning in Higher Education, 11*(2), 126–152. DOI: 10.54337/ojs.jpblhe.v11i2.7767

Chevalier, M., Giang, C., El-Hamamsy, L., Bonnet, E., Papaspyros, V., Pellet, J.-P., & Mondada, F. (2022). The Role of Feedback and Guidance as Intervention Methods to Foster Computational Thinking in Educational Robotics Learning Activities for Primary School. *Computers & Education, 180*, 1–15. DOI: 10.1016/j.compedu.2022.104431

Choi, H., Jovanovic, J., Poquet, O., Brooks, C., Joksimović, S., & Williams, J. J. (2023). The Benefit of Reflection Prompts for Encouraging Learning with Hints in an Online Programming Course. *The Internet and Higher Education, 58*, 1–10. DOI: 10.1016/j.iheduc.2023.100903

Cochran-Smith, M., & Lytle, S. L. (2009). *Inquiry as Stance: Practitioner Research for the Next Generation*. Teachers College Press. https://eric.ed.gov/?id=ED527594

Conklin, S., Ovarzun, B., Kim, S., & Dikkers, A. G. (2024). Exploring the Relationships of Learners and Instructors in Online Courses. *Online Learning : the Official Journal of the Online Learning Consortium, 28*(4), 257–281. DOI: 10.24059/olj.v28i4.3934

Córdova-Esparza, D.-M., Romero-González, J.-A., Córdova-Esparza, K.-E., Terven, J., & López-Martínez, R.-E. (2024). Active Learning Strategies in Computer Science Education: A Systematic Review. *Multimodal Technologies and Interaction, 8*(6), 1–20. DOI: 10.3390/mti8060050

Detmer, R., Li, C., Dong, Z., & Hankins, J. (2010). Incorporating Real-World Projects in Teaching Computer Science Courses. *Proceedings of the 48th annual ACM Southeast Conference*. https://doi.org/DOI: 10.1145/1900008.1900042

Ellis, H. J. C., Hislop, G. W., Goldweber, M., Rebelsky, S., Pearce, J., Ordonez, P., & Gordon, N. (2024). Computing for Social Good in Education. *ACM Inroads, 15*(4), 47–57. DOI: 10.1145/3699719

Fan, G., Liu, D., Zhang, R., & Pan, L. (2025). The Impact of AI-Assisted Pair Programming on Student Motivation, Programming Anxiety, Collaborative Learning, and Programming Performance: A Comparative Study with Traditional Pair Programming and Individual Approaches. *International Journal of STEM Education, 12*(1), 1–17. DOI: 10.1186/s40594-025-00537-3

Gantalao, L. C., Calzada, J. G. D., Capuyan, D. L., Lumantas, B. C., Acut, D. P., & Garcia, M. B. (2025). Equipping the Next Generation of Technicians: Navigating School Infrastructure and Technical Knowledge in the Age of AI Integration. In *Pitfalls of AI Integration in Education: Skill Obsolescence, Misuse, and Bias*. IGI Global., DOI: 10.4018/979-8-3373-0122-8.ch009

Garcia, M. B. (2023). Facilitating Group Learning Using an Apprenticeship Model: Which Master is More Effective in Programming Instruction? *Journal of Educational Computing Research*, *61*(6), 1207–1231. DOI: 10.1177/07356331231170382

Garcia, M. B. (2025). Teaching and Learning Computer Programming Using ChatGPT: A Rapid Review of Literature Amid the Rise of Generative AI Technologies. *Education and Information Technologies*, *30*, 16721–16745. DOI: 10.1007/s10639-025-13452-5

Garcia, M. B., & Revano, T. F., Jr. (2021). Assessing the Role of Python Programming Gamified Course on Students' Knowledge, Skills Performance, Attitude, and Self-Efficacy. *2021 IEEE 13th International Conference on Humanoid, Nanotechnology, Information Technology, Communication and Control, Environment and Management (HNICEM)*. https://doi.org/DOI: 10.1109/HNICEM54116.2021.9731935

Gill, S. S., Wu, H., Patros, P., Ottaviani, C., Arora, P., Pujol, V. C., & Buyya, R. (2024). Modern Computing: Vision and Challenges. *Telematics and Informatics Reports*, *13*, 1–38. DOI: 10.1016/j.teler.2024.100116

Goetze, T. S. (2023). Integrating Ethics into Computer Science Education: Multi-, Inter-, and Transdisciplinary Approaches. *Proceedings of the 54th ACM Technical Symposium on Computer Science Education* V. 1. https://doi.org/DOI: 10.1145/3545945.3569792

Graél, I., Musliu, X., & Fraser, G. (2025). Programming Art: Does Creative Programming Shift Girls' Stereotypes, Affections, and Comprehension of Programming? *Proceedings of the ACM Global on Computing Education Conference 2025* Vol 1. https://doi.org/DOI: 10.1145/3736181.3747161

Grover, S. (2021). Toward A Framework for Formative Assessment of Conceptual Learning in K-12 Computer Science Classrooms. *Proceedings of the 52nd ACM Technical Symposium on Computer Science Education*. https://doi.org/DOI: 10.1145/3408877.3432460

Gupta, V., & Nguyen-Duc, A. (2021). *Real-World Software Projects for Computer Science and Engineering Students*. CRC Press., DOI: 10.1201/9781003119883

Han, J., Yang, Y., Li, Y., & Ren, B. (2022). Students' Responses to a HyFlex Course: A Case Study in the Educational Technology Setting. *Proceedings of the 5th International Conference on Big Data and Education.* https://doi.org/DOI: 10.1145/3524383.3524394

Hedayati-Mehdiabadi, A. (2022). How do Computer Science Students Make Decisions in Ethical Situations? Implications for Teaching Computing Ethics based on a Grounded Theory Study. *ACM Transactions on Computing Education, 22*(3), 1–24. DOI: 10.1145/3483841

Holly, M., Hildebrandt, J., & Pirker, J. (2025). *A Computer-Supported Collaborative Learning Environment for Computer Science Education.* Immersive Learning Research Network., DOI: 10.1007/978-3-031-80475-5_21

Huang, W., & Looi, C.-K. (2021). A Critical Review of Literature on "Unplugged" Pedagogies in K-12 Computer Science and Computational Thinking Education. *Computer Science Education, 31*(1), 83–111. DOI: 10.1080/08993408.2020.1789411

Jarzemsky, J., Paup, J., & Fiesler, C. (2023). "This Applies to the Real World": Student Perspectives on Integrating Ethics into a Computer Science Assignment. *Proceedings of the 54th ACM Technical Symposium on Computer Science Education* V. 1. https://doi.org/DOI: 10.1145/3545945.3569846

Keith, P. K., Sullivan, F. R., & Pham, D. (2019). Roles, Collaboration, and the Development of Computational Thinking in a Robotics Learning Environment. In Kong, S.-C., & Abelson, H. (Eds.), *Computational Thinking Education* (pp. 223–245). Springer Singapore., DOI: 10.1007/978-981-13-6528-7_13

Kopcha, T. J., & Ocak, C. (2023). Children's Computational Thinking as the Development of a Possibility Space. *Computers and Education Open, 5*, 1–14. DOI: 10.1016/j.caeo.2023.100156

Kubincová, Z., Dropcová, V., & Homola, M. (2016). Students' Acceptance of Peer Review in Computer Science Course. *EAI Endorsed Transactions on e-Learning, 16*(10), 1-8. https://doi.org/DOI: 10.4108/eai.11-4-2016.151153

Kumar, A. N. (2012). A Study of Stereotype Threat in Computer Science. *Proceedings of the 17th ACM Annual Conference on Innovation and Technology in Computer Science Education.* https://doi.org/DOI: 10.1145/2325296.2325361

Latulipe, C., & Jaeger, A. D. (2022). Comparing Student Experiences of Collaborative Learning in Synchronous CS1 Classes in Gather.Town vs. Zoom. *Proceedings of the 53rd ACM Technical Symposium on Computer Science Education* - Volume 1. https://doi.org/DOI: 10.1145/3478431.3499383

Liu, Z., Gearty, Z., Richard, E., Orrill, C. H., Kayumova, S., & Balasubramanian, R. (2024). Bringing Computational Thinking into Classrooms: A Systematic Review on Supporting Teachers in Integrating Computational Thinking into K-12 Classrooms. *International Journal of STEM Education, 11*(1), 1–18. DOI: 10.1186/s40594-024-00510-6

Loksa, D., Margulieux, L., Becker, B. A., Craig, M., Denny, P., Pettit, R., & Prather, J. (2022). Metacognition and Self-Regulation in Programming Education: Theories and Exemplars of Use. *ACM Transactions on Computing Education, 22*(4), 1–31. DOI: 10.1145/3487050

Lynch, M., Sage, T., Hitchcock, L. I., & Sage, M. (2021). A Heutagogical Approach for the Assessment of Internet Communication Technology (ICT) Assignments in Higher Education. *International Journal of Educational Technology in Higher Education, 18*(1), 1–16. DOI: 10.1186/s41239-021-00290-x PMID: 34778541

Maesschalck, S. (2024). Critical Thinking: The Code to Crack Computer Science Education. *Journal of Information Technology Education: Innovations in Practice, 23*, 1–20. DOI: 10.28945/5387

Mansour, K. H., Jackson, D. K., Bievenue, L., Voight, A., & Sridhar, N. (2023). Understanding the Impact of Peer Instruction in CS Principles Teacher Professional Development. *ACM Transactions on Computing Education, 23*(2), 1–21. DOI: 10.1145/3585077

Matejić, J., & Milenković, A. (2025). Impact of Peer Feedback in a Web Programming Course on Students' Achievement. *International Journal of Cognitive Research in Science* [IJCRSEE]. *Engineering and Education, 13*(1), 33–49. DOI: 10.23947/2334-8496-2025-13-1-33-49

Moghaddam, R. Z., Bailey, B., & Fu, W.-T. (2012). Consensus Building in Open Source User Interface Design Discussions. *Proceedings of the SIGCHI Conference on Human Factors in Computing Systems*. https://doi.org/DOI: 10.1145/2207676.2208611

Moore, M., & Urness, T. (2024). Inclusive Practices and Universal Design in the Computer Science Classroom. *Journal of Computing Sciences in Colleges, 39*(6), 93–102.

Nathaniel, J., Oyelere, S. S., Suhonen, J., & Tedre, M. (2025). Investigating the Impact of Generative AI Integration on the Sustenance of Higher-Order Thinking Skills and Understanding of Programming Logic. *Computers and Education: Artificial Intelligence, 9*, 1–19. DOI: 10.1016/j.caeai.2025.100460

Öqvist, M., & Nouri, J. (2018). Coding by Hand or on the Computer? Evaluating the Effect of Assessment Mode on Performance of Students Learning Programming. *Journal of Computers in Education*, *5*(2), 199–219. DOI: 10.1007/s40692-018-0103-3

Pan, Z., Cui, Y., Leighton, J. P., & Cutumisu, M. (2023). Insights into Computational Thinking from Think-Aloud Interviews: A Systematic Review. *Applied Cognitive Psychology*, *37*(1), 71–95. DOI: 10.1002/acp.4029

Pournaghshband, V., & Medel, P. (2020). Promoting Diversity-Inclusive Computer Science Pedagogies: A Multidimensional Perspective. *Proceedings of the 2020 ACM Conference on Innovation and Technology in Computer Science Education*. https://doi.org/DOI: 10.1145/3341525.3387360

Revano, T. F., Jr., & Garcia, M. B. (2020). Manufacturing Design Thinkers in Higher Education Institutions: The Use of Design Thinking Curriculum in the Education Landscape. *2020 IEEE 12th International Conference on Humanoid, Nanotechnology, Information Technology, Communication and Control, Environment and Management (HNICEM)*. https://doi.org/DOI: 10.1109/HNICEM51456.2020.9400034

Roehrig, G. H., Dare, E. A., Ring-Whalen, E., & Wieselmann, J. R. (2021). Understanding Coherence and Integration in Integrated STEM Curriculum. *International Journal of STEM Education*, *8*(1), 1–21. DOI: 10.1186/s40594-020-00259-8

Srinivasan, K. R., Rahman, N. H. A., & Ravana, S. D. (2025). Reskilling and Upskilling Future Educators for the Demands of Artificial Intelligence in the Modern Era of Education. In *Pitfalls of AI Integration in Education: Skill Obsolescence, Misuse, and Bias*. IGI Global., DOI: 10.4018/979-8-3373-0122-8.ch008

Suleiman, A. D., Hou, D., Liu, Y., DeWaters, J., Shepherd, D. C., & Souza, J. G. D. (2025). Systematic Literature Review on Project-Based Learning in Computing Education. *ACM Transactions on Computing Education*, *25*(4), 1–53. DOI: 10.1145/3743684

Sunday, A. O., Agbo, F. J., & Suhonen, J. (2025). Co-Design Pedagogy for Computational Thinking Education in K-12: A Systematic Literature Review. *Technology. Knowledge and Learning*, *30*(1), 63–118. DOI: 10.1007/s10758-024-09765-y

Tariq, R., Aponte Babines, B. M., Ramirez, J., Alvarez-Icaza, I., & Naseer, F. (2025). Computational Thinking in STEM Education: Current State-of-the-Art and Future Research Directions. *Frontiers of Computer Science*, *6*, 1–19. DOI: 10.3389/fcomp.2024.1480404

Tegegn, D. A. (2024). The Role of Science and Technology in Reconstructing Human Social History: Effect of Technology Change on Society. *Cogent Social Sciences, 10*(1), 1–10. DOI: 10.1080/23311886.2024.2356916

Thangaraj, J., Ward, M., & O'Riordan, F. (2023). A Systematic Review of Formative Assessment to Support Students Learning Computer Programming. *4th International Computer Programming Education Conference (ICPEC 2023)*. https://doi.org/DOI: 10.4230/OASIcs.ICPEC.2023.7

Tromp, C., & Baer, J. (2022). Creativity from Constraints: Theory and Applications to Education. *Thinking Skills and Creativity, 46*, 1–11. DOI: 10.1016/j.tsc.2022.101184

Tsai, C.-W., Lee, L., Yu-Ching Lin, M., Cheng, Y.-P., Lin, C.-H., & Tsai, M.-C. (2025). Effects of Integrating Self-Regulation Scaffolding Supported by Chatbot and Online Collaborative Reflection on Students' Learning in an Artificial Intelligence Course. *Computers & Education, 232*, 1–19. DOI: 10.1016/j.compedu.2025.105305

Tubino, L., Cain, A., Schneider, J.-G., Thiruvady, D., & Fernando, N. (2020). Authentic Individual Assessment for Team-Based Software Engineering Projects. *Proceedings of the ACM/IEEE 42nd International Conference on Software Engineering: Software Engineering Education and Training*. https://doi.org/DOI: 10.1145/3377814.3381702

Tucker, M. C., Wang, X., Son, J. Y., & Stigler, J. W. (2024). Prediction Versus Production for Teaching Computer Programming. *Learning and Instruction, 91*, 1–13. DOI: 10.1016/j.learninstruc.2023.101871

von Briesen, E., Dutton, R., Duvall, S., Hutchings, D., Mattfeld, R., & Spurlock, S. (2025). Interventions for Increasing Belonging and Inclusion in Undergraduate Computer Science Classrooms. *Proceedings of the 56th ACM Technical Symposium on Computer Science Education* V. 1. https://doi.org/DOI: 10.1145/3641554.3701941

Xia, L., Wang, L., & Huang, C. (2024). Implementing a Social Presence-Based Teaching Strategy in Online Lecture Learning. *European Journal of Investigation in Health, Psychology and Education, 14*(9), 2580–2597. DOI: 10.3390/ejihpe14090170 PMID: 39329838

Xiao, J., Bozkurt, A., Nichols, M., Pazurek, A., Stracke, C. M., Bai, J. Y. H., & Themeli, C. (2025). Venturing into the Unknown: Critical Insights into Grey Areas and Pioneering Future Directions in Educational Generative AI Research. *TechTrends, 69*, 582–597. DOI: 10.1007/s11528-025-01060-6

Xu, Z., Zhao, Y., Liew, J., Zhou, X., & Kogut, A. (2023). Synthesizing Research Evidence on Self-Regulated Learning and Academic Achievement in Online and Blended Learning Environments: A Scoping Review. *Educational Research Review*, *39*, 1–17. DOI: 10.1016/j.edurev.2023.100510

Yeni, S., Grgurina, N., Saeli, M., Hermans, F., Tolboom, J., & Barendsen, E. (2024). Interdisciplinary Integration of Computational Thinking in K-12 Education: A Systematic Review. *Informatics in Education*, *23*(1), 223–278. DOI: 10.15388/infedu.2024.08

Zarestky, J., Bigler, M., Brazile, M., Lopes, T., & Bangerth, W. (2022). Reflective Writing Supports Metacognition and Self-regulation in Graduate Computational Science and Engineering. *Computers and Education Open*, *3*, 1–12. DOI: 10.1016/j.caeo.2022.100085

Zhou, C., & Zhang, W. (2024). Computational Thinking (CT) towards Creative Action: Developing a Project-Based Instructional Taxonomy (PBIT) in AI Education. *Education Sciences*, *14*(2), 1–14. DOI: 10.3390/educsci14020134

KEY TERMS AND DEFINITIONS

Active Learning: An instructional approach that engages students in the learning process through meaningful activities, reflection, and collaboration.

Computing Education: The field of study and practice concerned with teaching and learning the principles, processes, and applications of computing.

Computer Science: The systematic study of computation, algorithms, and information processing, encompassing the theory, design, and application of computer systems.

Equitable Education: A framework for ensuring that all learners, regardless of background or circumstance, have fair access to the resources, opportunities, and support.

Interdisciplinary Learning: An educational approach that integrates concepts, methods, and perspectives from multiple disciplines to deepen understanding, foster creativity, and enable learners to address complex real-world problems through connected knowledge.

Pedagogical Innovation: The intentional development and application of novel teaching approaches, tools, or frameworks that enhance learning effectiveness and engagement.

Teaching Strategies: Structured methods and techniques employed by educators to facilitate learning, foster critical thinking, and adapt instruction to diverse learner needs and contexts.

Chapter 2

Interdisciplinary Approaches in Computer Science Teaching:

Foundations, Integration, and Transformation of Education

Qurrotul Aini
https://orcid.org/0000-0002-2722-4755
UIN Syarif Hidayatullah Jakarta, Indonesia

Fitroh Fitroh
UIN Syarif Hidayatullah Jakarta, Indonesia

ABSTRACT

This section highlights the importance of an interdisciplinary approach in teaching Computer Science (CS). This approach integrates various disciplines such as social sciences, mathematics, and technology to create holistic learning that is relevant to complex real-world challenges. An integrated curriculum model guides students in understanding the relationships between concepts from various fields, thereby increasing their engagement and deepening their understanding. This approach also encourages character and competency development, as well as supporting innovation in solving social and environmental problems. Although it offers many benefits, interdisciplinary implementation requires careful planning and sufficient resources, as well as addressing concerns related to technical depth. Overall, this approach is key to preparing graduates who are able to face global dynamics and advance the field of computer science in a sustainable manner.

DOI: 10.4018/979-8-3373-6546-6.ch002

INTRODUCTION

The rapid evolution of technology demands that Computer Science (CS) education transcends its traditional technical boundaries to address complex socio-technical challenges. While the value of interdisciplinary approaches is widely acknowledged, a critical gap persists between theoretical advocacy and the practical, evidence-based guidance needed for curriculum design. This chapter addresses this gap by providing a critical, structured analysis of interdisciplinary curriculum models specifically for CS education. Its primary contribution is a novel analytical framework that synthesizes, contrasts, and critiques five integrated curriculum models (Shared, Webbed, Integrated, Sequenced, and Threaded) within the authentic context of CS. Moving beyond descriptive aggregation, this chapter argues for a contextual and critical selection of models, driven by clear pedagogical objectives rather than trends. The analysis is grounded in a structured narrative review of literature and offers practical insights for educators and curriculum developers seeking to implement interdisciplinary CS education with rigor and depth.

The teaching of CS uses interdisciplinary approaches, which involve the incorporation of ideas or techniques from different areas for the enhancement of comprehension, interpretation, or application of computational ideas. Teaching or learning CS, for instance, will be made even more beneficial with the following explanation on the definition, scope, or application of the teaching principle. To have a well-rounded view of technology, its impacts, and its implementations, the field of CS uses an interdisciplinary method involving notions from different areas, including economics, neuroscience, philosophy, or psychology (Mishra & Siy, 2020). This leads to better comprehension of computing systems, with greater stress on the integration of theoretical notions with practical implementations (Krüger et al., 2024).

The interdisciplinary approach provides the students with complex, interest-driven problems, hence increasing their involvement in the study of CS, especially those from disadvantaged backgrounds (Happe & Marquardt, 2023). The interdisciplinary approach also leads to cooperation between different disciplines, for example, the merging of law with technology to create programs that equip the current workforce with the necessary skills required in the current work environment (Otoyo et al., 2022). Socio-scientific problems, as well as the enhancement of computer science educational methodologies, are explored in the interdisciplinary approach (Lorenzo, 2020).

MAIN FOCUS OF THE CHAPTER

The interdisciplinary approach provides significant advantages, a robust academic discourse must also acknowledge its documented critiques and challenges. Scholars have raised substantive concerns that the breadth required may come at the expense of technical depth, potentially diluting the core algorithmic and systems competencies that define the discipline (Heikkinen & Räisänen, 2018). Others caution that without careful pedagogical design, interdisciplinary courses risk fostering superficial understanding across multiple domains rather than cultivating deep mastery in one (Kuzmenko et al., 2024). Furthermore, significant logistical and structural barriers, such as departmental silos, misaligned faculty incentives, and complex assessment methods, often impede effective implementation (Klein, 2010; Mansilla & Duraising, 2007). Acknowledging these potential shortcomings is not a rejection of interdisciplinarity but a necessary precondition for its rigorous and effective integration into CS curricula, which is the central focus of this chapter's analytical framework. Therefore, this chapter focus on integrated curriculum models (Shared, Webbed, Integrated, Sequenced, Threaded) within the CS context. This framework not only describes but also critiques their implementation, supporting evidence, and suitability for various contemporary CS education objectives. Consequently, the central argument of this chapter is that the selection and implementation of such models must be contextual and critical, driven by clear research questions regarding disciplinary integration rather than by trends alone.

LITERATURE REVIEW

The essence of the approach is to equip learners with context-related knowledge of ideas, which will be beneficial in solving practical problems (Sharma & Shukla, 2023; Pouso et al., 2020). Contextual relevance emphasizes understanding phenomena within their social, economic, or legal contexts to ensure solutions apply to real-life issues (Anatoly, 2024; Parshyna et al., 2022). Also, methodological diversity allows for a wider perspective by employing various methodologies (Parshyna et al., 2022).

To tackle complex problems effectively or enhance learning outcomes, there are many salient aspects or components of the interdisciplinary approach, but the vital parts are: (1) Knowledge synthesis, the integration of theoretical and practical knowledge acquired in interdisciplinary studies (Kuzmenko et al., 2022); (2) Collaborative learning, wherein students, teachers, and the learners are required to work collaboratively (Nugraha et al., 2024; Shepitko et al., 2023); (3) Real-life problem-solving, which promotes the application of their knowledge by the students in real-life situations (Nugraha et al., 2024); and (4) Interdisciplinary studies help students gain diverse learning outcomess (Holley, 2024).

In educational contexts, the interdisciplinary approach uses knowledge from different fields to create well-rounded educational methodologies and curriculum structures. Problem-based learning (PjBL) is one of the learning approaches often used in an interdisciplinary curriculum design. The main advantage of these approaches is that the students are able to participate actively in the process by solving real-life problems (Retscher et al., 2024; Gabela & Retscher, 2023). The interdisciplinary approach links knowledge, skills, and principles from different disciplines, hence facilitating the advancement of broad skills. The approach can be used both horizontally between disciplines of similar levels of study or vertically between disciplines of different levels of study (Avram, 2024).

The essence of interdisciplinarity lies in epistemological integration, the synthesis of methods, perspectives, and knowledge from two or more disciplines to generate new understanding or solutions that transcend the boundaries of a single field. While Project-Based Learning (PBL) or soft skills instruction often serve as effective vehicles for interdisciplinary work, they are not synonymous with it. A computer science project that includes a presentation (communication) remains monodisciplinary if it does not integrate frameworks from another discipline (e.g., sociology or design) into the core of its computational problem-solving. This chapter focuses on the substantive integration of knowledge, rather than solely on collaborative teaching methods.

An interdisciplinary approach is vital for the development and instruction of CS in the current complex world. This is because the approach promotes innovation, hence its usefulness in solving different problems since the approach brings different aspects of knowledge from different disciplines. Interdisciplinary approaches improve the understanding of computational systems by gathering information from different areas, including philosophy, neuroscience, or social sciences (Krüger et al., 2024; Mishra & Siy, 2020).Through the integration, there is improved comprehension of the bigger picture surrounding technology, which helps the students be better equipped for practical real-world problems, which mostly involve different aspects or viewpoints (Petrova & Vasichkina, 2021).

Combination degree programs involving CS with other areas of study have also proven successful in encouraging the involvement of minorities, including women, by relating these studies to practical problems from the world around them. The application of diverse study programs to engage more students in studying CS can lead to greater involvement, including diversity, in the field of CS (Happe & Marquardt, 2023). The solutions required in the contemporary environment must be grounded in the social and moral realms, implying the involvement of different fields in joint cooperation(Walker, 2017). In situations involving complexity, relying on reductionist methods is unlikely to provide the necessary solutions, so the application of holistic thinking implies the possibility of efficient, creative solutions (Krüger et al., 2024).

The integration of different domains, such as art, science, or engineering, will result in advanced computational work, novel ideas (Benedicenti et al., 2013).Interdisciplinary computer science will also help ensure that technological developments are linking with the needs of society by developing just rules for the future (Vasichkina & Petrova, 2021). Research has also disclosed the fact that the well-rounded approach involving different domains delivers greater scientific impact, which will help policymakers (Chakraborty, 2018).

METHODS

This section employs a structured narrative review methodology to examine interdisciplinary approaches in CS education. The review is designed to synthesize current knowledge, identify trends, and present conceptual and practical models for integrating interdisciplinary strategies into CS curricula. The methodological process consisted of three main phases: literature identification and selection, thematic analysis, and synthesis and model development.

Literature Search and Selection Criteria

A literature search was conducted using academic databases including IEEE Xplore, ACM Digital Library, SpringerLink, Scopus, and Google Scholar. Keywords and phrases such as "interdisciplinary computer science education," "integrated curriculum model," "CS and mathematics integration," "project-based learning in CS," and "ethics in CS education" were used to identify relevant publications. The search was limited to peer-reviewed articles, conference proceedings, book chapters, and institutional reports published between 2002 and 2025, with an emphasis on recent studies (2020–2025) to ensure contemporary relevance. A total of 87 references were included, selected based on their contribution to theoretical frameworks, curriculum models, case studies, or empirical findings related to interdisciplinary CS education.

Thematic Analysis and Framework Development

The selected literature was analyzed using a thematic content analysis approach. Initial coding identified recurring themes such as curriculum integration models, skill development, ethical considerations, and interdisciplinary partnerships. These themes were then organized into a coherent conceptual framework that structures the chapter into five core sections: (1) Foundations of Interdisciplinary Approaches,

(2) Urgency in Modern CS, (3) Connections with Other Disciplines, (4) Integrated Curriculum Models, and (5) Current Trends. Within each theme, sub-themes such as "shared model," "webbed model," and "threaded model" were extracted and illustrated with case studies drawn from the literature.

Case Study Compilation and Comparative Analysis

To enhance practical relevance, exemplary case studies were extracted from the literature and synthesized into comparative tables (Tables 2–6 in the chapter). Each case study was analyzed based on its interdisciplinary focus, implementation process, advantages, and challenges. This comparative approach allows for a nuanced understanding of how different interdisciplinary models operate in varied educational contexts, from higher education to vocational training.

RESULTS AND DISCUSSION

Education 4.0 refers to a higher education model, which proposes novel learning processes, innovative tools, and intelligence infrastructure enabled by Information and Communication Technology (ICT), which aims at improving the knowledge-generation and knowledge-transfer process (Miranda et al., 2021). The goal of Education 4.0 is to equip and generate highly competent future working professionals, competent enough to make use of available resources, both human and technological, to provide novel solutions to the modern challenges faced by society.

The integrated curriculum model can be fragmented, loosely connected, nested, as well as other categories (Khozin et al., 2021). The approach can be utilized based on a blend combined with religious values, characters, as well as computational thinking. The approach has been supported by Halimah (2018),as well as (Marifah (2022). Meanwhile, the development of the integrated model on the subject of the role of the laboratory is equally significant, especially within the context of computer science. The respective laboratory involves a research & development/final project lab. Additionally, it can be combined with entrepreneurship characters' teaching & training, where not only knowledge is gained but actual experiences in the respective areas are gained as well, opening a related venture according to their interests (Basti, 2022). The paradigm shifts as it attempts to produce graduates having characters as well as competence, focusing on having a noble character & competence as well, as written in the explanation from Abelha et al. (2020). Figure 1 presents an original conceptual model developed for this chapter to synthesize the core components of an integrated CS curriculum.

Figure 1. Integrated Model of Computer Science Curriculum

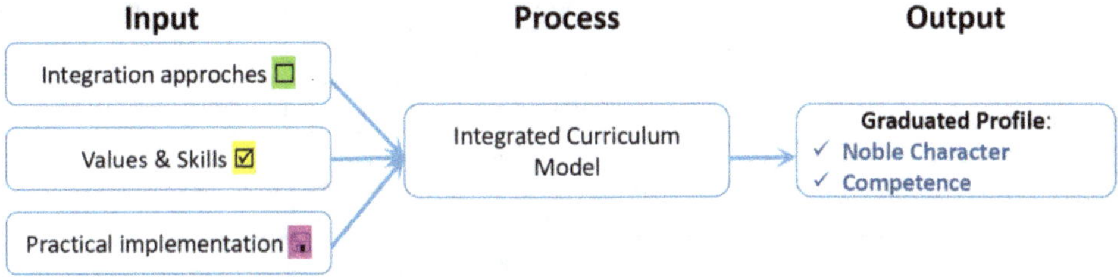

Implementation and Integrated Model in Computer Science Curriculum

Establishing an integrated curriculum model in Computer Science requires the combination of subjects such as Mathematics, Business Ethics, Social Sciences, and Philosophy. Currently, this integration in higher education is nascent and faces challenges like lecturer expertise and curriculum structure. However, it can be achieved through lecturer training, development of materials, and sound policy formulation. Under the integrated curriculum model for Computer Science, specifically the model of an Integrated Science discipline, there are five sub-models, namely shared, webbed, integrated, sequenced, and threated (Winarno et al., 2020; Fogarty & Pete, 2009). Table 1 is adapted from the foundational taxonomy of integrated curriculum models by Fogarty & Pete (2009), reinterpreted and specifically contextualized within the domain of Computer Science by the authors.

Table 1. Interdisciplinary Models of CS Curriculum

No.	Dimension	Model	Description	Design
1	Two or more disciplines	Shared	Collaborative planning occurs in two fields where intersecting thoughts or ideas arise as fundamental components.	
2		Webbed	The thematic approach to integrating topic matter is represented by curricula that are built on the web.	
3		Integrated	The integrated curricular model represents a cross-disciplinary approach similar to the shared model.	
4		Sequenced	Topic or units of study are rearranged and sequenced to coincide with one another. Similar ideas are taught in concert while remaining separate subjects.	
5		Threaded	Standard, thinking skills, social skills, graphic organizers, technology, and a multiple intelligences approach to learning thread through all disciplines.	

Shared model in CS

The shared model curriculum in CS, within higher education, can be referred to as an approach increasingly being implemented today, looking forward to a collaborative relationship between higher education establishments and industries. The idea of shared curriculum models within computer science involves a range of collaborative, integrated, and shared curriculum developments. Recent curriculum changes in computer science reflect a trend towards flexibility, emphasizing the integration of student and industry needs. This was highlighted in a review by Price et al. (2021), which identifies community development as a key component in implementing inquiry-based curriculum development. In a shared model curriculum, overlapping concepts from two other subjects are used as organizers for learning. The idea involves lecturers from two distinct subjects, such as two lecturers from computer science and philosophy, working on a collaborative, joint learning process based on the concept of organizing ideas from both subjects, teaching these concepts from both subjects in a combined approach. For example, two subjects, Computer Science and Ethics (Philosophy), are brought together using a shared model curriculum approach. The topic of interest lies within "Ethics in the Development of AI Systems," while the corresponding courses would be Computer Science, Technology Ethics, and Philosophy. The shared concepts would involve algorithmic fairness, privacy, AI accountability, along with AI System Biases.

Meanwhile, Kumar et al. (2023) have proposed a Combined Knowledge & Competency model, integrating knowledge domains & competency frameworks, specifically for the Computer Science curriculum. Prihantoro (2021) discusses the wheeler-model based curriculum development process within Learning Management Systems, focusing on government policy compliance & demands within the context of vocational education. The case study proposed by Wahyuni et al. (2022) on English instruction within Computer Science relates to the PROSPER learning model, encompassing competencies in system thinking, critical thinking, & collaboration & project development phases. The discussion on constructivist learning processes as flexible curriculum design, aiming for & dealing with variances in implementation is investigated by Muslimin et al. (2022). All these studies show that shared curriculum models in computer science pull together different educational frameworks, use competency-based methods, encourage students to work together, and offer flexible ways to put things into practice. The goal is to meet the wide range of needs from both education and the tech industry.

The implementation of the shared model curriculum in Indonesian higher education differs across institutions. At Indraprasta PGRI University, the project-learning model is applied in the Information Technology program for first-semester students, allowing flexibility in the learning process. Literature analysis indicates that this shared model positively influences learning outcomes in integrated science, improving students' understanding, skills, and literacy in science (Juriyah, 2021; Lestari & Brahma, 2025).

The shared model promotes interdisciplinary integration in Computer Science (CS) by leveraging overlapping concepts, though its application requires strong evidence. The accompanying case studies are more illustrative than empirical, revealing a lack of longitudinal studies that confirm the model's effectiveness in enhancing students' understanding of both disciplines. Additionally, the model may result in superficial learning if integration is only thematic and lacks disciplinary depth. Its success hinges on genuine and sustained collaboration among lecturers from various fields. The main focus, case studies, advantages, and disadvantages of the shared model are synthesized in Table 2 (an original comparative analysis constructed by the authors based on the literature review and conceptual framework of this chapter).

Table 2. Shared Model in Computer Science

Main Focus
Using the same concept or idea as a link between disciplines allows students to perceive a direct and profound connection between the fields. The teaching and learning processes of both disciplines are combined simultaneously, typically through integrated teaching planning and implementation. Identifying and elaborating on the overlaps or connections between key concepts from both disciplines enhances students' understanding of cross-field interrelationships.
Case Study 1
Development of a Data Security System in Software Development **Shared concept**: "Data Security" as the main theme, involving the fields of computer science, mathematics, ethics, and social sciences. **Implementation:** Mathematics: Learn about encryption and decryption algorithms, as well as number theory. Information Technology: Programming security systems and data encryption. Ethics: Discussion about privacy, user rights, and legal regulations regarding personal data. Social: Analyze the social impact of data security on society. **Visible advantages:** Students not only learn how to code encryption but also understand the importance of data security in society. They are able to see the relationship between mathematical concepts, technology, and social aspects. **Potential weaknesses:** Lack of focus clarity without good management. Some students may find it difficult to understand all aspects at once due to their complexity.
Case Study 2
Applying machine learning techniques on sentiment analysis thru social media. Shared concept: "Sentiment analysis" as the main theme, involving the fields of data science, AI/Machine Learning, Language and Linguistic, IT, Psychology. **Implementation:** Data Science: Data processing, feature extraction techniques, and statistical analysis. Artificial Intelligence/Machine Learning: Sentiment classification modeling using machine learning or deep learning algorithms. Language and Linguistics: Dive into natural language analysis (NLP), text processing, figuring out what words really mean and the context behind them. Computer Science/Information Technology: Build systems, work with data processing algorithms, and actually put together the software needed to analyze all this stuff. Psychology and Communication: Understanding the interpretation of emotions, attitudes, and perceptions revealed from sentiment. Sociology and Social Sciences: Explore how society shapes public opinion and tracks the bigger trends in how people feel. **Potential weaknesses:** ● Coordinating different disciplines demands effective communication as well as resource management. ● NLP is still having some difficulty processing slang, emoticons, and other informal language. ● The data has to be adequate for a valid analysis. ● Not all teams or organizations have expertise in all areas being considered. In fact, contextually as well as culturally, interpreting sentiment can be quite difficult.

continued on following page

Table 2. Continued

Main Focus	
Advantages	**Disadvantages**
Strong integration of concepts to enhance understanding between disciplines since topics are treated across different disciplines, enabling clearer understanding of inter-disciplinary relationships. The method promotes interdisciplinary thinking since it encourages students to acknowledge interrelations between subjects, thus developing their holistic problem-solving skills. The linked concepts are easily adaptable to other areas due to possible skill/knowledge translation. Fostering interdisciplinary collaboration to teach students to collaboratively work together and value expertise not only in other disciplines but across disciplines. Enhancing the contextual understanding of learning in a real-world context with the intention to raise students' motivation and interest in learning.	The complex planning arising out of the integration of diverse disciplines requires mature planning together with effective collaboration between lecturers drawn from diverse disciplines. Potential for overlap or redundancy if not carefully planned—overlapping topics can result in confusion or redundancy. Constraints related to time and resources become challenges when integrating curricula in diverse disciplines to enable them to support one another. Evaluating its capability to measure inter-disciplinary understanding can pose a challenge since it encompasses more intricacies compared to normal evaluations. Those who are used to conventional methods in teaching or are studying in these faculties might show reluctance, and students could get confused if too many concepts related to various disciplines are presented simultaneously.

Webbed model in CS

The Webbed (or thematic) model structures learning around a central, broad theme, connecting various sub-disciplines of computer science (e.g., programming, networking, databases) to explore it from multiple technical angles. This model is particularly advocated for its potential to mirror the interconnected nature of real-world technological systems and enhance student engagement through relevance (Efendi, 2021; Saripudin et al., 2020). However, a critical examination reveals significant tensions between its theoretical appeal and practical implementation, especially concerning academic rigor and depth. The main focus, case studies, advantages, and disadvantages of the webbed model are synthesized in Table 3 (an original analytical table developed by the authors to present and critique the webbed model in a CS context).

Table 3. Webbed Model in Computer Science

<table>
<tr><th colspan="2">Main Focus</th></tr>
<tr><td colspan="2">Integrates various sub-disciplines and concepts in computer science through themes that touch on many areas.
Through this approach, learning does not simply focus on one area (e.g., algorithms alone) but links various topics such as programming, networking, database systems, robotics, etc., simultaneously.
A webbed curriculum aims to visualize the "network" among different concepts and fields, illustrating their relationships and how they interact in real contexts.</td></tr>
<tr><th colspan="2">Case Study 1</th></tr>
<tr><td colspan="2">Online Application Development for E-Commerce System

Description:
Students build a complete e-commerce system, which includes:
Web programming (frontend & backend): user interface, transaction logic.
Database: store products, users, transactions.
Information security: data encryption, user authentication.
Network and infrastructure: data transmission over the internet, access speed optimization.
Data Analytics: process datatransaction for business analytics.

Approach:
All these concepts are studied and developed simultaneously, closely related and complementary, in one whole integrative project.</td></tr>
<tr><th colspan="2">Case Study 2</th></tr>
<tr><td colspan="2">Development of a Data-Driven Application to Improve Energy Management in Schools

Project Description: The project involved designing an application that combines data concerning energy use in schools. The app's goal is to enable schools to conserve energy and promote sustainability.

Areas of science involved in the webbed model:
Computer science/IT: include data collection using sensors, processing, application development, user interface design, data analysis.
Mathematic/Statistics: Data pattern analysis, predictive modeling, and results interpretation.
Environmental science/sustainability: An understanding of renewable energy resources, conservation methods, and ecological effects that result from energy use.
Social science/education: Awareness campaigns, communication, and educational activities to engage the school community.
Engineering science/IoT (Internet of Things): Utilization of sensors or hardware components to monitor energy automatically.</td></tr>
<tr><th>Advantages</th><th>Disadvantages</th></tr>
<tr><td>Student are acquiring skills to enable them to incorporate their knowledge of field relationships into forming well-rounded solutions.
Describing or reflecting real-world relationships in which there are interdependencies amongst a variety of concepts or technology.
Emphasis needs to lie in developing understanding and insight into concepts, not merely to master a domain.
Encouraging creativity and innovation in students so that they learn to merge different concepts to come up with new solutions.</td><td>An integrated approach to a diverse curriculum calls for planning.
There are occasions when areas need to be explored in detail in limited periods of study.
Teachers are expected to possess expertise to teach more than one discipline.
If not well designed, students can feel confused by the sheer number of topics and relationships that must be understood at once.</td></tr>
</table>

Integrated model in CS

The Integrated model represents the most ambitious approach to interdisciplinary curricula, aiming not merely to connect but to fuse distinct disciplines into a unified, holistic framework of knowledge. In Computer Science, this model seeks to dissolve traditional boundaries, creating learning experiences where concepts from, for example, software engineering, ethics, and social science are inseparable in addressing complex socio-technical problems. This pursuit of deep synthesis is its core theoretical justification, aligning with contemporary calls for graduates who can navigate the intertwined ethical, social, and technical dimensions of technology (ACM, 2023; Khozin et al., 2023). Al Mahdiyin et al. (2025) showed that an integrated curriculum can combine Quranic learning, religious obligations, and science/technology using problem-based learning and computational thinking to optimize understanding of Islamic values as well as mathematical and digital skills. The main focus, case studies, advantages, and disadvantages of the integrated model are synthesized in Table 4 (an original synthesis created for this chapter, integrating theoretical justification with a critical case study analysis).

Table 4. Integrated Model in Computer Science

Main Focus
Connects various concepts and related fields of science in an integrated learning sequence. This approach emphasizes the importance of seeing connections and relationships between fields, such as technology, mathematics, and other sciences, so that students are able to understand the application of concepts holistically and contextually in the real world.
Case Study 1
Development of Network Security Detection and Recommendation System Using Machine Learning and Social Science Problem description: Network security is becoming a vital aspect for organizations. Students majoring in computer science were asked to develop a system capable of automatically detecting network security threats and providing prevention recommendations based on user behavior analysis. **Scientific area involvement:** Computer Science (Technology and Programming): Development of malware and cyberattack detection algorithms using machine learning. Mathematics (Statistics and Data Analysis): Network traffic data analysis, statistical model building to recognize threat patterns. Social Sciences (Psychology and User Behavior): Identifying user behavior which could pose a security risk and developing strategies to educate users.

continued on following page

Table 4. Continued

Main Focus	
Advantages	**Disadvantages**
The understanding that there are interrelationships between concepts across disciplines increases understanding and retention. This approach helps to train students in developing critical and creative thinking skills. It becomes more applicable because learning connects theoretical knowledge with practical applications..	Requires complex planning efforts because it has to involve coordination between various disciplines. May need increased resources. May involve joint planning between teachers. Can make it challenging to organize a curriculum that needs to address so many facets in a short period.

Sequenced model in CS

The sequenced model structures interdisciplinary topics in computer science curricula chronologically, balancing cognitive load and foundational learning. It ensures students grasp core concepts in one domain, such as data structures, before integrating them with others, like software engineering. The model is also adaptable to new technologies, with the 2023 Curriculum introducing Ethics in AI and Quantum Computing into its advanced pathway. The main focus, case studies, advantages, and disadvantages of the sequence model are synthesized in Table 5 (an original comparative framework developed by the authors, highlighting the structured logic and inherent trade-offs of the sequenced model).

Table 5. Sequenced Model in Computer Science

Main Focus
It structures learning materials in a sequence but not necessarily in an orderly fashion since each step or level of learning builds or relies on pre-existing experience/knowledge. This approach greatly stresses that learning itself should take place in a definite or specific sequence, like learning basic concepts first before advancing to more complex learnings.
Case Study 1
Learning Algorithms and Data Structures **Background:** In a university setting, for example, the computer science program used a model sequence approach to ensure that prior to advancing into complex development processes for applications or systems, students must first comprehensively learn algorithm basics or data structure basics. In other words, developing complex applications or systems starts after students learn algorithm basics or data structure basics. **Stages of Implementation:** Semester 1 - Algorithm Fundamentals: At this point, the student develops skills to interpret basic algorithms like sorting algorithms or searching algorithms. Also introduced here are algorithms' concepts like time complexity or space complexity. Semester 2 - Basic Data Structures: With a basic understanding of algorithm concepts, basic data structures like arrays, linked lists, stacks, and queues are introduced to the students. Programming exercises are prescribed for implementing these structures. Semester 3 - Advanced Algorithms and Complex Data Structures: At this stage, topics related to trees, graphs, efficient searches, sorts, recursion & dynamic programming are introduced. Semester 4 - The subjects are integrated with software development, for example creating apps using data structures and algorithms studied previously. The technique of sequencing is applicable in this situation because: ● It allows students to completely understand basic concepts before applying them to real-world situations ● When you've become proficient with one skill level, you can proceed to learn another. ● The data has become easier to interpret since it has been arranged in a logical manner.
Case Study 2

continued on following page

Table 5. Continued

<table>
<tr><th colspan="2">Main Focus</th></tr>
<tr><td colspan="2">Learning Operating Systems

Background:
In the university, the computer science course employs a sequenced model method to teach fundamental concepts in operating systems. The method seeks to ensure that basic concepts are understood before proceeding to learn complex details. As a result, there is effective understanding of the entire system architecture of an operating system.

Implementation:
Semester 1 - Basic Concepts of Computer Systems: Computer architecture, hardware basics, interactions between hardware and software.
Semester 2 - Introduction to Operating Systems: The topic includes basic functions related to an operating system like processes, memory management, and process scheduling.
Semester 3 - File Management & File Systems: Students learn about file system organization, file management, and related access & security mechanisms. It's an extension topic related to Processes & Memory.
Semester 4 - Process Synchronization and Troubleshooting: This topic constructs knowledge related to synchronization, deadlock, and resources based on prior knowledge related to processes and memory.

Benefits of the sequenced approach in this case:
● Students master the basic concepts of computer systems and processes first, before moving on to file management and process synchronization.
● Each stage helps form a foundation for understanding more complex mechanisms in operating systems.
● Students gradually and systematically enhance their analytical and problem-solving skills.</td></tr>
<tr><th>Advantages</th><th>Disadvantages</th></tr>
<tr><td>Assist in understanding the levels involved in learning, from basic to advanced. These enable students to learn in a systemized manner.
In a specific sequence, students are able to learn basic concepts like algorithms, data structures, computational theory, and so forth before advancing to more complex projects like system development or artificial intelligence.
Lecturers are able to organize learning materials in a way that guarantees completion of each step before proceeding to deliver the subsequent material.</td><td>This model could restrict creativity or innovation because it's based too much on a preplanned sequence. Students who are proficient in a particular area are not allowed to innovate or create due to holding to a set sequence.
This model does not possess enough flexibility to accommodate curricula according to interest areas of students. It can create a barrier to developing skills to a deeper extent.
As being too sequential, this model does not quite favor interdisciplinary integration or large project-based learning that needs flexibility to address diverse disciplines together.</td></tr>
</table>

Threaded model in CS

The model based on a thread in computer science education poses a methodology involving competency development based on a continuous skill set that encompasses various dimensions related to competency. It integrates skills and concepts, such as problem solving, logic, algorithms, and technology applications by embedding and reinforcing them iteratively through various learning activities and contexts (Fogarty & Pete, 2009). The threaded model focuses on three main approaches: (1) integrating competencies and concepts to help students see connections within computer science; (2) emphasizing repetition and reinforcement of concepts through diverse learning experiences like projects and discussions; and (3) utilizing strategies that promote deep, contextual understanding instead of isolated learning. The main focus, case studies, advantages, and disadvantages of the threaded model are synthesized in Table 6 (an original summary table constructed by the authors to elucidate the continuous integration aims and practical challenges of the threaded model).

Table 6. Threaded Model in Computer Science

Main Focus
It connects concepts and skills continuously so that students' understanding becomes more coherent and can be applied flexibly in various situations. Thus, the threaded model aims to create deep, integrated, and continuous learning in the computer science curriculum.
Case Study 1
Interactive educational app development Description: Students are placed in an educational app development project aimed at improving math learning for children. This project requires students to synthesize knowledge and abilities across a number of computer science areas and other related disciplines. **Implementation:** Programming concepts: Students learn to code using an appropriate programming language (e.g., Python or JavaScript) to create an attractive and functional interface. Database development: They design and manage databases to store questions, scores, and user information. User Experience (UX) Design: Students learn about ergonomics and design principles to create user-friendly and aesthetically pleasing applications. Math and educational content: Math-related content provided includes math concepts that are age-appropriate to cater to numerical or logical-based questioning. Learning objectives: The objectives are not merely to learn a set of skills to apply to software development but to learn design and pedagogy. The aim is to learn these concepts simultaneously. Benefits: This method encourages the student to realize how closely related software development techniques are to educational theories and user design experiences. At the same time, skills involving interdisciplinary thinking are fostered.
Case Study 2

continued on following page

Table 6. Continued

Main Focus	
Creating an interactive learning application using augmented reality (AR) technology Description: The groups formed by the students are assigned the task to design and develop an educational application using augmented reality technology that can improve the learning experience for students in the field of human anatomy. **Implementation:** AR technology: Students are taught AR technology like Unity3D, Vuforia, ARKit, or ARCore. Educational content design: They merge knowledge in human anatomy, which comes from biology and medicine, with graphic design. Software development: Students build and design an application which displays rotating models of 3D human organs. Data integration and interaction: They use programming logic to guide interactions so that data integration occurs naturally. Ethical and privacy aspects: Issues related to data privacy for users are discussed, along with ethical considerations related to developing highly advanced technology-based educational instruments. **Learning objectives:** The project requires understanding and integrating numerous areas of knowledge—AR technology, human biology, design skills, and programming. The threading method utilized in teaching makes possible simultaneous learning or integration of knowledge.	
Advantages	**Disadvantages**
This model makes possible competency development in a holistic manner. Students are allowed to see inter-relationships between concepts and skills. It's possible because "the concept of prediction" can be applied to math problems, science education, or reading tasks. There are numerous other concepts like prediction. This model promotes an understanding between interlinked concepts in a holistic manner. It increases the critical thinking skills of the students since they are made to learn multiple concepts together.	The implementation of this model needs meticulous planning. It is not possible to achieve integration without planning. In fact, there should not only be integration but collaboration amongst teachers belonging to various disciplines. Evaluation of competency attainment in an integrated and sustainable manner can pose a challenge because merely testing mastery of concepts is insufficient but determining a student's integration capacities in a collective sense is crucial.

A synthesized overview of strategic implementation considerations for each model is presented in Table 7 (adapted and expanded from Fogarty & Pete (2009) with additional strategic layers and challenges specific to Computer Science education, as identified in this review).

Table 7. Strategy and Challenge

Model	Strategy	Challenge
Shared	Begin with areas in which concepts can be gradually integrated. Teachers and lecturers should team up for planning relevant teaching resources to be shared.	Avoid fragmentation by ensuring regular communication and synchronization.
Integrated	Using a thematic and concept-based approach that connects different disciplines within the department. Involving cross-functional teams to develop interconnected and non-overlapping curricula.	Designing an integration that doesn't complicate the learning process, using flexible planning strategies, and regularly supporting interagency collaboration.
Webbed	Utilizing a broad theme that crosses various topics from different sub-disciplines, with the theme serving as the main framework.	Preventing confusion and maintaining the relevance of the theme so it doesn't become too broad, ensuring it remains focused and directed.
Threaded	Identifying "big ideas" and integrating them through meta-thinking to continuously thread concepts across subjects. It involves simultaneously focusing on developing thinking and social skills.	Ensure all parties understand and can identify the big ideas, and manage the extensive material to avoid confusion.
Sequenced	Organizing the learning sequence in a logical and progressive manner, with a focus on interdependent relationships between learning units. Organizing a work schedule that suits the developmental needs of the students.	Avoiding rigidity in the sequence while maintaining flexibility to dynamically adjust to learning needs.

Trends in Interdisciplinary Approaches to Computer Science Education

Higher education in computer science is shifting from a solely technical skill development focus towards an interdisciplinary approach, addressing job market demands. Recent studies highlight the importance of training graduates in programming and problem-solving across various fields, including digital humanities, bioinformatics, computational finance, and digital arts. This adaptation involves creating a collaborative curriculum and project-based education to foster innovation at the intersection of computer science and other disciplines, ensuring graduates are prepared for a technology-driven future.

Various studies have informed the development of computer science curricula. Greenberg & Rague (2022), for example, studied a teaching model which combined computational thinking with artistic materials like the performing arts. In addition to these studies, there are teaching experiences along with the benefits arising from linking artistic subjects to computer science that could increase creativity skills in computer science students. Cri an et al. (2023) introduced an interdisciplinary curriculum within computer science using embedded entrepreneurship education (EEE), proving that its implementation in computer science education should focus on project-based learning aligned with stakeholder collaboration. Some case studies show that using computer science education based on embedded EEE usually implements competency-based or hybrid demand-competence pedagogies. These are largely focused on complex problem-solving tasks, creating real-world products, or industry collaboration. Nonetheless, challenges to its implementation lie in the burden imposed upon students to undertake additional education or training to achieve these objectives. Also, there remains some concern to make these education-related concepts converge with computer science professionalization. Thus, DM includes consecutive implementation to attain organizational-level goals (Doboli et al., 2010), or address specific community-wide needs (Arias et al., 2018), alongside individual-level achievements.

Holland-Minkley et al. (2025) found that there was a need to strike a balance between national curriculum guidelines and institutional identity as well as specific art education objectives. The interdisciplinary curricula not only encompass technical skills but also cater to developing skills in critical thinking, interdisciplinary collaboration, or social-ethical awareness, depending upon integration with another discipline like art, humanities, or social sciences. The new curriculum involving computer science studies along with other areas of interest can include studying abroad or joint ventures with other parties.

Emphasis on soft skills and ethics

The latest curriculum encompasses not only technical skills but also includes training in soft skills like communication skills, teamwork skills, ethical skills, and social responsibility skills. Ethics in AI, data privacy, sustainability issues are emerging areas (Fincher & Robins, 2019). The need to focus on soft skills like problem-solving skills, teamwork skills, communication skills in higher education for IT students was asserted in another study conducted by Mohammed & Ozdamli (2024). IT graduates are found to fall short in terms of meeting job requirements due to a gap between academic training and expected skills. Based on PRISMA guidelines, a total of 69 papers related to soft skills in HE categorized between 2018 to 2024 were considered for analysis. The result shows that there exists an imperative need to modify curricula based upon a rapidly changing post-Industry 4.0 job market scenario since graduates possess desired technical skills but lack basic soft skills.

Project-based learning and experiential learning

Project-based learning and field experience (internships and industry collaboration) are emerging to become major trends. Students are encouraged to undertake projects related to real-world applications of cutting-edge technologies like AI, IoT, and blockchain. Project-based learning (PBL) assumes paramount significance to integrate theoretical education with industry knowledge in areas like computing. The effectiveness of PBL was assessed using 'Instructional Materials Motivation Survey' and 'Kirkpatrick's model' in a study which helped to improve problem solving skills, application skills, time management skills, and confidence level. Project management, methods of Workflow Strategies, and integrating specific domain knowledge are areas to be worked upon (Alsmadi et al., 2024).

Inclusion and diversity

Curriculum development encompasses inclusivity efforts to raise participation numbers among those groups (females and minorities), consisting of resources that address diverse needs. Increasing inclusivity to attract diverse participation includes strategies like proactive outreach recruitment efforts, cultivating a supportive environment for learning, organizing female/minority-only events or sessions, establishing access to mental or academic assistance. In other words, to improve inclusivity in computer science education:

- There needs to be system-level changes made to recruitment, instruction, and service.
- Humanistic, contextual, and relevant curricula.
- Involvement of teachers, schools, and communities to foster an environment that appreciates diversity.

In doing so, computer science will become more appealing to women and minorities, more creative field with a more positive influence in society (Margolis & Fisher, 2002).

Adaptation to technological developments

The curriculum continues to be updated to incorporate emerging areas like machine learning, data science, cybersecurity, and quantum computing. Research development trends in computing education related to increased emphases in cutting-edge areas like AI, ML, and quantum computing suggest that these areas are rapidly emerging to become highly relevant components in computer education curriculum development and are indicative of being incorporated into knowledge scaling within these curriculum developments to enable staying abreast with technology developments (Apiola et al., 2022).Case studies performed on a PER university illustrated that with curriculum adjustments based on internationalization using ACM/IEEE Computing Curricula guidelines introduced various major impacts like:

a. A rise in the proportion of students coming from lower and middle socioeconomic groups because of changes in the curriculum and improvement in scholarship programs.

b. A decline in dropout rates, where a more structured set of curriculum standards helped to reduce dropouts.

c. A globally uniform curriculum increases inclusivity and retention rates, though there was initial difficulty for less prepared students. Nonetheless, a uniform curriculum based on ACM/IEEE increases attraction to diverse groups and geographic areas. It can thus be concluded that changes in curricula to adapt to technological advancement and global standardization can offer benefits to education quality, inclusivity, and retention.

Online learning and hybrid learning

Online platforms, MOOCs (Massive Open Online Courses), or hybrid learning ecosystems are used to a great extent to make computer science education more accessible. Taking advantage of flexibility in curricula or non-regular semester options benefits those who want to repeat courses or fast track education. Online courses or self-learning modules are added benefits to these flexibility features in a hybrid or online model (Gutierrez-Pachas et al., 2022). Technology integration, innovation in teaching methods, academic strength, or involvement are significant parameters that define or shape hybrid online learning into a practical stepping stone for success (Gudoniene et al., 2025). In variants like online or hybrid teaching models to achieve tracking or assessment for value addition to interested candidates to become better computer science graduates in global markets or ecosystems, there exists an increased need to focus upon formative assessment to evaluate candidates growth or development in satisfactory or acceptable parameters. Emphasis upon online flexibility or motivational induction to reduce initial resistance or apprehensions related to face-to-face interactions enhances deeper 'motivational' participation or interest to address added benefits involving computer science education. Applying or using online teaching or training for ebasis or emergency situation challenges like COVID-19 experiences significant internet or awareness barriers to training or development involving face-to-face interaction status (Gudoniene et al., 2025).

CONCLUSION AND RECOMMENDATION

This chapter has argued that interdisciplinarity in CS education is a pedagogical imperative for preparing students to solve complex world problems. Through a structured review and critical analysis, it has synthesized and evaluated five key curriculum integration models, providing a framework to guide their contextual application rather than prescriptive adoption.

The primary conclusion is that there is no single optimal model. The selection between Shared, Webbed, Integrated, Sequenced, or Threaded approaches must be a strategic one, informed by specific program objectives, student readiness, and institutional capacity. The ultimate goal is to move beyond surface-level thematic connections toward meaningful epistemological integration, where students learn to wield CS knowledge in concert with insights from other disciplines to innovate and critique.

Recommendations

Adopt a phased approach that institutions new to interdisciplinary CS should begin with lower-intensity models (e.g., Sequenced or Shared modules) to build experience and collaboration before attempting Integrated or institution-wide Threaded programs. Also, invest in faculty development with creating dedicated support for educators through learning communities, team-teaching grants, and training focused on interdisciplinary pedagogy and partner-discipline literacy. Next, design evaluations that measure interdisciplinary synthesis, such as complex project portfolios, reflective journals, or assessments co-graded by faculty from different disciplines.

To advance interdisciplinary CS education from a well-intentioned concept to a rigorously evaluated practice, future research must prioritize closing critical evidence gaps through four key avenues: first, conducting longitudinal, empirical studies that track students from interdisciplinary programs into their careers to assess long-term impacts on problem-solving, innovation, and professional identity; second, undertaking controlled, comparative research to evaluate learning outcomes and student experiences across different integration models within similar institutional contexts; third, developing, validating, and disseminating reliable assessment methodologies and rubrics specifically designed to measure interdisciplinary learning outcomes in CS; and finally, investigating the systemic and policy barriers to the scalability of high-integration models, along with actionable strategies for overcoming institutional inertia. By systematically addressing these research priorities, the CS education community can build a robust evidence base to inform and refine effective, scalable interdisciplinary pedagogy.

REFERENCES

Abelha, M., Fernandes, S., Mesquita, D., Seabra, F., & Ferreira-Oliveira, A. T. (2020). Graduate Employability and Competence Development in Higher Education—A Systematic Literature Review using PRISMA. *Sustainability, 12*(15), 5900. Advance online publication. DOI: 10.3390/su12155900

Alsmadi, H., Kandasamy, G., Kafri, A. A., & Zahirah, K. F. (2024). Empowering computing students through multidisciplinary project based learning (PBL): Creating meaningful differences in the real world. *Social Sciences & Humanities Open, 10*, 101180. Advance online publication. DOI: 10.1016/j.ssaho.2024.101180

Apiola, M., López-Pernas, S., & Saqr, M. (2022). The evolving themes of Computing Education Research: Trends, topic models, and emerging research. SSRN *Electronic Journal*. DOI: 10.2139/ssrn.4190583

Arias, E., Barba-Sánchez, V., Carrión, C., & Casado, R. (2018). Enhancing Entrepreneurship education in a Master's Degree in Computer Engineering: A Project-Based Learning approach. *Administrative Sciences, 8*(4), 58. Advance online publication. DOI: 10.3390/admsci8040058

Association for Computing Machinery (ACM). IEEE-Computer Society. (2023). Computer Science Curricula 2023. https://csed.acm.org/wp-content/uploads/2023/03/Version-Beta-v2.pdf

Avram, A. I. (2024). Developing the interest for learning through interdisciplinariness in primary class students. *Studia Universitatis Moldaviae Seria tiin e Ale Educa iei, 9*(169), 176–182. DOI: 10.59295/sum9(169)2024_26

Basti, T. (2022). Model pendidikan karakter kewirausahaan terintegrasi di perguruan tinggi [An integrated entrepreneurial character education model in higher education]. *Prosiding Seminar Nasional Fakultas Tarbiyah Dan Ilmu Keguruan IAIM Sinjai, 1*, 7–14. DOI: 10.47435/sentikjar.v1i0.824

Benedicenti, L., Blachford, D., Chan, C. W., East, A. L. L., Gelowitz, C. M., Huang, G., Paranjape, R., Petty, S., Yao, J., & Yao, Y. (2013). Multidisciplinary approaches to computing. *Canadian Conference on Electrical and Computer Engineering*, 1–8. DOI: 10.1109/CCECE.2013.6567668

Chakraborty, T. (2018). Role of interdisciplinarity in computer sciences: Quantification, impact and life trajectory. *Scientometrics, 114*(3), 1011–1029. DOI: 10.1007/S11192-017-2628-Z

Cri an, E. L., Beleiu, I. N., Salan ă, I., Bordean, O. N., & Bunduchi, R. (2023). Embedding entrepreneurship education in non-business courses: A systematic review and guidelines for practice. *Management Learning*, *55*(4), 553–575. DOI: 10.1177/13505076231169594

Doboli, S., Tang, W., Ramnath, R., Impagliazzo, J., VanEpps, T., Agarwal, A., Romero, R., & Currie, E. H. (2010). Models of entrepreneurship education and its role in increasing creativity, innovation and leadership in computer science and engineering students. *2021 IEEE Frontiers in Education Conference (FIE), 15*, F1B-4. DOI: 10.1109/fie.2010.5673380

Efendi, F. K. (2021). Efektivitas model pembelajaran terpadu tipe webbed berbantuan media teknologi untuk meningkatkan kualitas pembelajaran IPS tema makanan sehat murid sekolah dasar gugus 29 campaga loe kabupaten bantaeng [The effectiveness of the webbed type integrated learning model assisted by technology media to improve the quality of social studies learning on the theme of healthy food for elementary school students in cluster 29 campaga loe bantaeng district]. *Journal of Teacher Education*, *2*(2), 58–65. DOI: 10.3100/jote.v2i2.1464

Fincher, S. A., Blikstein, P., Ko, A. J., Haden, P., Haden, P., Tenenberg, J., Margulieux, L. E., Robins, A. V., Shephard, K., Loui, M. C., Robins, A. V., Krishnamurthi, S., Lancaster, T., Falkner, K., & Lewis, C. M. (2019). *The Cambridge Handbook of Computing Education Research*. Cambridge University Press. DOI: 10.1017/9781108654555

Fogarty, R. J., & Pete, B. M. (2009). How to integrate the curricula. Corwin Press. http://us.corwin.com/en-us/nam/how-to-integratethe-curricula/book229128

Gabela, J. G. F., & Retscher, G. (2023). Interdisciplinary approach to curricula development in geomatics education: erasmus+ lbs2its project. *ISPRS Annals of the Photogrammetry, Remote Sensing and Spatial Information Sciences*, X-5/W1-2023, 19–26. DOI: 10.5194/isprs-annals-x-5-w1-2023-19-2023

Greenberg, J., & Rague, B. (2022). Computational thinking and the humanities: Interdisciplinary collaboration in computer science and theatre design. *INTED Proceedings*, *1*, 1769. Advance online publication. DOI: 10.21125/inted.2022.0530

Gudoniene, D., Staneviciene, E., Huet, I., Dickel, J., Dieng, D., Degroote, J., Rocio, V., Butkiene, R., & Casanova, D. (2025). Hybrid Teaching and Learning in Higher Education: A Systematic Literature review. *Sustainability*, *17*(2), 756. Advance online publication. DOI: 10.3390/su17020756

Gutierrez-Pachas, D. A., Garcia-Zanabria, G., Cuadros-Vargas, A. J., Camara-Chavez, G., Poco, J., & Gomez-Nieto, E. (2022). How do curricular design changes impact computer science programs?: A case study at San Pablo Catholic University in Peru. *Education Sciences*, *12*(4), 242. DOI: 10.3390/educsci12040242

Halimah, S. (2018). Integrasi nilai-nilai agama dan karakter dalam kurikulum pendidikan guru mengacu KKNI dan SNPT [Integration of religious values and characters in the teacher education curriculum refers to KKNI and SNPT]. *Jurnal Tarbiyah*, *24*(2), 201–225. DOI: 10.30829/tar.v24i2.214

Happe, J., & Marquardt, K. (2023). Authentic Interdisciplinary Online Courses for More Diversity in Computer Science. *SSRN*. DOI: 10.2139/ssrn.4632668

Heikkinen, K.-P., & Räisänen, T. (2018). Role of Multidisciplinary and Interdisciplinary Education in Computer Science: A Literature Review. *Managing Global Transitions*, *16*, 159–172. DOI: 10.26493/1854-6935.16.159-172

Holland-Minkley, A., Barnard, J. E., Barr, V., Braught, G., Davis, J., Reed, D., Schmitt, K., Tartaro, A., & Teresco, J. D. (2025). CS2023: Computer Science Curriculum Guidelines: A New Liberal Arts perspective. *ACM Inroads*, *16*(1), 40–52. DOI: 10.1145/3700773

Holley, K. A. (2024). *Interdisciplinary curricula*. Edward Elgar Publishing., DOI: 10.4337/9781035317967.ch66

Juriyah, N. (2021). Profil implementasi model shared pada pembelajaran ipa terpadu di indonesia: Kajian literatur (2012-2021) [Implementation profile of shared model in integrated science learning in indonesia: A literature review (2012-2021)]. *Jurnal Inovasi Penelitian Dan Pengabdian Masyarakat*, *1*(1), 32–46. DOI: 10.53621/jippmas.v1i1.6

Khozin, K., Haris, A., & Asrori, A. (2021). Pengembangan integrasi kurikulum [Development of curriculum integration]. *TADARUS*, *10*(1), 84–94. DOI: 10.30651/td.v10i1.9090

Klein, J. T. (2010). A Taxonomy of Interdisciplinarity. In Frodeman, R., Klein, J. T., & Mitcham, C. (Eds.), *The Oxford Handbook of Interdisciplinarity* (pp. 15–30). Oxford University Press.

Krüger, F. A., Queen, Z., Radelva, O., & Lawrence, N. D. (2024). Comparative Analysis of Scientific Approaches in Computer Science: A Quantitative Study. *International Transactions on Education Technology*, *2*(2), 120–128. DOI: 10.33050/itee.v2i2.567

Kumar, A. N., Becker, B. A., Pias, M., Oudshoorn, M., Jalote, P., Servin, C., Aly, S. G., Blumenthal, R. L., Epstein, S. L., & Anderson, M. D. (2023). A Combined Knowledge and Competency (CKC) model for computer science curricula. *ACM Inroads, 14*(3), 22–29. DOI: 10.1145/3605215

Kuzmenko, O., Tomchuk, M., & Kysiuk, D. (2024). The importance of interdisciplinary integration in training specialists to work in modern conditions. *Педагогіка Безпеки, 9*(1), 8–13. DOI: 10.31649/2524-1079-2024-9-1-008-013

Lorenzo, M. G. (2020). Abordaje interdisciplinar para la enseñanza de las ciencias y la actualización de profesores. Lorenzo, M. G. (2020). Abordaje interdisciplinar para la enseñanza de las ciencias y la actualización de profesores. *Revista Educación En Ciencias Biológicas, 5*(1), 1–9. DOI: 10.36861/recb.5.1.2

Mahdiyin, K. A., Zamzami, M. J., Silaban, M. R., & Suyudi, M. (2025). Pengembangan Kurikulum Integratif: Al-Qur'an, Faraidh, dan Ilmu Sains/Teknologi [Integrative Curriculum Development: Qur'an, Faraidh, and Science/Technology]. *Instructional Development Journal, 8*(1), 114. DOI: 10.24014/idj.v8i1.36340

Mansilla, V. B., & Duraisingh, E. D. (2007). Targeted assessment of students' interdisciplinary work: An empirically grounded framework proposed. *The Journal of Higher Education, 78*(2), 215–237. DOI: 10.1353/jhe.2007.0008

Margolis, J., & Fisher, A. (2002). *Unlocking the clubhouse: Women in Computing*. MIT Press.

Marifah, S. N. (2022). Systematic literatur review: Integrasi computational thinking dalam kurikulum sekolah dasar di indonesia [Systematic literature review: Integration of computational thinking in the Indonesian primary school curriculum] [Creative of Learning Students Elementary Education]. *COLLASE, 5*(5), 928–938. DOI: 10.22460/collase.v5i5.12148

Miranda, J., Navarrete, C., Noguez, J., Molina-Espinosa, J., Ramírez-Montoya, M., Navarro-Tuch, S. A., Bustamante-Bello, M., Rosas-Fernández, J., & Molina, A. (2021). The core components of education 4.0 in higher education: Three case studies in engineering education. *Computers & Electrical Engineering, 93*, 107278. Advance online publication. DOI: 10.1016/j.compeleceng.2021.107278

Mishra, A., & Siy, H. (2020). An Interdisciplinary Approach for Teaching Artificial Intelligence to Computer Science Students. *Proceedings of the 21st Annual Conference on Information Technology Education (SIGITE '20)*. Association for Computing Machinery, New York, NY, USA. DOI: 10.1145/3368308.3415440

Mohammed, F. S., & Ozdamli, F. (2024). A Systematic Literature review of Soft skills in Information Technology education. *Behavioral Sciences (Basel, Switzerland)*, *14*(10), 894. Advance online publication. DOI: 10.3390/bs14100894 PMID: 39457766

Muslimin, J., Reksiana, R., & Munawar, W. (2022). Constructivism and Teaching Design: In search of an appropriate learning Process of Sharia Entrepreneurship for Pesantren-Based University. *MIQOT Jurnal Ilmu-ilmu Keislaman*, *46*(2). Advance online publication. DOI: 10.30821/miqot.v46i2.969

Nugraha, M. G., Kidman, G., & Tan, H. (2024). Interdisciplinary STEM education foundational concepts: Implementation for knowledge creation. *Eurasia Journal of Mathematics, Science and Technology Education*, *20*(10), em2523. Advance online publication. DOI: 10.29333/ejmste/15471

Otoyo, L., Russell, A., Silver, K., & Unger, A. (2022). *Legal Education Meets Computer Science: An interdisciplinary Approach to teaching LawTech*. Routledge. DOI: 10.4324/9780429351082-11

Parshyna, O. A., Parshyna, M., & Chumak, T. V. (2022). Conceptual aspects of the interdisciplinary approach to regional studies in the global economy system. *Êvropejs kij Vektor Ekonomìčnogo Rozvitku, 1*(32), 80–90. DOI: 10.32342/2074-5362-2022-1-32-8

Petrova, J., & Vasichkina, O. (2021). Computer aspect of interdisciplinary research in philosophy of education and computer science. *SHS Web of Conferences, 109*, Article 01029. DOI: 10.1051/shsconf/202110901029

Pouso, S., Borja, Á., & Uyarra, M. C. (2020). An Interdisciplinary Approach for Valuing Changes After Ecological Restoration in Marine Cultural Ecosystem Services. *Frontiers in Marine Science*, *7*, 1–16. DOI: 10.3389/FMARS.2020.00715

Price, E., Lau, A. C., Goldberg, F., Turpen, C., Smith, P. S., Dancy, M., & Robinson, S. (2021). Analyzing a faculty online learning community as a mechanism for supporting faculty implementation of a guided-inquiry curriculum. *International Journal of STEM Education*, *8*(1), 17. Advance online publication. DOI: 10.1186/s40594-020-00268-7 PMID: 33643775

Prihantoro, C. R. (2021). Examining the use of Wheeler-Model based curriculum development in a learning management system for vocational study program. *International Journal of Education and Practice*, *9*(3), 507–519. DOI: 10.18488/journal.61.2021.93.507.519

Retscher, G., Gabela, J., & Gikas, V. (2024). Lessons Learned from the LBS2ITS Project—An Interdisciplinary Approach for Curricula Development in Geomatics Education. *Geomatics*, *5*(1), 2. Advance online publication. DOI: 10.3390/geomatics5010002

Saripudin, S., Djohar, A., Rohendi, D., & Abdullah, A. G. (2020). Developing Information Technology in OpenCourseWare: From movements to opportunities in Asia. *Indonesian Journal of Science and Technology*, *5*(3), 308–320. DOI: 10.17509/ijost.v5i3.24886

Sharma, B. K., & Shukla, V. K. (2023). Interdisciplinary Approach to Education with Special Reference to Social Science at Secondary Schools. *BSSS Journal of Education*, *12*(01), 41–51. DOI: 10.51767/je1203

Shepitko, V. I., Sherstyuk, O. O., Boruta, N., Tykhonova, O., Tarasenko, Y. A., Skotarenko, T. A., & Levchenko, O. A. (2023). Interdisciplinary Integration as a Main Factor in the Development of Clinical and Professional Thinking of Students of Medical Higher Education Institutions of Ukraine. *Ukraïns kij Žurnal Medicini. Bìologìï Ta Sportu*, *8*(1), 268–272. DOI: 10.26693/jmbs08.01.268

Wahyuni, D. S., Rozimela, Y., Ardi, H., Mukhaiyar, M., & Darmansyah, D. (2022). PROSPER (Project, Sustainability, and Perseverance) learning model in English for computer science. *Sustainability*, *14*(24), 16749. DOI: 10.3390/su142416749

Walker, H. M. (2017). Classroom Vignettes Connecting computing with other disciplines and the wider community. *ACM Inroads*, *8*(2), 29–32. DOI: 10.1145/3078315

Winarno, N., Rusdiana, D., Riandi, R., Susilowati, E., & Afifah, R. M. A. (2020). Implementation of Integrated Science Curriculum: A Critical Review of the Literature. *Journal for the Education of Gifted Young Scientists*, *8*(2), 795–817. DOI: 10.17478/jegys.675722

KEY TERMS AND DEFINITIONS

Artificial Intelligence: The capability of computer systems or algorithms to imitate intelligent human behavior, such as problem-solving, decision- making, and pattern recognition, with applications in education, automation, and workforce training.

Education 4.0: Digital applications designed to educate, train, or change behavior through engaging and interactive gameplay, going beyond mere entertainment.

Epistemological Integration: The intentional combination of philosophical, theoretical, and practical knowledge-generation methods into computing curricula, moving beyond simple technical skill acquisition. It focuses on understanding how knowledge is created, validated, and applied in computer science, while often integrating ethical and social perspectives.

Chapter 3
Recentering Computer Science Education on Problem-Solving:
Pedagogical Foundations and Curriculum Design

Mustafa Kayyali
https://orcid.org/0000-0003-3300-262X
Maaref University of Applied Sciences, Syria

ABSTRACT

This chapter explores the centrality of problem-solving in computer science education through the dual lenses of project-based learning (PjBL) and problem-based learning (PBL). While both approaches emphasize inquiry, collaboration, and real-world engagement, they differ in scope, structure, and outcomes. PjBL often immerses learners in extended projects that mirror professional practice, whereas PBL foregrounds open-ended problems that cultivate critical reasoning and adaptability. Anchored in the belief that computer science is not merely about mastering syntax or tools but about nurturing the ability to think computationally and creatively, the chapter argues for a "problem-solving first" philosophy in curriculum design. By examining practical applications, challenges, and emerging trends, it highlights how integrating PjBL and PBL can empower students to approach complexity with confidence, cultivate resilience in the face of ambiguity, and prepare for a rapidly evolving technological landscape.

DOI: 10.4018/979-8-3373-6546-6.ch003

INTRODUCTION

Computer science (CS) has always been more than the mastery of algorithms, programming languages, or hardware configurations. At its very core, it is the art and discipline of problem-solving: the persistent search for solutions in a world increasingly defined by complexity, uncertainty, and constant change. When we teach CS merely as the acquisition of technical tools, we risk reducing it to a mechanical exercise of syntax and commands, stripped of the deeper habits of mind that enable genuine creativity and resilience. Yet when we place problem-solving at the heart of the educational process, we begin to cultivate learners who can not only survive in a dynamic digital environment but also shape it with ingenuity and purpose. It is here that pedagogical approaches such as project-based learning (PjBL) and problem-based learning (PBL) come into sharp focus. Both methods reject the notion of education as passive reception of information, insisting instead that students must actively engage, inquire, and wrestle with authentic challenges. They transform the classroom into a laboratory of thinking, where knowledge is not handed down in neat packages but is discovered, contested, and applied in messy, real-world contexts. For CS, a field where the distance between theory and practice is often razor-thin, such approaches are not merely desirable but essential.

The turn toward problem-solving as the organizing principle of curriculum design reflects broader shifts in educational philosophy. Across disciplines, there is a growing recognition that the traditional lecture-dominated model, while efficient for transmitting large volumes of information, is ill-suited to fostering the critical thinking and adaptability demanded by contemporary societies (Gopal, 2025). Employers, too, increasingly seek graduates who can navigate ambiguity, collaborate across disciplines, and devise creative solutions rather than simply replicate existing methods. In CS, this demand is particularly acute. Software development, data science, cybersecurity, and emerging fields like artificial intelligence require not only technical competence but also the capacity to ask the right questions, frame problems thoughtfully, and imagine multiple pathways toward resolution (Kolosnjaji et al, 2024). PjBL and PBL are often spoken of in the same breath, and with good reason (Moore, 2025). Both share a commitment to student-centered pedagogy, collaborative inquiry, and the integration of knowledge across domains. Yet their nuances matter. PjBL tends to emphasize extended projects that culminate in tangible outputs that mirror professional practice. PBL, on the other hand, begins with a deliberately ill-structured problem, encouraging learners to analyze, hypothesize, and explore possible solutions before formal instruction provides additional scaffolding. One approach is expansive, often spanning weeks or months; the other is iterative, focused on cultivating the habits of inquiry and critical reasoning that underpin effective problem-solving.

Placing these approaches within CS education raises several pressing questions: How do we prepare students for a discipline where the boundaries between theory and application are fluid? What kinds of problems best capture the essence of computational thinking? How can educators design projects that challenge without overwhelming, or problems that stretch students' reasoning without descending into chaos? These are not simply methodological questions; they are philosophical ones, bound up with our understanding of what it means to teach and learn in a world defined by rapid technological change (Hanstedt, 2023).

MAIN FOCUS OF THE CHAPTER

This chapter situates PjBL and PBL within the larger narrative of CS education, arguing that problem-solving should not be a by-product of instruction but the primary organizing principle around which curricula are built. By exploring the theoretical foundations, practical implementations, and potential synergies between the two approaches, it makes the case for a "problem-solving first" philosophy that equips students not only with technical expertise but with the intellectual flexibility to thrive in unpredictable contexts. Along the way, the discussion engages with challenges, from assessment difficulties to resource constraints, while also pointing toward future directions in curriculum innovation. In doing so, the chapter invites educators, researchers, and practitioners alike to reimagine what it means to teach CS in an era where knowledge is abundant, but wisdom in applying it remains scarce.

PEDAGOGICAL FOUNDATIONS

Theoretical Foundations of Problem-Based and Project-Based Learning

The idea that learning should begin with a real problem did not arrive with modern laptops or slick frameworks. It has a much older lineage, woven through the pragmatism of John Dewey, the project method of William Heard Kilpatrick, the spiral of discovery set loose by Jerome Bruner, and the social fabric of Lev Vygotsky's zone of proximal development (Pomelov, 2021). These names aren't ornamental citations; they signal a way of thinking about education that refuses to separate knowing from doing. Knowledge, in this view, is not stockpiled content; it's enacted, negotiated, and stress-tested in practice. Put a different way: the classroom is not a warehouse but a workshop.

Dewey's influence is the bedrock. He insisted that learning is rooted in experience and that schools should mirror the problem spaces of the wider world (Landorf & Wadley, 2022). Kilpatrick, a student of Dewey, gave this philosophy a navigable shape by championing the "project" as the central unit of curriculum: an activity with purpose, social value, and outcomes that reach beyond the classroom walls. Their shared intuition, still radical beneath the surface, is that human beings don't truly understand by reciting definitions; they understand by trying to change something, by encountering friction, by revising a plan when reality pushes back.

PBL and PjBL inherit this ethos but channel it differently (Silma et al, 2024). PBL starts with an ill-structured problem that is real enough to matter and vague enough to require interpretation. Learners identify what they know, what they don't know, and how they plan to figure it out. The aim is not to sprint toward a tidy solution but to develop a disciplined way of inquiring: hypothesize, seek evidence, argue, reframe, iterate. PjBL, by contrast, typically stretches across a longer arc. There is a defined artifact or outcome that focalizes the work (Eswaran, 2024). The artifact is never just a thing; it's the crystallization of many decisions, trade-offs, and lines of reasoning. Both approaches are unapologetically social. Students learn with and through one another: arguing about assumptions, splitting tasks, sharing partial results, and producing something they can stand behind.

The modern shape of PBL owes a debt to medicine. In the 1960s, Howard Barrows and colleagues reshaped medical education by giving students clinical cases before lectures (Klamen et al, 2022). The shock was intentional. First encounter the problem, then backfill the theory as you need it. That inversion spreads quickly once tasted, because it changes what counts as understanding. Education becomes less about recall and more about judgment. In CS, the move is even more natural. Code doesn't care how many glossary terms live in memory; code demands decisions about data structures, time complexity, failure modes, and user constraints. Put a novice in front of a thorny debugging session and watch how quickly a taxonomy of misconceptions emerges; watch, too, how the skill of asking the right question becomes the oxygen of progress.

Papert, working under the banner of constructionism, added a crucial ingredient. Build things, not to display mastery, but to have a conversation with the world: tangible artifacts that talk back. A student's project becomes a partner in thought, sometimes adversarial, always honest (Yang et al, 2022). Vygotsky's insight explains why mentorship, peer explanation, and code reviews do so much heavy lifting in PBL/PjBL contexts. The "zone of proximal development" in computing feels almost literal: that uncomfortable space where the next step is just barely out of reach until a teammate's hint, a guiding question, or a well-timed test unlocks it.

There is also Kolb's experiential cycle: concrete experience, reflective observation, abstract conceptualization, active experimentation. CS maps tidy onto this. Build a feature (experience), reflect on the unexpected bug (observation), formulate a general rule about asynchronous calls or state management (abstraction), then revise and test again (experimentation). The cycle is not a classroom gimmick; it is the rhythm of actual software practice, condensed.

Designing Problem-First Computer Science Learning

Translating these theoretical commitments into classroom practice requires intentional instructional design that foregrounds authentic problems, carefully calibrated scaffolding, and meaningful assessment. A problem worthy of PBL must be underspecified enough to provoke genuine inquiry but bounded enough that students can move (Woolard, 2022). In CS education, this often means real data with real noise, a user story that contains internal tensions, or a system constraint that forces trade-offs. "Build a route-planner for emergency services that prioritizes both travel time and road reliability after a storm," for instance. Immediately the class must juggle graph algorithms, probabilistic modeling, and human factors. Nobody can "cover" such a problem with a single lecture. Nor should they. The quarrel with teaching of monoculture starts here: complexity is not the enemy of learning; it is the habitat in which durable understanding evolves.

PjBL thrives when the project is public. When students must present to an audience that includes someone beyond the instructor their attention to credibility and clarity spikes (Alharthi, 2024). Peer code reviews stop feeling like ceremonial hoops and start functioning like intellectual guardrails. Version control systems become more than tools; they become chronicles of reasoning, evidence of how ideas morphed over time. Agile rituals, when adapted thoughtfully, bring cadence: short iterations, visible backlogs, retrospectives that reward honest appraisal of what worked and what did not. The "definition of done" grows teeth. Tests become a way of thinking, not a late-night panic.

There is a danger, of course, in romanticizing projects and problems as if they were pedagogical cure-alls. Cognitive load matters. Unstructured challenges, without scaffolding, can tilt quickly into confusion. But scaffolding is not micromanagement. It is the design of ramps that support ascent without carrying the learner to the summit (Neves, 2024). And because CS contains many invisible moves (mental models of memory, execution paths, recursion depth), making those moves visible becomes part of the craft: whiteboard traces, interactive debuggers, think-alouds, and small-group "code whispering" sessions where teams narrate intentions before touching the keyboard.

Assessment often ruins the party if it's clumsy. Traditional exams have their place but they miss the soul of PBL/PjBL if used alone. Better to blend artifacts with process evidence: commit histories, issue threads, test coverage, design rationales, code readability, and after-action reviews that name both triumphs and missteps. Rubrics should breathe. Evaluate not merely whether a program works today, but how maintainable it is, how gracefully it fails, how ethically it treats data, how clearly the team communicates to future maintainers. In other words, judge the work the way a professional community would.

The ethical layer isn't optional anymore. Problems in CS are entangled with human lives—privacy decisions in a database schema, bias in a classifier, accessibility in an interface. PBL that quarantines ethics in a separate week misreads the moment. Better to bake it into the problem statement and grading: the routing algorithm that must prioritize ambulances without marginalizing certain neighborhoods; the language model that must balance accuracy with transparency; the data visualization that must not erase uncertainty. When students tussle with these tensions during design rather than after implementation, the lesson lands in muscle memory.

Equity is another stubborn, necessary thread. High-quality PBL/PjBL often asks for resources that are not evenly distributed (Tweeten & Hung, 2023). Without careful design, group work can reproduce hierarchies: one loud expert commanders the hard problems, others drift to the periphery. Roles help (lead developer, tester, documentation owner, product liaison), rotated frequently. Peer assessment that counts, coaching inclusive collaboration, and explicit norms around airtime are not niceties but structural supports. The promise of problem-centered pedagogy is wasted if only the already-confident reap the real benefits.

A quiet shift happens when courses adopt a problem-first stance across the curriculum rather than as an occasional capstone. Introductory programming can launch with contextually rich micro-problems instead of a tour of syntax. Data structures can anchor around competing designs for a real system like a messaging platform where latency, memory footprint, and fairness collide (Ortiz, 2023). Systems courses can run on performance budgets and energy constraints, not just correctness. Even theory can be problem-first: reduction proofs as design conversations, probabilistic bounds as negotiated guarantees for living systems. The syllabus becomes less a map of topics and more a set of increasingly sophisticated negotiations with reality. This way of teaching changes the role of the instructor. Less oracle, more architect. A designer of problem spaces, a curator of exemplars, a critic who asks dangerous questions at just the right moment, and a mentor who normalizes uncertainty (Michela, 2022). There is also humility baked into the role: in authentic projects, surprises are not bugs in the syllabus; they are part of the learning. Plans will wobble. That wobble is productive if acknowledged and mined.

For all the romance surrounding "real-world" problems, it helps to remember that school has its own realities. Calendars are choppy. Cohorts are diverse in preparation. Grading must converge at specific times. A practical compromise is the problem studio: a repeating cadence in which students move through problem scoping, investigation, build, critique, and reflection, all within a course-friendly rhythm. Studios can host both PBL and PjBL: short, sharp problem cycles for conceptual muscles; longer build cycles for integrative work (Yau, 2021). Over a term, students accumulate a portfolio that reveals growth not only in what they can make, but in how they reason and collaborate when things go sideways.

There's also the matter of transfer. The holy grail isn't proficiency on the project at hand; it's the ability to carry ways of thinking into unfamiliar domains. PBL nurtures transfer by practicing problem framing (what is this problem really?), assumption surfacing (what am I taking for granted?), and strategy selection (which approach makes sense given the constraints?). PjBL strengthens transfer through design patterns, architectural thinking, and the discipline of testing hypotheses in code (Jiang & Pang, 2023). Together, they seed a stance: approach novelty with curiosity, structure the unknown, move forward with a provisional plan, listen to the feedback, and adjust without melodrama.

In CS education, a near-spiritual lesson hides inside debugging. The machine is relentless, but not cruel. It gives back exactly what it was asked to do, not what was intended. Tracing that gap demands a particular kind of attention: precise, patient, hypothesis-driven. PBL turns debugging into epistemology (*how do we know what we think we know?)* while PjBL elevates it into culture (*how do we, as a team, build systems that are debuggable, observable, and resilient?)* When students start to narrate their debugging moves with the same confidence they narrate a solution, the pedagogy has sunk in.

All of this suggests a practical recipe—more orientation than formula. Start with a problem that matters (to someone, somewhere, not just the grader). Make the constraints explicit and real. Offer scaffolds that fade. Insist on artifacts that are read by others so that accountability is social as much as evaluative. Weave reflection throughout, not as an afterthought but as a parallel track where students name their strategies, misjudgments, and next experiments. Evaluate the product and the process. Give ethics a seat at the design table. Rotate roles. Use version control and tests as thinking tools, not only technical ones. And, crucially, keep the loop tight: frequent feedback, short iterations, visible progress.

If the theory feels lofty, the practice is earthy. Sticky notes on a whiteboard. A failing unit test pinned to a bug nobody saw coming. A teammate realizing the elegant algorithm is starving a minority of requests. A sprint retrospective that admits the estimate was fantasy. The instructor's question, "*What would break if the input doubled?*," landing at just the right time. These details are not peripheral; they are how the theory breathes.

Problem-based and project-based approaches are not competing fads. They are two dialects of a language that education speaks when it reminds us that knowledge is alive. In that language, CS stops being a museum of techniques and becomes a studio for disciplined imagination. Students don't merely learn to make things work; they learn to make sense, to make choices, to make amends when their systems fail. The lineage stretches from Dewey's workshop to today's collaborative repos, from Kilpatrick's purposeful activity to a team's public demo, from Vygotsky's scaffolded dialogue to a well-timed code review comment that turns a corner (Baltoski, 2024). Theory gives the compass. Practice gives the miles. And somewhere in the walking, learners become the kind of problem-solvers a volatile world quietly hopes will graduate and get to work.

PROBLEM-SOLVING IN COMPUTER SCIENCE

Problem Framing and Decomposition

Strip away the gloss—frameworks with short half-lives, languages that wax and wane, the never-ending parade of tools—and something sturdier remains at the center of CS: a disciplined way of confronting the unknown. Problem-solving is not a unit wedged between loops and recursion, nor a soft skill tacked onto the end of a syllabus (Nadir, 2021). It is the spine. How a learner frames ambiguity, decomposes a tangle, invents structure where there was none, and tolerates the stubbornness of reality when elegant ideas misbehave—this is the durable education that survives version bumps and shifting paradigms.

Start with the deceptively simple act of problem framing. Before the first line of code, there's a quieter craft: clarifying the question. What is actually being asked? Which hidden assumptions are silently steering the design? Where are the constraints that matter, and which constraints are convenient myths? Students who jump straight to implementation often find themselves sprinting in a circle, dutifully crafting a solution to a misread question. Teaching problem framing is slow work; it thrives on examples that sting a little. A recommender system that "works" until fairness is measured. A scheduling algorithm that dazzles on average but punishes edge cases. The lesson isn't that code lies; it's that problems are social creatures, thick with context, and the thinker who rushes past that texture signs up for rework.

Decomposition follows, though not as a mechanical checklist (Daby-Seesaram et al, 2025). Splitting a large task into parts is less like carving a statue and more like proposing temporary boundaries: here is a module that might hold, here is an interface that buys freedom for teams to work in parallel, here is a responsibility that should not be shared. In early coursework, decomposition often masquerades as "write three functions," but that undersells it. In authentic settings, decomposition is strategic; it anticipates change and localizes risk. The student who learns to identify volatile regions, to isolate them behind stable contracts, is already thinking at the level of architecture and long-term maintainability, even if the artifact is "just" a class project.

Abstraction, Heuristics, and Algorithmic Pattern Recognition

Now abstraction, the unsung habit that keeps minds from drowning in detail. Abstraction has a reputation for loftiness, yet in practice it's a survival tactic (Lopatecki, 2022). Choose the right level of description, and complexity becomes navigable. Choose poorly, and everything feels brittle. A data structure is an abstraction, so is a network protocol, so is a test harness that pretends the world is kinder than it is. Problem-solving in CS means shuttling between levels—bit operations to algorithmic patterns to system-level behaviors—without getting lost. This movement isn't innate. It can be taught by asking students to model the same problem at two levels in quick succession, to feel the heat of granularity and the cool of generalization, and to articulate why a particular vantage point helps. To make these dimensions explicit for learners and instructors alike, Table 1 presents a problem-solving skills rubric that operationalizes framing, decomposition, abstraction, debugging, collaboration, ethical awareness, and metacognitive reflection across developmental levels.

Table 1. Problem-Solving Skills Rubric for CS Students

Problem-Solving Skill	Emerging	Developing	Proficient
Problem framing	Restates problem as given; key constraints and stakeholders are often missed or oversimplified.	Identifies core requirements, constraints, and some stakeholders; begins to question assumptions.	Frames problems in context, articulating stakeholders, success criteria, and open questions.
Decomposition	Breaks tasks into pieces mainly by following examples; boundaries between parts are ad hoc.	Plans modules or components with basic interfaces; can justify some decomposition choices.	Designs coherent, modular decompositions that localise change and support parallel work.
Abstraction	Focuses on surface details of problems and code; struggles to generalise beyond current task.	Can move between a specific example and a more general description with instructor support.	Chooses appropriate abstraction levels; can justify representations and modelling choices.

continued on following page

Table 1. Continued

Problem-Solving Skill	Emerging	Developing	Proficient
Debugging and iteration	Debugs reactively by trial-and-error edits without a clear plan or logging of attempts.	Uses simple strategies (e.g., print statements, small tests); begins to form and test hypotheses.	Plans debugging systematically, logs experiments, and uses tools and tests to narrow fault locations.
Collaboration and communication	Contributes mainly to isolated coding tasks; limited sharing of reasoning or feedback.	Shares partial reasoning with peers; participates in reviews; takes on rotating project roles.	Leads or facilitates collaboration; communicates decisions clearly to technical and non-technical audiences.
Ethical and stakeholder awareness	Rarely considers how solutions affect users or society unless explicitly prompted.	Recognises obvious ethical issues and trade-offs; can describe who benefits and who may be harmed.	Integrates ethical and stakeholder analysis into design; documents trade-offs and rationale.
Metacognitive reflection	Reflects mainly on grades or outcomes; rarely names specific strategies or misjudgments.	Articulates what worked or failed in a task; can name at least one alternative strategy to try next time.	Maintains a deliberate learning journal; identifies personal patterns in problem-solving and sets goals.

There's also heuristic reasoning, the repertoire of moves used when formal methods are overkill or impossible under the clock (Thomsen, 2024). Estimate first, refine later. Try a greedy approach, measure, then replace with dynamic programming if the profile screams. Use a sketch implementation to probe a design space before committing. Heuristics are often treated like guilty secrets—informal, second-class compared to theorem-backed solutions—but competent engineers live on them. What matters pedagogically is to surface these moves, to treat them as discussable and improvable, not as private wizardry. When students narrate their heuristics ("start simple, instrument relentlessly, bias toward readability until data says otherwise"), they are apprenticing into a culture of explicit thinking.

Algorithmic thinking sits nearby but is not the whole story. Yes, learners should explore canonical families—divide-and-conquer, graph search, probabilistic methods, streaming—yet the aim isn't to memorize recipes (Petropoulos et al, 2024). It's to recognize patterns of structure across domains, to sense when a problem smells like bipartite matching or when it whispers for a suffix array. Pattern recognition, in this academic sense, is a cultivated sensitivity. It grows through cases and countercases, through the discipline of asking, "What is this *like*?" without forcing a fit. When students misapply a known algorithm and then carefully diagnose the mismatch, they are strengthening the very muscles that make novelty survivable. These differences in emphasis across instructional approaches are summarized in Figure 1, which contrasts how core learning dimensions are foregrounded in lecture-based, problem-based, and project-based contexts.

Figure 1. Illustrative Emphasis of Key Learning Dimensions Across CS Teaching Approaches

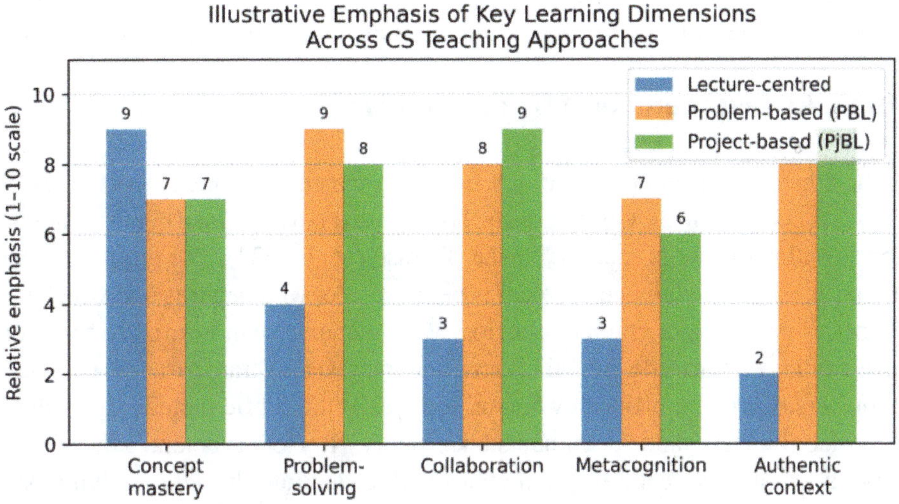

Debugging and Collaborative Sensemaking

Enter debugging, which might be the most honest teacher in the building. Debugging reframes problem-solving as epistemology: what do we know, how do we know it, what evidence would actually change our mind? A failing test is not a personal attack; it's a clue (Hennessy Elliott et al, 2024). The best debugging habits—reproducible cases, binary search through the state space, tracing with minimal disturbance, hypotheses stated out loud—can be taught early and reinforced until they become reflexes. Teams can ritualize them: keep a "bug diary," predict the cause before opening the debugger, time-box hunches, celebrate the boring fix that removes a class of errors instead of the flashy patch that silences one. Debugging also reveals temperament. Patience without passivity. Skepticism without cynicism. A willingness to be wrong in public. These are not just techniques; they are dispositions that shape a career.

Problem-solving also lives in collaboration, although the word can sound like a euphemism for "group assignment." Real collaboration is division of *thought*, not only division of *labor*. One person frames hypotheses while another sets up instrumentation; a third rewrites the thorny loop with a clearer invariant. Rotating roles teaches students to step outside habitual comfort. The deft coder takes on documentation; the design-minded teammate writes performance tests; the quiet analyst facilitates the retrospective (Werder & Otis, 2023). When a team treats its repository as a conversation—commit messages that read like micro-essays, issues that include reasoning, pull requests with questions rather than edicts—problem-solving becomes shared memory rather than private brilliance. The long-term effect is subtle but huge: students learn to build artifacts that another human can inhabit.

Ethics, Assessment, and Metacognitive Practice

The ethical layer belongs here, not bolted to the end. Problems worth solving come with consequences. Optimizing a classifier that labels human beings is not the same as optimizing an in-memory cache (Donisch et al, 2024). The problem solver who never asks *for whom* the problem is being solved, who benefits and who bears the cost, is practicing a cramped version of CS. Courses can normalize trade-off conversations that include ethical claims: accuracy versus transparency, personalization versus privacy, efficiency versus equity. Let the rubric include "articulates stakeholder impacts" and "documents uncertainty." Let teams defend a decision to *not* build a requested feature. When ethics is threaded into the act of solving, students learn that responsibility is not an add-on; it is part of the definition of done.

Assessment often reveals whether a program actually values problem-solving or merely pays lip service. Exams that reward speed on toy exercises can be useful for fluency but risk distorting priorities. A richer picture blends product and process: the working system, the test suite, the design rationale, the trail of iterations, the quality of collaboration. Ask for a two-page failure report that names the three worst decisions and what triggered them. Grade the clarity of commit history. Credit the removal of code as a positive act. Instructors sometimes fear that such criteria are "subjective." They are, in the sense that professional practice is full of judgment. Teaching students how such judgments are made—by criteria, evidence, and community norms—prepares them for a world where correctness is necessary and rarely sufficient.

Metacognition is the silent engine underneath. Learners who monitor their own strategies, who name when they are stuck and can switch tactics, make better progress than those who grind in place (Erwin, 2024). Prompting metacognition can be lightweight: a five-minute "strategy snapshot" at the halfway point of a lab ("what are we trying, why, what else could we try if this stalls?"), or short reflection prompts after a sprint. This isn't busywork. It's the discipline of keeping the problem-solving *process* in the foreground, not just the product. Over time, these reflections become a personal library: a map of prior struggles and how they were navigated.

What about the presence of AI tools and automated help that whisper suggestions before a student has fully formed a thought? It's tempting to frame this as a threat to problem-solving (Aymen et al, 2024). The more interesting stance is to treat such tools as collaborators with very specific strengths and blind spots. A student who leans on a code assistant without understanding is outsourcing cognition; a student who uses it to surface alternatives, generate edge cases, or test a conceptual model is amplifying cognition. The curriculum can teach this discernment explicitly: when to consult, how to verify, how to identify hallucination or shallow pattern match, how to remain the author of the reasoning even when not the typist of every token. In that light, AI becomes a new setting for an old lesson: delegation without abdication.

Transfer, Resilience, and Professional Identity

Transfer is the litmus test for whether problem-solving has taken root. Can a student carry habits from one domain to another, or do they collapse outside familiar patterns? Designing for transfer means varying surface features while preserving deep structure (Tokuhama-Espinosa, 2021). Today the task is route planning on weighted graphs; next week it's dependency resolution in a package manager; the underlying reasoning travels. Instructors can cultivate this by asking students to write "pattern memos" that generalize beyond the current assignment: What class of problems does your solution template address? Where would it break? Which assumptions are brittle, which are safe? A course that builds this habit graduates thinkers who, when faced with a fresh mess, instinctively reach for structure rather than panic.

The emotional texture of problem-solving deserves more direct attention than it usually gets (Güss & Starker, 2023). Frustration isn't a sign of failure; it's data. The dip between naive optimism and hard-won clarity shows up in every serious project, and naming it helps. Teams can pre-commit to rituals that metabolize the low points: time-boxed spikes, "rubber duck" sessions, and, crucially, the permission to step away for perspective rather than grinding into diminishing returns. Resilience is teachable, not as cheerleading but as technique: deliberate rest, diversified approaches, tactical scope reduction, the grace to abandon sunk costs. Shaping these habits prepares students for the long arc of real work, where setbacks are not detours but the road itself.

When curricula truly center problem-solving, topic order starts to change. Instead of marching from syntax to control flow to data structures in a pristine sequence, courses loop through these elements in the context of problems that pressure them. A unit on concurrency might begin with the lived pain of a race condition and only then formalize locks, semaphores, and memory models. A lesson on complexity can start from a time-budget a system must meet—"responses under 200 ms at the 95th percentile"—and pull the mathematics into focus as a tool for keeping that promise. Theory is not devalued; it is moved closer to the heat of practice where its elegance becomes visible.

There's a final, less quantifiable dividend. Treating problem-solving as the core of CS education changes the identity students build (Friend et al, 2022). Instead of "a Python programmer" or "a front-end developer," they start to say, "a person who can make sense of complexity." That identity travels across jobs, tools, and eras. It also grounds humility: mastery becomes less about having the answer and more about knowing how to move when there isn't one yet. The graduates most trusted by colleagues aren't the ones who never err; they are the ones whose errors are discoverable, whose reasoning is legible, whose choices are principled under constraint.

So the case is simple and demanding. Put problem-solving at the center, and everything else arranges around it with more integrity. Problems come first, not as gimmicks but as the natural habitat of understanding. Abstraction and decomposition become instruments rather than slogans. Debugging becomes a philosophy, not a chore. Collaboration becomes a way of thinking, not a calendar requirement (Alaboudi & LaToza, 2023). Ethics sits at the table where decisions are made, not on a poster. Assessment honors process as well as product. Metacognition turns reflection into fuel. AI assistance is absorbed thoughtfully, without surrendering authorship. Transfer is engineered, not hoped for. Emotional skill is treated as part of the work, not an extracurricular.

The result is a different kind of classroom—less museum, more studio; less itinerary, more expedition. Students leave with artifacts, yes, but more importantly with habits of mind that persist when the codebase is archived and the next problem arrives. And it will arrive, indifferent to the comfort of old answers, asking again: what exactly is the question, where are the constraints, which abstractions fit, how will we know if we're wrong, and who is affected by our choice? An education built on problem-solving doesn't promise to make those questions easy. It offers something rarer: the confidence to face them with clarity and care.

PEDAGOGICAL MODELS IN PRACTICE

Comparing Project-Based and Problem-Based Approaches

At first glance, PjBL and PBL look like siblings separated by little more than a hyphen (Yau, 2021). Both emphasize student-centered inquiry, both resist the passivity of lecture-dominated instruction, and both situate learning in contexts that feel alive rather than abstract. Yet anyone who has actually designed or facilitated them knows the differences run deeper. They operate on distinct rhythms, cultivate different habits of mind, and sometimes clash when imported uncritically into CS education. At the same time, they can complement each other in unexpected ways, producing a pedagogical duet richer than either solo. For a concise overview of how these approaches differ in drivers of learning, time scale, instructor roles, student activities, and assessment practices, Table 2 provides a comparative summary of lecture-centered instruction, PBL, and PjBL in computer science education.

Table 2. Comparison of Lecture, PBL, and PjBL in CS Education

Dimension	Lecture-centred	PBL	PjBL
Primary driver of learning	Transmission of concepts and worked examples from instructor to students.	Ill-structured problems that reveal knowledge gaps and drive inquiry.	Extended projects culminating in tangible artifacts (systems, apps, prototypes).
Typical time scale	Single class sessions or short units focused on specific topics.	Short to medium cycles (from one session to a couple of weeks).	Longer cycles (several weeks to a full term or capstone).
Role of instructor	Expert explainer; designs examples and controls pacing.	Facilitator of inquiry; prompts students to surface and test hypotheses.	Coach and design architect; supports planning, checkpoints, and reviews.
Typical student activity	Listening, note-taking, replicating patterns on similar exercises.	Analyzing scenarios, asking questions, planning investigations, revisiting ideas.	Designing, implementing, testing, documenting, and presenting artifacts.
Nature of problems/tasks	Well-structured textbook problems with clear, single solutions.	Ill-structured, authentic problems with multiple plausible approaches.	Complex, multi-step tasks with technical, social, and ethical dimensions.
Evidence of learning	Correct answers on quizzes, exams, and short programming tasks.	Quality of reasoning, group discussions, learning issues, and reflective notes.	Quality of artifacts, demos, documentation, tests, and peer/client feedback.
Main strengths	Efficient coverage of foundational knowledge; predictable structure.	Strong development of framing, inquiry habits, and metacognition.	Integration of concepts, collaboration, and professional-like practice.
Typical risks if poorly designed	Shallow problem-solving, low transfer to authentic contexts, passive engagement.	Cognitive overload, drifting discussions, uneven participation without scaffolding.	Scope creep, uneven workload, focus on product over learning without explicit reflection.

PjBL tends to stretch across time like a long horizon. Its currency is the artifact—a website, a database, a simulation, a game engine—that captures weeks of planning, iteration, and revision. The artifact isn't just evidence of learning; it becomes a conversation partner, a stubborn object that reveals whether ideas hold water. Students pour energy into designing, building, debugging, and presenting something that stands outside themselves. In CS, this aligns almost uncannily with professional practice. Industry rewards those who can ship, maintain, and explain systems that work in the wild. A semester-long project echoes this ethos, immersing learners in the mess of version control, collaboration, scope creep, testing, and the soft skills of negotiation. The learning emerges not in isolated bursts but in the slow accretion of decisions—many of them imperfect—across time.

PBL, on the other hand, has a different texture. It begins not with an artifact to be produced but with a thorny question that defies simple resolution. Students are thrown into ambiguity early, asked to define the contours of the problem before even sketching a solution. This requires a different mindset: instead of saying, "Here's what we'll build," the group asks, "What's really being asked of us?" A medical student faced with a puzzling case, a CS novice tasked with designing an algorithm for dynamic scheduling under uncertain inputs—these learners must hypothesize, gather evidence, test lines of reasoning, and often return to square one. PBL is about cultivating inquiry and adaptability more than producing a polished end product. In CS, this can mean confronting algorithmic puzzles, ethical dilemmas in data usage, or architecture trade-offs where no option is obviously best.

The divergence becomes clearer when examining their temporal scales. PjBL thrives on extended cycles. Deadlines come in milestones, sprints, and final showcases. The pacing mirrors industry timelines, albeit compressed. PBL, by contrast, favors shorter, recursive loops (Smith et al, 2024). A case is introduced, hypotheses fly, dead ends emerge, and knowledge gaps become explicit. Instruction swoops in to scaffold what's missing, then the group returns to the problem with sharper tools. PjBL feels like a marathon with checkpoints; PBL feels like interval training where intensity spikes repeatedly. Both exhaust and energize, but in different registers.

There's also a contrast in their epistemic emphasis. PjBL pushes students to integrate knowledge across domains to make something coherent (Sánchez-García & Reyes-de-Cózar, 2025). The learning lies in orchestration: tying together databases, interfaces, algorithms, and design principles into one functioning system. PBL, meanwhile, sharpens diagnostic reasoning. Its essence is not integration but dissection: What's the crux of the problem? Which variables matter most? Which assumptions are untested? In a sense, PjBL asks, "Can you build something real and valuable?" while PBL asks, "Can you think through uncertainty with rigor?" One trains systems thinking, the other problem-framing discipline. In CS, both matter desperately. One without the other produces either elegant reasoning with no practical grip or working systems built on shallow understanding.

And yet, the synergies between them are striking. Many educators find that PjBL benefits from being seeded with PBL (Silma et al, 2024). A project launched with a raw, ill-structured problem sets the stage for deeper motivation: the project becomes the response to a lived puzzle, not a detached assignment. Likewise, PBL can find its limits if it never transitions into building. A group might generate brilliant hypotheses and theoretical models, but until those models are tested in code, the reasoning risks floating above ground. Marrying them—problem to spark inquiry, project to ground it—yields a sequence truer to professional life. Real work rarely begins with a perfect spec or ends with a thought experiment. It swings between wrestling with problems and producing artifacts that embody tentative solutions.

One might imagine a semester-long course where the two approaches alternate like inhaling and exhaling (Wang & Flory, 2024). Early weeks introduce messy problems: a network that collapses under unpredictable loads, a dataset riddled with bias, an algorithm whose performance deteriorates at scale. Students wrestle with these problems in PBL mode, mapping knowledge gaps, speculating, and articulating what they need to learn next. Then the course shifts into PjBL mode, asking students to design, build, and present a system that addresses the problem at least partially. Later, a new ill-structured problem is introduced, cycling them back into inquiry mode. Over time, learners internalize a rhythm: question deeply, design tentatively, test concretely, reflect honestly, repeat.

Another dimension where the two diverge is assessment. PjBL outputs are visible and often spectacular—demos, prototypes, presentations—but they can mask uneven understanding within teams (Eswaran, 2024). A dazzling app can conceal that one student carried the logic while others orbit at the periphery. PBL's assessment is subtler: it rewards reasoning trails, quality of questions, and iterative refinement of ideas. But PBL artifacts are often intangible; outsiders may struggle to see what was accomplished. The synergy lies in blending their evaluative strategies. Projects can be graded not just on polish but on the problem-framing and diagnostic reasoning that preceded them. Problems can be assessed not only on thought process but on how insights transfer into a concrete system.

Tensions emerge as well. One is cognitive load. PjBL demands stamina over long timelines; PBL demands tolerance for ambiguity in the short term (Amiri, 2025). Students unused to uncertainty may panic in PBL sessions, longing for clear instructions. Students new to extended work may flag under the sustained effort of PjBL, succumbing to procrastination or uneven contributions. Teachers must recognize these pressures and design scaffolds that don't dilute the challenge. Another tension is scope management. Projects can balloon uncontrollably; problems can sprawl into the philosophical. The art of teaching lies in keeping both challenging but navigable, resisting the twin temptations of over-structuring and under-supporting. Figure 2 illustrates how core problem-solving subskills tend to develop differently across PBL and PjBL contexts, highlighting their complementary contributions to student learning trajectories.

Figure 2. Illustrative Development of Problem-Solving Subskills in PBL and PjBL Contexts

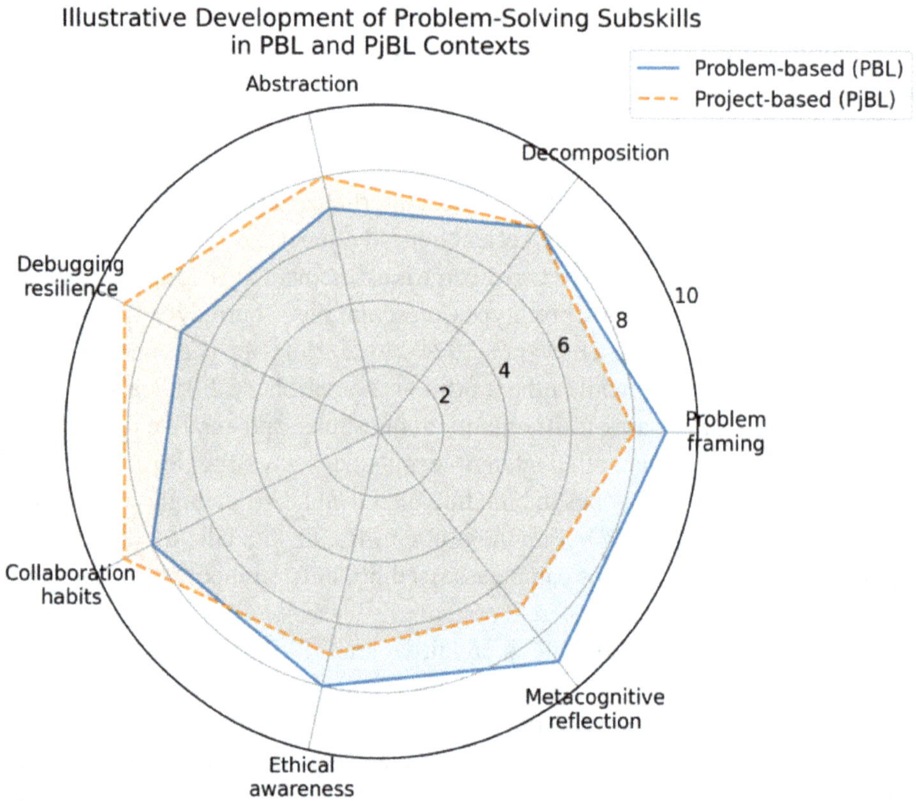

An underexplored synergy lies in their affective impact. Projects often generate pride. Students see something running, clickable, demonstrable, and feel the satisfaction of creation. Problems often generate humility. Students confront the limits of their knowledge and must articulate confusion before progress occurs (Hall, 2021). Pride without humility risks arrogance; humility without pride risks despair. Together, they balance the emotional ecology of learning. A student who can feel both—proud of what they built, humbled by what they don't yet know—has tasted something close to the real spirit of CS.

Critics sometimes argue that PjBL veers into vocationalism, preparing students for industry deliverables at the expense of theoretical depth. Others counter that PBL can feel too academic, mired in endless questioning without producing usable skills. The truth is less binary. Both approaches can be superficial if poorly executed, and both can be profound if nurtured well. A project can devolve into paint-by-numbers if the problem at its root is trivial (O'Reilly III & Tushman, 2021). A problem can devolve into guesswork if it never connects to practice. The measure of their quality is not the label but the integrity of the design: Does the activity invite real thinking? Does it connect knowledge to action? Does it stretch without breaking?

In comparing them, it becomes clear that they illuminate different faces of problem-solving. PjBL is about carrying ideas forward into tangible form, making thinking visible and accountable in public. PBL is about slowing down, interrogating assumptions, and letting uncertainty breathe before rushing into construction. If CS education is to cultivate graduates who can both build responsibly and think critically, then it cannot afford to privilege one at the expense of the other. It must weave them, letting their divergences sharpen different skills and their synergies create richer learning trajectories.

Perhaps the best metaphor is musical. PjBL is the sustained chord, resonant and layered, requiring patience to let its harmonies unfold (Nan, 2025). PBL is the improvisational riff, fast and searching, full of tension and release. Alone, each is compelling. Together, they create a pedagogy that sounds more like the real work of CS: sometimes steady, sometimes improvisational, always negotiating between clarity and complexity. And maybe that is the point: students who learn to dance between them carry forward not just content knowledge, but a posture toward learning itself—active, adaptive, willing to build, willing to question, and ready for a world that will keep presenting problems without neat answers.

Designing Authentic Learning Environments for Computational Thinking

The phrase *computational thinking* has been stretched so thin in recent years that it sometimes risks collapsing under its own popularity. Everyone seems to invoke it, yet the lived experience of teaching it often feels far from the buzzwords. At its best, computational thinking is not a slogan but a set of deeply human habits: learning how to deconstruct messy situations, noticing patterns across seemingly unrelated problems, abstracting away irrelevant noise, and then building solutions that can be scaled, tested, and adapted. If one accepts this as the essence, then the question shifts from definitions to environments. Where, and under what conditions, do these habits actually flourish? And how might educators design spaces that feel authentic—not contrived drills or prepackaged exercises, but living contexts where thinking computationally becomes necessary rather than decorative?

Authenticity in education is a slippery notion. It does not mean simply dragging the "real world" into the classroom, because the so-called real world is vast and unruly, and classrooms are bounded by time, resources, and institutional rituals (Rychly, 2024). What it does mean is constructing problems and projects that carry a genuine sense of consequence, where students feel their work matters beyond the gradebook, and where shortcuts to memorization or rote pattern application collapse under the weight of the task (Kayyali, 2026). In CS, this authenticity often emerges when learners face constraints that mirror professional practice: incomplete data, unpredictable users, limited resources, and the moral weight of decisions that affect others.

Consider the difference between asking students to implement a sorting algorithm versus asking them to design a system that organizes incoming emergency alerts by urgency, reliability, and relevance to different stakeholders. The first can be reduced to mechanics; the second resists trivialization. Suddenly questions of efficiency, scalability, fairness, and transparency intersect. Students must decide which properties to optimize and which to relax. Here, computational thinking is not an abstract checklist but the air required to breathe. The environment has shifted from artificiality toward authenticity, and with it, the learner's mindset begins to change.

Designing such environments requires acknowledging that computational thinking is rarely solitary. Too often, assignments are framed as private duels between student and compiler. Yet real computational work happens in networks of collaboration, where code reviews, design critiques, and peer debates sharpen ideas (Barros et al, 2021). An authentic environment must, then, be social. This doesn't mean every project needs a sprawling group structure, but it does mean cultivating rituals that mirror professional communities: documenting reasoning in version control, writing test cases that future teammates can inherit, or holding reflective conversations about design choices. These practices make the thinking visible, and visibility is the lifeblood of collective problem-solving.

There is also the matter of risk. Authenticity withers if students are never allowed to fail meaningfully (Cronin, 2024). If every task is engineered so tightly that success is almost guaranteed, then computational thinking remains shallow. Environments that cultivate depth must permit the possibility of real setbacks—bugs that take days to isolate, projects that collapse under scope creep, or ethical dilemmas where no option is fully clean. The educator's role here is paradoxical: to design safety nets that prevent despair while leaving enough slack that struggle retains its instructional power. Students should taste frustration, but also learn that frustration is a stage, not an endpoint. This requires courage from the teacher, who must resist the urge to over-scaffold and instead trust the process of iterative learning.

Authenticity also depends on context. A system that feels authentic in one cultural or institutional setting may feel hollow elsewhere. Designing for computational thinking in a resource-rich university lab is not the same as doing so in a classroom where hardware is scarce and connectivity unreliable (Nemadziva, 2023). Authentic design, then, must adapt to circumstance. Sometimes this means scaling down the technology but preserving the problem's richness—using pen-and-paper simulations of algorithms when machines are limited, or relying on community data sets that resonate locally rather than glossy, imported case studies. The principle is less about the sophistication of tools and more about preserving the integrity of the intellectual challenge.

Ethics cannot be bolted on as an afterthought. Authentic computational environments demand that learners grapple with the implications of their solutions. A seemingly neutral technical decision—how to compress data, how to prioritize processes, how to represent categories—can ripple outward into questions of bias, access, and justice. If computational thinking is reduced to efficiency alone, its educational purpose shrivels. Designing authentic spaces means embedding ethical considerations into the very fabric of problems. Students asked to build a scheduling system for a hospital, for instance, must weigh not only throughput but fairness to vulnerable populations. They should be encouraged to articulate trade-offs, defend them, and reflect on the human stakes of technical elegance. This weaving of ethics into computation is what separates authentic thinking from sterile optimization.

One overlooked dimension is time. Authentic environments often require longer arcs than traditional assignments allow. Computational thinking unfolds slowly: hypotheses formed, tested, discarded, revisited (Peel et al, 2022). Short, decontextualized exercises rarely permit the reflective looping that deep learning requires. Designing authentic contexts, then, means carving out temporal space—projects that span weeks rather than days, opportunities to revisit earlier decisions with fresh understanding, cycles of revision that mirror how real systems evolve. Authenticity thrives on duration because duration allows for change, and change allows for reflection.

A crucial ingredient is *uncertainty*. Too many instructional settings scrub away the mess, leaving problems so sanitized they no longer resemble life. Authentic computational environments invite the mess back in: data that contains outliers, specifications that shift midway, stakeholders who disagree on priorities (Jubi, 2024). Students learn to navigate ambiguity not by being told that ambiguity exists, but by inhabiting it. The discomfort that follows is precisely the crucible in which flexible, adaptive habits of computational thinking emerge. What matters is that ambiguity is not left to fester aimlessly; it is framed, discussed, and mined for insight.

The role of technology itself must be interrogated. Authentic environments do not fetishize the newest tools; they choose technology that serves the problem, not the other way around (Beerends & Aydin, 2021). Sometimes that means cutting-edge machine learning platforms; sometimes it means pseudocode and sticky notes. The goal is not to impress with gadgetry but to cultivate discernment: can students select appropriate tools, justify their choices, and understand the implications? Authentic computational thinkers are not dazzled by novelty; they are anchored by judgment.

Assessment in such environments cannot rely solely on correctness. A perfectly functioning program may conceal shallow understanding, while a broken prototype may contain profound insights. Authentic evaluation looks beyond output to process: how students framed the problem, how they decomposed it, how they adapted when strategies failed, how they documented their reasoning. Portfolios, reflective journals, annotated code histories—all of these can capture dimensions of thinking that a unit test alone misses. Assessment, in other words, becomes a mirror not only of what was built but of how the building transformed the builder.

One might ask whether all this talk of authenticity risks romanticizing the classroom, expecting students to behave like miniature professionals when they are still novices. The danger is real. Authenticity should not be confused with mimicry. Students are not software engineers yet; they are learners (Lovellette et al, 2024). The task is not to replicate the industry wholesale but to curate experiences that echo its intellectual challenges without overwhelming with its burdens. An authentic environment is, in the end, a crafted illusion—structured enough to be safe, open enough to be unpredictable, and resonant enough to feel like it matters.

There is a subtle beauty in watching computational thinking emerge under these conditions. Students begin to ask different questions. Instead of "What's the right answer?" they ask "Which assumptions am I making?" Instead of "Does the code run?" they ask "What happens if the input shifts?" Instead of "What's the fastest way?" they ask "Fast for whom, and at what cost?" These shifts in discourse are signs that the environment is working—that the learners have crossed from compliance into genuine engagement.

In the long arc of CS education, designing authentic learning environments may be the most important work educators can do. Languages will change, frameworks will come and go, paradigms will rotate through their cycles of hype and decline (Meihami & Alexander, 2024). But the habits of mind cultivated in authentic spaces—patience with complexity, courage in ambiguity, humility in the face of error, and imagination in design—will endure. Computational thinking is not taught through definition; it is grown in environments where it is indispensable. The challenge, and the opportunity, is to design such spaces with care, creativity, and an unflinching respect for the messy beauty of real problems.

FUTURE DIRECTIONS

To talk about the future of CS education is to walk into contested terrain. Every few years, new calls arise to prioritize this or that: data science as the new lingua franca, artificial intelligence as the inevitable centerpiece, cybersecurity as the ethical imperative (Shafik, 2024). Each trend brings urgency, and each has some truth. But beneath these waves, the deeper current remains unchanged: the discipline's enduring gift is not mastery of ephemeral tools but the ability to navigate problems—ill-defined, shifting, and consequential. If the curriculum is to remain relevant in ten, twenty, or fifty years, it must be reimagined with problem-solving not as an ornament but as the central skeleton around which everything else attaches.

This reimagining cannot simply be cosmetic, swapping in buzzwords or rearranging a few elective modules. It requires questioning the very architecture of CS programs (Twarek et al, 2024). Why do so many curricula still begin with a semester on syntax and control structures divorced from context, as though memorizing grammar alone could ignite curiosity? Why are problems too often treated as afterthoughts, tucked into the final weeks in the form of capstone projects or competitive contests? The inversion needed is radical yet simple: begin with problems, let the problems demand the concepts, and allow the discipline's technical apparatus to emerge as the vocabulary for describing and attacking those problems.

Imagine a first-year CS student not greeted by a lecture on variables but by a real dilemma: how to design an application that allocates scarce hospital resources during a crisis, or how to detect misinformation spreading through a social network. They would not know the tools yet. They would stumble. They would need scaffolding, guidance, and well-placed mini-lessons. But the logic of sequencing shifts. Instead of covering loops for their own sake, the student discovers loops because the problem requires iteration. Instead of introducing recursion as a sterile trick, it arises because a fractal-like structure in the data makes recursion the natural lens. Knowledge becomes motivated rather than imposed, contextual rather than detached.

This shift also reshapes assessment. A curriculum anchored in problem-solving cannot be satisfied with exams that merely test recall of definitions or the ability to code short snippets under time pressure (DeDecker, 2025). Such tasks measure a kind of fluency but miss the heart of the discipline. Instead, evaluation must capture the messier dimensions: the clarity of problem framing, the ingenuity of decomposition, the honesty of debugging logs, the quality of collaboration, the ability to articulate trade-offs when perfection is impossible. A problem-first curriculum would recognize partial successes, thoughtful failures, and well-reasoned pivots as equally rich evidence of learning.

There's an irony here worth acknowledging: problem-solving is harder to teach than content. It is unpredictable, messy, and resistant to standardization. A problem-first curriculum demands more from faculty, who must act as mentors, designers, and provocateurs rather than mere transmitters of content (Lim, 2023). It demands more from institutions, which must resist the ease of multiple-choice grading at massive scale and instead invest in environments that support dialogue, iteration, and reflection. It demands more from students, who cannot hide behind memorization but must confront the discomfort of not knowing. Yet precisely because it is demanding, it has transformative potential.

The design of such curricula must also reckon with interdisciplinarity. Real problems rarely respect disciplinary boundaries. Climate modeling involves algorithms, yes, but also environmental science and policy trade-offs (Douville, 2025). Designing inclusive social platforms requires not just databases but sociological awareness and sensitivity to cultural nuance. A problem-first CS curriculum would necessarily blur the walls, inviting students to partner with peers in medicine, economics, or design. This doesn't dilute CS; it deepens it, forcing students to practice computational thinking as one instrument in a broader orchestra of knowledge. It also guards against the arrogance that sometimes shadows technical fields—the illusion that all problems are code-shaped.

Looking forward, one can envision curricula that operate less like conveyor belts and more like studios. Instead of moving lockstep through topics, students rotate through problem studios: labs where pressing challenges are introduced, inquiry is scaffolded, and technical knowledge is acquired on demand. One studio might focus on sustainable energy optimization, another on ethical AI, another on accessibility in human-computer interaction. Students cycle through these studios across their years, gradually layering expertise while maintaining the sense that their work addresses questions larger than the classroom.

Technology itself complicates the picture. With AI code assistants now capable of generating boilerplate, the rationale for exercises built on routine implementation grows weaker (Lharoui, 2025). Why waste weeks memorizing syntax when tools autocomplete it in seconds? The problem-solving first paradigm absorbs this shift rather than resists it. The focus tilts toward higher-order tasks: specifying problems clearly enough that tools can assist meaningfully, critiquing outputs, stress-testing generated solutions, and integrating multiple strands into coherent systems. Far from undermining education, AI makes the case for problem-centric curricula even stronger, since what cannot be automated easily is the very art of problem formulation and judgment. This curricular reorientation toward a problem-first model across a four-year CS program is conceptualized in Figure 3.

Figure 3. Illustrative Shift Toward Problem-First Curriculum Design Across a Four-Year CS Program

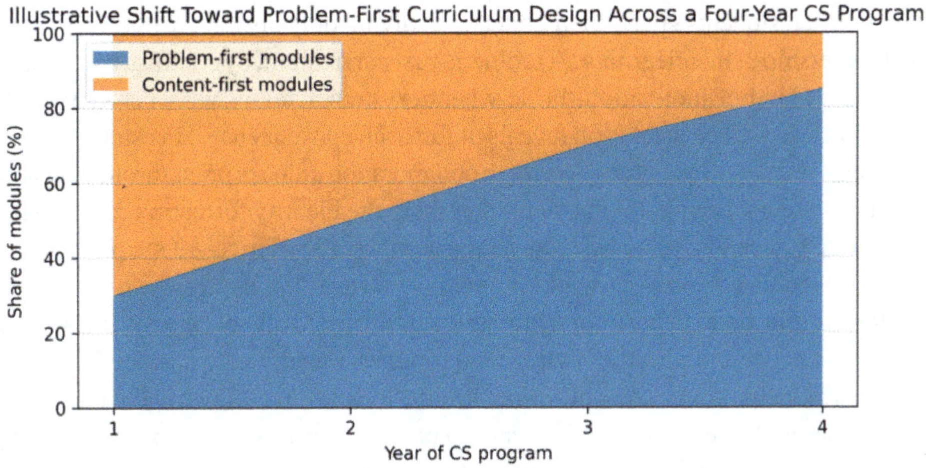

Authenticity must remain the guiding principle. Too many current curricula fall into the trap of toy problems—sanitized inputs, contrived goals, contrived constraints. The future lies in messier authenticity: data sets that misbehave, requirements that shift, stakeholders that disagree. Students should learn that a "correct" algorithm is often less important than a robust, adaptable one. They should experience the weight of ethical decisions as they code, not in a detached ethics seminar but in the living pulse of their projects. The curriculum must create repeated opportunities for students to confront the question: "What does it mean to solve this problem responsibly?"

Equity also demands attention. A problem-solving first curriculum must not privilege only those with prior exposure or those comfortable with ambiguity. Structures must be built to support novices—transparent rubrics, clear scaffolds, peer mentoring, and spaces where asking "naïve" questions is safe. Otherwise, the very students most in need of empowerment may be the ones most alienated. Authentic environments can be inclusive if designed with intention, but without care, they risk amplifying inequities.

Looking at the horizon, the notion of curricular flexibility becomes essential. The problems worth solving shift rapidly. Five years ago, few predicted the urgency of AI ethics at today's scale (Elamin, 2024). A decade ago, cybersecurity was peripheral in many curricula; now it is central. A problem-first design accepts this volatility as normal. Instead of trying to predict every future trend, it creates adaptive structures—modular studios, interdisciplinary problem labs, flexible electives—that can absorb new challenges without tearing the curriculum apart. The stability resides not in specific topics but in the underlying pedagogy: the conviction that students learn best when confronting authentic, consequential problems.

There's also something to be said about the emotional dimension of this reimagining. When students spend their education solving only abstract drills, they rarely feel ownership of their learning. A problem-first curriculum, by contrast, can awaken a different kind of motivation. Pride when a system actually serves a community need. Humility when a solution reveals unforeseen consequences. Frustration when problems resist quick answers. Joy when collaboration unlocks breakthroughs. These emotions are not peripheral; they are integral to the identity formation of computer scientists. Education, at its best, doesn't just impart knowledge—it shapes dispositions, sensibilities, and a sense of belonging to a field that matters.

Reimagining curricula around problem-solving first will not be easy. Institutions may resist because it unsettles entrenched routines. Faculty may hesitate because it requires more improvisation and vulnerability. Students may flinch at the uncertainty it imposes. Yet if education is meant to prepare learners for a world defined by complexity, uncertainty, and relentless change, then anything less than a problem-first approach feels like a betrayal (Fleming, 2021). The future demands more than technicians who can implement instructions; it demands thinkers who can frame, navigate, and resolve problems responsibly.

Perhaps the ultimate test of this vision lies not in the immediate outcomes but in what graduates do a decade later. Do they approach new domains with curiosity rather than fear? Do they collaborate across differences with respect and clarity? Do they design systems that account for unintended consequences? Do they see themselves as problem-solvers in the fullest sense: technical, ethical, and human? If so, then the curriculum has done its work. What's being imagined here is less a reform and more a reorientation. CS education, viewed through this lens, is not primarily about producing code but about producing capacity—the capacity to wrestle with difficult questions, to invent structures where none exist, to design responsibly under constraint. By re-centering curricula around problem-solving, the discipline can move past the churn of tools and trends and return to its deeper promise: equipping people not just to work in a digital world, but to shape it thoughtfully.

CONCLUSION

As CS education continues to expand its reach and redefine its boundaries, one insight emerges with striking clarity: the most enduring contribution of the field to learners is not proficiency in a specific programming language or familiarity with the latest software framework, but the cultivation of problem-solving as a way of thinking and being. Tools and technologies will shift with dizzying speed; today's cutting-edge innovations may become tomorrow's relics. What remains constant is the human capacity to confront novel challenges, to break them down into manageable parts, and to navigate the unknown with creativity, logic, and persistence. For this reason, anchoring CS curricula in problem-solving is not just a pedagogical preference but a necessity for meaningful, future-oriented education.

In examining PjBL and PBL, this chapter has underscored their shared commitment to authentic, student-centered inquiry. Each offers a distinctive yet complementary pathway toward embedding problem-solving in educational practice. PjBL allows students to immerse themselves in extended tasks, developing both technical expertise and professional-like habits of collaboration and design. PBL sharpens the cognitive skills of framing, questioning, and hypothesizing, fostering a mindset attuned to ambiguity and intellectual risk. When seen together, these approaches enrich one another, offering educators a toolkit for cultivating both the breadth and depth of computational thinking.

Yet the adoption of these pedagogies is not without challenges. They demand more of students, who must take greater responsibility for their own learning, and more of instructors, who must act as facilitators, designers, and mentors rather than conveyors of fixed knowledge. Institutions must grapple with questions of assessment, curriculum alignment, and resource allocation. There are no simple answers, only evolving practices shaped by context, culture, and the willingness of educators to experiment and reflect. Still, it is precisely within this complexity that the transformative potential of PjBL and PBL resides. By embracing rather than avoiding ambiguity, educators mirror the realities of CS itself—a discipline perpetually engaged in solving problems that resist easy resolution.

Looking ahead, the integration of PjBL and PBL into CS education is more than a matter of methodology; it is a call to reimagine the very purpose of education in a digital age. Instead of producing graduates narrowly trained in technical proficiency, we must aspire to nurture thinkers, creators, and problem-solvers who can contribute responsibly to a world reshaped by technology. The "problem-solving first" philosophy gestures toward this broader vision, reminding us that the goal is not to prepare students for the tools of today but to empower them for the challenges of tomorrow.

In the end, the measure of success in CS education will not be the number of lines of code a student can produce, nor the speed at which they can learn a new framework, but their ability to encounter unfamiliar problems with curiosity, resilience, and creativity. Project-based and problem-based approaches, in their different ways, point us toward this horizon. They invite us to see education not as the transmission of static knowledge but as the cultivation of living, adaptive intelligence. If we can embrace this shift fully, CS classrooms will cease to be places where students simply learn about technology; they will become spaces where the future of problem-solving itself is imagined, tested, and continually renewed.

REFERENCES

Alaboudi, A., & LaToza, T. D. (2023). What constitutes debugging? An exploratory study of debugging episodes. *Empirical Software Engineering*, *28*(5), 117.

Alharthi, M. (2024). Voices in Crisis: High-Salience Stakeholders' Experiences and Perceptions of Communication During Educational Management Crisis. Studies in Educational Management (SEM), 16.

Amiri, S. M. H. (2025). Project-Based Learning Pedagogy: Bridging Theory and Practice for Real-World Impact. Available at *SSRN* 5333995.

Aymen, D. I. F., & Zakarya, B. O. U. S. I. O. U. D. (2024). The Influence of Artificial Intelligence on Students' Critical Thinking (Doctoral dissertation, university center of abdalhafid boussouf-MILA).

Baltoski, M. (2024). Counting Connections: Exploring Preschool Numeracy, Early Interventions and Parent-Child Relationships (Doctoral dissertation, University of Wollongong).

Barros, B., Conejo, R., Ruiz-Sepulveda, A., & Triguero-Ruiz, F. (2021). I explain, you collaborate, he cheats: An empirical study with social network analysis of study groups in a computer programming subject. *Applied Sciences (Basel, Switzerland)*, *11*(19), 9328.

Beerends, S., & Aydin, C. (2021). Negotiating authenticity in technological environments. *Philosophy & Technology*, *34*(4), 1665–1685.

Cronin, K. S. (2024). The Intentional Pursuit of Purpose: Nurturing Students' Authentic Motivation for Practicing Law. Legal Writing. *J. Legal Writing Inst.*, *28*, 159.

Daby-Seesaram, A., Škardová, K., & Genet, M. (2025). Finite element neural network interpolation: Part II—hybridisation with the proper generalised decomposition for non-linear surrogate modelling. *Computational Mechanics*, •••, 1–26.

DeDecker, S. (2025). The Impact of Instructors' Assessment Design on Undergraduate Student Motivation and Learning Approach within STEM Problem-Solving Learning Environments.

Donisch, L., Schacht, S., & Lanquillon, C. (2024). Inference optimizations for large language models: Effects, challenges, and practical considerations. arXiv preprint arXiv:2408.03130.

Douville, H. (2025). Doing better rather than promising more: A basic principle applicable to both climate modelling and climate policies. *PLOS Climate*, *4*(1), e0000466.

Elamin, M. O. I. (2024). AI through the ages: Unlocking key opportunities and navigating challenges in the history and future of artificial intelligence. *International Journal of Religion*, *5*(12), 1152–1166.

Erwin, J. C. (2024). *The Classroom of Choice: 100+ Strategies to Reach and Teach Every Learner*. ASCD.

Eswaran, U. (2024). Project-based learning: Fostering collaboration, creativity, and critical thinking. In *Enhancing education with intelligent systems and data-driven instruction* (pp. 23–43). IGI Global Scientific Publishing.

Fleming, P. (2021). *Dark academia: How universities die*. Pluto Books.

Friend, M., Mcgill, M., & Reinking, A. (2022, November). Solve this! K-12 CS education teachers' problems of practice. In Proceedings of the 22nd Koli Calling International Conference on Computing Education Research (pp. 1-13).

Gopal, B. C. (2025). Cognitive, Motivational, and Pedagogical Factors Influencing Effective Teaching and Learning in Math Education. *Journal of Musikot Campus*, *3*(1), 186–199.

Güss, C. D., & Starker, U. (2023). The influence of emotion and emotion regulation on complex problem-solving performance. *Systems*, *11*(6), 276.

Hall, M. E. L. (2021). Teaching students to doubt well: The roles of intellectual humility and uncertainty tolerance. *Christian Scholar's Review*, *50*(3), 261–279.

Hanstedt, P. (2023). *Creating wicked students: Designing courses for a complex world*. Routledge.

Hennessy Elliott, C., Nixon, J., Gendrau Chakarov, A., Bush, J. B., Schneider, M. J., & Recker, M. (2024). Characterizing teacher support of debugging with physical computing: Debugging pedagogies in practice. ACM transactions on computing education, 24(4), 1-28.

Jiang, C., & Pang, Y. (2023). Enhancing design thinking in engineering students with project-based learning. *Computer Applications in Engineering Education*, *31*(4), 814–830.

Jubi, R. (2024). *Business analytics-unleashing data driven decision making*. NEHAS PUBLICATIONS.

Kayyali, M. (2026). The Rationales Behind the Creation of Applied Models for Problem Solving. In Building Applied Models for Problem Solving (pp. 123-152). IGI Global Scientific Publishing.

Klamen, D., Suh, B., & Tischkau, S. (2022). Problem-based learning. In *An introduction to medical teaching: The foundations of curriculum design, delivery, and assessment* (pp. 115–131). Springer International Publishing.

Kolosnjaji, B., Xiao, H., Xu, P., & Zarras, A. (2024). *Artificial Intelligence for Cybersecurity: Develop AI approaches to solve cybersecurity problems in your organization*. Packt Publishing Ltd.

Landorf, H., & Wadley, C. (2022). The importance of John Dewey's philosophy for global learning theory and practice. *Social Studies Research & Practice*, *17*(1), 6–18.

Lharoui, M. (2025). Role-specific AI use cases for enhancing daily operations in energy upgrades projects.

Lim, W. K. (2023). Problem based learning in medical education: Handling objections and sustainable implementation. *Advances in Medical Education and Practice*, •••, 1453–1460. PMID: 38164409

Lopatecki, D. (2022). The Body Navigated Through Moments of Abstraction.

Lovellette, E., Bouvier, D. J., & Matta, J. (2024). Contextualization, authenticity, and the problem description effect. *ACM Transactions on Computing Education*, *24*(2), 1–32.

Meihami, H., & Alexander, C. (2024). Adopting Gartner's hype cycles to investigate the lifespan of computer assisted language learning from EFL learners' perspectives. *Asian-Pacific Journal of Second and Foreign Language Education*, *9*(1), 31.

Michela, E. (2022). This Uncertain Space of Teaching": How Design Studio Instructors Talk about Design Critiques along with Themselves When Giving Critiques. *The Journal of Scholarship of Teaching and Learning*, *22*(1), 48–66.

Moore, D. J. (2025). Motivating Students Through Problem-Based and Project-Based Learning.

Nadir, H. M. (2021). *Investigating a Teacher's Scaffolding for Design Problem Solving in Project-Based Learning*. Indiana University.

Nan, J. (2025). In-Depth Practice and Strategic Exploration of Project-Based Learning in Primary and Secondary School Music Teaching. *OAlib*, *12*(6), 1–9.

Nemadziva, B. (2023). Using science communication strategies to close the resource gap in under-resourced schools: A focus on rural schools in South Africa (Doctoral dissertation, University of Otago).

Neves, R. (2024). The Engineering Leadership Playbook: Strategies for Team Success and Business Growth. Apress.

O'Reilly, C. A.III, & Tushman, M. L. (2021). *Lead and disrupt: How to solve the innovator's dilemma.* Stanford University Press.

Ortiz, I. (2023). Integrating advanced data handling approaches in modern architectural designs to optimize efficiency and scalability. Journal of Sustainable Technologies and Materials.

Peel, A., Sadler, T. D., & Friedrichsen, P. (2022). Algorithmic explanations: An unplugged instructional approach to integrate science and computational thinking. *Journal of Science Education and Technology, 31*(4), 428–441. PMID: 35535350

Petropoulos, F., Laporte, G., Aktas, E., Alumur, S. A., Archetti, C., Ayhan, H., & Zhao, X. (2024). Operational Research: Methods and applications. *The Journal of the Operational Research Society, 75*(3), 423–617.

Pomelov, V. B. (2021). The William Heard Kilpatrick's Project Method: on the 150th anniversary of the American educator. Перспективы науки и образования, (4), 436-447.

Rychly, L. (Ed.). (2024). *What Do We Mean by That?: Interrogating Familiar Expressions in Education.* Stylus Publishing, LLC.

Sánchez-García, R., & Reyes-de-Cózar, S. (2025). Enhancing Project-Based Learning: A Framework for Optimizing Structural Design and Implementation—A Systematic Review with a Sustainable Focus. Sustainability (2071-1050), 17(11).

Shafik, W. (2024). Artificial intelligence and machine learning with cyber ethics for the future world. In *Future communication systems using artificial intelligence, internet of things and data science* (pp. 110–130). CRC Press.

Silma, N., Maulida, I., Wulan, A. P., Merawati, J., & Hasan, M. K. (2024). A comprehensive review of Project-Based Learning (PBL): Unravelling its aims, methodologies, and implications. Journal of Education, Social &. *Communication Studies, 1*(1), 10–19.

Smith, R., Liggett, W., Niewola, J., & Hegarty, K. (2024, March). From Dimes to Deadlines: What Project Management Techniques Are Right for You? In *2024 IEEE Aerospace Conference* (pp. 1-17). IEEE.

Thomsen, K. (2024). A heuristic sketch how it could fit all together with time. arXiv preprint arXiv:2405.10335.

Tokuhama-Espinosa, T. (2021). *Bringing the neuroscience of learning to online teaching: an educator's handbook*. Teachers College Press.

Twarek, B., Koressel, J., Smith, J. M., & McGill, M. M. (2024). Reimagining CS Pathways Interim Report# 2: Defining Pathways Beyond a Foundational High School CS Course.

Tweeten, J., & Hung, W. (2023). Design-Based Research Method in PBL/PjBL: A Case in Nursing Education. *The Interdisciplinary Journal of Problem-Based Learning*, *17*(2), n2.

Wang, H., & Flory, J. (2024). Room for Breathing: Mindfulness, Currere, and Contemplative Practices in Teacher Education. *Journal of Contemplative and Holistic Education*, *2*(1), 3.

Werder, C., & Otis, M. M. (Eds.). (2023). *Engaging student voices in the study of teaching and learning*. Taylor & Francis.

Woolard, T. (2022). No Teacher Left Behind: The Science (and Psychology) of Sustaining PBL PD (Doctoral dissertation, Morgan State University).

Yang, X., Zhao, G., Yan, X., Chao, Q., Zhao, X., Lu, T., & Dong, Y. (2022). Presetting stances for students during collaborative argumentation: Parallel thinking versus adversarial thinking. *Research in Science Education*, *52*(6), 1829–1850.

Yau, C. B. (2021). Interaction of Scientist-Teacher-Students in Problem-Project Based Learning (Master's thesis, University of Malaya (Malaysia)).

KEY TERMS AND DEFINITIONS

Authentic Learning Environments: designed contexts where problems, constraints, stakeholders, and risks mirror real-world CS practice rather than simplified textbook exercises.

Computational Thinking: a set of habits including decomposition, abstraction, pattern recognition, and algorithmic design used to make sense of complex situations and build testable solutions.

Debugging Culture: the shared attitudes, practices, and strategies that treat debugging as disciplined inquiry and epistemic practice, not just error-fixing.

Problem Studio: a recurring course structure in which students cycle through problem scoping, investigation, building, critique, and reflection, blending PBL and PjBL over time.

Problem-Based Learning (PBL): a pedagogy that begins with ill-structured, authentic problems which drive inquiry, self-directed learning, and iterative reasoning before formal instruction.

Problem-Solving First: a curriculum philosophy that treats structured problem-solving as the core of computer science education rather than a side outcome of content coverage.

Project-Based Learning (PjBL): an approach where students work over extended periods on complex projects that culminate in tangible artifacts such as applications, simulations, or systems.

Chapter 4
Formative Epistemics and Inclusive Design Approach Using Constructive Alignment and Metacognition: Sociotechnical Pedagogy for Computer Education

Ashraf Alam
https://orcid.org/0000-0001-6178-1187
Alliance University, Bengaluru, India

ABSTRACT

This chapter proposes a pedagogy first architecture for computing assessment that couples formative routines with minimalist analytics and equity by design. It argues for alignment to disciplinary big ideas, visible success criteria, short revision cycles, and multimodal evidence including code histories, test rationales, diagrams, and oral defenses. Peer and self-judgment are cultivated as disciplined practices, supported by universal design and culturally sustaining tasks. Analytics remain small, interpretable, and privacy preserving, answering concrete instructional questions within hours. Capacity is built through coaching, lesson study, micro credentials, and calibrated observation, with change managed through protected schedules and toolkits. Comparative cases from K to 8, secondary, undergraduate, and reskilling contexts show feasibility and impact. An improvement science agenda links logic models to measurable gains in competence, fairness, and credible external signaling.

DOI: 10.4018/979-8-3373-6546-6.ch004

INTRODUCTION

Computer science education often valorizes syntax recall, isolated correctness, and speeded quizzes while contemporary software practice prizes underdetermined problem framing, systematic debugging, evidentiary testing, literate documentation, and collaborative governance (Yue et al., 2022). The resulting construct misalignment distorts study behaviors and grading heuristics, privileging brittle performance over transferable competence (Susanto et al., 2020). Convergent evidence shows that learning trajectories steepen when teachers elicit and act on in-course evidence rather than tally end states, that high yield feedback is timely, specific, and task or process oriented, and that mastery learning treats time as elastic and quality as invariant (Tzafilkou et al., 2023). Strong effects accrue when success criteria are public, revision is routine, and design rationales are examinable. In programming this means criteria for decomposition, naming, invariants, test coverage, and ethical data use, accompanied by staged submissions and brief oral defenses. The chapter advances an integrated architecture in which assessment for learning, inclusion by design, and interpretable analytics operate as a single cybernetic system that stabilizes measurement validity, accelerates remediation, and renders intermediate reasoning inspectable (Dai et al., 2024).

The chapter functions as a narrative synthesis across learning sciences, computing education, human computer interaction, program evaluation, organizational change, and information law, translating theory into deployable routines for classrooms, departments, and systems (Choi et al., 2023). Instructors receive design patterns such as visible criteria, peer and self-calibration with anchor exemplars, and guaranteed resubmission windows that credit growth. Leaders receive schedule and incentive blueprints that protect critique, moderation, and double marking. Policymakers receive implementable guardrails that normalize formative use of data while honoring privacy by design, with consent, minimization, role bounded access, auditability, and retention limits aligned with statutory regimes whose enforceability for European general data protection began in 2018 alongside longstanding frameworks such as FERPA and COPPA and recent national statutes (Papadakis, 2022). Students and industry partners receive a portfolio logic that foregrounds code with history, test rationales, design tradeoffs, and reflective narratives that better index reliability, maintainability, and collaborative judgment than isolated scores.

Analytics is positioned as an attentional prosthesis for pedagogy rather than as an oracle (Fagerlund et al., 2021). Signals are proportional to the instructional question, interpretable in a brief conference, and paired with candidate teacher moves to close a sense make act loop. A three-item exit probe on loop invariants often outperforms exhaustive telemetry, and a spike in compile failures warrants different action depending on whether the goal is conceptual consolidation, productive struggle, or test discipline. Inclusion is treated as a first principle not a retrofit. Universal Design for Learning improves inference fidelity by diversifying representational and expression pathways, culturally sustaining design aligns tasks and datasets with learner communities, and trauma aware routines reduce noise from surprise penalties and opaque rules (Saputra et al., 2023). Boundary conditions are explicit. Bias reviews and moderation improve reliability, workload is contained by short cycles and capped comments, integrity is safeguarded through individualized traces such as commit histories and micro-orals, and governance prohibits opaque rankings while favoring distributional reporting with uncertainty. The system thereby converts classroom evidence into rapid instructional adjustments, program evidence into iterative improvement, and public evidence into credible signals for progression and employment.

MAIN FOCUS OF THE CHAPTER

This chapter focuses on redesigning computer science assessment so that the evidence students generate during learning becomes the primary driver of instruction, equity, and credible progression decisions. It advances an integrated architecture in which assessment for learning, inclusion by design, and pedagogy-first analytics operate as one closed-loop system. The chapter reorients assessment away from speeded syntax recall and toward underdetermined problem framing, systematic debugging, evidentiary testing, literate documentation, and collaborative governance. It specifies how visible success criteria, short-cycle feedback, peer and self-calibration, and guaranteed revision windows convert formative evidence into measurable growth while improving inter-rater reliability. It also defines a multimodal evidence model that combines code, version history, tests and rationales, diagrams, short oral defenses, and response-to-reviewer logs, enabling portfolios that index reliability and maintainability better than isolated scores.

Equally, the chapter concentrates on governing data and analytics so they remain interpretable, purpose-bound, and privacy compliant. Analytics is positioned as an attentional aid that uses the smallest sufficient traces such as time to first passing test, compile-error streaks, commit cadence, and topic-tagged help requests, each paired with bounded teacher actions in rapid sense make act cycles. Equity is treated as a validity condition through Universal Design for Learning, culturally sustaining task contexts, and trauma-aware logistics, alongside bias reviews and moderation that prevent opaque ranking. Finally, the chapter translates the architecture into implementation routines and toolkits, including scheduling and incentive designs, coaching and PLC protocols, procurement guardrails, and evaluation logic that tracks revision uptake, equity deltas, workload variance, and program improvement over time.

THEORETICAL FOUNDATIONS AND THEORY OF CHANGE

A coherent account of learning in computing begins with the formative tradition synthesized by Paul Black and Dylan Wiliam in 1998, which demonstrated that achievement accelerates when instruction continually elicits evidence and adapts in real time rather than stockpiling terminal marks. John Hattie and Helen Timperley in 2007 articulated feedback as feed up against explicit intentions, feedback on present performance, and feed forward as concrete next moves, while Valerie Shute in 2008 showed that task and process level information delivered promptly and stripped of ego judgments yields the largest effects (Vitaliy et al., 2022; Kadirbergenovna, 2022). Benjamin Bloom's learning for mastery in 1968 argued that time should be elastic and quality invariant, which justifies reassessment windows and staged submissions in programming where debugging and refactoring constitute central epistemic games (Qureshi, 2023). Sociocultural work from Lev Vygotsky in 1978 and from Jean Lave and Etienne Wenger in 1991 repositioned learning as guided participation inside a community of practice, which in computing legitimizes code talk, pair programming, and studio style review as primary sites of cognitive apprenticeship (Yue et al., 2022; Zhan et al., 2022). Barry Zimmerman in 2002, Paul Pintrich in 2000, and Philip Winne in 2011 established self-regulation and metacognition as teachable cycles of forethought, monitoring, and reflection, operationalized in CS by decomposition planning, pre run failure prediction, and revision logs that bind comments to code changes (Ogegbo & Ramnarain, 2022). Motivation and identity research from Edward Deci and Richard Ryan in 2000, Jacquelynne Eccles and Allan Wigfield in 2002, Carol Dweck in 2006, and Claude Steele with Joshua Aronson in 1995 explains why autonomy, expectancy, and belonging shape persistence, which renders transparent criteria, choiceful datasets, and person neutral critique indispensable.

Table 1. Foundations-to-Practice Matrix for Feedback-Rich, Equitable CS Assessment

Macro-Domain & Provenance	**Key Constructs & Claims (Validated)**	**CS-Specific Operationalization (Tasks, Rubrics, Routines)**	**Instructional Analytics & Measurement Hooks**	**Risks, Limitations, and Mitigations**
Assessment for Learning & Feedback Theory	Formative evidence accelerates achievement; task and process feedback outperforms ego feedback; mastery is criterion referenced with time as the free variable; feed up, feedback, feedforward close the loop.	Publish student-readable criteria for correctness, design, testing, documentation, ethics; staged submissions with guaranteed revision; two-stage checks; response-to-reviewer linkage; growth-weighted scoring.	Time-to-first-passing-test; comment-uptake rate; calibration delta between self-scores and rubric; mutation and boundary coverage over iterations; feedback-to-change latency.	Comment overload curbed by two high-leverage notes; inter-rater reliability via moderation; inflate-deflate grading guarded by fixed cut-scores; integrity via commit history and micro-orals.
Sociocultural & Constructivist Views	Learning as guided participation; epistemic apprenticeship; authentic tool mediation; dialogic reasoning externalizes tacit knowledge.	Normalized code review and pair roles; design charrettes; think-aloud debugging; version control, issues, tests as first-class tasks; sentence-stemmed critique.	Specificity density of peer comments; criterion citation rate; peer-to-peer uptake; participation entropy in studios; traceability of design rationales to diffs.	Social loafing mitigated by rotating roles and accountable artifacts; discourse bias reduced through anonymized anchors and tone scripts; equitable turns enforced by quotas.
Self-Regulated Learning & Metacognition	Forethought–monitor–reflect cycles trainable; calibration improves with exemplar scoring; agency evidenced in plan–predict–test–explain routines; portfolios show transfer.	Pre-submit self-rating; prediction before test run; design decision memos in commits; before–after artifacts with concise rationales; exemplar calibration rehearsals.	Prediction accuracy vs outcomes; self-rubric agreement coefficients; proportion of explanatory commits; revision depth index favoring structural over cosmetic edits.	Reflection drag minimized by sub-100-word micro-prompts; ego threat avoided with work-focused language; novice scaffolds provided through templates.

continued on following page

Table 1. Continued

Macro-Domain & Provenance	Key Constructs & Claims (Validated)	CS-Specific Operationalization (Tasks, Rubrics, Routines)	Instructional Analytics & Measurement Hooks	Risks, Limitations, and Mitigations
Motivation & Identity in CS	Autonomy, competence, relatedness drive persistence; expectancy–value–cost governs effort; fixed-ability cues depress engagement; belonging buffers identity threat.	Constrained choice of datasets; public criteria and exemplars; recognition of diverse excellence; penalty-free revision; critique targets work not person.	Help-request taxonomy by topic; revision attempt counts; micro-belonging pulses around milestones; conversion from first-attempt fail to criterion attainment.	Identity threat reduced via alternate contexts and public celebration of revision; perceived cost lowered with staged deadlines; redistribute access to office hours.
Equity-Centered Design	UDL increases construct fidelity; culturally sustaining contexts elevate participation; trauma-aware routines reduce measurement noise.	Diversified evidence paths: code, tests, diagrams, orals, prototypes; prompt and dataset bias scans; quiet options and flexible timing where construct permits; grading for growth.	Subgroup participation and attainment contrasts; modality-performance correlations controlling prior; test-to-code ratios as equity sentinels; completeness under low-bandwidth or assistive tech.	Accommodation by design reduces retrofits; opt-out contexts of equal rigor; invariant criteria avoid soft expectations; publish accessibility checklists.
Constructive Alignment & TPACK for CS	Outcomes, activities, assessments must cohere or learners optimize to points; tool–pedagogy–content interactions can reveal or occlude constructs; validity rises when affordances surface what is scored.	If testing discipline is an outcome students write, justify, run tests; choose environments exposing debugging moves; linting and formatters operationalize readability; make APIs and VCS scorable.	Coverage and mutation aligned to rubric; lint compliance as readability proxy; alignment audits mapping each criterion to a task action and artifact; misalignment flags when correctness lacks tests.	Under-representation corrected by adding artifacts not points; avoid tool lock-in; periodic alignment reviews; temper auto-grading with design judgment.

continued on following page

Table 1. Continued

Macro-Domain & Provenance	Key Constructs & Claims (Validated)	CS-Specific Operationalization (Tasks, Rubrics, Routines)	Instructional Analytics & Measurement Hooks	Risks, Limitations, and Mitigations
Cognitive Considerations	Manage intrinsic, extraneous, germane load; worked-example fading accelerates schemata; retrieval and spacing strengthen retention; deliberate practice targets weak subskills.	Worked examples of decomposition and invariants then fade; short oral retrieval before execution; spaced revisit of iteration, recursion, state; micro-diagnostics with targeted mini-lessons.	Spaced-item correctness trajectories; pre–post error taxonomy shifts; time-on-transition for example to problem; forgetting slopes on core patterns.	Split-attention reduced with single-pane instructions; redundancy pruned; diagnostics capped to protect momentum; ensure example–problem isomorphism.
Learning Analytics & Ethics	Proportional, interpretable, purpose-bound analytics; smallest sufficient data; governance via consent, minimization, role access, retention, auditability; avoid opaque risk scores for formative use.	Minimal traces: first-test latency, compile-error streaks, help-request topics, commit cadence; pair each indicator with candidate teaching moves; cohort prediction confined to program review; intervention logs.	Classroom cycles: daily sense–make–act; Program cycles: bottleneck, workload, equity trends; dashboards show uncertainty and action templates; deletion and access trails.	Human-in-the-loop thresholds; no league tables; vendor contracts ban secondary use; present distributions not ranks; plain-language notices and correction rights.
Theory of Change (Operational Logic)	Inputs to outcomes chain with explicit boundary conditions; continuous improvement via short cycles; equity and privacy constraints integral.	Inputs: PD on criteria and critique, vetted blueprints, lightweight analytics, protected checkpoints. Activities: co-create criteria, calibrate, peer and self review, concise feedback, record moves. Outputs: documented revisions, higher boundary coverage, clearer decomposition. Outcomes: durable transfer, narrowed gaps, stabilized workload, program refinement.	Leading indicators: revision uptake, criterion trajectories, workload variance, equity deltas. Lagging indicators: completion, progression, portfolio adoption.	Boundary conditions: data minimization, governed peer review, guaranteed revision rights, achievement separated from behavior, PDSA cycles to scale what works and retire what does not.

Equity oriented design frameworks supply the normative guardrails that make inference credible across populations (Hall et al., 2024; Tang et al., 2020). Universal Design for Learning from CAST advances multiple means of representation, action and engagement, while Gloria Ladson Billings in 1995 and Django Paris in 2012 argue that culturally relevant and culturally sustaining pedagogy align tasks with community knowledge rather than treating culture as backdrop. Trauma informed practice popularized by federal guidance in 2014 cautions against high surprise penalties and opaque rules that inject extraneous variance. Constructive alignment from John Biggs in the 1990s and technological pedagogical content knowledge from Punya Mishra and Matthew Koehler in 2006 require outcomes, activities, tools, and rubrics that cohere, aided by editors that surface readability through linting and environments that expose debugging strategies.

Cognitive science contributes load theory from John Sweller in 1988, multimedia design from Richard Mayer, retrieval and spacing from Henry Roediger and Jeffrey Karpicke in 2006 and from Nicholas Cepeda and colleagues in 2008, and deliberate practice from K Anders Ericsson, which together justify worked example fading, brief diagnostics, cumulative quizzes, and short oral reconstructions before execution. Learning analytics is framed as proportional decision support rather than surveillance, with George Siemens and Phil Long in 2011 and Ryan Baker with Kalina Yacef in 2009 emphasizing interpretable traces such as time to first passing test, while privacy by design from Ann Cavoukian and data protection law adopted in 2016 with application commencing in 2018 in Europe require consent, minimization, role bound access, and purpose clarity. The theory of change aggregates these strands into inputs such as professional learning, vetted blueprints, lightweight instruments, and protected time, into activities such as calibrated peer review and focused comments, into outputs such as documented revisions and improved coverage, and into outcomes such as durable competence, narrowed gaps, stabilized workload, and iterative program improvement under explicit boundary conditions.

DESIGN PRINCIPLES FOR FEEDBACK-RICH AND INCLUSIVE CS ASSESSMENT

A coherent design for feedback rich and inclusive computing assessment privileges disciplinary reasoning over superficial syntax and treats authenticity as quotidian professional praxis rather than theatrical case dressing (Lamrani & Abdelwahed, 2020). Alignment begins with outcomes rewritten as observable verbs that name abstraction, decomposition, algorithmic evaluation, data representation, state invariants, verification, and principled trade-offs, then proceeds to tasks that compel these moves through version control, code review, unit and property testing, literate documentation, and reliable API use (Tkachuk et al., 2020; Ashraf et al., 2020). Construct validity rises when the highest scoring pathway coincides with the workflow that yields dependable software in a team setting (Lyon & Magana, 2020; Sanusi et al., 2022). Precision in success criteria converts tacit norms into scorable signals and compresses feedback into concise directives that point to missing invariants, untested boundaries, or unjustified structures (Yilmaz Ince & Koc, 2021). Iterative cadence operationalizes learning as control theory in miniature, using short sprints with checkpoints that surface intermediate cognition through decomposition sketches, minimal viable implementations, and first pass test suites (Prather et al., 2023; Fincher et al., 2020). Revision is guaranteed and growth weighted so that quality remains invariant while time becomes elastic. Evidence is multimodal and designed rather than improvised, combining code with history, test rationales, diagrams of state and flow, oral defenses, debugging screencasts, and reflective memos that tie comments to changes, which increases inferential fidelity and reduces modality bias.

Table 2. Design Principles Matrix for Feedback-Rich Inclusive Computing Assessment

Macro-Domain & Provenance	Key Constructs & Claims (Validated)	CS-Specific Operationalization (Tasks, Rubrics, Routines)	Instructional Analytics & Measurement Hooks	Risks, Limitations, and Mitigations
Alignment to Big Ideas and Authentic Practice	Construct validity rises when targets include abstraction, decomposition, algorithmics, data models, state invariants, verification, Pareto tradeoffs; authenticity equals professional praxis; optimal path aligns with reliable software.	Outcomes recast as observable verbs; tasks mandate VCS, issue tracking, peer review, unit and property tests, API hygiene, literate docs, reliability engineering; alternatives compared via asymptotics and failure modes; puzzle items excised.	Alignment matrices; percent tasks with mandatory tests and rationales; alternative comparison frequency; post-merge defect density; mean time to restore.	Under-representation and construct-irrelevant variance mitigated through blueprints, anchor artifacts, rubric pruning; anti-gaming via scorable workflows; feasibility checked with grading time audits.
Visible Success Criteria and Student Calibration	Transparency elevates calibration and feedback uptake; dimensions operationalize readability, design quality, testing discipline, responsible data use; precise criteria compress comment length and increase actionability.	One-page student-readable criteria with exemplars and counter-exemplars; pre-review calibration on anonymized work; criterion-keyed comment banks; micro-comments on invariants and boundary coverage.	Self–rubric concordance; comment-to-revision linkage; feedback-to-change latency; lint compliance and identifier entropy; coverage and mutation thresholds.	Over-specification, rater drift, lexical bias curtailed via moderation bursts, de-biased descriptors, compact rubrics.
Iterative Sprints and Short-Cycle Feedback	Rapid cycles expose intermediate reasoning and smooth workload; mastery treats time as elastic and quality as invariant; cadence reduces end-loaded superficial fixes.	Two-week sprints with 2–3-day checkpoints; MVIs and first-pass tests; guaranteed revision and growth-weighted scoring; micro retros embedded.	Progress velocity; commit cadence regularity; time-to-first passing test; criterion growth curves; last-day commit share.	Feedback overload and churn constrained by high-leverage comment caps, time-boxed revision, structural-change indices, schedule protection.

continued on following page

Table 2. Continued

Macro-Domain & Provenance	Key Constructs & Claims (Validated)	CS-Specific Operationalization (Tasks, Rubrics, Routines)	Instructional Analytics & Measurement Hooks	Risks, Limitations, and Mitigations
Multimodal Evidence Architecture	Triangulation across modalities heightens inferential fidelity and reliability; captures implementation, failure anticipation, conceptual models, metacognition.	Portfolio with code history, test rationales, data-flow diagrams, short orals, debugging screencasts, prototypes where relevant, reflective memos linking comments to edits.	Cross-modal convergence indices; test-to-code ratios; diagram–implementation consistency; oral explanatory adequacy; debugging event traces.	Busywork and modality privilege minimized via minimal sufficient sets, language and motor audits, required code realization.
Peer and Self-Assessment Protocols	Distributed epistemic judgment emerges through trained peer review and self-assessment; calibration institutionalizes communal standards and increases uptake.	Structured roles and timed studios; sentence-stemmed critique; response-to-reviewer logs; mandatory self-ratings with next-step plans; sampled peer comment quality with micro-coaching.	Comment specificity density; peer-attributable uptake; interrater agreement on anchors; self-prediction accuracy; participation entropy to detect dominance.	Loafing, tone drift, inequitable help mitigated by artifact accountability, discourse scripts, redistributed office hours.
Closed-Loop Revision Logistics	Feedback yields value only when work changes; policy and workflow must guarantee and visualize revision; revision culture normalizes improvement.	Review window then revision window and mini retrospective; three-column change logs linking comment, change, rationale; priority-limited comments; mini-lessons triggered by recurrent gaps.	Revision depth index favoring structural edits; comment resolution rate per cycle; mini-lesson effect sizes on error families; persistence of gains across tasks.	Procrastination and noncompliance reduced via scheduled checkpoints, visible logs, paced resubmissions, templated responses.
Accessibility and Cultural Relevance by Design	Universal design and culturally sustaining contexts increase measurement fidelity and participation; trauma-aware routines attenuate extraneous stress signals.	Multiple representations and expressions; alternate rigorous contexts; quiet zones and flexible timing where constructs permit; dataset and prompt audits; individualized accommodations atop accessible baselines.	Subgroup participation and attainment differentials; modality–performance correlations controlling prior; bandwidth sensitivity of submissions; opt-out parity checks.	Soft expectation bias prevented by invariant standards; retrofit debt avoided through upfront accessibility; equivalent alternatives provided; transparency via published checklists.

continued on following page

Table 2. Continued

Macro-Domain & Provenance	Key Constructs & Claims (Validated)	CS-Specific Operationalization (Tasks, Rubrics, Routines)	Instructional Analytics & Measurement Hooks	Risks, Limitations, and Mitigations
Multidimensional Rubrics and Reliability Engineering	Orthogonal dimensions prevent halo effects; reliability depends on clear thresholds, rater training, moderation; language must be observable and bias resistant.	Five-dimension rubric for correctness, design, tests, documentation, ethics; anchors per level per criterion; rapid calibration rituals; bias scrub to operational descriptors.	Weighted kappa for interrater reliability; outlier audit trails; criterion-level dispersion to detect compression; time-per-artifact benchmarks.	Over-granularity and construct drift mitigated by collapsing redundancies and rubric–outcome audits; section variance reduced through standardized TA calibration.
Toolkits Workload Integrity and External Signaling	Codified toolkits enable scale and workload control; individualized traces safeguard integrity; portfolios translate classroom evidence into credible external signals.	Templates for task design, criteria, critique, bias review, analytics plans, revision logs, portfolio curation; automation with linters and harnesses; micro orals on sampled functions; standardized showcase tasks.	Teacher workload variance over term; automation hit rates on low-level defects; integrity fingerprints via commit granularity and defense scores; external portfolio uptake.	Burnout, plagiarism, signaling noise mitigated by scheduled moderation, traceable histories, common showcase artifacts, iterative PDSA cycles.

Equity and feasibility are engineered from the start through universal design, culturally sustaining prompts, and trauma aware logistics that remove extraneous variance while preserving rigor (Chen et al., 2023). Rubrics separate orthogonal dimensions such as correctness, design, testing, documentation, and ethical reasoning, with anchors that stabilize rater judgment and moderation rituals that protect reliability at scale (Troussas et al., 2020b). Practitioner toolkits codify routines into one-page blueprints, critique protocols, bias audits, minimal analytics plans, revision logs, and portfolio guides so that setup cost declines and cognitive energy moves to high leverage decisions. Workload remains tractable through scheduled critique blocks, capped comments, assistant calibration, and automation at the appropriate granularity for formatting and regression checks. Integrity and fairness are safeguarded by individualized traces such as frequent small commits and micro-orals, transparent policies for proportionate responses, and even access to help (Zhang et al., 2020; Troussas et al., 2020a). Classroom artifacts are curated into portfolios that signal reliability, maintainability, and collaboration to external audiences more credibly than isolated correctness scores (Chang et al., 2020). The stance is simple and demanding, namely that small interpretable data must serve pedagogy, that judgment is distributed through trained peer and self-review, and that leadership aligns schedules, procurement, and evaluation so that these routines become ordinary rather than exceptional.

PEDAGOGY-FIRST LEARNING ANALYTICS

Pedagogy first analytics begins with questions that instructors actually confront mid unit and only then with measurements that can redirect instruction within hours (Johnson & Elliott, 2020; Dudyrev & Maksimenkova, 2020). The discipline is parsimony, not telemetry accumulation. A three-item exit probe on sentinel-controlled loops yields a faster corrective than a week of keystroke logs, while a stand up record that tags environment blockers versus conceptual blockers triggers a targeted clinic for a small subset (Alam & Mohanty, 2023a). Minimal traces carry disproportionate value when they map cleanly to teachable moves. Time to first passing test indicates harness fluency and assertion craft, compile error streaks without code deltas signal path or dependency confusion, rolling commit cadence separates steady progress from deadline spikes that correlate with superficial fixes, topic tagged help requests surface reteach needs with precision (Vakil, 2020). Traces differ by environment and demand careful hermeneutics. Block sequences and reuse patterns in K to 8 reveal structure seeking but can overcount productive tinkering, text courses benefit from coverage and mutation trajectories, lint compliance, and added to deleted line ratios, physical computing requires photos, wiring diagrams, and safety checklists, unplugged tasks rely on structured observation of strategy use and turn taking (El-Hamamsy et al., 2021; Abichandani et al., 2022). Early warning remains local, auditable, and human in the loop, with simple triggers such as three inactive days during a sprint or two checkpoints without new tests followed by documented interventions and review.

Table 3. Pedagogy First Learning Analytics Matrix for Actionable and Ethical Instruction

Domain Focus & Scope	Principle and Empirical Rationale	Operationalization in CS Settings	Signals and Quantification	Risks and Governance Safeguards
Inquiry-Driven Analytics	Pedagogy sets the question before measurement; parsimony maximizes signal to noise; rapid sense make act cycles outcompete static dashboards	For each sprint predefine two or three high leverage decisions with approved responses; identify viewers instructor learner team; run same day micro retros that log action and effect	Three item exit checks on focal constructs; stand up blocker tags environment or concept; micro confidence probes; immediate pre post deltas recorded	Metric theater curtailed by preregistered decisions and time boxes; require short reflection logs; forbid nonactionable vanity visualizations
Minimal Sufficiency of Data	Data minimization heightens ethics and interpretability; direct traces dominate exhaustive telemetry; transparency preserves autonomy	Harvest traces from extant tools not keystrokes; two-minute self reports for help topic and blocker class; publish retention windows access roles and deletion cadence	Time to first passing test; compile error streaks without code diffs; rolling commit cadence; topic frequency and dwell time in help tickets	Overcollection averted by minimal schemas and least privilege access; rotating deletion schedules; user visible data inventories and audit trails
Cross-Environment Learning Traces	Traces are modality contingent; indicators serve as conversational prompts not verdicts; triangulation reduces inference error	Blocks use drag sequence and reuse plus text transition tasks; text uses coverage mutation linting added to deleted line ratios; physical uses photos wiring diagrams safety checklists; unplugged uses structured observation rubrics	Coverage and mutation trajectories; commit dispersion indices; diagram to implementation isomorphism checks; prototype readiness tallies; strategy use counts	Tinkering overcount controlled by multimodal corroboration and brief conferences; no punitive action from single indicators; explicit interpretive notes archived
Early Warning without Overreach	Thresholds remain local and auditable; human in the loop decisions prevent stigmatizing labels; explanations precede intervention	Triggers include no commits across three active days, two checkpoints without new tests, repeated identical compiler faults; instructors log intervention type time and outcome	Binary trigger flags; intervention uptake; time to recovery curves; counterfactual notes on preventive moves	Labeling and automation bias constrained by ban on individual risk scorers; require explanation interfaces; consequential actions need instructor signoff

continued on following page

Table 3. Continued

Domain Focus & Scope	Principle and Empirical Rationale	Operationalization in CS Settings	Signals and Quantification	Risks and Governance Safeguards
Equity and Bias Auditing	Equity requires routine disparate impact scans; instruments inspected for construct irrelevance; peer discourse monitored for tone and specificity	Monitor office hour access by subgroup and slot; compare test to code ratios at equal correctness; anonymize artifacts where feasible; coach reviewers who show evaluative drift	Participation and attainment deltas with uncertainty bands; lexical specificity scores; review assignment entropy; parity of optional support attendance	Spurious causality mitigated by contextual memos and design changes to times formats datasets; publish parity plans; re audit after interventions
Privacy by Design and Data Governance	Consent minimization purpose clarity role restricted access retention control encryption by default; default to the strictest applicable regime	Plain language notices; impact assessments; vendor clauses banning secondary use and mandating deletion at exit with audit rights; secure key management and breach drills	Access logs with actor and purpose; deletion receipts and timers; compliance attestations; recovery time objectives validated	Data sprawl and endogeneity reduced by schema minimization de identification where feasible least privilege matrices external audits and red team tests
Interpretability and Actionability	Indicators must be explainable in minutes and map to bounded pedagogical moves; shared semantics prevent heteroscedastic interpretation	Define class wide meanings for meaningful commit failing boundary test stale branch; narrative dashboards pair each signal with candidate actions and exemplars; learner self dashboards tied to rubric	Failing boundary flag; commits per day within phase envelope; plan artifacts referencing a signal and intended move; micro effects measured next session	Misreadings curbed by glossaries anchor exemplars short conferences and periodic semantic calibration across sections

continued on following page

Table 3. Continued

Domain Focus & Scope	Principle and Empirical Rationale	Operationalization in CS Settings	Signals and Quantification	Risks and Governance Safeguards
Classroom Scale and Program Scale Use	Classroom cycles operate on day scale and drive reteach regroup practice; program cycles operate on term scale and reshape structures; distributional reporting replaces ranks	Daily or alternate day sense making with quick reteach or regroup; program reviews align prerequisites criteria and deadlines and expand supports for part time learners	Next day performance shifts; trendlines on bottlenecks last day commit spikes portfolio completion by track; workload peaks mapped	Perverse incentives avoided by privileging process indicators with narrative annotations; ban league tables; require instructor commentary with aggregates
Research and Continuous Improvement	Improvement science frames analytics as disciplined experimentation; design based methods iterate instruments; replication accelerates diffusion; null results are assets	For each unit set an aim a change idea feasible measures and a review timeline; run small randomized or quasi experimental tests where ethical; archive prompts rubrics scripts and notebooks	Effect sizes with confidence intervals; fidelity checks; negative result registries; reuse rates of replication packages; time to adoption across sections	Experiment fatigue and inequity bounded by consent fairness checks predefined stop rules and governance that prioritizes teacher judgment over algorithmic prescription

Equity, privacy, interpretability, and scale constitute the governing constraints that keep analytics ethical and effective (Kanika et al., 2020). Equity reviews examine participation, test to code ratios at comparable correctness, and access to optional supports by subgroup, and they audit peer discourse for tone and specificity, with structural remedies when disparities appear (Belmar, 2022). Privacy by design mandates consent, minimization, role restricted access, encryption, and deletion on a published timetable, and cross border programs default to the strictest applicable regime under long standing education privacy law and contemporary data protection statutes. Interpretability requires signals that can be explained in minutes and that map to bounded libraries of pedagogical actions, with shared semantics for meaningful commits, failing boundary tests, and stale branches, and with narrative dashboards that pair each indicator with candidate next steps for teachers and learners (Caeli & Yadav, 2020; Kong et al., 2020). Classroom use runs on a day scale with rapid reteach, regroup, or practice, while program use aggregates across cohorts to locate bottlenecks and workload peaks without ranking teachers, preferring distributions with contextual memo. Improvement science closes the loop through clear aims, narrow change ideas, feasible measures, short review cycles, and replication packages that include prompts, rubrics, anchors, and scripts, so that gains spread and null results prevent wasteful repetition.

CAPACITY, CHANGE, AND PRACTITIONER TOOLKITS

Durable capacity in computing assessment begins with precise teacher knowledge that travels from seminar to classroom through modeling, rehearsal, coaching, and calibrated observation (Otterborn et al., 2020). The Joyce and Showers synthesis reported that stand alone theory rarely transfers, whereas demonstration with guided practice and coaching yields near universal enactment, a pattern echoed by the Yoon and colleagues estimate that multi session professional development exceeding roughly fifty hours is associated with gains near one fifth of a standard distribution (Alam & Mohanty, 2023b). For computing, assessment literacy becomes operational when instructors write student legible criteria that partition correctness, design, testing, documentation, and data responsibility, facilitate calibrated peer review with anonymized anchors, guarantee structured revision windows, and read a compact set of traces such as time to first passing test and commit cadence (Bertram, 2020). Coaching magnifies uptake, with the Kraft, Blazar, and Hogan meta-analysis indicating large effects on practice and smaller but meaningful effects on achievement when caseloads are constrained and routines are concrete. Weekly professional learning communities that score artifacts against a common rubric, reconcile disagreements with evidence pointing, and plan short reteaches convert individual skill into collective capacity (Happe et al., 2021). Micro credentials and observation rubrics render growth auditable through artifacts such as anchor annotated rubrics, critique videos with consent, response to reviewer logs, and one-page analytics plans that bind signals to actions.

Table 4. Operational Capacity Matrix for Practitioner Led Assessment Reform in Computing

Strategic Domain	Principle and Empirical Rationale	High-Fidelity Operationalization in CS Programs	Quantification and Performance Indices	Risks and Mitigations
Assessment Literacy Accretion	Transfer scales when theory couples with modeling, rehearsal, feedback, and coaching; literacy spans criteria design, moderation, uptake tracking, trace reading	Draft student-legible criteria partitioning correctness, design, testing, documentation, ethics; rehearse anchored critiques; guarantee revision windows; interpret minimal traces time-to-first-test, commit cadence, boundary error mix	PD dosage hours; share of tasks with visible criteria and revision rights; interrater agreement coefficients; median feedback-to-change latency; boundary coverage deltas across iterations	Training dilution countered by coached trials; rubric drift tempered via anchor refresh; comment fatigue reduced by two high-leverage notes; trace overreach checked with teacher prompts
Instructional Coaching and Collaborative Inquiry	Coaching shifts practice; PLCs and lesson study convert individual skill into collective capacity; narrow foci heighten effect sizes	Twelve-minute coached critiques with stems; elicitation of test rationales in code review; weekly PLC artifact reads; cyclic research lessons with shared observation and revision	Coaching contact hours; observed practice change indices; PLC throughput and actionables; TA calibration variance; criterion attainment gains post coaching	Coach overload limited by caseload caps; initiative sprawl pruned by focus charters; observer bias reduced with video anchors; stagnation avoided via rotating foci
Micro-Credentials and Observation Rubrics	Competency badging renders growth auditable; behaviorally anchored rubrics raise reliability; micro-calibration sustains signal integrity	Badge stack criteria writing, calibration, peer facilitation, revision policy, equity audit, minimal analytics; observation rubric indexing visible criteria, structured peer or self-review, signal-to-move use, documented revision	Badge attainment rate; weighted kappa targets; outlier audit frequency; indicator hit rate; credential turnaround time	Badge inflation constrained by artifact audits; over-granularity collapsed to orthogonal factors; rater drift corrected by micro-calibrations; privacy preserved with consented media
Change Management and Implementation Science	Diffusion requires competency, organizational, leadership drivers; short PDSA cycles outperform episodic rollouts; early wins anchor culture	One-year arc with checkpoints; protected critique blocks and mid-sprint moderation; leaders model routines; PDSA on narrow change ideas with rapid readouts; readiness and fidelity rubrics published	Adoption penetration by cohort; fidelity scores on core routines; cycle time from idea to decision; checkpoint SLA adherence; year-over-year sustainability index	Announcement-only rollout avoided by staging; fatigue offset with visible wins; fidelity erosion flagged via run charts; ownership built through teacher-led refinements

continued on following page

Table 4. Continued

Strategic Domain	Principle and Empirical Rationale	High-Fidelity Operationalization in CS Programs	Quantification and Performance Indices	Risks and Mitigations
Administrative Architecture and Incentive Design	Time structures and incentives determine enactment quality; workload smoothness predicts persistence; procurement aligned with pedagogy lowers friction	Weekly PLC block; midweek double-mark micro moderation; checkpoints every two or three lessons; TA caseload caps with shared rubrics; comment caps using criterion shorthand; tools that support revision and export	Workload variance profiles; moderation throughput and agreement; TA comment quality indices; tool export rates; revision participation ratios	Peak overload buffered by cadence; misaligned incentives reset to reward uptake and exemplars; vendor lock-in averted by open export; opaque scores barred in favor of interpretable indicators
Practitioner Toolkits and Templates	Codified artifacts compress setup cost and standardize cognition; minimalism preserves feasibility; versioning enables continuous refinement	One-page task blueprint, student criteria sheet, critique protocol, bias and equity audits, minimal analytics plan, revision log, portfolio guide with commit history and micro oral	Toolkit utilization; template completeness; share of submissions with revision logs; portfolio readiness audits; cross-course reuse rates	Template bloat prevented by minimal necessary sets; performative compliance deterred by spot checks; accessibility ensured by plain-language variants; version creep governed by releases
Risk Management Wellbeing and Integrity	Sustainability requires bounded effort and ethical guardrails; trauma-aware routines reduce extraneous variance; individualized traces deter misconduct	Scheduled checkpoints, capped comments, paced resubmissions; opt-out equivalents for sensitive contexts; integrity fingerprints frequent small commits, micro-orals, response-to-reviewer linkage	Effort minutes per artifact; opt-out equivalence verifications; incident rate and resolution time; subgroup help uptake distributions; privacy compliance checks	Burnout mitigated via rota weeks and boundaries; inequity addressed through structural supports; violations resolved with learning recovery; data minimized with role-restricted access

continued on following page

Table 4. Continued

Strategic Domain	Principle and Empirical Rationale	High-Fidelity Operationalization in CS Programs	Quantification and Performance Indices	Risks and Mitigations
Ownership Routinization and Culture	Normed routines and shared language stabilize practice; cultural internalization yields bottom-up refinement and resilience under turnover	Openings revisit key criteria; predictable peer review cadence; universal response-to-reviewer attachments; short observation rubric for peer walkthroughs and self-audits	Share of classes running structured review; teacher-initiated refinements logged; survivability through staff changes; exemplar library growth; student requests for critique time	Backslide prevented by cadence guardians; dependency risk reduced by distributed leadership; ritual fatigue eased with periodic refresh; transparency through public exemplars
Policy Coherence and External Accountability	System alignment converts routines into defaults; evaluation privileges process quality and interpretability; externals value portfolios over isolated scores	Evaluation rubrics mirror classroom dimensions; reassessment authorized; privacy by design mandated; procurement favors revision workflows and open export; recognition for exemplars and uptake gains	Policy compliance audits; reassessment utilization; external portfolio adoption; procurement conformance scores; process quality indicators on reviews	Policy practice gaps closed with audits and coaching; perverse incentives countered by process weighted evaluation; compliance costs limited by shared templates; clauses reviewed for fit continuously

Implementation succeeds when leaders treat assessment reform as system design rather than messaging (Druga et al., 2022). Rogers diffusion proportions forecast adoption tempo, so leaders stage innovators and early adopters into visible pilots that produce short term wins in the Kotter sequence while building competency, organizational, and leadership drivers articulated in implementation science (Vakil, 2020). Schedules reserve weekly critique blocks, midweek micro moderation, and recurring calibration so that reliability is routine not discretionary. Incentives reward exemplar quality and feedback uptake rather than only terminal scores, and procurement favors tools that support revision workflows, open export, interpretable indicators, and privacy by design (Vogel et al., 2020). Practitioner toolkits compress friction through one page task blueprints, critique protocols, bias and equity audits, minimal analytics templates, revision logs, and portfolio guides (Raji et al., 2021; Goode et al., 2021). Risk management protects wellbeing and integrity with capped comment loads, paced resubmissions, individualized traces such as frequent small commits and micro-orals, proportionate responses to violations, and transparent data retention with role restricted access (Ni et al., 2023; Ryoo et al., 2020). Ownership emerges as routines become ordinary, visible in teacher-initiated refinements and student requests for critique time (Alam, 2022). The result is a program where evidence is generated by design, acted upon quickly, governed ethically, and legible to external audiences that prize reliability, collaboration, and judgment.

MODELS, TASKS, CASES, AND EVIDENCE OF IMPACT

Programs that treat assessment as the engine of learning rely on pedagogical models that manufacture analyzable evidence as a byproduct of ordinary work rather than as a separate bureaucracy. Project based and problem-based computing yields this effect when milestones are choreographed to externalize intermediate reasoning through decomposition sketches, minimal running versions, student written tests, and reflective trade off narratives scored against crisp criteria for design, readability, testing, and responsible data use (Agbo et al., 2021; Nancy et al., 2020). Studio adaptations transform code review into a public seminar where peers cite criteria, point to screen level evidence, and record concrete next moves, which stabilizes discourse and generates reusable anchors for moderation (Garcia, 2021). Mastery learning enters through guaranteed reassessment windows with growth weighted reporting so that quality remains invariant while time flexes. Two stage examinations compress assessment for learning into a single sitting by pairing an individual attempt with an immediate collaborative reprise and a short metacognitive memo. Pair programming with rotating roles, micro planning, and post session self reports extends the social dimension of evidence without diluting individual accountability. Cross curricular computational thinking broadens acceptable artifacts through data narratives, creative coding performances, and ethical analyses that preserve disciplinary rigor while widening audience legibility (Paiva et al., 2022; Videnovik et al., 2023). Task libraries become living repositories of fully specified blueprints with success criteria, evidence paths, and grading time estimates that render feasibility visible.

Table 5. Models Tasks Cases and Impact Matrix for Evidence Centric CS Assessment

Model or Case Label	Mechanism and Rationale	Task and Evidence Architecture	Metrics and Quantitative Indices	Constraints and Mitigations
Integrated Pedagogical Models and Task Libraries	PBL studio mastery and two stage checks instantiate continuous formative control, externalize intermediate reasoning, and stabilize workload through sprint cadence and calibrated critique	Decomposition sketch minimal running version student written tests with rationale structured code review brief oral defense ethics reflection reusable blueprint library with concise success criteria	Share of tasks with mandatory tests and rationales commit cadence regularity coverage and mutation trajectories review specificity density revision uptake rate post merge defect density	Remove puzzle prompts weight growth to reward refactors protect critique blocks publish criteria to reduce gaming enforce feasibility by grading time audits
Blueprint Specification and Moderation Architecture	Didactic contract makes expectations inspectable reduces construct ambiguity and elevates interrater reliability via anchors and micro calibration	Brief with stakeholder and constraints competencies mapped to big ideas two or three criteria per dimension minimal diversified evidence code history tests rationale diagram oral defense explicit scaffolds revision policy anchor artifacts per level	Weighted kappa reliability rubric dispersion indices time per artifact benchmarks completeness of change logs anchor reuse frequency	Bias scrub of language minimize evidence set require individualized traces commit history and micro orals schedule quick calibrations before grading
Case A: K to 8 Computational Storytelling	Dialogic critique plus block prototyping elicits conceptual models and state reasoning without heavy telemetry supports heterogeneous learners	Sprint checkpoints decomposition first scene state table transitions sentence stem critique circles paired oral justifications revision logs attached to artifacts	Time to first working scene count of testable transitions criterion citation rate in critiques rate of state explanations without execution	Moderate language load provide quiet options use exemplar anchors keep metrics minimal offer alternate contexts of equal rigor
Case B: Rural Secondary Physical Computing	Authentic constraints with low-cost sensors yield reliable inference through multimodal artifacts while foregrounding safety and inclusion	Wiring diagram safety checklist annotated code listing indoor dry run outdoor test with logs stakeholder demo neighbor team verification rotating roles to equalize participation	Consecutive days without working prototype power stability incidents checklist pass rate oral explanation adequacy parity of role participation	Offline first submissions spare kits structural supports for limited writing proportionate resubmission after faults targeted help on recurrent power issues

continued on following page

Table 5. Continued

Model or Case Label	Mechanism and Rationale	Task and Evidence Architecture	Metrics and Quantitative Indices	Constraints and Mitigations
Case C: Undergraduate CS1 CS2 Hybrid Assessment	Automation handles format and baseline correctness human feedback targets design naming decomposition and test rationale two stage quizzes elicit pre tool reasoning	Modular assignments student written failing tests visible autograder suite documented refactor after review biweekly two stage quiz weekly TA calibration with anchors	Time to first passing student written test readability renaming commits per assignment presence of property based tests last day commit share inter section comment consistency	Cap TA caseload standardize rubrics with anchors forbid opaque risk scores reserve time for moderation credit documented refactor quality
Case D: Professional Reskilling Industry Aligned Briefs	Authentic briefs weekly demos and recorded defenses align evidence with hiring signals while assessment control remains academic	Stable criteria correctness design tests documentation stakeholder communication individual attempt then team extension consented micro oral defenses PR review participation tracked	Attendance adherence commit frequency and burst ratio review participation response time to mentor comments portfolio completeness and showcase readiness	No keystroke logging explicit consent boundary partner influence separated from grading protect critique time prefer open licensed datasets
Cross Case Synthesis and Design Invariants	Visible criteria short cycles multimodal evidence individualized traces and minimal question driven analytics explain efficiency equity and integrity	Public criteria predictable checkpoints response to reviewer linkage small environment appropriate traces weekly moderation to reduce variance	Revision depth structural versus cosmetic participation entropy equity deltas for test to code at equal correctness workload variance across term	Guard cadence and coaching monitor discourse tone redistribute optional support access keep retention minimal publish interpretive memos

continued on following page

Table 5. Continued

Model or Case Label	Mechanism and Rationale	Task and Evidence Architecture	Metrics and Quantitative Indices	Constraints and Mitigations
Evaluation Framework and Evidence of Impact	Logic model ties inputs activities and outputs to proximal and distal outcomes with mixed measures and feasible validity safeguards	Inputs PD hours blueprints scripts protected checkpoints activities peer review count revision window prevalence calibration frequency outputs documented revisions test rationales change logs	Short term design explanation without execution coverage and mutation gains decline in deadline spikes long term completion progression internship conversion external portfolio adoption	Address maturation with cohort comparisons reduce selection bias via full sequence adoption version rubrics to prevent drift interpret diffusion with context
Improvement Cycles Replication and Reporting	Improvement science frames change ideas as disciplined experiments replication packages compress diffusion audience aligned reporting drives action	Set aim change idea feasible measures rapid review test live demo plus boundary checklist archive prompts rubrics scripts anchors report to teachers leaders externals with artifacts	Effect size with confidence bounds fidelity checks negative result registry replication reuse rate time to adoption stakeholder action taken rate	Consent and fairness checks stop rules governance that centers teacher judgment shared repositories to limit reinvention periodic refresh to avoid ritual fatigue

Comparative cases indicate that these models travel across age bands, resource profiles, and delivery modes when logistics are disciplined. A K to 8 computational storytelling unit shows how dialogic critique and block-based prototyping elicit state reasoning without heavy telemetry, with teachers tracking time to first working scene and the count of testable transitions. A rural secondary physical computing unit demonstrates reliability through multimodal artifacts that include wiring diagrams, safety checklists, annotated listings, and short stakeholder demos, while offline first submissions maintain participation under bandwidth constraints. A large undergraduate CS sequence combines visible autograder suites with human narrative feedback on design and testing and uses biweekly two stage quizzes to elicit algorithmic reasoning without tools, producing steadier commit cadences and more consistent comments across sections (Hazzan et al., 2020). A professional reskilling program aligns weekly demos and recorded micro-orals with hiring signals while retaining academic control of judgment, and placement gains track portfolios that integrate code history, test rationales, and design defenses (Madkins et al., 2020; Huang & Looi, 2021). Evaluation links inputs and activities to outcomes through logic models, double marked rubrics, minimal analytics tied to instructional questions, and improvement cycles that adopt successful change ideas and archive null results, thereby producing cumulative gains in competence, fairness, and credibility.

CONCLUSION

Durable assessment reform in computing requires coherence across policy, curriculum, and institutional logistics so that classroom routines are reinforced rather than contradicted. Competency frameworks must articulate decomposition, invariants, testing discipline, documentation, and responsible data use in forms that are directly scorable, which allows instructors to align artifacts with outcomes without guesswork. Policy should authorize reassessment within bounded windows so that quality remains the invariant and time becomes elastic, with reporting systems that separate achievement from behavior to credit documented improvement rather than punctuality alone. Data governance must be legible and proportionate, with plain language notices that specify collection purpose and deletion timetables, role-based access controls, encryption at rest and in transit, and vendor agreements that guarantee open export and prohibit secondary use. Procurement should prefer tools that enable revision workflows, expose test results in interpretable formats, and interoperate with portfolio systems, which prevents shadow infrastructures and reduces clerical burden. Timetables need recurring critique blocks, short moderation windows, and protected time for professional learning communities so that feedback and reliability are routine rather than discretionary. Quality assurance should examine anchors, moderation notes, and evidence of revision, not only terminal marks, thereby signaling that formative use of evidence constitutes institutional doctrine.

A pragmatic roadmap allocates actions to actors and measures progress with artifacts rather than aspirations. Instructors begin with a single unit, rewrite outcomes into two or three student friendly criteria per dimension, and script a two-week cadence that includes a decomposition sketch, a minimal running version, a first test suite with rationale, and a brief oral defense. They guarantee a revision window and cap comments to one or two high leverage moves, then attach response to reviewer logs that bind feedback to change. Program leaders secure a weekly block for critique or moderation, train assistants on the same rubrics, require a small double marked sample per assignment, and maintain an anchor repository for calibration. They track the proportion of tasks with revision rights, the average number of documented revisions per student, and the frequency of calibration meetings. Policymakers publish consent and retention templates, authorize reassessment, and recognize portfolios that include code history and test rationales as legitimate evidence. Industry partners contribute compact authentic briefs, attend critiques as mentors while abstaining from grading, and provide small, licensed datasets. Students use rubrics to plan, request specific feedback, document revisions carefully, and curate portfolios that include code with history, test rationales, design diagrams, and short recorded defenses.

A focused research and development program should build concise indicators that practitioners can explain in minutes and that predict revision uptake within days, derive agency measures that link predictions, monitoring decisions, and post revision evaluations to code histories, and construct equity diagnostics that inspect participation, test to code ratios at comparable correctness, and temporal patterns of commits across subgroups. Cost and workload must be measured with the same rigor as attainment, including minutes per artifact for feedback, moderation time, and weekly variance profiles. Specific design moves merit randomized or quasi experimental tests where ethical, such as two stage quizzes with immediate oral reflection or primers that raise property-based testing and mutation scores. Replication packages that include prompts, criteria, anchors, and collection scripts accelerate diffusion and reduce reinvention, while tool development should prioritize lightweight rubric editors, response to reviewer generators tied to commits, small analytics panels that pair each indicator with candidate actions, and portfolio exporters that yield compact, navigable bundles. The closing synthesis is straightforward and exacting, namely that programs should align tasks to big ideas and authentic practice, make success criteria visible, shorten cycles, guarantee revision, diversify evidence, distribute judgment through peer and self-review, govern data ethically, and lead with schedules and procurement that entrench these routines.

REFERENCES

Abichandani, P., Sivakumar, V., Lobo, D., Iaboni, C., & Shekhar, P. (2022). Internet-of-things curriculum, pedagogy, and assessment for stem education: A review of literature. *IEEE Access : Practical Innovations, Open Solutions*, *10*, 38351–38369.

Agbo, F. J., Sanusi, I. T., Oyelere, S. S., & Suhonen, J. (2021). Application of virtual reality in computer science education: A systemic review based on bibliometric and content analysis methods. *Education Sciences*, *11*(3), 142.

Alam, A. (2022, March). Educational robotics and computer programming in early childhood education: a conceptual framework for assessing elementary school students' computational thinking for designing powerful educational scenarios. In *2022 International Conference on Smart Technologies and Systems for Next Generation Computing (ICSTSN)* (pp. 1-7). IEEE.

Alam, A., & Mohanty, A. (2023a). Discerning the application of virtual laboratory in curriculum transaction of software engineering lab course from the lens of critical pedagogy. In *Sentiment analysis and deep learning* [Singapore: Springer Nature Singapore.]. *Proceedings of ICSADL, 2022*, 53–68.

Alam, A., & Mohanty, A. (2023b). Design, development, and implementation of software engineering virtual laboratory: A boon to computer science and engineering (CSE) education during Covid-19 pandemic. In *Proceedings of third international conference on sustainable expert systems: ICSES 2022* (pp. 1-20). Singapore: Springer Nature Singapore.

Ashraf, M., Zaman, M., & Ahmed, M. (2020). An intelligent prediction system for educational data mining based on ensemble and filtering approaches. *Procedia Computer Science*, *167*, 1471–1483.

Belmar, H. (2022). Review on the teaching of programming and computational thinking in the world. *Frontiers of Computer Science*, *4*, 997222.

Bertram, L. (2020). Digital learning games for mathematics and computer science education: The need for preregistered RCTs, standardized methodology, and advanced technology. *Frontiers in Psychology*, *11*, 2127. PMID: 33178055

Caeli, E. N., & Yadav, A. (2020). Unplugged approaches to computational thinking: A historical perspective. *TechTrends*, *64*(1), 29–36.

Chang, C. S., Chung, C. H., & Chang, J. A. (2020). Influence of problem-based learning games on effective computer programming learning in higher education. *Educational Technology Research and Development*, *68*(5), 2615–2634.

Chen, P., Yang, D., Metwally, A. H. S., Lavonen, J., & Wang, X. (2023). Fostering computational thinking through unplugged activities: A systematic literature review and meta-analysis. *International Journal of STEM Education*, *10*(1), 47.

Choi, S., Jang, Y., & Kim, H. (2023). Influence of pedagogical beliefs and perceived trust on teachers' acceptance of educational artificial intelligence tools. *International Journal of Human-Computer Interaction*, *39*(4), 910–922.

Dai, Y., Lin, Z., Liu, A., & Wang, W. (2024). An embodied, analogical and disruptive approach of AI pedagogy in upper elementary education: An experimental study. *British Journal of Educational Technology*, *55*(1), 417–434.

Druga, S., Otero, N., & Ko, A. J. (2022, July). The landscape of teaching resources for AI education. In *Proceedings of the 27th ACM Conference on on Innovation and Technology in Computer Science Education* Vol. 1 (pp. 96-102).

Dudyrev, F., & Maksimenkova, O. (2020). Training simulators in vocational education: pedagogical and technological aspects. *Voprosy obrazovaniya/Educational Studies Moscow*, (3), 255-276.

El-Hamamsy, L., Chessel-Lazzarotto, F., Bruno, B., Roy, D., Cahlikova, T., Chevalier, M., & Mondada, F. (2021). A computer science and robotics integration model for primary school: Evaluation of a large-scale in-service K-4 teacher-training program. *Education and Information Technologies*, *26*(3), 2445–2475. PMID: 33162777

Fagerlund, J., Häkkinen, P., Vesisenaho, M., & Viiri, J. (2021). Computational thinking in programming with Scratch in primary schools: A systematic review. *Computer Applications in Engineering Education*, *29*(1), 12–28.

Fincher, S., Jeuring, J., Miller, C. S., Donaldson, P., Du Boulay, B., Hauswirth, M., & Petersen, A. (2020). Notional machines in computing education: The education of attention. In *Proceedings of the working group reports on innovation and technology in computer science education* (pp. 21-50).

Garcia, M. B. (2021). Cooperative learning in computer programming: A quasi-experimental evaluation of Jigsaw teaching strategy with novice programmers. *Education and Information Technologies*, *26*(4), 4839–4856.

Goode, J., Ivey, A., Johnson, S. R., Ryoo, J. J., & Ong, C. (2021). Rac (e) ing to computer science for all: How teachers talk and learn about equity in professional development. *Computer Science Education*, *31*(3), 374–399.

Hall, B., Grantham, S., & Whyte, R. (2024, January). Embedding culturally relevant pedagogy in practice: Considerations for training and resource development. In *Proceedings of the 8th Conference on Computing Education Practice* (pp. 29-32).

Happe, L., Buhnova, B., Koziolek, A., & Wagner, I. (2021). Effective measures to foster girls' interest in secondary computer science education: A literature review. *Education and Information Technologies*, *26*(3), 2811–2829.

Hazzan, O., Lapidot, T., & Ragonis, N. (2020). *Guide to teaching computer science*. Springer International Publishing.

Huang, W., & Looi, C. K. (2021). A critical review of literature on "unplugged" pedagogies in K-12 computer science and computational thinking education. *Computer Science Education*, *31*(1), 83–111.

Johnson, A., & Elliott, S. (2020). Culturally relevant pedagogy: A model to guide cultural transformation in STEM departments. *Journal of Microbiology & Biology Education*, *21*(1), 10–1128. PMID: 32431767

Kadirbergenovna, B. L. (2022). Teaching computer graphics as a pedagogical problem on the basis of massive open online courses in information conditions. *World Bulletin of Social Sciences*, *8*, 71–74.

Kanika, Chakraverty, S., & Chakraborty, P. (2020). Tools and techniques for teaching computer programming: A review. *Journal of Educational Technology Systems*, *49*(2), 170–198.

Kong, S. C., Lai, M., & Sun, D. (2020). Teacher development in computational thinking: Design and learning outcomes of programming concepts, practices and pedagogy. *Computers & Education*, *151*, 103872.

Lamrani, R., & Abdelwahed, E. H. (2020). Game-based learning and gamification to improve skills in early years education. *Computer Science and Information Systems*, *17*(1), 339–356.

Lyon, J. A., & Magana, J., A. (2020). Computational thinking in higher education: A review of the literature. *Computer Applications in Engineering Education*, *28*(5), 1174–1189.

Madkins, T. C., Howard, N. R., & Freed, N. (2020). Engaging equity pedagogies in computer science learning environments. *Journal of Computer Science Integration*, *3*(2), 1. PMID: 37547748

Nancy, W., Parimala, A., & Livingston, L. M. (2020). Advanced teaching pedagogy as innovative approach in modern education system. *Procedia Computer Science*, *172*, 382–388.

Ni, L., Bausch, G., & Benjamin, R. (2023). Computer science teacher professional development and professional learning communities: A review of the research literature. *Computer Science Education, 33*(1), 29–60.

Ogegbo, A. A., & Ramnarain, U. (2022). A systematic review of computational thinking in science classrooms. *Studies in Science Education, 58*(2), 203–230.

Otterborn, A., Schönborn, K. J., & Hultén, M. (2020). Investigating preschool educators' implementation of computer programming in their teaching practice. *Early Childhood Education Journal, 48*(3), 253–262.

Paiva, J. C., Leal, J. P., & Figueira, Á. (2022). Automated assessment in computer science education: A state-of-the-art review. [TOCE]. *ACM Transactions on Computing Education, 22*(3), 1–40.

Papadakis, S. (2022). Apps to promote computational thinking and coding skills to young age children: A pedagogical challenge for the 21st century learners. [EDUPIJ]. *Educational Process: International Journal, 11*(1), 7–13.

Prather, J., Denny, P., Leinonen, J., Becker, B. A., Albluwi, I., Craig, M., & Savelka, J. (2023). The robots are here: Navigating the generative ai revolution in computing education. In *Proceedings of the 2023 working group reports on innovation and technology in computer science education* (pp. 108-159).

Qureshi, B. (2023). Exploring the use of chatgpt as a tool for learning and assessment in undergraduate computer science curriculum: Opportunities and challenges. *arXiv preprint arXiv:2304.11214*.

Raji, I. D., Scheuerman, M. K., & Amironesei, R. (2021, March). You can't sit with us: Exclusionary pedagogy in ai ethics education. In *Proceedings of the 2021 ACM conference on fairness, accountability, and transparency* (pp. 515-525).

Ryoo, J. J., Tanksley, T., Estrada, C., & Margolis, J. (2020). Take space, make space: How students use computer science to disrupt and resist marginalization in schools. *Computer Science Education, 30*(3), 337–361.

Sanusi, I. T., Oyelere, S. S., & Omidiora, J. O. (2022). Exploring teachers' preconceptions of teaching machine learning in high school: A preliminary insight from Africa. *Computers and Education Open, 3*, 100072.

Saputra, I., Astuti, M., Sayuti, M., & Kusumastuti, D. (2023). Integration of Artificial Intelligence in Education: Opportunities, Challenges, Threats and Obstacles. A Literature Review. *The Indonesian journal of computer science, 12*(4).

Susanto, R., Rachmadtullah, R., & Rachbini, W. (2020). Technological and Pedagogical models. *Journal of Ethnic and Cultural Studies*, *7*(2), 1–14.

Tang, K. Y., Chou, T. L., & Tsai, C. C. (2020). A content analysis of computational thinking research: An international publication trends and research typology. *The Asia-Pacific Education Researcher*, *29*(1), 9–19.

Tkachuk, V., Yechkalo, Y., & Khotskina, S. (2020). Selection of mobile ICT for learning informatics of future professionals in engineering pedagogy.

Troussas, C., Krouska, A., & Sgouropoulou, C. (2020). A novel teaching strategy through adaptive learning activities for computer programming. *IEEE Transactions on Education*, *64*(2), 103–109.

Troussas, C., Krouska, A., & Sgouropoulou, C. (2020). Collaboration and fuzzy-modeled personalization for mobile game-based learning in higher education. *Computers & Education*, *144*, 103698.

Tzafilkou, K., Perifanou, M., & Economides, A. A. (2023). Assessing teachers' digital competence in primary and secondary education: Applying a new instrument to integrate pedagogical and professional elements for digital education. *Education and Information Technologies*, *28*(12), 16017–16040. PMID: 37361819

Vakil, S. (2020). "I've always been scared that someday I'm going to sell out": Exploring the relationship between political identity and learning in computer science education. *Cognition and Instruction*, *38*(2), 87–115.

Videnovik, M., Vold, T., Kiønig, L., Madevska Bogdanova, A., & Trajkovik, V. (2023). Game-based learning in computer science education: A scoping literature review. *International Journal of STEM Education*, *10*(1), 54.

Vitaliy, K., Nataliia, V., Ievgen, B., Volodymyr, S., & Anna, K. (2022). Innovative educational technologies in management training: Experience of EU countries. *International Journal of Computer Science & Network Security*, *22*(6), 45–50.

Vogel, S., Hoadley, C., Castillo, A. R., & Ascenzi-Moreno, L. (2020). Languages, literacies and literate programming: Can we use the latest theories on how bilingual people learn to help us teach computational literacies? *Computer Science Education*, *30*(4), 420–443.

Yilmaz Ince, E., & Koc, M. (2021). The consequences of robotics programming education on computational thinking skills: An intervention of the Young Engineer's Workshop (YEW). *Computer Applications in Engineering Education*, *29*(1), 191–208.

Yue, M., Jong, M. S. Y., & Dai, Y. (2022). Pedagogical design of K-12 artificial intelligence education: A systematic review. *Sustainability, 14*(23), 15620.

Zhan, Z., He, L., Tong, Y., Liang, X., Guo, S., & Lan, X. (2022). The effectiveness of gamification in programming education: Evidence from a meta-analysis. *Computers and Education: Artificial Intelligence*, *3*, 100096.

Zhang, A., Olelewe, C. J., Orji, C. T., Ibezim, N. E., Sunday, N. H., Obichukwu, P. U., & Okanazu, O. O. (2020). Effects of innovative and traditional teaching methods on technical college students' achievement in computer craft practices. *SAGE Open*, *10*(4), 2158244020982986.

KEY TERMS AND DEFINITIONS

Constructive Alignment: Constructive alignment is a curriculum design principle in which intended learning outcomes, learning activities, and assessment tasks are systematically aligned. "Constructive" highlights learners actively constructing meaning, while "alignment" requires assessments to directly measure the targeted outcomes. It strengthens validity by reducing mismatch between goals and evidence.

Equity in Computing Education Assessment: Equity in computing education assessment refers to designing and using assessment practices so that opportunities to demonstrate competence are not systematically constrained by identity, language, disability, prior access, or social position. It requires attention to differential access, cultural relevance, bias in judgment, and fair supports. Equity is evaluated by examining distributional outcomes and lived experiences.

Formative Assessment: Formative assessment refers to ongoing, low-stakes processes used to elicit evidence of student learning during instruction in order to adapt teaching and support improvement. Its defining function is feedback for learning rather than judgment of learning. It relies on clear success criteria, timely feedback loops, and opportunities for revision.

Learning Analytics: Learning analytics is the measurement, collection, analysis, and reporting of data about learners and learning contexts to understand and improve learning and the environments in which it occurs. Analytically, it links observed traces to interpretable constructs and decisions. Ethically, it requires proportionality, transparency, and context-sensitive interpretation.

Metacognition: Metacognition is the capacity to monitor and regulate one's own thinking, learning strategies, and performance. It includes metacognitive knowledge (about tasks, strategies, self) and metacognitive control (planning, monitoring, evaluating). In assessment, it is operationalized through reflection, self-explanation, and evidence-based revision.

Privacy by Design: Privacy by design is a governance approach in which privacy protections are embedded into systems and practices from the outset rather than added after deployment. It prioritizes data minimization, purpose limitation, security safeguards, and user transparency. In educational settings, it also includes clear consent boundaries and proportionality of data collection to pedagogical need.

Universal Design for Learning: Universal Design for Learning (UDL) is a framework for designing instruction that anticipates learner variability and reduces barriers to participation. It emphasizes providing multiple means of engagement, representation, and action or expression. UDL shifts accommodation from reactive to proactive design, supporting accessibility and equitable opportunity.

Validity in Educational Assessment: Validity is the degree to which evidence and theory support the interpretations and uses of assessment scores or judgments for a specific purpose. It is not a property of a test alone but of the inferences drawn from evidence. Validity arguments consider construct representation, bias, consequences, and the fit between claims and evidence.

Section 2
Inclusivity, Ethics, and Social Responsibility in CS Education

Chapter 5
Transforming Computer Science Education:
Inclusivity, Ethics, and Emerging Technologies

Hanh Le
https://orcid.org/0009-0007-8172-0809
University of the Cumberlands, USA

ABSTRACT

Computer science education is undergoing a profound transformation at the intersection of inclusivity, ethics, and rapidly evolving technologies. This chapter explores how innovative pedagogical approaches can effectively address the diverse needs of contemporary learners while simultaneously addressing the ethical, social, and societal challenges posed by technological advancements. Interdisciplinary models such as STEAM (Science, Technology, Engineering, Arts, and Mathematics), along with open-source tools and collaborative platforms, enhance experiential learning, creativity, and critical thinking skills. Central to this vision is the integration of ethical reasoning and responsible computing practices, equipping students to make principled, informed decisions in an increasingly automated and AI-driven world. The chapter concludes with actionable recommendations for educators, administrators, and policymakers, emphasizing the importance of professional development for computer science education.

INTRODUCTION

Over the past several decades, computer science (CS) education has evolved from a specialized focus on programming languages and algorithmic efficiency into

DOI: 10.4018/979-8-3373-6546-6.ch005

a foundational discipline shaping economic systems, social interaction, and civic life. Computational technologies now mediate decision-making across healthcare, finance, education, and governance, while artificial intelligence (AI) increasingly performs tasks once assumed to require skilled human judgment. In this context, CS education occupies a critical role: it not only prepares future technologists but also shapes how learners understand knowledge, agency, and responsibility in an increasingly automated world. Despite this expanded significance, dominant paradigms of CS education continue to emphasize technical proficiency and procedural mastery. Success is often measured through correctness, efficiency, and task completion, under the assumption that these indicators reliably reflect conceptual understanding. While such foundations remain essential, they are increasingly insufficient in learning environments where intelligent systems can generate code, diagnose errors, and optimize solutions with minimal human intervention. As automation becomes embedded in the learning process itself, traditional markers of competence grow ambiguous, leaving instructors and learners alike uncertain about what is truly understood and how expertise develops.

These dynamics place CS education at a pedagogical crossroads. The challenge is no longer simply integrating new tools into instruction but designing learning environments in which students remain responsible for thinking, reasoning, and problem-solving when automation can perform much of the cognitive labor. One pressing issue is pedagogical deskilling, the gradual erosion of learners' conceptual understanding, judgment, and problem-solving agency as intellectual work is redistributed to automated systems. Unlike traditional labor-focused analyses of deskilling, in CS education, this phenomenon occurs within the learning process itself: students may produce correct, polished outputs while remaining disengaged from the reasoning processes that give those outputs meaning. Compounding this challenge, CS education continues to grapple with persistent inequities. Women, racially minoritized students, first-generation learners, and neurodiverse students remain underrepresented across computing pathways. Instructional models that prioritize speed, competition, or narrow definitions of competence may exacerbate these disparities. Automation does not automatically mitigate such inequities; in some cases, it can obscure conceptual differences behind superficially successful outputs, making gaps less visible while potentially widening them.

This chapter argues that addressing these challenges requires treating deskilling as a central pedagogical problem rather than as a secondary labor-market concern or unintended consequence of technological change. Drawing on qualitative insights from CS students, the chapter examines how automation redistributes cognitive responsibility, how learning environments mediate conceptual engagement, and how these dynamics shape students' readiness for future software engineering practice. Rather than offering a comprehensive empirical study or prescriptive solutions, the chapter adopts an interpretive, design-oriented approach to surface the tensions, uncertainties, and dilemmas that arise when intelligent systems participate in learning. The focus of this work is fundamentally pedagogical and ethical. It frames CS education as a space where automation is critically examined rather than uncritically adopted, and where learning is intentionally structured to preserve human understanding, judgment, and responsibility. By foregrounding cognitive responsibility as a central concern, the chapter highlights the choices educators and institutions face in preparing students to become capable, reflective, and ethically aware software engineers in a world increasingly shaped by intelligent automation.

MAIN FOCUS OF THE CHAPTER

The central focus of this chapter is on CS students as emerging software engineers and on how AI-assisted and automated systems reshape the cognitive work involved in learning to program, reason, and make judgments. Rather than framing automation as a question of tool adoption or efficiency, the chapter foregrounds pedagogical deskilling, the gradual redistribution of responsibility for reasoning, conceptual understanding, and ethical decision-making from students to intelligent systems. Specifically, the chapter examines how automation influences who thinks, who decides, and who learns in technology-mediated learning environments. When AI tools generate code, diagnose errors, or optimize solutions, students may produce functionally correct outputs while disengaging from the underlying reasoning that constitutes professional expertise. These dynamics raise critical questions about the development of durable conceptual understanding, ethical judgment, and readiness for professional software engineering practice. Guided by the Deskilling of Jobs Theory (Braverman, 1974), the chapter investigates how cognitive labor is allocated between students and machines and how this allocation is shaped by instructional design. Attention is given to four interrelated dimensions:

1. Cognitive Responsibility: How automation affects students' ownership of reasoning, problem-solving, and decision-making.
2. Conceptual Engagement: The extent to which students engage with underlying principles and abstract thinking rather than relying solely on machine-generated outputs.
3. Ethical and Professional Judgment: How responsibility for evaluating consequences, making decisions, and practicing accountability may be displaced by automation.

4. Equity and Access to Expertise: How reliance on automation may differentially impact learners, potentially masking gaps in understanding and limiting opportunities to develop critical skills.

By framing CS education as a site of active negotiation between human and machine cognition, this chapter emphasizes that learning is not merely affected by automation—it is reorganized by it. The chapter explores how students navigate this reorganization, highlighting opportunities to preserve agency, deepen conceptual understanding, and cultivate professional competence in an era of intelligent automation.

LITERATURE REVIEW

Pedagogical Deskilling in Computer Science Education

The rapid integration of AI and automation into educational settings has prompted a growing body of scholarship exploring their implications for teaching, learning, and skill development. In CS education, this attention has intensified as AI-assisted development tools, intelligent tutoring systems, and automated assessment platforms have become increasingly prevalent. Research has examined these technologies from multiple perspectives, including learning outcomes, student engagement, instructional efficiency, and equity. Collectively, this work underscores the transformative potential of automation to support learners and democratize access to computing. At the same time, it highlights significant tensions regarding human judgment, conceptual understanding, and learner agency within technology-mediated environments.

Despite this growing body of literature, much research remains oriented toward instrumental questions, such as whether tools improve performance, reduce cognitive load, or scale instruction. Far less attention has been paid to deeper pedagogical concerns about how learning itself is reorganized under conditions of automation. As intelligent systems increasingly assume responsibility for problem-solving, feedback, and decision-making, traditional markers of learning—such as correctness, speed, and task completion—become increasingly ambiguous. Students may appear successful while engaging less directly with the conceptual reasoning, problem-solving, and ethical judgment essential to future software engineering practice. This review addresses this gap by synthesizing scholarship through the lens of pedagogical deskilling. Rather than treating automation as a discrete intervention or neutral enhancement, the review examines how intelligent systems redistribute cognitive labor, shaping who thinks, who decides, and who learns. Drawing on research from CS education, the learning sciences, and critical technology studies, the review identifies recurring concerns related to automation, conceptual understanding, ethical reasoning, and inclusion.

Deskilling of Jobs Theory (Braverman, 1974) provides the unifying analytical framework for this synthesis. By foregrounding the allocation of cognitive responsibility, the theory enables disparate strands of research to be connected coherently, emphasizing the pedagogical consequences of automation beyond surface-level outcomes. The sections that follow elaborate on these dynamics, highlighting how deskilling manifests in CS education and the implications for the development of students' expertise, agency, and ethical judgment.

From Labor Deskilling to Pedagogical Deskilling

The Deskilling of Jobs Theory originated in analyses of industrial automation and managerial control, emphasizing how technological systems fragment skilled work, externalize expertise, and shift decision-making authority from workers to machines or organizational structures, while maintaining or increasing productivity. Braverman (1974) argued that automation rarely eliminates labor outright; instead, it reorganizes work so that individuals remain active participants while losing responsibility for judgment, interpretation, and understanding. A central insight of the Deskilling of Jobs Theory is that deskilling cannot be equated simply with reduced effort, visible inactivity, or diminished output. In fact, deskilled labor often appears efficient, productive, and highly aligned with organizational or institutional performance metrics. Workers—or, in the case of education, learners—may complete tasks successfully and meet expected standards without apparent difficulty. Yet beneath this surface-level competence lies a significant loss of agency: the individual's responsibility for reasoning, problem-solving, judgment, and critical decision-making is eroded. In other words, while performance may remain intact or even improve, the intellectual ownership of the work is transferred elsewhere—to technological systems, procedural guidelines, or automated processes. This distinction underscores the subtlety of deskilling: it is not a decline in observable activity, but a reorganization of cognitive labor in which the capacity to understand, analyze, and control the task is diminished, even as outputs continue to meet expectations.

Recent scholarship suggests that similar dynamics are emerging in educational contexts. As intelligent systems automate aspects of problem-solving, feedback, and evaluation, learning itself may be reorganized. Students may remain engaged and productive while ceding responsibility for reasoning that traditionally defined mastery. These changes are often subtle and difficult to detect, particularly when automated outputs appear correct, polished, or sophisticated. In CS education, this concern is particularly pronounced. Computing serves not only as the subject matter but also as the medium through which automation operates. As students learn to design intelligent systems, they simultaneously learn with smart systems that perform core cognitive tasks on their behalf. Without deliberate pedagogical design, these conditions create fertile ground for pedagogical deskilling, with potential long-term consequences for students' development as skilled software engineers.

Automation and Learning: From Cognitive Support to Cognitive Substitution

A substantial body of research has examined how AI-assisted tools affect learning in programming and computational thinking. Studies consistently report that automated code generation, intelligent tutoring systems, and adaptive feedback platforms reduce syntactic burden, accelerate novice progress, and lower barriers to participation (Crowston & Bolici, 2025; Rinta-Kahila et al., 2023). These tools are frequently framed as scaffolds, enabling learners to focus on higher-order problem-solving rather than low-level implementation details. On the surface, such tools appear pedagogically advantageous. Students complete tasks more quickly, experience less frustration, and produce functional artifacts earlier in the learning process. However, a growing body of scholarship cautions that automation can function as cognitive substitution rather than cognitive support if learners are not required to engage with underlying concepts.

When intelligent systems generate solutions, diagnose errors, or recommend optimizations automatically, students may succeed in completing tasks while remaining disengaged from the reasoning processes essential for expertise development. This observation aligns closely with Braverman's (1974) analysis of deskilling, which emphasizes that automation can preserve productivity while hollowing out understanding. In pedagogical contexts, efficiency and correctness alone are unreliable indicators of learning. Empirical studies indicate that AI tools are most effective when instructional designs require learners to interrogate, modify, or justify automated outputs (Garcia, 2024; Julien, 2024; Stefaniak & Moore, 2024). In these cases, automation prompts reflection rather than replacing reasoning. Conversely, when automation operates transparently—producing correct outputs without explanation, students may bypass the cognitive work central to conceptual learning and software engineering practice.

These findings underscore a critical insight: the pedagogical impact of automation is not intrinsic to the technology itself but is highly contingent on how responsibility for thinking is allocated within learning environments. Automation can either function as a cognitive scaffold that prompts reflection, problem-solving, and reasoning, or as a cognitive substitute that performs intellectual work on behalf of the learner. From a deskilling perspective, the way this distribution is structured determines whether students retain meaningful ownership of cognitive labor—or gradually cede it to automated systems.

When learners are required to interrogate, modify, or justify machine-generated outputs, automation can support engagement and deepen understanding. Conversely, when systems produce correct solutions with minimal student intervention, conceptual reasoning, abstraction, and judgment are diminished, even if learners remain behaviorally active. This distinction highlights that pedagogical deskilling is a design-contingent phenomenon, emerging not from the presence of intelligent tools alone, but from the ways in which tasks, assessments, and instructional expectations mediate who thinks, who decides, and who ultimately learns.

Proceduralization and the Erosion of Conceptual Depth

Another concern in literature is the increasing proceduralization of CS education as automation handles higher-order tasks. When learners rely on tools to select algorithms, optimize code, or diagnose errors, conceptual understanding can degrade to pattern recognition or tool navigation rather than robust conceptual construction. This proceduralization mirrors patterns identified in classic deskilling analyses of labor, where workers execute predefined processes without understanding the systems that structure their work. In educational contexts, such patterns raise critical questions about what constitutes mastery and how it should be assessed when automation mediates learning. Several studies report that learners who rely heavily on automation struggle with knowledge transfer, applying concepts to novel or ill-structured problems despite strong performance on scaffolded or tool-mediated tasks (Rinta-Kahila et al., 2023; Crowston & Bolici, 2025). These findings suggest that exposure to sophisticated tools does not guarantee conceptual depth; learners must still reason about why solutions work, not merely whether they do. Scholars argue that preserving conceptual depth requires pedagogical strategies that slow problem-solving, foreground explanation, and make reasoning visible, even when automation could render such steps unnecessary. From a deskilling lens, these strategies represent pedagogical resistance, preserving human cognitive labor in environments optimized for efficiency.

Ethics, Responsibility, and the Outsourcing of Judgment

Ethical computing has become a central focus in CS education, encompassing issues such as algorithmic bias, data governance, and societal impact. However, research suggests that ethics is often treated as a discrete domain, separate from technical reasoning, rather than as integral cognitive labor. From a deskilling perspective, ethical responsibility can itself be outsourced when automation is treated as neutral or authoritative. When students rely on AI-generated recommendations without questioning assumptions, limitations, or consequences, ethical judgment is displaced alongside technical reasoning. Studies indicate that ethical engagement is most effective when integrated directly into technical decision-making, such as dataset selection, model evaluation, or deployment—rather than isolated in standalone ethics modules (Century & Weisberg, 2023; Ferraioli et al., 2025). When ethics is decoupled from practice, it risks becoming abstract, performative, or easily sidelined. This body of literature reinforces a central claim of this chapter: ethical judgment is a form of cognitive work. Without deliberate pedagogical design, ethics risks being deskilled alongside technical understanding, with implications for both student learning and their development as responsible software engineers.

Inclusion, Equity, and Uneven Deskilling

Persistent inequities in CS education have prompted extensive calls for inclusive pedagogy. Automation is often positioned as a leveling force, supporting diverse learners through personalization, adaptive scaffolding, and just-in-time guidance. While this potential is real, research suggests that automation may obscure rather than eliminate inequities. Learners with stronger prior knowledge are more likely to leverage automation strategically, extending their reasoning, whereas learners with less prior experience may rely on it as a compensatory mechanism (Banwo et al., 2024). Over time, these dynamics can widen conceptual gaps, even if outputs appear superficially similar, making inequities less visible and more difficult to address. From a deskilling perspective, inclusion is not only about access to tools but about access to meaningful cognitive work. When automation substitutes for reasoning, learners who most need opportunities for cognitive engagement may be disproportionately affected. Inclusive design strategies, such as Universal Design for Learning, multimodal instruction, and flexible pacing, are effective only when automation is designed to amplify, rather than replace, learners' thinking (Julien, 2024).

Fragmentation in the Existing Literature

Despite increasing attention to AI in CS education, much of the literature remains fragmented. Studies frequently examine automation, ethics, motivation, or inclusion in isolation, focusing on tool efficacy, student attitudes, or performance outcomes without addressing **how** automation redistributes cognitive labor. Few frameworks explicitly consider pedagogical deskilling as a unifying concern. As a result, guidance is often piecemeal: adopt tools to increase engagement, add ethics modules to address responsibility, implement inclusive practices to support diversity, without a coherent framework for reasoning about how these elements interact in automated learning environments.

Contribution of the Present Chapter

This chapter addresses these gaps by advancing a deskilling-oriented conceptual framework grounded in empirical insights from CS education. Rather than proposing new technologies or interventions, it offers a way of thinking about pedagogy that foregrounds responsibility, agency, and conceptual understanding as central design concerns. By situating CS education within a broader tradition of deskilling analysis, the chapter reframes automation not as a neutral enhancement or existential threat, but as a structural condition that reshapes learning by redistributing cognitive labor. This orientation provides the foundation for the empirical analysis and conceptual framework that follow, emphasizing the preparation of students for future software engineering practice in which conceptual reasoning, ethical judgment, and cognitive agency remain indispensable.

RESEARCH QUESTIONS

Building on the literature review and the theoretical framing of Deskilling of Jobs Theory (Braverman, 1974), this chapter examines how cognitive responsibility is redistributed in CS education as intelligent systems and automation are embedded in learning environments. Unlike studies that evaluate tool efficacy, student satisfaction, or task completion, this inquiry emphasizes how students—both traditional learners and returning software engineers—experience, negotiate, and respond to automation's influence on their learning and skill development. The research questions are designed to illuminate the subtle and often invisible processes of pedagogical deskilling, including shifts in reasoning, conceptual understanding, and ethical judgment. They aim to surface tensions, uncertainties, and design dilemmas rather than stable patterns or prescriptive solutions.

RQ1: How do CS students describe the ways AI-assisted and automated systems reshape their cognitive responsibility and conceptual engagement?

This question focuses directly on the student experience of deskilling. It seeks to understand how learners perceive the division of cognitive labor between themselves and automated tools, and how these perceptions affect engagement with problem-solving, abstraction, and conceptual reasoning. The goal is to capture what students are learning—and what they are not learning, when automation mediates core aspects of computational tasks.

RQ2: How do CS students respond to or attempt to maintain ownership of thinking in technology-rich learning environments?

Rather than asking which instructional strategies are "effective," this question examines the strategies, behaviors, and reflective practices students employ to preserve their agency and responsibility for reasoning when AI performs tasks that were previously central to skill development. This addition includes both traditional students and software engineers returning to study, who may bring prior professional experience and expectations that shape how they engage with automation.

RQ3: How do CS students perceive the relationship between automation, inclusion, and unequal access to meaningful cognitive work?

This question investigates how deskilling pressures may be experienced unevenly across learners. Some students may rely on automation to compensate for knowledge gaps, while others use it to extend conceptual reasoning. Over time, automation can mask differences in understanding, producing superficially similar outputs that conceal unequal mastery of core skills. This question emphasizes equity and access to expertise development, asking how learners themselves perceive the impact of automated systems on their learning trajectories.

Rational and Theoretical Alignment

Together, these questions foreground who thinks, who decides, and who learns in contemporary CS education. Table 1 presents the alignment of each research question with Deskilling of Jobs Theory and highlights the student-centered emphasis of the inquiry. They align with the Deskilling of Jobs Theory by emphasizing the redistribution of cognitive labor: the shift of intellectual and ethical responsibility from learners to systems. By explicitly focusing on the student perspective, including professionals returning to formal education, the questions extend deskilling analysis beyond labor markets into the classroom and the broader educational ecosystem.

Table 1. Alignment of Research Questions with Deskilling of Jobs Theory and Student-Centered Focus

Research Question (RQ)	Deskilling Focus	Student-Centered Emphasis
RQ1: How do CS students describe the ways AI-assisted and automated systems reshape their cognitive responsibility and conceptual engagement?	Examines how automation reallocates reasoning and understanding from learners to systems.	Captures learners' experiences of what they are actually thinking, learning, and understanding in technology-mediated tasks.
RQ2: How do CS students respond to or attempt to maintain ownership of thinking in technology-rich learning environments?	Investigates students' strategies to resist or mitigate pedagogical deskilling, preserving agency and judgment.	Focuses on student behaviors, reflective practices, and engagement—especially for learners with prior professional experience (returning software engineers).
RQ3: How do CS students perceive the relationship between automation, inclusion, and unequal access to meaningful cognitive work?	Explores how deskilling pressures may differentially affect learners, potentially obscuring gaps in conceptual understanding.	Highlights learners' perspectives on equity, access to expertise development, and the impact of automation on diverse learning trajectories.

THEORETICAL FRAMEWORK

Contemporary CS education unfolds within a rapidly evolving sociotechnical landscape in which intelligent systems increasingly participate in human thinking. Across professional domains, AI and automation have moved far beyond routine or mechanical tasks to perform functions traditionally associated with skilled human judgment, including analysis, diagnosis, optimization, and creative problem-solving. These developments have generated sustained scholarly attention to how automation reshapes work, expertise, and authority. Yet comparatively little attention has been given to how similar dynamics unfold in educational contexts where learners are simultaneously studying intelligent systems and learning alongside them. This chapter argues that understanding the pedagogical implications of automation requires a shift in analytical focus. Instead of asking whether intelligent technologies improve learning outcomes, increase efficiency, or enhance engagement, educators and researchers must confront a more foundational question: how does automation redistribute cognitive responsibility within learning environments? When automated systems generate solutions, provide feedback, or guide decision-making, they inevitably reshape who is responsible for reasoning, judgment, and understanding. These shifts matter not only for what students learn but also for how their expertise develops, how professional habits form, and how they are prepared for future software engineering practice.

To examine these dynamics, this chapter adopts the Deskilling of Jobs Theory (Braverman, 1974) as its central theoretical framework. Deskilling is not used as a metaphor or retrospective label, but as a pedagogical design lens for analyzing how instructional environments allocate cognitive labor between learners and machines. This lens allows the chapter to connect classroom-level experiences with broader sociotechnical patterns of automation while maintaining conceptual coherence and analytic focus. The sections that follow elaborate on this theoretical stance, first by situating deskilling historically and then by extending it into the pedagogical domain of CS education.

Deskilling of Jobs Theory: Historical Foundations and Core Concepts

The deskilling of Jobs Theory emerged from critical analyses of industrial automation and managerial control in the twentieth century. Braverman (1974) argued that technological systems rarely eliminate labor outright. Instead, they reorganize work by fragmenting complex tasks, externalizing expertise, and transferring decision-making authority from workers to machines, standardized procedures, or managerial structures. Workers may remain active and productive while gradually losing control over the intellectual content of their work. A central insight of the theory is that deskilling is not synonymous with reduced effort or visible inactivity. On the contrary, deskilled labor can appear efficient, orderly, and successful when measured by conventional performance metrics. What is diminished is not output, but agency, specifically, the worker's responsibility for judgment, interpretation, and decision-making. This distinction is crucial for educational analysis. If deskilling is defined solely in terms of reduced performance, it isn't easy to detect in learning environments where automation improves speed, correctness, or functional output. Braverman's framework, by contrast, directs attention to who thinks, who decides, and who understands, making it exceptionally well-suited for analyzing learning environments shaped by intelligent systems.

Extending Deskilling from Labor to Learning

Although the Deskilling of Jobs Theory was initially developed to analyze labor, its conceptual logic extends directly to education. Learning, like work, involves the distribution of cognitive labor: identifying problems, selecting strategies, evaluating outcomes, and adapting understanding. Increasingly, educational technologies participate in these processes. In CS education, this participation is especially pronounced. AI-assisted coding tools generate functional programs, automated debuggers identify errors, and adaptive platforms guide learners through problem spaces. These systems can reduce frustration and lower barriers to participation, yet they also assume responsibility for forms of reasoning that were once central to learning. From a deskilling perspective, the pedagogical risk is not that students stop working, but that they stop owning the thinking. Learners may complete assignments successfully while disengaged from conceptual understanding, abstraction, and judgment. Over time, expertise risks being embedded in systems rather than cultivated within learners. In this chapter, pedagogical deskilling refers to the gradual shift of cognitive responsibility from learners to automated systems—a process shaped primarily by instructional design decisions rather than by students' individual effort, aptitude, or motivation.

Deskilling as a Pedagogical Design Lens

Treating deskilling as a pedagogical design lens shifts attention away from tool efficacy and toward questions of responsibility, agency, and cognitive ownership. Rather than asking whether automation "works," the lens foregrounds questions such as:

- What cognitive work is required of learners in this task?
- Which decisions are made by students, and which are delegated to systems?
- How visible is learners' reasoning—to themselves, peers, and instructors?
- Which forms of understanding are developed, and which are bypassed?

From this perspective, pedagogical deskilling is not an inherent feature of technology, but a design-contingent outcome that emerges through everyday instructional choices, including task framing, assessment structures, and the positioning of automation within learning activities.

In CS education, where efficiency, correctness, and functional output are often prioritized, these choices carry particular weight. Automated systems can generate correct solutions faster than students can reason through them. Without deliberate design constraints, the path of least resistance may gradually redirect learners away from the cognitive work that underpins durable understanding and professional competence.

Ethical Responsibility and the Deskilling of Judgment

A critical extension of the Deskilling of Jobs Theory in this chapter concerns ethical responsibility. In labor contexts, deskilling reduces workers' accountability by relocating judgment elsewhere. In educational contexts, similar dynamics emerge when students treat automated outputs as authoritative or neutral. When learners rely on intelligent systems to recommend solutions, optimize designs, or flag errors, ethical judgment can be displaced alongside technical reasoning. Responsibility for outcomes becomes diffuse: is it the learner's decision, the tool's recommendation, or the designer's intent? From a deskilling perspective, ethical reasoning is itself a form of cognitive labor. Suppose pedagogy does not require students to exercise judgment, accountability, and reflection, ethics risks being deskilled alongside technical understanding. Ethical engagement, therefore, should not be treated as an add-on, but as integral to preserving human agency in AI-mediated learning environments.

Deskilling, Inclusion, and Access to Expertise

Deskilling of Jobs Theory also provides a lens for examining inclusion in CS education. Traditional equity frameworks emphasize access to courses, tools, and resources. While access remains necessary, a deskilling perspective highlights a more profound concern: access to meaningful cognitive work and expertise development. When automation substitutes for reasoning, learners may produce correct outputs without developing the conceptual foundations needed for long-term growth. Students with less prior computing experience are particularly likely to rely on automation as a compensatory strategy. Over time, differences in understanding can be masked by superficially similar outputs, making inequities harder to detect and address. From this standpoint, inclusive pedagogy requires more than providing tools. It requires designing learning environments where all students retain opportunities to think, decide, struggle, and understand, ensuring that automation amplifies, rather than replaces, cognitive engagement.

The Role of Deskilling in This Chapter

Throughout this chapter, Deskilling of Jobs Theory functions as an analytic orientation rather than a retrospective label. It draws attention to moments when students experience uncertainty, when automation reshapes responsibility, and when conceptual understanding is bypassed or obscured. By foregrounding deskilling, the chapter reframes CS education as a site where the politics of automation is enacted not only in workplaces but also in classrooms. Learning becomes a form of work whose organization matters pedagogically, ethically, and socially. This theoretical framework provides the foundation for the empirical analysis and conceptual model that follow, enabling a coherent examination of how automation reshapes CS education not merely by changing tools, but by transforming who thinks, who decides, and who learns.

METHODOLOGY/ RESEARCH APPROACH

This chapter draws on qualitative interview data to inform a practice-oriented pedagogical argument about deskilling in CS education. The empirical component is intentionally exploratory and illustrative, serving to ground the conceptual framework in lived professional contexts rather than to produce generalizable findings or formal theory. This chapter draws on qualitative interview data to develop a practice-oriented pedagogical argument about deskilling in CS education, with a focus on learners themselves—both traditional CS students and software engineers returning to study. The empirical component is intentionally exploratory and illustrative designed to ground the conceptual framework in learners' lived experiences navigating automated and AI-assisted educational environments, rather than generating generalizable findings or formal theory.

Study Design

The study employed an interpretive qualitative approach, using semi-structured interviews to explore how learners make sense of automation, cognitive responsibility, and conceptual engagement in CS education. The approach is not phenomenological or hermeneutic in the strict sense; instead, it emphasizes thematic sensemaking by identifying recurring tensions, contradictions, and dilemmas in learners' experiences of technology-mediated instruction. Deskilling of Jobs Theory (Braverman, 1974) guided the analytic stance, directing attention to who is thinking, how expertise is distributed, and where judgment resides in automated learning contexts. Importantly, the theory functioned as an interpretive lens rather than a rigid coding template, shaping how learners' experiences were read and contextualized. This approach ensures alignment between the empirical scope and the analytical claims about pedagogical deskilling.

Participants

Fifteen individuals participated in the study, selected for their engagement with CS learning under conditions of automation:

- Traditional CS students, enrolled in undergraduate or graduate programs, are navigating AI-assisted learning platforms and automated coding tools.
- Software engineers returning to study, seeking to update skills, or pivot to new areas of technology often balance professional experience with engagement in automated learning environments.

Participants were chosen to reflect a range of backgrounds, prior experience, and levels of familiarity with automation, providing a rich view of how deskilling pressures emerge across diverse learners. This study intentionally centers learners' perspectives rather than educators' or platform designers' alone. While instructors and technology professionals influence learning environments, this chapter prioritizes how students experience responsibility for thinking, problem-solving, and ethical reasoning in AI-mediated education. The accounts of software engineers returning to study are particularly instructive, as these learners navigate **tensions** between prior professional expertise and automated scaffolds, highlighting the subtle erosion or reinforcement of conceptual understanding in contexts intended to enhance professional practice.

Data Collection

Data were collected through semi-structured interviews conducted via video conferencing over six weeks. Interviews lasted approximately 45–70 minutes and focused on:

- Experiences interacting with AI-assisted coding tools, automated debugging, and adaptive learning platforms.
- Perceptions of personal understanding, cognitive engagement, and ownership of problem-solving.
- Strategies learners used to maintain reasoning, abstraction, and ethical judgment when automation intervened.
- Reflections on inclusion, equity, and the impact of automation on learning relative to peers with different prior experience.
- All interviews were conducted with participants' informed consent, ensuring that they understood the purpose of the study and their right to withdraw at any time. Each session was recorded to capture the full depth and nuance of participants' reflections, and the recordings were transcribed verbatim to preserve accuracy and fidelity to their accounts. To protect confidentiality, all identifying information was removed, and transcripts were anonymized using unique codes. The data were stored securely on encrypted devices, and access was restricted to the research team, in accordance with ethical guidelines for handling sensitive qualitative data. These measures ensured that participants' perspectives could be analyzed rigorously while maintaining privacy and trust.

Analytical Strategy

Analysis proceeded through iterative cycles of inductive coding and interpretive **refinement**. Initial coding focused on moments where participants expressed uncertainty, tension, or contradiction regarding automation and their own learning. Subsequent analysis clustered these moments around deskilling-related concerns, including:

- Diminished engagement with reasoning, where automation performed tasks that traditionally required conceptual understanding.
- Hidden conceptual gaps, where learners completed tasks successfully without developing transferable knowledge.
- Shifts in cognitive responsibility, where decision-making and judgment were implicitly ceded to automated systems.

Analytic memos documented interpretive decisions, ensuring that emerging themes remained grounded in participants' experiences rather than abstract theoretical assumptions. Qualitative analysis software supported data organization and retrieval but did not determine analytic outcomes.

Trustworthiness and Limitations

Interpretive rigor was supported through multiple strategies. Reflexive journaling allowed the researcher to continuously examine assumptions, biases, and interpretive choices throughout the analytic process. Triangulation across different types of learners—including traditional students and software engineers returning to study—helped ensure that emerging themes reflected a range of experiences rather than a single perspective. Selective member checking was also employed, providing participants with opportunities to review and confirm that the interpretations resonated with their lived experiences.

Given the study's exploratory focus, the findings are not presented as exhaustive or universally representative of all CS learners. Instead, they offer practice-informed insights into how students experience and navigate the pressures of pedagogical deskilling, particularly in learning environments where AI-assisted tools mediate key aspects of problem-solving, reasoning, and assessment. By centering students' perspectives, the study highlights not only what learners accomplish but also how their cognitive agency, conceptual understanding, and ethical reasoning are shaped—or, in some cases, diminished—by the integration of automated systems in CS education. These insights aim to inform both instructional design and future research on supporting meaningful learning in technology-rich environments.

FINDINGS

This chapter investigates how AI-assisted and automated systems reshape CS students' learning, engagement, and preparation for future software engineering practice. Data were analyzed to understand the redistribution of cognitive responsibility, conceptual engagement, and access to meaningful work. Participants included both traditional CS students and software engineers returning to study, highlighting experiences across diverse learner profiles.

RQ1: How do CS students describe the ways AI-assisted and automated systems reshape their cognitive responsibility and conceptual engagement?

Participants consistently reported that automation profoundly reshapes the ways they engage with computational tasks, influencing not only the strategies they employ but also their deeper conceptual reasoning and sense of ownership over problem-solving. Many students noted that AI-assisted tools can accelerate task completion and reduce frustration, yet these benefits come with trade-offs that affect how they interact with core computational concepts. Across the interviews, three overarching themes emerged that capture the nuanced ways automation mediates cognitive responsibility, shapes engagement with abstraction and reasoning, and influences learners' confidence in independent problem-solving:

Theme 1.1: Shift from Reasoning to Output Verification

Both traditional students and returning software engineers described a transition from active problem construction to verifying AI-generated solutions. AI-assisted tools frequently produced functionally complete and syntactically correct code, positioning students as reviewers rather than originators of logic. Traditional students reported spending less time designing algorithms themselves, focusing instead on checking whether the output "worked." Returning software engineers noted that even with prior experience, repeated exposure to automated code generation led to reduced engagement with low-level logic and algorithmic reasoning, as they relied on AI to handle repetitive or complex tasks. Across groups, this shift diminished opportunities to articulate reasoning, explain decisions, or explore alternative approaches, which are critical for developing transferable expertise in software engineering.

Theme 1.2: Episodic and Reactive Conceptual Engagement

Students reported that conceptual reasoning occurred primarily in response to errors or unexpected AI outputs, rather than as part of sustained cognitive effort. Traditional learners highlighted that their engagement was triggered only when outputs failed to meet expectations, producing reactive learning cycles punctuated by rapid automated production. Returning software engineers observed similar patterns but noted that their prior professional experience allowed them to interpret failures more strategically, sometimes using them to reconnect with underlying principles. Nevertheless, both groups agreed that this episodic engagement was inconsistent, leaving gaps in durable conceptual understanding and abstract reasoning that underpin software engineering expertise.

Theme 1.3: Correct Outputs Mask Uncertainty and Understanding Gaps

A recurring concern among participants was that successful automated outputs gave a false sense of mastery. Traditional students often completed assignments efficiently but were uncertain about whether they could reproduce or explain solutions independently. Returning software engineers recognized similar risks, noting that polished AI-generated solutions could mask misunderstandings about system behavior, algorithmic efficiency, or debugging strategies. This disconnect between task completion and genuine understanding complicates learners' ability to assess readiness for real-world software engineering, where independent reasoning and problem-solving are essential.

RQ2: How do CS students respond to or attempt to maintain ownership of thinking in technology-rich learning environments?

Findings reveal that learners actively employ a variety of strategies to preserve their cognitive agency, maintain conceptual engagement, and assert ownership over problem-solving, even when AI-assisted systems handle core aspects of computational work. The effectiveness of these strategies, however, is not uniform; it depends heavily on the design of learning tasks, the availability of structured opportunities for reflection, and learners' prior experience with coding or professional software development. Students with previous industry experience often approached automation differently from novices, strategically leveraging AI to extend rather than replace their reasoning. In contrast, less experienced learners were more likely to defer to automated outputs. Across the data, three primary themes emerged that illuminate the ways learners negotiate, resist, or adapt to the redistribution of cognitive responsibility in technology-mediated learning environments:

Theme 2.1: Justification and Explanation Preserve Cognitive Ownership

Participants reported that requiring explanations, modifications, or defenses of AI-generated solutions increased cognitive engagement. Traditional students indicated that written reflections, annotations, or peer discussions forced active engagement with underlying concepts, transforming AI outputs into opportunities for learning. Returning software engineers leveraged prior professional experience to critically evaluate and extend AI solutions, connecting assignments to broader software engineering principles. Across both groups, tasks that required reasoning articulation served as a mechanism to counteract deskilling and reinforce ownership of cognitive labor.

Theme 2.2: Efficiency-Oriented Environments Encourage Delegation to Automation

Students noted that time pressure, emphasis on speed, and task volume strongly influenced reliance on AI. Traditional learners frequently prioritized completing assignments efficiently, especially in large courses, leading them to delegate reasoning to automated systems. Returning software engineers sometimes leveraged AI to streamline routine problem-solving, freeing time for higher-level design thinking but also introducing the risk that conceptual engagement would be bypassed. In both populations, when external incentives reward speed and correctness over understanding, students' cognitive ownership is systematically reduced, reinforcing deskilling dynamics.

Theme 2.3: Visibility of Reasoning Reinforces Engagement

Ownership was most robust when learning environments made intermediate steps explicit, allowing students to trace AI outputs back to underlying logic. Traditional students highlighted that visualizations, stepwise debugging, and algorithmic flow charts strengthened understanding. At the same time, returning professionals emphasized that transparent decision points allowed them to integrate prior knowledge while remaining actively engaged. When automation obscured reasoning pathways, learners in both groups reported difficulty in identifying where to intervene cognitively, often resulting in superficial engagement and reliance on AI-generated outputs.

The degree to which reasoning is visible thus emerges as a critical determinant of cognitive agency.

RQ3: How do CS students perceive the relationship between automation, inclusion, and unequal access to meaningful cognitive work?

Participants highlighted that automation can amplify existing differences in prior knowledge, technical skill, and professional experience, thereby shaping unequal access to meaningful conceptual learning. Learners noted that while some students can use AI tools strategically to explore, experiment, and deepen understanding, others rely primarily on automation to complete tasks, often bypassing the reasoning that underpins mastery. Over time, these patterns can produce superficially similar outputs that conceal substantial variation in understanding, making it difficult for both learners and instructors to identify gaps in expertise. Across the interviews, three interrelated themes emerged that illustrate how automation interacts with prior experience, learning behavior, and access to cognitive challenge:

Theme 3.1: Unequal Access to Cognitive Challenge

Students with strong prior knowledge, including returning software engineers, used AI strategically to explore alternatives, test hypotheses, and accelerate routine coding, retaining responsibility for core reasoning. In contrast, learners with less experience relied on AI to substitute for reasoning, often completing tasks without engaging deeply with underlying principles. Participants described this divergence as producing systematic differences in access to meaningful cognitive work, even when all students received identical instruction and tools.

Theme 3.2: Superficially Uniform Outputs Conceal Learning Differences

Students noted that AI-generated solutions often masked differences in understanding. Traditional learners who relied heavily on AI produced outputs indistinguishable from peers with deeper engagement, while returning engineers recognized that even proficient coders could have gaps hidden by automation. This concealment delayed feedback and prevented targeted support, creating long-term implications for skill transfer and readiness for professional software engineering tasks.

Theme 3.3: Deskilling Erodes Confidence in Independent Practice

Reliance on AI influenced learners' confidence in performing tasks without automated assistance. Traditional students reported uncertainty about debugging or designing systems independently, while returning professionals reflected on the risk that automation could weaken judgment and critical thinking. Participants across both groups emphasized that sustained reliance on AI might hinder the development of professional autonomy and self-efficacy, essential traits for successful software engineers.

Summary of Findings

Across all three research questions, findings reveal that pedagogical deskilling in CS education manifests as a redistribution of cognitive responsibility rather than a reduction **in** activity. AI-assisted and automated systems reshape what learners think about, when they engage in reasoning, and how much ownership they retain over problem-solving and conceptual understanding.

- RQ1 emphasizes that automation shifts engagement toward output validation, creates reactive reasoning cycles, and masks understanding gaps.
- RQ2 demonstrates that students actively employ strategies to preserve reasoning, but cognitive ownership is fragile and highly dependent on task design and visibility of reasoning.
- RQ3 highlights equity implications: automation produces uneven access to cognitive challenge, conceals learning disparities, and can undermine confidence in independent software engineering practice.

Both traditional CS students and returning software engineers experience these dynamics, though prior experience shapes the ways learners interact with AI. Collectively, these findings underscore the need for instructional designs that preserve conceptual engagement, visible reasoning, and equitable access to cognitive work.

DISCUSSION AND IMPLICATIONS

The findings indicate that integrating AI-assisted and automated systems into CS education fundamentally reshapes how students learn, reason, and prepare for professional practice. Pedagogical deskilling does not manifest as a lack of effort, motivation, or engagement; instead, it emerges as a subtle yet consequential redistribution of cognitive responsibility from learners to automated tools. This shift affects not only students' ability to construct and apply conceptual knowledge but also their capacity to exercise ethical judgment and maintain professional autonomy.

Students frequently described that while automation accelerates task completion and reduces technical friction, it simultaneously obscures the reasoning processes that underlie expertise. Correct outputs can create the impression of mastery, even when learners are only superficially engaging with core concepts. For students returning from professional experience, this tension is particularly salient: prior knowledge and expectations can either buffer against deskilling—when automation is used strategically—or exacerbate it, when learners defer judgment to AI tools.

Interpreted through the lens of the Deskilling of Jobs Theory (Braverman, 1974), these findings suggest that cognitive labor is not eliminated in learning but reallocated. Just as workers in industrial settings may remain active while losing decision-making responsibility, students remain behaviorally engaged. At the same time, their agency for reasoning, problem-solving, and ethical reflection is diminished. The result is a learning environment that prioritizes efficiency, correctness, and output visibility, sometimes at the expense of deep conceptual understanding and professional readiness.

From a pedagogical perspective, these findings underscore the importance of designing learning experiences that explicitly preserve student ownership of cognitive work. Tasks that require explanation, justification, or modification of AI-generated outputs can counteract deskilling by forcing learners to re-engage with underlying reasoning. Reflection prompts, peer discussion, and iterative problem-solving exercises also help maintain cognitive responsibility and reinforce conceptual depth.

From an equity and inclusion perspective, the study highlights that automation does not affect all students equally. Learners with more prior knowledge or professional experience can leverage AI tools to extend their understanding and explore complex problem spaces. In contrast, others may rely on automation as a substitute for reasoning. Without deliberate instructional strategies, these dynamics can widen gaps in conceptual mastery and access to expertise, producing superficially similar outputs that mask underlying inequities.

Overall, the findings illustrate that AI and automation in CS education are neither inherently beneficial nor harmful. Their pedagogical impact is contingent on how responsibility for thinking, decision-making, and ethical reasoning is distributed within learning environments. Recognizing and addressing these dynamics is essential for cultivating students who are not only technically proficient but also capable of independent reasoning, ethical judgment, and professional autonomy in software engineering practice.

Pedagogical Deskilling and Conceptual Understanding

Automation shifts the locus of reasoning from students to systems, often reducing sustained engagement with fundamental computational concepts. While tools accelerate task completion and reduce cognitive load, they can inadvertently transform learning into a reactive process, with conceptual reasoning occurring only in response to system failures. For future software engineers, this episodic engagement risks superficial mastery: students may generate working code without fully understanding algorithmic design, debugging strategies, or system behaviors.

Implications for Practice:

- Design for active reasoning: Educators should structure tasks that require students to explain, justify, or modify automated outputs, ensuring engagement with underlying principles.
- Scaffold conceptual reflection: Instructional strategies such as reflective journaling, peer discussion, or code walkthroughs can reinforce durable understanding.
- Integrate breakdown analysis: Prompting learners to analyze why automation fails or produces suboptimal outputs encourages proactive problem-solving and deeper conceptual engagement.

For returning software engineers, scaffolds should integrate prior knowledge with new learning, helping them critically interrogate AI outputs rather than rely on automated solutions as shortcuts.

Cognitive Ownership and Professional Autonomy

Ownership of reasoning is highly contingent on instructional conditions and visibility of thought processes. Where intermediate steps are abstracted by automation, students may disengage cognitively, even while producing correct outputs. This finding has direct implications for professional readiness: software engineers entering or returning to the workforce must be able to exercise independent judgment rather than rely on automated tools. Over-reliance risks eroding confidence in decision-making, debugging, and system design.

Implications for Practice:

- Make reasoning visible: Tools and assignments should reveal decision points, algorithmic choices, and trade-offs, fostering ownership of thinking.
- Prioritize process over product: Assessment strategies should emphasize reasoning, explanation, and design justification, rather than correctness alone.

- Support autonomy through challenge: Tasks should balance efficiency with cognitive demand, encouraging learners to tackle problems that cannot be fully automated.

Returning professionals may benefit from bridging exercises that explicitly connect AI-assisted learning to independent problem-solving scenarios typical in industry, maintaining confidence and reinforcing professional autonomy.

Equity, Inclusion, and Access to Expertise

Automation has the potential to both amplify and obscure inequities in CS education. Students with prior experience or stronger conceptual foundations can use AI strategically, while others may depend on it as a substitute for reasoning. Superficially similar outputs mask these differences, potentially perpetuating gaps in understanding and long-term professional readiness.

Implications for Practice:

- Design equitable cognitive opportunities: Ensure all students, regardless of prior experience, have access to meaningful problem-solving tasks.
- Monitor learning beyond outputs: Assess understanding through explanatory tasks, project reflections, or collaborative problem-solving, rather than relying solely on automated outputs.
- Use automation as amplification, not replacement: Tools should support diverse learners by extending thinking, providing scaffolds, or enabling exploration, rather than completing work for them.

For returning engineers, equity considerations also include differences in familiarity with contemporary tools or updated programming paradigms. Targeted support can prevent automation from creating uneven professional development trajectories.

Ethics, Responsibility, and the Redistribution of Judgment

The findings highlight that ethical reasoning can be deskilled alongside technical understanding. Students may defer to automated recommendations without interrogating assumptions, biases, or broader implications, undermining ethical judgment and accountability—skills crucial for software engineers.

Implications for Practice:

- Embed ethics into technical work: Rather than standalone modules, ethical reflection should be integrated into coding, system design, and debugging tasks.
- Prompt critique of automation: Students should assess outputs for correctness, fairness, and unintended consequences, reinforcing responsibility alongside reasoning.
- Develop reflective routines: Incorporating structured reflection on both technical and ethical dimensions fosters holistic professional judgment.

Returning software engineers can particularly benefit from scenarios that simulate real-world ethical decision-making in technology-mediated environments, bridging classroom learning with professional responsibility.

Strategic Use of Automation in Learning

The research underscores that automation itself is not inherently deskilling; its effects are contingent on how responsibility is structured within learning environments. When tasks demand active engagement with outputs, automation can serve as a cognitive amplifier—enhancing problem-solving without replacing reasoning. Conversely, when outputs are treated as authoritative or when speed and volume dominate learning goals, automation becomes a cognitive substitute, reducing engagement with core concepts and professional skills.

Implications for Practice:

- Define boundaries of automation: Clearly specify which tasks students must solve independently and which can be scaffolded.
- Integrate automation as a partner: Position AI as a collaborator rather than a replacement, prompting learners to interrogate, debug, and justify outputs.
- Encourage iterative learning cycles: Use automation to accelerate practice while embedding reflection, explanation, and problem decomposition into task cycles.

Preparing Students for Professional Software Engineering

Ultimately, pedagogical deskilling has long-term implications for professional readiness. Students who rely excessively on automation risk entering the workforce with gaps in independent problem-solving, debugging, system design, and ethical reasoning. For returning software engineers, this dynamic is compounded by differences between previous professional experience and current tool paradigms.

Implications for Practice:

- Simulate real-world constraints: Assignments should mimic professional challenges where automation cannot fully resolve uncertainty, requiring critical thinking.
- Foster adaptive expertise: Encourage students to use AI tools strategically while maintaining the ability to reason independently and transfer knowledge across contexts.
- Reinforce reflective professional practice: Reflection on decision-making, successes, and failures bridges academic learning with industry readiness.

Summary of Discussion and Implications

This chapter highlights that automation reshapes CS education not by reducing effort, but by redistributing cognitive responsibility. Pedagogical deskilling is context-dependent and influenced by task design, the visibility of reasoning, prior knowledge, and reflective practice. For students and returning professionals alike:

1. Conceptual engagement must be deliberately structured to avoid reactive or episodic learning.
2. Cognitive ownership and autonomy should be supported through tasks that require explanation, critique, and decision-making.
3. Equitable access to expertise requires scaffolds and assessment practices that make understanding visible beyond automated outputs.
4. Ethical reasoning must be integrated directly into technical work to preserve judgment and accountability.
5. Automation should amplify, not replace, thinking, providing a platform for reflection, experimentation, and skill development.
6. Professional readiness depends on preparing students to operate independently in contexts where automation may not provide reliable guidance.

By foregrounding these considerations, educators can harness AI-assisted learning to strengthen rather than erode cognitive and professional competencies, ensuring students and returning software engineers develop the judgment, understanding, and resilience necessary for contemporary software engineering practice.

CONCLUSION

This chapter argued that the central challenge for contemporary CS education is not simply whether to adopt intelligent technologies, but how to cultivate learning environments in which students retain meaningful cognitive responsibility, conceptual engagement, and ethical agency. By applying the Deskilling of Jobs Theory as a pedagogical design lens, automation is reframed not as a neutral tool or a threat, but as a structural condition that reorganizes who thinks, who decides, and who learns. Rather than focusing solely on technical proficiency or measurable outputs, this perspective draws attention to the subtle redistribution of cognitive labor, the potential erosion of conceptual understanding, and the risks to equitable access to expertise. The contribution of this chapter lies in articulating a practice-informed framework that illuminates how pedagogical deskilling emerges and can be anticipated, mitigated, or redirected through deliberate instructional design. This framework emphasizes the interdependence of reasoning, judgment, and ethical responsibility, providing educators with a lens for assessing when automation supports learning and when it displaces it. In highlighting these dynamics, the work underscores that CS education remains a fundamentally human endeavor. Learning is not merely about producing correct outputs or efficient code; it is about fostering students' ability to think critically, reason independently, and engage ethically—skills that remain essential even as intelligent systems take on increasingly sophisticated tasks.

Moreover, the chapter situates these insights within the broader context of inclusion and equity. It highlights that the effects of automation are not uniform: learners' prior knowledge, professional experience, and access to reflective opportunities shape how they engage with AI-assisted systems. By making visible the differential impacts of automation, the framework encourages educators to design interventions that preserve access to meaningful cognitive work for all students, ensuring that technology amplifies rather than diminishes opportunities for learning, conceptual growth, and professional readiness. Ultimately, this chapter positions pedagogical design as the decisive factor in shaping the future of CS education. By centering students' cognitive agency and ethical engagement, it offers a lens for rethinking instruction in an era of intelligent automation, emphasizing that the human dimension of learning must remain at the core of educational practice.

REFERENCES

Banwo, B. O., Navarrete-Burks, L., McGee, S., & McGee-Tekula, R. (2024). Building Bridges in STEM Education: Minoritized Secondary School Student Computer Science Pathways and Experiences. *Education in Science, 14*(8), 831. DOI: 10.3390/educsci14080831

Braverman, H. (1974). *Labor and monopoly capital.* Monthly Review Press.

Century, J., & Weisberg, L. (2023). Growing Knowledge about Using Culturally Responsive Pedagogy and Universal Design for Learning in Computer Science Education. *2023 Conference on Research in Equitable and Sustained Participation in Engineering, Computing, and Technology (RESPECT).* https://doi.org/DOI: 10.1109/RESPECT60069.2023.00013

Crowston, K., & Bolici, F. (2025). Deskilling and upskilling with AI Systems. *nformation Research an International Electronic Journal, 30*(iConf), 1009-1023. https://doi.org/DOI: 10.47989/ir30iconf47143

Ferraioli, V., Mondada, F., & Abou-Khalil, V. (2025). Reframing Computational Thinking for AI Education. https://doi.org/DOI: 10.1007/9

Garcia, M. B. (2024). Profiling the skill mastery of introductory programming students: A cognitive diagnostic modeling approach. *Education and Information Technologies, 30*, 6455–6481. DOI: 10.1007/s10639-024-13039-6

Julien, G. (2024). How Artificial Intelligence (AI) impacts inclusive education. *Educational Research Review, 19*(6), 95–103. DOI: 10.5897/ERR2024.4404

Rinta-Kahila, T., Penttinen, E., Salovaara, A., Soliman, W., & Ruissalo, J. (2023). The vicious circles of skill erosion: A case study of cognitive automation. *Journal of the Association for Information Systems, 24*(5), 1378–1412. DOI: 10.17705/1jais.00829

Stefaniak, J., & Moore, S. (2024). The Use of Generative AI to Support Inclusivity and Design Deliberation for Online Instruction. *Online and Blended Learning in the Age of Generative AI, 28*(3), 181–205. DOI: 10.24059/olj.v28i3.4458

Toto, G. A., Marinelli, C. V., Cavioni, V., Furia, M. d., Traetta, L., Iuso, S., & Petito, A. (2024). *What is the Role of Technologies for Inclusive Education? A Systematic Review.* Springer., DOI: 10.1007/9

KEY TERMS AND DEFINITIONS

Academic Integrity: Commitment to honesty, trust, fairness, respect, and responsibility in educational work. It includes avoiding plagiarism, cheating, and unauthorized assistance, and correctly using AI-generated content.

Artificial Intelligence (AI): A field of computer science focused on creating systems capable of performing tasks that typically require human intelligence, such as reasoning, learning, problem-solving, and language understanding.

Bias in AI: Systematic and unfair discrimination that occurs in AI outputs due to biased training data, algorithms, or system design often affects marginalized groups disproportionately.

Chatbot: An AI-powered program designed to simulate human conversation through text or voice. Chatbots are commonly used in customer service, education, and healthcare applications.

Computer Science (CS) Students: Learners enrolled in computer science programs, including both traditional undergraduate and graduate students, **and** returning software engineers who engage in formal study to update or expand their knowledge. These students vary in prior experience, motivation, and exposure to professional software development, which shapes how they interact with AI-assisted tools.

Deskilling: A process by which automation or technological tools reduce the need for human skills, often leading to diminished expertise, confidence, or ownership over work processes.

Ethical AI Use: The responsible and informed use of AI tools that align with moral principles, institutional policies, and social values. It includes fairness, accountability, transparency, and respect for privacy and user well-being.

Ethics-by-Design: An approach to system development in which ethical principles are embedded into the design process from the outset, ensuring that technology aligns with human values and social good.

Generative AI: A subset of AI technologies that can generate content—including text, code, images, or audio—based on input prompts. Examples include ChatGPT, GitHub Copilot, and other large language models (LLMs).

Ownership of Thinking: The degree to which learners retain agency, control, and accountability over reasoning and decision-making in tasks mediated by AI or automated systems. High ownership requires students to interrogate, justify, and modify AI-generated solutions, maintaining intellectual engagement and critical judgment.

Prompt Engineering: The practice of crafting effective input prompts to optimize the responses generated by AI models, especially in natural language and code generation contexts.

Returning Software Engineers: Professionals with prior experience in software development or IT who return to formal education to acquire new skills, transition careers, or update their technical knowledge. Their previous professional experience influences their engagement with automation, critical reasoning, and conceptual reflection in CS learning environments.

Chapter 6
Gender-Inclusive Pedagogies in Computer Science Education:
Insights, Implications, and Future Directions

Narcisan S. Galamiton
Cebu Technological University, Philippines

Mary Jane C. Sim
Cebu Technological University, Philippines

Dharel P. Acut
https://orcid.org/0000-0002-9608-1292
Cebu Technological University, Philippines

Damola Olugbade
https://orcid.org/0000-0003-3938-6273
First Technical University, Nigeria

Asegul Hulus
https://orcid.org/0000-0001-8797-450X
University of Nicosia, Cyprus

Ramesh Chander Sharma
https://orcid.org/0000-0002-1371-1157
Dr. B.R. Ambedkar University, Delhi, India

Ari Happonen
https://orcid.org/0000-0003-0744-1776
LUT University, Finland

Manuel B. Garcia
https://orcid.org/0000-0003-2615-422X
FEU Institute of Technology, Philippines

ABSTRACT

Despite growing demand for computing professionals, women remain significantly underrepresented in computer science education and technology careers. This chapter presents a narrative review of literature on gender-inclusive pedagogies, examining classroom practices, curriculum design, assessment strategies, mentorship,

DOI: 10.4018/979-8-3373-6546-6.ch006

and institutional initiatives that support female learners' engagement, persistence, and sense of belonging. Drawing on international and regional studies, the review identifies effective approaches such as collaborative learning, identity-affirming and real-world curricula, formative assessment, and structured support systems, while highlighting persistent gaps including Western-centric perspectives, limited intersectional analyses, and misalignment between policy rhetoric and classroom practice. Grounded in technofeminist theory, the chapter discusses implications for educators, institutions, policymakers, and future research aimed at advancing equity in computing education.

INTRODUCTION

In an era defined by rapid digital transformation, gender disparities in computing remain a persistent global concern (Ashlock & Tufekci, 2024; Fietta et al., 2023; Perez-Felkner et al., 2024). Despite substantial progress in access to education and workforce participation, women continue to be underrepresented in computing fields both in academia and in industry. According to the World Economic Forum (2023), women comprise only about 28% of the global STEM workforce, with their participation particularly low in computing-related roles. In the technology industry, women account for roughly 25% of technical positions and an even smaller share of leadership roles (Forbes, 2024). Within software development, the imbalance is even more pronounced as over 90% of developers identify as male.

These figures are often interpreted through the lens of a persistent "leaky pipeline," where women's representation diminishes progressively from education to employment, as access to computing fields remains shaped by gendered cultural capital, socialization patterns, and institutional pathways that disproportionately advantage male-dominated trajectories. However, recent critical scholarship cautions that this metaphor risks producing static and deficit-oriented accounts of women's participation in computing. Vitores and Gil-Juárez (2016) argue that decades of research framed around the leaky pipeline have paradoxically contributed to a sense of inevitability by focusing on women's attrition rather than interrogating how computing itself is socially constructed and institutionally organized. They highlight that, despite growing participation of women across most STEM fields, computing remains an outlier and that the problem lies with entrenched disciplinary cultures, research assumptions, and policy framings that continue to reproduce gendered exclusions.

These global patterns are mirrored at regional levels. Within the European Union, for instance, women comprise 52% of the overall science and technology workforce yet remain significantly underrepresented in information and communication technology (ICT) professions (Eurostat, 2024). Eurostat (2023) data show that men account for approximately 84% of ICT specialists, leaving women with only a 15.9% share. The European Institute for Gender Equality (2024) links this imbalance to persistent sociocultural stereotypes, unequal access to digital skills development, and the limited presence of women in technology-related leadership roles. Likewise, the United Nations Economic Commission for Europe (2025) notes that despite progressive policy frameworks, structural inequalities continue to shape women's participation across education, employment, and innovation systems in Europe.

Similar dynamics are evident across Asia and the Pacific, where gendered barriers to digital access and participation continue to constrain women's engagement with technology. Centuries of patriarchy, discrimination, and harmful stereotypes have shaped a persistent digital gender divide, with only 54% of women in Asia and the Pacific having digital access (United Nations Economic and Social Commission for Asia and the Pacific, 2023). Women and girls remain less likely than men and boys to use the internet or own a smartphone, and gender-based violence (both offline and increasingly online) further compounds their exclusion. Consistent with these findings, Galpaya and Zainudeen (2022) emphasize that barriers extend beyond connectivity, encompassing limited opportunities for digital skill development, constrained participation in technology-related learning, and socio-cultural expectations that discourage engagement with ICT fields. UNICEF (2023) likewise reports that in low-income countries, 90% of adolescent girls and young women aged 15–24 remain offline compared to 78% of boys and young men, with the largest gap in South Asia, favoring males by 27 percentage points. Furthermore, for every 100 male youth possessing digital skills, only 65 female youth do, and across 41 countries, young women are nearly 13% less likely to own a mobile phone. These intersecting disadvantages reveal that the gender gap in ICT extends far beyond issues of access or infrastructure. Instead, it is deeply rooted in structural inequalities and sociocultural barriers that shape women's digital participation and perpetuate broader patterns of exclusion in computing and technology-related fields (Kovaleva et al., 2024a; Kovaleva et al., 2024c).

While the literature identifies a range of pedagogical, institutional, and policy-oriented approaches that can foster greater inclusivity for women in higher education computing contexts (Ashlock & Tufekci, 2024; Fietta et al., 2023; Lopes, 2022; Perez-Felkner et al., 2024; Wu & Uttal, 2024), such practices remain unevenly adopted and are far from being embedded as standard practice. This systemic exclusion from digital participation also translates into underrepresentation within the technology workforce. A persistent paradox emerges in that, although users of technology are nearly evenly distributed by gender, the creators of technology (e.g., software engineers, systems designers, and computing professionals) remain predominantly male (European Institute for Gender Equality, 2024; Eurostat, 2023). This imbalance has far-reaching implications. When technological systems are designed primarily by men, the resulting products, algorithms, and digital infrastructures risk embedding implicit gender biases (DeCook, 2020). Design decisions shaped by narrow assumptions about users can marginalize diverse users in subtle but consequential ways. Research in inclusive and user-centered design demonstrates that broadening design perspectives not only improves equity but also enhances usability, efficiency, and sustainability for all users. In this sense, increasing diversity among computing professionals is not solely a matter of representation but a critical condition for producing technologies that are responsive to evolving practices, contexts, and user needs.

In the context of education, gendered disparities in computing are visible early in the pipeline. Although girls and women are active technology users, they remain underrepresented in computing programs at secondary and tertiary levels (UNESCO, 2017). Studies attribute this to a combination of factors including cultural stereotypes, lack of role models, implicit classroom biases, and learning environments that unconsciously privilege male participation (Adams & Morgan, 2021; Kurti et al., 2024; Sulla et al., 2025). Pedagogical practices that emphasize competition and individual performance may further discourage participation among female learners, while inclusive teaching strategies (e.g., collaborative learning, mentoring, and real-world project engagement) are shown to improve belonging and persistence (Dost, 2024; Guo et al., 2025). These patterns highlight the urgent need to examine not only who participates in computing education but also how pedagogical structures, classroom cultures, and curriculum designs shape participation, persistence, and inclusion by reproducing or challenging gendered norms.

MAIN FOCUS OF THE CHAPTER

This chapter addresses a critical gap in computing education research by synthesizing existing scholarship on gender disparities with a focused examination of gender-inclusive pedagogical approaches in computer science education. While prior studies have extensively documented women's underrepresentation in computing, less attention has been given to systematically analyzing which pedagogical practices effectively foster inclusion, belonging, and persistence among female learners, and why these practices work across diverse educational contexts. Moreover, existing reviews often privilege structural or policy-level explanations, leaving pedagogical dynamics underexplored. Responding to this gap, the chapter adopts a narrative review supported by expert-informed synthesis to (1) identify and categorize gender-inclusive pedagogical strategies reported in the literature, (2) examine how these approaches address sociocultural, instructional, and institutional barriers in computing education, and (3) distill actionable implications for educators, institutions, and policymakers. Foregrounding pedagogy as a central lever for change, this chapter aims to contribute a coherent, practice-oriented framework that informs inclusive teaching, curriculum design, and future research directions in computer science education.

METHODOLOGY

Approach and Analytical Lens

This chapter adopts a narrative review approach with expert-informed synthesis to examine gender-inclusive pedagogies in computer science education. Unlike systematic or PRISMA-style reviews that prioritize exhaustive coverage and procedural replication (Page et al., 2021), a narrative review foregrounds conceptual depth, interpretive coherence, and pedagogical relevance. This approach is particularly suited to examining the multifaceted and context-dependent factors shaping women's participation, persistence, and progression in computing education and related technology pathways (Kovaleva et al., 2023).

The synthesis draws on a broad corpus of empirical studies, conceptual and theoretical papers, policy documents, and practitioner-oriented literature. Importantly, the review is informed by the combined professional and research expertise of the authors who collectively bring approximately 5 to 25 years of experience in higher education teaching, research, curriculum development, and academic leadership within computer science, information technology, and STEM education. This expertise includes sustained engagement in gender equity work, including current administrative leadership roles such as directing institutional Gender and Development (GAD) initiatives, which provide direct insight into policy implementation, faculty development, and equity-driven educational reform. This cumulative knowledge, spanning more than two decades of engagement with gender-focused and multi-gendered educational settings at national and international levels, supports a critical and contextually grounded interpretation of the literature. While the review does not follow a formal PRISMA protocol, principles of transparency, rigor, and reflexivity associated with systematic reviewing were applied through collaborative source selection, cross-checking of key themes, and iterative synthesis informed by the authors' diverse educational experiences.

The analytical framework is guided by technofeminist theory and gender-inclusive pedagogical perspectives. Technofeminism, as articulated by Wajcman (2004), conceptualizes technology and technological knowledge as socially constructed rather than neutral, shaped by historically situated gendered power relations. Applied to computing education, this lens foregrounds how curricula, classroom cultures, assessment practices, and institutional norms may reproduce exclusionary assumptions or, alternatively, serve as sites for resistance and transformation. Complementing this perspective, gender-inclusive pedagogy emphasizes relational, collaborative, and equity-oriented instructional approaches, including mentorship, project-based and community-engaged learning, and culturally responsive teaching (Dost, 2024; Guo et al., 2025). Across the chapter, the synthesis is organized around three interrelated analytical dimensions: (1) pedagogical practices, (2) learning environments and cultures, and (3) structural and sociocultural conditions that intersect with classroom-level practices to shape female learners' engagement, identity formation, and persistence in computer science education.

Conceptual and Theoretical Perspectives

The conceptual foundation of this review draws on interdisciplinary scholarship from computing education, gender studies, and STEM pedagogy. Technofeminism provides a lens for interpreting how gendered power dynamics permeate technology development, learning environments, and classroom interactions (DeCook, 2020; Wajcman, 2004). The chapter also incorporates social constructivist principles (Vygotsky, 1978), which position learning as socially situated and relational, emphasizing collaborative knowledge-building and peer interaction as key mechanisms for fostering inclusion. Gender-inclusive pedagogy frameworks further inform the analysis, highlighting strategies that enhance belonging, representation, and equity in STEM classrooms (Kurti et al., 2024; Sulla et al., 2025). These frameworks guide the identification and interpretation of pedagogical interventions (e.g., collaborative problem-solving, real-world projects, mentoring, and inclusive assessment practices) enabling the synthesis to move beyond descriptive accounts toward actionable insights for educational practice and policy.

Literature Search and Source Selection

Relevant literature was identified through a targeted search strategy across multiple databases, including Scopus, Web of Science, ERIC, and Google Scholar. Keywords included combinations of "*gender-inclusive pedagogy*," "*female students*," "*computing education*," "*STEM*," "*classroom inclusion*," and "*technofeminism*." The search prioritized sources published in the last decade, supplemented with foundational and policy-oriented documents from organizations such as UNESCO, the European Institute for Gender Equality (EIGE), UNICEF, and the World Economic Forum. Selection of studies followed a structured, expert-informed process. Initially, titles and abstracts were screened for relevance to gender-inclusive pedagogical practices, learning outcomes, and equity in computing education. Full texts were then critically appraised using a checklist that assessed three dimensions: relevance, methodological rigor, and applicability to higher education contexts. The scoring was conducted independently by three contributing authors, and final ratings were determined through inter-rater agreement discussions to ensure consistency and reliability. Critical appraisal techniques (e.g., evaluation of study design, sample characteristics, analytical methods, and context specificity) were applied to ensure inclusion of high-quality and impactful studies. Both empirical studies and conceptual or theoretical contributions were included, reflecting the contributors' combined 5–25 years of experience in national and international gender-focused and multi-gendered educational settings.

The selected studies are summarized in Table 1, which presents the study type, key contributions, checklist scores, and inclusion rationale. The literature synthesis is thematic and interpretive, aiming to identify patterns, gaps, and tensions across contexts rather than quantify studies or produce meta-analytic estimates. This approach enables a critical, practice-oriented examination of gender-inclusive pedagogical strategies and provides a foundation for actionable recommendations for educators, institutions, and policymakers.

Table 1. Summary of Selected Literature on Gender-Inclusive Pedagogical Practices in Computing Education

No	Author (s) & Year	Key Focus/Contribution	Checklist Scores	Inclusion Rationale
1	Choi (2014)	Compares gender pair combinations in pair programming; examines collaboration and performance outcomes	Relevance – 3 Rigor – 3 Applicability – 3	Demonstrates how structured pairing can reduce isolation, support peer learning, and enhance equitable participation in CS classrooms
2	Lee (2015)	Examines the effect of secondary-level CS education on STEM major selection in postsecondary institutions	Relevance – 3 Rigor – 2 Applicability – 3	Highlights how early CS learning environments influence female students' persistence in STEM; informs design of inclusive secondary CS curricula
3	Lubin (2016)	Provides frameworks for intentional ICT curriculum and pedagogy	Relevance – 3 Rigor – 2 Applicability – 3	Offers foundational principles for designing inclusive computing curricula and instructional practices
4	Spieler et al. (2018)	Analyzes female teenagers' coding performance; identifies pedagogical practices that reinforce gender equality	Relevance – 3 Rigor – 3 Applicability – 3	Provides evidence on classroom practices that support female learners; supports identity-affirming, engagement and inclusive strategies

continued on following page

Table 1. Continued

No	Author (s) & Year	Key Focus/Contribution	Checklist Scores	Inclusion Rationale
5	Arawjo and Mogos (2021)	Discusses community-oriented computing projects and intercultural perspectives	Relevance – 3 Rigor – 2 Applicability – 3	Provides guidance for embedding social relevance and real-world problem-solving in collaborative pedagogies
6	Kallia and Cutts (2021)	Examines inequalities in CS participation using a Bourdieusian lens; identifies structural and cultural barriers	Relevance – 3 Rigor – 3 Applicability – 3	Highlights the sociocultural dynamics influencing female learners' access and belonging in computing; informs identity-affirming curriculum design
7	Salguero et al. (2021)	Identifies sources of student struggle in early CS courses, highlighting barriers for female learners	Relevance – 3 Rigor – 3 Applicability – 3	Provides insights into structural and instructional factors that affect persistence and participation, informing support strategies
8	Davis et al. (2022)	Explores educators' needs for building inclusive classrooms; identifies strategies for policy and practice	Relevance – 3 Rigor – 3 Applicability – 3	Directly addresses inclusive classroom practices, teacher support, and policy implications; highly relevant for fostering belonging and engagement
9	Kovaleva et al. (2022c)	Explores gender balance strategies in intensive CS events; identifies inclusive practices for female participation	Relevance – 3 Rigor – 2 Applicability – 3	Highlights practical applications of collaborative pedagogies in short-term, high-intensity educational settings, supporting inclusion and peer support
10	Kovaleva et al. (2022a)	Analyzes pros and cons of gender-neutral hackathon design; addresses implementation challenges	Relevance – 3 Rigor – 2 Applicability – 3	Informs best practices for gender-balanced events, demonstrating the need to balance inclusivity with practical constraints
11	Kovaleva et al. (2022b)	Explores design of gender-neutral software engineering programs; identifies stereotypes and social pressures	Relevance – 3 Rigor – 2 Applicability – 3	Supports broader program-level design insights; highlights systemic approaches to making CS and engineering programs inclusive for all genders
12	Lagesen et al. (2021)	Discusses inclusion of women in ICT engineering; evaluates curriculum and program design lessons	Relevance – 3 Rigor – 2 Applicability – 3	Highlights the role of curriculum representation, diverse role models, and program structures in supporting female learners
13	Yates and Plagnol (2021)	Investigates female CS students' experiences in UK universities; focuses on classroom climate and curriculum impact	Relevance – 3 Rigor – 3 Applicability – 3	Provides qualitative insight into authentic student experiences, reinforcing the need for inclusive, socially relevant, and representative curriculum design

continued on following page

Table 1. Continued

No	Author (s) & Year	Key Focus/Contribution	Checklist Scores	Inclusion Rationale
14	Patel et al. (2023)	Examines implementation of inclusive software design practices in CS courses	Relevance – 3 Rigor – 3 Applicability – 3	Direct evidence on strategies to integrate gender-inclusive and socially relevant examples into computing curriculum
15	Garcia et al. (2024)	Presents the Matchmaker inclusive design curriculum to enable faculty to teach inclusive design across undergrad CS	Relevance – 3 Rigor – 3 Applicability – 3	Presents the Matchmaker inclusive design curriculum to enable faculty to teach inclusive design across undergrad CS
16	Kovaleva et al. (2024b)	Provides evidence-based strategies for female-inclusive CS program design	Relevance – 3 Rigor – 2 Applicability – 3	Summarizes actionable design practices for inclusive computing education, bridging curriculum, pedagogy, and institutional policies
17	Ko and Stephens-Martinez (2024)	Characterizes students' individual help-seeking approaches in computing education	Relevance – 3 Rigor – 3 Applicability – 3	Shows how collaborative structures like pair programming normalize help-seeking, reduce isolation, and improve retention for female learners
18	Kurti et al. (2024)	Investigates women's motivations for pursuing ICT higher education; examines barriers and enablers	Relevance – 3 Rigor – 2 Applicability – 3	Offers insights into female learners' pathways in higher education CS programs; informs identity-affirming strategies and institutional initiatives
19	Napier and Bourgeois (2024)	Evaluates a cohort-based community for Black women in computing	Relevance – 3 Rigor – 3 Applicability – 3	Highlights the value of learning communities and peer networks for fostering identity, belonging, and retention
20	O'Brien et al. (2025)	Assesses gender bias in software used for CS and software engineering education	Relevance – 3 Rigor – 3 Applicability – 3	Highlights how instructional tools themselves can embed bias; informs equitable software and assessment practices
21	Ackerman et al. (2025)	Explores an internship for teaching design research, emphasizing real-world engagement	Relevance – 3 Rigor – 3 Applicability – 3	Shows how experiential learning and industry-linked programs provide mentorship and role modeling to support female students' professional pathways
22	Garcia (2025a)	Uses self-coded digital portfolios as authentic assessment in web development courses	Relevance – 3 Rigor – 3 Applicability – 3	Shows alternative assessment methods that value diverse learning pathways and competencies beyond exams
23	Heath et al. (2025)	FLARE framework for code comprehension and formative assessment in block-based programming	Relevance – 3 Rigor – 3 Applicability – 3	Demonstrates structured formative assessment strategies that promote inclusive learning and iterative feedback

continued on following page

Table 1. Continued

No	Author (s) & Year	Key Focus/Contribution	Checklist Scores	Inclusion Rationale
24	McLaughlin et al. (2025)	Explores mentors' and mentees' experiences in K-12 CS classrooms	Relevance – 3 Rigor – 3 Applicability – 3	Demonstrates the impact of structured mentoring on confidence, belonging, and skill development for female students
25	Moura et al. (2025)	Explores cooperation and competition dynamics in computing education	Relevance – 3 Rigor – 3 Applicability – 3	Explores cooperation and competition dynamics in computing education
26	O'Leary et al. (2025)	Evaluates "Care Pathways," a culturally informed co-design program for Black American women	Relevance – 3 Rigor – 3 Applicability – 3	Illustrates community-engaged initiatives that reinforce mentorship, inclusion, and socially responsive computing education
27	Robinson (2025)	Investigates effects of mentoring programs for CS students with disabilities	Relevance – 3 Rigor – 3 Applicability – 3	Provides evidence of inclusive mentorship approaches that support underrepresented groups, including female learners with intersecting identities
28	Wali and Hooshangi (2025)	Examines barriers, success metrics, and research gaps for transfer students in CS	Relevance – 3 Rigor – 3 Applicability – 3	Emphasizes institutional factors and structural supports needed to promote equity and inclusion for female learners and nontraditional students
29	Yeom et al. (2025)	Examines gender disparities in collaborative learning; highlights effective group-based pedagogies	Relevance – 3 Rigor – 3 Applicability – 3	Emphasizes group and project-based approaches to enhance belonging, confidence, and participation of female learners
30	Palvia et al. (2026)	Explores global patterns of women leaving IT professions; analyzes curricular and cultural factors	Relevance – 3 Rigor – 2 Applicability – 3	Emphasizes the importance of sustained representation and curriculum strategies to retain women in computing fields

Notes. Checklist scores range from 1 to 3, with 1 = low, 2 = medium, and 3 = high, reflecting relevance, methodological rigor, and applicability. Abbreviations used: CS = Computer Science; ICT = Information and Communication Technology; IT = Information Technology; STEM = Science, Technology, Engineering, and Mathematics.

SYNTHESIS OF GENDER-INCLUSIVE PEDAGOGICAL PRACTICES

This section synthesizes findings from the reviewed literature to articulate key pedagogical practices that support gender inclusion in computer science education. Rather than treating inclusion as a single instructional strategy, the synthesis conceptualizes gender-inclusive pedagogy as a multilevel and interconnected set of practices that operate across classroom environments, instructional approaches, curriculum design, assessment, and institutional support structures. As illustrated in Figure 1, these practices collectively shape learners' experiences by addressing both the social and structural dimensions of participation in computing. The figure highlights five interrelated domains that emerged consistently across studies, underscoring that fostering gender inclusion requires coordinated efforts at multiple levels of the educational ecosystem. The subsections that follow elaborate on each domain, beginning with the creation of inclusive learning environments and a strong sense of belonging, which the literature identifies as a foundational condition for equitable participation in computer science.

Figure 1. Multilevel Gender-Inclusive Pedagogical Practices in Computer Science Education

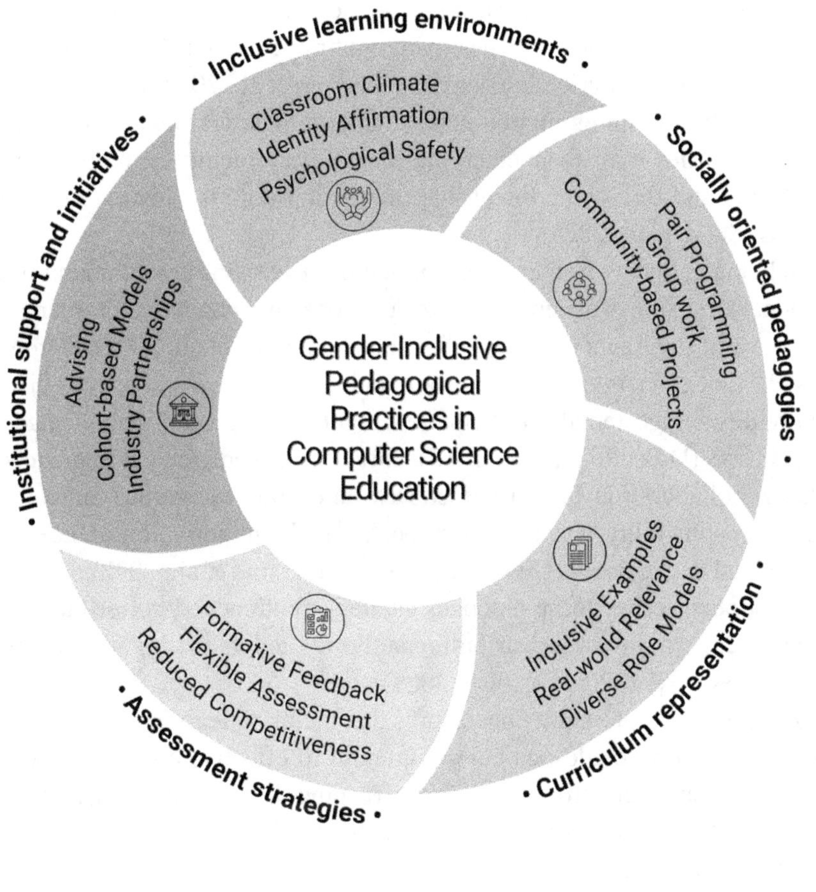

Creating Inclusive Learning Environments and Sense of Belonging

Creating inclusive learning environments is a foundational component of gender-inclusive pedagogies in computer science education, particularly in fostering a sense of belonging among female learners. Research consistently shows that classroom climate plays a critical role in shaping students' engagement, persistence, and identity development in computing fields (Cheryan et al., 2017; Davis et al., 2022; Kurti et al., 2024). When learning environments are perceived as welcoming, respectful, and inclusive, female students are more likely to participate actively, take intellectual risks, and envision themselves as legitimate members of the computing community (Spieler & Girvan, 2025).

A central dimension of inclusive classroom climate is identity affirmation, wherein students' gender identities, experiences, and perspectives are recognized and valued within the learning process. Studies indicate that pedagogical practices that normalize diversity (e.g., inclusive language use, diverse examples and case studies, and visible representation of women in computing) can counteract stereotypes that frame computing as a masculine domain (Cheryan et al., 2017; Fisher & Margolis, 2003). Identity-affirming environments enable female learners to reconcile their personal identities with their emerging disciplinary identities, reducing feelings of alienation and stereotype threat that often contribute to attrition in computing programs (Sulla et al., 2025).

Psychological safety further underpins inclusive learning environments by allowing students to express uncertainty, ask questions, and engage in problem-solving without fear of judgment or marginalization (Mangubat et al., 2025). Competitive, high-stakes, or error-intolerant classroom cultures have been shown to disproportionately discourage female participation, reinforcing perceptions of inadequacy and exclusion (Dost, 2024; Lee, 2015). In contrast, pedagogical approaches that emphasize collaboration, formative feedback, and iterative learning promote a shared sense of responsibility and mutual respect, which supports confidence-building and sustained engagement (Guo et al., 2025; Valderama et al., 2022). From a technofeminist perspective, these practices challenge entrenched power hierarchies in computing classrooms by redistributing authority and validating multiple ways of knowing (DeCook, 2020; Wajcman, 2009).

Collectively, the literature underscores that inclusive learning environments are not merely supportive add-ons but are integral to effective computing pedagogy. Cultivating positive classroom climates, affirming diverse identities, and fostering psychological safety can disrupt exclusionary norms and create conditions that enable female learners to thrive. Such environments form a critical foundation for subsequent pedagogical innovations aimed at promoting equity, persistence, and success in computer science education.

Collaborative and Socially Oriented Pedagogies

Collaborative and socially oriented pedagogies have been widely identified as effective strategies for promoting gender inclusion in computer science education. Traditional computing instruction often emphasizes individual performance, competition, and solitary problem-solving, practices that may inadvertently marginalize students who value relational and social learning contexts (Cheryan et al., 2017; Fisher & Margolis, 2003). In contrast, pedagogical approaches that foreground collaboration and shared knowledge construction align more closely with inclusive learning principles and have been shown to enhance engagement, confidence, and persistence among female learners.

Pair programming is one of the most extensively studied collaborative practices in computing education (Garcia, 2023a). Research suggests that structured pair programming, when intentionally implemented, supports equitable participation, reduces anxiety, and fosters peer support, particularly for students who may feel less confident in technical environments (Choi, 2014). Also, in the context of intensive educational events such as Code Camps and Hackathons, these practices provide opportunities to promote more gender-balanced participation, with peer support, structured pairing, and reduced "working alone" culture serving as key tools for success (Garcia, 2023b; Kovaleva et al., 2022c; Revano & Garcia, 2020). Female students often report that pair programming mitigates feelings of isolation and helps normalize help-seeking behaviors, contributing to stronger learning outcomes and increased retention in computing courses (Ko & Stephens-Martinez, 2024). However, studies also caution that without clear role rotation and instructor guidance, gendered power dynamics may persist within pairs, indicating yet again that proper implementations must consider both the advantages and limitations of running educational events, courses, and programs in gender-specific ways (Kovaleva et al., 2022a; Lubin, 2016).

Beyond dyadic collaboration, group work and peer learning create opportunities for dialogue, collective problem-solving, and distributed expertise. Social constructivist perspectives emphasize that learning is inherently social, shaped through interaction and shared meaning-making (Vygotsky, 1978). In computing classrooms, group-based activities enable female learners to engage in multiple roles, such as planning, debugging, and explaining (Yeom et al., 2025). When instructors explicitly value communication, reflection, and teamwork, these pedagogies challenge dominant norms that equate competence solely with speed or individual mastery. Community-based and project-oriented learning further extend collaborative pedagogies by situating computing within meaningful, real-world contexts. Projects that address social issues, local community needs, or interdisciplinary challenges have been shown to increase relevance and motivation among female students, who often express a desire to see the social impact of computing work (Arawjo & Mogos, 2021; Dost, 2024; Kurti et al., 2024). From a technofeminist perspective, such approaches disrupt the notion of computing as a purely technical endeavor, reframing it as a socially embedded practice shaped by values, ethics, and human needs (DeCook, 2020; Wajcman, 2004).

Collectively, collaborative and socially oriented pedagogies foster learning environments that value interdependence, dialogue, and shared agency (Sharma et al., 2021). When thoughtfully designed and supported, these approaches not only enhance learning outcomes but also contribute to a stronger sense of belonging and identity among female learners, reinforcing their sustained participation in computer science education. On a larger scope, what is needed are considerations, means, and methods combined into broader, gender-neutral program designs that make engineering and computing programs less stereotypical, more inclusive of all genders, and genuinely "designed for all," inspired and guided by inclusive principles (Kovaleva et al., 2022b, 2024b).

Curriculum Design and Representation

Curriculum design plays a critical role in shaping students' perceptions of who belongs in computer science and whose knowledge and experiences are valued. Research consistently demonstrates that curricula which rely on narrow, abstract, or gender-stereotypical examples can inadvertently reinforce the perception of computing as a masculine and socially detached field (Fisher & Margolis, 2003; Kallia & Cutts, 2021). In contrast, inclusive curriculum design foregrounds relevance, representation, and contextualized learning, creating opportunities for female learners to meaningfully connect with computing concepts and practices (Garcia et al., 2024; Patel et al., 2023).

One key dimension of inclusive curriculum design is the use of gender-inclusive and socially relevant examples. Studies indicate that when programming tasks and problem sets are situated in real-world contexts (e.g., health, education, sustainability, or community development), female students report higher levels of engagement and perceived value in computing courses (Mills et al., 2024; Peters et al., 2024). These contextualized examples challenge dominant narratives that frame computing as detached from social concerns. Instead, they position computing as a tool for addressing real societal challenges. Education can be connected across multiple domains at the same time (e.g., teaching both the technical aspects of computer science and physical fitness and exercise together; Garcia et al., 2023). From a technofeminist perspective, previously discussed curricular choices resist the notion of technological neutrality by explicitly acknowledging the social implications and ethical dimensions of computing (Wajcman, 2004).

Representation of diverse role models within the curriculum further contributes to gender-inclusive learning environments. Visibility of women and other underrepresented groups in computing (through case studies, biographies, guest speakers, or historical narratives) has been shown to positively influence students' sense of belonging and self-efficacy (Lagesen et al., 2021; Palvia et al., 2026). Exposure to diverse pathways and career trajectories helps disrupt stereotypes about who can succeed in computing, enabling female learners to envision themselves as legitimate contributors to the field. Importantly, research emphasizes that representation must be authentic and sustained, rather than tokenistic, to meaningfully impact student perceptions (Kurti et al., 2024; Yates & Plagnol, 2021).

Inclusive curriculum design also involves critically examining the hidden curriculum, which refers to the implicit values, assumptions, and norms embedded within course content and assessment practices. When curricula privilege speed, individualism, or competition as markers of competence, they may marginalize learners whose strengths lie in collaboration, reflection, or contextual problem-solving (Lunn et al., 2021). Revising curricular structures to value multiple forms of expertise and learning pathways can help counteract exclusionary norms and support more equitable participation.

Collectively, these findings underscore that curriculum design is not a neutral or purely technical endeavor but a powerful site for advancing gender equity in computer science education. Integrating inclusive examples, real-world relevance, and diverse representation allows educators to reshape curricular narratives in ways that affirm female learners' identities, broaden participation, and foster more inclusive computing cultures.

Instructional Practices and Assessment

Instructional practices and assessment strategies are central to shaping students' learning experiences and perceptions of competence in computer science education. Research suggests that traditional assessment models can disproportionately disadvantage female learners by amplifying anxiety, reinforcing stereotype threat, and privileging narrow demonstrations of technical ability (Garcia, 2025b; O'Brien et al., 2025; Spieler et al., 2018). Gender-inclusive pedagogies therefore emphasize instructional approaches that support growth, reflection, and equitable participation.

Formative feedback is a key instructional practice that contributes to inclusive learning environments. Frequent, low-stakes feedback allows students to identify misconceptions, build confidence, and view learning as an iterative process rather than a fixed measure of ability. In computing classrooms, formative feedback mechanisms (e.g., code reviews, reflective journals, and iterative project checkpoints) have been shown to reduce fear of failure and encourage persistence among female learners (Araujo et al., 2025; Garcia & Revano Jr, 2021; Heath et al., 2025; Jamal & Renzella, 2024). Such practices align with social constructivist perspectives by emphasizing learning as a process of continuous improvement supported through dialogue and interaction (Vygotsky, 1978).

Flexible assessment strategies further support gender-inclusive learning by accommodating diverse learning styles, prior experiences, and pathways to demonstrating competence. Alternatives to traditional timed examinations (e.g., portfolio-based assessments, collaborative projects, and applied problem-solving tasks) allow students to showcase both technical skills and higher-order competencies, including communication, collaboration, and ethical reasoning (Córdova-Esparza et al., 2024; Gamusa et al., 2025; Garcia, 2024, 2025a). These approaches challenge deficit-oriented views of ability and broaden the definition of success in computing education.

Reducing excessive competitiveness in instructional settings also plays a critical role in fostering inclusion. Competitive classroom cultures that emphasize speed, individual ranking, or "weed-out" mentalities have been linked to decreased belonging and increased attrition among women in computing programs (Wolz & Taylor, 2019). In contrast, instructional practices that prioritize mastery, cooperation, and shared achievement contribute to psychological safety and sustained engagement (El-Hamamsy et al., 2023; Moura et al., 2025). From a technofeminist perspective, such shifts in assessment and instruction disrupt entrenched power hierarchies by valuing relational, process-oriented, and context-sensitive forms of learning (DeCook, 2020; Wajcman, 2004).

Collectively, the literature highlights that inclusive instructional practices and assessment are not merely evaluative tools but pedagogical levers for advancing gender equity in computer science education. By emphasizing formative feedback, flexibility, and reduced competitiveness, educators can create learning environments that support diverse learners and promote more equitable outcomes.

Mentorship, Support Structures, and Institutional Initiatives

Beyond classroom-level pedagogy, institutional support structures play a critical role in sustaining female students' participation and success in computer science education. Mentorship, advising systems, and structured learning communities provide relational and structural support that complements inclusive instructional practices, addressing both academic and psychosocial dimensions of student experience (Al-Hunaiyyan et al., 2020; Herckis & Oden Choi, 2025). Research consistently shows that the presence of these supports significantly aids female learners in male-dominated computing environments, where isolation and limited access to informal networks can reduce persistence (Salguero et al., 2021).

Mentorship and academic advising have been identified as powerful mechanisms for fostering confidence, career clarity, and belonging among women in computing. Formal mentoring programs (whether peer-based, faculty-led, or industry-linked) offer guidance, role modeling, and affirmation that counteract stereotypes and self-doubt (Stoeger et al., 2013). Studies indicate that access to mentors who share similar identities or experiences can be especially impactful, as they provide visible pathways for success and normalize challenges encountered in computing education (McLaughlin et al., 2025; Robinson, 2025). From a technofeminist perspective, mentorship disrupts hierarchical and exclusionary knowledge structures by legitimizing experiential knowledge and relational forms of support (Wajcman, 2004).

Learning communities and cohort-based models further strengthen institutional efforts toward gender inclusion by creating sustained spaces for peer interaction and collective learning. Programs that intentionally group students across courses or provide dedicated spaces for collaboration have been shown to improve retention, academic performance, and social integration among underrepresented students in computing (Napier & Bourgeois, 2024; Wali & Hooshangi, 2025). These communities promote shared identity formation and reduce the competitive isolation often associated with traditional computing programs.

Institutional initiatives that extend beyond academia, particularly industry partnerships and experiential learning opportunities, also contribute to gender-inclusive pathways in computing. Internships, mentorships with industry professionals, and community-engaged projects expose female students to real-world applications of computing and diverse professional role models, reinforcing the relevance and social impact of their learning (Ackerman et al., 2025; O'Leary et al., 2025). Such initiatives help bridge the gap between education and employment while challenging narrow conceptions of who belongs in the computing workforce.

Collectively, mentorship, support structures, and institutional initiatives function as critical enablers of gender-inclusive computing education. When aligned with inclusive pedagogical practices, these structures contribute to more equitable learning ecosystems that support female learners' persistence, professional identity development, and long-term success in computer science fields.

DISCUSSION

Across the reviewed literature, several consistent patterns emerge regarding what supports female learners' participation and persistence in computer science education. Inclusive classroom climates, collaborative pedagogies, representative curricula, formative assessment practices, and robust mentoring structures repeatedly appear as central enablers of engagement and belonging (Garcia et al., 2024; Heath et al., 2025; McLaughlin et al., 2025; Spieler & Girvan, 2025; Yeom et al., 2025). These practices share a common orientation toward relational learning, contextual relevance, and psychological safety, suggesting that gender inclusion in computing is not driven by isolated interventions but by coherent pedagogical ecosystems. When teaching, assessment, and institutional support are aligned around equity-oriented values, female learners are more likely to develop sustained identification with computing disciplines.

Despite these consistencies, the literature also reveals persistent tensions and gaps in current pedagogical approaches. Many studies document the benefits of inclusive practices while noting uneven implementation, superficial adoption, or resistance within traditionally structured computing programs (Davis et al., 2022; Wolz & Taylor, 2019). For example, collaborative learning may be introduced without addressing underlying power dynamics, leading to gendered role segregation rather than equitable participation (Yeom et al., 2025). Similarly, curricular efforts to diversify examples or role models risk becoming tokenistic when not embedded within broader institutional commitments to inclusion (Garcia et al., 2024; Kurti et al., 2024). These tensions highlight a critical gap between pedagogical intent and pedagogical transformation, underscoring the need to interrogate not only what practices are adopted but how and why they are enacted.

Viewed collectively, gender-inclusive pedagogies fundamentally challenge dominant norms in computer science education, particularly those that privilege individualism, competition, speed, and technical purity as markers of competence (Kallia & Cutts, 2021; Ko & Stephens-Martinez, 2024). Such norms are often framed as value-neutral or meritocratic, yet the literature demonstrates that they disproportionately advantage learners who already align with masculine-coded expectations of computing identity (Lunn et al., 2021; Wolz & Taylor, 2019). Inclusive pedagogical approaches disrupt these assumptions by redefining competence to include collaboration, reflection, ethical awareness, and social impact (Garcia et al., 2024). In doing so, they invite a reimagining of computer science not merely as a technical discipline but as a socially embedded practice shaped by human values and power relations.

These findings strongly align with technofeminist theory, which argues that technologies—and by extension, technological education—are neither neutral nor inevitable but are produced within gendered social structures (DeCook, 2020; Wajcman, 2004). From a technofeminist perspective, inclusive pedagogies function as sites of resistance, making visible the gendered assumptions embedded in computing curricula, assessment regimes, and classroom cultures (Hulus, 2025). By foregrounding lived experience, relational learning, and critical engagement with technology, gender-inclusive pedagogies expose how educational practices can either reproduce or contest existing power hierarchies. Collectively, the literature suggests that advancing gender equity in computer science education requires more than increasing participation or access. It demands a critical reorientation of pedagogical values, one that questions long-standing disciplinary norms and embraces more inclusive, reflexive, and socially responsive forms of computing education. Such a shift has implications not only for who participates in computing but also for how the field itself evolves in response to increasingly diverse societal needs.

Drawing on the convergent patterns and tensions identified across the reviewed literature, the following guidelines are proposed to inform the design, enactment, and evaluation of gender-inclusive pedagogies in computer science education. These guidelines are not intended as a fixed checklist but as evidence-informed considerations that educators, curriculum designers, and institutions can adapt to their specific contexts.

1. **Cultivate inclusive classroom climates as a foundational pedagogical condition.** Instructors should prioritize psychological safety, respectful discourse, and identity-affirming practices from the outset of computing courses. Explicit norms that value questioning, collaboration, and diverse perspectives help counter exclusionary climates that disproportionately marginalize female learners.
2. **Align collaborative pedagogies with explicit equity goals.** Collaborative learning should be intentionally structured to address power dynamics within groups, including role assignment, accountability mechanisms, and reflective debriefing. Without such scaffolding, collaboration risks reproducing gendered participation patterns rather than disrupting them.
3. **Design curricula around relevance, representation, and social context.** Computing curricula should integrate socially meaningful problems, diverse role models, and interdisciplinary contexts that reflect the breadth of computing applications. Representation should be sustained and authentic, embedded across courses rather than confined to isolated examples or units.
4. **Adopt formative and flexible assessment practices that broaden definitions of competence.** Assessment strategies should emphasize learning as an iterative process through formative feedback, portfolios, project-based work, and reflective tasks. Reducing reliance on high-stakes, speed-oriented evaluations supports diverse demonstrations of competence and mitigates stereotype threat.
5. **Embed mentoring and support structures within institutional ecosystems.** Mentoring programs, learning communities, and cohort-based initiatives should be integrated into departmental and institutional structures rather than positioned as optional or peripheral supports. Access to mentors with shared or affirming identities can be particularly impactful for sustaining persistence and belonging.

6. **Interrogate hidden curricular and disciplinary norms.** Educators and institutions should critically examine implicit values embedded in computing education (e.g., individualism, competition, and notions of technical "purity") and consider how these norms shape participation and success. Making these assumptions visible is a necessary step toward pedagogical transformation.
7. **Approach gender inclusion as an ongoing, reflexive process rather than a one-time intervention.** The literature underscores that inclusive pedagogies require continuous reflection, evaluation, and adaptation. Institutions should support professional learning and reflective practice that enable educators to move beyond superficial adoption toward sustained cultural change.

Implications for Practice and Policy

The synthesis of the literature underscores that advancing gender equity in computer science education requires coordinated action across classroom practice, institutional leadership, and policy frameworks, in alignment with global commitments to sustainable development. For computer science educators and curriculum designers, the findings highlight the importance of embedding inclusive pedagogical principles (e.g., collaborative learning, identity-affirming curricula, formative assessment, and flexible learning pathways) into everyday teaching practices, directly supporting SDG 4 (Quality Education) by promoting equitable and inclusive learning opportunities. At the institutional level, leadership plays a critical role in sustaining these efforts through investments in faculty development, mentoring programs, and learning communities that foster inclusive teaching cultures and address structural barriers faced by female learners, thereby advancing SDG 5 (Gender Equality).

From a policy perspective, gender equity in computing education requires alignment between educational policy, workforce development strategies, and digital inclusion initiatives, ensuring that equity goals are reflected in curriculum standards, funding priorities, and accountability mechanisms that contribute to SDG 9 (Industry, Innovation, and Infrastructure). Collectively, these implications suggest that meaningful progress depends not only on pedagogical innovation but also on systemic commitment to rethinking how computing education is designed, supported, and governed to promote inclusive and sustainable technological futures.

Limitations of the Existing Literature

Despite the growing body of research on gender-inclusive pedagogies in computer science education, several notable limitations persist. Much of the literature is heavily Western-centric, with findings from North America and Europe dominating discourse, which limits the transferability of recommendations to diverse cultural, social, and institutional contexts. Additionally, intersectional perspectives remain underexplored, resulting in an incomplete understanding of the varied experiences and needs of female learners. Finally, a persistent gap exists between policy rhetoric and classroom practice, where institutional or governmental commitments to equity often fail to translate into meaningful pedagogical change, mentorship structures, or inclusive curricula at the course level. Collectively, these limitations highlight the need for research that is globally representative, intersectionally informed, and attentive to the translation of policy into actionable, context-sensitive strategies for equity in computing education.

Future Directions for Research and Innovation

Based on the synthesis and guidelines suggested, future research in gender-inclusive computer science education should prioritize qualitative and longitudinal studies that capture the nuanced experiences of female learners over time, moving beyond cross-sectional surveys to understand persistence, identity development, and the long-term impact of pedagogical interventions. There is a pressing need to incorporate intersectional perspectives and amplify voices from the Global South, where sociocultural, economic, and infrastructural factors shape unique barriers and opportunities for equity in computing. Co-designing curricula and learning environments with students themselves offers a promising avenue for creating responsive, contextually relevant pedagogies that reflect learners' needs and aspirations. Moreover, bridging education, industry, and policy through collaborative partnerships can ensure that equity-focused initiatives are reinforced across academic programs, workforce pipelines, and governmental frameworks, translating inclusive intentions into tangible outcomes. Collectively, these directions point toward a research agenda that is participatory, globally aware, and capable of informing systemic innovation in computing education.

CONCLUSION

This chapter underscores that advancing gender equity in computer science education demands sustained pedagogical, curricular, and institutional transformation that foregrounds inclusion, representation, and learner agency. Across the reviewed literature, consistent evidence highlights the importance of inclusive classroom climates, collaborative and socially oriented pedagogies, identity-affirming curricula, flexible and formative assessment practices, and robust mentorship and support structures in fostering female learners' engagement, persistence, and sense of belonging in computing education. Responding to the gaps identified at the outset of this chapter, this chapter (1) systematically identified and categorized gender-inclusive pedagogical strategies reported across empirical, theoretical, and policy-oriented literature; (2) examined how these strategies address sociocultural, instructional, and institutional barriers shaping female learners' experiences in computing education; and (3) synthesized cross-cutting patterns, tensions, and design principles that inform actionable guidance for educators, institutions, and policymakers.

At the same time, the review reveals persistent limitations in the field. Overreliance on Western contexts, limited intersectional analyses, and recurring gaps between policy intentions and classroom-level enactment continue to constrain progress toward equitable computing education. These shortcomings point to the need for more globally representative, context-sensitive, and participatory research designs that meaningfully engage learners and educators as co-constructors of inclusive practice. Importantly, the chapter situates gender equity within the broader context of the contemporary expansion of artificial intelligence (AI) across education and the computing workforce. As AI increasingly shapes learning environments, assessment practices, and professional pathways, its role in reproducing or mitigating gender bias must be critically examined. Ethical and effective integration of AI in education and subsequent work-life contexts requires heightened awareness of bias embedded in training data, algorithmic design, and large language models, alongside deliberate efforts to counteract these inequities through inclusive pedagogical and institutional strategies. Without such critical engagement, emerging technologies risk reinforcing the very disparities that gender-inclusive education seeks to address.

Collectively, the findings reaffirm that pedagogy functions as a central lever for change, but only when aligned with institutional commitment and policy coherence. Advancing gender equity in computer science education is not the result of isolated interventions but of systemic efforts that integrate teaching practices, curriculum design, assessment, mentorship, and governance. Fostering inclusive futures in computing therefore requires sustained, reflexive, and equity-driven approaches that ensure technology is both produced and shaped by a diverse and socially responsive community of learners.

REFERENCES

Ackerman, M. K., Armour, V., Najeeb, Z., & Mendoza, N. (2025). Experiential Learning Internship for Teaching Design Research. *Proceedings of the Extended Abstracts of the CHI Conference on Human Factors in Computing Systems*. https://doi.org/DOI: 10.1145/3706599.3707654

Adams, M., & Morgan, K. (2021). Relational Sensibilities and Women's Participation in Computer Science and Information Technology Degrees: A Cultural-Historical Approach. *Learning, Culture and Social Interaction*, *28*, 100464. DOI: 10.1016/j.lcsi.2020.100464

Al-Hunaiyyan, A. A., Bimba, A. T., & Alsharhan, S. (2020). A Cognitive Knowledge-based Model for an Academic Adaptive e-Advising System. *Interdisciplinary Journal of Information, Knowledge, and Management*, *15*, 247–263. DOI: 10.28945/4633

Araujo, L., Lopez-Ostenero, F., Plaza, L., & Martinez-Romo, J. (2025). Automated Formative Feedback for Algorithm and Data Structure Self-Assessment. *Electronics (Basel)*, *14*(5), 1034. DOI: 10.3390/electronics14051034

Arawjo, I., & Mogos, A. (2021). Intercultural Computing Education: Toward Justice Across Difference. *ACM Transactions on Computing Education*, *21*(4), 1–33. DOI: 10.1145/3458037

Ashlock, J. M., & Tufekci, Z. (2024). Gender Differences in Computing Interest: The Role of Social Constructs in Early Paths. *Computer Science Education*, •••, 1–33. DOI: 10.1080/08993408.2024.2433354

Cheryan, S., Ziegler, S. A., Montoya, A. K., & Jiang, L. (2017). Why Are Some STEM Fields More Gender Balanced Than Others? *Psychological Bulletin*, *143*(1), 1–35. DOI: 10.1037/bul0000052 PMID: 27732018

Choi, K. S. (2014). A Comparative Analysis of Different Gender Pair Combinations in Pair Programming. *Behaviour & Information Technology*, *34*(8), 825–837. DOI: 10.1080/0144929x.2014.937460

Córdova-Esparza, D.-M., Romero-González, J.-A., Córdova-Esparza, K.-E., Terven, J., & López-Martínez, R.-E. (2024). Active Learning Strategies in Computer Science Education: A Systematic Review. *Multimodal Technologies and Interaction*, *8*(6), 50. DOI: 10.3390/mti8060050

Davis, K., Twarek, B., Becton-Consuegra, D., & Koshy, S. (2022). The Needs of K-12 Computer Science Educators towards Building an Inclusive Classroom. *Proceedings of the 53rd ACM Technical Symposium on Computer Science Education* V. 2. https://doi.org/DOI: 10.1145/3478432.3499229

DeCook, J. R. (2020). A [White] Cyborg's Manifesto: The overwhelmingly Western ideology driving technofeminist theory. *Media, Culture &amp. Society*, *43*(6), 1158–1167. DOI: 10.1177/0163443720957891

Dost, G. (2024). Students' Perspectives on the 'STEM Belonging' Concept at A-Level, Undergraduate, and Postgraduate Levels: An Examination of Gender and Ethnicity in Student Descriptions. *International Journal of STEM Education*, *11*(1), 1–33. DOI: 10.1186/s40594-024-00472-9

El-Hamamsy, L., Bruno, B., Audrin, C., Chevalier, M., Avry, S., Zufferey, J. D., & Mondada, F. (2023). How Are Primary School Computer Science Curricular Reforms Contributing to Equity? Impact on Student Learning, Perception of the Discipline, and Gender Gaps. *International Journal of STEM Education*, *10*(1), 1–43. DOI: 10.1186/s40594-023-00438-3

European Institute for Gender Equality. (2024). *Gender Equality Index 2024 – Sustaining Momentum on a Fragile Path*. Publications Office of the European Union., DOI: 10.2839/9523460

Eurostat. (2023). *Men Represented 84% of People Employed with an ICT Education*. https://ec.europa.eu/eurostat/web/products-eurostat-news/w/ddn-20231016-1

Eurostat. (2024). *Women Make Up 52% of Science & Technology Employment*. https://ec.europa.eu/eurostat/web/products-eurostat-news/w/ddn-20240613-2

Fietta, V., Navarin, N., Monaro, M., & Gaggi, O. (2023). Women and Gender Disparities in Computer Science: A Case Study at the University of Padua. *Proceedings of the 2023 ACM Conference on Information Technology for Social Good*. https://doi.org/DOI: 10.1145/3582515.3609521

Fisher, A., & Margolis, J. (2003). Unlocking the Clubhouse: Women in Computing. *ACM SIGCSE Bulletin*, *35*(1). Advance online publication. DOI: 10.1145/792548.611896

Forbes. (2024). *Women in Tech Stats: How the Industry Can Provide Equal Opportunities*. https://www.forbes.com/sites/cherylrobinson/2024/06/18/women-in-tech-stats-how-the-industry-can-provide-equal-opportunities/

Galpaya, H., & Zainudeen, A. (2022). Gender and Digital Access Gaps and Barriers in Asia: But What About After Access? *LIRNEasia*. http://hdl.handle.net/10625/61914

Gamusa, E. V., Sim, M. J. C., Medina, J. B., Acut, D. P., Garcia, M. B., & Lahby, M. (2025). From Chalkboards to Chatbots: The Role of Generative AI in Philippine Teacher Education Assessment. In *Innovative Educational Assessment with Generative AI: Opportunities, Challenges, and Practical Case Studies* (Vol. 70, pp. 245-274). Springer Nature. https://doi.org/DOI: 10.1007/978-3-032-05306-0_12

Garcia, M. B. (2023a). Facilitating Group Learning Using an Apprenticeship Model: Which Master is More Effective in Programming Instruction? *Journal of Educational Computing Research*, *61*(6), 1207–1231. DOI: 10.1177/07356331231170382

Garcia, M. B. (2023b). Fostering an Innovation Culture in the Education Sector: A Scoping Review and Bibliometric Analysis of Hackathon Research. *Innovative Higher Education*, *48*(4), 739–762. DOI: 10.1007/s10755-023-09651-y PMID: 37361114

Garcia, M. B. (2024). Profiling the Skill Mastery of Introductory Programming Students: A Cognitive Diagnostic Modeling Approach. *Education and Information Technologies*, *30*(5), 6455–6481. DOI: 10.1007/s10639-024-13039-6

Garcia, M. B. (2025a). Self-Coded Digital Portfolios as an Authentic Project-Based Learning Assessment in Computing Education: Evidence from a Web Design and Development Course. *Education Sciences*, *15*(9), 1150. DOI: 10.3390/educsci15091150

Garcia, M. B. (2025b). Teaching and Learning Computer Programming Using ChatGPT: A Rapid Review of Literature Amid the Rise of Generative AI Technologies. *Education and Information Technologies*, *30*, 16721–16745. DOI: 10.1007/s10639-025-13452-5

Garcia, M. B., & Revano, T. F., Jr. (2021). Assessing the Role of Python Programming Gamified Course on Students' Knowledge, Skills Performance, Attitude, and Self-Efficacy. *2021 IEEE 13th International Conference on Humanoid, Nanotechnology, Information Technology, Communication and Control, Environment and Management (HNICEM)*. https://doi.org/DOI: 10.1109/HNICEM54116.2021.9731935

Garcia, M. B., Yousef, A. M. F., Pereira de Almeida, R. P., Arif, Y. M., Happonen, A., & Barber, W. (2023). Teaching Physical Fitness and Exercise Using Computer-Assisted Instruction: A School-Based Public Health Intervention. In Garcia, M. B., Lopez Cabrera, M. V., & de Almeida, R. P. P. (Eds.), *Handbook of Research on Instructional Technologies in Health Education and Allied Disciplines* (pp. 177–195). IGI Global Scientific Publishing., DOI: 10.4018/978-1-6684-7164-7.ch008

Garcia, R., Morreale, P., Verdi, G., Garcia, H., Noa, G. J., Madsen, S. P., & Burnett, M. (2024). The Matchmaker Inclusive Design Curriculum: A Faculty-Enabling Curriculum to Teach Inclusive Design Throughout Undergraduate CS. *Proceedings of the CHI Conference on Human Factors in Computing Systems*. https://doi.org/DOI: 10.1145/3613904.3642475

Guo, C., Wu, W., Hu, T., & Gao, T. (2025). Unequal Access, Equal Outcomes? Gender Differences in the Relationship Between University-Led STEM Program Factors and Undergraduates' Career Commitment in STEM. *International Journal of STEM Education*, *12*(1), 1–21. DOI: 10.1186/s40594-025-00569-9

Heath, J., Whyte, R., & Sentance, S. (2025). FLARE: A Framework Supporting Code Comprehension and Formative Assessment in Block-Based Programming Education. *Proceedings of the 9th Conference on Computing Education Practice*. https://doi.org/DOI: 10.1145/3702212.3702219

Herckis, L., & Oden Choi, J. (2025). Portable Pedagogy: Teaching Computer Science Across Institutions. *Proceedings of the 56th ACM Technical Symposium on Computer Science Education* V. 2. https://doi.org/DOI: 10.1145/3641555.3705229

Hulus, A. (2025). Execute_reboot(): Defining MetaTech feminism as a unified framework for FemTech approaches. *Sustainable Futures : An Applied Journal of Technology, Environment and Society*, *10*, 101172. DOI: 10.1016/j.sftr.2025.101172

Jamal, R., & Renzella, J. (2024). Enhancing Formative Feedback at Scale with the Intelligent Feedback Assistant. *Proceedings of the 55th ACM Technical Symposium on Computer Science Education* V. 2. https://doi.org/DOI: 10.1145/3626253.3635482

Kallia, M., & Cutts, Q. (2021). Re-Examining Inequalities in Computer Science Participation from a Bourdieusian Sociological Perspective. *Proceedings of the 17th ACM Conference on International Computing Education Research*. https://doi.org/DOI: 10.1145/3446871.3469763

Ko, S.-H., & Stephens-Martinez, K. (2024). The Trees in the Forest: Characterizing Computing Students' Individual Help-Seeking Approaches. *Proceedings of the 2024 ACM Conference on International Computing Education Research* - Volume 1. https://doi.org/DOI: 10.1145/3632620.3671099

Kovaleva, Y., Happonen, A., Garcia, M. B., & Kasurinen, J. (2024a). Female-Inclusive Practices for Software Engineering and Computer Science Higher Education: A Literature Review. *Proceedings of the Annual Doctoral Symposium of Computer Science 2024*. https://ceur-ws.org/Vol-3776/paper08.pdf

Kovaleva, Y., Happonen, A., & Hasheela-Mufeti, V. (2022a). Pros and Cons of Running Educational Hackathons in a Gender-Neutral Fashion. *Proceedings of the Third Workshop on Gender Equality, Diversity, and Inclusion in Software Engineering.* https://doi.org/DOI: 10.1145/3524501.3527603

Kovaleva, Y., Happonen, A., & Kindsiko, E. (2022b). Designing Gender-Neutral Software Engineering Program. Stereotypes, Social Pressure, and Current Attitudes Based on Recent Studies. *Proceedings of the Third Workshop on Gender Equality, Diversity, and Inclusion in Software Engineering.* https://doi.org/DOI: 10.1145/3524501.3527600

Kovaleva, Y., Happonen, A., & Kindsiko, E. (2024b). *Literature-Based Practices for Designing Female-Inclusive Software Engineering and Computer Science Programs.* Intelligent Sustainable Systems., DOI: 10.1007/978-981-99-8111-3_23

Kovaleva, Y., Happonen, A., & Mbogho, A. (2022c). Towards Gender Balance in Modern Hackathons: Literature-Based Approaches for Female Inclusiveness. *Proceedings of the Third Workshop on Gender Equality, Diversity, and Inclusion in Software Engineering.* https://doi.org/DOI: 10.1145/3524501.3527594

Kovaleva, Y., Hyrynsalmi, S., Saltan, A., Happonen, A., & Kasurinen, J. (2023). Becoming an Entrepreneur: A Study of Factors with Women from the Tech Sector. *Information and Software Technology, 155*, 107110. DOI: 10.1016/j.infsof.2022.107110

Kovaleva, Y., Kasurinen, J., Kindsiko, E., & Happonen, A. (2024c). State-of-the-Art Review on Current Approaches to Female Inclusiveness in Software Engineering and Computer Science in Higher Education. *IEEE Access : Practical Innovations, Open Solutions, 12*, 1360–1373. DOI: 10.1109/ACCESS.2023.3346767

Kurti, E., Ferati, M., & Kalonaityte, V. (2024). Closing the Gender Gap in ICT Higher Education: Exploring Women's Motivations in Pursuing ICT Education. *Frontiers in Education, 9*, 1–13. DOI: 10.3389/feduc.2024.1352029

Lagesen, V. A., Pettersen, I., & Berg, L. (2021). Inclusion of Women to ICT Engineering – Lessons Learned. *European Journal of Engineering Education, 47*(3), 467–482. DOI: 10.1080/03043797.2021.1983774

Lee, A. (2015). Determining the Effects of Computer Science Education at the Secondary Level on STEM Major Choices in Postsecondary Institutions in the United States. *Computers & Education, 88*, 241–255. DOI: 10.1016/j.compedu.2015.04.019

Lopes, A. G. (2022). Women in Computing: Attitudes and Experiences. *International Journal of Technology and Human Interaction, 18*, 1–11. DOI: 10.4018/IJTHI.302663

Lubin, I. A. (2016). *Intentional ICT: Curriculum, Education and Development.* UNESCO International Bureau of Education. https://unesdoc.unesco.org/ark:/48223/pf0000244081

Lunn, S., Ross, M., Hazari, Z., Weiss, M. A., Georgiopoulos, M., & Christensen, K. (2021). How Do Educational Experiences Predict Computing Identity? *ACM Transactions on Computing Education, 22*(2), 1–28. DOI: 10.1145/3470653

Mangubat, R., Calasang, V., Espina, R. C., Capuyan, D. L., Gamusa, E. V., Pernaa, J., & Garcia, M. B. (2025). Understanding the Role of Technological Self-Efficacy in Fostering Creative Problem-Solving and Curiosity in Teacher Education: A Structural Equation Modeling Approach. *Journal of Technology and Science Education, 15*(2), 456–478. DOI: 10.3926/jotse.3233

McLaughlin, G., Ahmadi, S., Novak, E., & Borgerding, L. (2025). Mentoring in K-12 Computer Science Classrooms: Exploring Mentors' and Mentees' Experiences. *ACM Transactions on Computing Education, 26*(1), 1–20. DOI: 10.1145/3772073

Mills, K. A., Cope, J., Scholes, L., & Rowe, L. (2024). Coding and Computational Thinking Across the Curriculum: A Review of Educational Outcomes. *Review of Educational Research, 95*(3), 581–618. DOI: 10.3102/00346543241241327

Moura, W., Delbem, E., França, J., & Dias, A. (2025). Exploring Cooperation and Competition in Computer Science Education: An Investigation Based on Game Theory. *Proceedings of the 17th International Conference on Computer Supported Education.* https://doi.org/DOI: 10.5220/0013216700003932

Napier, N. P., & Bourgeois, A. G. (2024). RISE in Computing Scholars: A Cohort-Based Community for Black Women. *Proceedings of the 2024 on RESPECT Annual Conference.* https://doi.org/DOI: 10.1145/3653666.3656100

O'Brien, L., Kanij, T., & Grundy, J. (2025). Assessing Gender Bias in the Software Used in Computer Science and Software Engineering Education. *Journal of Systems and Software, 219*, 112225. DOI: 10.1016/j.jss.2024.112225

O'Leary, T. K., Batti, V., Dhindsa, S., Krishnan, V. H., Wilcox, L., Woods-Giscombe, C. L., . . . McCall, T. (2025). "It was Empowering": Care Pathways a Novel Culturally Informed Inspiration Card Game for Community-Engaged Co-Design with Black American Women and Clinicians. *Proceedings of the Extended Abstracts of the CHI Conference on Human Factors in Computing Systems.* https://doi.org/DOI: 10.1145/3706599.3720056

Page, M. J., McKenzie, J. E., Bossuyt, P. M., Boutron, I., Hoffmann, T. C., Mulrow, C. D., & Moher, D. (2021). The PRISMA 2020 Statement: An Updated Guideline for Reporting Systematic Reviews. *BMJ (Clinical Research Ed.)*. Advance online publication. DOI: 10.1136/bmj.n71 PMID: 33782057

Palvia, P., Cooper, V., & Kakhki, M. D. (2026). The Flight of Women from the Information Technology Profession: Nuances and Global Perspectives. *Information &amp. Management*, *63*(3), 104299. DOI: 10.1016/j.im.2025.104299

Patel, P., Chu, J., Kumar, Y., Kwak, D., Morreale, P., Garcia, R., & Burnett, M. (2023). Implementing Inclusive Software Design in the CS Curriculum. *Proceedings of the 54th ACM Technical Symposium on Computer Science Education*. https://doi.org/DOI: 10.1145/3545947.3573254

Perez-Felkner, L., Erichsen, K., Li, Y., Chen, J., Hu, S., Ramirez Surmeier, L., & Shore, C. (2024). Computing Education Interventions to Increase Gender Equity from 2000 to 2020: A Systematic Literature Review. *Review of Educational Research*, *95*(3), 536–580. DOI: 10.3102/00346543241241536

Peters, A.-K., Capilla, R., Coroamă, V. C., Heldal, R., Lago, P., Leifler, O., & Venters, C. C. (2024). Sustainability in Computing Education: A Systematic Literature Review. *ACM Transactions on Computing Education*, *24*(1), 1–53. DOI: 10.1145/3639060

Revano, T. F., & Garcia, M. B. (2020). Manufacturing Design Thinkers in Higher Education Institutions: The Use of Design Thinking Curriculum in the Education Landscape. *2020 IEEE 12th International Conference on Humanoid, Nanotechnology, Information Technology, Communication and Control, Environment and Management (HNICEM)*. https://doi.org/DOI: 10.1109/HNICEM51456.2020.9400034

Robinson, R. (2025). Investigating the Impact of a Mentoring Program for Computer Science Students with Disabilities. *Proceedings of the 30th ACM Conference on Innovation and Technology in Computer Science Education* V. 2. https://doi.org/DOI: 10.1145/3724389.3730808

Salguero, A., Griswold, W. G., Alvarado, C., & Porter, L. (2021). Understanding Sources of Student Struggle in Early Computer Science Courses. *Proceedings of the 17th ACM Conference on International Computing Education Research*. https://doi.org/DOI: 10.1145/3446871.3469755

Sharma, K., Torrado, J. C., Gómez, J., & Jaccheri, L. (2021). Improving Girls' Perception of Computer Science as a Viable Career Option Through Game Playing and Design: Lessons from a Systematic Literature Review. *Entertainment Computing*, *36*, 100387. DOI: 10.1016/j.entcom.2020.100387

Spieler, B., & Girvan, C. (2025). The PECC Framework: Promoting Gender Sensitivity and Gender Equality in Computer Science Education. *Computers*, *14*(7), 249. DOI: 10.3390/computers14070249

Spieler, B., Hummel, D., Herbertz, S., & Mädche, A. (2018). Reinforcing Gender Equality by Analysing Female Teenagers' Performances in Coding Activities. *Proceedings of the 4th Conference on Gender & IT - GenderIT '18*. https://doi.org/ DOI: 10.1145/3196839.3196871

Stoeger, H., Duan, X., Schirner, S., Greindl, T., & Ziegler, A. (2013). The Effectiveness of a One-Year Online Mentoring Program for Girls in STEM. *Computers & Education*, *69*, 408–418. DOI: 10.1016/j.compedu.2013.07.032

Sulla, F., Agueli, B., Lavanga, A., Logrieco, M. G. M., Fantinelli, S., & Esposito, C. (2025). Analysis of the Development of Gender Stereotypes and Sexist Attitudes Within a Group of Italian High School Students and Teachers: A Grounded Theory Investigation. *Behavioral Sciences (Basel, Switzerland)*, *15*(2), 230. DOI: 10.3390/bs15020230 PMID: 40001861

UNESCO. (2017). *Cracking the Code: Girls' and Women's Education in Science, Technology, Engineering and Mathematics*. STEM., DOI: 10.54675/QYHK2407

United Nations Children's Fund. (2023). *Bridging the Gender Digital Divide: Challenges and an Urgent Call for Action for Equitable Digital Skills Development*. UNICEF. https://data.unicef.org/wp-content/uploads/2023/05/Bridging-the-Gender-Digital-Divide-1.pdf

United Nations Economic and Social Commission for Asia and the Pacific. (2023). *Bridging the Digital Gender Divide: How Girls and Women Can Lead the Way*. UNESCAP. https://www.unescap.org/story/bridging-digital-gender-divide-how-girls-and-women-can-lead-way

United Nations Economic Commission for Europe. (2025). *Moving Forward in Gender Statistics in the EU*. UNECE. https://unece.org/sites/default/files/2025-03/WP3%20Eur%20GenderstatsEU.pdf

Valderama, A. M. C., Tuazon, J. B. D., & Garcia, M. B. (2022). Promoting Student Thinking and Engagement Through Question-Based and Gamified Learning. *2022 IEEE 14th International Conference on Humanoid, Nanotechnology, Information Technology, Communication and Control, Environment and Management (HNICEM)*. https://doi.org/DOI: 10.1109/HNICEM57413.2022.10109470

Vitores, A., & Gil-Juárez, A. (2016). The Trouble with 'Women in Computing': A Critical Examination of the Deployment of Research on the Gender Gap in Computer Science. *Journal of Gender Studies, 25*(6), 666–680. DOI: 10.1080/09589236.2015.1087309

Vygotsky, L. S. (1978). *Mind in Society: Development of Higher Psychological Processes.* Harvard University Press., DOI: 10.2307/j.ctvjf9vz4

Wajcman, J. (2004). *TechnoFeminism.* Polity. https://www.wiley.com/en-sg/TechnoFeminism-p-9780745630434

Wajcman, J. (2009). Feminist Theories of Technology. *Cambridge Journal of Economics, 34*(1), 143–152. DOI: 10.1093/cje/ben057

Wali, N., & Hooshangi, S. (2025). Transfer Students in Computer Science: Examining Barriers, Success Metrics, and Research Gaps. *Proceedings of the 30th ACM Conference on Innovation and Technology in Computer Science Education* V. 1. https://doi.org/DOI: 10.1145/3724363.3729118

Wolz, U., & Taylor, S. R. (2019). Towards a More Inclusive Tech Culture. *Proceedings of the 50th ACM Technical Symposium on Computer Science Education.* https://doi.org/DOI: 10.1145/3287324.3293742

World Economic Forum. (2023). *Global Gender Gap Report 2023.* WEF. https://www3.weforum.org/docs/WEF_GGGR_2023.pdf

Wu, J., & Uttal, D. H. (2024). Diversifying Computer Science: An Examination of the Potential Influences of Women-in-Computing Groups. *Science Education, 108*(3), 957–980. DOI: 10.1002/sce.21861

Yates, J., & Plagnol, A. C. (2021). Female Computer Science Students: A Qualitative Exploration of Women's Experiences Studying Computer Science at University in the UK. *Education and Information Technologies, 27*(3), 3079–3105. DOI: 10.1007/s10639-021-10743-5

Yeom, S., Herbert, N., & Ryu, R. (2025). Exploring Gender Disparities and Collaborative Learning in IT Education. *Proceedings of the 27th Australasian Computing Education Conference.* https://doi.org/DOI: 10.1145/3716640.3716645

KEY TERMS AND DEFINITIONS

Gender-Inclusive Pedagogy.: Teaching approaches, curriculum designs, and learning environments intentionally structured to promote equitable participation, representation, and success of learners across all genders, particularly addressing barriers faced by women in computing education.

Inclusive Curriculum Design.: The intentional integration of diverse perspectives, real-world relevance, and representative role models into course content and learning activities to support equitable participation and identity affirmation.

Mentorship and Support Structures.: Formal or informal relationships, learning communities, and institutional initiatives that provide guidance, role modeling, and relational support to enhance learners' academic, professional, and psychosocial outcomes.

Sense of Belonging.: The psychological experience of acceptance, inclusion, and recognition within a learning environment, which positively influences motivation, engagement, and persistence in computing programs.

Technofeminism.: A theoretical perspective that examines how technology and technological practices are socially constructed, gendered, and influenced by power dynamics, emphasizing the role of pedagogy and institutional practices in either reproducing or challenging gender inequities in technology fields.

Chapter 7
Inclusive Pedagogy in Computer Science Education:
A Critical Pedagogical Framework for Computational Access

Akshara Singh
https://orcid.org/0009-0002-4363-927X
Christ University, India

Lawrence Kujur
https://orcid.org/0000-0002-2704-0825
Christ University, India

ABSTRACT

Computer science (CS) inclusive teaching provides an opportunity for everyone to learn in a way that is fair and accessible. Through the traditional approaches, neurodiverse and disadvantaged learners are often cut off due to the strictness of the instruction and the surrounding limitations on support. UDL (Universal Design for Learning) and CRP (Culturally Responsive Pedagogy) are the two major strategies for inclusive teaching that facilitate flexible, engaging, and relevant learning. UDL allows you to choose different ways to learn and to express your understanding, and CRP connects the content with the students' cultural backgrounds. Gallaudet University and AccessCSforAll are some of the initiatives that have been proving that learners are more engaged when using assistive tools and through the application of adaptive methods. Supported by educating CS for all, U.N. SDG 4, inclusivity in computer sciences education not only narrows the digital gap but also opens up the door for every student to thrive in a diverse and tech-savvy world.

DOI: 10.4018/979-8-3373-6546-6.ch007

INTRODUCTION

The global industry's digitization has made computer science (CS) an essential literacy (Ryoo, 2019). On the other hand, the traditional teaching methods—stiffly structured lectures and standardized tests—gradually push out the learners with different cognitive styles or cultural backgrounds than the "norm" (Pournaghshband & Medel, 2020). Those students who belong to the neurodivergent category (e.g., with ASD, ADHD, or dyslexia) usually find it hard to learn in a still-and-unyielding classroom setting that does not use and thus oppresses their innate cognitive strengths (Bonnette et al., 2022). Marginalized populations suffer more from the inequities caused by the institutional inertia and structural barriers (Israel et al., 2022).

The Inclusive pedagogy, which is the merging of Universal Design for Learning (UDL) and Culturally Responsive Pedagogy (CRP), is the one that can break down the walls of systemic inequities (Madkins et al., 2020, Kooli & Chakraoui, 2025) Although UDL helps in the creation of a communication environment that meets the needs of all learners with the help of a range of media, CRP in its turn fosters through recognition and trust the learner's culture the identity and the motivation necessary for the learner to stay on (Goode et al., 2020). Even though there are global laws like UNESCO's Sustainable Development Goal 4 (SDG 4) which promote inclusion in education, the goal of equal opportunities in CS teaching is still often blocked by a big "Policy-Practice Gap," which is characterized by the discrepancy between the lack of institutional support and resources and the theoretical aspirations (Ferguson & Roofe, 2020)

MAIN FOCUS OF THE CHAPTER

This chapter contributes to the field by introducing the Critical Pedagogy of Computational Access (CPCA)—a conceptual framework that does not stop at the analysis of "access" but rather probes the power relations and the reasons for the failures of an inclusive CS implementation. The CPCA framework does not only map out a set of the best practices but also interprets how models such as UDL can turn into "compliance checklists" without any structural changes. The main goals of the framework are to: (a) critical analysis of CS access and retention placing emphasis on systemic and structural barriers; (b) failure of implementation and unintentional consequences of applying foundational theories in resource-poor or culturally diverse contexts being the target of scrutiny; and (c) development of an analytically grounded roadmap for stakeholders to convert inclusive policy into practicable steps (Israel et al., 2022, Bonnette et al., 2022)

The chapter, via this critical analysis, points out inclusive pedagogy as a tactical and ethical requirement that facilitates learning in terms of better cognitive processing, social-emotional development, and self-efficacy (Kooli & Chakraoui, 2025). Inclusive CS education that focuses on neurodiverse and minority students merges equity with quality thus, by making students ready for the coming technological and societal changes, it serves the future better (Afzal et al., 2023). To move from theoretical necessity to practical application, the following section outlines the qualitative framework synthesis used to build the CPCA model.

METHODOLOGY

The CPCA framework came out of a Qualitative Framework Synthesis that combined three pillars to connect the gap between policy and practice:

1. **Theoretical Synthesis:** Combining UDL, CRP, and Constructivism.
2. **Empirical Analysis:** Drawing on international program data and UNESCO SDG 4 reports.
3. **Comparative Case Analysis:** Uncovering systemic tensions in Gallaudet University (specialized/high-resource), *AccessCSforAll* (scalable/policy-driven), and I-STEM India (resource-light).

This method takes us from just describing the situation to an analytically grounded framework for inclusive CS education globally.

UNDERSTANDING INCLUSIVE PEDAGOGY

Inclusive pedagogy in CS is student-centered so it values and caters to the varying learning needs of each student (Mullens & Hoffman, 2023). In contrast to the one-size-fits-all principle commonly adopted by traditional methods, inclusive teaching offers equitable experiences by recognizing the differences in learning styles, cultural backgrounds, and social-economic factors (Lopez-Fernandez et al., 2021, Vrieler & Salminen-Karlsson, 2022)

Theoretical Frameworks

Universal Design for Learning

A flexible approach that guarantees through various ways of representation, expression, and engagement that all learners with different needs have equal opportunities (Bhattacharya et al., 2022). In CS, it makes possible for neurodiverse students to learn complicated computational concepts using visual programming tools, adaptive interfaces, and multimodal instructions (Smith & McGill, 2025)

Culturally Responsive Pedagogy

Recognizes the impact of students' cultural, linguistic, and socio-economic backgrounds on learning (Salgarayeva & Makhanova, 2024). By utilizing familiar examples, collaborative problem-solving, and localized content, CRP fosters motivation and comprehension in CS learners, ensuring academic and social relevance globally (Vrieler & Salminen-Karlsson, 2022)

Critical Pedagogy

It allows learners to examine social injustices in parallel with computational problem-solving, which is rooted in Freirean values. It nurtures a digital literacy that is critically aware, thereby helping learners to realize the ethical and cultural barriers that hinder the development of technology. UDL, CRP, and critical pedagogy unite to provide the theoretical foundation for inclusive CS education (Bhattacharya et al., 2022)

The Inclusive CS Education Matrix

Instead of discussing separately the individual frameworks, the Inclusive CS Education Matrix is the key idea behind the CPCA. The matrix shows that inclusive CS education that takes into account the diverse aspects of society and culture, has to apply at the same time, the corresponding pedagogical and equity approaches along the two basic axes of diversity: Cognitive Diversity and Cultural Diversity. The model illustrates that frameworks like UDL and CRP are inadequate if considered alone; rather, their convergence is where real equity is reached. It is to be considered how policies, curricula, and tools perform across all four resulting quadrants in the evaluation of their application. (Leonard & Sentance, 2021)

Comparison with Traditional Pedagogy in CS Education

Traditional CS pedagogy is based on the assumptions of the same level of knowledge and the same way of thinking among students (Salgarayeva & Makhanova, 2024). This can be very taxing for neurodiverse and students from less privileged families (Tshukudu et al., 2022). The combination of fixed pacing and high-stakes assessments can lead to even bigger disparities in learning (Lopez-Fernandez et al., 2021, Martin et al., 2020). On the other hand, inclusive pedagogy gives priority to the instructor's differentiated instruction, group learning, and continuous assessment (Warner et al., 2021). Use of the strategies like project-based learning, gamified instruction, and peer mentorship not only attract diverse students but also keep them in the learning process. This clearly signifies the superiority of learner-centered models in comparing with the strictness of traditional methods (Local Burden of Disease Collaborators, 2019)

Core Principles of Inclusive Pedagogy

Four principles define inclusive pedagogy in CSE:

1. **Equity:** Removing structural barriers, including hardware and connectivity issues, to guarantee equal chances for all students (García-Holgado et al., 2022).
2. **Accessibility:** The creation of teaching materials and the arrangement of classrooms so that they are in line with the sensory, cognitive or motor skills of the students through the use of assistive technology and multimodal content (Zheng et al., 2023, Smith & McGill, 2025).
3. **Diversity:** Appreciating differences in student identities and experiences, fostering a culture of respect by including diverse viewpoints in problem-solving (Vrieler & Salminen-Karlsson, 2022).
4. **Adaptability:** The use of adaptive technologies, modular course structures and scaffolded tasks that enable students to learn core computational concepts at their own pace (Warner et al., 2021).

This mix of elements is what builds the resilience necessary to deal with the problems of access and quality (Mathrani et al., 2021). Not only access but also inclusive teaching opens the door to 21st-century skills like computational thinking—that is, the ability to analyse complex problems and find systematic solutions (Vrieler & Salminen-Karlsson, 2022). Flexible and collaborative methods let the students use technology easier, which in turn fosters digital participation and an understanding of the social and ethical dimensions of technology (Schreffler et al., 2019). While these core principles provide a blueprint for inclusion, their implementation is often obstructed by structural and systemic barriers within traditional CS education.

BARRIERS IN TRADITIONAL CS EDUCATION

CS education is one of the main pillars of modern digital literacy, yet traditional teaching methods often create difficult-to-overcome barriers that restrict equal access for different global students. These barriers are not confined to particular regions, but come out as a complicated mix of cognitive, financial, and institutional factors (Frawley et al., 2020, Yu, 2018).

Cognitive and Neurodiverse Barriers

The conventional CS learning environment—distinguished by teacher-centered lecturing, strict timetabling, and the use of single standard tests—often overlooks the individual learning needs of students with different abilities, for example, those diagnosed with Autism Spectrum Disorder (ASD), Attention Deficit Hyperactivity Disorder (ADHD), and dyslexia. Research has shown that these students struggle the most when the abstract nature of computing is expressed only through verbal or written language (Moriña, 2020). Therefore, if the instruction is not multimodal, neurodiverse learners suffer from a higher cognitive load which eventually leads them to lose interest in the subject matter, and their self-confidence in the classical classroom diminishes (Charteris et al., 2021) In addition, the lack of technology and personalized teaching in standard labs guarantees that the differences in learning are part of the system and not merely incidental (Moriña, 2020)

Socioeconomic and Structural Hurdles

Access to CS education is still largely determined by the socio-economic condition of the students. In the case of low-income and rural areas, electricity cuts, poor internet, and lack of computers have turned the situation into a "Resource Ceiling" (Tshukudu et al., 2022, Chada et al., 2025) The *AccessCSforAll* project in the United States has pointed out that even in developed countries with plenty of resources, students from underprivileged communities still need a lot of help and tools to pass the Advanced Placement (AP) courses. Likewise, studies in India show that kids in poorly funded schools are at a "double disadvantage": they lack the physical tools and the curriculum does not even include the most basic computer usage examples relevant to their lives [38, 39]. The extremely high price of proprietary software adds insult to injury and further creates a digital divide between the urban rich and the rural poor (Doyle & Zakrajsek, 2023)

Cultural, Linguistic, and Gender Barriers

Cultural congruence is not a typical feature of a traditional CS teaching practice since such practices use examples and problem-solving situations that mainly reflect the major cultural groups while the minority and indigenous learners are left out (Frawley et al., 2020). This cultural disconnect is generally accompanied by gender inequities. The 2024 UNESCO GEM Report points out a 'participation paradox' although parity in school enrollment has improved. On the global scale, the representation of women among the STEM graduates has not changed over the last ten years and it still stands at a mere 35% [UNESCO, 2024]. The difference is even more pronounced in CS where women account for only 40% of the graduating classes and are a minority of just 25% in the ICT sector. (Kesler et al., 2021). This exclusion is reinforced by a 'Hidden Curriculum' of biased social norms that manifest as mathematics anxiety and a lack of female mentorship, deterring girls from advanced CS pathways as early as age 15. In addition, in Africa and other areas of the Global South, students go through a "double-cognitive load," since they have to learn both English and complex computational logic at the same time (Fovet, 2020) This is exacerbated by the fact that **130 million fewer women** than men own a mobile phone globally, creating a physical 'Access Gap' alongside the linguistic one [UNESCO, 2024]. Thus, technologically-dependent assessments that disregard such linguistic and cultural disparities, will ensure that the conventional CS education system will keep on reinforcing its structural inequities (Doyle & Zakrajsek, 2023)

As table 1 suggests, such barriers are specifically influenced by gender and linguistic factors.

Table 1. Global Synthesis of Barriers to Inclusive CS (Based on 2024 UNESCO Data)

Barrier Type	Key Statistical Driver	Underlying Cause	Inclusion Impact
Gender Gap	35% female STEM grads	"Hidden Curriculum" & Age 15 drop-off	Participation Paradox
Linguistic	"Double-Cognitive Load"	English-centric coding syntax	Socio-cultural exclusion
Workforce	25% female ICT participation	Lack of mentorship & biased algorithms	Lack of role models
Policy	'Digital Uzbekistan 2030' focus	Need for Linguistic Adaptation	Transitioning to Sovereignty

Identifying these global barriers provides the necessary context for developing the frameworks required to bridge the policy-practice gap.

FRAMEWORKS FOR INCLUSIVE PEDAGOGY

CS education that is effective and inclusive is rooted in proper frameworks and thus the factors of teaching and curriculum designing are not only covered but also the integration of technology is also considered. (Wille et al., 2017) Hence, the development of computational skills will be among all the learners. The UDL framework is based on three core principles, which direct the design of teaching, curriculum, and evaluation in such a way that diverse learning profiles are proactively addressed in table 2:

Table 2. Functions in Inclusive CS Education

Principle	Function in Inclusive CS Education
I. Multiple Means of Engagement	Providing various options to foster interest, motivation, and self-regulation (e.g., choice in programming projects, team roles, and assessment timing).
II. Multiple Means of Representation	Presenting information and content in different formats (e.g., visual block coding, captioned videos, text-to-speech) to accommodate different sensory and cognitive styles.
III. Multiple Means of Action & Expression	Offering varied ways for students to demonstrate knowledge (e.g., project-based assessment, verbal explanation, traditional exam) rather than a single method.

With the UDL approach, educators are driven to design evaluations that are not limited to the traditional exams, but rather, it allows the students to demonstrate their comprehension through various means like projects, fun activities, or even different media. Not only does this practice foster inclusiveness but it also requires more thorough assessment of students' learning—thus, equity is brought up as a major pedagogical issue instead of merely being an idea that is postponed to the next stage. (Goldan et al., 2021)

Culturally Responsive Pedagogy

CRP is a methodology that goes to the extreme of UDL by placing the pupil's cultural background, life experiences, and socio-economic status at the core. In CS, this method incorporates storytelling from the students' cultures and problem-solving scenarios that represent the learners' immediate environment. By connecting the abstract computational concepts to local knowledge and global issues, CRP not only draws the students' real-life experiences closer to the digital world but also makes sure that the underprivileged learners are not, in any way, excluded by the Western-oriented teaching materials (Yu, 2018)

The digital initiative paves the way for the globalization of Cultural Resources Preservation as seen through the 'Digital Uzbekistan 2030' project. Thus, teachers have progressed from merely translating Western textbooks to 'Linguistic Adaptation.' The software, through matching the computational logic with the distinct syntactic structure of Uzbek, lightens the 'double cognitive load' imposed on students who are, in fact, pricked with the same two (a new language, English, and coding) learning tasks, one of which is very difficult, the other quite new. By this regional method, CRP is shown as a social not only but a psychological tool for the country in its quest for digital independence.

Constructivism and Active Learning

Constructivist methods, which place inquiry and hands-on problem-solving above passive information reception, further fortify inclusive CS education. Student-cantered approaches—flipped classrooms, peer instruction, and project-based learning—enable students to find and improve solutions at their pace (Dewsbury et al., 2022). Such methods are very effective in eliminating the disparities due to the different levels of prior exposure to computing, since they permit individualized interventions and scaffolded support (Li & Singh, 2022)

Critical Tensions and SWOT Analysis

While UDL and CRP offer powerful pathways for inclusion, their application is not without systemic challenges. To ensure analytical rigor, Table 3 presents a SWOT analysis evaluating the implementation of these frameworks within the CS ecosystem.

Table 3. SWOT Analysis of Implementing UDL and CRP Frameworks in the CS Ecosystem

Category	Key Factors	Impact on CS Pedagogy
Strengths	Cognitive Scaffolding	Reduces the "syntax barrier" for neurodiverse learners, focusing on high-level logic.
Weaknesses	Resource Intensity	Requires significant "design tax" (upfront time/expertise) for faculty to create multimodal materials.
Opportunities	Linguistic Sovereignty	Localizing code blocks (e.g., Swahili/Yoruba) eliminates the "Double-Cognitive Load" for non-native speakers.
Threats	Pedagogical Dilution	Risk of over-simplifying abstract concepts (e.g., recursion) instead of making the complexity accessible.

Critical Note: If not examined critically, UDL runs the risk of becoming just a "Compliance Checklist," where universities and colleges give preference to having accessibility features in place instead of considering whether the marginalized learners have really succeeded. It is the perspective of "expert learners," who are co-designers of their own technical environments, rather than the mere recipients of accommodations that the CPCA framework's positioning is suggested for resolving these tensions (Spandagou, 2021).

These strategic insights from the SWOT analysis provide the evaluative lens needed to examine the real-world application of inclusive pedagogy in our selected case studies.

Case Studies of Inclusive Practices

The UDL and CRP frameworks are empirically supported across diverse contexts. This section examines these principles within specialized US tertiary environments, Indian national resource-sharing, and African linguistic adaptations.

Gallaudet University: UDL and the Visual-Spatial Advantage

Gallaudet University, the only university in the world that provides English and ASL education side by side, has adopted the Visual Language and Visual Learning (VL2) framework for the D/HH students' visual-spatial processing strengths (Simms et al., 2013). This framework combines the use of specialized instructional technology with the UDL principle of Multiple Means of Representation, thus opening up the visual channels the most for problem-solving (Huff et al., 2020). The outcome of the research leads to the conclusion that D/HH students fluent in ASL tend to have the best visual-spatial processing; therefore, Gallaudet University translates the hard concepts like data structures, graph theory, and parallel programming to visual-driven activities so that these cognitive benefits can be tapped (Simms et al., 2013).

The most important new feature is that block-based languages like Snap! have been combined with motion-sensing technology Students interacting with code by signing gestures, for example, using a "looping" sign to control loop structures, are in harmony with the UDL principle of Multiple Means of Action and Expression (Simms et al., 2013). This is an example of CRP where computational logic is based on the students' primary cultural communication that results in greatly increased engagement and self-esteem. Besides, Gallaudet's Artificial Intelligence, Accessibility and Sign Language Center (AIASL) empowers students to be the ones who create accessibility tools instead of being the ones who only consume them which in turn helps to develop their technical skills profoundly (Simms et al., 2013).

AccessCSforAll: UDL for K-12 Neuro- and Physically Diverse Learners

AccessCSforAll (formerly AccessCS10K) is a nationwide U.S. initiative scaling inclusive CS for K-12 students with visual, physical, and neuro-cognitive disabilities (Simms et al., 2013). The program prioritizes systemic inclusion over individual retrofitting through two core objectives:

- **Teacher Capacity Building:** Professional Development (PD) training equips educators—who often lack experience in disability-inclusive pedagogy—to apply UDL guidelines systematically. This involves providing Multiple Means of Representation for visual/cognitive barriers, Multiple Means of Action and Expression for motor/executive function barriers, and Multiple Means of Engagement for motivational barriers (Wille et al., 2017).
- **Curricular Adaptation and Scaffolding:** By integrating UDL into the design of the AP CS Principles course, accessibility is established during the planning stage. Scaffolding strategies—including simplified language, task decomposition, and visual organizers—support students with learning disabilities (SLDs) and executive function challenges while preserving the rigor of computational thinking (Simms et al., 2013)

Accessible Tool Integration and Systematic Impact

AccessCSforAll mitigates technical barriers through evidence-based tools that facilitate multimodal engagement. *Quorum*, a programming language with "human-readable" syntax, eliminates the syntactic "noise" (semicolons/braces) that often hinders screen-reader and dyslexic users. Additionally, *CodeJumper*—a physical coding system—enables visually impaired students to collaborate directly with sighted peers on coding logic. These measures produce a "curb-cut effect," where simplified syntax and multimodal tools benefit not only sensory-impaired learners but also ELLs and neurodiverse students (Tsai, 2023).

Critical Tensions and Limitations

Although they were successful, the models highlighted three system barriers that were considered by the CPCA framework:

1. **Policy and Funding Dependency**: The dependence on temporary grants (such as NSF) and U.S.-specific legal protections (ADA) makes it difficult to replicate in other areas which do not have the same rules or the same level of money for a long time.
2. **The Scalability Gap:** The expensive nature of specialized equipment and extensive PD barriers create a "resource ceiling" preventing schools from unwrapping the transition of pilot programs into sustainable initiatives.
3. **Industry Alignment**: The problem between the educational tools (for example, Quorum) and the languages that are used in industries (like Python) still remains in the form of a "glass ceiling." The professional IDEs that lack user-friendliness pose a barrier to the entry of diverse learners into the workforce and spotlighting the risks of "techno-solutionism."

Global South: Resource-Sharing and Linguistic Sovereignty

To move from high-resource proofs-of-concept to models that can be economically sustained requires the attention to shared infrastructure and equality in languages:

- **Shared-Resource Infrastructure (India):** The I-STEM (Indian Science, Technology, and Engineering facilities Map) portal provides a cloud-based "One Nation, One Portal" gateway to publicly financed scientific tools and software. This means that students from Socio-Economically Disadvantaged Groups (SEDGs) in rural or tier-2 colleges are able to use advanced tools that are usually too expensive for local institutions (Spandagou, 2021).
- **Linguistic Inclusion and "Double-Cognitive Load" (Africa):** Programs like Africa Code Week help to eliminate the problem of having students learn English first before learning computational logic—a "double-cognitive load." Projects that are localized are developing vernacular coding blocks in languages such as Swahili and Yoruba by using the CRP method to ensure

coding logic is connected to the learner's primary cultural and cognitive language (Bray et al., 2023).

Despite these limitations, the successful elements of these models highlight the significant benefits that inclusive pedagogy brings to the classroom.

BENEFITS OF INCLUSIVE PEDAGOGY

The shift of inclusive pedagogy, which combines UDL and CRP, is seen in UDL's step of "deficits" to proactive design and in the teacher's consideration of diverse learners as an asset (Ryoo, 2019). The combination leads to measurable benefits not only in academics but also in the social and professional areas (Madkins et al., 2020).

Academic Benefits

It is a proven fact that the implementation of inclusive strategies not only boosts academic achievement but also increases the completion rates in challenging CS programs to 60% to 64% at least. The use of multimodal instruction which includes visual aids, tactile experiments, and verbal scaffolding indeed aligns the content perfectly with the various cognitive strengths of the students thereby creating an environment for deep conceptual understanding rather than just rote recall (Huff et al., 2020). The transition from high-stakes, single-format exams to various assessments (e.g., portfolios, multimedia projects) not only lowers test anxiety but also stimulates intellectual risk-taking. In addition, the differentiated group work taps into the students' talents and utilizes them as collaborative resources (Spandagou, 2021).

The impact of institutional inclusivity on the retention of students in a positive way is direct. The closure of the "Policy-Practice Gap" meanwhile, results in the high dropout rates in STEM being viewed as a failure on part of the institutions rather than a lack of ability in students. An adaptive curriculum is of utmost importance for the technical fields to attract and retain the underrepresented groups (Lapidot-Lefler, 2025).

Social-Emotional Benefits

The success of CS as a field is largely dependent on non-cognitive factors such as identity acceptance and mental health (Paju et al., 2021). Inclusive teaching methods merge different case studies to create "cultural capital," aiding the development of a strong STEM identity (NCERT, n.d.). Granting learners the freedom to choose their own learning paths and the tools to work with, caters to the psychological needs of mastery and self-regulation. The provision of effort-based feedback leads to an increase in both academic self-efficacy and technical confidence (Kieran & Anderson, 2019). Moreover, it is inclusiveness that reduces the impact of stereotype threat, while formative assessments are not seen as "unproductive failures," but rather, help infants to develop the growth mindset and resilience that are vital for tech learning (Gale et al., 2022, Araujo et al., 2023). While the advantages of this approach are clear, several practical challenges must be addressed to ensure successful implementation in diverse classrooms.

CHALLENGES IN IMPLEMENTATION

Transitioning to inclusive CS teaching methods necessitates facing the power dynamics within the institution and the resistance to the change. Implementation often fails due to a "Policy-Practice Gap," where ambitious equity goals collide with bureaucratic inflexibility and financial constraints (Memon & Memon, 2024).

Resource Constraints and Social Stigmas

The global digital divide, particularly in the Global South, is a major factor that trumps the technology-dependent UDL frameworks. Unreliable electricity supplies and limited Internet bandwidth in rural or low-income urban neighborhoods greatly reduce the possibility of real-time instructional adjustments (CAST, 2024). Besides, the steep pricing of specialized assistive software transforms access to education into a "pay-wall for inclusion" that is dependent on one's socioeconomic status (Memon & Memon, 2024).

Moreover, social stigma around neurodiversity is one of the factors that contribute to the ineffectiveness of the situation. In several countries, low expectations from school administrators and parents result in the misconception that inclusive practices "lower standards." Without narratives specific to the community, CS is still seen as an elite and Western-oriented field. This can be overcome by changing the perception of neurodiversity as a unique computational resource that provides different perspectives for solving problems (Borsotti et al., 2024).

Policy, Institutional, and Assessment Barriers

Institutional Inertia and the emphasis on physical modifications (e.g., ramps) usually neglect the cognitive, cultural, and socio-economic needs of various learners. The lack of specific budgeting and management through top leaders to reform administration results in the situation where the burden of inclusion is unjustly shifted to teachers individually (Pournaghshband & Medel, 2020).

A major risk in the structure is the mismatch between the use of innovative teaching and assessment methods that are standardized. The entire educational systems in the world are dependent on timed, high-stakes summative exams that promote rote learning and put the students under stress, hence discouraging neuro-diverse students. When the performance of teachers is appraised using these strict standards, they are likely to feel the need to "teach to the test," thus disregarding the principles of UDL and CRP. Moreover, inclusive practices are likely to be viewed as "supplementary" unless accreditation systems monitor equitable outcomes specifically (Shi et al., 2025).

Educator Resistance: Workload and Training

Teaching staff resistance is frequently a misunderstanding of their personal getting in the way rather than being a lot more back and forth between the system and them. The design of UDL is a proactive method that takes a lot of time; often, the teachers' contracts won't cover the preparation of varied content and the technologies that support various learning profiles (Shi et al., 2025)

The situation is made worse by the lack of a continuous Professional Development (PD) system. A lot of teachers are not able to make moving from minimal accommodations like providing extra time to designing culturally relevant accessible problem sets through skill development. The inability to abolish the standardized pressures while imposing the inclusion requirements results in "Inclusion by Addition" and "Pedagogical Tokenism," where UDL is implemented superficially for compliance purposes while the exclusionary core of the CS curriculum remains unchanged (Reid et al., 2025)

CPCA Operational Framework:

The logic for these actions, as well as the potential risks involved in each layer, is detailed in Table 4.

Table 4. Implementation Logic

Implementation Layer	Strategic Component	Decision Logic / Actionable Step	Critical Tension (The "R2" Edge)
Pedagogical	Dynamic Scaffolding	If learners face high cognitive load, then utilize modular, block-based logic before syntax-heavy coding.	Risk of UDL becoming a "compliance checklist."
Technological	Resource-Light IDEs	If hardware/bandwidth is limited, then prioritize browser-based, mobile-friendly compilers.	Risk of "Techno-solutionism."
Structural	Policy Alignment	If standardized tests conflict with UDL, then pilot "Portfolio-as-Assessment" models.	Confronting "Institutional Inertia."

Translating this operational framework into lasting change requires a shift from individual classroom practice toward broad systemic reform.

THE CPCA OPERATIONAL FRAMEWORK: STRATEGIES FOR SYSTEMIC REFORM

In order to make CS education a totally inclusive domain, it is necessary to implement a very large-scale, multi-level strategy that will not only eliminate individual teachers' adjustments but also require systemic change to governing bodies, educational institutions, and technology development sectors. This change will call for a series of interventions at the policy level that are well-coordinated, long-term allocated resources, and a strong widespread commitment to taking evidence-based design as the way forward. (DeMatthews et al., 2021) t will be necessary to speak about the equity and access goals in a way that they can be traced back from the macro-level of international law and government funding down to the micro-level of curriculum design and technological development. (Borsotti et al., 2024)

Global and National Governance

The UN Convention on the Rights of Persons with Disabilities (CRPD) calls for profound changes in the system by proclaiming accessible education as a universal human right. This makes it the duty of the states to assure that there is accessibility in all the communications, both the physical and the digital one. Global initiatives are supported by the knowledge-sharing networks that are formed from the collaboration of civil society and advocacy groups, which make sure that the policies are in tune with the people's experiences (Bisson et al., 2022). At the national level, the implementation of these mandates is done through policies like the one in India, called Equitable and Inclusive Education policy, which defines minimum enrolment quotas for SEDGs. The governments employ fiscal instruments and performance-based funding to reduce the gap between policy and practice. The educational institutions are given incentives for reducing the differences in attainment and for importing global best practices, which results in a continuous flow of innovations that are backed by long-term resource allocation (Asbell-Clarke et al., 2024).

Institutional Embedding and Leadership

Institutional policy must shift from individual accommodations toward a "margins-to-mainstream" organizational culture (DeMatthews et al., 2021). Annual modular curriculum audits ensure compliance with UDL and CRP, integrating the cultural capital of diverse learners into CS design. Continuous Professional Development (PD) is integrated into teaching diplomas to foster faculty empathy and reduce implicit bias. Crucially, this transition cultivates student agency, positioning learners as co-partners in developing the independence necessary to become "expert learners" (DeMatthews et al., 2021).

Technology and the Design of Accessible Tools

In the CS sector, it is necessary for developers to adopt a proactive attitude in designing for inclusivity rather than just conforming to the minimum required standards. The digital applications created should, right from the start, have the capability to work with assistive technologies (AT), and support different types of content consumption (Leonard & Sentance, 2021). The use of artificial intelligence (AI) and data from adaptive learning can provide personalized pathways based on individual achievements. Nevertheless, the application of an ethical design approach is critical in reducing the impact of algorithmic biases in the VR and AR fields, which are considered to be among the emerging technologies, and in making technology a means of economic mobility rather than a barrier (Ravet & Mtika, 2021)

Research and Evaluation for Evidence-Based Practice

Sustainability is a process that demands strict, evidence-based evaluations. Teaching Effectiveness Frameworks (TEFs) offer a multidimensional quality approach, which is not limited to biased metrics only but also encompasses peer reflection and student voice. These frameworks motivate continuous reflection, enabling institutions to change teaching methods according to the real-time data (May & Bridger, 2010). In the end, impact measurement has to monitor the reductions in the achievement gaps and the increase of the non-cognitive skills such as self-efficacy and belonging, thus giving the data support for the continuation of the institutional funding (Moriña, 2020).

Systemic Barriers to Policy Implementation

Even with these frameworks in place, a constant Policy-Practice Gap is still there because of three reasons. First, equity mandates are mostly considered "unfunded mandates," which means that most institutions do not have the specific money allocated to them for specialized equipment or hiring. Second, Teacher PD Attrition is a situation that can occur when a one-time workshop is conducted and it is not followed by long-term, constant mentorship that is necessary to master complicated assistive tools. Last, Metric Fixation gives priority to the scores of standardized tests instead of long-term equity goals. As a result, inclusive CS initiatives are often branded as "optional extras," which in turn gives rise to what CPCA framework has termed the "token inclusion" and which has been criticized.

In order to overcome these obstacles, it is essential to have a clear operational rationale which can bring into line the different levels of the CS ecosystem. The necessary strategic actions to shift from aspirational policy to practical, systemic inclusion are summarized in the below table 5:

Table 5. Operationalizing Inclusive CS Alignment

Stakeholder	Primary Action	Decision Logic (The "Why" & "When")
Policymakers	Ring-fenced Funding	If mandates are "unfunded," then allocate specific CS-AT (Assistive Tech) budgets to prevent "Token Inclusion."
Administrators	Modular Audits	If UDL is treated as an "extra," then embed it into the mandatory course approval/accreditation cycle.
Developers	Native Accessibility	If tools require "reactive patching," then enforce "Accessibility-First" builds at the prototype stage.
Faculty	Iterative Mentorship	If "one-off workshops" fail, then transition to long-term mentorship-based teaching diplomas.

Overcoming these policy barriers enables a shift toward future directions and the global implications of inclusive computational access.

FUTURE DIRECTIONS AND GLOBAL IMPLICATIONS

The path of inclusive CS education is marked by the inevitable crossing of changing technology, increasing pedagogical theory, and a global economic necessity coming with the awareness of the latter. (Nazarova, 2020) The growth of the area will not just lead the future research to focus on improving the existing models but also on expanding the diversity of the inclusion and using AI to enable delivering customized and culturally sensitive learning experiences worldwide (Ahmad et al., 2024) Consequently, the planet will be more rich in talents and technologically innovative due to such endeavors. (Baglieri, 2022)

Cross-National Adaptability of Inclusive Pedagogy

The proper use of UDL and CRP depends on their incorporation into various national and cultural contexts (Tuitt, 2023). UDL has its global principles but its success still needs Linguistic Sovereignty. The 2024 UNESCO Global Education Monitoring Report proposes a "context-sensitive practice," which means using local languages and indigenous philosophies even in coding syntax for making inclusiveness really happen (Nazarova, 2020).

Research worldwide has shown that the advantages of inclusive education are still very limited due to the use of very narrow definitions of disability which do not take into account things like ethnicity, language, and socioeconomic status (Bray et al., 2023). Moving away from Western-centric models will entail the localization of educational philosophies and expertise (Obiakor et al., 2022). Research in the future should create professional development models that are informing worldwide but are executed locally, thus creating a vibrant connection between global research and local practice (Pagliara et al., 2024).

Role of AI and Adaptive Learning in Inclusive CS Education

AI and machine learning play a pivotal role in inclusive computing science, offering individualized and flexible educational experiences that conquer the barriers of traditional instruction (Obiakor et al., 2022). There is a real-time transformation of the computational abstraction through AI Dynamic Scaffolding. By observing the cognitive load, the system will automatically reduce or increase the difficulty of the recursion logic or data structures depending on the neurodivergent learner's executive functioning profile (Kieran & Anderson, 2019). This movement constitutes a change from "accommodation" to a biopsychosocial model, where the software environments are trained for the neural diversity and not to the students following the rigid interface standards (Pagliara et al., 2024).

Nonetheless, the use of AI-supported education holds the danger of "Algorithmic Stratification." According to studies, AI tutors that have been trained on neurotypical data may lead to the creation of a "Deficit Loop" by failing to interpret the non-linear problem-solving of ADHD or Autistic students as true cognitive variations rather than errors (3.1, 3.2). The realization of "Algorithmic Justice" will require initiatives similar to India's BharatGen project, scheduled for 2025/26. BharatGen is creating multimodal large language models for the 22 scheduled languages to ensure that the "data plantation" scenario does not happen, where the Global North benefits by extracting data while the Global South struggles with the application of flawed models.

AI is not only providing basic support but also enabling creation of Culturally Responsive curricula by identifying and mitigating Eurocentric biases in the prevalent CS datasets and recommending examples that are appropriate and contextual for that specific site. Hence, computational concepts will be anchored in the particular cultural and linguistic heritage of the learners. To tackle Digital Colonialism, which happens when the Western-trained models impose foreign linguistic standards through AI, Algorithmic Justice would demand 'a human-in-the-loop' policy. This way, the AI would be a supplement to—rather than a replacement of—the teacher-student relationship, which brings along the cultural and emotional factors of mentoring (Pagliara et al., 2024, Salas-Pilco et al., 2022)

Expanding Inclusivity Beyond Neurodiverse and Marginalized Learners

In the future, a shift must occur in disability inclusion from a charity model that aids specific groups to a gradual and complete adoption of a Disability Studies viewpoint, which sees disability as human diversity rather than a flaw (Besic, 2020). This change of perspective will demand a transition to a biopsychosocial model: by 2026, the curriculum should be the "disabled entity," not the student, if it does not accommodate neural diversity (Besic, 2020). Inclusion in CS education must also benefit non-traditional learners such as first-generation students and working adults. Utilization of sociological insights in pedagogy not only contributes to "cognitive empathy" among teachers but also to the realization of belonging that is so important for complicated topics (Obiakor et al., 2022). By turning differences into strengths, educational institutions are employing a strategy that will lead the graduates to be ready for a global workforce that is diverse.

Global Workforce Implications: Diversity and Innovation in Tech Sectors

Diverse and inclusive CS education creates a versatile and varied pool of graduates, which in turn, directly strengthens the workforce pipeline (Besic, 2020). The diversity of a team prevents "groupthink" and allows the creation of better products and fairer algorithms (Pagliara et al., 2024). Besides technical skills, inclusive practices train students in the cultural sensitivity required for global cooperation

(Pagliara et al., 2024). The whole inclusive CS process turns out to be a cost to the economy, as the students are empowered to create technologies that remove, rather than support, social barriers (Besic, 2020). The 2026 strategic matrix for these pillars is shown in Table 6.

Table 6. 2026 Inclusive CS Strategic Matrix

Pillar	Status (2026)	Critical Risk (The "Depth")	Future Action
Neurodiversity	Moderate (UDL)	Data Bias (Deficit Loop)	Inclusive Dataset Training
Linguistic Equity	Emerging	Digital Colonialism	Vernacularized LLM Interfaces
Gender Parity	Stagnant (35% grads)	Hidden Curriculum (Age 15)	Early Mentorship & Role Models
Workforce	Transitioning	Syntax Obsolescence	Focus on Human-Centric Ethics

These global insights and future trajectories lead to the final synthesis and concluding thoughts on the necessity of inclusive computational access.

CONCLUSION

Synthesis of Key Insights and Strategic Mandates

The transformation of CS is dependent on radical changes in the existing structure through cooperation of all the stakeholders involved at different levels (Tuitt, 2023). The chapter delineates the four future global mandates for equity:

1. **Cognitive Access through Pedagogical Flexibility:** UDL has scientifically proven to remove obstacles through various means of communication and understanding (Pagliara et al., 2024). The combining of UDL and CRP leads to greater interest in the curriculum and lower dropout rates for underrepresented students (Obiakor et al., 2022; Besic, 2020). Full justice requires moving from "compliance-based" approaches to a CPCA, which integrates cognitive, pedagogical, and cultural aspects (Besic, 2020).
2. **Policy as a Driver for Systemic Change**: Governments and international organizations, in line with the UN CRPD, will have to pivot to proactive policy-making (Tuitt, 2023). Public funding should only be granted to countries that require computer literacy for the economically disadvantaged, thereby making

inclusive programs financially sustainable instead of just temporary (Salas-Pilco et al., 2022).

3. **Technology as a Remedy:** The UDL principles must be integrated into the design of the digital platforms right from the start by the developers (Ahmad et al., 2024). The AI and adaptive learning technologies will be able to deliver personalized instruction on a large scale, but at the same time, there should be strict ethical guidelines that would prohibit any form of discrimination by the algorithms. It is expected that the technological gadgets of the future will be accessible, aware of the cultural differences, and open-source (Salas-Pilco et al., 2022).
4. **Evidence-Based Evaluation:** Institutions should implement equity-centered evaluations—similar to the TEF—that measure both reduced attainment gaps and the growth of non-cognitive traits like student resilience (Nazarova, 2020).

A Unified Call to Action

Fulfilling the demand for fully inclusive CS pedagogy, it is necessary to take immediate and persistent measures:

1. **Educators:** Literally should, among other things, reject the myth of 'average student' completely, be committed to constant UDL/CRP professional development, and change curricula to the extent of centering around life resources and issues that are important to a varied student population (Kieran & Anderson, 2019)
2. **Policymakers:** Are required to include inclusive design as a condition in educational procurement, provide subsidies for UDL/CRP teachers' professional training, and create an entire system of national metrics that focus on the equity of outcomes as the main goal (Obiakor et al., 2022)
3. **Researchers:** Are invited to explore the inclusive practices, i.e., the datamined researches to find out the specific connections between these practices and student success rates in CS (Pagliara et al., 2024)
4. **Technology Developers:** Must give "design equity" the first priority instead of comfort and ease, so that AI tools are built to include human variance rather than intensifying social barriers (Adamu et al., 2025)

Synthesis of Contribution

The chapter has gone past merely recounting inclusive educational practices to the point of setting up the CPCA. The synthesis through triangulation framework has indicated that inclusive CS education is not simply a supplementary 'accommodation' but rather, a fundamental and structural necessity. The data from well-resourced places such as Gallaudet University, compared to the under-resourced regions of the Global South (I-STEM and Africa Code Week), presents the same final point: inclusion will not succeed if treated as an 'optional extra.' The real equity will need the transition from 'Pedagogical Tokenism' to the systemic integration—where the policy dictates are matched with the specially allocated funding and UDL is deeply rooted in the curriculum and code structure. The CPCA framework is, in the end, the operational logic that is required to fill the gap between policy and practice. In an age where new technologies might create digital stratifications, the strategies specified here can serve as a guide for educators and policymakers to ensure that the 'Computational Revolution' is inclusive of all students irrespective of their sensory, cognitive, or economic backgrounds.

REFERENCES

Adamu, A. (Ed.). R., Okebukola, P., Assistants, E., Gbeleyi, O., Oladejo, A., Agbanimu, D., Onowugbeda, F., Foreword, E., & Jackson-Hammond, C. (2025). *AI and Curriculum Development for the Future Book in honour of.* Retrieved November 11, 2025, from https://eprints.gouni.edu.ng/4428/1/Volume%202-AI%20and%20Quality%20Higher%20Education%20Handbook-January%202025.pdf#page=74

Afzal, A., Khan, S., Daud, S., Ahmad, Z., & Butt, A. (2023). Addressing the Digital Divide: Access and Use of Technology in Education. *Journal of Social Sciences Review, 3*(2), 883–895. DOI: 10.54183/jssr.v3i2.326

Ahmad, I., Sharma, S., Singh, R., & Gehlot, A., Lovi Raj Gupta, Amit Kumar Thakur, Neeraj Priyadarshi, & Bhekisipho Twala. (2024). Inclusive learning using industry 4.0 technologies: Addressing student diversity in modern education. *Cogent Education, 11*(1). Advance online publication. DOI: 10.1080/2331186x.2024.2330235

Asbell-Clarke, J., Ibrahim Dahlstrom-Hakki, Voiklis, J., Attaway, B., Barchas-Lichtenstein, J., Edwards, T., Bardar, E., Robillard, T., Paulson, K., Grover, S., Israel, M., Ke, F., & Weintrop, D. (2024). Including neurodiversity in computational thinking. *Frontiers in Education, 9*. Advance online publication. DOI: 10.3389/feduc.2024.1358492

Baglieri, S. (2022). *Disability Studies and the Inclusive Classroom.* https://doi.org/DOI: 10.4324/9781003138808

Besic, E. (2020). Intersectionality: A pathway towards inclusive education? *Prospects, 49*(49), 111–122. DOI: 10.1007/s11125-020-09461-6

Bhattacharya, P., Joshi, S., Bandyopadhyay, S., & Mittal, R. (2022). Virtual Computer Science Education in India: Challenges and Opportunities. SSRN *Electronic Journal.* https://doi.org/DOI: 10.2139/ssrn.4026251

Bisson, L., Grindstaff, L., Brazil-Cruz, L., & Barbu Editors, S. (2022). *Uprooting Bias in the Academy Lessons from the Field.* https://library.oapen.org/bitstream/handle/20.500.12657/51948/1/978-3-030-85668-7.pdf#page=36

Bonnette, R., Abramovich, S., Decker, A., & Fabiano, G. A. (2022). Building Ecosystems of Belonging for Neurodiverse Students. *Proceedings of the 53rd ACM Technical Symposium on Computer Science Education* v. 2, 1192–1192. https://doi.org/DOI: 10.1145/3478432.3499182

Borsotti, V., Begel, A., & Bjørn, P. (2024). Neurodiversity and the Accessible University: Exploring Organizational Barriers, Access Labor and Opportunities for Change. *PACM on Human-Computer Interaction, 8*(CSCW1). https://doi.org/ DOI: 10.1145/3641011

Bray, A., Devitt, A., Banks, J., & Sanchez Fuentes, S., Marta Sandoval Mena, Katerina Riviou, Byrne, D., Flood, M., Reale, J., & Terrenzio, S. (2023). What next for universal design for learning? A systematic literature review of technology in UDL implementations at second level. *British Journal of Educational Technology, 55*(1). Advance online publication. DOI: 10.1111/bjet.13328

CAST. (2024). *Universal Design for Learning*. CAST. https://www.cast.org/what-we-do/universal-design-for-learning/

Charteris, J., Anderson, J., & Page, A. (2021). Psychological safety in innovative learning environments: Planning for inclusive spaces. *International Journal of Inclusive Education, 28*(5), 1–17. DOI: 10.1080/13603116.2021.1974108

DeMatthews, D. E., Serafini, A., & Watson, T. N. (2021). Leading inclusive schools: Principal perceptions, practices, and challenges to meaningful change. *Educational Administration Quarterly, 57*(1), 3–48. DOI: 10.1177/0013161x20913897

Dewsbury, B. M., Swanson, H. J., Moseman-Valtierra, S., & Caulkins, J. (2022). Inclusive and active pedagogies reduce academic outcome gaps and improve long-term performance. *PLoS One, 17*(6), e0268620. DOI: 10.1371/journal.pone.0268620 PMID: 35704639

Doyle, T., & Zakrajsek, T. D. (2023). *Learner-Centered Teaching*. https://doi.org/ DOI: 10.4324/9781003445630

Ferguson, T., & Roofe, C. G. (2020). SDG 4 in higher education: Challenges and opportunities. *International Journal of Sustainability in Higher Education, 21*(5), 959–975. DOI: 10.1108/ijshe-12-2019-0353

Fovet, F. (2020). Universal Design for Learning as a Tool for Inclusion in the Higher Education Classroom: Tips for the Next Decade of Implementation. *Education Journal, 9*(6), 163. DOI: 10.11648/j.edu.20200906.13

Gale, L., Bhushan, P., Eidnani, S., Graham, L., Harrison, M., McKay-Brown, L., Pande, R., Shreeraman, S., & Sivashunmugam, C. (2022). Overcoming barriers to inclusion in education in India: A scoping review. *Social Sciences & Humanities Open, 5*(1), 100237. DOI: 10.1016/j.ssaho.2021.100237

García-Holgado, A., Soledad, C., Silveira, I. F., & García-Peñalvo, F. J. (2022). A Case Study in Brazil and Spain about the Students' Perception of the Gender Gap in Computing. *International Journal of Engineering Education*, *38*(3), 663–672. https://www.researchgate.net/publication/360912221_A_Case_Study_in_Brazil_and_Spain_about_the_Students%27_Perception_of_the_Gender_Gap_in_Computing

Goode, J., Skorodinsky, M., Hubbard, J., & Hook, J. (2020). *Article 162 Citation. 4*. https://doi.org/DOI: 10.3389/feduc.2019.00162

Huff, E., Koushik, V., Ladner, R., Ludi, S., Milne, L., College, M., Mountapmbeme, A., Perkoff, M., & Stefik, A. (2020). *Accessible Tools and Curricula for K-12 Computer Science Education*. https://www.microsoft.com/en-us/research/wp-content/uploads/2021/02/Accessible-Tools-and-Curricula-for-K-12-Computer-Science-Education_Group-A.pdf

Israel, M., Kester, B., Williams, J. J., & Ray, M. J. (2022). *Equity and Inclusion through UDL in K-6 Computer Science Education: Perspectives of Teachers and Instructional Coaches*. ACM Transactions on Computing Education., DOI: 10.1145/3513138

Goldan, J. Hoffmann, L., & Schwab, S. (2021). A Matter of Resources? – Students' Academic Self-Concept, Social Inclusion and School Well-being in Inclusive Education. *Emerald Publishing Limited EBooks*, 89–100. https://doi.org/DOI: 10.1108/s1479-363620210000015008

Kesler, A., Shamir-Inbal, T., & Blau, I. (2021). Active Learning by Visual Programming: Pedagogical Perspectives of Instructivist and Constructivist Code Teachers and Their Implications on Actual Teaching Strategies and Students' Programming Artifacts. *Journal of Educational Computing Research*, *60*(1), 073563312110177. DOI: 10.1177/07356331211017793

Kieran, L., & Anderson, C. (2019). Connecting universal design for learning with culturally responsive teaching. *Education and Urban Society*, *51*(9), 1202–1216. DOI: 10.1177/0013124518785012

Lapidot-Lefler, N. (2025). Teacher Responsiveness in Inclusive Education: A Participatory Study of Pedagogical Practice, Well-Being, and Sustainability. *Sustainability*, *17*(7), 2919. DOI: 10.3390/su17072919

Leonard, H. C., & Sentance, S. (2021). Culturally-relevant and responsive pedagogy in computing: A Quick Scoping Review. *International Journal of Computer Science Education in Schools*, *5*(2), 3–13. DOI: 10.21585/ijcses.v5i2.130

Li, Y., & Singh, C. (2022). Inclusive learning environments can improve student learning and motivational beliefs. *Physical Review. Physics Education Research, 18*(2). Advance online publication. DOI: 10.1103/physrevphyseducres.18.020147

Lopez-Fernandez, D., Gordillo, A., Alarcon, P. P., & Tovar, E. (2021). Comparing Traditional Teaching and Game-Based Learning Using Teacher-Authored Games on Computer Science Education. *IEEE Transactions on Education, 64*(4), 1–7. DOI: 10.1109/te.2021.3057849

Madkins, T. C., Howard, N. R., & Freed, N. (2020). Engaging Equity Pedagogies in Computer Science Learning Environments. *Journal of Computer Science Integration*, •••, 1–27. DOI: 10.26716/jcsi.2020.03.2.1 PMID: 37547748

Martin, F., Chen, Y., Moore, R. L., & Westine, C. D. (2020). Systematic review of adaptive learning research designs, context, strategies, and technologies from 2009 to 2018. *Educational Technology Research and Development, 68*(4), 1903–1929. DOI: 10.1007/s11423-020-09793-2 PMID: 32837122

Mathrani, A., Sarvesh, T., & Umer, R. (2021). Digital Divide framework: Online Learning in Developing Countries during the COVID-19 Lockdown. *Globalisation, Societies and Education, 20*(5), 1–16. DOI: 10.1080/14767724.2021.1981253

May, H., & Bridger, K. (2010). *Developing and embedding inclusive policy and practice in higher education Developing and embedding inlcusive policy and practice in higher education*. https://www.aau.org/wp-content/uploads/sites/9/2018/04/Developing-Embedding-Inclusive-Policy-Practice-Report-final.pdf

Memon, F. N., & Memon, S. N. (2024). Digital Divide and Equity in Education. *Advances in Educational Technologies and Instructional Design Book Series*, 107–130. https://doi.org/DOI: 10.4018/979-8-3693-1854-6.ch004

Moriña, A. (2020). Faculty members who engage in inclusive pedagogy: Methodological and affective strategies for teaching. *Teaching in Higher Education, 27*(3), 1–16. DOI: 10.1080/13562517.2020.1724938

Nazarova, N. M. (2020). Comparative analysis of the inclusive education paradigm implementation in Russia and abroad. *Perspectives of Science and Education, 44*(2), 354–365. DOI: 10.32744/pse.2020.2.28

Obiakor, F. E., Aluka, I. J., Obiakor, G. C., & Obi, S. O. (2022). Educating culturally and linguistically diverse students with disabilities in inclusive settings: Beyond debates. *Multicultural Learning and Teaching, 0*(0). Advance online publication. DOI: 10.1515/mlt-2022-

Pagliara, S. M., Gianmarco Bonavolontà, Pia, M., Falchi, S., Antioco Luigi Zurru, Gianni Fenu, & Mura, A. (2024). The Integration of Artificial Intelligence in Inclusive Education: A Scoping Review. *Information (Basel)*, *15*(12), 774–774. DOI: 10.3390/info15120774

Paju, B., Kajamaa, A., Pirttimaa, R., & Kontu, E. (2021). Collaboration for Inclusive Practices: Teaching Staff Perspectives from Finland. *Scandinavian Journal of Educational Research*, *66*(3), 1–14. DOI: 10.1080/00313831.2020.1869087

Pournaghshband, V., & Medel, P. (2020). Promoting Diversity-Inclusive Computer Science Pedagogies: A Multidimensional Perspective. *Proceedings of the 2020 ACM Conference on Innovation and Technology in Computer Science Education*. https://doi.org/DOI: 10.1145/3341525.3387360

Ravet, J., & Mtika, P. (2021). Educational inclusion in resource-constrained contexts: A study of rural primary schools in Cambodia. *International Journal of Inclusive Education*, *28*(1), 1–22. DOI: 10.1080/13603116.2021.1916104

Reid, J., Ahmadian, M., & Jennings, D., Anathea Abad Pepperl, Adkins, A., Anthony, K. C., Volkan Aytar, Basu, M., Bosworth, K., Bristow, A. S., Cannon, L., Cario, C., Carpenter, E., Coston, E., Crenshaw, J., Davis, J. L., Durfee, R., Gandhi, P., Ghahramani, Z. N., & Gibson, R. (2025). Saying It Aloud: Inclusive Teaching Statements Impact on Sense of Belonging and Engagement. *Journal of College Science Teaching*, •••, 1–14. DOI: 10.1080/0047231x.2025.2487437

Ryoo, J. J. (2019). Pedagogy that Supports Computer Science for All. *ACM Trans. Comput. Educ.*, *19*(4). Advance online publication. DOI: 10.1145/3322210

Salas-Pilco, S. Z., Xiao, K., & Oshima, J. (2022). Artificial Intelligence and New Technologies in Inclusive Education for Minority Students: A Systematic Review. *Sustainability*, *14*(20), 13572. DOI: 10.3390/su142013572

Schreffler, J., Vasquez, E.III, Chini, J., & James, W. (2019). Universal Design for Learning in postsecondary STEM education for students with disabilities: A systematic literature review. *International Journal of STEM Education*, *6*(1). Advance online publication. DOI: 10.1186/s40594-019-0161-8

Shi, Y. R., Sin, K. F. K., & Wang, Y. Q. (2025). Teacher professional development of digital pedagogy for inclusive education in post-pandemic era: Effects on teacher competence, self-efficacy, and work well-being. *Teaching and Teacher Education*, *168*, 105230. DOI: 10.1016/j.tate.2025.105230

Simms, L., Baker, S., & Clark, M. D. (2013). The Standardized Visual Communication and Sign Language Checklist for Signing Children. *Sign Language Studies, 14*(1), 101–124. DOI: 10.1353/sls.2013.0029

Smith, J. M., & McGill, M. M. (2025). How Should We Measure Race, Ethnicity, and Gender Equity in Undergraduate CS Programs? *Proceedings of the 56th ACM Technical Symposium on Computer Science Education* v. 2, 1625–1626. https://doi.org/DOI: 10.1145/3641555.3705196

Tsai, Y.-C. (2023). Empowering Learner-Centered Instruction: Integrating ChatGPT Python API and Tinker Learning for Enhanced Creativity and Problem-Solving Skills. *Lecture Notes in Computer Science*, •••, 531–541. DOI: 10.1007/978-3-031-40113-8_52

Tuitt, F. (2023). Conclusion. *Race, Equity, and the Learning Environment*, 205–221. https://doi.org/DOI: 10.4324/9781003446637-16

United Nations. (2025). Goal 4 | Ensure Inclusive and Equitable Quality Education and Promote Lifelong Learning Opportunities for All. United Nations. https://sdgs.un.org/goals/goal4

Visual Language and Visual Learning (VL2). (n.d.). Gallaudet University. https://gallaudet.edu/visual-language-visual-learning/

Vrieler, T., & Salminen-Karlsson, M. (2022). *A Sociocultural Perspective on Computer Science Capital and its Pedagogical Implications in Computer Science Education*. ACM Transactions on Computing Education., DOI: 10.1145/3487052

Warner, J. R., Childs, J., Fletcher, C. L., Martin, N. D., & Kennedy, M. (2021). *Quantifying Disparities in Computing Education: Access*. Participation, and Intersectionality., DOI: 10.1145/3408877.3432392

Wille, S., Century, J., & Pike, M. (2017). Exploratory Research to Expand Opportunities in Computer Science for Students with Learning Differences. *Computing in Science & Engineering, 19*(3), 40–50. DOI: 10.1109/mcse.2017.43

Yu, E. (2018). The Impact of Culturally Inclusive Pedagogy on Student Achievement in a Multicultural Urban School Setting. *Urban Education, 57*(1), 004208591880401. DOI: 10.1177/0042085918804013

Zheng, Q., Li, Y., Yin, Q., Zhang, N., Wang, Y., Li, G., & Sun, Z. (2023). The effectiveness of problem-based learning compared with lecture-based learning in surgical education: A systematic review and meta-analysis. *BMC Medical Education, 23*(1). Advance online publication. DOI: 10.1186/s12909-023-04531-7 PMID: 37528406

KEY TERMS AND DEFINITIONS

Critical Pedagogy of Computational Access (CPCA): A theoretical framework that combines UDL and CRP to tackle the issue of marginalization in computer science by addressing the power dynamics related to structure, technology, and education.

Culturally Responsive Pedagogy (CRP): A teaching method that promotes the idea of incorporating students' cultural references and primary languages in every aspect of learning to create a feeling of belonging and academic identity.

Double-Cognitive Load: The major impediment faced by the students of the Global South who have to learn a foreign language (usually English) and at the same time master computational logic.

Inclusion by Addition: It is a management error that the inclusive demands are piled up on a teacher's job without the removal of prior standardized strain, thus, the teacher falls into the state of exhaustion and gives up.

Pedagogical Tokenism: The implementation of inclusive strategies for compliance that is merely surface-level, while the exclusionary curriculum and assessments remain unchanged at the core.

Techno-solutionism: The incorrect assumption that only the provision of hardware or software can eliminate the systemic educational inequalities without the need for any pedagogical and structural reforms.

The "Curb-Cut Effect": The accessibility feature phenomenon where the specific user group (e.g., dyslexic users and simplified coding syntax) not only gets the benefit of the feature but also the rest of the population such as English Language Learners and neurotypical students.

Universal Design for Learning (UDL): An educational framework consisting of three principles—Multiple Means of Representation, Action/Expression, and Engagement—that aim to provide equal learning opportunities for all students by eliminating barriers at the planning stage.

Chapter 8
Ethics and Responsible Computing in the Classroom:
Embedding Ethical Reasoning in Computer Science Education

Bright Keswani
https://orcid.org/0000-0003-1464-0431
Poornima University, Jaipur, India

ABSTRACT

Rapid growth in computing technologies has been witnessed in recent decades. Along with progress, serious ethical concerns have been raised. Issues of privacy, security, algorithmic bias, digital well-being, and the responsible use of artificial intelligence have become common. Students of computer science are expected to become future designers and innovators. They must be trained not only in technical knowledge but also in ethical responsibility. However, traditional curricula have placed more focus on programming, systems, and theory. Ethical aspects have often been left out or given little attention. To build responsible digital citizens, ethics must be included in classroom learning. This chapter focuses on the need to integrate ethics into computing education, and pedagogical practices, challenges, and strategies for responsible teaching have been discussed.

DOI: 10.4018/979-8-3373-6546-6.ch008

INTRODUCTION

Background: Computing Technologies and Ethical Concerns

The fast development of computing technologies has essentially changed the educational, industrial, and social aspects, reforming the decision-making process, knowledge creation, and provision of services. The field of artificial intelligence, data science, cybersecurity, and human-computer interaction is becoming an increasingly more mediating force in the allocation of resources and the human behavior, usually in large numbers and with little to no transparency (Khan et al., 2021; Holmes et al., 2022). With the integration of computing systems into educational institutions and daily living, ethical imperatives have ceased to be a professional idealistic pursuit to actual design and governance limitations that determine the material manifestation (Baumer, 2022; Belitz et al., 2024).

Professional organizations and policy groups are placing more emphasis on the idea that computing education should not just teach the student technical skills but also equip them with the ability to predict the effects of the computing technology, ethically assess trade-offs, and be responsible in relations to the complex socio-technical environment. The change reflects the increasingly high demands that ethics and responsible computing are not peripheral or optional subjects in modern computing programs but are now considered core subjects of computer science. The statistical data and tables in this chapter are intended as analysis tools and not description summaries. Rather than repeating narrative content, these artefacts are intended to support comparison across instructional models, clarify tensions between competing curricular priorities, and make explicit the structural implications of different pedagogical designs. Such use of visuals as conceptual scaffolds is consistent with design-based and framework-oriented scholarship in computing education, where diagrams and matrices are employed to support reasoning and curriculum planning rather than to present empirical measurements (Holmes et al., 2022; Brown et al., 2024).

Figure 1. Growth of computing technologies and emerging ethical concerns

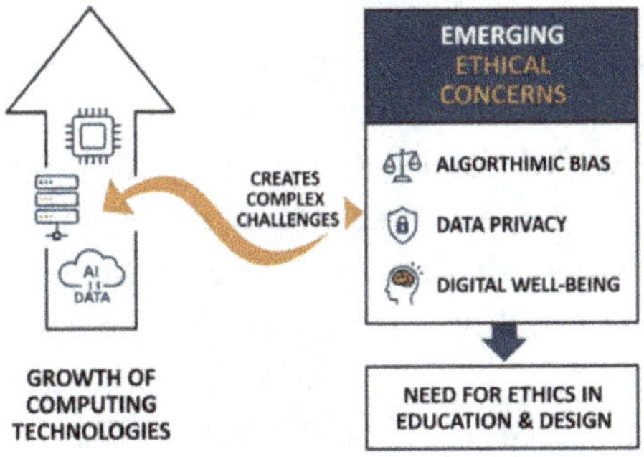

Human-computer Interaction also traverse deeply with ethical questions. The growing commonness of new and emerging technologies has sparked multiple debates about freedom, social responsibility, and digital well-being (Holmes et al., 2022; Vartiainen et al., 2024). Technologies change the way of learning between students and educators. It changes the way in learning environment and personal behavior, underlining the need of ethics in design and implementation (Neagu et al., 2025). Addressing ethical issues is not optional, it has become a necessity for future to navigate to a greater digital society. Ethical reasoning skills enable students to getting a deep understanding of how to implement technologies and understand their role in shaping responsible computing systems (Brown et al., 2024; Goetze, 2023).

Figure 2. Comparison of traditional vs. modern computer science curriculum focus

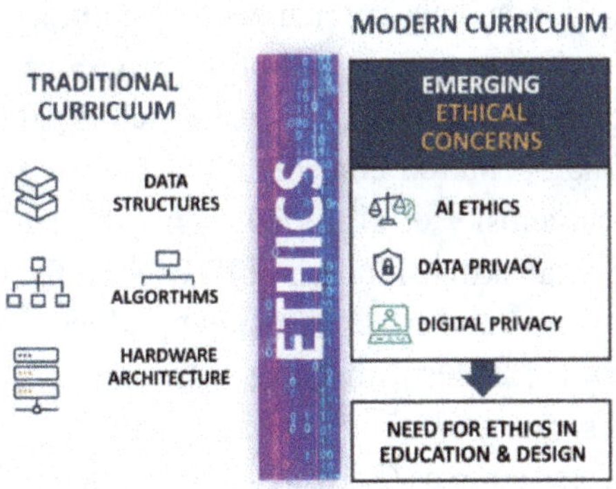

Importance of Ethics for Future Designers and Innovators

In today's technology-driven world, designers and innovators have unmatched influence over society through the systems and applications they create. Computing technologies such as AI, ML, and data analytics shape human decision-making and access to resources. As a result, the ethical responsibilities of future designers is increased to more than writing efficient code (Khan et al., 2021; Brown et al., 2024). The ethical responsibility is preventing unintentional harm. For example, algorithmic biasness in educational systems or hiring platforms cause social inequities without the intention (Bird et al., 2023; Idowu, 2024). Students are trained to identify such biasness during early stages in their education and are guided to use the gained knowledge to create systems which are fair, and are socially responsible. In the same way, privacy concerns in applications also need innovators to use secure and ethical data-handling practices (Baumer, 2022; Matei & Bertino, 2023). Responsible innovation is also majorly required in ethical awareness. Designers who consider human implications of technology create systems that promote equity and well-being (Holmes et al., 2022; Williams et al., 2023, Flechais & Chalhoub, 2023). Developing ethical awareness in computing education builds societal trust and accountability. Graduating students who use ethics in their daily professional practices are more likely to build systems that users trust and rely on responsibly (Neagu et al., 2025).

Current Gaps in Traditional Computer Science Curriculum

Even after the increasing recognition of ethics as an important part of computing education, many computer science curriculars still continue to treat ethics as not up important as other technical parts. Most of the programs give more importance to programming, algorithms, and system design while ethical reasoning, social responsibility, and human-centered considerations are treated as optional courses (Brown et al., 2024; Jarzemsky et al., 2023). This discrimination creates a gap between student's technical skills and their ability to see the consequences of their work. One of the major gaps is the lack of using of ethics with core technical subject. Students can learn algorithms, machine learning, or cybersecurity in depth, still they rarely discuss using of biased datasets, privacy violations, or security vulnerabilities within these courses (Bird et al., 2023; Idowu, 2024). Another major challenge is limitations of exposure to real-world ethical misconceptions. Many curriculars heavily depends on theoretical frameworks without making students use opportunities to apply ethics to real worlds scenarios, such as predictive analytics in education, automated decision-making systems, or AI-driven recommendation engines (Holmes et al., 2022; Khan et al., 2021). All the educators do not have the required knowledge of ethics (Flechais & Chalhoub, 2023). This gap result in major inconsistency in the teaching ethical concepts.

Further limitations extend to insufficient attention to emerging domains like AI fairness, digital well-being and cybersecurity ethics. The traditional modules and curriculars lack ethical challenges (Neagu et al., 2025). Graduates may enter into workplace with technical skills but will lack in complex ethical scenarios. Most Programs choose students primarily on technical skills, but there a minimal measure for reasoning, reflection, or ethical decision-making (Williams et al., 2023). Using this approach, it can improve critical thinking and can be beneficial in responsible practices.

MAIN FOCUS OF THE CHAPTER

Chapter Scope, Methodological Positioning, and Guiding Questions

This chapter does not report on an empirical experiment or statistical study. Instead, it is positioned as a design-based, evidence-informed pedagogical framework for ethics and responsible computing education. The objective is to synthesize peer-reviewed scholarship, international curriculum standards, and documented instructional practices to articulate design principles, pedagogical trade-offs, and implementation pathways for computing education.

The primary aim of this chapter is to study how ethics and responsible computing could be taught in a systematic way in the computer science learning environment. The focus is on pedagogical approaches, curriculum design issues, and teaching models that incorporate ethical reasoning in technical classes. Aspects of design trade-offs, implementation issues and context sensitive strategies focused on nurturing ethical awareness and responsibility in computing education are brought out in the chapter.

The chapter is guided by the following research-informed questions:

- RQ1: How can ethics and responsible computing be meaningfully embedded within technical computing courses without diluting disciplinary rigor?
- RQ2: Are there any pedagogical trade-offs between stand-alone ethics courses and embedded ethics modules?
- RQ3: How is it possible to reconcile ethics education with international curriculum and accreditation frameworks with context-sensitive, at the same time?

Pedagogical Contribution and Novelty of This Chapter

Although the significance of ethics in computing education has been widely reported in the previous literature, this chapter makes a step forward in arguing this by providing a design-based model of learning that explicitly connects moral values to the way the curriculum is designed, the type of learning strategies and assessment systems, as well as the readiness of the faculties. Instead of repeating the available recommendations, the chapter takes them and condenses them into a comprehensive, practically-oriented model that identifies design tensions and choice points that educators must address. The contribution that the chapter makes is in three areas:

(1) defining ethics as a design limitation that is part of technical computing education and not a peripheral subject;
(2) determining pedagogical trade-offs between embedded and stand-alone ethics teaching; and
(3) linking ethics education to curriculum alignment and assessment practices in a manner that will offer long-term sustainability.

With the preemptive planning of such design considerations, the chapter transcends descriptive review to a form-of constructive pedagogical intervention based on existing scholarship (Holmes et al., 2022; Brown et al., 2024).

Scope Delimitation and Domain Focus

Even though the topic of ethics in computing is multi-disciplinary, in this chapter, it is purposefully chosen to consider the area of artificial intelligence, data science, and cybersecurity education as a representative field where ethical issues may be both technically difficult and pedagogically relevant. Such areas are applied as referent anchor points in all parts of the chapter, and other domains, including HCI and digital well-being, have a supporting function. This narrow area of interest allows considering the ways in which ethics can be incorporated into courses that are technically intensive, and the trade-offs between the depth of the curriculum and its ethical coverage are most critical.

METHODS

Methodological Note on Figures and Conceptual Models

The numbers used in this chapter are not empirical data visualizations, but conceptual and analytical models. They are meant to combine information in the previous literature, curriculum frameworks and teaching practice into organized forms to facilitate reasoning, comparison and curriculum design decisions. They are not supposed to be statistical reports; the figures are supposed to serve as design artefacts, which shows a relationship between ethical principles, pedagogical strategies, and learning objectives. (Holmes et al., 2022; Brown et al., 2024).

Evidence Base and Use of Secondary Sources

Primary data collection is not mentioned in the chapter. Rather it is based on a systematic review of peer-reviewed articles, curricula models, accreditation, and recorded educational practices in computing education. The reasons behind the choice of sources were due to being relevant in their ethics integration, pedagogical design, and curriculum implementation as opposed to being empirical data to analyze statistically. Tables and summaries provided in the chapter may thus be interpreted as analytical summaries that summarize recurring themes, design dimensions, and pedagogical considerations as found throughout the literature. This method corresponds to the accepted traditions of conceptual and design-based scholarship in which secondary evidence is systematized in order to contribute to framework formation, but not hypothesis testing (Brown et al., 2024; Holmes et al., 2022).

Methodological Approach

Instead of hypothesis testing, the chapter uses an approach of analytic synthesis, and it incorporates convergent evidence in form of curriculum frameworks, accreditation guidelines and peer-reviewed educational research to prove its arguments.

ETHICAL ISSUES IN MODERN COMPUTING

Ethics in Artificial Intelligence and Algorithmic Bias

AI is giving new shapes to decision making in the various sectors which include education, healthcare and finance. AI give efficiency, increases power and scalable solutions but it also raises some ethical concerns like fairness, accountability, transparency and its impact to socials (Khan et al., 2021; Bird et al., 2023). The issue which arrives the most in AI ethics is biasness of Algorithm which are trained on the previous historical data. If these datasets reflect existing social inequalities, the AI systems can amplify them Automatically (Idowu, 2024; Vartiainen et al., 2024). Education in AI ethics should go include societal implications and students should think about the possible results of decisions took by AI on human behavior, equity and well-being. Engagement is practically much needed for learning ethics in AI. Project-based approaches, case studies, and real-world simulations allow students to differentiate between biasness and evaluate outcomes in various environments (Williams et al., 2023; Jarzemsky et al., 2023). Using AI ethics cultivates a mindset of responsibility. Students will get trained to recognize biasness, lookup for social consequences, and design unbiased systems are better and prepared to make their way in technological environments (Flechais & Chalhoub, 2023; Matei & Bertino, 2023).

Figure 3. Common ethical challenges in AI, cybersecurity, and data science

Privacy and Security in Data Science

Computing is reaching new heights by the adoption of various data-driven technologies, but it has also brought some major ethical concerns which related to privacy and security. Educational institutions, healthcare providers, financial organizations, and social platforms continuously collect, store, a huge amount personal data. This helps them for personalized learning, predictive analytics, and enhanced decision-making, they also increase risks of unauthorized access, and violations of the private data of users. (Baumer, 2022; Matei & Bertino, 2023). Students and educators generate large amounts of data. If this data is not secured, it can be on the verge or multiple risks and breaches. (Kozhuharova et al., 2022; Flechais & Chalhoub, 2023). Ensuring confidentiality, integrity, and availability of data is now becoming a major and necessary responsibility.

Data privacy requires a more careful approach. Students should be able to understand the process of how their data will be collected, stored, and used, and they should have control over these processes (Neagu et al., 2025). Ethical education ensures that data scientists must take care of privacy-by-design principles, and should ensure that the privacy is safe and security measures from the earliest stages of development. Security measure extends beyond multiple measures and implementations of ethical decision-making. (Holmes et al., 2022; Khan et al., 2021).

Ethical Challenges in Cybersecurity

Cybersecurity is an emerging domain which make organization and institutions store private and sensitive information on digital systems which grows the stakes of ethics in cybersecurity (Kozhuharova et al., 2022; Flechais & Chalhoub, 2023). Future professionals should understand the importance of ethics in the field of cyber security. Professionals are trusted with sensitive information that can lead to major threats which shows major ethical challenge of responsible handling of sensitive data (Matei & Bertino, 2023). Ensuring traits like confidentiality, integrity and availability while maintaining accountability in a major ethical responsibility. Ethical use of hacking and penetration testing techniques is another major concern. These skills are important in the field of cybersecurity but can also be used for malicious purposes. So, it increases the importance of teaching the ethics in the field of cybersecurity. (Lallie et al., 2022; Kozhuharova et al., 2022).

Rapid evolution of cyber threats introduces new ethical complexities. Emerging of new technologies like AI raises questions about accountability (Flechais & Chalhoub, 2023; Matei & Bertino, 2023). It increases need of evaluating social consequences by students before deploying certain technologies. Using of project-based learning, simulations, and case studies have proven effective in addressing these challenges (Williams et al., 2023; Jarzemsky et al., 2023). Responsible data stewardship, professional integrity, societal trust, and accountability should be taught before technical parts of the curricular (Kozhuharova et al., 2022; Matei & Bertino, 2023; Lallie et al., 2022).

Human-Computer Interaction and Social Responsibility

Human-Computer Interaction is very important part in developing the user experience and accessibility. Ethical considerations in HCI includes social responsibility, inclusivity, and human well-being (Holmes et al., 2022). Inclusive and equitable design major HCI concern. Failing to accommodate diverse user needs by systems can reinforce inequalities (Vartiainen et al., 2024; Williams et al., 2023). Using universal design principles and user centered research make sure that technologies turn out to be usable and beneficial for society.

Transparency and informed consent are also a key component. Users should know how their data is collected, processed, and utilized in applications that track behavior or personalize content (Baumer, 2022). Technologies can result in change in social behaviors and learning outcomes (Neagu et al., 2025; Holmes et al., 2022). For example, algorithmic content in education can put impact on student motivation, engagement, and access to multiple perspectives. Educating students to consider these effects increases awareness of responsibility to society.

Project-based learning, usability studies, and participatory design exercises are very good strategies for teaching ethical HCI (Williams et al., 2023; Jarzemsky et al., 2023). Students actively getting involved in designing systems with real users through which educators can bring forward ethical challenges such as biasness and multiple social consequences. A true ethical HCI education make sure that the technology should serve as a tool for empowerment instead of causing harm. HCI cannot be separated from social responsibility. Using ethical considerations in HCI education make students ready to design systems that are transparent, socially conscious, and aligned with human values, ensuring the integrity of the broader mission of responsible computing (Holmes et al., 2022; Vartiainen et al., 2024; Neagu et al., 2025).

Digital Well-being and Responsible Technology Use

Using of digital technologies into daily life, promoting digital well-being has become an important ethical practice in computing education. Digital well-being points to physical, psychological, and social health of users in relation to their technology use (Neagu et al., 2025). Using of technology in responsible way includes minimizing harm from improper technology exposure and also promote ethical relationship with digital systems.

Figure 4. Conceptual framework for digital responsibility and student impact

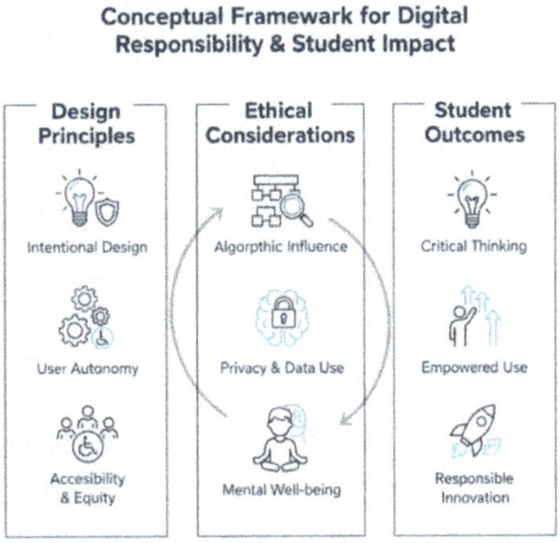

Overreliance on digital platforms is also a concern which is to be noted. Increasing usage of online learning systems and social media among students and professionals can result in learning overload, decreased attention, and reducing real-world social interactions (Vartiainen et al., 2024; Holmes et al., 2022). Increasing engagement and taking out valuable outcomes also involves the risk of unforeseen results which are not suitable (Bird et al., 2023; Idowu, 2024).

Equity and accessibility also come along with digital well-being. Using technology in ethical manner requires considering multiple needs of user (Williams et al., 2023; Vartiainen et al., 2024). Using these principles in classroom projects or case studies can help students increase their understanding of the social impact of their designs. Reflection, discussion, and experiential learning also get involved while promoting user well-being. self-assessment of digital habits and analyzing ethical scenarios encourage students to engage with the human consequences towards technology (Jarzemsky et al., 2023; Holmes et al., 2022). Digital well-being and responsible use of technology are very important in ethical computing education. (Neagu et al., 2025; Vartiainen et al., 2024; Bird et al., 2023).

Table 1. Analytical synthesis of ethical design dimensions across computing domains

Domain	Key Ethical Concerns	Examples / Issues Highlighted
Artificial Intelligence (AI)	Algorithmic bias, transparency, accountability	Biased predictive models, black-box decision systems
Data Science	Privacy, security, responsible data handling	Unauthorized access, data misuse, lack of consent
Cybersecurity	Integrity, responsible use of skills, accountability	Ethical hacking misuse, threats to confidentiality
Human-Computer Interaction (HCI)	Inclusivity, accessibility, social responsibility	Inequitable design, manipulation of user behavior

Table 1 does not present empirical variables or measured outcomes. Instead, it synthesizes ethical design dimensions that recur across computing education literature and professional frameworks. Concepts such as algorithmic bias, transparency, and accountability are treated as analytical categories used to structure curriculum design, instructional activities, and assessment criteria rather than as operationalized variables.

These dimensions are widely used in ethics and responsible computing scholarship to guide pedagogical reasoning and curriculum alignment, particularly in framework-based and design-oriented educational research (Brown et al., 2024). This table summarizes the major ethical concerns across different computing domains. While AI faces issues of bias and transparency, data science struggles with privacy and security. Cybersecurity highlights responsible use of sensitive data, whereas HCI emphasizes inclusivity, accessibility, and social responsibility.

PEDAGOGICAL APPROACHES FOR INTEGRATING ETHICS

Pedagogical Scaffolding and Design Logic

Pedagogical strategies addressed in this chapter are not suggested to be universal and effective solutions but design strategies based on the documented educational practice and theory. Their integration follows a scaffolding rationale that ties learning activities (e.g., case analysis, project-based learning, reflection) with particular learning goals, e.g., ethical awareness, reasoning, and decision justification. This scaffolding focuses on progression: students initially gain conceptual knowledge about the principles of ethics, and then they combine this knowledge into technical contexts, and last, they reflect on trade-offs and implications. The design of such a staged learning process is common in computing education and the ethics pedagogy as a process of promoting sustainable ethical competence and not merely superficial compliance (Holmes et al., 2022; Jarzemsky et al., 2023; Brown et al., 2024). The effectiveness of pedagogical methods in this chapter is referred to in a contextualized and qualified manner based on the documented results written in the literature of computing education instead of general causal assertion. Studies cited typically assess effectiveness through qualitative indicators such as student reflection, ethical awareness, reasoning quality, and engagement, often within specific institutional or curricular contexts (Jarzemsky et al., 2023; Williams et al., 2023).

Accordingly, this chapter does not claim that particular instructional methods "work" in all settings. Instead, it identifies conditions under which certain approaches are more likely to support ethical learning, while acknowledging limitations related to curriculum time, faculty expertise, and assessment practices (Holmes et al., 2022; Brown et al., 2024).

Teaching Methods for Embedding Ethics with Technical Content

Modern curricular should include ethics directly into technical part instead of including it as an optional topic, which allows students to adapt principles of responsible computing with practical system design (Holmes et al., 2022). One of the major approaches includes case-based learning, in which students learn to real-world scenarios (Bird et al., 2023; Idowu, 2024).

Project-based learning is another highly effective method in PBL, students design and evaluate systems while implementing ethical challenges like fairness and security (Williams et al., 2023; Jarzemsky et al., 2023). Using discussion and reflection exercises alongside technical courses increases the knowledge of ethical awareness (Flechais & Chalhoub, 2023). Students getting involved in projects that inclines with social sciences, law, or healthcare which helps them get experience of the technical work (Holmes et al., 2022). Ethical reasoning can be used in multiple aspects like design decisions team communication, stakeholder analysis, and policy awareness. Using technology-enabled teaching tools as an advantage for tasks like simulations, interactive modules, and ethical decision-making platforms gives multiple beneficial ways to implement ethics in technical courses (Khan et al., 2021; Neagu et al., 2025).

Stand-alone Ethics Courses vs. Embedded Modules

The embedding of ethics into computing education can use two primary approaches: stand-alone ethics courses and including ethics modules within technical courses. Each way offers new and unique advantages and challenges, and it is necessary to understand the impact of each way which is essential for designing effective curricular that encourage responsible computing practices (Holmes et al., 2022). Stand-alone ethics courses mainly focus on ethical theory, professional codes of conduct, social responsibility, and broader societal implications of computing. A dedicated space to explore philosophical principles, legal frameworks, and case studies is provided to students through these courses Where the immediate pressure of technical application is not required (Brown et al., 2024; Jarzemsky et al., 2023). Stand-alone courses is beneficial because it can used to build a strong base of knowledge of ethical reasoning which grant advantage for multiple discussion and reflection. A limitation which can be possible is disconnecting from technical coursework, which can result in taking ethics as secondary course (Bird et al., 2023; Idowu, 2024).

Including ethics modules is process which it is directly included in technical courses such as algorithms, AI, cybersecurity, or human-computer interaction. This approach is beneficial in the context of practical challenges, making it suitable to students' technical work (Williams et al., 2023; Neagu et al., 2025). Advantage includes normalizing ethical reasoning as part of the engineering process, which encourage students to use moral values along with technical problem-solving. Embedded modules can also have some challenges such as time constraints and inconsistent faculty expertise (Flechais & Chalhoub, 2023). Students will be able to receive only a limited exposure without careful design of curricular. Educators who are in support of hybrid approach are getting benefits of both methods. Stand-alone courses can be a base for Introductory ethical knowledge and embedded modules can support and expand pathways through this gained knowledge (Jarzemsky et al., 2023). Using both approaches helps computing programs in producing graduates who are good in technical skills and have ethical knowledge. Educators can ensure that ethics becomes a core, actionable component of computing courses instead of a optional course (Bird et al., 2023; Williams et al., 2023). While stand-alone courses offer conceptual depth, they risk isolation from practice when not reinforced through embedded application (Holmes et al., 2022; Jarzemsky et al., 2023; Brown et al., 2024).

Project-Based Learning and Case Study Approaches

Project-based learning and case study methods are stated as important and effective strategies for using ethics within computing education. These methods help students to solve real-world problems and helps them to apply their technical knowledge while reflecting on ethical implications (Williams et al., 2023; Jarzemsky et al., 2023). Project-based learning helps students gain hands-on experiences which teach them how ethics should be used with technical challenges. For example, educational platform with AI-Integration developed by students can figure out algorithmic bias and data privacy issues (Bird et al., 2023; Idowu, 2024). PBL encourages critical thinking, moral reflection, and practical accountability, that helps students understand effect of their design decisions on society (Holmes et al., 2022; Khan et al., 2021). Also, it encourages team-based ethical decision-making.

Case studies provide a real-world example of ethical challenges in computing. Students evaluate and analyze real-world scenarios, such as data breaches, algorithmic discrimination, or cybersecurity to figure out the results of design choices, choosing different approaches, and give solutions with respect to ethical principles (Flechais & Chalhoub, 2023). Case studies also benefit in discussion and reflection, which enables students to explore different and multiple views to understand the societal, legal, and cultural dimensions (Neagu et al., 2025). Combining PBL and case studies increases the connection strength between theory and practice. case studies give the conceptual framework for ethical analysis, Students experiment with solutions and lookout for outcomes in various type of environments (Williams et al., 2023; Jarzemsky et al., 2023).

Table 2. Comparative analysis of teaching methods: lectures, projects, case studies, and PBL

Teaching Method	Strengths	Limitations
Lectures	Provide theoretical foundation, structured knowledge	Passive learning, limited critical engagement
Projects	Encourage hands-on application and problem-solving	Resource intensive, requires close supervision
Case Studies	Expose real-world dilemmas, encourage reflection	May lack generalization beyond specific context
Project-Based Learning (PBL)	Integrates technical + ethical reasoning, promotes collaboration	Demands high faculty expertise and student time

This table compares four teaching methods for integrating ethics into computing. While lectures provide foundational knowledge, projects and case studies allow practical application and ethical reflection. PBL stands out by combining technical learning with ethical decision-making but requires strong facilitation.

Encouraging Reasoning, Reflection, and Ethical Decision-Making

Literacy in ethics for computing is necessary for students to actively reason, reflect, and make informed decisions real-world scenarios. Using these skills develop prepares future designers and innovators to observe how technology can increase its efficiency and figure out how to increase it, which aligning multiple technical solutions with various societal values (Holmes et al., 2022).

Ethical reasoning makes students analyze situations in various ways and prepare of possible results of technical actions (Bird et al., 2023; Idowu, 2024). This practice inspires students to treat design decisions in a systematic and ethical way instead of entirely depending on technical aspects. Reflection helps increase self-awareness and moral sensitivity. Activities such as journals, guided discussions, or peer review session encourage students figure out multiple ethical aspects about projects, and figure out the result of their work on various communities (Flechais & Chalhoub, 2023). Ethical decision-making maintains the reasoning and reflection in practical challenges. Students face challenges such as user privacy versus data utility or accessibility versus security which must be balanced (Holmes et al., 2022; Khan et al., 2021). The systematic way of making decisions makes the learners explain their decisions and seek alternative solutions that equip them with real-world duties. Such approaches as simulations, role-playing, and scenario-based exercises, give students various experience to make ethical decisions (Williams et al., 2023; Jarzemsky et al., 2023).

Measuring Student Engagement and Learning Outcomes

Ethical training in computing is also significant so that students may acquire knowledge and ethical reasoning, reflective skills, and responsible decision-making abilities. The quantification of student engagement and learning outcomes lead to informative feedback that aids in a revision of future decisions and changes (Holmes et al., 2022). It is possible to examine student engagement in ethics in a variety of ways that involve participating in discussions, making contributions to case studies, and engaging in project-based learning (Williams et al., 2023; Jarzemsky et al., 2023). High level of engagement shows good reaction to the practice of the real-life computing tasks (Flechais and Chalhoub, 2023). Learning outcome determines the skill acquired to recognize ethical concerns, evaluate the effects of the stakeholders, implement professional codes of conduct, and make well-informed decisions (Bird et al., 2023; Idowu, 2024).

Figure 5. Flowchart showing how reasoning and reflection can be incorporated into learning

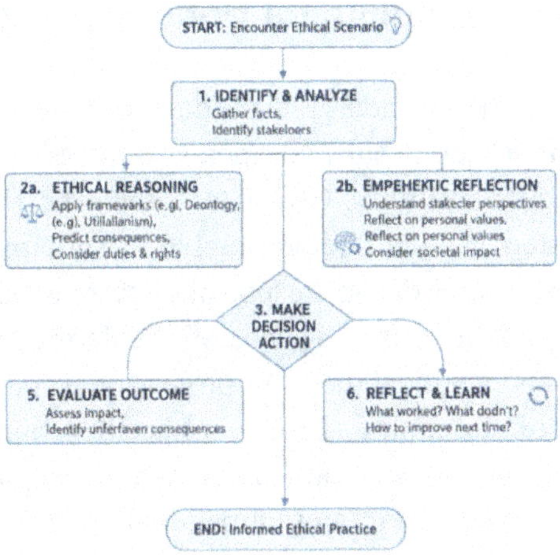

Assessment reliability and consistency are some of the benefits of rubrics and systematic evaluation frameworks. It establishes some criteria such as identifying ethical concerns, weighing the outcomes and analysis of stakeholders with the help of which educators can juxtapose the performance of both the individual and the group (Holmes et al., 2022; Neagu et al., 2025). Technology-assisted assessment presents a number of possibilities as well. The platforms and simulations used online document all the interactions that occurred between the students, their decision-making paths, and the outcome of a situation, which offers data-driven insights (Khan et al., 2021; Matei and Bertino, 2023).

Table 3. Metrics for measuring student engagement and learning outcomes in ethical education

Metric Category	Indicators
Engagement	Participation in discussions, contributions to projects, involvement in simulations
Ethical Reasoning	Ability to identify ethical issues, apply frameworks, and analyze stakeholder impact
Reflection	Depth of self-assessment journals, quality of peer reviews, critical debate skills
Decision-Making	Balancing trade-offs, justifying choices, proposing responsible solutions

This table outlines the metrics used to measure student engagement and learning outcomes in ethics education. The indicators range from active participation to the demonstration of ethical reasoning, reflective thinking, and structured decision-making.

CURRICULUM DESIGN AND IMPLEMENTATION

Designing Ethics Curriculum for Undergraduate Programs

Using ethics as a subject into undergraduate computing programs needs a strategic curriculum design which keeps a balance among technical skill development, moral reasoning and social responsibility. Graduates should be fluent in programming and analytical competencies and dhould be able to anticipate ethical challenges, evaluate societal impact, and design responsible systems (Holmes et al., 2022). Foundational courses are the base of a successful undergraduate ethics curriculum which teach students about ethical theories, professional codes of conduct, and the societal implications of computing (Brown et al., 2024; Jarzemsky et al., 2023). Important topics which should be included are algorithmic fairness, privacy, cyber security ethics, digital well-being, and human-computer interaction (Bird et al., 2023; Vartiainen et al., 2024). Involving ethical subjects with technical courses is very important for giving support to ethical application. Using these modules with subjects like programming, AI, data science, and systems design gain students experience of real-work ethical challenges (Williams et al., 2023; Idowu, 2024).

Assessment strategies evaluate both ethical reasoning and technical competency. Rubrics differentiate students on their ability of finding ethical issues, analyzing stakeholder impact and give responsible solutions (Neagu et al., 2025; Flechais & Chalhoub, 2023).

Integrating Responsible Computing in Postgraduate Studies

Computing programs of postgraduate level gives benefits to students who are assuming leadership roles in technology development, research, and policy implementation. (Holmes et al., 2022). The postgraduate programs need to include advanced coursework to cover the more complicated ethical issues posed by a variety of emerging technologies like Cybersecurity, Artificial Intelligence, Cloud Computing, and Bigdata Analytics (Bird et al., 2023; Matei and Bertino, 2023). Some of the topics may be algorithmic transparency, mitigation of bias, privacy-preserving data architecture, responsible AI governance, and the impact of automated systems on society (Idowu, 2024; Vartiainen et al., 2024). This especially applies to the postgraduate level of inter-disciplinary cooperation. The students have an opportunity to communicate with professionals in the fields of law, social sciences, business ethics, and policy studies to have a holistic view of the regulatory, cultural, and social aspects of technology implementation (Holmes et al., 2022).

Responsible computing can be studied through research oriented learning which provides post graduate students with such a platform. Real-life practical experience is provided by projects that require some ethical assessment of experimental approaches, data gathering, algorithm development, or cybersecurity culture (Williams et al., 2023; Jarzemsky et al., 2023). Simulated technologies in the real world such as simulation, policy analysis exercises and case studies challenges students to consider alternatives, analyze, and provide responsible solutions (Flechais and Chalhoub, 2023). In this manner, postgraduate students are able to gain strategic thinking and leadership skills.

Figure 6. Curriculum framework integrating ethics across undergraduate and postgraduate programs

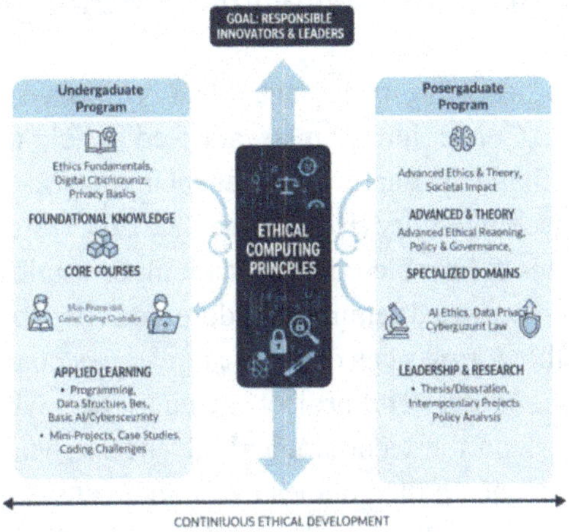

Faculty Preparedness and Training

Faculty readiness and continuous professional growth are critical to the successful implementation of ethics and responsible computing into the curricula. Teachers should not only be technologically skilled but also need to be aware of ethical values, social consequences, and teaching approaches that would help them educate the students to follow responsible computing habits (Holmes et al., 2022). Ethical competency among faculty lies in its basis. They are expected to know the issues of privacy, cybersecurity, algorithmic bias, digital well-being, and human-computer interaction ethics (Bird et al., 2023; Idowu, 2024). Knowledge of professional code of conduct, regulations, and international standards can guarantee that faculty members can impart ethics in a way that would be acceptable in the world as people have to deal with, and in new technological issues (Matei and Bertino, 2023). Pedagogical training is as well significant. Faculty should use the abilities to teach ethics into technical classes, conduct a reflective conversation, conduct a case-based examination, and apply project-based learning (Williams et al., 2023; Jarzemsky et al., 2023). Organized training, workshops, seminars equip the instructor with approaches to insert the ethical information into programming courses, AI courses, data science courses, and cybersecurity courses in an almost transparent manner (Flechais and Chalhoub, 2023).

Faculty preparedness is increased by interdisciplinary exposure. By working with professionals in social sciences, law, and public policy, instructors can have a wider lens and apply it to the societal and cultural aspects of computing in a responsible manner (Holmes et al., 2022).

Curriculum Flexibility and Assessment Strategies

Ethics curriculum designing must have a balance between structured learning and adaptive learning. Curriculum changes adopted to help the students be able to contemplate real-life challenges, and assessment plans that track the level of technical mastery and ethical accountability (Holmes et al., 2022). Curriculum flexibility ensures that the new issues of AI ethics, data privacy, algorithmic responsibility, digital well-being, and cybersecurity dilemma are addressed (Bird et al., 2023; Matei and Bertino, 2023). Flexible formats can comprise of elective courses, integrated ethics courses with technical courses and project learning. This will enable the teachers to instruct the learners on the technological advances, social issues and local or international developments in the policies (Vartiainen et al., 2024).

The assessment strategies follow the capacity of the students to reason, reflect and make responsible decisions. Sufficient evaluations involve case study analyses, reflective journals, scenario-based evaluations, project presentations, as well as peer reviews (Williams et al., 2023; Jarzemsky et al., 2023). Rubrics present a clear criterion, according to which an ethical reasoning, stakeholder analysis, social impact, and adoption of ethical principles in relation to technical decisions should be judged (Neagu et al., 2025; Flechais and Chalhoub, 2023).

Figure 7. Outline of curriculum flexibility and assessment strategy.

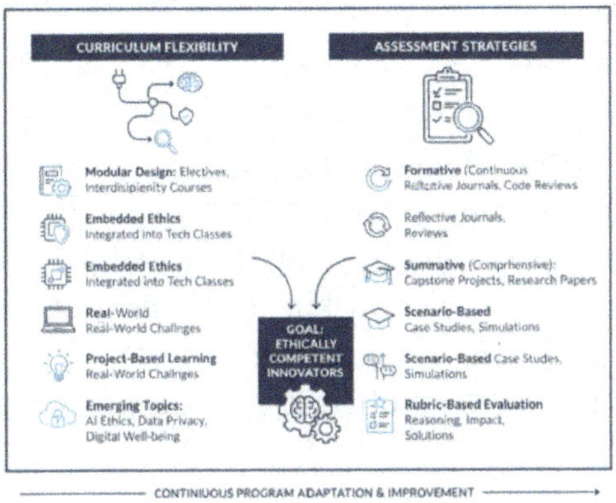

Alignment with International Guidelines (ABET, ACM/IEEE)

The mention of professional and policy associations in this chapter like the ACM, IEEE, ABET, and OECD are not meant to be normative approvals but rather analytical referencing points when aligning the curriculum. These frameworks were reviewed to find out the recurring expectation with regards to ethical reasoning, societal impact, professional responsibility and learning outcomes in computing education. The evaluation was on three dimensions:

(1) how ethics fits in curriculum arrangements,
(2) the types of competencies that are stressed (e.g., ethical reasoning, accountability, social impact), and
(3) implications for assessment and design of instructions.

This comparative reading allows the chapter to trace the pedagogical strategies in the literature to the commonly followed curriculum expectations, to indicate areas of overlap and practical usefulness. Ensuring that ethics education is in line with the international standards and guidelines is highly essential to graduates of international competence, social responsibility and professional accountability. According to the following organizations such as ABET, ACM, and IEEE, there are structured models that indicate an incorporation of ethical reasoning, social impact, and professional responsibility in computing curricular (Holmes et al., 2022). ABET accreditation standards shows the value of professional and ethical responsibility. Computing programs looking for ABET recognition are proposed to show how students can analyze the impact of computing solutions, including ethical, legal, and cultural considerations into their process of decision-making (Bird et al., 2023; Matei & Bertino, 2023).

Following these standards maintains consistency and quality in education of ethics. Following these internationally recognized frameworks, students can be provided comparable ethical foundations (Flechais & Chalhoub, 2023). Practical implementation includes keeping track of learning, inclusion of ethics into both core and elective courses, and building assessment tools which measures the ethical reasoning and responsible decision-making (Jarzemsky et al., 2023). case studies, simulations, and project-based exercises can also be used by Institutions to showcase students that are technically proficient, ethically competent and socially aware.

Table 4. Alignment of curriculum components with ABET and ACM/IEEE standards

Curriculum Component	ABET Focus	ACM/IEEE Focus
Core Courses	Ethical responsibility as part of learning outcomes	Professional ethics, privacy, security, fairness
Embedded Ethics Modules	Applying ethical reasoning in technical work	Integration into AI, HCI, cybersecurity, data science
Project-Based Learning	Societal impact analysis in design projects	Experiential learning and interdisciplinary collaboration
Assessment Strategies	Evaluation of ethical decision-making skills	Rubrics for fairness, transparency, and accountability
Capstone/Research Projects	Comprehensive ethical + technical integration	Demonstrating responsible innovation practices

This table compares curriculum components with ABET and ACM/IEEE standards, showing how international frameworks emphasize professional responsibility, fairness, transparency, and accountability within computing education.

CASE STUDIES AND BEST PRACTICES

Examples of Successful Ethics Integration in Classrooms

Including ethics into computing education is proven most effective. Various documented approaches show how classrooms can encourage responsible computing (Holmes et al., 2022).

One example which can be noted is the inclusion of ethics modules with AI and data science courses at some of the leading universities. Students in these programs analyze algorithmic biasness, privacy concerns, and social implications (Bird et al.,

2023; Idowu, 2024). By practicing ethical reflection with hands-on projects students can develop ability to consider social impact during system design.

Project-based learning showcases the proof of success. For example, cybersecurity courses encourage students in simulations that based on real-world security breaches. These exercises teach them about balancing of technical solutions with ethical responsibility (Williams et al., 2023; Jarzemsky et al., 2023). Students develop problem-solving skills and learn importance of ethical decision-making.

Curriculars containing case-studies is beneficial in teaching related to ethics in HCI, software engineering, and data analytics. Courses which use detailed case studies on topics such as digital well-being, algorithmic discrimination, and responsible AI deployment can inspire students' interest on stakeholder interests, social implications, and long-term consequences of technical design (Flechais & Chalhoub, 2023). Programs that include peers from law, social sciences, or business ethics in student's curriculum which allow participants to view technical decisions from various perspectives and multiple factors (Holmes et al., 2022). These projects can increase engagement and ethical awareness.

Table 5. Examples of successful ethics integration in computer science courses worldwide

Institution/Region	Integration Approach	Outcomes Achieved
Leading AI Programs (US/ Europe)	Embedded ethics modules in AI/ Data Science courses	Students design fairer, transparent models
Cybersecurity Courses	Real-world simulations of breaches	Students balance technical fixes with ethical responsibility
HCI and Software Engineering	Case studies on digital well-being and inclusivity	Increased awareness of user diversity and societal impact
Interdisciplinary Programs	Collaboration with law/social sciences	Students develop holistic ethical reasoning

This table showcases global examples of ethics integration. Inclusion of ethics in AI, cybersecurity, HCI, and interdisciplinary settings shows that students gain technical proficiency, ethical awareness and accountability.

Comparative Analysis of Teaching Models

Inclusion of ethics in computing education can be done by various teaching models. A comparative analysis shows strategies which are more beneficial in encouraging in ethical reasoning, reflective practice, and responsible decision-making (Holmes et al., 2022).

Stand-alone ethics courses focus more on ethical principles, professional standards, and social implications (Brown et al., 2024; Jarzemsky et al., 2023). These courses give discussion on topics such as algorithmic bias, cybersecurity ethics, and digital well-being. However, it lacks hands-on technical practice, which results in students considering it as an additional course.

Embedded ethics modules include ethical modules with technical courses such as AI, data science, or software engineering (Williams et al., 2023; Idowu, 2024). This approach state ethical reasoning as an important part in the process of designing.

Technical development with ethical reflection is combined in Project-based learning model through hands-on assignments (Bird et al., 2023; Jarzemsky et al., 2023). Students facing real-world challenges like designing of fair algorithms or secure systems benefits in developing skills like critical thinking, collaboration, case study analyses and accountability (Flechais & Chalhoub, 2023).

Lessons Learned from Curriculum Implementation

The application of ethics and responsible computing within classroom environments has shown that there are a number of important lessons that are taught about pedagogy, student involvement, and curriculum. Lessons can assist in informing the best practices in creating programs that produce technically proficient and ethically conscious graduates (Holmes et al., 2022). Among all, it has been confirmed that ethics education is more effectively implemented as a part of technical courses, instead of being taught separately (Williams et al., 2023; Idowu, 2024). The students react better to the situations when the ethical reasoning is properly linked to practical projects: the algorithm design, AI implementation, or cybersecurity simulation.

Case studies, project-based learning, and interactive simulation are some of the best methods to enhance reflection, reasoning, and decision-making abilities among students (Bird et al., 2023; Jarzemsky et al., 2023). The focus on practical uses of curriculum helps students think about the effects on the society and the opinions of the stakeholders, which develops a greater significance between the ethics and the technical competency (Flechais and Chalhoub, 2023). It requires successful execution of instructions by instructors that are both technically skilled and familiar with ethical concepts and teaching methods (Holmes et al., 2022). Measures of ethical learning outcome, such as rubrics, scenario-based tests, reflective journals, and peer review, will make sure that measures of technical competence are matched with ethical competence (Neagu et al., 2025; Khan et al., 2021).

Results states that combination of frequent feedback and summative evaluation encourages ethical reasoning. Flexibility and adaptability are necessary because of the fast evolution of technology and societal norms which requires curricular that can contain emerging topics such as AI ethics, data privacy, and digital well-being (Vartiainen et al., 2024).

Figure 8. Stepwise implementation of ethics modules in a classroom

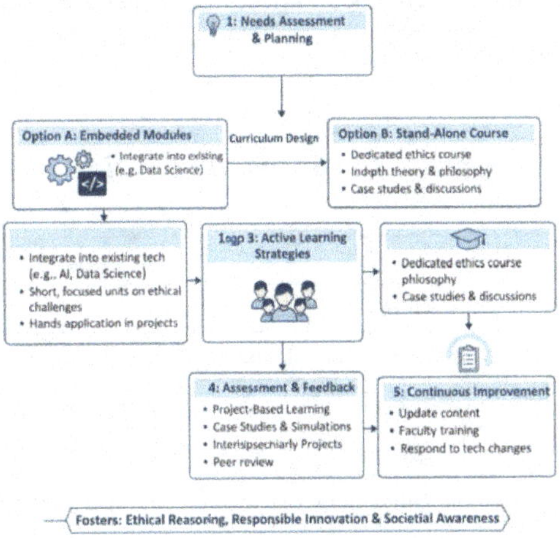

RECOMMENDATIONS FOR RESPONSIBLE COMPUTING EDUCATION

Practical Recommendations for Building Ethical Awareness

Spreading ethical awareness among computing students' needs various strategies, structures curricular design, and constant support from institutions. These strategies increase moral reasoning and get students prepared to make responsible decisions in professional and social contexts (Holmes et al., 2022). Ethical awareness is most effective when students encounter real-worlds ethical challenges (Williams et al., 2023; Idowu, 2024).

Project-based learning, real-world case studies and simulations increases critical thinking and reflective practice (Bird et al., 2023; Jarzemsky et al., 2023). Encouraging students for hands-on projects to make them face real-worlds consequences and design responsible solutions. Guiding students to work with peers from law, social sciences, and policy disciplines increases their understanding of the regulatory, cultural, and social dimensions of technology (Holmes et al., 2022). Interdisciplinary projects emphasize the social impact of technical choices and assist students to value different viewpoints in the process of ethical thinking. The self-awareness and moral judgment are achieved through reflection activities, such as journals, discussion boards, and peer feedback (Flechais and Chalhoub, 2023Narrative frameworks also assist the students in dealing with complicated scenarios in which the technical, social, and legal factors interconnect. These tools provide students with an opportunity to test their ethical decision-making according to the controlled conditions with instant feedback about the outcomes of responsible and irresponsible computing (Neagu et al., 2025; Khan et al., 2021).

Table 6. Practical recommendations for building ethical awareness and inclusive perspectives

Recommendation Area	Strategies
Curriculum Design	Embed ethics into technical courses, not as optional add-ons
Active Learning	Use projects, simulations, and case studies for hands-on ethical challenges
Interdisciplinary Learning	Collaborate with law, policy, and social sciences for broader perspectives
Reflection Practices	Encourage journals, peer reviews, and debates for self-awareness
Global/Inclusive Approach	Use multicultural case studies, inclusive design, and accessibility standards
Faculty & Institutional Support	Provide training, resources, and incentives for ethics integration

This table summarizes practical steps for fostering ethical awareness. It demonstrates the incorporation of ethics, dynamic, interdisciplinary learning, and the encouragement of inclusive global attitudes, in the curriculum directly.

Strategies for Promoting Global and Inclusive Perspectives

Although the global responsibility is a major theme in the computing ethics, there is a wide range of difference in teaching of ethics in different regions, types of institutions and regulation. Ethical instruction in computing can be integrated into curriculum through different means, depending on differences in accreditation systems, cultural norms, resource availability and policy frameworks. Interdisciplinary projects such as collective AI ethics tasks make students think about the rules, accessibility and fairness worldwide. Courses encourage designing of systems which contain users with different abilities and languages (Flechais & Chalhoub, 2023).

Reflection activities, like discussion boards or journals help students analyze the impact of technology on various communities (Williams et al., 2023; Jarzemsky et al., 2023). This practice increases empathy, global awareness, and ethical sensitivity in process of decision-making. Introduction of students to international standards like the OECD AI Principles or ACM/IEEE ethical codes, allows them to take global norms under considerations in the process of designing of technology (Matei &

Bertino, 2023; Vartiainen et al., 2024). Interactive platforms and scenario-based simulations grant students various social contexts to test systems and observe possible ethical results of their choices of design (Neagu et al., 2025; Khan et al., 2021). These exercises develop practical skills in designing solutions that are used by global populations.

Roadmap for Connecting Ethics Education with Workforce and Society

Ethics education usage in real-world need a clear roadmap which joins classroom learning with professional practice and social responsibility. Future graduates who are ethically aware and workforce-ready needs a professionally developed learning path (Holmes et al., 2022). Ethics education should be included with the codes of conduct and proper guidelines by professional bodies, such as ACM and IEEE, to teach students about research pracices (Bird et al., 2023; Matei & Bertino, 2023). Incorporating these standards into assignments, projects, and assessments is a way of training the students to handle ethical dilemmas they will face in their careers. Working with technology firms, startups, and governmental entities can give students a practical experience of ethical issues in the real world (Williams et al., 2023; Jarzemsky et al., 2023). The internships, mentorship programs, and capstone projects enable students to implement ethical thinking over practical issues, e.g., privacy-not-violating data processing, conscious AI application, or mitigation of cybersecurity attacks. Students are expected to consider larger-scale impact of their technical solutions on stakeholders, communities, and the environment (Idowu, 2024; Flechais and Chalhoub, 2023). As an illustration, examining the impact that an AI-based service can have on marginalized groups promotes responsible innovation and creates the conditions in which technology is created to the advantage of the society.

Figure 9. Roadmap for implementing ethics education from classroom to global workforce

Professional reflection organized around professional experiences, simulation, and scenario-based exercises help fill in the knowledge gap between theory and practice (Neagu et al., 2025; Khan et al., 2021). Students are exposed to how to foresee ethics threats, defend decisions, and realize repercussions in a safe but realistic environment which will increase readiness to workforce issues. They should develop an ethics education that instills a culture of lifelong moral thinking, ready students to deal with new technologies, new social norms, and new regulatory demands (Holmes et al., 2022). When ethical principles are internalized by graduates, they are in a better position to promote responsible practices, shape organizational culture and be a positive influence to the society. The involvement of students in ethically responsible professionals and alumni opens new possibilities of guidance and discussion, as well as mentoring, which supports the practical significance of ethics in professional life (Bird et al., 2023; Williams et al., 2023).

Preparing Students for Ethical Challenges in a Digital Society

The swift emerging digital technologies have established a situation where the computing profession encounters sophisticated ethical dilemmas, including those of AI decision-making and the privacy of personal data, as well as cybersecurity issues and the effects of technology on the society. The training of students to work in this environment will need a complex strategy including knowledge, critical thinking, and reflexivity (Holmes et al., 2022). Learn to reason critically on ethical matters. The learners should be taught how to recognize ethical dilemmas, dissect competing interests, and how to predict the possible outcomes of technological interventions (Bird et al., 2023; Idowu, 2024).

Incorporation of both scenario-based exercises, case studies and real-world problem-solving activities in courses also provide students with the ability to identify the ethical aspect of the work they do and to make effective decisions. Educating students on inclusivity, accessibility, and social responsibility will make sure that they comprehend the overall implications of their designs and uses (Flechais and Chalhoub, 2023).

Multiple perspectives from law, social sciences, and public policy increase students' skill to figure out social implications, use ethical decision-making frameworks, provide structured approaches which helps in responsible decisions making (Holmes et al., 2022; Khan et al., 2021). Activities such as reflective journals, peer discussions, and immersive simulations enable students to experiment with digital technologies while taking care of ethical consequences (Neagu et al., 2025; Williams et al., 2023). Students should be prepared for current and future challenges by including courses like AI ethics, cyber security, data privacy, algorithmic biasness, digital well-being, and environmental sustainability in curricular (Matei & Bertino, 2023; Vartiainen et al., 2024).

Figure 10. Framework connecting ethics education with societal and professional expectations

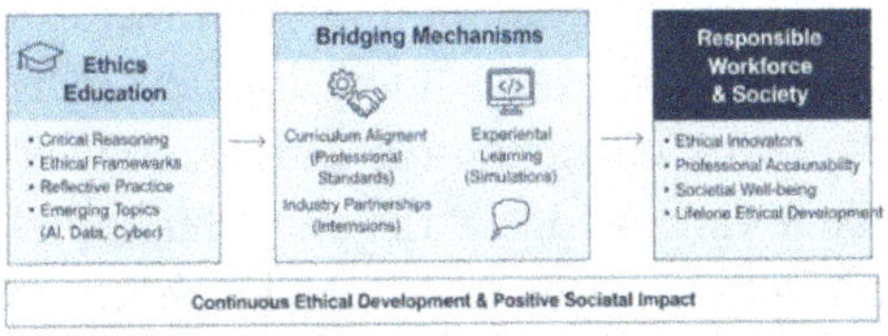

CONCLUSION

This chapter does not purport to be able to empirically show learning outcomes or teaching effectiveness. Rather, it represents a conceptualized pedagogical case of how ethics and responsible computing should be infused in technical education by employing design-oriented curriculum approaches. Combining the available literature and professional paradigms, the chapter helps to make sense of the major pedagogical decisions, trade-offs, and implementation strategies that teachers have to take.

This work has a contribution of being able to facilitate informed curriculum design and not reporting the evaluative results. The empirical studies that are yet to be carried out in the future must evaluate the effects of certain applications of these design principles on student learning and professional practice in different learning settings.

Recap of Key Findings

This chapter suggests that ethics and responsible computing should be a core issue in computing education and not a peripheral or optional subject in computing education. By means of organised synthesis of curriculum guidelines, pedagogical studies and reports on the educational practices, the chapter shows how ethical reasoning can be systematically incorporated in technical computing curricula. Instead of stating empirical evidence, the chapter outlines a conceptual and pedagogic framework in explaining the manner in which ethics education can be integrated, evaluated and maintained at undergraduate and postgraduate levels. The research demonstrates that the ethics education should be combined with technical courses, which provides individual modules of basic knowledge and apply the project-based and case-study methodology to the practical knowledge (Bird et al., 2023; Williams et al., 2023). Result of active learning strategies, reflective exercises, and scenario-based simulations shows increase in critical thinking, moral reasoning, and decision-making skills.

Faculty preparedness turned out as an important factor of success. Instructors should have technical expertise with ethical literacy (Matei & Bertino, 2023; Jarzemsky et al., 2023). Also, curriculum updation and well-designed assessment strategies develop student's knowledge with new technologies and ethical challenges (Neagu et al., 2025). International standards, including ABET and ACM/IEEE guidelines, should be used for updating curriculum and assessment to global level. These Programs make sure that students should graduate with ethically informed and socially responsible skills (Bird et al., 2023; Idowu, 2024).

Table 7. Key takeaways linking objectives, pedagogy, and expected outcomes

Objective	Pedagogical Approach	Expected Outcomes
Build ethical literacy	Stand-alone ethics modules, lectures	Foundational knowledge of principles, codes
Integrate ethics in practice	Embedded modules, project-based learning	Application of ethics in technical projects
Foster critical reflection	Case studies, journals, guided discussions	Improved moral sensitivity and reasoning
Enhance decision-making	Scenario-based exercises, role-play, simulations	Consistent, responsible solutions to dilemmas
Ensure global relevance	Inclusive case studies, alignment with ABET/ACM/IEEE	Graduates ready for diverse professional contexts

This table provides a holistic link between ethics education objectives, pedagogical approaches, and learning outcomes. It represents working of structured teaching models through which skills like technically proficient, ethically aware, and globally competent graduates can be developed.

Figure 11. Summary model of ethics integration for responsible computing education

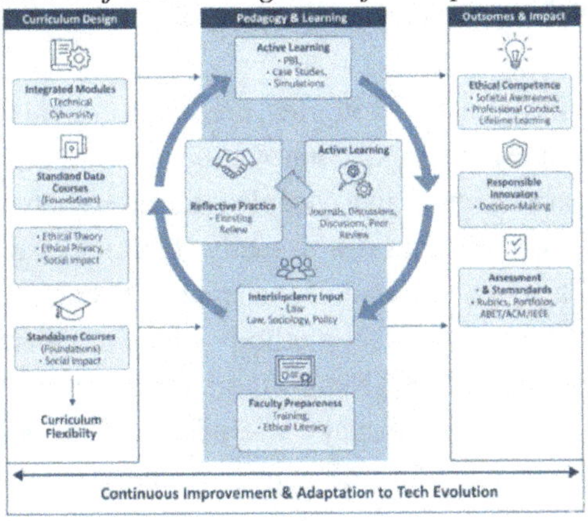

Ethics as a Core Component of Computing Education

The findings of this research state that ethics should not be treated as an optional topic in computing education and should be treated as important as technical knowledge and technical skills (Holmes et al., 2022). Computing professionals regularly face complex decisions that affects privacy, fairness, security, and social welfare, making ethical competence essential for responsible practice (Bird et al., 2023; Idowu, 2024).

Including ethics in the curriculum make sure that all students should use moral reasoning as an important part of technical problem-solving. Ethical considerations should be included in courses like AI, cyber security, HCI and data analytics (Williams et al., 2023; Jarzemsky et al., 2023). This creates a mindset in students regularly analyze the social implications, biasness, and possible harms linked with their technical work. Professional foundation of ethics organized computing education with international standards and workforce expectations. (Matei & Bertino, 2023; Bird et al., 2023).

Active learning and reflection are important for setting up ethics as an important component. Project-based learning, case studies, simulations, and reflective exercises encourage students to face real-world challenges (Flechais & Chalhoub, 2023). Inclusion of Ethics in law, social sciences, and policy studies develops student's way of approaching computing challenges (Holmes et al., 2022).

Future Directions for Pedagogical Innovation and Interdisciplinary Approaches

The fast evolving of digital technologies, predicted ethical challenges in computing education should have pedagogical innovation and interdisciplinary approaches. Students getting prepared to enter in a complex digital society will need a curricular that is adaptive, collaborative, and future ready (Holmes et al., 2022).

Gaming based learning, simulations, scenario-based exercises, and new AI platforms are Innovative pedagogical methods which are turning as effective tools in the process of teaching ethics (Neagu et al., 2025; Khan et al., 2021). These approaches encourage students to make use of ethical principles in processes of decision-making while increase engagement and retention in students. Project-based and experiential learning models also holds importance for linking technical skills with ethical reasoning in practical contexts (Bird et al., 2023; Jarzemsky et al., 2023). Ethical challenges in computing is also included with law, sociology, public policy, environmental science, and business. Future curricular should encourage collaborations and disciplines, which help students in analyzing technical problems from multiple perspectives and give responsible solutions (Holmes et al., 2022).

Technologies like AI, machine learning, blockchain, and IoT requires often changes in the curricular. Ethical training should point out challenges like algorithmic biasness, privacy of data, digitally enabled surveillance, and autonomous decision-making make sure that preparation of students is enough to figure out the results of cutting-edge technologies (Idowu, 2024; Vartiainen et al., 2024). Including ethics with technical innovation helps students forecast and handle risks before its deployment.

REFERENCES

Baumer, B. S. (2022). Integrating data science ethics into an undergraduate major. *ACM Inroads, 13*(2), 34–41. DOI: 10.1145/3524188

Belitz, C., Lee, H., & Nasiar, N.. (2024). Hierarchical dependencies in classroom settings influence algorithmic bias metrics. In *Proceedings of the 14th International Conference on Learning Analytics and Knowledge (LAK 2024)* (pp. 1–10). Association for Computing Machinery. https://doi.org/DOI: 10.1145/3583780

Bird, K. A., Castleman, B. L., Denning, J. T., Goodman, J., & Lamberton, C. (2023). Are algorithms biased in education? Exploring racial bias in predictive models. *Educational Researcher, 52*(2), 1–12. DOI: 10.3102/0013189X231157201

Brown, N., Xie, B., Sarder, E., Fiesler, C., & Wiese, E. S. (2024). Teaching ethics in computing: A systematic literature review of ACM computer science education publications. *ACM Transactions on Computing Education, 24*(1), 1–29. DOI: 10.1145/3610217

Flechais, I., & Chalhoub, G. (2023). Practical cybersecurity ethics: Mapping CyBOK to ethical concerns. *ACM Computing Surveys, 56*(4), 1–28. DOI: 10.1145/3595312

Goetze, T. S. (2023). Integrating ethics into computer science education: Multi-, inter-, and transdisciplinary approaches. In *Proceedings of the 54th ACM Technical Symposium on Computer Science Education (SIGCSE '23)* (pp. 645–651). Association for Computing Machinery. https://doi.org/DOI: 10.1145/3545945.3569797

Holmes, W., Porayska-Pomsta, K., & Holstein, K.. (2022). *Ethics of AI in education: Towards a community-wide framework*. Springer., DOI: 10.1007/978-3-031-10427-0

Idowu, J. A. (2024). Investigating algorithmic bias in student progress monitoring systems. *Computers & Education: Artificial Intelligence, 5*, 100156. DOI: 10.1016/j.caeai.2023.100156

Jarzemsky, P., Fiesler, C., & Payne, B. (2023). Student perspectives on integrating ethics into a computer science course. *Proceedings of the ACM on Human-Computer Interaction, 7*(CSCW2), 1–27. https://doi.org/DOI: 10.1145/3610105

Khan, A. A., Badshah, S., & Liang, P.. (2021). Ethics of artificial intelligence: A systematic literature review of principles and challenges. *AI and Ethics, 1*(4), 351–366. DOI: 10.1007/s43681-021-00081-7

Kozhuharova, D., Kirov, A., & Al-Shargabi, Z. (2022). *Ethics in cybersecurity: Challenges and approaches*. Springer., DOI: 10.1007/978-3-030-93699-5

Lallie, H. S., Sinclair, J., & Joy, M.. (2022). Pedagogic challenges in teaching cybersecurity: A UK perspective. *Education and Information Technologies*, *27*(5), 6657–6680. DOI: 10.1007/s10639-021-10834-3

Matei, S. A., & Bertino, E. (2023). Educating for AI cybersecurity work and research: Ethics, systems thinking, and communication requirements. *IEEE Security and Privacy*, *21*(2), 75–83. DOI: 10.1109/MSEC.2022.3226902

Neagu, S., Vasile, S., & Costache, R. (2025). Digital and psychological well-being among technical students: Implications for ethics education. *Education Sciences*, *15*(2), 112. DOI: 10.3390/educsci15020112

Organisation for Economic Co-operation and Development. (2023). *Algorithmic bias and education: Policy considerations*. OECD Publishing., DOI: 10.1787/7c9c7c8a-

Organisation for Economic Co-operation and Development. (2024). *Ethical AI in education and workforce development*. OECD Publishing., DOI: 10.1787/4c7e4f8f-

Vartiainen, H., Kahila, J., Tedre, M., López-Pernas, S., & Pope, N. (2024). Enhancing children's understanding of algorithmic biases with generative AI. *Learning, Media and Technology*, *49*(1), 1–16. DOI: 10.1080/17439884.2023.2283475

Williams, R., Ali, S., & Devasia, N.. (2023). AI + ethics curricula for middle school youth: Lessons learned from project-based curricula. *Computer Science Education*, *33*(3), 257–281. DOI: 10.1080/08993408.2023.2193942

KEY TERMS AND DEFINITIONS

Algorithmic Bias: Algorithmic bias refers to systematic and unfair outcomes produced by computational models due to biased data, design choices, or contextual assumptions.

Curriculum Alignment: The purposeful alignment of learning objectives, instructional strategies, assessment strategies and accreditation standards in order to provide a coherent, effective design of educational programs.

Curriculum Development: Curriculum development is the systematic design and organization of educational content, pedagogy, and assessment to achieve defined learning outcomes and academic standards.

Digital Well-Being: The physical, psychological, and social well-being with regard to the use of digital technology with consideration to user autonomy, balanced use, and reduction of the adverse cognitive or behavioral consequences.

Ethical Reasoning: Ethical reasoning is the cognitive process through which individuals evaluate situations, assess consequences, and justify decisions based on ethical principles and values.

Ethics in Computing: Ethics in computing involves the application of moral principles and professional responsibilities to guide decisions related to computing technologies and their societal impact.

Pedagogical Scaffolding: A teaching model that organizes learning tasks in such a way that students learn to become ethically conscious, reason, and make decisions with the help of the instructor and their reflections on them.

Responsible Computing: The practice of designing and using computing technologies in ways that prioritize social responsibility, transparency, human well-being, and long-term societal consequences alongside technical performance.

Section 3
Teaching, Learning, and Assessment in the Age of Artificial Intelligence

Chapter 9
Assessment of Coding Skills and Programming Knowledge in the Age of Generative AI:
Best Practices and Effective Strategies for Computer Science Education

Manuel B. Garcia
https://orcid.org/0000-0003-2615-422X
FEU Institute of Technology, Philippines

Ramesh Chander Sharma
https://orcid.org/0000-0002-1371-1157
Dr. B.R. Ambedkar University, Delhi, India

Ahmed Mohamed Fahmy Yousef
https://orcid.org/0000-0003-0522-0734
Fayoum University, Egypt

Thomas K. F. Chiu
Chinese University of Hong Kong, Hong Kong

Ramazan Yılmaz
Bartın University, Turkey

Robertas Damaševičius
https://orcid.org/0000-0001-9990-1084
Vytautas Magnus University, Lithuania

ABSTRACT

The rapid emergence of artificial intelligence (AI) and generative AI tools poses a significant threat to the validity of traditional programming assessments. As the boundary between authored and AI-generated code becomes increasingly indiscernible, long-standing assessment models centered on output correctness and code submission are at risk of obsolescence. Despite its urgency, prior work has largely

DOI: 10.4018/979-8-3373-6546-6.ch009

concentrated on detection, with limited emphasis on reimagining assessment design. This chapter addresses that gap by proposing strategies for assessing programming proficiencies in an AI-mediated context. Its objective is to help educators move beyond surveillance-based models and adopt approaches that emphasize uniquely human cognitive capacities. These pedagogical strategies advance the field by shifting the discourse from reactive prevention to proactive, pedagogically aligned assessment design. In doing so, the chapter affirms that the future of programming assessment is not about resisting AI but about designing systems that assess human thinking over code output.

INTRODUCTION

Perhaps nowhere outside of computer programming can a simple typographical error result in hours of failure and introspection. Such an experience reveals the blend of linguistic, logical, and design precision the discipline requires. Programming demands not only technical acuity but also the capacity for abstraction, problem decomposition, and iterative reasoning (Garcia, 2024). As software systems permeate nearly every domain of modern life, the ability to write and comprehend code has become a foundational skill across both academic and professional contexts. Consequently, the evaluation of programming proficiency holds significant importance to cultivate a culture of computational rigor and innovation. Accurate assessments help ensure that learners internalize not just how to code, but why specific design choices, algorithms, and structures matter in diverse contexts. In the era of artificial intelligence (AI), however, the landscape of programming assessment has undergone a profound shift (Lepp & Kaimre, 2025; Wilson & Nishomoto, 2023). Tools such as ChatGPT and other large language models (LLMs) are now capable of generating syntactically valid and semantically plausible code with minimal human prompting. As emphasized by Bringula (2024) and Garcia (2025), the increasing adoption of these AI technologies in educational settings is reshaping how programming is taught and learned. Novice programmers may rely on LLMs not as scaffolds but as surrogates for the reasoning process, which obscures the boundary between assistance and authorship. The practice of assessing programming knowledge is, therefore, undergoing urgent and necessary scrutiny due to the disruptive capabilities of generative AI.

While generative AI offers promising enhancements to programming instruction, its integration into learning environments introduces substantial challenges to assessment validity. According to rapid review of programming education literature (Garcia, 2025), issues such as plagiarism, over-reliance on AI-generated outputs, and the attenuation of individual cognitive engagement pose serious risks to skill development. These concerns manifest in observable shifts in student behavior, where engagement with foundational problem-solving may be supplanted by superficial interaction with AI tools. Moreover, the traditional indicators of programming competence (e.g., syntactic correctness, output accuracy, and completion time) are increasingly inadequate in distinguishing between work produced through authentic understanding and work generated or heavily augmented by AI. The opacity of generative models, combined with their fluency in mimicking human-like problem solving, makes it exceedingly difficult to detect academic dishonesty using conventional evaluative methods. Left unaddressed, this threatens to undermine both the credibility of assessment outcomes and the reliability of programming credentials. Preserving the integrity of programming education consequently requires a recalibration of assessment strategies that can distinguish between genuine comprehension and passive consumption. Institutions must now develop and adopt methodologies that promote authentic learning, reward process over product, and uphold the core pedagogical goals of computing curricula. Therefore, there is a pressing need to update programming assessment strategies to remain aligned with both technological realities and educational imperatives.

MAIN FOCUS OF THE CHAPTER

In computational disciplines where correctness, efficiency, and algorithmic thinking are paramount, rigorously designed assessments are indispensable. Effective evaluation in programming education is not solely about verifying whether a student can produce syntactically correct or functionally adequate code. Rather, it must determine whether the learner possesses the conceptual depth required to design, analyze, and refine software systems under real-world constraints. Although scholarly interest in the pedagogical implications of generative AI has grown in recent years, a pronounced research gap persists in the domain of educational assessment (Garcia et al., 2025). Most prior works have concentrated on the instructional affordances of AI tools, while comparatively few have addressed the design of assessment practices capable of withstanding the epistemological, ethical, and procedural challenges introduced by such technologies. There is also a notable absence of structured guidance on how to assess programming knowledge and skills in ways that maintain authenticity, safeguard academic integrity, and account for the evolving dynamics of human-AI code collaboration.

Therefore, the primary objective of this chapter is to address this critical gap by articulating a set of best practices and effective strategies for assessing programming competencies in the age of generative AI. It seeks to examine how traditional assessment paradigms are being disrupted by AI-assisted code generation and to offer educators and institutions a set of evidence-informed recommendations that reflect both pedagogical rigor and technological realism. This study is timely and relevant as the absence of a principled redefinition of assessment frameworks creates a tangible risk of accrediting competencies that have not been authentically acquired. As generative AI becomes increasingly ubiquitous and sophisticated, conventional assessments lose their discriminatory capacity to evaluate deep understanding. Unchecked reliance on these AI tools threatens not only the credibility of academic outcomes but also the readiness of graduates to meet the complex demands of professional software development. By addressing this emerging challenge, this chapter contributes to sustaining excellence, trust, and accountability in computer programming education.

METHODS

This chapter adopted an integrative approach to identify and articulate best practices and effective strategies for assessing programming competencies in the age of generative AI (Bozkurt et al., 2024). The methodological orientation is grounded in expert-informed synthesis, drawing upon a broad and interdisciplinary foundation that includes practitioner knowledge, empirical literature, and instructional artifacts. The primary source of insights stems from the authors' cumulative experiences as educators, researchers, and practitioners in the field of computer programming, educational technology, and AI. This experiential knowledge served as a foundational lens for identifying emerging challenges, pedagogical tensions, and practical interventions relevant to assessment in AI-mediated learning environments. In parallel, a wide-ranging review of published case studies, instructional reports, and teaching reflections was conducted. These papers included materials disseminated through academic journals, conference proceedings, institutional white papers, and open-access repositories where faculty and instructional designers have shared implementation strategies and observed outcomes.

To ensure methodological robustness and relevance, the study also incorporated an analysis of contemporary trends in computing education literature. This involved examining recent scholarship on the integration of LLMs in the classroom, the evolving discourse on academic integrity in the age of AI, and pedagogical innovations aimed at promoting authentic learning (e.g., Garcia, 2025; Mahon et al., 2024). Sources were selected based on their scholarly rigor, contextual relevance, and contribution to ongoing conversations in computer science education, learning sciences, and AI ethics. Additionally, perspectives from peer educators and instructional technologists were solicited through informal interviews, community forums, and reflective blogs. This supplementary evidence offers situated knowledge of classroom-level implications that may not yet be fully captured in peer-reviewed publications. These varied inputs were not treated in isolation but were critically evaluated, triangulated, and synthesized into a coherent framework of recommended practices. The methodological intent of this chapter is not to produce generalizable empirical claims, but rather to construct a well-informed, practice-oriented guide that bridges the gap between theoretical discourse and pedagogical implementation. By integrating diverse sources of evidence and expertise, this work seeks to advance the field's understanding of how programming assessment can be both resilient and responsive in the face of rapidly evolving technological capabilities.

BEST PRACTICES AND STRATEGIES

Emphasize Problem-Solving and Conceptual Understanding

As generative AI systems increasingly possess the capacity to synthesize syntactically valid and functionally accurate code with minimal human input, the pedagogical imperative shifts from assessing rote code production to evaluating higher-order cognitive competencies. In this new paradigm, assessments must interrogate learners' abstract conceptualization, algorithmic reasoning, and procedural metacognition to ensure authentic learning. Emphasizing process over product allows educators to discern genuine computational thinking from superficial correctness.

Emphasize Algorithmic Reasoning and Logical Structure

To circumvent the superficial mimicry afforded by LLMs, assessments should foreground algorithmic construction and the logical architecture of solutions ((Wilson & Nishimoto, 2024). Requiring students to explicate their design rationale (e.g., through structured pseudocode, annotated flow representations, or formal logic statements) elicits evidence of deliberate problem decomposition and heuristic selection. This approach engages learners in cognitive processes aligned with revised Bloom's taxonomy (Krathwohl, 2002), particularly within the domains of "*analyzing*," "*evaluating*," and "*creating*." By privileging algorithmic reasoning over syntactic fidelity, instructors can appraise the depth of students' procedural schemata and their capacity to adapt algorithms to novel problem constraints. For instance, rather than asking learners to implement a sorting algorithm, a more revealing prompt might be: "*Compare the asymptotic behavior of your chosen approach against a divide-and-conquer alternative and justify your selection under memory-limited conditions.*" Such practices promote schema-based learning, foster transfer, and decenter the code artifact in favor of the cognitive operations that precede it.

Assess Conceptual Understanding Through Explanatory Reasoning

A robust indicator of programming proficiency lies in the ability to articulate foundational principles abstracted from specific implementations. Conceptual assessments that require explanatory reasoning (e.g., distinguishing recursion from iteration, delineating stack versus heap memory behavior, or critiquing object-oriented versus functional paradigms) surface the learner's ontological grasp of programming constructs. These prompts transcend surface-level recognition and necessitate semantic elaboration, aligning with constructivist views of learning in which knowledge is actively constructed and contextually grounded. Moreover, they provide a mechanism for assessing the learner's epistemic positioning, whether programming is perceived as a rule-based technical activity or as a conceptual discipline governed by theoretical principles and design trade-offs. For example, a question such as "*Why might tail-recursive functions be preferable in functional languages but largely irrelevant in imperative languages?*" demands a deliberate understanding that is difficult to synthesize without deep disciplinary engagement.

Require Manual Code Tracing and Execution Simulation

Among the most cognitively diagnostic assessment techniques is manual code tracing, wherein learners simulate the runtime behavior of a given code segment to determine outputs, identify latent bugs, or describe the evolution of memory state (Andrei & Nabi, 2023). This practice elicits procedural knowledge and exposes the learner's mental model of execution flow, particularly in the presence of control structures, recursion, and dynamic data handling. Code tracing is underpinned by dual-process theories of reasoning. While novices may rely on heuristic shortcuts, expert performance requires deliberate, system-2 engagement to logically simulate state transitions. Tasks might involve predicting variable values at specific execution points, annotating call stacks, or identifying off-by-one errors in iteration constructs. All these tasks demand meticulous attention to operational semantics. By disallowing reliance on code-generation tools, code tracing compels learners to internalize the causal mechanics of computation. Importantly, it reinforces the bidirectional relationship between code construction and comprehension, which is a pedagogical objective often overlooked in output-focused assessments.

Implement Robust AI-Resistant Assessment Strategies

With generative AI systems increasingly obfuscating the boundary between authored and synthesized code, educators must adopt assessment modalities that render unauthorized algorithmic assistance less feasible or pedagogically irrelevant

(Damaševičius, 2024; Xu & Sheng, 2024). AI-resistant assessments are epistemically aligned with evaluating authentic cognitive labor, design intentionality, and expressive fluency in programming. These modalities foreground human explanation, adaptive reasoning, and real-time synthesis, which are capacities that remain outside the operational scope of current generative models. Traditional assessment practices that overemphasize syntactic correctness and direct implementation are no longer adequate to capture the depth of learners' computational understanding (Kendon et al., 2023). The goal is not to eliminate the presence of AI but to elevate the evidentiary threshold of understanding such that its covert use becomes pedagogically inert (Pan et al., 2024).

Facilitate Live Code Reviews to Evaluate Design Intent

Live code reviews serve as powerful instruments for eliciting authentic evidence of comprehension, decision-making, and iterative reasoning (Selvaraj et al., 2021). These activities are structured dialogues wherein learners present and defend their code to an evaluator. Unlike static code submission, this format requires the learner to articulate the motivations behind architectural choices, algorithmic trade-offs, and stylistic conventions in real time (Indriasari et al., 2020). For example, a student tasked with implementing a pathfinding algorithm might be prompted to justify the choice of A* over Dijkstra's algorithm in a game development context, including an explanation of heuristic admissibility and computational overhead. These interactions surface the learner's depth of conceptual integration and reveal the extent to which the submitted code reflects deliberate construction rather than passive replication. Moreover, code reviews mirror professional software engineering practices that foster industry-aligned competencies (e.g., code readability, maintainability, and peer critique). This format also provides dynamic feedback loops, which allows instructors to probe for conceptual weaknesses, detect overfitting to templates, and challenge overreliance on superficial correctness.

Conduct Oral Defenses to Probe Algorithmic Reasoning

Oral examinations, or viva voce assessments, provide a discursive medium through which learners are invited to externalize their algorithmic thought processes, design logic, and computational intuitions. These examinations are particularly potent in assessing the learner's ability to reason adaptively, respond to critical inquiry, and articulate non-obvious design decisions (Ardito, 2024). For instance, after solving a problem involving backtracking, a student might be asked: "*Under what conditions would a greedy algorithm suffice in this domain, and why might backtracking offer a more generalizable solution?*" Such questions require comparative reasoning, contextual awareness, and the ability to navigate abstract algorithmic paradigms. The oral format disrupts the possibility of answer pre-generation via AI tools, as learners must synthesize responses dynamically and demonstrate genuine fluency in the conceptual grammar of programming. This assessment type also encourages the cultivation of verbal articulation in computational contexts, which is a vital yet often underdeveloped skill in the discipline.

Administer Controlled-Environment Programming Assessments

While not inherently innovative, in-person programming assessments administered in AI-restricted environments are regaining relevance as a baseline safeguard against unauthorized augmentation. Conducting such assessments in supervised laboratories, with network access disabled and development environments monitored, ensures that learners operate solely on internalized knowledge and procedural memory. However, to transcend mere constraint, such assessments should incorporate open-ended prompts that resist brute-force memorization. For example, rather than requesting the implementation of a standard binary search, instructors might ask: "*Design a modified search algorithm for a rotated sorted array and analyze its time complexity*." This type of prompt engages analytical thinking, adaptability, and creative recombination of prior knowledge, which are dimensions of competence that are also difficult to fabricate extemporaneously (Taeb et al., 2024). Controlled-environment tasks also provide valuable data on the learner's coding fluency, debugging approach, and efficiency under cognitive load, all of which are key indicators of real-world programming readiness.

Integrate Constructive AI Use into Assessment Design

The pedagogical response must evolve from prohibition to principled integration as generative AI becomes increasingly embedded in the programming workflow. Rather than viewing AI tools solely as threats to academic integrity, educators can leverage them as metacognitive amplifiers, provided their use is governed by clear parameters and assessed with epistemic nuance (Acut et al., 2025; Gantalao et al., 2025). Integrating AI-use policies and tasks into assessment design promotes transparency, encourages critical engagement with machine-generated outputs, and cultivates students' ability to distinguish between augmentation and automation. This approach reframes AI not as an end but as a catalyst for reflective practice, comparative evaluation, and human-AI collaboration (Boguslawski et al., 2025).

Evaluate Proficiency in AI-Augmented Problem Solving

Assessments can be structured to explicitly permit the use of AI tools during designated stages of the problem-solving process. Rather than penalizing reliance, instructors can evaluate the learner's discernment in how, when, and why such tools were employed—and whether their outputs were critically interrogated or blindly accepted. For example, a programming task might instruct students to use an AI assistant to brainstorm algorithmic approaches to a constraint satisfaction problem (e.g., Sudoku solving). Students would then implement one strategy and annotate their code to indicate which elements were AI-derived and which were their own refinements. Evaluation would center on how effectively the student adapted, optimized, or rejected AI suggestions based on context-specific reasoning and correctness constraints. This mode of assessment positions generative AI as a design interlocutor where students must critically evaluate rather than emulate. It also mirrors contemporary industry practices, where AI-enhanced development requires discernment, ethical awareness, and domain-specific validation.

Elicit Reflective Metacognition Through AI-Use Documentation

Requiring students to submit structured reflections detailing their interaction with AI systems cultivates both metacognitive awareness and academic accountability (Adler & Shani, 2026). These reflective artifacts serve as qualitative evidence of students' decision-making processes, error-correction strategies, and evaluative judgments regarding AI reliability. Reflection prompts might include: "*Describe a point during the task where you considered AI output but chose an alternative approach. What guided your decision?*" Such reflective scaffolds encourage learners to operationalize critical thinking and to engage with AI as a tool to be scrutinized. They also allow educators to assess cognitive independence and epistemic vigilance, which are central to cultivating trustworthy and resilient programmers in AI-augmented contexts.

Compare Human and AI Solutions to Cultivate Evaluative Judgment

An advanced form of critical engagement involves assigning parallel problem-solving tasks (e.g., one completed manually and the other with AI assistance) followed by a comparative analysis of the two solutions. This task structure enables learners to develop evaluative judgment regarding code quality, elegance, robustness, and adherence to problem constraints. For instance, students might be asked to implement a dynamic programming solution to a combinatorial optimization problem (e.g., the knapsack problem) unaided, and then to generate an AI-based solution for the same task. Their comparative reflection could address computational efficiency, code readability, use of abstractions, and error propagation. This strategy serves dual purposes: it demystifies AI capabilities and limitations while simultaneously deepening learners' own analytical competencies. By situating human cognition and machine output in dialogic tension, educators can foster the development of hybrid intelligence wherein students learn not only to program but to reason about programming with and against machines.

Design Open-Ended and Creative Programming Tasks

In contrast to narrowly scoped programming problems that can be trivially solved or replicated by generative AI, open-ended and creative tasks foreground the learner's capacity for innovation, judgment, and integrative thinking. These tasks emphasize originality over replication, process over product, and justification over mere functionality (Silva et al., 2024). By introducing ambiguity, multiple solution paths, and authentic constraints, such assessments compel learners to engage in design-oriented reasoning. In this context, success is defined not by a single correct answer, but by the coherence, viability, and expressiveness of their solution. These tasks are critical in preserving human agency in a landscape increasingly mediated by automated outputs.

Implement Project-Based Assessments to Foster Creative Synthesis

Project-based assessments serve as expansive formats in which students are required to design, implement, and iteratively refine a software artifact that reflects both technical competency and creative agency. These projects typically extend beyond textbook exercises, involving user-centric design, integration of external libraries or APIs, and adherence to real-world constraints. For instance, students may be asked to develop an educational application for language learners that adapts content based on performance metrics, or to create a simulation tool for visualizing algorithm performance under varying conditions. Such projects require learners to define their own specifications, navigate ambiguous requirements, and make trade-offs across performance, usability, and maintainability. Critically, project-based tasks enable the assessment of not only coding ability but also architectural thinking, version control fluency, collaborative skills (if team-based), and reflective documentation.

Assess Real-World Problem Solving Through Multivariate Scenarios

Designing assessments around authentic, real-world problems invites learners to contend with complexity, multiplicity, and imperfection (Obaidellah et al., 2020). These problems are intentionally underdetermined, offering several plausible solutions, each with its own set of trade-offs. The assessment, therefore, hinges not only on the solution's efficacy but also on the rationale underpinning design decisions. A representative prompt might be: "*Develop a data visualization dashboard for municipal waste management using publicly available datasets. Your solution should balance performance, interpretability, and accessibility for non-technical stakeholders.*" Here, students must justify choices about data preprocessing, visualization libraries, UI design, and even ethical considerations in data presentation. This form of assessment prioritizes evaluative reasoning, stakeholder awareness, and system-level thinking, which are core attributes of creative problem-solving. Furthermore, it renders AI-generated solutions insufficient unless they are strategically adapted and substantiated by the learner's design rationale.

Engage Learners Through Code Customization and Extension

Rather than presenting students with blank slates or fully specified problems, instructors can provide scaffolded or partially completed codebases and require learners to customize or extend them in meaningful, context-aware ways. This format disrupts pattern-matching strategies employed by generative AI tools and shifts the cognitive load onto the learner's ability to interpret existing logic, identify constraints, and design contextually appropriate modifications. For example, a student might receive a minimal version of a two-dimensional (2D) physics simulation engine and be asked to implement new object behaviors (e.g., friction or elasticity), refactor the code for modularity, or enhance its performance through algorithmic optimizations. Alternatively, students might be tasked with internationalizing a web application to support right-to-left languages or integrating new accessibility features into a user interface. These tasks assess a blend of comprehension, synthesis, and reengineering, which are also competencies central to real-world development and difficult to automate. They also encourage students to engage with legacy code, interface specifications, and pre-existing design decisions, preparing them for the complexities of collaborative and inherited software environments.

Leverage Automated Tools and Code Quality Metrics

In an educational landscape increasingly shaped by automation, the strategic deployment of automated analysis tools provides instructors with scalable, objective mechanisms for evaluating code authenticity, development behavior, and software quality (Chen et al., 2022; Gambo et al., 2025; Novak et al., 2019). These tools do not merely function as surveillance instruments, but as pedagogical supports that can uncover patterns of engagement, reveal deviations from normative coding practices, and offer diagnostic insights into the learner's developmental trajectory. When judiciously applied, automated tools complement qualitative assessment by enabling the continuous monitoring of both code provenance and structural integrity, which are domains that are susceptible to obfuscation in the age of generative AI.

Detect Anomalous Code Similarity Through Algorithmic Plagiarism Analysis

Automated similarity detection tools (e.g., Measure of Software Similarity, JPlag, or Codequiry) offer robust methods for identifying textual or structural overlap across student submissions and known code corpora. These tools apply token-based, tree-based, or fingerprinting algorithms to detect semantic equivalence or suspicious convergence in code artifacts, even when superficial modifications (e.g., variable renaming, control flow inversion) are introduced to evade detection. In the context of generative AI, such tools become particularly relevant for flagging artifacts that exhibit high degrees of similarity with publicly available training data or canonical code templates. For instance, an introductory assignment on linked list implementation that yields structurally identical solutions across cohorts may warrant further inspection, especially when accompanied by limited verbal justification from the learner. While such tools should never serve as the sole arbiter of academic misconduct, they provide empirical grounds for initiating reflective dialogue and further investigation. Their integration into the assessment pipeline promotes a culture of originality and attribution that are essential in both academia and industry.

Analyze Version Control Histories to Evaluate Development Authenticity

Mandating the use of distributed version control systems such as *Git* not only inculcates professional software engineering practices but also provides a temporal record of development activity that can be pedagogically invaluable. Commit histories, branch structures, and diff logs offer insight into the evolution of student work, revealing whether code was developed iteratively or submitted as a monolithic artifact. This aspect is an indicator often associated with last-minute synthesis or potential AI intervention. For example, an analysis of commit logs may show a student progressively implementing modules across several days, interspersed with debugging and refactoring activities. In contrast, a single commit containing the entirety of a completed project, followed by negligible activity, may suggest copy-paste behavior or generative augmentation. Instructors may further operationalize version control analysis through rubrics that reward process transparency, granular development, and meaningful commit messages. These metrics reflect not only the student's technical proficiency but also their reflective engagement.

Employ Static Code Analysis to Measure Software Quality

Automated tools that assess code quality (e.g., *SonarQube*, *ESLint*, or *Pylint*) offer quantitative indicators of software robustness, readability, and adherence to language-specific idioms. These tools can detect issues ranging from cyclomatic complexity and dead code to naming convention violations and poor modularization, all of which serve as proxies for maintainability and technical debt. Importantly, while generative AI can often produce syntactically valid code, it does not consistently enforce idiomatic best practices, context-specific conventions, or maintainable architectural patterns. Thus, integrating code quality metrics into assessment schemes allows educators to reward not just functional correctness, but also craftsmanship and discipline. For example, a student might submit a fully functional web scraper that passes all tests but contains hard-coded dependencies, nested loops with excessive complexity, and poor documentation. Static analysis would flag these issues, and the student's grade could reflect the difference between merely working code and professionally viable code. These metrics can be transparently shared with learners to support formative feedback, enabling them to iteratively improve code hygiene and internalize best practices over time.

Assess Debugging Proficiency and Maintenance Skills

While traditional programming assessments often emphasize code generation, real-world software development disproportionately involves debugging, refactoring, and maintaining existing systems. These maintenance-oriented tasks demand not only fluency in program comprehension but also critical thinking, error localization, and architectural foresight. In the age of generative AI, where functional code can be synthesized rapidly (Garcia, 2025; Garcia et al., 2023), the ability to diagnose, improve, and sustain code quality over time emerges as a distinctive marker of human expertise. Assessing these capacities foregrounds the learner's ability to engage with the full lifecycle of code to ensure robustness, clarity, and longevity.

Assess Debugging Proficiency Through Fault Localization and Resolution Tasks

Deliberately introducing semantic, logical, or structural errors into code and tasking students with identifying and resolving them serves as a rigorous diagnostic for their debugging acumen. Unlike generative code synthesis, debugging requires granular comprehension of control flow, data dependencies, and potential side effects. Programmers are expected to possess such competencies that are cognitively intensive and pedagogically revealing. For example, students might receive a recursive implementation of a depth-first search algorithm that fails on edge cases due to incorrect base conditions or mutable default arguments. The assessment would require them not only to correct the behavior but to articulate the source of the failure, propose a fix, and validate it through targeted testing. Such tasks align with real-world software engineering practices, where the ability to efficiently isolate faults and deploy minimally invasive corrections distinguishes competent programmers from novice coders. They also shift the focus from generation to explanation, which AI tools currently struggle to perform authentically.

Evaluate Code Maturity Through Structured Refactoring Exercises

Refactoring tasks assess a learner's capacity to enhance the internal structure of code without altering its external functionality. This activity involves applying design principles (e.g., modularity and abstraction), as well as identifying and eliminating code smells (i.e., suboptimal patterns that may impede scalability, readability, or maintainability). A representative task might involve presenting students with a monolithic data processing script and asking them to refactor it into a series of modular, reusable functions, each with clearly defined input-output contracts. Alternatively, students could be required to introduce design patterns (e.g., strategy, observer) into an object-oriented system to improve extensibility. These assessments surface the student's architectural thinking and ability to transform working but inelegant code into a maintainable artifact, which is an essential skill in collaborative, long-term software projects. Moreover, unlike AI-generated code, which often prioritizes minimal working examples, human-led refactoring reflects deeper comprehension of maintainability as a core software quality attribute.

Assess Documentation and Testing as Markers of Software Reliability

The ability to produce clear, coherent documentation and comprehensive test suites constitutes a critical yet often neglected component of programming proficiency. While AI can generate plausible docstrings or test stubs, it lacks the context sensitivity and domain judgment required for high-quality specification and coverage assurance. In assessment contexts, students may be tasked with writing module-level documentation that explains code behavior, design rationale, and expected usage patterns for a non-expert developer. Concurrently, they could be evaluated on their ability to develop unit, integration, or boundary tests using frameworks such as *pytest*, *JUnit*, or *Mocha*, with attention to test coverage, assertions, and edge case handling. For example, a task might involve augmenting an existing codebase with meaningful inline comments, API documentation, and a suite of parameterized tests that achieve at least 80% coverage. Evaluation would consider not only completeness but also clarity, consistency, and pedagogical value, which are attributes essential to maintainable and collaborative code. This mode of assessment reinforces the notion that high-quality software is not merely code that runs, but code that communicates intent, resists regression, and invites reuse.

Facilitate Collaborative and Peer-Based Assessments

Collaboration is not ancillary but foundational in software development. Modern programming environments are inherently social, with tools and practices designed to facilitate shared code ownership, distributed problem-solving, and continuous integration (Garcia, 2023). As such, assessments must capture individual technical proficiency and evaluate interpersonal and collaborative competencies that are central to real-world programming practice. Collaborative and peer-based assessment strategies cultivate dialogic reasoning, expose learners to diverse design perspectives, and reinforce metacognitive reflection (Prather et al., 2024). These dimensions of learning are both resistant to automation and essential to professional formation.

Evaluate Collaborative Fluency Through Structured Pair Programming

Pair programming is an agile practice wherein two programmers work in tandem, alternating between "driver" and "navigator" roles. According to prior studies, this strategy offers a pedagogically rich context for assessing both technical execution and real-time collaborative discourse. In academic settings, this modality can be structured to ensure role rotation, equitable participation, and reflective accountability. Assessment can include observational rubrics evaluating communication quality, task division, and responsiveness to feedback, supplemented by post-session reflections that document problem-solving strategies, conflict resolution, and individual learning gains. For instance, students might be assigned a problem involving concurrent data access in a multithreaded environment, where one partner implements synchronization primitives while the other audits for race conditions and data integrity. This format promotes code comprehension as a social process, reinforcing the development of soft skills (e.g., active listening, articulation of technical rationale, and shared debugging) that are essential in collaborative engineering contexts but often neglected in traditional assessments.

Assess Critical Engagement Through Peer Code Reviews

Peer code review exercises expose students to diverse programming styles, implementation strategies, and design rationales, fostering evaluative judgment and collective learning. Instructors can scaffold this process with review templates that prompt analysis along key dimensions: correctness, readability, modularity, adherence to conventions, and potential for optimization. Tools such as *PuzzleMe* and *AI-Lab* have been shown to support live peer discussion and feedback, enabling students to collaboratively debug, optimize, and understand alternate implementation strategies in real time (Dickey et al., 2024). For example, students may be tasked with reviewing a peer's implementation of a machine learning model pipeline, offering comments on data preprocessing practices, feature selection, and hyperparameter tuning logic. Each reviewer would be assessed on the technical validity of their critique, constructiveness, specificity, and ability to justify suggestions with reference to established practices. This approach encourages learners to articulate tacit knowledge, surface latent misconceptions, and internalize quality benchmarks through exposure to both exemplary and flawed code. Moreover, the reciprocal nature of peer reviews fosters a culture of accountability and reflective refinement that AI-driven assessments cannot replicate (Wang et al., 2021; Yang et al., 2024).

Design Team-Based Projects to Simulate Professional Development Ecosystems

Team projects, especially those structured to emulate real-world development cycles (Garcia, 2021), represent a comprehensive assessment format. They capture a wide spectrum of learning outcomes, from systems thinking and division of labor to conflict negotiation and integration testing. Empirical evidence suggests that such collaborative and open-ended prototyping tasks produce more engaged learners and superior learning outcomes compared to instructor-led feedback models (Soomro et al., 2024). These projects should be sufficiently complex to necessitate genuine collaboration, interdependence, and project management. For example, students might be assigned the task of developing a cross-platform mobile application with back-end integration, requiring the delineation of roles such as front-end development, API design, database modeling, and deployment automation. Assessment rubrics can incorporate peer evaluation, role-based deliverables, shared repositories, and sprint reviews to capture both individual accountability and collective output (Alipour et al., 2024). By engaging in sustained collaboration under authentic constraints, students develop not only technical and architectural skills but also professional habits of mind. These skills include version control etiquette, asynchronous coordination, and codebase stewardship, which can prepare them for industrial software ecosystems. These competencies remain beyond the scope of generative AI and affirm the human-centered nature of complex problem-solving.

Ensure Submission Authenticity through Structural Design

In the current educational climate, where generative AI can produce seemingly original code artifacts instantaneously, safeguarding the authenticity of student submissions is an urgent pedagogical imperative. The challenge is not simply one of detection, but of designing assessment protocols that promote transparency, traceability, and evidentiary accountability. Authenticity must be verified through punitive measures and structural features that render inauthentic shortcuts impractical or pedagogically ineffective. By embedding temporal markers, requiring multimodal demonstrations, and diversifying input conditions, educators can foster a setting where authentic engagement becomes the most viable path to success (Velicea et al., 2025).

Document Development Through Progressive Snapshots

Requiring students to submit incremental versions of their work (e.g., design sketches, pseudocode drafts, partial implementations, and early test results) provides a temporal footprint of their problem-solving trajectory. These progress snapshots serve both formative and forensic purposes (Garcia & Revano Jr, 2021; Obaidellah et al., 2020; Semenov et al., 2025). They encourage iterative development while simultaneously furnishing instructors with evidence of authentic authorship. For example, in a two-week assignment on developing a file encryption utility, students might be required to submit: (1) a design outline detailing algorithm choice and file handling logic, (2) a mid-project codebase with placeholder functions, and (3) a final implementation with testing scripts. This approach not only deters last-minute AI-generated submissions but also reinforces habits of incremental problem-solving and reflection. Furthermore, instructors can analyze changes in naming conventions, code structuring, and logic refinement to identify whether the work exhibits evidence of authentic intellectual labor. In effect, progress documentation transforms authenticity verification into a pedagogical opportunity for intervention and growth. This scaffolding approach also facilitates early intervention, which allows instructors to provide targeted feedback before the final submission. This strategy consequently transforms authenticity enforcement into a pedagogical support mechanism.

Elicit Verbal Explanation Through Code Walkthrough Videos

Video demonstrations wherein students record themselves explaining and executing their programs provide a compelling mechanism for verifying conceptual ownership. Unlike static code, which may be copied or generated, the ability to fluently articulate design decisions, control flow, and edge case behavior in real time serves as a proxy for internalized understanding (Hutson et al., 2024). A typical requirement might be a 5-minute screen recording in which the student walks through the code structure, explains key functions and their interactions, and narrates a test run using example input data (Xue et al., 2024). Evaluators can use rubrics to assess not only technical accuracy but also fluency, precision of terminology, and responsiveness to hypothetical variations. Such demonstrations are difficult to outsource or fabricate using generative tools and offer a human-centered form of assessment that privileges explanation over artifact.

Mitigate Plagiarism Through Input Randomization and Individualization

One of the most effective design-based deterrents to AI-assisted plagiarism is the incorporation of randomized or individualized parameters into assessment prompts. By modifying datasets, function specifications, or constraint sets across students, instructors reduce the feasibility of sharing solutions or querying generic AI tools for problem-specific code (Karnalim, 2023). For example, in a data processing task, students might receive structurally distinct CSV files, compelling them to customize parsing routines. Tools such as *CodeRunner* (Hickman et al., 2023), when integrated into LMS environments, can automate the generation of customized task variants, making the deployment of randomized assessments scalable and consistent. Furthermore, evidence suggests that generative models like ChatGPT perform poorly on algorithmically complex or highly contextualized problems, especially when compared to generic tasks (Dunder et al., 2024). In one study involving 127 Kattis-style problems, ChatGPT succeeded on only 19, underscoring the effectiveness of complexity and variation in preserving assessment integrity. Randomization thus accomplishes multiple objectives: it deters plagiarism, promotes problem decomposition and abstraction, and upholds fairness by distributing unique but conceptually aligned problems across a cohort (Zhang et al., 2024). When combined with verbal explanations and process documentation, it forms a triadic model of AI-resilient assessment that is grounded in reasoning, originality, and individualized challenge.

SYNTHESIS AND FUTURE DIRECTIONS

The rapid diffusion of generative AI has irrevocably altered the epistemological terrain of programming education. These systems have blurred traditional boundaries between production and reproduction, authorship and assistance, rendering obsolete any assessment approach that relies solely on syntactic generation or surface-level correctness. As argued throughout this chapter, the imperative now is to reorient programming assessments toward the elicitation of epistemic authenticity, or evidence that learners can reason algorithmically, reflect metacognitively, and engage critically with computational tools. This shift must not be viewed as a defensive posture but rather as a reimagining of educational design for an era of human–AI collaboration (Bozkurt et al., 2024; Xiao et al., 2025). In this emerging paradigm, assessments must interrogate students' capacity to curate, evaluate, and contextualize AI-generated outputs rather than merely replicate or reject them (Yilmaz & Karaoglan Yilmaz, 2023). The most meaningful metrics of programming proficiency will increasingly reside not in code artifacts themselves, but in the cognitive and ethical sophistication with which those artifacts are critiqued and refined. To support this reorientation, Figure 1 presents the AI-Resilient Programming Assessment Framework that offers a coherent structure for designing assessments that are not only resistant to generative AI misuse but also pedagogically enriching.

Figure 1. AI-Resilient Programming Assessment Framework

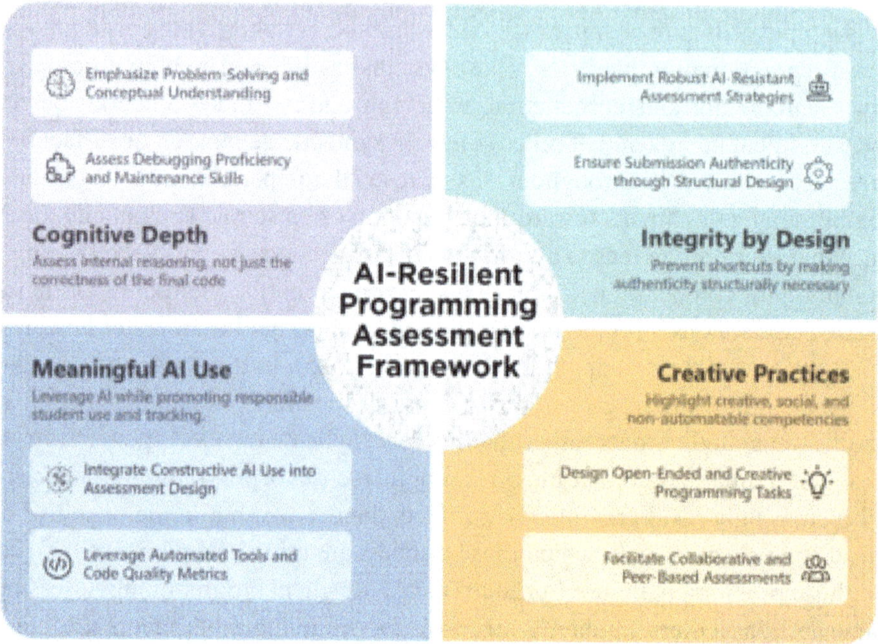

Adaptive Platforms and Personalized Learning Trajectories

Short-term trends already point to the mainstream adoption of AI-driven instructional systems capable of dynamically tailoring task difficulty, feedback, and pacing based on granular learner data (Hasanah et al., 2025). These platforms leverage reinforcement learning and predictive modeling to scaffold student progress in real-time, resulting in a shift from static curricula to adaptive cognitive ecologies. While such systems hold promise for reducing attrition and enhancing personalization, they simultaneously raise critical concerns regarding algorithmic opacity, data privacy, and pedagogical accountability. As Garcia et al. (2023) emphasized, it is essential that adaptive systems be governed by design principles that foreground transparency, auditability, and inclusiveness. Without such safeguards, personalization may inadvertently entrench digital privilege or reinforce deficit-based learning models.

Elevating Higher-Order Cognitive and Ethical Competencies

As generative systems automate increasingly complex coding tasks, human value will shift toward competencies that resist automation: abstraction, self-regulation, interdisciplinary integration, and ethical reasoning. Assessment frameworks must evolve accordingly to center these higher-order constructs. For instance, tasks that ask students to deconstruct flawed AI-generated code, anticipate emergent behavior, or mitigate algorithmic bias provide opportunities to assess computational judgment as distinct from code proficiency. Moreover, the ethical dimensions of programming must be re-centered. This aspect includes evaluating how students reason about fairness, sustainability, intellectual responsibility, and unintended consequences. Interdisciplinary assessments (Garcia et al., 2025), such as designing socially impactful systems in domains like health informatics or environmental modeling, can serve as platforms for holistic evaluation, connecting code to context and logic to lived reality.

Blockchain for Verifiable Learning and Academic Integrity

Blockchain infrastructures offer a novel mechanism for decentralizing credentialing and preserving the integrity of student-generated work (Babu et al., 2026; El Koshiry et al., 2023). By embedding time-stamped, tamper-evident records of student contributions (e.g., code commits, design iterations, and peer feedback), blockchain systems enable the construction of verifiable learning transcripts that transcend static summative evaluations. Such architectures are particularly potent in countering the obfuscation introduced by generative AI, as they provide granular evidence of developmental progression rather than isolated end products. From an institutional perspective, blockchain may further function as a deterrent to academic misconduct and an enabler of scalable, trust-based assessment in distributed learning ecosystems.

Immersive Technologies and Experiential Assessment

The affordances of immersive technologies, particularly virtual and augmented reality, enable assessment modalities that go beyond what traditional screen-based environments can capture (Alexander et al., 2022). These platforms allow for embodied coding experiences where learners interact with algorithms spatially, engage in real-time collaboration, or co-program alongside AI agents in 3D simulations. In such contexts, the scope of assessment can be extended to include spatial reasoning, situated problem-solving, and real-time decision-making. For example, debugging a robot's pathfinding routine in a virtual warehouse or explaining machine logic to a simulated stakeholder offers a multidimensional view of learner competence that integrates communication, systems thinking, and performance under uncertainty.

Continuous, Modular, and Stackable Credentialing

The linearity of traditional academic credentialing systems is increasingly misaligned with the rapid skill turnover in computing fields. Micro-credentialing and modular assessment frameworks address this disconnect by offering granular, just-in-time verification of competencies across the learning continuum (Alenezi et al., 2024; Gamage & Dehideniya, 2025; Ralston, 2021). These systems enable students to assemble credential portfolios over time, validated through rigorously assessed modules (e.g., secure coding, testing automation, or algorithmic ethics), often in partnership with external platforms such as *GitHub* or *Coursera.* Beyond providing flexibility, these models promote learning as a lifelong, recursive process that emphasizes depth, adaptability, and evidence-based progress. When integrated with institutional standards and assessment rigor, stackable credentials can complement formal qualifications while making learning trajectories more transparent and transferrable (Louder, 2025).

Governance, Regulation, and Faculty Preparedness

The incorporation of AI into programming assessment requires not only pedagogical innovation but also structural reform (Garcia, 2025). Regulatory bodies must address emerging concerns around liability for AI-generated outputs, attribution of authorship, and intellectual property rights (Mangubat et al., 2025). Without such frameworks, the legitimacy of assessment systems will remain contested. Equally critical is the professionalization of the academic workforce in response to these shifts. Faculty must be equipped with the conceptual tools and technical fluency necessary to design, manage, and interpret AI-integrated assessments. Institutions should prioritize sustained in-service training that spans ethical AI use, data literacy, and the design of human-centered evaluation systems (Azevedo et al., 2025; Barus et al., 2025; Luo, 2024). Finally, ensuring equitable access to emerging tools and infrastructure must remain a central priority. In a global education system still marked by digital stratification, efforts to innovate must be accompanied by commitments to inclusion—lest the benefits of AI-enhanced assessment accrue only to those with privileged access to connectivity and computational resources. Finally, digital equity remains a non-negotiable imperative. Ensuring that all students, regardless of geography or socioeconomic status, have reliable access to high-quality tools and connectivity is essential to prevent the amplification of existing educational inequities.

CONCLUSION

The stark reality confronting programming education today is that generative AI can now produce correct, efficient, and stylistically coherent code on demand and at scale. This new normal threatens to collapse long-standing assessment frameworks that equate output with understanding, and performance with authorship. In this rapidly shifting terrain, educators are no longer asking whether students can write code, but whether they understand what it means, where it comes from, and why it matters. This chapter contributes a timely and necessary intervention into the emerging literature on programming assessment by proposing a comprehensive framework for evaluating coding knowledge and skills in an era saturated by AI augmentation. While prior studies have largely focused on AI's pedagogical affordances in isolation, this work foregrounds the intersections of cognitive authenticity, technological disruption, and ethical design. In doing so, it responds to an urgent need for research-informed guidance on how assessment practices must evolve alongside technological capabilities.

The proposed strategies speak to multiple constituencies. Educators gain concrete, implementable models for designing assessments that foreground learner intent, cognitive process, and reflective capacity. Institutional leaders are equipped with a roadmap for developing resilient, future-oriented assessment infrastructures. Students, in turn, benefit from a learning environment that recognizes and rewards metacognitive engagement and ethical judgment, not just technical output. Meanwhile, the framework calls on policymakers to enact regulatory measures and infrastructural investments that uphold academic integrity and equitable access in digitally mediated contexts. The implications extend far beyond classroom practice. From curricular innovation and credentialing models to global conversations on AI governance in education, the future of programming assessment will demand continuous dialogue between pedagogy, policy, and technological development. Without deliberate recalibration, there is a risk that AI will erode the very conditions under which meaningful learning occurs. But with thoughtful design, these same tools can elevate assessment from a measure of output to a demonstration of human thought, purpose, and values.

REFERENCES

Acut, D. P., Gamusa, E. V., Pernaa, J., Yuenyong, C., Pantaleon, A. T., Espina, R. C., & Garcia, M. B. (2025). AI Shaming Among Teacher Education Students: A Reflection on Acceptance and Identity in the Age of Generative Tools. In *Pitfalls of AI Integration in Education: Skill Obsolescence, Misuse, and Bias*. IGI Global., DOI: 10.4018/979-8-3373-0122-8.ch005

Adler, I., & Shani, Y. (2026). Hybrid Human-GenAI Cognitive Apprenticeship: Encouraging Pre-Service Teachers to Implement Instructional Practices to Support Students' Self-Regulated Learning. *Teaching and Teacher Education*, *169*, 1–19. DOI: 10.1016/j.tate.2025.105268

Alenezi, M., Akour, M., & Alfawzan, L. (2024). Evolving Microcredential Strategies for Enhancing Employability: Employer and Student Perspectives. *Education Sciences*, *14*(12), 1–24. DOI: 10.3390/educsci14121307

Andrei, O., & Nabi, S. W. (2023). On Students' Experiences with Algorithm Tracing using Pair Programming. *Proceedings of the 2023 ACM Conference on International Computing Education Research* - Volume 2. DOI: 10.1145/3568812.3603477

Ardito, C. G. (2024). Generative AI Detection in Higher Education Assessments. *New Directions for Teaching and Learning*. Advance online publication. DOI: 10.1002/tl.20624

Azevedo, L., Robles, P., Best, E., & Mallinson, D. J. (2025). Institutional Policies on Artificial Intelligence in Higher Education: Frameworks and Best Practices for Faculty. *New Directions for Adult and Continuing Education*, *2025*(188), 70–78. DOI: 10.1002/ace.70013

Babu, S., & Anbumozhi, A. S, P., N, V., & Kaliamoorthy, V. (2026). Blockchain for Credentialing and Academic Record-Keeping. In J. Moore, S. Gupta, M. Sharma, A. Garg, & H. Josephine V. L (Eds.), *Transforming Education With Data Science in the AI Era* (pp. 407-448). IGI Global Scientific Publishing. DOI: 10.4018/979-8-3373-2185-1.ch014

Barus, O. P., Hidayanto, A. N., Handri, E. Y., Sensuse, D. I., & Yaiprasert, C. (2025). Shaping Generative AI Governance in Higher Education: Insights from Student Perception. *International Journal of Educational Research Open*, *8*, 1–12. DOI: 10.1016/j.ijedro.2025.100452

Boguslawski, S., Deer, R., & Dawson, M. G. (2025). Programming Education and Learner Motivation in the Age of Generative AI: Student and Educator Perspectives. *Information and Learning Science, 126*(1/2), 91–109. DOI: 10.1108/ILS-10-2023-0163

Bozkurt, A., Xiao, J., Farrow, R., Bai, J. Y. H., Nerantzi, C., Moore, S., & Asino, T. I. (2024). The Manifesto for Teaching and Learning in a Time of Generative AI: A Critical Collective Stance to Better Navigate the Future. *Open Praxis, 16*(4), 487–513. DOI: 10.55982/openpraxis.16.4.777

Bringula, R. (2024). ChatGPT in a Programming Course: Benefits and Limitations. *Frontiers in Education, 9*, 1–6. DOI: 10.3389/feduc.2024.1248705

Chen, H.-M., Nguyen, B.-A., & Dow, C.-R. (2022). Code-Quality Evaluation Scheme for Assessment of Student Contributions to Programming Projects. *Journal of Systems and Software, 188*, 1–18. DOI: 10.1016/j.jss.2022.111273

Damaševičius, R. (2024). ChatGPT-Supported Student Assessment – Can we rely on it? *Journal of Research in Innovative Teaching & Learning, 17*(2), 414–416. DOI: 10.1108/JRIT-09-2024-195

Dickey, E., Bejarano, A., & Garg, C. (2024). AI-Lab: A Framework for Introducing Generative Artificial Intelligence Tools in Computer Programming Courses. *SN Computer Science, 5*(6), 720. DOI: 10.1007/s42979-024-03074-y

Dunder, N., Lundborg, S., Wong, J., & Viberg, O. (2024). Kattis vs ChatGPT: Assessment and Evaluation of Programming Tasks in the Age of Artificial Intelligence. *Proceedings of the 14th Learning Analytics and Knowledge Conference.* DOI: 10.1145/3636555.3636882

El Koshiry, A., Eliwa, E., Abd El-Hafeez, T., & Shams, M. Y. (2023). Unlocking the Power of Blockchain in Education: An Overview of Innovations and Outcomes. *Blockchain: Research and Applications, 4*(4), 1–19. DOI: 10.1016/j.bcra.2023.100165

Gamage, K. A. A., & Dehideniya, S. C. P. (2025). Unlocking Career Potential: How Micro-Credentials Are Revolutionising Higher Education and Lifelong Learning. *Education Sciences, 15*(5), 1–18. DOI: 10.3390/educsci15050525

Gambo, I., Abegunde, F.-J., Gambo, O., Ogundokun, R. O., Babatunde, A. N., & Lee, C.-C. (2025). GRAD-AI: An Automated Grading Tool for Code Assessment and Feedback in Programming Course. *Education and Information Technologies, 30*(7), 9859–9899. DOI: 10.1007/s10639-024-13218-5

Gantalao, L. C., Calzada, J. G. D., Capuyan, D. L., Lumantas, B. C., Acut, D. P., & Garcia, M. B. (2025). Equipping the Next Generation of Technicians: Navigating School Infrastructure and Technical Knowledge in the Age of AI Integration. In *Pitfalls of AI Integration in Education: Skill Obsolescence, Misuse, and Bias*. IGI Global., DOI: 10.4018/979-8-3373-0122-8.ch009

Garcia, M. B. (2021). Cooperative Learning in Computer Programming: A Quasi-Experimental Evaluation of Jigsaw Teaching Strategy with Novice Programmers. *Education and Information Technologies*, *26*(4), 4839–4856. DOI: 10.1007/s10639-021-10502-6

Garcia, M. B. (2023). Facilitating Group Learning Using an Apprenticeship Model: Which Master is More Effective in Programming Instruction? *Journal of Educational Computing Research*, *61*(6), 1207–1231. DOI: 10.1177/07356331231170382

Garcia, M. B. (2024). Profiling the Skill Mastery of Introductory Programming Students: A Cognitive Diagnostic Modeling Approach. *Education and Information Technologies*, *30*(5), 6455–6481. DOI: 10.1007/s10639-024-13039-6

Garcia, M. B. (2025). Teaching and Learning Computer Programming Using ChatGPT: A Rapid Review of Literature Amid the Rise of Generative AI Technologies. *Education and Information Technologies*, •••, 1–25. DOI: 10.1007/s10639-025-13452-5

Garcia, M. B., & Revano, T. F., Jr. (2021). Assessing the Role of Python Programming Gamified Course on Students' Knowledge, Skills Performance, Attitude, and Self-Efficacy. *2021 IEEE 13th International Conference on Humanoid, Nanotechnology, Information Technology, Communication and Control, Environment and Management (HNICEM)*. DOI: 10.1109/HNICEM54116.2021.9731935

Garcia, M. B., Revano, T. F., Jr., Maaliw, R. R., III, Lagrazon, P. G. G., Valderama, A. M. C., Happonen, A., . . . Yilmaz, R. (2023). Exploring Student Preference Between AI-Powered ChatGPT and Human-Curated Stack Overflow in Resolving Programming Problems and Queries. *2023 IEEE 15th International Conference on Humanoid, Nanotechnology, Information Technology, Communication and Control, Environment and Management (HNICEM)*. DOI: 10.1109/HNICEM60674.2023.10589162

Garcia, M. B., Rosak-Szyrocka, J., Yılmaz, R., Metwally, A. H. S., Acut, D. P., Ofosu-Ampong, K., & Bozkurt, A. (2025). Rethinking Educational Assessment in the Age of Generative AI: Actionable Strategies to Mitigate Academic Dishonesty. In *Pitfalls of AI Integration in Education: Skill Obsolescence, Misuse, and Bias*. IGI Global., DOI: 10.4018/979-8-3373-0122-8.ch001

Hasanah, N. A., Aziza, M. R., Junikhah, A., Arif, Y. M., & Garcia, M. B. (2025). Navigating the Use of AI in Engineering Education Through a Systematic Review of Technology, Regulations, and Challenges. In *Pitfalls of AI Integration in Education: Skill Obsolescence, Misuse, and Bias*. IGI Global., DOI: 10.4018/979-8-3373-0122-8.ch016

Hickman, H., McKeown, P., & Bell, T. (2023). Beyond Question Shuffling: Randomization Techniques in Programming Assessment. *2023 IEEE Frontiers in Education Conference (FIE)*. DOI: 10.1109/FIE58773.2023.10342976

Hutson, J., Fulcher, B., & Ratican, J. (2024). Enhancing Assessment and Feedback in Game Design Programs: Leveraging Generative AI for Efficient and Meaningful Evaluation. *IJERI: International Journal of Educational Research and Innovation*, (22), 1–20. DOI: 10.46661/ijeri.11038

Indriasari, T. D., Luxton-Reilly, A., & Denny, P. (2020). A Review of Peer Code Review in Higher Education. *ACM Transactions on Computing Education*, *20*(3), 1–25. DOI: 10.1145/3403935

Karnalim, O. (2023). Maintaining Academic Integrity in Programming: Locality-Sensitive Hashing and Recommendations. *Education Sciences*, *13*(1), 1–23. DOI: 10.3390/educsci13010054

Kendon, T., Wu, L., & Aycock, J. (2023). AI-Generated Code Not Considered Harmful. *Proceedings of the 25th Western Canadian Conference on Computing Education*. DOI: 10.1145/3593342.3593349

Krathwohl, D. R. (2002). A Revision of Bloom's Taxonomy: An Overview. *Theory into Practice*, *41*(4), 212–218.

Lepp, M., & Kaimre, J. (2025). Does Generative AI Help in Learning Programming: Students' Perceptions, Reported Use and Relation to Performance. *Computers in Human Behavior Reports*, *18*, 1–12. DOI: 10.1016/j.chbr.2025.100642

Louder, J. R. (2025). Alternative Educational Pathways: Stackable and Micro-Credentials to Bridge Education and Employment. In *The Emerald Handbook on International Higher Education: Navigating Workforce and Leadership Changes in a Digital Age*. Emerald Publishing Limited., DOI: 10.1108/978-1-83549-788-320251007

Luo, J. (2024). A Critical Review of GenAI Policies in Higher Education Assessment: A Call to Reconsider the "Originality" of Students' Work. *Assessment & Evaluation in Higher Education*, *49*(5), 651–664. DOI: 10.1080/02602938.2024.2309963

Mahon, J., Namee, B. M., & Becker, B. A. (2024). Guidelines for the Evolving Role of Generative AI in Introductory Programming Based on Emerging Practice. *Proceedings of the 2024 on Innovation and Technology in Computer Science Education* V. 1. DOI: 10.1145/3649217.3653602

Mangubat, J. C., Mangubat, M. R., Uy, T. B. L., Acut, D. P., & Garcia, M. B. (2025). Safeguarding Educational Innovations Amid AI Disruptions: A Reassessment of Patenting for Sustained Intellectual Property Protection. In *Pitfalls of AI Integration in Education: Skill Obsolescence, Misuse, and Bias*. IGI Global., DOI: 10.4018/979-8-3373-0122-8.ch013

Novak, M., Joy, M., & Kermek, D. (2019). Source-Code Similarity Detection and Detection Tools Used in Academia: A Systematic Review. *ACM Transactions on Computing Education, 19*(3), 1–37. DOI: 10.1145/3313290

Obaidellah, U., Blascheck, T., Guarnera, D. T., & Maletic, J. (2020). A Fine-Grained Assessment on Novice Programmers' Gaze Patterns on Pseudocode Problems. *ACM Symposium on Eye Tracking Research and Applications*. DOI: 10.1145/3379156.3391982

Pan, W. H., Chok, M. J., Wong, J. L. S., Shin, Y. X., Poon, Y. S., Yang, Z., & Lim, M. K. (2024). Assessing AI Detectors in Identifying AI-Generated Code: Implications for Education. *Proceedings of the 46th International Conference on Software Engineering: Software Engineering Education and Training*. DOI: 10.1145/3639474.3640068

Prather, J., Reeves, B. N., Leinonen, J., MacNeil, S., Randrianasolo, A. S., Becker, B. A., & Briggs, B. (2024). The Widening Gap: The Benefits and Harms of Generative AI for Novice Programmers. *Proceedings of the 2024 ACM Conference on International Computing Education Research*. DOI: 10.1145/3632620.3671116

Ralston, S. J. (2021). Higher Education's Microcredentialing Craze: A Postdigital-Deweyan Critique. *Postdigital Science and Education, 3*(1), 83–101. DOI: 10.1007/s42438-020-00121-8 PMID: 40476912

Selvaraj, A., Zhang, E., Porter, L., & Raj, A. G. S. (2021). Live Coding: A Review of the Literature. *Proceedings of the 26th ACM Conference on Innovation and Technology in Computer Science Education* V. 1. DOI: 10.1145/3430665.3456382

Semenov, S., Kolomiitsev, O., Hulevych, M., Mazurek, P., & Chernyk, O. (2025). An Intelligent Method for C++ Test Case Synthesis Based on a Q-Learning Agent. *Applied Sciences (Basel, Switzerland), 15*(15), 1–31. DOI: 10.3390/app15158596

Silva, C. A., Ramos, F. N., de Moraes, R. V., & Santos, E. L. (2024). ChatGPT: Challenges and Benefits in Software Programming for Higher Education. *Sustainability, 16*(3), 1–23. DOI: 10.3390/su16031245 PMID: 38756353

Soomro, S. A., Nanjappan, V., Casakin, H., & Georgiev, G. V. (2024). Fostering Technical Skills and Creativity in the Digital Fabrication Spaces: An Open-Ended Prototyping Approach. *International Journal of Technology and Design Education*. Advance online publication. DOI: 10.1007/s10798-024-09940-3

Taeb, M., Chi, H., & Bernadin, S. (2024). Assessing the Effectiveness and Security Implications of AI Code Generators. *Journal of The Colloquium for Information Systems Security Education, 11*(1), 1–6. DOI: 10.53735/cisse.v11i1.180

Velicea, F. P., Ghimbă an, A. E., Filip, R. C., Danciu, G. M., & Kertész, C. Z. (2025). *Programming Examination Platform: Generative AI-Driven Evaluation Tool for Computer Programming Classes*. Futureproofing Engineering Education for Global Responsibility., DOI: 10.1007/978-3-031-83520-9_33

Wang, A. Y., Chen, Y., Chung, J. J. Y., Brooks, C., & Oney, S. (2021). PuzzleMe: Leveraging Peer Assessment for In-Class Programming Exercises. *Proceedings of the ACM on Human-Computer Interaction*. DOI: 10.1145/3479559

Wilson, S., & Nishomoto, M. (2023). Assessing Learning of Computer Programing Skills in the Age of Generative Artificial Intelligence. *Journal of Biomechanical Engineering, 146*(5), 1–6. DOI: 10.1115/1.4064364 PMID: 38140801

Wilson, S. E., & Nishimoto, M. (2024). Assessing Learning of Computer Programing Skills in the Age of Generative Artificial Intelligence. *Journal of Biomechanical Engineering, 146*(5), 1–6. DOI: 10.1115/1.4064364 PMID: 38140801

Xiao, J., Bozkurt, A., Nichols, M., Pazurek, A., Stracke, C. M., Bai, J. Y. H., & Themeli, C. (2025). Venturing into the Unknown: Critical Insights into Grey Areas and Pioneering Future Directions in Educational Generative AI Research. *TechTrends*, •••, 1–16. DOI: 10.1007/s11528-025-01060-6

Xu, Z., & Sheng, V. S. (2024). Detecting AI-Generated Code Assignments Using Perplexity of Large Language Models. *Proceedings of the AAAI Conference on Artificial Intelligence, 38*(21), 23155–23162. DOI: 10.1609/aaai.v38i21.30361

Xue, Y., Chen, H., Bai, G. R., Tairas, R., & Huang, Y. (2024). Does ChatGPT Help With Introductory Programming?An Experiment of Students Using ChatGPT in CS1. *Proceedings of the 46th International Conference on Software Engineering: Software Engineering Education and Training*. DOI: 10.1145/3639474.3640076

Yang, S., Zhao, H., Xu, Y., Brennan, K., & Schneider, B. (2024). Debugging with an AI Tutor: Investigating Novice Help-seeking Behaviors and Perceived Learning. *Proceedings of the 2024 ACM Conference on International Computing Education Research*. DOI: 10.1145/3632620.3671092

Yilmaz, R., & Karaoglan Yilmaz, F. G. (2023). Augmented Intelligence in Programming Learning: Examining Student Views on the Use of ChatGPT for Programming Learning. *Computers in Human Behavior: Artificial Humans*, *1*(2), 1–7. DOI: 10.1016/j.chbah.2023.100005

Zhang, W., Guan, Y., & Hu, Z. (2024). The Efficacy of Project-Based Learning in Enhancing Computational Thinking Among Students: A Meta-Analysis of 31 Experiments and Quasi-Experiments. *Education and Information Technologies*, *29*(11), 14513–14545. DOI: 10.1007/s10639-023-12392-2

KEY TERMS AND DEFINITIONS

AI-Assisted Coding: The use of generative AI tools (e.g., ChatGPT, GitHub Copilot) to support programming tasks such as code generation, debugging, refactoring, and documentation, which can improve productivity but also influence learning and assessment validity.

Artificial Intelligence: A broad field of computer science focused on creating systems capable of performing tasks that normally require human intelligence, such as reasoning, learning, decision-making, perception, and language understanding.

Assessment Integrity: The assurance that the outcomes of an evaluation genuinely reflect a learner's own knowledge, effort, and skill, free from unauthorized or unacknowledged assistance.

Ethical Programming: An evaluative lens that considers the societal, legal, and moral implications of software design that emphasize issues such as algorithmic fairness, data privacy, bias mitigation, and responsible AI use.

Generative AI: A class of artificial intelligence models (e.g., LLMs like ChatGPT or Codex) capable of producing code, text, or other artifacts based on learned patterns.

Human-AI Collaboration: A pedagogical and professional paradigm where learners or developers work alongside AI systems to enhance productivity, problem-solving, and creativity, while maintaining human oversight and critical judgment.

Programming Education: A structured teaching-and-learning process that develops learners' ability to understand computational concepts and apply programming skills such as algorithm design, debugging, code comprehension, and software development practices.

Chapter 10
Pedagogical Promise and Peril of AI:
A Text Mining Analysis of ChatGPT Research Discussions in Programming Education

Juvy C. Grume
https://orcid.org/0009-0007-0744-4121
Pampanga State University, Philippines

Mark Anthony A. Castro
https://orcid.org/0009-0007-2610-3605
Pampanga State University, Philippines

John Paul P. Miranda
https://orcid.org/0000-0003-2059-972X
Pampanga State University, Philippines

Vernon Grace M. Maniago
https://orcid.org/0009-0009-5076-5400
Pampanga State University, Philippines

Aileen P. De Leon
https://orcid.org/0009-0002-5419-1722
Pampanga State University, Philippines

Joel D. Canlas
https://orcid.org/0009-0001-3880-6582
Pampanga State University, Philippines

Jordan L. Salenga
https://orcid.org/0009-0006-6371-3018
Pampanga State University, Philippines

Joel B. Quiambao
https://orcid.org/0009-0008-1581-8012
Pampanga State University, Philippines

Hilene E. Hernandez
https://orcid.org/0009-0008-9356-8178
Pampanga State University, Philippines

ABSTRACT

GenAI systems such as ChatGPT are increasingly discussed in programming education, but the ways in which the research literature conceptualizes and frames their

DOI: 10.4018/979-8-3373-6546-6.ch010

role remain unclear. This chapter applies text mining to publications indexed in a leading academic database to map scholarly discourse on ChatGPT in programming education. Term frequency analysis, phrase pattern extraction, and topic modeling reveal four dominant themes: pedagogical implementation, student-centered learning and engagement, AI infrastructure and human–AI collaboration, and assessment, prompting, and model evaluation. The literature prioritizes classroom practice and learner interaction, with comparatively limited attention to assessment design and institutional governance. Across studies, ChatGPT is positioned both as a learning aid that supports explanation, feedback, and efficiency and as a pedagogical risk linked to overreliance, unreliable outputs, and academic integrity concerns. These findings support responsible integration and highlight the need for stronger assessment and governance mechanisms.

INTRODUCTION

Programming remains one of the most demanding subjects in computer science education. Despite continued curriculum and pedagogical reforms, many students still struggle to learn programming effectively. Studies across multiple institutions report failure and withdrawal rates ranging from 30 to 50% in introductory programming courses (Margulieux et al., 2020; Simon et al., 2019). Students often describe programming as abstract and mentally challenging because it requires logical reasoning, syntax accuracy, and problem decomposition (Dirzyte et al., 2023; Malik & Coldwell-Neilson, 2017). These challenges lower confidence and increase anxiety, which frequently result in disengagement and attrition (Dirzyte et al., 2023; Garcia, 2024). These persistent difficulties motivate educators to seek approaches that provide timely feedback, guided practice, and individualized support for novice programmers.

Earlier responses to these difficulties included intelligent tutoring systems and automated assessment platforms. These tools adapted feedback and evaluated student work through structured mechanisms. They improved performance in topics such as loops, recursion, and data structures (Crow et al., 2018; Kouam & William, 2024). However, they were limited in scale and unable to support complex or open-ended programming tasks. The steady growth of class sizes in computer science programs reduced the capacity of instructors to deliver individualized assistance. This situation created a need for scalable systems capable of providing interactive and immediate instructional support.

The emergence of large language models, particularly ChatGPT, redirected this pursuit. ChatGPT produces explanations, examples, and code corrections through natural conversation. Instructors now integrate it into lessons to help students understand logic and structure in programming, while learners use it to receive guidance, generate code, and verify solutions (Xiao et al., 2025). Several studies report that ChatGPT supports motivation, coding accuracy, and self-efficacy when used with structured pedagogical frameworks (Garcia, 2025a; Wang & Fan, 2025). Other studies caution that unstructured use can lead to dependency, incorrect understanding, and ethical concerns regarding originality and fairness (Agbo et al., 2025; Muringa, 2025).

Within programming education, ChatGPT now functions as a tutor, debugging assistant, and feedback tool (Agbo et al., 2025; Gleeson, 2024). Students appreciate its accessibility and responsiveness, while researchers note issues related to plagiarism, misinformation, and unequal access to advanced versions (Reihanian et al., 2025; Tong, 2024). These perspectives demonstrate both optimism and caution, showing that ChatGPT combines pedagogical potential with ethical uncertainty.

This chapter examines this dual character through a text mining analysis of research on ChatGPT in programming education. It describes how recent publications discuss its educational applications and clarifies how ChatGPT can operate as both a productive learning aid and a source of academic and ethical challenges. The chapter aims to provide direction for teachers, researchers, and policymakers in creating responsible and effective strategies for integrating generative AI into programming instruction.

BACKGROUND

Artificial intelligence has supported programming education for several decades through systems that provide adaptive feedback and automated assessment. Early tools such as intelligent tutoring systems and code visualization platforms improved learning performance but were limited in flexibility and coverage (Crow et al., 2018; Kouam & William, 2024). Automated graders improved efficiency by comparing program outputs with expected solutions, but they could not evaluate problem-solving logic or coding style (Garcia, 2025b). These earlier systems established the groundwork for AI-supported instruction but lacked the conversational and contextual capacity of current large language models (Agbo et al., 2025; Franklin et al., 2025).

Generative AI offers a more interactive and context-aware approach to programming instruction. ChatGPT responds to questions, explains code, and produces examples aligned with the learner's level of understanding. Current literature documents its use in tutoring, content development, and automated assessment (Franklin et al., 2025; Garcia, 2025b; Gleeson, 2024). Studies in programming education show that ChatGPT can generate functional code, clarify compiler messages, and simplify complex programming structures in different languages such as Python, Java, and

C++ (Kosar et al., 2024; Phung et al., 2023; Shanto et al., 2025; Sun et al., 2024). Controlled applications report higher motivation, engagement, and self-perceived competence among students who use ChatGPT as a supplement to teacher-led instruction (Sun et al., 2024; Villegas-Ch et al., 2025). This body of evidence suggests that generative AI strengthens student participation and supports comprehension of difficult programming concepts.

Despite these advantages, concerns remain about ethical use and educational quality. Many students rely on AI-generated code without understanding its logic (Cotton et al., 2023; Silva et al., 2024). Teachers continue to face challenges in confirming authorship and ensuring that assessment practices remain fair and valid (Reihanian et al., 2025; Shafii & Berger, 2025; Swiecki et al., 2022). Some researchers note that excessive reliance on ChatGPT reduces persistence and limits independent debugging ability (Humble et al., 2024; Monib et al., 2024). These concerns demonstrate the need for structured guidelines and institutional policies that define appropriate AI use in academic settings.

The growing body of literature on ChatGPT remains limited in scope. Most studies focus on small classes or isolated instructional settings and seldom connect pedagogical and ethical dimensions within one analytical framework (Garcia et al., 2023; Kosar et al., 2024). Evidence about learning benefits and dependency patterns remains inconsistent, and institutional readiness for AI integration continues to vary (Agbo et al., 2025; Taheri et al., 2025). Few studies discuss ChatGPT's role as a long-term instructional partner or supervised learning resource in programming courses.

A comprehensive synthesis is needed to explain the dual role of ChatGPT in programming education. This chapter addresses that need through text mining of published studies to identify recurring educational and ethical themes. It provides a consolidated perspective on how researchers describe the advantages and risks of using ChatGPT in programming instruction. This background establishes the context for the text mining analysis that follows.

MAIN FOCUS OF THE CHAPTER

This chapter examines how scholarly research conceptualizes the use of ChatGPT in programming education. It analyzes dominant themes, recurring concepts, and structural patterns in academic discourse through text mining techniques applied to a curated corpus of Scopus-indexed publications. Rather than evaluating learning outcomes or system performance, the chapter concentrates on how research frames ChatGPT within teaching practice, learner engagement, assessment processes, and institutional contexts. This focus directs attention to both instructional opportunities and systemic considerations associated with generative AI in computer science education.

The chapter is anchored in a sociotechnical perspective, which treats educational technologies as components of interconnected systems that include students, teachers, pedagogical practices, institutional structures, and governance arrangements. From this perspective, ChatGPT is examined not only as an instructional support tool but also as a sociotechnical element shaped by classroom norms, assessment expectations, and policy conditions. This theoretical framing guides the interpretation of text mining outputs by situating discourse patterns within broader educational systems rather than viewing ChatGPT as a neutral or isolated instructional resource.

Guided by this perspective, the chapter examines how research discourse emphasizes classroom implementation and student engagement while giving comparatively less attention to assessment practices and institutional governance. It interprets these patterns as indicators of how agency, responsibility, and innovation are positioned within programming education research. By foregrounding these dimensions, the chapter clarifies how current scholarship situates ChatGPT within the evolving landscape of computer science education and highlights areas where pedagogical and institutional considerations remain underdeveloped.

METHODS

The dataset consisted of 229 documents retrieved from Scopus using the search query TITLE-ABS-KEY(chatgpt AND ("programming education" OR "teaching programming" OR "computer science education")). Only open-access journal articles and conference papers were included to ensure transparency and accessibility of research sources. After the removal of duplicate, irrelevant, and incomplete entries, 81 documents remained for initial review. A second validation excluded 12 documents that did not address programming education or the educational use of ChatGPT. The final dataset contained 69 documents that represented distinct academic discussions related on ChatGPT in programming and computer science education. The dataset captures research discussions indexed in Scopus and accessible through open-access publication channels, which define the scope of analysis in this chapter.

Each document underwent text preprocessing to prepare the corpus for analysis. All text was converted to lowercase, and punctuation marks, digits, and non-alphabetic symbols were removed. The corpus was tokenized to separate words, and standard English stopwords were removed to retain only semantically relevant terms. Porter stemming was applied to normalize word variations, such as reducing students and student to a single root form. These steps produced a clean and consistent dataset suitable for computational text analysis.

Three analytical procedures were applied. Term frequency analysis identified the most frequently occurring words to determine dominant research concepts. Phrase pattern analysis using bigrams and trigrams examined co-occurring terms that represented conceptual relationships such as "AI tools," "programming education," and "problem-solving skills." Latent Dirichlet Allocation (LDA) topic modeling was employed to identify underlying themes in the dataset. Topic solutions ranging from two to six topics were evaluated using perplexity, average topic overlap, and topic dominance. The four-topic model achieved a substantial reduction in semantic overlap, with an average Jaccard similarity of 0.393 compared with 0.667 for two topics and 0.581 for three topics, while maintaining a high mean maximum topic probability of 0.937. Models with more than four topics showed lower topic dominance and fragmented thematic structures. Based on these quantitative diagnostics and interpretability checks, the four-topic configuration was selected. The resulting topics were further reviewed by two professors with backgrounds in educational technology and programming, who independently examined topic coherence and alignment with established research themes in programming education. Each document was assigned to a primary topic based on the highest probability score, and representative authors were recorded to link computational patterns with corresponding scholarly discussions. In addition, each document was examined manually to identify reported opportunities, challenges, and limitations, ensuring that the interpretation reflected both quantitative patterns and contextual meaning within the academic discourse through informed author judgment.

RESULTS

Term Frequency Analysis

The term frequency analysis showed a consistent focus on students, AI integration, and programming education (Table 1). The most frequent words were student, ChatGPT, AI, education, and program. These terms indicate that researchers describe ChatGPT as both a learning companion and a pedagogical tool. The presence of tool, learn, and use shows that ChatGPT is often discussed as an instructional support that encourages engagement and assists in understanding programming concepts. The dominance of learner-oriented and tool-related terms suggests that research discourse frames ChatGPT primarily as an individual support resource, while instructional design and institutional roles are less explicitly emphasized. This pattern confirms that programming education remains the main context of scholarly attention and that AI integration is viewed as a significant component of teaching and learning in computer science.

Table 1. Top 10 Stemmed Terms

Rank	Term	Frequency
1	student	443
2	chatgpt	324
3	ai	291
4	educ	255
5	program	254
6	use	224
7	learn	222
8	studi	192
9	tool	149
10	code	143

Phrase Pattern Analysis

The phrase pattern analysis identified key relationships among concepts within the corpus (Table 2). Phrases such as programming education, AI tools, and use ChatGPT appeared most frequently, showing that research often centers on formal classroom environments where AI supports coding practice and instruction. Phrases including problem solving, learning outcomes, and future research demonstrate that authors combine pedagogical interest with evaluation and reflection. The trigram ChatGPT programming education occurred most frequently, linking pedagogical themes with the technological basis of generative AI. The repetition of AI generated content and AI generated code indicates continuing attention to originality and plagiarism. The co-occurrence of pedagogical, ethical, and evaluative phrases suggests that research discourse treats instructional opportunity, ethical risk, and learning impact as parallel concerns rather than as integrated design considerations. These patterns reveal that current discussions are organized around three central areas: pedagogy, ethics, and learning outcomes.

Table 2. Top 10 Bigrams and Trigrams

Rank	Bigram	Frequency	Trigram	Frequency
1	programming education	59	chatgpt programming education	12
2	ai tools	38	large language models	9
3	use chatgpt	33	ai generated content	8

continued on following page

Table 2. Continued

Rank	Bigram	Frequency	Trigram	Frequency
4	computer science	32	computer science education	8
5	using chatgpt	24	tools like chatgpt	6
6	chatgpt programming	21	problem solving skills	6
7	ai generated	20	chatgpt computer programming	6
8	future research	19	benefits negative impacts	5
9	problem solving	19	potential benefits negative	5
10	learning outcomes	18	ai generated code	5

Topic Modeling Results

The LDA topic modeling analysis produced four themes that describe how research conceptualizes the use of ChatGPT in programming education (Table 3). These themes are *Pedagogical Use and Classroom Implementation, Student-Centered Learning and Engagement, AI Infrastructure and Human-AI Collaboration, and Assessment, Prompting, and Model Evaluation.* The first two topics account for most of the corpus and foreground classroom practice and learner interaction, while the latter two reflect institutional and evaluative concern. The uneven distribution of topics suggests that research discourse prioritizes immediate instructional practice over systemic and assessment-related considerations.

The topic *Pedagogical Use and Classroom Implementation* includes works by Husain (2024), Stoyanova et al. (2025), López-Fernández and Vergaz (2025), Yang et al. (2025), and Penney et al. (2025). These studies emphasize teacher facilitation, structured integration, and ethical awareness. This topic suggests that ChatGPT is framed primarily as a pedagogical instrument whose effectiveness depends on instructional orchestration rather than institutional regulation. Although these discussions acknowledge ethical considerations, they remain situated at the classroom level, reinforcing a practice-oriented framing of AI adoption.

The topic *Student-Centered Learning and Engagement* includes studies by Annuš (2025), Boudia and Krismadinata (2024), Raihan et al. (2025), Güner and Er (2025), and Troussas et al. (2025). These studies describe ChatGPT as an interactive tutor that supports motivation, engagement, and coding performance. Across this topic, students are positioned as primary agents of AI use, while responsibility for oversight is implicitly delegated to instructors rather than institutional systems. This focus on learner-centered discourse indicates that research assigns agency to individual users and pedagogical design, while structural constraints and assessment validity receive less sustained attention

The themes *AI Infrastructure and Human-AI Collaboration* and *Assessment, Prompting, and Model Evaluation* expand the discussion to institutional and technical aspects. Habiballa et al. (2025), Dunder et al. (2024), da Silva et al. (2024), Phung et al. (2024), and Aruleba et al. (2025) examine how transparency, readiness, and accountability influence the integration of ChatGPT into institutional systems. Grandel et al. (2025), Lee and Song (2024), Cowan et al. (2023), Lau and Guo (2023), and Leinonen et al. (2023) address assessment-related issues through studies on prompt design, feedback generation, and model accuracy. Parallel discussions from Habiballa et al., da Silva et al., and Aruleba et al. describe AI systems as educational resources that require teacher preparation and ethical oversight, while Grandel et al., Lee and Song, and Lau and Guo explain how human moderation enhances the reliability of AI-assisted evaluation. The smaller proportion of these topics suggests that assessment validation and institutional governance are treated as secondary considerations rather than central components of pedagogical innovation. This imbalance highlights a gap between rapid instructional adoption and slower development of evaluative and regulatory frameworks.

Table 3. Top Terms per Topic and their Distribution

Topic	Label	Representative Terms	Count	Proportion
0	Pedagogical Use and Classroom Implementation	chatgpt, student, use, educ, learn, studi, ai, tool, implement, teach	13	0.19
1	Student-Centered Learning and Engagement	student, program, ai, chatgpt, learn, educ, use, studi, tool, task	34	0.49
2	AI Infrastructure and Human-AI Collaboration	ai, educ, student, llm, human, gener, model, code, program, task	16	0.23
3	Assessment, Prompting, and Model Evaluation	code, model, llm, perform, prompt, evalu, gpt, test, gener, feedback	6	0.09

BENEFITS AND OPPORTUNITIES OF USING CHATGPT IN PROGRAMMING EDUCATION

Enhanced Learning and Skill Development

ChatGPT strengthens programming proficiency when integrated through structured instructional frameworks. The R5E model presented by Abouelenein et al. (2025) improved student performance and critical thinking compared with unstructured use. PyChatAI developed by Alanazi et al. (2025) delivered real-time bilingual feedback that improved debugging and conceptual understanding among Python learners. The mobile learning system examined by Atta et al. (2025) enhanced motivation, self-efficacy, and coding accuracy through guided learning activities. The GPT-based code review system designed by Lee and Joe (2025) reduced academic dishonesty and increased precision in feedback, while Yilmaz and Yilmaz (2023) reported gains in computational thinking and programming confidence. These studies align with the text mining results, which show frequent attention to teaching practice, learning support, and classroom use of ChatGPT. Furthermore, these studies show that ChatGPT contributes to programming education when supported by pedagogical guidance and teacher facilitation.

Personalized Learning and Accessibility

ChatGPT supports adaptive and personalized learning that responds to individual progress and skill level. The R5E model developed by Abouelenein et al. (2025) produced higher post-test gains in computational thinking and coding performance. The automated grading study by Bernik et al. (2025) showed that ChatGPT-4 achieved a 0.91 correlation with instructor ratings and generated consistent and fair feedback. PyChatAI in Alanazi et al. (2025) improved examination scores through bilingual and adaptive guidance. The fuzzy memory model introduced by Troussas et al. (2025) generated feedback based on learner progress and achieved high retrieval accuracy. Studies by Lee and Joe (2025) and Lee and Song (2024) demonstrated that ChatGPT provided clear and relatable explanations for abstract programming concepts. Research by Abdulla et al. (2024), Liao et al. (2024), and Barambones et al. (2024) showed that ChatGPT-based scaffolding enhanced problem-solving and expanded opportunities for practice in simulated programming environments. This focus reflects the frequent use of student- and learning-related terms identified in the text mining analysis. In addition, these studies indicate that ChatGPT supports accessibility and individualized learning through adaptive feedback and context-sensitive guidance.

Instructor and Institutional Efficiency

The integration of ChatGPT improves instructional efficiency and reduces workload for teachers and institutions. Bernik et al. (2025) demonstrated that ChatGPT-4 graded programming submissions with a 0.91 correlation to instructor scores while completing evaluations faster than manual grading. Grandel et al. (2025) reported that the GreAIter system decreased grading time by over 75 percent without compromising accuracy. The GPT-based code review module developed by Lee and Joe (2025) improved error detection, supported large classroom management, and reduced repetitive teacher feedback. The SQL exam design study conducted by Aerts et al. (2024) showed that ChatGPT-3.5 generated coherent exam questions and reduced preparation time for instructors. These discussions correspond with assessment- and evaluation-related terms identified in the topic modeling results. Likewise, these results demonstrate that ChatGPT assists in improving efficiency, consistency, and scalability in programming assessment and feedback.

CHALLENGES, RISKS, AND LIMITATIONS

Academic Integrity and Misuse Risks

Concerns about academic integrity remain central to the discussion of ChatGPT in programming education. The survey conducted by Stoyanova et al. (2025) showed that teachers regarded ChatGPT as a major factor contributing to exam dishonesty, while students expressed more neutral perspectives. The experiment by Akçapınar and Sidan (2024) reported that students who received ChatGPT assistance obtained higher grades but often copied inaccurate outputs from the model. Shirazi et al. (2025) developed an outlier detection method to identify irregular grade patterns, but their approach could not confirm individual cases of cheating. Pan et al. (2024) evaluated AI-content detectors and observed poor accuracy in distinguishing AI-generated code from human-written submissions. Aligned with the text mining analysis, it shows that discussions of integrity often appear alongside teaching and learning topics rather than as separate debates. In addition, these studies show that ChatGPT can both improve and distort performance results, reinforcing the need for institutional policies, clear ethical frameworks, and monitoring mechanisms that maintain fairness in programming education.

Negative Cognitive and Educational Impacts

Cognitive dependency and reduced persistence represent continuing challenges in the use of ChatGPT for programming education. Stoyanova et al. (2025) reported that both teachers and students observed risks related to memorizing incorrect explanations and losing motivation to solve problems independently. Sun et al. (2024) noted that students who used ChatGPT showed higher satisfaction but no measurable improvement in learning outcomes. Mezzaro et al. (2024) found that students who relied heavily on ChatGPT produced fewer and less effective software tests. Gandhi and Muldner (2025) observed limited reasoning when students explained AI-generated code, which is comparable to other studies (Miranda et al., 2025). Aruleba et al. (2025) and Azoulay-Schwartz et al. (2024) emphasized that frequent reliance on AI weakens problem-solving effort and deep understanding. These issues appear less frequently in the text mining results compared with instructional discussions which means that they receive less emphasis in current research. Furthermore, these studies demonstrate that while ChatGPT supports comprehension, unmoderated use may restrict the development of independent reasoning and persistence in programming (Lepp & Kaimre, 2025).

Technical Limitations and Unreliability

Technical limitations affect the accuracy, reliability, and consistency of ChatGPT's outputs in programming tasks. Annuš (2025) reported that students frequently encountered incomplete or incorrect code responses. Lepp and Kaimre (2025) found a negative correlation between frequent ChatGPT use and programming test performance. Husain (2024) noted that instructors experienced inconsistent or irrelevant responses when using ChatGPT for code generation. Troussas et al. (2025) observed that the fuzzy memory model maintained better contextual accuracy than standard ChatGPT but remained constrained during extended sessions. Mezzaro et al. (2024) and Frankford et al. (2024) identified repeated errors in code explanations and hallucinated responses. Cowan et al. (2023) found that only 30% of ChatGPT outputs were fully usable, while failed conversations occurred frequently. These technical issues align with the smaller set of studies focused on evaluation and model performance identified in the topic analysis. These studies also emphasize that ChatGPT requires additional human supervision, algorithmic refinement, and contextual calibration to ensure dependable integration into programming education (Izquierdo-Álvarez & Jimeno-Postigo, 2025; Olugbade, 2025).

Ethical and Social Concerns

Ethical and social concerns influence how ChatGPT is perceived and implemented in programming education. The survey conducted by Da Silva et al. (2024) showed that while most students valued ChatGPT for its instructional support, they also raised issues of plagiarism, privacy, and unequal access. Boudia and Krismadinata (2024) reported that both teachers and students expressed reservations about dependency, misinformation, and reduced creativity. Abdulla et al. (2024) observed that students favored institutional monitoring to ensure responsible use. Aruleba et al. (2025) documented uncertainty about authorship and the ethical use of AI-generated work. Their study also showed that ChatGPT assisted learners with disabilities, which raised questions about equity when access was limited. Teachers in Boudia and Krismadinata (2024) emphasized that AI could support learning but could not replace human creativity and judgment. The text mining results indicate that ethical concerns are often discussed separately from assessment and curriculum design. At the same time, these studies demonstrate the need for institutional frameworks, equitable access, and ethical awareness programs that guide responsible use of ChatGPT in computer science education (Stoyanova et al., 2025).

SOLUTIONS AND RECOMMENDATIONS

The text mining results show that research discourse frequently frames ChatGPT around student use and instructional support, which places agency primarily at the learner–tool level. In response, programming courses should define clear instructional boundaries that guide how students engage with ChatGPT during learning activities and assessments. Course-level guidelines should specify when ChatGPT may support exploration, explanation, or debugging, and when independent problem solving is required. Instructors can reinforce these expectations through structured checkpoints such as code walkthroughs, explanation tasks, or short oral reviews that require students to articulate their reasoning. These practices align pedagogical control with observed discourse patterns while preserving academic integrity. By making student responsibility explicit, instructors can reduce ambiguity around acceptable AI use and support authentic engagement with programming concepts.

Pedagogical integration should emphasize reasoning, evaluation, and reflection rather than output generation (Bozkurt et al., 2024). The prominence of learner-centered terms in the corpus suggests that ChatGPT is often treated as a learning aid rather than an instructional authority. Instructors can respond by designing activities that require students to compare AI-generated solutions with their own code, identify errors, and justify algorithmic decisions. Such tasks shift attention from correctness to process and support the development of computational thinking. ChatGPT can also assist instructors in preparing guided practice materials, debugging prompts, and formative feedback examples. To ensure effective implementation, teachers should receive training in AI literacy, prompt formulation, and critical evaluation of AI-supported outputs.

The relatively limited attention to assessment and institutional infrastructure in the text mining results indicates an instructional gap that warrants pedagogical action. Programming courses should adapt assessment practices to account for the presence of generative AI by prioritizing explanation, reasoning, and code interpretation over final output alone. Institutions can support this shift by providing shared access to AI tools, documentation on responsible use, and technical support for monitoring student interaction patterns. Faculty collaboration can further promote consistency in assessment design and instructional expectations across courses. Accessibility features such as multilingual feedback and adaptive interfaces can support diverse learners and align AI use with inclusive teaching goals. Through targeted pedagogical design informed by discourse patterns, computer science education can integrate ChatGPT in ways that strengthen learning while maintaining instructional rigor.

FUTURE RESEARCH DIRECTIONS

Future research should investigate the long-term influence of ChatGPT on learning behavior, programming competence, and self-regulated learning among students in computer science education. Most current studies are limited to short-term classroom experiments. Longitudinal research can assess how consistent exposure to ChatGPT affects problem-solving skills, code quality, and persistence over multiple courses. These studies can determine whether regular use of AI assistance strengthens or reduces students' independent reasoning and debugging abilities. Research in this area can also evaluate how ChatGPT influences the development of higher-order skills such as abstraction, design thinking, and algorithmic reasoning.

Further research should compare instructional frameworks that integrate ChatGPT with existing programming pedagogy. Experimental and quasi-experimental designs can assess which combinations of AI-assisted and teacher-led instruction produce the most balanced outcomes in learning and motivation. Studies can analyze course implementations in areas such as software development, algorithms, and database systems to identify effective approaches for using ChatGPT as a learning partner rather than a replacement for instructor guidance. Research on assessment models can explore how reflective documentation, oral defense, or version-controlled project submissions maintain authenticity while accommodating AI-supported work.

Cross-institutional and cross-cultural research can expand understanding of equity, readiness, and policy adoption in AI-assisted learning environments. Comparative studies can reveal how resource differences, teacher confidence, and institutional infrastructure shape the quality of ChatGPT integration. Partnerships between educators and developers can improve prompt accuracy, reduce bias, and enhance the interpretability of AI-generated explanations in programming tasks. Studies that combine learning analytics with behavioral observation can identify usage patterns and inform intervention strategies. These research directions can advance responsible and data-informed practices for integrating ChatGPT into computer science education.

CONCLUSION

ChatGPT has become an important development in computer science education because of its capacity to generate, explain, and evaluate code in real time. Its use in programming courses presents opportunities for personalized instruction, immediate feedback, and improved engagement. When integrated through structured pedagogical frameworks, ChatGPT can strengthen computational thinking, self-efficacy, and problem-solving performance. However, unregulated use can create dependency and reduce independent reasoning. These contrasting effects emphasize the need for well-defined integration that upholds academic integrity and authentic learning. The patterns discussed in this chapter reflect how these issues are represented within the research corpus examined.

The role of institutions and educators remains central in achieving responsible implementation. Clear policies, transparent assessment procedures, and teacher training ensure that ChatGPT enhances instruction rather than replaces the learning process. Courses should align AI use with active learning strategies that require justification, code evaluation, and reflection. Institutions should also provide equitable access to AI resources and technical support to prevent inequality among students. Through careful regulation and guided use, universities can balance technological assistance with the goal of developing independent and competent programmers. These considerations emerge from research discussions indexed in Scopus and accessible through open-access publication channels.

In the broader context of computer science education, ChatGPT represents both innovation and responsibility. Its integration challenges traditional ideas about authorship, creativity, and expertise in programming. Continued collaboration among educators, researchers, and developers is essential to ensure that generative AI supports human learning objectives. With ethical governance, sound pedagogy, and institutional readiness, computer science education can adopt ChatGPT as a constructive partner that enhances understanding and promotes reflective and meaningful learning.

REFERENCES

Abdulla, S., Ismail, S., Fawzy, Y., & Elhaj, A. (2024). Using ChatGPT in Teaching Computer Programming and Studying its Impact on Students Performance. *Electronic Journal of e-Learning*, *22*(6), 66–81. DOI: 10.34190/EJEL.22.6.3380

Abouelenein, Y. A. M., Ghazala, A. F. A., Mahdy, E. M. M., & Khalaf, M. H. R. (2025). The R5E pattern: Can artificial intelligence enhance programming skills development? *Education and Information Technologies*, *30*(15), 22177–22205. DOI: 10.1007/s10639-025-13616-3

Aerts, W., Fletcher, G., & Miedema, D. (2024). *A Feasibility Study on Automated SQL Exercise Generation with ChatGPT-3.5*. 13–19. DOI: 10.1145/3663649.3664368

Agbo, F. J., Olivia, C., Oguibe, G., Sanusi, I. T., & Sani, G. (2025). Computing education using generative artificial intelligence tools: A systematic literature review. *Computers and Education Open*, *9*, 100266. 10.1016/j.caeo.2025.100266

Akçapınar, G., & Sidan, E. (2024). AI chatbots in programming education: Guiding success or encouraging plagiarism. *Discover Artificial Intelligence*, *4*(1), 87. DOI: 10.1007/s44163-024-00203-7

Alanazi, M., Soh, B., Samra, H., & Li, A. (2025). PyChatAI: Enhancing Python Programming Skills—An Empirical Study of a Smart Learning System. *Computers*, *14*(5). Advance online publication. DOI: 10.3390/computers14050158

Annuš, N. (2025). Investigation of Generative AI Adoption in IT-Focused Vocational Secondary School Programming Education. *Education Sciences*, *15*(9). Advance online publication. DOI: 10.3390/educsci15091152

Aruleba, K., Sanusi, I. T., Obaido, G., Ogbuokiri, B., & Mienye, I. D. (2025). *Beyond the Prompt: Student Strategies, Ethical Reflections, and Learning with ChatGPT in Computer Science*. Technology, Knowledge and Learning., DOI: 10.1007/s10758-025-09899-7

Atta, A., Esmat, M., Amasha, N., Elayat, E., & Elsaid, W. K. (2025). A Smart ChatGPT Mobile Application for Improving C# Programming Skills for Students in Educational Institutions. *Qubahan Academic Journal*, *5*(2), 49–62. DOI: 10.48161/qaj.v5n2a1772

Azoulay-Schwartz, R., Hirst, T., & Reches, S. (2024). Academia and Industry Synergy: Addressing Integrity Challenge in Programming Education. *International Conference on Agents and Artificial Intelligence, 3*, 1135–1143. DOI: 10.5220/0012451000003636

Barambones, J., Moral-Martos, C., De Antonio, A., Imbert, R., Martínez-Normand, L., & Villalba-Mora, E. (2024). ChatGPT for Learning HCI Techniques: A Case Study on Interviews for Personas. *IEEE Transactions on Learning Technologies, 17*, 1486–1501. DOI: 10.1109/TLT.2024.3386095

Bernik, A., Radošević, D., & Čep, A. (2025). A Comparative Study of Large Language Models in Programming Education: Accuracy, Efficiency, and Feedback in Student Assignment Grading. *Applied Sciences (Switzerland), 15*(18). Advance online publication. DOI: 10.3390/app151810055

Boudia, C., & Krismadinata, K. (2024). Early insights into SLA with chatGPT: Navigating CS teachers and student perspectives in an opinion-based exploration. *Edelweiss Applied Science and Technology, 8*(5), 648–661. http://dx.doi.org/10.55214/25768484.v8i5.1729

Bozkurt, A., Xiao, J., Farrow, R., Bai, J. Y. H., Nerantzi, C., Moore, S., & Asino, T. I. (2024). The Manifesto for Teaching and Learning in a Time of Generative AI: A Critical Collective Stance to Better Navigate the Future. *Open Praxis, 16*(4), 487–513. DOI: 10.55982/openpraxis.16.4.777

Cowan, B., Watanobe, Y., & Shirafuji, A. (2023). *Enhancing Programming Learning with LLMs: Prompt Engineering and Flipped Interaction*. 10–16. DOI: 10.1145/3634814.3634816

Crow, T., Luxton-Reilly, A., & Wuensche, B. (2018). Intelligent tutoring systems for programming education: a systematic review. *Proceedings of the 20th Australasian Computing Education Conference*, 53–62. DOI: 10.1145/3160489.3160492

Da Silva, C. A. G. D., Ramos, F. N., de Moraes, R. V., & Dos Santos, E. L. D. (2024). ChatGPT: Challenges and Benefits in Software Programming for Higher Education. *Sustainability (Switzerland), 16*(3). Advance online publication. DOI: 10.3390/su16031245

Dirzyte, A., Perminas, A., Kaminskis, L., Žebrauskas, G., Sederevičiūtė-Pačiauskienė, Ž., Šliogerienė, J., Suchanova, J., Rimašiūtė-Knabikienė, R., Patapas, A., & Gajdosikiene, I. (2023). Factors contributing to dropping out of adults' programming e-learning. *Heliyon, 9*(12), e22113. DOI: 10.1016/j.heliyon.2023.e22113 PMID: 38107286

Dunder, N., Lundborg, S., Wong, J., & Viberg, O. (2024). Kattis vs ChatGPT: Assessment and Evaluation of Programming Tasks in the Age of Artificial Intelligence. *Proceedings of the 14th Learning Analytics and Knowledge Conference*, 821–827. DOI: 10.1145/3636555.3636882

Frankford, E., Sauerwein, C., Bassner, P., Krusche, S., & Breu, R. (2024). AI-Tutoring in Software Engineering Education Experiences with Large Language Models in Programming Assessments. *Proceedings - International Conference on Software Engineering*, 309–319. DOI: 10.1145/3639474.3640061

Franklin, D., Denny, P., Gonzalez-Maldonado, D. A., & Tran, M. (2025). *Generative AI in Computer Science Education: Challenges and Opportunities*. Cambridge University Press., DOI, DOI: 10.1017/9781009581738

Gandhi, A., & Muldner, K. (2025). Beyond verbal self-explanations: Student annotations of a code-tracing solution produced by ChatGPT. *British Journal of Educational Technology*. Advance online publication. DOI: 10.1111/bjet.13600

Garcia, M. B. (2025a). Profiling the skill mastery of introductory programming students: A cognitive diagnostic modeling approach. *Education and Information Technologies, 30*(5), 6455–6481. DOI: 10.1007/s10639-024-13039-6

Garcia, M. B. (2025b). Teaching and learning computer programming using ChatGPT: A rapid review of literature amid the rise of generative AI technologies. *Education and Information Technologies*, *30*(12), 16721–16745. DOI: 10.1007/s10639-025-13452-5

Garcia, M. B., Revano Jr, T. F., Maaliw Iii, R. R., Lagrazon, P. G. G., Valderama, A. M. C., Happonen, A., . . . Yilmaz, R. (2023). Exploring Student Preference Between AI-Powered ChatGPT and Human-Curated Stack Overflow in Resolving Programming Problems and Queries. *2023 IEEE 15th International Conference on Humanoid, Nanotechnology, Information Technology, Communication and Control, Environment and Management (HNICEM)*. DOI: 10.1109/HNICEM60674.2023.10589162

Gleeson, M. (2024). Exploring the Use of Generative AI in Computer Science Education in a Technological University in Ireland. *European Journal of Open. Distance and E-Learning*, *26*(1), 107–118. DOI: 10.2478/eurodl-2025-0004

Grandel, S., Schmidt, D. C., & Leach, K. (2025). Applying Large Language Models to Enhance the Assessment of Java Programming Assignments. *Proceedings of the ACM SIGSOFT Symposium on the Foundations of Software Engineering*, 789–799. DOI: 10.1145/3696630.3727236

Güner, H., & Er, E. (2025). AI in the classroom: Exploring students' interaction with ChatGPT in programming learning. *Education and Information Technologies*. Advance online publication. DOI: 10.1007/s10639-025-13337-7

Habiballa, H., Kotyrba, M., Volna, E., Bradáč, V., & Dusek, M. (2025). Artificial Intelligence (ChatGPT) and Bloom's Taxonomy in Theoretical Computer Science Education. *Applied Sciences (Switzerland), 15*(2). Advance online publication. DOI: 10.3390/app15020581

Haji Amin Shirazi, S. H. A., Pang, A., Knight, A., Salloum, M., & Vahid, F. (2025). *Midterm Exam Outliers Efficiently Highlight Potential Cheaters on Programming Assignments., 1*, 437–442. DOI: 10.1145/3641554.3701883

Humble, N., Boustedt, J., Holmgren, H., Milutinovic, G., Seipel, S., & Östberg, A.-S. (2024). Cheaters or AI-Enhanced Learners: Consequences of ChatGPT for Programming Education. *Electronic Journal of e-Learning, 22*(2), 16–29. 10.34190/ejel.21.5.3154

Husain, A. (2024). Potentials of ChatGPT in Computer Programming: Insights from Programming Instructors. *Journal of Information Technology Education, 23*, 1–25. 10.28945/5240

Izquierdo-Álvarez, V., & Jimeno-Postigo, C. (2025). Challenges and Opportunities of Integrating Generative Artificial Intelligence in Higher Education: A Systematic Review. In *Pitfalls of AI Integration in Education: Skill Obsolescence, Misuse, and Bias*. IGI Global., DOI: 10.4018/979-8-3373-0122-8.ch017

Kosar, T., Ostojič, D., Liu, Y. D., & Mernik, M. (2024). Computer Science Education in ChatGPT Era: Experiences from an Experiment in a Programming Course for Novice Programmers. *Mathematics, 12*(5). Advance online publication. DOI: 10.3390/math12050629

Kouam, F., & William, A. (2024). The effectiveness of intelligent tutoring systems in supporting students with varying levels of programming experience. *Discover Education, 3*(1), 278. DOI: 10.1007/s44217-024-00385-3

Lau, S., & Guo, P. (2023). From "Ban It Till We Understand It" to "Resistance is Futile": How University Programming Instructors Plan to Adapt as More Students Use AI Code Generation and Explanation Tools such as ChatGPT and GitHub Copilot. 106–121. DOI: 10.1145/3568813.3600138

Lee, D.-K., & Joe, I. (2025). A GPT-Based Code Review System With Accurate Feedback for Programming Education. *IEEE Access : Practical Innovations, Open Solutions, 13*, 105724–105737. DOI: 10.1109/ACCESS.2025.3581139

Lee, S., & Song, K.-S. (2024). Teachers' and students' perceptions of AI-generated concept explanations: Implications for integrating generative AI in computer science education. *Computers and Education: Artificial Intelligence*, *7*. Advance online publication. DOI: 10.1016/j.caeai.2024.100283

Leinonen, J., Denny, P., MacNeil, S., Sarsa, S., Bernstein, S., Kim, J., Tran, A., & Hellas, A. (2023). Comparing Code Explanations Created by Students and Large Language Models. *Annual Conference on Innovation and Technology in Computer Science Education, ITiCSE, 1*, 124–130. DOI: 10.1145/3587102.3588785

Lepp, M., & Kaimre, J. (2025). Does generative AI help in learning programming: Students' perceptions, reported use and relation to performance. *Computers in Human Behavior Reports*, *18*. Advance online publication. DOI: 10.1016/j.chbr.2025.100642

Liao, J., Zhong, L., Zhe, L., Xu, H., Liu, M., & Xie, T. (2024). Scaffolding Computational Thinking With ChatGPT. *IEEE Transactions on Learning Technologies*, *17*, 1668–1682. DOI: 10.1109/TLT.2024.3392896

López-Fernández, D., & Vergaz, R. (2025). ChatGPT in Computer Science Education: A Case Study on a Database Administration Course. *Applied Sciences (Switzerland)*, *15*(2). Advance online publication. DOI: 10.3390/app15020985

Malik, S. I., & Coldwell-Neilson, J. (2017). Comparison of Traditional and ADRI Based Teaching Approaches in an Introductory Programming Course. *Journal of Information Technology Education*, *16*, 267–283. 10.28945/3793

Margulieux, L. E., Morrison, B. B., & Decker, A. (2020). Reducing withdrawal and failure rates in introductory programming with subgoal labeled worked examples. *International Journal of STEM Education*, *7*(1), 19. DOI: 10.1186/s40594-020-00222-7

Mezzaro, S., Gambi, A., & Fraser, G. (2024). *An Empirical Study on How Large Language Models Impact Software Testing Learning*. 555–564. DOI: 10.1145/3661167.3661273

Miranda, J. P. P., Cruz, M. A. D., Fernandez, A. B., Balahadia, F. F., Aviles, J. S., Caro, C. A., & Gaña, E. P. (2025). Erosion of Critical Academic Skills Due to AI Dependency Among Tertiary Students: A Path Analysis. In *Pitfalls of AI Integration in Education: Skill Obsolescence, Misuse, and Bias*. IGI Global., DOI: 10.4018/979-8-3373-0122-8.ch002

Monib, W. K., Qazi, A., Apong, R. A., Azizan, M. T., De Silva, L., & Yassin, H. (2024). Generative AI and future education: A review, theoretical validation, and authors' perspective on challenges and solutions. *PeerJ. Computer Science, 10*, e2105. DOI: 10.7717/peerj-cs.2105 PMID: 39650462

Muringa, T. P. (2025). Exploring ethical dilemmas and institutional challenges in AI adoption: a study of South African universities. *Frontiers in Education, Volume 10-2025*. https://www.frontiersin.org/journals/education/articles/10.3389/feduc.2025.1628019

Olugbade, D. (2025). A Systematic Review of the Role of AI-Enabled Chatbots in Modern Education: Benefits, Risks, and Implementation Complexity. In *Pitfalls of AI Integration in Education: Skill Obsolescence, Misuse, and Bias*. IGI Global., DOI: 10.4018/979-8-3373-0122-8.ch018

Pan, W. H., Chok, M. J., Wong, J. L. S., Shin, Y. X., Poon, Y. S., Yang, Z., Chong, C. Y., Lo, D., & Lim, M. K. (2024). Assessing AI Detectors in Identifying AI-Generated Code: Implications for Education. *Proceedings - International Conference on Software Engineering*, 1–11. DOI: 10.1145/3639474.3640068

Penney, J., Acharya, P., Hilbert, P., Parekh, P., Sarma, A., Steinmacher, I., & Gerosa, M. A. (2025). *Outcomes, Perceptions, and Interaction Strategies of Novice Programmers Studying with ChatGPT*. DOI: 10.1145/3719160.3736625

Phung, T., P\uadurean, V.-A., Cambronero, J., Gulwani, S., Kohn, T., Majumdar, R., Singla, A., & Soares, G. (2023). Generative AI for Programming Education: Benchmarking ChatGPT, GPT-4, and Human Tutors. *Proceedings of the 2023 ACM Conference on International Computing Education Research* - Volume 2, 41–42. DOI: 10.1145/3568812.3603476

Phung, T., P durean, V.-A., Singh, A., Brooks, C., Cambronero, J., Gulwani, S., Singla, A., & Soares, G. (2024). Automating Human Tutor-Style Programming Feedback: Leveraging GPT-4 Tutor Model for Hint Generation and GPT-3.5 Student Model for Hint Validation. 12–23. DOI: 10.1145/3636555.3636846

Raihan, N., Goswami, D., Puspo, S. S. C., Siddiq, M. L., Newman, C., Ranasinghe, T., Santos, J. C. S., & Zampieri, M. (2025). On the performance of large language models on introductory programming assignments. *Journal of Intelligent Information Systems*. Advance online publication. DOI: 10.1007/s10844-025-00968-y

Reihanian, I., Hou, Y., Chen, Y., & Zheng, Y. (2025). A Review of Generative AI in Computer Science Education: Challenges and Opportunities in Accuracy, Authenticity, and Assessment. In Arabnia, H. R., Deligiannidis, L., Shenavarmasouleh, F., Amirian, S., & Ghareh Mohammadi, F. (Eds.), *Computational Science and Computational Intelligence* (pp. 144–158). Springer Nature Switzerland.

Shafii, R. A., & Berger, J.-L. (2025). Teacher assessment literacy, formative assessment practices, and their perceived efficacy in Tanzania: A scoping review. *Studies in Educational Evaluation, 86*, 101496. 10.1016/j.stueduc.2025.101496

Shanto, S. S., Ahmed, Z., & Jony, A. I. (2025). Generative AI for Programming Education: Can ChatGPT Facilitate the Acquisition of Fundamental Programming Skills for Novices? *Proceedings of the 3rd International Conference on Computing Advancements*, 685–692. DOI: 10.1145/3723178.3723268

Simon, L.-R. A., Ajanovski, V. V, Fouh, E., Gonsalvez, C., Leinonen, J., Parkinson, J., Poole, M., & Thota, N. (2019). Pass Rates in Introductory Programming and in other STEM Disciplines. *Proceedings of the Working Group Reports on Innovation and Technology in Computer Science Education*, 53–71. DOI: 10.1145/3344429.3372502

Stoyanova, D., Stoyanova-Petrova, S., & Mileva, N. (2025). Exploring Students' and Teachers' Perceptions about Using ChatGPT in Programming Education. *International Journal of Engineering Pedagogy, 15*(2), 15–41. DOI: 10.3991/ijep.v15i2.50607

Sun, D., Boudouaia, A., Zhu, C., & Li, Y. (2024). Would ChatGPT-facilitated programming mode impact college students' programming behaviors, performances, and perceptions? An empirical study. *International Journal of Educational Technology in Higher Education, 21*(1), 14. DOI: 10.1186/s41239-024-00446-5

Swiecki, Z., Khosravi, H., Chen, G., Martinez-Maldonado, R., Lodge, J. M., Milligan, S., Selwyn, N., & Gašević, D. (2022). Assessment in the age of artificial intelligence. *Computers and Education: Artificial Intelligence, 3*, 100075. 10.1016/j.caeai.2022.100075

Taheri, R., Nazemi, N., Pennington, S. E., Clark, J. A., & Dadgostari, F. (2025). Factors influencing educators' AI adoption: A grounded meta-analysis review. *Computers and Education: Artificial Intelligence, 9*, 100464. 10.1016/j.caeai.2025.100464

Tong, A. (2024). OpenAI launches free AI training course for teachers. *Reuters*. https://www.reuters.com/technology/artificial-intelligence/openai-launches-free-ai-training-course-teachers-2024-11-20/

Troussas, C., Krouska, A., Mylonas, P., Sgouropoulou, C., & Voyiatzis, I. (2025). Fuzzy Memory Networks and Contextual Schemas: Enhancing ChatGPT Responses in a Personalized Educational System. *Computers, 14*(3). Advance online publication. DOI: 10.3390/computers14030089

Villegas-Ch, W., Buenano-Fernandez, D., Navarro, A. M., & Mera-Navarrete, A. (2025). Adaptive intelligent tutoring systems for STEM education: Analysis of the learning impact and effectiveness of personalized feedback. *Smart Learning Environments, 12*(1), 41. DOI: 10.1186/s40561-025-00389-y

Wang, J., & Fan, W. (2025). The effect of ChatGPT on students' learning performance, learning perception, and higher-order thinking: Insights from a meta-analysis. *Humanities & Social Sciences Communications, 12*(1), 621. DOI: 10.1057/s41599-025-04787-y

Xiao, J., Bozkurt, A., Nichols, M., Pazurek, A., Stracke, C. M., Bai, J. Y. H., & Themeli, C. (2025). Venturing into the Unknown: Critical Insights into Grey Areas and Pioneering Future Directions in Educational Generative AI Research. *TechTrends, 69*, 582–597. DOI: 10.1007/s11528-025-01060-6

Yang, T.-C., Hsu, Y.-C., & Wu, J.-Y. (2025). The effectiveness of ChatGPT in assisting high school students in programming learning: Evidence from a quasi-experimental research. *Interactive Learning Environments, 33*(6), 3726–3743. DOI: 10.1080/10494820.2025.2450659

Yilmaz, R., & Karaoglan Yilmaz, F. G. (2023). The effect of generative artificial intelligence (AI)-based tool use on students' computational thinking skills, programming self-efficacy and motivation. *Computers and Education: Artificial Intelligence, 4*, 100147. 10.1016/j.caeai.2023.100147

KEY TERMS AND DEFINITIONS

Academic Integrity: An ethical standard that ensures honesty and originality in AI-assisted programming work.

AI Literacy: The knowledge and ability to understand, evaluate, and apply AI tools in programming education.

ChatGPT: An AI system that generates code, explanations, and feedback through natural language interaction.

Computational Thinking: A problem-solving process involving abstraction, decomposition, and algorithmic reasoning.

GenAI: An AI technology that creates new content such as text, code, or images based on learned data patterns.

Human-AI Collaboration: A cooperative framework where teachers and ChatGPT jointly support learning and evaluation.

Pedagogical Integration: The structured inclusion of ChatGPT in programming instruction to support learning and assessment.

Programming Education: The structured teaching of coding, algorithmic reasoning, and problem-solving in computer science.

Prompt Engineering: The design of precise input prompts that guide ChatGPT to produce accurate programming responses.

Student-Centered Learning: An instructional approach that promotes active participation and individualized guidance through ChatGPT.

Chapter 11
Pedagogical Framework for Developing Students' Python Programming Competencies Using Intelligent Systems

Kasim Khusanov
https://orcid.org/0000-0002-5491-7071
Turin Polytechnic University, Uzbekistan

Ravshanjon Kakharov
https://orcid.org/0009-0002-3324-6472
Namangan State University, Uzbekistan

Xoshimjon Erkinjonovich Xolmirzayev
https://orcid.org/0009-0001-4526-9949
Namangan State University, Uzbekistan

Akhrorbek Abdullayev
https://orcid.org/0009-0005-9798-4206
Namangan State University, Uzbekistan

ABSTRACT

This chapter explores the use of intelligent learning systems to develop students' Python programming competencies in higher education. The research highlights how these systems provide automated assessment, personalized feedback, and gamified learning experiences that foster programming literacy, learner independence, and motivation. By demonstrating the effectiveness of intelligent systems in enhancing

DOI: 10.4018/979-8-3373-6546-6.ch011

Python programming competencies, this chapter underscores the transformative role of artificial intelligence and machine learning in education. The results of this study clearly demonstrate that integrating intelligent learning systems into Python programming education significantly improves both the quality and efficiency of the learning process. The use of intelligent systems transforms traditional instructional models into adaptive, interactive, and learner-centered environments that align with the pedagogical demands of the digital age.

INTRODUCTION

In the twenty-first century, the rapid development of information and communication technologies (ICT) has had a profound impact on all sectors of society, including education. The increasing digitalization of modern economies has placed new demands on educational institutions to prepare specialists who are not only technically proficient but also capable of critical thinking, problem-solving, and adaptive learning. Among these emerging competencies, programming literacy has become a fundamental component of the digital skill set required in the contemporary workforce. Programming is now regarded not merely as a technical activity but as a universal cognitive skill that enables individuals to design, analyze, and implement solutions across diverse domains, such as artificial intelligence (AI), big data analytics, cybersecurity, cloud computing, and the Internet of Things (IoT).

The growing importance of programming education has prompted higher education institutions worldwide to reassess their curricula and instructional strategies. Traditional lecture-based and teacher-centered approaches often fail to address the diverse learning needs of students, particularly in large classes or online learning environments. As a result, there is an increasing need to adopt innovative pedagogical models and intelligent technologies capable of personalizing learning, automating assessment, and delivering timely feedback to enhance the overall learning experience.

Despite its accessibility, Python education continues to face several challenges. Traditional instructional methods, which rely heavily on lectures, manual code review, and static assessments, are often time-consuming and lack scalability. Instructors must devote substantial effort to evaluating assignments and providing individualized feedback, a task that becomes increasingly difficult as class sizes grow. Additionally, students learning under these conventional approaches often receive delayed or insufficient feedback, which can lead to frustration and diminished motivation. This mismatch between instructional demands and pedagogical capacity highlights the need for intelligent learning technologies that can effectively support both instructors and learners throughout the educational process.

In this context, the integration of Intelligent Tutoring Systems (ITS) has emerged as a promising approach to enhancing programming education. ITS platforms are designed to simulate one-on-one tutoring by employing artificial intelligence algorithms to analyze learner behavior, identify errors, and deliver adaptive guidance. In programming education, such systems can automatically evaluate code submissions, detect syntactical and logical errors in real time, and generate personalized feedback based on individual performance and learning progress. This immediate and adaptive interaction encourages active learner engagement, promotes reflection on errors, and supports the development of self-regulated learning skills.

Despite the growing adoption of intelligent educational technologies, their effectiveness remains highly dependent on contextual and pedagogical adaptation. In many developing countries, including Uzbekistan, the digital transformation of higher education is uneven and often constrained by limited infrastructure, insufficient teacher training, and varying levels of digital literacy among students. Consequently, there is a pressing need to design localized methodologies that align intelligent learning systems with specific cultural, linguistic, and institutional contexts.

The novelty of this research lies in the proposal of a comprehensive methodology that integrates AI-based tutoring mechanisms into Python programming education while maintaining sensitivity to learner diversity and pedagogical principles. Rather than merely automating assessment or providing generic feedback, the proposed approach seeks to establish a synergistic relationship between human instructors and intelligent systems, in which AI functions as a co-facilitator rather than a substitute for human teaching. This balance ensures that the advantages of automation—such as objectivity, efficiency, and scalability—are realized while preserving the emotional, motivational, and social dimensions of learning under instructor guidance.

Furthermore, this study contributes to the theoretical foundations of digital pedagogy by integrating principles of constructivism, adaptive learning, and self-regulated learning into a unified framework for programming education. Within this model, learners are positioned as active participants who construct knowledge through continuous interaction with both intelligent systems and peers. The intelligent system supports this process by providing timely scaffolding, formative feedback, and adaptive challenges that foster deeper cognitive engagement.

Unlike general advocacy for Intelligent Tutoring Systems, this chapter introduces a structured Human–AI co-facilitation framework. The novelty of this methodology lies in its integrated feedback loop that combines automated assessment, dynamic feedback granularity, and instructor-led pedagogical intervention, specifically optimized for resource-constrained higher education environments.

MAIN FOCUS OF THE CHAPTER

This chapter focuses on the development of students' Python programming competencies through the integration of intelligent learning systems. It examines how artificial intelligence–based tools, particularly Intelligent Tutoring Systems (ITS), enhance learning by automating assessment, providing personalized and real-time feedback, and supporting self-regulated learning processes. The research highlights that such systems strengthen students' algorithmic thinking, problem-solving abilities, and independent learning skills, while simultaneously reducing instructors' workload through objective and efficient evaluation mechanisms. Furthermore, the chapter demonstrates, through experimental findings, that intelligent learning systems significantly improve learning efficiency, motivation, and student engagement when compared with traditional instructional methods.

Recent trends in educational technology emphasize not only the cognitive dimension of learning but also its affective and behavioral components. Intelligent learning systems support this multidimensional approach by fostering emotional engagement and learning persistence through gamification, adaptive difficulty levels, and positive reinforcement strategies. In addition, the integration of learning analytics enables instructors to visualize learner progress patterns and implement timely pedagogical interventions. These data-informed practices facilitate a shift from reactive to proactive education, in which instruction dynamically adapts to learner behavior and performance.

From a pedagogical perspective, the instructor's role evolves from that of a "knowledge transmitter" to a "learning architect," responsible for designing enriched digital environments that promote inquiry, reflection, and collaboration. This transformation reflects the core principles of digital pedagogy, wherein technology serves not as an end but as a means of supporting human-centered, competency-based education.

From a macroeconomic perspective, programming literacy is increasingly recognized as a critical component of national innovation capacity. Countries that invest in computational education tend to demonstrate higher levels of technological competitiveness, digital entrepreneurship, and knowledge-based economic growth. Consequently, educational reforms aimed at strengthening programming competencies fulfill a dual purpose: they equip individuals with market-relevant skills while simultaneously fostering systemic innovation within the broader economy.

Contemporary labor markets increasingly demand hybrid professionals who combine domain-specific expertise with computational fluency. This convergence—often describes computational interdisciplinary requires higher education institutions to embed coding skills across non-technical disciplines, enabling economists, linguists, and social scientists to apply data-driven reasoning within their respective fields. When effectively implemented, intelligent learning systems can accelerate this integration by adapting learning pathways to accommodate learners from diverse academic backgrounds.

BACKGROUND OF THE STUDY

Although Intelligent Tutoring Systems (ITS) have demonstrated substantial potential in improving programming education, their implementation presents several challenges. These systems, which rely on artificial intelligence algorithms, have been shown to enhance students' learning performance and motivation by providing personalized feedback and adaptive support (Fodouop Kouam, 2024). Automated grading and feedback tools streamline instructors' tasks, ensure objectivity, and promote independent learning; however, they require continuous maintenance and specialized technical expertise to function effectively (Messer, Brown, Kölling, & Shi, 2023). Similarly, fuzzy logic–based ITS models have proven effective in tailoring learning pathways to individual needs, yet their successful deployment depends on advanced infrastructure and careful calibration to maintain accuracy and reliability (Chrysafiadi & Virvou, 2023).

Furthermore, research indicates that ITS play a significant role in fostering students' self-regulation and positive learning attitudes, although their effectiveness is closely tied to adequate institutional support and user training (Ilić, Ivanović, & Klašnja-Milićević, 2024). Adaptive systems that dynamically adjust content based on learner activity have been shown to improve learning efficiency; however, the management of large datasets and the protection of learner data privacy remain critical challenges (Ouyang & Spitzer, 2025). Platforms such as Dodona, which analyze Python code in real time, function as virtual co-instructors by delivering interactive feedback, yet their integration into conventional curricula often requires substantial pedagogical adaptation and technical readiness (Van Petegem et al., 2022). In addition, studies on the development of electronic courses within adaptive training systems provide a theoretical basis for ITS implementation, emphasizing the importance of tailoring instructional content to individual learner needs (Khusanov & Kakharov, 2023).

Adaptive learning technologies have also been shown to reduce learning difficulties and increase student engagement; however, disparities in accessibility and resource availability continue to hinder widespread adoption (Al-Azawei & Alshahrani, 2022). Interactive feedback mechanisms enhance computational thinking and conceptual understanding, but their effectiveness depends heavily on the timeliness and relevance of the feedback provided (Shaffer & Resnick, 2021). Personalized feedback models can lead to performance improvements of up to 20%, yet they require ongoing monitoring and regular algorithmic refinement to remain effective (Nouri, Zhang, & Mannila, 2022). Moreover, while AI-assisted evaluation systems improve the precision of error detection and correction, their deployment necessitates rigorous validation procedures to mitigate bias and ensure transparency (Bhatnagar & Singh, 2023).

Despite these advantages, integrating Intelligent Tutoring Systems into programming curricula remains complex. Although ITS have been shown to enhance student engagement and learning outcomes through adaptive feedback and personalized learning trajectories (Graesser & McNamara, 2022; Li & Chen, 2023), their successful adoption often depends on the availability of advanced technological infrastructure and institutional expertise. The development and maintenance of AI-driven educational systems also require substantial financial investment and continuous updates to ensure reliability, fairness, and scalability in assessment processes (Ullrich & Gütl, 2024; Wang & Zhao, 2023).

In addition, while ITS significantly support the development of algorithmic thinking and problem-solving skills, their effectiveness is influenced by institutional readiness and equitable access to digital resources (Al-Mutairi & Al-Muqbil, 2021; Kim & Lee, 2022). Designing effective feedback strategies remains particularly challenging, as intelligent systems must balance cognitive, emotional, and motivational dimensions to sustain learner engagement and long-term educational impact (Park & Choi, 2023; Ahmed & Ismail, 2024). Furthermore, although intelligent feedback mechanisms can enhance creativity and motivation, they may also increase learner dependence on technology and raise ethical concerns related to data privacy, transparency, and learner autonomy (Zhao & Liu, 2023; Chou & Huang, 2022).

The analysis of the reviewed literature clearly indicates that Intelligent Tutoring Systems are highly effective in programming education, particularly in the instruction of the Python programming language. These systems transform the educational process into an individualized, interactive, and analytically driven experience, thereby enhancing learners' motivation, autonomy, and algorithmic thinking skills.

The primary advantages of ITS include automated assessment, personalized feedback, adaptive content delivery, and data-driven instructional decision-making. As a result, the integration of ITS into Python programming education is increasingly recognized as a strategic direction in modern pedagogy, promoting efficiency, personalization, and learner engagement in the digital era. The principles underlying the development of adaptive electronic courses closely align with the ITS paradigm, as both aim to maximize learning outcomes through individualized instruction and timely support (Khusanov & Kakharov, 2023).

The theoretical foundations of Intelligent Tutoring Systems are grounded in several established learning paradigms. Constructivist learning theory, as advanced by Piaget and Vygotsky, posits that learners actively construct knowledge through exploration, experimentation, and reflection. Intelligent systems operationalize these principles by enabling learners to test hypotheses through coding, observe outcomes, and iteratively refine their understanding. In programming education, this process aligns with the "learning by doing" approach, where errors and debugging activities are treated as integral learning opportunities rather than failures.

Adaptive learning theory further extends this framework by emphasizing the personalization of educational experiences. Intelligent systems continuously analyze learner performance, identify cognitive patterns, and adjust task difficulty to maintain an optimal level of challenge. This approach is closely aligned with Vygotsky's concept of the Zone of Proximal Development (ZPD), in which learning is most effective when tasks slightly exceed a learner's independent capabilities but remain achievable with appropriate support. Within this context, ITS function as digital scaffolding mechanisms that guide learners toward mastery.

The self-regulated learning (SRL) framework also provides a critical psychological foundation for ITS. SRL theory suggests that learners who actively monitor and regulate their cognition, motivation, and behavior achieve superior academic outcomes. Intelligent systems foster SRL by offering learning analytics dashboards, progress indicators, and performance feedback that encourage reflection and strategic adjustment. These tools empower learners to set goals, monitor progress, and refine learning strategies—competencies essential for lifelong learning in a rapidly evolving digital environment.

From a cognitive perspective, ITS are informed by information processing theory, which conceptualizes learning as the transformation of information into long-term memory through processes of encoding, storage, and retrieval. The immediate feedback provided by ITS reinforces correct responses and addresses misconceptions before they become entrenched, thereby enhancing knowledge retention and skill transfer.

Pedagogically, the integration of intelligent systems aligns with blended learning and flipped classroom models, in which technology complements human instruction. In such models, intelligent systems manage routine tasks—such as grading and diagnostic assessment—while instructors focus on higher-order pedagogical activities, including conceptual discussion, mentoring, and facilitation of collaborative learning. This synergy between AI-driven automation and human expertise creates a balanced educational ecosystem that combines efficiency with pedagogical sensitivity.

In conclusion, the literature suggests that Intelligent Tutoring Systems are not merely technological tools, but comprehensive pedagogical frameworks rooted in established theories of cognition, motivation, and instructional design. Their continued refinement and contextual adaptation hold significant potential to redefine programming education in the digital age.

THE NEED FOR DEVELOPING STUDENTS' PROGRAMMING COMPETENCIES

In the contemporary era of globalization and digital transformation, the labor market is undergoing profound and rapid changes driven by continuous technological advancement. Emerging industries are reshaping professional requirements, demanding a workforce equipped not only with traditional domain-specific expertise but also with strong computational and analytical capabilities. As the global digital economy expands and technologies such as artificial intelligence (AI), big data analytics, cybersecurity, and automated control systems are integrated into nearly all sectors of society, programming competence has become a core skill that determines professional adaptability and success in the modern workplace.

According to the World Economic Forum (2020), by 2025 the most in-demand skills will include analytical thinking, algorithmic reasoning, technological literacy, and programming proficiency. These competencies are central to the emerging paradigm of the Fourth Industrial Revolution, in which automation and intelligent systems fundamentally transform how individuals work, learn, and communicate. Consequently, the development of programming competencies among students should be viewed not merely as instruction in a technical discipline, but as a strategic investment in national human capital and long-term innovation capacity.

Importantly, programming competence is no longer confined to computer scientists or information technology professionals. In the digital age, it has evolved into a transdisciplinary skill that enables innovation across a wide range of academic and professional domains. For example, economists employ programming and data analysis tools such as Python and R for econometric modeling and financial forecasting; engineers use programming to simulate complex processes, design automated systems, and optimize production technologies; biologists and medical researchers apply programming techniques in bioinformatics, medical imaging, and the management of large-scale health data; and social scientists rely on programming tools to process, analyze, and visualize data derived from surveys, experiments, and social media platforms.

Within this broader context, programming competence can be regarded as a universal intellectual skill that supports interdisciplinary integration, promotes analytical reasoning, and enhances problem-solving abilities. The development of such competencies not only improves students' employability but also strengthens their capacity for creative and critical thinking, thereby preparing them to address complex real-world challenges in an increasingly technology-driven society.

Core Components of Programming Competence

The development of programming competence involves the acquisition of several interrelated components that collectively form the foundation of computational literacy. These components include:

- *Algorithmic Thinking* – the ability to decompose complex problems into smaller, logical steps and to design efficient algorithms that can be implemented computationally.
- *Coding Skills* – mastery of the syntax, semantics, and logical structures of programming languages, enabling learners to write clear, correct, and efficient code.
- *Problem-Solving Ability* – the capacity to apply programming principles to address practical and theoretical problems across diverse domains.
- *Technological Adaptability* – the flexibility to work with multiple programming environments, libraries, and platforms, as well as the ability to rapidly adopt emerging technologies.
- *Collaboration and Teamwork* – competence in cooperative software development practices, including version control, code review, and technical documentation, which are essential in professional programming contexts.
- *Self-Directed Learning* – the ability to independently acquire new programming skills, explore evolving technologies, and continuously update professional knowledge.

Together, these components constitute a comprehensive programming competency framework that aligns with the broader objectives of lifelong learning and digital literacy in the twenty-first century.

The Case of Uzbekistan

In Uzbekistan, the enhancement of programming competencies has been identified as a national priority within the country's long-term development agenda. The *Digital Uzbekistan–2030* strategy emphasizes the expansion of digital literacy, the strengthening of youth competencies in information technology, and the cultivation of a new generation of specialists capable of driving innovation in both the public and private sectors.

To achieve these objectives, the government has implemented several strategic initiatives. Early programming education has been introduced in Presidential Schools and specialized IT lyceums, where students are exposed to coding concepts from an early age. Higher education institutions have incorporated programming languages such as Python, Java, and C++ into their core curricula, ensuring alignment with international educational standards. In addition, national programs and platforms—including IT Park and the *One Million Uzbek Coders* initiative—aim to provide accessible programming education for young people and to promote entrepreneurship within the digital economy.

Despite these advancements, students continue to face significant challenges in mastering programming skills. Common difficulties include the complexity of programming syntax, the gradual development of algorithmic thinking, and psychological barriers associated with early learning failures, which may reduce motivation and persistence. Moreover, large class sizes often restrict opportunities for individualized instruction, while traditional assessment methods are frequently characterized by subjectivity, inconsistency, and delayed feedback. These challenges underscore the need for more adaptive, scalable, and learner-centered approaches to programming education.

The Role of Intelligent Systems in Enhancing Programming Education

To address these challenges, the adoption of intelligent educational systems has become increasingly important. Such systems offer a range of pedagogical and technological advantages that significantly enhance the effectiveness of programming education. These advantages include:

- *Automated Code Analysis* – students' code is analyzed in real time, enabling the immediate detection of syntactic and logical errors.
- *Personalized Feedback* – learners receive individualized recommendations based on their performance, thereby supporting differentiated instruction.
- *Efficient and Objective Assessment* – the assessment process becomes faster, more transparent, and less susceptible to human bias.
- *Support for Self-Regulated Learning* – students are empowered to independently monitor their progress and identify areas requiring improvement.

By integrating intelligent tutoring systems into the instructional process, higher education institutions can create student-centered, adaptive, and data-driven learning environments that foster engagement, reduce cognitive load, and enhance the long-term retention of programming knowledge.

Accordingly, the development of programming competencies constitutes a strategic objective of modern education, ensuring not only students' professional preparedness but also their capacity for creative innovation and competitiveness within the global digital economy.

METHODS

Assessment is a fundamental component of the educational process, serving as a key mechanism for identifying students' knowledge, skills, and competencies, as well as for monitoring academic progress and supporting the continuous improvement of educational quality. In programming education, assessment assumes particular significance, as it reflects not only learners' theoretical understanding but also their ability to apply computational logic, algorithmic reasoning, and problem-solving strategies in practical contexts.

Traditional assessment methods in programming instruction are typically based on manual grading, in which instructors evaluate code for syntactic correctness, algorithmic efficiency, execution accuracy, and functional performance. Although this approach enables a nuanced understanding of students' reasoning processes, it is time-consuming, subject to evaluator bias, and difficult to scale—especially in large classes or online learning environments. The growing demand for individualized instruction and timely feedback in programming courses therefore necessitates more efficient, scalable, and objective assessment approaches.

Within the context of the national education system, research on the development of e-learning evaluation systems based on learning management systems (LMS) in Uzbekistan highlights the critical importance of objectivity and efficiency in assessment practices (Kakharov, Khusanov, & Jamolov, 2023). In this regard, the integration of automated assessment systems within intelligent learning environments offers substantial pedagogical and technological advantages, enabling consistent evaluation, rapid feedback, and enhanced support for learner development.

Advantages of Assessment in Intelligent Systems

Assessment methods integrated into Intelligent Tutoring Systems (ITS) and other intelligent learning platforms introduce automation, personalization, and data-driven analysis into the evaluation process. The primary advantages of these assessment methods include:

- *Automated Analysis* – Students' code is automatically compiled and executed by the system, with outputs compared against predefined solutions or test cases. This immediate analysis enables rapid detection of both syntactic and logical errors.
- *Personalized Feedback* – Intelligent systems go beyond simply identifying mistakes; they provide targeted recommendations for correction, guiding students toward conceptual understanding rather than rote debug-

ging. Personalized feedback fosters reflection and enhances metacognitive awareness.

- *Objectivity* – By eliminating human bias in grading, intelligent systems ensure a fair and consistent assessment process. All students are evaluated according to the same criteria and computational standards. The automated assessment mechanisms of ITS effectively address the issues highlighted in research on e-learning evaluation, eliminating subjectivity and ensuring high consistency in grading programming assignments (Kakharov, Khusanov, & Jamolov, 2023).
- *Efficiency and Real-Time Feedback* – Assessment results are generated instantaneously, allowing students to observe the outcomes of their work in real time. This immediacy supports iterative learning, sustains engagement, and accelerates the development of programming skills.
- *Data-Driven Insights* – Intelligent systems automatically record and store assessment results in centralized databases. This structured data facilitates statistical analysis, identification of learning patterns, and evidence-based decision-making to inform instructional improvement.

By integrating these capabilities, intelligent learning systems transform assessment from a static measurement tool into an interactive, adaptive mechanism that continuously informs and enhances the educational process. Such systems not only evaluate performance but also actively support learning, making assessment an integral component of the instructional experience rather than a separate, summative activity.

Automated Assessment in Programming Education

In programming education, automated assessment systems employ advanced algorithms and testing frameworks to evaluate code quality across multiple dimensions. These systems typically assess:

- *Syntactic Accuracy* – the correct use of programming language syntax.
- *Semantic Validity* – the logical coherence and correctness of code structure.
- *Algorithmic Efficiency* – execution performance in terms of time and resource utilization.
- *Code Readability and Structure* – adherence to programming standards, including naming conventions, formatting, and modular design.
- *Functional Correctness* – the alignment of program outputs with expected results.

This multi-level evaluation provides instructors and students with a comprehensive understanding of programming proficiency, effectively bridging the gap between automated evaluation and pedagogical objectives. Furthermore, automated assessment fosters self-directed learning, enabling students to iteratively test, refine, and optimize their solutions without waiting for external grading. Table 1 presents a detailed set of criteria for assessing Python programming competencies.

Table 1. Criteria for Assessing Python Programming Competencies

N°	Competency Component	Description	Assessment Criterion (0–5 scale)	Indicator of Achievement
1	Algorithmic Thinking	Ability to decompose problems into logical steps and construct algorithms.	Logical accuracy, task completion rate	Correct design of algorithms and logical flow
2	Coding Accuracy	Writing syntactically correct and efficient code.	Syntax and execution success	Number of errors per task
3	Problem-Solving Skills	Applying programming to solve real-world and theoretical problems.	Creativity and efficiency	Optimization of code and correct output
4	Debugging Skills	Identifying, analyzing, and fixing logical or runtime errors.	Error analysis speed	Reduction of repetitive errors
5	Independent Learning	Self-directed study and exploration of programming tools.	Learning autonomy	Ability to complete additional tasks independently
6	Collaboration	Working effectively in a coding team.	Peer contribution	GitHub commit activity and teamwork efficiency

The Role of Statistical Analysis: Application of the Student's t-Test

Beyond automated grading, statistical methods play an essential role in validating the outcomes of pedagogical innovations and research experiments conducted within intelligent learning environments. Among these, the Student's t-test is one of the most widely used tools for evaluating whether differences between the performance indicators of two groups–typically an experimental group using intelligent systems and a control group following traditional instruction–are statistically significant.

The Student's t-test assesses whether the difference between two sample means arises from random variation or reflects a genuine effect of the intervention. In educational research, this test is applied to compare students' achievement scores, learning rates, or performance metrics after exposure to a specific teaching method. When the calculated p-value is below the chosen significance threshold (commonly

0.05), the null hypothesis of equality is rejected, indicating that the observed difference is statistically significant.

By employing such statistical techniques, researchers can quantitatively substantiate the effectiveness of intelligent tutoring systems in improving students' programming competencies. Combining automated assessment data with inferential statistical analysis strengthens the empirical foundation of educational studies and provides objective evidence for pedagogical decision-making.

The assessment process involves:

1. Formulating hypotheses:
   - o Null hypothesis (H_0): There is no significant difference between the results of the control group (CG) and the experimental group (EG).
   - o Alternative hypothesis (H_1): The results of the EG differ significantly from those of the CG.
2. Statistical analysis of results

To evaluate the effectiveness of the proposed methodology, the Student's t-test for independent samples was employed. This statistical analysis was conducted by comparing the average scores of the experimental and control groups, while considering the variances within each group and the total number of participants. This approach allows for a rigorous determination of whether the differences in learning outcomes are statistically significant and attributable to the use of intelligent systems.

3. Analysis of the pedagogical experiment results

The study conducted at Namangan State University involved 30 students in the experimental group and 28 students in the control group. This phase was specifically designed to validate the Human-AI Co-facilitation Framework by evaluating the hybrid interaction between instructors and intelligent systems. The statistical analysis of the final test results, using a significance level of 0.05 and 56 degrees of freedom, showed that the calculated t-value (4.07) significantly exceeded the critical table value (2.003). Consequently, the null hypothesis was rejected. This means that the performance of the experimental group is significantly higher than that of the control group, proving that the use of intelligent systems led to a statistically significant improvement in students' Python programming competencies.

The statistical validation through the Student's t-test provides not only numerical confirmation but also epistemological rigor to the study's findings. In empirical educational research, statistical significance ensures that the improvements observed are not the result of random variation but reflect the actual impact of the intervention. However, beyond statistical metrics, it is equally important to examine the pedagogical significance of the results, that is, the extent to which observed improvements translate into meaningful learning outcomes.

In this study, the effect size derived from the t-test indicates a substantial improvement in the experimental group's programming competence. This suggests that intelligent systems contribute not merely to performance metrics but also to deeper conceptual understanding. Additionally, triangulation of data—combining quantitative results with qualitative observations and learner feedback—strengthens the internal validity of the research.

Reliability is another critical consideration. Automated systems minimize human bias and grading inconsistency, enhancing measurement reliability. Nonetheless, researchers must also ensure that algorithms are transparent, explainable, and ethically sound. In recent academic discourse, there is growing emphasis on "explainable AI" (XAI) in education, which promotes algorithmic transparency to foster trust among students and instructors.

Finally, the generalizability of these findings depends on replication across diverse contexts. Future research should include larger samples, multiple programming languages, and varying institutional environments to verify the scalability of this methodology. By embedding statistical analysis into pedagogical inquiry, the study demonstrates how data-driven validation can transform educational innovation into scientifically grounded practice.

Therefore, the effectiveness of teaching Python programming using intelligent systems is statistically confirmed. Figure 1 shows comparison of results between the control group and experimental groups in graphical form.

Figure 1. Comparison of results between the control group and experimental group in graphical form

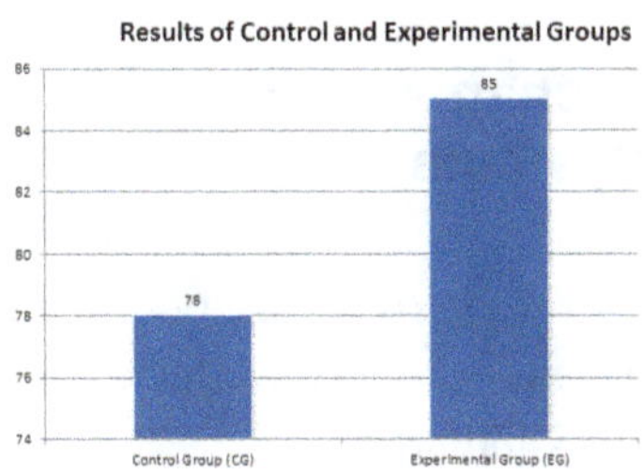

Statistical analysis conducted using Student's t-test revealed that students who learned with the assistance of the intelligent system acquired programming competencies more effectively compared to those who received traditional education. The results demonstrate that the use of intelligent systems not only automates the assessment process but also ensures the scientific rigor of the learning process.

FEEDBACK MECHANISMS IN INTELLIGENT LEARNING SYSTEMS

As discussed in the previous section, intelligent learning systems (ILS) provide a dynamic and adaptive environment for developing students' programming competencies. The effectiveness of these systems, however, depends largely on the presence and quality of feedback mechanisms. Feedback serves as the communicative bridge between the learner and the system, enabling reflection, correction, and continuous improvement. Without timely and meaningful feedback, the learning process becomes fragmented and less effective, as students struggle to identify, understand, or correct their mistakes.

In educational theory, feedback is defined as the process of providing learners with information about their performance relative to learning objectives, allowing them to regulate their behavior and improve outcomes (Hattie & Timperley, 2007). Within intelligent systems, feedback serves not only as a corrective function but also diagnostic, motivational, and developmental roles, guiding learners toward deeper conceptual understanding.

Feedback mechanisms are particularly critical in programming education. Programming inherently involves problem-solving through iterative trial and error, and students frequently encounter logical errors, syntactic ambiguities, and algorithmic inefficiencies that can impede progress if left unaddressed. Traditional classroom feedback is often delayed due to instructor workload, which can diminish both motivation and learning momentum. In contrast, modern AI-powered intelligent tutoring systems (ITS) can instantly analyze code, detect error patterns, explain their underlying causes, and generate personalized, adaptive recommendations, thereby enhancing both learning efficiency and conceptual clarity.

Types of Feedback Mechanisms in Intelligent Learning Systems

Intelligent learning systems employ a variety of feedback types, each serving a specific pedagogical purpose and supporting the learner's self-regulated development. The most common types include:

1. *Automated Diagnostics and Analysis*
    a) The system automatically executes the student's code, verifies the output against expected results, and immediately highlights errors detected.
    b) Instead of providing generic messages such as "Incorrect answer," intelligent systems identify the precise cause of the problem, for example, "undeclared variable," "syntax error," or "incorrect function call."

This level of specificity transforms feedback into a learning opportunity, enabling students to understand the underlying logic of their errors.

2. *Personalized Recommendations*
   a) The system analyzes the student's historical performance and error patterns to identify recurring conceptual difficulties.
   b) Based on these insights, it generates an individualized learning trajectory, recommending targeted exercises and resources tailored to the learner's specific needs.

This personalized approach not only enhances mastery but also sustains motivation by ensuring that learning challenges are neither too easy nor too difficult.

3. *Adaptive Feedback*

Intelligent systems dynamically adjust the level of detail and complexity of feedback according to the learner's proficiency:

a) For beginners, the system provides step-by-step guidance and detailed explanations.
b) For advanced learners, it offers concise hints or performance metrics, allowing greater autonomy.

This adaptive mechanism ensures that feedback remains appropriately challenging, fostering scaffolded learning and the gradual development of independence.

4. *Motivational Feedback*

Beyond correction, intelligent systems can deliver encouraging and reinforcing feedback to sustain learner engagement. Examples include messages such as "Great job! Your code runs 15% faster than before" or "You've successfully completed 90% of this module." Such motivational cues appeal to students' intrinsic motivation, reinforcing perseverance and fostering a sense of achievement.

5. *Visual and Interactive Feedback*
   a) Progress tracking tools—such as graphs, dashboards, and progress bars—enable students to visualize their learning trajectory and improvement over time.
   b) These visual elements promote self-assessment and goal setting, helping learners identify strengths and areas for improvement.

Visualization also enhances transparency, allowing both students and instructors to monitor development in real time.

6. *Peer Feedback (Mutual Evaluation)*

Many intelligent platforms incorporate peer-assessment features, enabling students to review, comment on, and evaluate each other's code. This process reinforces coding and debugging skills while cultivating critical thinking, collaboration, and communication competencies that are essential in professional programming environments.

Educational Significance of Feedback Mechanisms

Feedback mechanisms in intelligent learning environments serve multiple interrelated educational functions:

- *Monitoring Function* – Feedback enables students to continuously assess their performance and track their knowledge acquisition in real time.
- *Developmental Function* – It helps learners identify weaknesses, clarify misconceptions, and apply corrective strategies, transforming errors into opportunities for growth.
- *Motivational Function* – Timely and supportive feedback enhances students' enthusiasm and persistence, promoting sustained engagement in learning activities.
- *Communicative Function* – Feedback facilitates interaction between learners and the system, as well as between students and instructors, thereby strengthening the overall pedagogical relationship in blended and online learning contexts.

Together, these functions elevate feedback from a simple evaluative tool to a central pedagogical mechanism that supports the cognitive, emotional, and behavioral dimensions of learning.

The Impact of Feedback Mechanisms on Programming Competencies

The integration of advanced feedback mechanisms within intelligent systems exerts a measurable and positive impact on the development of programming competencies. The effects can be summarized as follows:

- *Accelerated Error Identification* – Students receive immediate insights into their coding mistakes, enabling faster correction and reducing frustration.
- *Enhanced Logical and Algorithmic Thinking* – Through iterative feedback loops, learners internalize structured problem-solving processes and algorithmic reasoning.
- *Improved Independent Learning Skills* – Continuous feedback supports self-regulation, empowering students to autonomously identify, analyze, and resolve challenges.
- *Personalized Learning Pathways* – Adaptive, data-driven feedback ensures that each learner progresses according to their proficiency and cognitive style.

Ultimately, feedback mechanisms within intelligent systems not only reduce instructors' workload but also foster a more active, reflective, and autonomous learning culture among students. By transforming assessment into an ongoing dialogue between the learner and the system, intelligent feedback bridges the gap between evaluation and instruction, ensuring that learning remains meaningful, personalized, and effective.

Feedback mechanisms thus serve as the pedagogical foundation upon which subsequent assessment systems and learning analytics frameworks are built, linking the cognitive development of learners to data-informed educational decision-making, as explored in the following section.

The transition from traditional instruction to intelligent, data-driven learning environments requires a systematic approach to change management within educational institutions. Faculty members must be equipped not only with technical competence but also with digital pedagogical literacy, the ability to integrate technology meaningfully into teaching strategies. Moreover, institutional policies must guarantee equitable access to digital resources to prevent widening the digital divide among students.

Successful implementation of intelligent systems also depends on continuous evaluation and iterative improvement. Feedback loops connecting system performance, instructor observations, and student outcomes create a dynamic ecosystem of educational innovation. This iterative cycle aligns with design-based research principles, emphasizing experimentation, reflection, and continuous refinement in authentic learning contexts.

EXPERIENCE IN APPLYING INTELLIGENT SYSTEMS IN PYTHON PROGRAMMING COURSES

The experience of teaching Python programming using intelligent learning systems (ILS) demonstrates that this approach offers substantial pedagogical and methodological advantages over traditional instructional methods. Intelligent systems can automate core elements of the learning process, providing real-time performance monitoring, personalized instruction, and adaptive feedback tailored to each student's individual learning trajectory.

Beyond these efficiency gains, ILS enhances the pedagogical quality of programming education by diagnosing learning challenges, explaining the underlying logic of errors in an accessible manner, and supporting the gradual, systematic acquisition of programming knowledge and skills. Consequently, integrating intelligent systems into Python programming courses represents a strategic innovation that aligns with the principles of competency-based, learner-centered, and data-informed education.

Outcomes of Applying Intelligent Systems in Python Education

Automated Code Testing and Error Identification

One of the most persistent challenges in programming education is debugging—the process of identifying and correcting errors in students' code. Traditional approaches often rely on basic compiler messages such as "Error exists" or "Syntax invalid," which provide little context for meaningful learning.

Intelligent systems, however, employ automated code analysis that extends far beyond simple error detection. They execute code line by line, diagnose specific error types, and explain their causes in a pedagogically meaningful way. For example, in the case of an *IndexError* in Python—triggered when an index is out of range—the system not only flags the error but also reminds the student of Python's indexing rules, highlights the relevant code segment, and suggests possible corrections.

This explanatory feedback loop transforms debugging from a frustrating obstacle into a valuable learning opportunity. Students begin to internalize logical reasoning patterns, strengthen their understanding of programming semantics, and enhance their ability to anticipate and prevent similar errors in the future. Consequently, the learning process becomes more reflective, analytical, and self-directed.

Time Efficiency and Rapid Visualization of Results

In traditional programming instruction, instructors devote a substantial amount of time to manually reviewing, grading, and commenting on each student's code.

This process can be labor-intensive and inefficient, particularly in large classes. Intelligent systems, however, automate much of this work, instantly processing code submissions and providing real-time feedback.

This automation not only reduces instructors' workload but also allows them to focus on higher-order pedagogical activities, such as mentoring, designing complex projects, and supporting students in developing conceptual understanding rather than addressing routine technical issues.

For students, the benefits are equally significant. Immediate feedback enables them to correct mistakes promptly, observe the effects of their modifications, and iteratively refine their solutions. This continuous feedback cycle enhances learning efficiency, fosters motivation, and cultivates the iterative problem-solving mindset essential for professional programmers.

Independent Assignments with Immediate Feedback and Recommendations

Independent learning forms a cornerstone of modern, competency-based education. Intelligent systems support this process by providing students with automatically generated tasks that vary in complexity—from simple syntax exercises to advanced algorithmic challenges.

Upon completion of each task, the system evaluates the submission, delivers immediate feedback, and offers contextualized recommendations, such as:

- Explaining the logical or structural cause of an error.
- Suggesting supplementary learning materials or examples.
- Highlighting specific topics that may require further review.

Through this process, students learn to self-assess, regulate their learning pace, and reinforce conceptual understanding even outside of classroom hours. The system's adaptability ensures that learners receive appropriately challenging tasks, maintaining engagement while preventing cognitive overload. This approach contributes to the development of lifelong learning competencies, including autonomy, self-regulation, and reflective practice.

Monitoring Student Progress through Enhanced Statistical Data

Another major benefit of intelligent systems is their capacity for continuous monitoring and analytics of the learning process. These systems not only identify errors but also collect and analyze detailed data related to student performance and engagement. For example, they can track:

- The topics or concepts where students most frequently encounter difficulties.
- The average time spent solving types of problems.
- Learning efficiency over time, visualized through graphs and dashboards.

These data-driven insights empower instructors to make informed pedagogical decisions, such as redesigning course modules, introducing supplementary workshops, or providing individualized guidance to students who struggle with specific concepts.

At the same time, students benefit from transparent progress tracking, which enables them to visualize their improvement, set realistic learning goals, and maintain a sense of ownership over their educational journey. Visualizing learning dynamics such as weekly or monthly progress—transforms assessment into an ongoing diagnostic tool that supports metacognitive development and self-evaluation.

Pedagogical and Practical Implications

The cumulative experience of integrating intelligent systems into Python programming courses highlights several key implications for modern educational practice:

- *Pedagogical Efficiency* – Intelligent systems optimize instructional time, allowing both teachers and students to focus on higher-level cognitive activities.
- *Personalization and Adaptivity* – Each learner follows an individualized progression path, promoting inclusivity and differentiated learning.
- *Enhanced Engagement* – Immediate, constructive feedback sustains student motivation and encourages persistence in problem-solving.
- *Empirical Evaluation* – Built-in analytics support evidence-based assessment of learning effectiveness, aligning with contemporary educational research standards.
- *Skill Deepening* – Students develop not only technical proficiency but also higher-order cognitive competencies, including abstraction, reasoning, and algorithmic thinking.

Integrating intelligent systems into Python programming education significantly transforms both teaching and learning processes. By automating assessment, providing adaptive feedback, and enabling data-driven course management, these systems enhance the efficiency, precision, and interactivity of programming instruction.

The Proposed Human-AI Co-Facilitation Framework

To move beyond the general application of Intelligent Tutoring Systems (ITS), this chapter introduces a Human-AI Co-Facilitation Framework. This methodology operates through a four-stage cycle:

1. *Diagnostic Phase* – The instructor establishes the conceptual framework, while the ITS identifies students' baseline logic and syntax errors.
2. *Adaptive Scaffolding* – Rather than providing direct answers, the ITS offers tiered hints that guide students toward the solution, maintaining engagement within the Zone of Proximal Development.
3. *Instructor-Led Intervention* – Using real-time analytics dashboards, the instructor identifies students who are struggling and provides targeted, personalized support.
4. *Feedback Integration* – Data generated by the ITS is analyzed and used to adjust the curriculum for subsequent lessons, ensuring continuous improvement and learner-centered instruction.

Table 2 presents methodological differences between standard ITS and the proposed approach.

Table 2. Methodological differences between standard ITS and the proposed approach

Feature	Standard ITS Implementation	Proposed Methodology
Instructional Role	Stand-alone digital tutor	Co-facilitation (Hybrid model)
Feedback Logic	Rule-based (Right/Wrong)	Adaptive Scaffolding (Hints)
Teacher Presence	Passive monitoring	Active (Data-driven intervention)
Contextual Focus	General software usage	Educational outcome focus

For instructors, intelligent systems function as pedagogical assistants, reducing routine workload and enabling greater focus on creative and strategic teaching activities. For students, these systems foster an active, self-paced, and personalized learning environment that encourages exploration, autonomy, and continuous improvement.

Consequently, the integration of intelligent systems into Python programming education supports the development of highly competent, self-regulated, and innovative learners who are well equipped to meet the challenges of the digital era and contribute effectively to the knowledge-based economy.

RESULTS AND DISCUSSION

The findings of the pedagogical experiment conducted at Namangan State University demonstrate that the implementation of intelligent learning systems (ILS) in Python programming courses results in significantly higher learning efficiency and enhanced competence development compared to traditional instructional approaches. Students who learned through intelligent systems demonstrated faster mastery of programming concepts, greater independence in problem-solving, and a deeper understanding of algorithmic principles. Table 3 presents a comparative analysis of the results obtained from the experimental and control groups.

Table 3. Comparative Results Between Experimental and Control Groups

Group	N (students)	Mean Score (Initial)	Mean Score (Final)	Growth (%)	Standard Deviation
Experimental Group (EG)	30	56.4	84.2	+49.3	6.0
Control Group (CG)	28	54.7	68.1	+24.5	7.0

Table 3 compares the initial and final performance of students in the experimental and control groups, highlighting the overall improvement achieved using intelligent learning systems.

The primary advantage of intelligent systems lies in their capacity to evaluate code in real time, immediately identify errors, and provide clear, context-specific explanations. This automated and adaptive feedback mechanism reduced students' reliance on direct instructor intervention. Instead, learners were able to analyze, interpret, and correct errors autonomously—an essential competency for proficient programmers. Over time, this process strengthened students' self-directed learning skills and fostered greater confidence in addressing complex coding challenges.

Development of Independent Learning Competence

A notable improvement in students' ability to work independently was observed during the experiment. Learners in the experimental group demonstrated an increased capacity for self-assessment, identifying weaknesses in their code and applying corrections without relying on instructor support.

The continuous and immediate feedback provided by intelligent systems encouraged students to engage actively with the learning material. As a result, learners repeatedly refined their solutions, reinforcing knowledge through practical application and iterative experimentation.

This interactive learning cycle contributed to substantial growth in analytical thinking, algorithmic reasoning, and problem-solving competence. In contrast, students in the control group, who followed traditional instructional approaches, relied more heavily on teacher guidance for clarification and validation. This reliance led to slower progress toward learner autonomy and reduced engagement in independent learning activities. Table 4 presents the weekly dynamics of learning progress.

Table 4. Weekly Dynamics of Learning Progress

Week	Average Score	Weekly Growth (%)	Observed Change	Pedagogical Interpretation
1st Week	56.0	–	Baseline	Students started with minimal algorithmic understanding
2nd Week	65.0	+16.1	Improved syntax accuracy	Feedback loops supported faster code correction
3rd Week	72.0	+10.8	Logical problem-solving improved	Increased use of adaptive tasks
4th Week	79.0	+9.7	Stronger debugging skills	Learners began to self-correct errors
5th Week	84.0	+6.3	Mastery phase	Competency stabilization and autonomy achieved

Table 4 shows the weekly development of students' competencies in the experimental group, indicating continuous improvement due to adaptive feedback mechanisms.

Statistical Validation of Experimental Results

The quantitative analysis of the collected data provides empirical evidence supporting the effectiveness of intelligent systems in programming education. Statistical methods, including the Student's t-test, were employed to compare the performance of the experimental and control groups, confirming that the observed differences were statistically significant.

The key outcomes are summarized as follows:

- *Mastery Level* – The experimental group's average performance indicators were 15–20% higher than those of the control group.
- *Error Reduction* – The number of syntactic and logical errors in the experimental group decreased by 25–30% compared to the control group receiving traditional instruction.

- *Task Completion Speed* – Students in the experimental group completed programming tasks approximately 1.5 times faster, on average, than those in the control group.

These quantitative findings indicate that integrating intelligent systems substantially improves learning outcomes by enhancing accuracy, efficiency, and cognitive engagement. Table 5 presents the results of the Student's *t*-test analysis.

Table 5. Results of Student's t-Test Analysis

Variable	Experimental Group (EG)	Control Group (CG)	Statistical Measure
Mean (M)	84.2	68.1	–
Variance (S^2)	6.0	7.0	–
Sample Size (n)	30	28	–
Calculated t-value (t_exp)	**4.07**	–	–
Critical t-value (t_crit, α=0.05)	–	–	**2.003**
Result	–	–	**Significant**

Since t_exp (4.07) > t_crit (2.003), the difference between the groups is statistically significant. Table 5 presents the results of the *t*-test analysis, confirming that the difference between the experimental and control groups is statistically significant.

The intelligent learning system demonstrably enhances students' academic performance. Beyond quantitative measures, qualitative feedback from both students and instructors revealed meaningful behavioral and attitudinal changes. Students reported increased self-efficacy, reduced anxiety toward programming tasks, and a stronger sense of ownership over their learning processes. Instructors, in turn, observed higher levels of classroom participation and collaboration, with students more frequently discussing debugging strategies and sharing insights during peer-based activities.

These behavioral shifts reflect the socio-cognitive benefits of intelligent learning systems, which extend beyond measurable test outcomes. Such systems cultivate resilience, curiosity, and reflective practice—core components of lifelong learning. Moreover, the learning data generated provides valuable opportunities for educational analytics, enabling predictive modeling of student success and the early identification of learners at risk of underperformance.

Further analysis of learning logs revealed that students using intelligent systems demonstrated more consistent progress patterns, shorter error-correction cycles, and higher retention of key programming concepts over time. These data-driven insights confirm that continuous feedback and adaptive assessment mechanisms directly contribute to improved programming performance and cognitive development.

Influence on Motivation and Engagement

In addition to academic improvement, students in the experimental group demonstrated markedly higher levels of motivation and engagement. The intelligent systems incorporated gamification elements—such as point accumulation, badges, leaderboards, and level progression—that created a stimulating and competitive learning environment.

These features encourage learners to complete additional exercises voluntarily, explore programming problems beyond the prescribed curriculum, and persist in the face of challenging tasks. Consequently, the motivational design of the intelligent systems fostered intrinsic motivation, transforming learning from a teacher-driven process into a self-directed one.

In contrast, students in the traditional instruction group relied predominantly on external motivation and instructor supervision. Their engagement was largely confined to assigned tasks, and they exhibited lower persistence when encountering programming difficulties. Table 6 presents students' feedback on the Intelligent Learning System.

Table 6. Students' Feedback on the Intelligent Learning System

Survey Item	Positive (%)	Neutral (%)	Negative (%)	Interpretation
The system helped me learn Python faster	87	9	4	Students benefited from real-time error detection
Automated grading was fair and transparent	90	6	4	Objective assessment increased learner trust
Personalized feedback was useful	92	7	1	Feedback improved conceptual understanding
Gamification increased motivation	85	10	5	Reward system encouraged persistence
Visual analytics helped me track progress	88	8	4	Learners gained greater self-awareness

Table 6 summarizes students' feedback on the use of intelligent systems, reflecting positive attitudes, enhanced motivation, and engagement with adaptive learning technologies.

The feedback data supports the quantitative findings, showing high student satisfaction, increased motivation, and stronger engagement with intelligent systems.

Benefits for Instructors

From the instructors' perspective, the introduction of intelligent systems significantly enhanced teaching efficiency. Tasks that previously required substantial manual efforts such as code review, grading, and the provision of feedback—were largely automated.

This automation enabled educators to concentrate on more creative and strategic aspects of teaching, including curriculum design, the development of advanced programming challenges, and the provision of individualized support to students who required additional assistance.

Moreover, access to statistical dashboards and learning analytics allowed instructors to identify at-risk students at an early stage, personalize interventions, and adjust instructional strategies in a timely and evidence-based manner.

Consequently, intelligent systems not only improved student learning outcomes but also offered considerable pedagogical support and professional benefits for educators.

Summary of Findings

Overall, the experimental results indicate that Python programming courses supported by intelligent systems produce significant positive changes in students' learning behaviors and outcomes. Specifically, the study confirms the following:

- Faster and more efficient acquisition of programming knowledge and skills.
- A reduction in coding errors and the development of cleaner, more structured coding practices.
- Enhanced independent learning capabilities and sustained learner motivation.
- Simplified and more objective assessment processes for instructors.

Collectively, these findings validate the pedagogical and technological effectiveness of intelligent systems as transformative tools in modern programming education. By fostering automation, adaptivity, and interactivity, intelligent systems contribute to the development of competent, motivated, and self-regulated learners who are well prepared for the demands of the digital economy. Figure 2 presents a comparative table and graphical representation of the results for the control and experimental groups.

Figure 2. Comparison of results table and graph for Control and Experimental groups

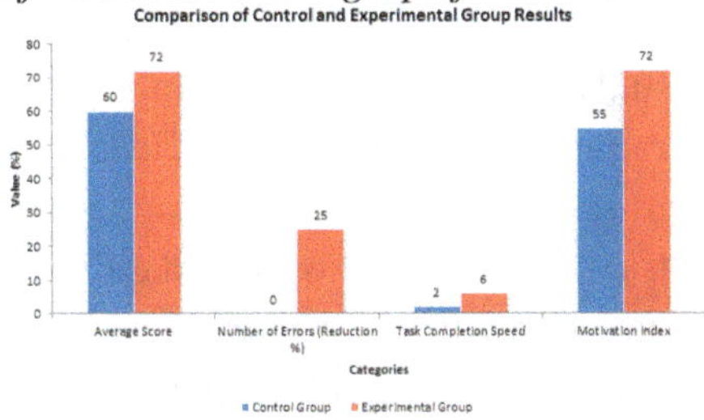

Thus, the experiments conducted confirm that the use of intelligent systems is highly effective in developing programming competencies and underscore the need for the wider implementation of this approach within educational practice.

Broader Implications and Future Directions

The implications of this research extend beyond the domain of Python programming education. The proposed methodology represents a scalable model that can be applied to other STEM disciplines, where logical reasoning, algorithmic problem-solving, and adaptive learning are essential. Moreover, the integration of intelligent systems aligns with global trends in digital education reform, which emphasize personalization, inclusivity, and evidence-based pedagogy.

From a practical perspective, this approach can inform national initiatives aimed at fostering digital literacy and computational thinking among young learners. By integrating intelligent tutoring systems into existing curricula, educational institutions can help reduce disparities in learning outcomes, particularly between urban and rural regions. In addition, the analytical capabilities of these systems can support institutional decision-making by providing insights into learner performance, curriculum effectiveness, and instructional impact.

From a theoretical standpoint, this study contributes to the emerging field of human–AI collaboration in education. Rather than positioning artificial intelligence as a substitute for teachers, the findings highlight its role as a pedagogical partner that enhances human creativity, instructional insight, and empathy through automation and adaptivity.

Ultimately, the widespread adoption of intelligent learning systems will require not only robust technological infrastructure but also cultural and organizational transformation. Continuous professional development, ethical governance of educational data, and inclusive design principles will be essential to ensuring that the benefits of intelligent learning systems are accessible to all learners, regardless of background or ability.

CONCLUSION AND RECOMMENDATIONS

The findings of this study indicate that integrating intelligent learning systems (ILS) into Python programming education can significantly enhance both the quality and efficiency of the learning process. The use of intelligent systems facilitates a shift from traditional instructional models toward adaptive, interactive, and learner-centered environments that align with the pedagogical demands of the digital age.

By incorporating automated assessment, real-time feedback, and personalized learning trajectories, intelligent systems enable students to identify and correct errors promptly, reinforce conceptual understanding, and engage in continuous self-improvement. This approach not only strengthens students' technical proficiency but also fosters essential competencies such as independent learning, logical reasoning, problem-solving, and the development of a disciplined programming mindset.

From an instructional perspective, intelligent systems offer substantial benefits for educators. The automation of assessment processes reduces the time and effort required for grading and evaluation, while ensuring greater objectivity, transparency, and consistency. As a result, instructors can devote more time to creative pedagogical design, methodological innovation, and individualized student mentoring—activities that directly enhance the overall quality of education.

Furthermore, the study confirms that intelligent systems not only improve academic achievement but also enhance students' intrinsic motivation. The integration of interactive and gamified elements—such as progress tracking, achievement badges, and peer competition—encourages sustained engagement and supports a positive learning experience. As students move from passive recipients of information to active participants in their learning journey, they develop increased confidence, persistence, and ownership of their educational outcomes.

Recommendations for Future Development

To build on the positive results of this study and strengthen the use of intelligent systems in programming education, several recommendations are proposed.

1. Future efforts should focus on developing specialized intelligent assessment platforms for Python that can automatically evaluate tasks ranging from basic syntax exercises to complex project-based work, combining formative and summative assessments for comprehensive evaluation.
2. Feedback mechanisms should be humanized by addressing not only technical accuracy but also emotional, psychological, and pedagogical aspects, providing motivational support that sustains student confidence.

3. Expanding self-assessment and reflection tools would enable learners to track progress, identify recurring errors, and develop personalized learning plans, enhancing metacognitive and lifelong learning skills.
4. The successful use of intelligent systems in Python suggests strong potential for integration across other programming languages and STEM disciplines, fostering an interconnected digital learning ecosystem.
5. Continuous professional development is essential to ensure educators have the digital and pedagogical competencies needed to effectively implement and interpret intelligent systems.

Final Considerations

In conclusion, the application of intelligent systems in programming education represents a transformative innovation in contemporary pedagogy. These systems bridge the gap between technology and learning, fostering dynamic educational environments where automation, adaptivity, and human-centered design converge to enhance both teaching and learning outcomes.

The study confirms that intelligent systems not only improve students' technical proficiency but also play a critical role in cultivating motivation, creativity, and independent thinking—competencies essential for success in the rapidly evolving digital economy.

Looking forward, the continued refinement and expansion of intelligent educational technologies will be instrumental in shaping the future of computer science education. By leveraging artificial intelligence, data analytics, and personalized feedback, educators can design learning environments that are efficient, objective, inspiring, inclusive, and deeply human-centered.

In the long term, the success of intelligent systems in education will depend on interdisciplinary collaboration among computer scientists, educators, psychologists, and policymakers. The development of ethical frameworks for AI-driven learning environments is equally crucial. Issues such as data privacy, algorithmic fairness, and student autonomy must be addressed through transparent governance and public dialogue.

Future iterations of intelligent learning systems should also incorporate advances in affective computing, enabling systems to recognize learners' emotions and adapt instruction accordingly. Such emotionally intelligent systems would bridge the gap between technological precision and human empathy, ensuring that the future of education remains authentically human-centered despite increasing automation.

While the findings of this study provide encouraging evidence, further research involving larger and more diverse cohorts is necessary to generalize the impact of the proposed framework.

REFERENCES

Al-Azawei, A., & Alshahrani, S. (2022). The Role of Adaptive Learning Technologies in Enhancing Programming Education. *Education and Information Technologies*, *27*(9), 12451–12468.

Bhatnagar, R., & Singh, P. (2023). AI-Assisted Evaluation Systems for Programming Education: Opportunities and Challenges. *International Journal of Artificial Intelligence in Education*, *33*(2), 288–305.

Chrysafiadi, K., & Virvou, M. (2023). Evaluating the User's Experience, Adaptivity and Learning Outcomes of a Fuzzy-Based Intelligent Tutoring System for Computer Programming for Academic Students in Greece. *Education and Information Technologies*, *28*, 6453–6483.

Fodouop Kouam, A. W. (2024). The Effectiveness of Intelligent Tutoring Systems (ITS) in Supporting Students with Varying Levels of Programming Experience. *Discover Education*, *3*, 278.

Graesser, A. C., & Mcnamara, D. S. (2022). The Evolution of Intelligent Tutoring Systems: From Cognitive Models to AI-Driven Education. *Computers & Education*, *184*, 104497I.

Kakharov, R., Khusanov, K., & Jamolov, O. (2023). Some Aspects of Development of E-Learning Evaluation System Based on LMS in Uzbekistan. *The 17th IEEE International Conference on Application of Information and Communication Technologies (AICT2023) to be held on 18-20 October 2023 in Baku, Azerbaijan*. https://doi.org/DOI: 10.1109/AICT59525.2023.10313202

Khusanov, K., & Kakharov, R. (2023). Development of Electronic Course as the Element of Adaptive Training System. *The 17th IEEE International Conference on Application of Information and Communication Technologies (AICT2023)*, 1–5. https://DOI: <ALIGNMENT.qj></ALIGNMENT>10.1109/AICT59525.2023.10313159

Li, Y., & Chen, J. (2023). Gamified Intelligent Tutoring for Python Programming: Motivating Students Through Adaptive Challenges. *Journal of Interactive Learning Research*, *34*(1), 12–29.

Lić, J., Ivanović, M., & Klašnja-Milićević, A. (2024). The Impact of Intelligent Tutoring Systems and Artificial Intelligence on Students' Motivation and Achievement in STEM Education: A Systematic Literature Review. *Journal of Educational Studies in Mathematics and Computer Science*, *1*(2), 5–18.

Messer, M., Brown, N. C. C., Kölling, M., & Shi, M. (2023). Automated Grading and Feedback Tools for Programming Education: A Systematic Review. *ACM Transactions on Computing Education*, *23*(4), 45–67.

Nouri, J., Zhang, L., & Mannila, L. (2022). Personalized Feedback in Programming Education Using Intelligent Systems: A Design-Based Study. *Computers in Human Behavior*, *134*, 107324.

Ouyang, X., & Spitzer, M. (2025). *Adaptive Intelligent Tutoring Systems for STEM Education: Analysis of Design and Evaluation*. Smart Learning Environments.

Shaffer, D., & Resnick, M. (2021). Developing Computational Thinking Through Interactive Feedback Systems in Programming Courses. *Journal of Educational Computing Research*, *59*(3), 495–518.

Ullrich, C., & Gütl, C. (2024). AI-Enhanced Assessment and Feedback in Computer Science Education: A Comprehensive Review. *Computers & Education: Artificial Intelligence*, *5*, 100146.

Van Petegem, C., & Maertens, R.. (2022). Dodona: Learn to Code with a Virtual Co-Teacher that Supports Active Learning. *Computers & Education*, *190*, 104610.

Wang, L., & Zhao, T. (2023). Data-Driven Feedback Mechanisms in Online Programming Environments. *Journal of Learning Analytics*, *10*(1), 45–63.

KEY TERMS AND DEFINITIONS

Adaptive Learning System: A digital learning environment that dynamically adjusts the difficulty, pace, and content of instruction according to the learner's individual needs.

Automated Assessment: The process of evaluating students' code or assignments automatically using intelligent algorithms that ensure accuracy, consistency, and efficiency in grading.

Intelligent Tutoring System (ITS): An AI-based learning platform that provides personalized guidance, automatic assessment, and adaptive feedback to students during the learning process.

Personalized Feedback: Customized guidance and suggestions generated by intelligent systems based on each student's learning progress and performance data.

Programming Competence: A combination of algorithmic thinking, coding skills, and problem-solving ability that enables learners to design, implement, and evaluate computational solutions.

Python Programming: A high-level, versatile programming language widely used in education, data analysis, artificial intelligence, and software development due to its simplicity and readability.

Self-Regulated Learning: A learner's ability to independently plan, monitor, and evaluate their learning progress through continuous reflection and feedback.

Section 4

Emerging Learning Environments and Educational Media

Chapter 12
Game Development as a Pedagogical Innovation for Project-Based Learning in Computer Graphics and Gaming

Rachana Yogesh Patil
https://orcid.org/0000-0001-9973-6998
Pimpri Chinchwad College of Engineering, India

Yogesh Patil
https://orcid.org/0000-0001-9968-8287
D.Y. Patil College of Engineering, India

ABSTRACT

The advent of project-based learning (PBL) as a pedagogical method has made the Computer Graphics and Gaming course a practical, real-life learning experience to undergraduate computer engineers. Creating and producing their own video games, students combined the knowledge of graphics programming, storytelling, user interface design, animation, and game mechanics. It was a step-by-step process, starting with basic ideas and going into practice, and ending with demonstrations judged on technical implementation, creativity, interactivity and teamwork. The approach incorporated use of iterative design, peer feedback, and reflective practices and was inspired by the experiential learning cycle and multiple intelligences of Kolb and Gardner respectively. The chapter provides planning, implementation and evalua-

DOI: 10.4018/979-8-3373-6546-6.ch012

tion approaches, discusses possible obstacles like resource shortage and diversity of learners, and provides flexible information on transferring this PBL model to other STEM fields involving creativity, technical skill and teamwork.

INTRODUCTION

Engineering education has undergone a major change in the last twenty years (Kamp, 2023). As a result of the recent rapid technological development, an enlarged interdisciplinary convergence, and the constantly changing industry demand, there is now a greater need to have academic institutions re-engineer their pedagogical approach (Froyd et al., 2012). Computer Graphics and Gaming, which constitutes a subject that sits at the border of mathematics, programming, design, and visualization, provides a special opportunity to apply and take advantage of innovative instructional models in the context (Jayakanthan, 2002). Nevertheless, the conventional lecture-practical divide does not always allow making the most out of this discipline, including its ability to engage students in a way that goes beyond algorithmic knowledge (Du & Yang, 2017).

Having taught and researched engineering education for more than 20 years and published over 100 research articles in the leading journals, we have noticed a very long time ago that there was a gap between theoretical knowledge and the application of this knowledge in technical subjects (Hatlevik, 2012). Students learn in a disjointed manner--doing assignments, attending labs, passing exams--and never really internalizing ideas and seeing their larger significance (Everwijn et al., 1993). This disjuncture is especially problematic in Computer Graphics, where the ability to know algorithmic solutions to drawing a line (Bresenhams, Bezier curves, etc.) does not imply the ability to be creative or competent in the real world.

The contrast between the conventional teaching techniques and PBL is quite radical, including the style of learning and evaluation, the intensity of student engagement and acquisition of skills (Lavado-Anguera et al., 2024). Traditional approaches tend to be based on passive learning and uniform assessment as shown in figure 1, whereas PBL promotes active, student-centered investigations and real-life assessments that are relevant to practice.

Figure 1. Comparison between Traditional Teaching and Project-Based Learning approaches in engineering education

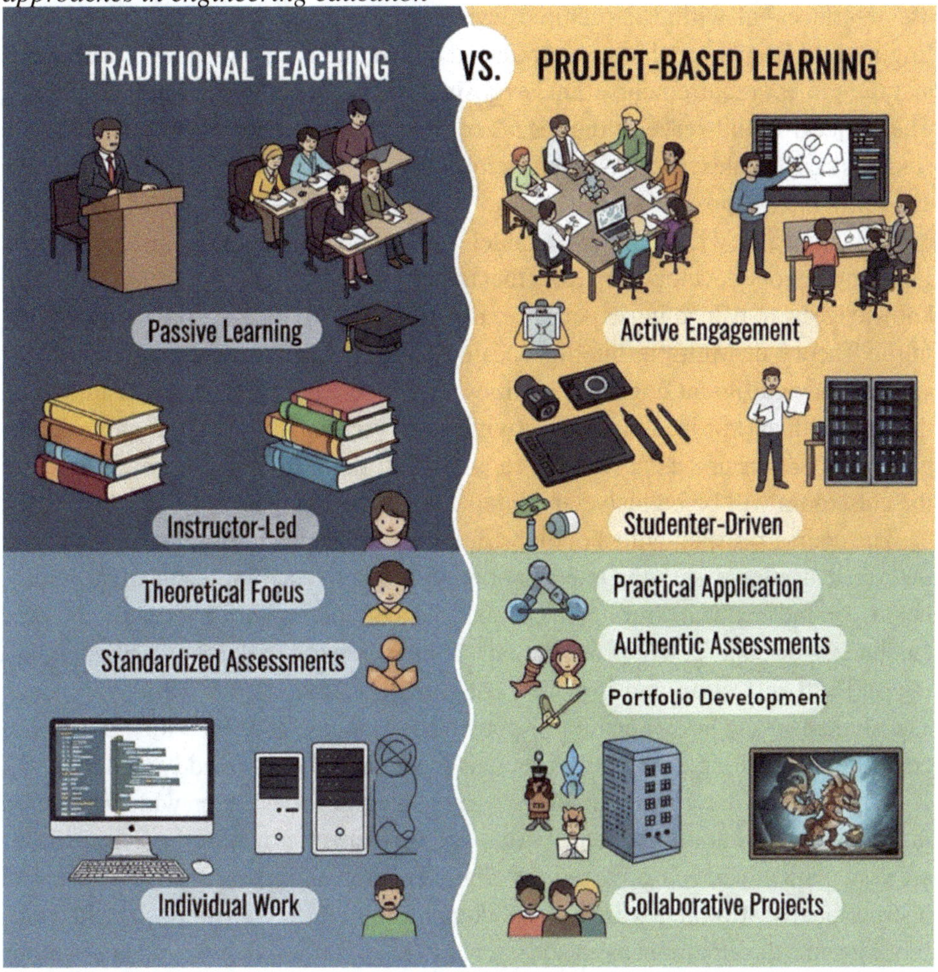

In order to deal with this issue, we proposed a PBL framework in the undergraduate course on CGG, which targets third-year students in the Computer Engineering program. The essence of the matter was that it was time to stop the passive process of knowledge consumption and start learning actively, through experiences (Li et al., 2019; Bubenkova & Pietrikova, 2024). Students did not simply learn computer graphics but were motivated to use their knowledge to build their own, complete video games. Game development was selected not only due to its multidisciplinary depth but due also to the inherent fit with the learning outcomes of computer graphics: rendering, animation, interaction and visual storytelling.

This method allowed students to collaborate in teams, develop storylines, characters and scenes, apply graphics algorithms, generate animation effects, and build user interfaces--all within a structured development lifecycle. OpenGL, Unity, Unreal Engine, and Blender tools were introduced depending on the readiness of students and the project requirements, thus, exposing them to what is used in the industry. The projects would serve as the means of experiential learning which would give students a rich context in which to participate in ideation, experimentation, feedback, and refinement loops.

Pedagogically, what makes this model strong is that it fits within the Experiential Learning Theory developed by Kolb that focuses on learning as a process of creating knowledge by transforming experience (Kolb & Kolb, 2017). It also takes inspiration in the Theory of Multiple Intelligences by Howard Gardner who recognizes that students have different cognitive abilities, some students perform better in logical thinking, others in visual-spatial activities, storytelling, or group dynamics. The game production process is related to almost all these dimensions, and therefore the classroom will be inclusive and intellectually engaging.

The course finished with a demonstration of the games in front of a crowd, and the rubric used to assess the games not only took into account technical accuracy, but also creativity, teamwork and user experience. The reflective journals and peer feedback, as well as poster presentations, contributed to the depth of critical thinking and self-reflection and provided enrichment of the overall learning process. The students grew in ownership, responsibility, and confidence, which traditional engineering teaching does not focus on as much as it should (Reddy et al., 2024).

While project-based learning and game development have been widely explored in computing education, the contribution of this chapter lies in how these approaches are systematically operationalized and aligned with learning theory, assessment, and instructional scaffolding within a core computer graphics course. Rather than presenting game development as an add-on or motivational activity, this work positions it as a structured pedagogical vehicle for teaching foundational graphics concepts, supported by explicit phase mapping, theory-informed design choices, and rubric-based evaluation. The chapter thus advances existing practice by offering a replicable instructional design pattern that integrates creativity, technical rigor, and reflective learning, making it applicable beyond a single course or institutional context.

MAIN FOCUS OF THE CHAPTER

The purpose of this chapter is to give a full description of this pedagogical experiment. It presents the theoretical basis, the course design, implementation plan, student results, and practice issues that appeared in the process. More to the point, it challenges teachers to question the way such subjects as Computer Graphics can be taught not as disjointed units of knowledge but as dynamic student-centered learning experiences. Allowing technical learning to be a part of a creative and project-based ecosystem, we can not only help students gain more conceptual knowledge, but also skills that are critical in a 21st-century work place: collaboration, innovation, communication, and self-directed learning.

Although project-based learning is widely advocated in computer science education, there remains a gap between its theoretical support and the availability of well-articulated, transferable instructional designs for core technical courses such as Computer Graphics. Existing studies often emphasize outcomes or isolated classroom practices, offering limited insight into pedagogical decision-making, scaffolding, and assessment alignment.

This chapter addresses the need for a practice-informed yet theoretically grounded approach that demonstrates how game development can be effectively used to teach foundational graphics concepts without compromising technical rigor. It also responds to the lack of reflective discussion on implementation challenges such as learner diversity, assessment fairness, instructional workload, and scalability. The primary objective of the chapter is to present and analyze a structured PBL-based instructional design for a Computer Graphics and Gaming course. Rather than serving as a project showcase, the chapter focuses on the pedagogical rationale behind design choices, the integration of experiential learning principles, and the role of rubric-aligned evaluation.The chapter contributes to existing knowledge by framing PBL-based game development as a deliberate pedagogical strategy supported by theory and reflective practice. It offers educators generalizable design principles and assessment insights that can be adapted to other graphics-intensive and design-oriented STEM courses, while aligning with broader educational priorities emphasizing experiential, creative, and skill-integrated learning.

METHODS

This chapter adopts a practice-informed, design-oriented methodological approach rather than an experimental research design. No original empirical data were collected through controlled interventions or pre–post measurements. Instead, the chapter is grounded in the systematic documentation and reflective analysis of a project-based learning implementation within an undergraduate Computer Graphics and Gaming course.

The methodological basis consists of instructional design analysis, artifact review, rubric-based evaluation outcomes, and structured instructor reflection. Course design decisions were informed by established learning theories, while evidence of learning and engagement was derived from student-created artifacts, project demonstrations, assessment rubrics, and observational insights gathered during multiple iterations of the course.

Analysis was conducted through qualitative synthesis, identifying recurring patterns related to student engagement, creativity, collaboration, and technical skill development. Conclusions were reached by triangulating these observations with relevant educational literature and accreditation-aligned learning objectives, allowing the chapter to contribute pedagogical insights while maintaining methodological transparency and scope clarity.

THEORETICAL FRAMEWORK

This section outlines the educational theories and pedagogical frameworks that form the foundation of the course design. By aligning the curriculum with research-based learning theories, the project-based game development approach ensures both deep learning and skill-building, essential for 21st-century engineers.

PBL Principles

PBL is a pedagogical approach that emphasizes learning through active exploration of real-world problems and challenges. It transforms students from passive recipients of information into active creators of knowledge. In this course, PBL is implemented through game development projects, aligning learning outcomes with technical competencies in computer graphics (Caratozzolo et al., 2021).

- **Driving Questions:** The theme-based game concept is assigned or developed by each team and makes them learn and utilize the main principles of rendering, animation, object modeling, and interaction design.
- **Sustained Inquiry:** Over a number of weeks, students ask questions, do research, design, prototype, and test their games, getting feedback and iterating based on peer and faculty feedback.
- **Authenticity:** The projects reflect the real-life situation and procedures in the gaming industry, such as utilization of the tools, such as Unity, Blender, and GitHub, as a version control tool.
- **Student Voice and Choice:** The teams have their own freedom of choosing the genre of the game (e.g., arcade, puzzle, adventure), programming language (e.g., Python, C++), and art style, which makes them more ownership and motivated.

- **Rephrase & Edit:** The review sessions that are held each week and peer-testing enable iterative refinement, and they also train students how to accept and use feedback, which is also given constructively.
- **Public Product:** Games are demonstrated in the form of public demos, college symposiums, and portfolio websites. Students also make posters that describe their design process, technical stack, and narrative arc (Wijnen-Meijer et al., 2022).

This method does not only develop technical competence but also problem-solving, creativity, and collaboration, which are very appreciated by the industry.

Integration of Kolb's Experiential Learning Cycle

David Kolb's Experiential Learning Theory (1984) proposes that learning is a cyclical process involving four stages as shown in table 1. This model is ideal for structuring project-based game development modules:

Table 1. Stages of Kolb's Experiential Learning Cycle

Kolb's Stage	Course Application
Concrete Experience	Students begin by engaging directly with game development environments, such as creating characters or rendering scenes using OpenGL or Blender.
Reflective Observation	During code reviews, students analyze gameplay elements, debug rendering issues, and reflect on user feedback from peer testing.
Abstract Conceptualization	Students relate their experience to theoretical models—like Phong shading, Bézier curves, or game loop mechanics—taught in lectures.
Active Experimentation	Learners implement refinements, change interaction logic, or apply new shaders and UI layouts based on their insights.

By integrating all four phases, students not only "learn by doing" but also develop metacognitive awareness—critical for independent problem-solving and innovation (Matthews, 1988). Figure 2 demonstrates how Kolb's learning cycle was embedded in the course design, allowing students to experience, reflect, conceptualize, and experiment through their game development tasks.

Figure 2. Kolb's Experiential Learning Cycle in Game Development-based Project-Based Learning

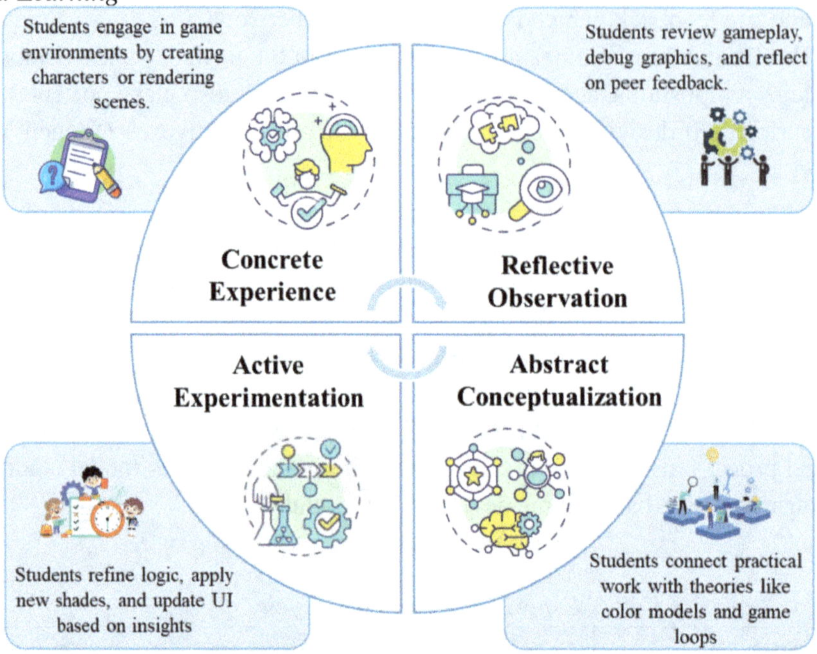

Application of Gardner's Theory of Multiple Intelligences in Evaluation

Howard Gardner's theory (1983) recognizes that intelligence is not a single measurable ability but a combination of different modalities. Game development projects offer a unique opportunity to engage and evaluate multiple intelligence simultaneously (Lai & Yap, 2016).

- **Visual-Spatial Intelligence:** Used in designing game environments, avatars, icons, level maps, and animations using tools like Photoshop, Blender, or 3D Studio Max.
- **Logical-Mathematical Intelligence:** Applied in implementing algorithms for collision detection, physics engines, animation interpolation, and procedural content generation.
- **Linguistic Intelligence:** Demonstrated through writing storyboards, in-game dialogues, UI texts, and technical documentation.

- **Musical Intelligence:** Expressed in integrating background music, sound effects, and audio cues for feedback and immersion.
- **Bodily-Kinesthetic Intelligence:** In motion-sensitive games (e.g., using Unity with Kinect), or designing interaction mechanisms that respond to user gestures or controller movements.
- **Interpersonal Intelligence:** Activated through teamwork, collaboration, assigning roles (e.g., programmer, artist, tester), and managing group dynamics.
- **Intrapersonal Intelligence:** Reflected in personal learning journals, portfolio reflections, and self-assessments conducted at mid- and end-term reviews.

This inclusive framework ensures that evaluation is not limited to cognitive ability but extends to creative and social dimensions, making it more equitable and comprehensive. While Kolb's experiential learning cycle and Gardner's theory of multiple intelligences are well-established, they are not without critique, particularly regarding empirical validation in the case of Gardner's framework. In this work, these theories are used as design heuristics rather than evaluative models. Kolb's cycle informed the sequencing of activities from hands-on game creation to reflection and refinement, while Gardner's framework guided the inclusion of diverse expressive modes such as visual design, narrative, logical reasoning, and collaboration. These frameworks were chosen to support inclusive engagement and creative exploration, making them suitable for studio-style game development contexts.

COURSE DESIGN AND IMPLEMENTATION

Course Objectives and Learning Outcomes

The primary objective of this course is to provide students with foundational knowledge and practical skills in the field of computer graphics and game development. By engaging with a variety of tools and platforms, students learn to apply core graphics concepts, transformations, and design principles to develop interactive visual content. The learning experience is structured to build both technical proficiency and creative fluency.

After successful completion of the course, students will be able to:

1. Comprehend and apply fundamental graphics primitives and core concepts in computer graphics.
2. Implement 2D and 3D geometric transformations for designing visual scenes.
3. Apply polygon filling and clipping techniques for rendering complex shapes.

4. Design and develop simple animations and game prototypes using industry-standard graphics tools.

Mapping CO to Bloom's Taxonomy and Program Outcomes (POs)

To facilitate the formulation and efficiency of the curriculum, every CO is precisely aligned to relevant levels of Bloom Taxonomy and also to the already established POs of the Computer Engineering curriculum. Such mapping enables:

- **Progressive skill development**, from understanding to creating.
- **Alignment with accreditation criteria**, ensuring transparency in assessment and evaluation.
- **Outcome-based learning**, encouraging active participation and deeper comprehension.

Table 2. Cos of course CGG

CO No.	Course Outcome Description	Bloom's Level	Relevant Program Outcomes (POs)
CO1	Comprehend graphics primitives and fundamentals	Understand	PO1, PO2
CO2	Use transformation operations for visual applications	Apply	PO1, PO3
CO3	Apply polygon filling and clipping methods	Apply	PO1, PO5
CO4	Design animations and games using gaming tools and software	Create	PO3, PO5, PO9

This structured alignment ensures that students are not only evaluated on knowledge acquisition but also on the ability to apply, analyze, and create.

Structure of the Course

The course is structured in a step-by-step manner that corresponds to the growing complexity of the concepts of computer graphics and their use in the development of games. The framework is a combination of theory, lab-based practice, and project-based learning.

- **Phase 1: Foundations Fundamentals (Weeks 1-4)-** Presents simple graphics rules, color models, rasterization, and primitive drawing. Learners become conversant with the application of graphics in the digital systems.
- **Phase 2: Algorithms and transformations (Weeks 5 7)-** Focuses on geometric transformation and clipping. Students are taught about matrix representation, coordinate transformations and filling algorithms.
- **Phase 3: Tools and Environment (weeks 8 9)-** Discusses such industry tools as OpenGL, Unity, Blender, and Flash. Students are allowed to experiment with the design of simple scenes, character models and textures.
- **Phase 4: Game Design and Development (Weeks 10-12)-** Coverage of the game development life cycle: game ideation and storyboarding, prototyping, and interactivity. Students are organized into groups and start mini-projects.
- **Phase 5: Testing, Presentation and Reflection (weeks 13 15)-** Comprises bug fixing, demo day, poster presentation and reflective writing. Students assess their process and results in learning.

This module-based system promotes life-long learning and development as well as a combination of theory and practical results.

Tools, Technologies, and Platforms Used

The course applies to a combination of industry-relevant tools and open-source technologies that expose students to a variety of environments that are acceptable in academic research and professional practice. Tools include:

- **OpenGL** – for understanding low-level rendering and transformation.
- **Unity and Unreal Engine** – for creating interactive 2D/3D games and VR/AR experiences.
- **Blender and Maya** – for 3D modeling, rigging, and animation.
- **Photoshop or GIMP** – for sprite and texture design.
- **GLUT or SDL** – for building windowed graphics applications and managing user inputs.

These tools support the full pipeline of game development—from asset creation to rendering and interactivity.

Project Stages

The practical mini project is the central experiential part of the course. Students usually operate in groups, and they have a streamlined development process:

1. **Idea Generation**: Choosing an idea of a game that is related to social or educational topics.
2. **Storyboarding**: Drawing the visual story and characterizing or game.
3. **Prototyping**: Developing a playable minimum prototype with game engines or scripting.
4. **Development:** Adding game logic, interactivity, visuals, and sound.
5. **Testing and Finalization**: Fixing bugs, optimizing performance, and preparing for final presentation.

This structure mirrors industry workflows, promoting both collaboration and creativity.

Use of Multilingual Teaching Elements

To acknowledge the linguistic and regional background of the students of the Computer Engineering (Regional Language) program, multilingual teaching strategies are incorporated in the course and mainly make use of the mother tongue of the students in addition to English. This is based on the philosophy that students learn better, acquire a better conceptual knowledge and lasting knowledge when they are taught in a language that is most comfortable to them (Patil et al., 2025a).

Practically, it implies that technical terms will be presented in English, as it is demanded in the industry and academic requirements, yet will be immediately followed by the real-time explanations, analogies, and discussions in Marathi, so that they are perfectly clear and understandable. Google Docs, slides, and recorded lessons are offered as teaching aids in bilingual formats, which helps the students during the classroom and self-study. In the process of lab work and coding exercises, students practice syntax and structure of programming languages in English and communicate about the logic of algorithms or visual processing in Marathi, which contributes to the decrease in the gap between the knowledge and its implementation.

The assessments, especially those where design justifications, documentation or reflective writing are involved, give the students the freedom to write in either English or Marathi according to their comfort and clarity of expression. Group discussions, peer feedback, and presentations are also held in a mixed-language format in the classroom. This will make all the students, irrespective of their level of language proficiency, take part in the activities actively and without hesitation. The multilingual method does not only enrich the conceptual clarity and knowledge retention but also increases the level of confidence among the students, which promotes more classroom interaction and a more inclusive and encouraging learning environment.

PEDAGOGICAL STRATEGY

The course design adopts PBL as its central methodology, enabling students to learn by actively engaging in authentic, real-world tasks. This approach is complemented by scaffolding, where each phase of game development builds upon the previous one, guiding learners progressively from concept ideation to a fully developed and tested product (Aglen, 2016). The scaffolding is not purely technical; it is also cognitive and linguistic, given the unique learning environment of regional-language-speaking computer engineering students.

A core philosophy driving this course is that when students learn in their mother tongue alongside the technical language, comprehension improves significantly, and retention is prolonged. Therefore, technical terms are taught in English, but complex concepts, design thinking processes, and problem-solving discussions are often facilitated in the students' regional language (Patil et al., 2025b). This dual-language approach bridges the gap between conceptual understanding and technical expression, resulting in stronger learning outcomes.

The activity followed a structured, iterative framework as illustrated in figure 3, ensuring seamless integration of design, development, and evaluation phases. This pedagogical approach fostered both technical mastery and creative problem-solving in game development.

Figure 3. Pedagogical Approach for Game Development

Phase 1: Idea Generation

Table 3 presents an overview of the 14 project groups formed for the course. Each group selected a unique game concept, classified according to its project title, category (e.g., Educational, Narrative-Driven, Experimental, Puzzle-Based), genre (e.g., Adventure, Sci-Fi, Horror, Fantasy, Sports), and development type (2D or 3D). This classification highlights the diversity of ideas generated during the Idea Generation phase. From the table, it is evident that the projects span a wide creative spectrum — from conceptually rich narrative adventures to skill-based puzzle games, and from realistic simulations to imaginative fantasy worlds. The inclusion of both 2D and 3D development approaches demonstrates the students' adaptability in selecting technologies and tools that align with their creative vision and technical comfort.

This initial distribution of categories and genres provides a strong foundation for analyzing trends, such as the dominance of certain genres, the balance between educational and entertainment-focused projects, and the adoption rates of 2D versus 3D environments. These insights form the baseline for further evaluation in subsequent phases of the course.

Table 3. Overview of Project Groups with Categories, Genres, and Development Types

Group No.	Project Title	Category	Genre	Game Type
1	Math Quest	Educational / Simulation	Adventure & Quest-Based Games	2D
2	Cosmic Odyssey	Sci-Fi / Space-Themed	Adventure & Quest-Based Games	3D
3	Haunted Escape	Horror / Survival	Puzzle & Platformers	2D
4	Battle Bots	Action & Combat	Sci-Fi / Space-Themed	3D
5	StoryWeave	Narrative-Driven	Experimental / Creative Storytelling	2D
6	Eco City Builder	Educational / Simulation	Puzzle & Platformers	2D
7	Time Rift	Sci-Fi / Space-Themed	Action & Combat	3D
8	Mystery Manor	Horror / Survival	Narrative-Driven / Storytelling	2D
9	Galaxy Defender	Action & Combat	Sci-Fi / Space-Themed	2D
10	Rapid Rake	Experimental / Creative	Narrative-Driven / Storytelling	2D
11	Code Warriors	Educational / Simulation	Action & Combat	2D
12	Treasure Trails	Adventure / Quest-Based	Puzzle & Platformers	2D
13	Survival Island	Horror / Survival	Adventure & Quest-Based Games	3D
14	Rusty Cat	Narrative-Driven	Adventure & Quest-Based Games	3D

Genre Trends

The Adventure & Quest-Based Games genre is the most popular, with 4 projects (Groups 1, 12, 13, 14). This reflects students' preference for exploratory gameplay, storytelling, and multi-level challenges. Other notable genres as shown in figure 4 include Sci-Fi / Space-Themed and Action & Combat, each having 3 projects, showing an interest in futuristic narratives and dynamic mechanics. Horror / Survival appears in 3 projects, often blended with puzzle-solving or adventure elements, suggesting a focus on suspense-driven engagement.

Figure 4. Genre Trends

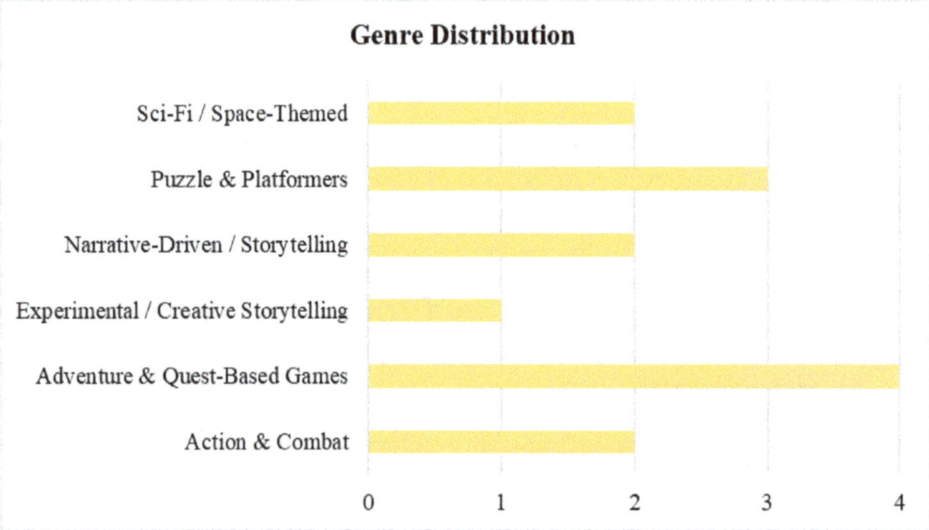

Category Representation

Educational / Simulation games (Groups 1, 6, 11) account for ~21% of the projects, highlighting an inclination toward learning-oriented designs. Narrative-Driven / Storytelling (Groups 5, 8, 10, 14) is well-represented, indicating a strong focus on immersive plot development. Experimental / Creative Storytelling appears twice (Groups 5, 10), often combined with narrative-driven gameplay, showing a trend toward creative and unconventional mechanics.

The category distribution of the 14 project groups is illustrated in figure 5. The representation shows a balanced spread across multiple categories, with certain genres emerging as more prominent. Horror / Survival and Educational / Simulation games are the most common, each accounting for 22% of the total projects, indicating a strong interest in immersive and instructive gameplay experiences. Action & Combat, Narrative-Driven / Storytelling, and Sci-Fi / Space-Themed each contribute 14%, reflecting the appeal of dynamic, plot-rich, and futuristic settings among the students. Meanwhile, Adventure & Quest-Based and Experimental / Creative

Storytelling games are the least represented, each with 7%, suggesting niche but creative project explorations in these genres.

This distribution highlights that while students explore a diverse range of game categories, they tend to favor genres that either provide strong narrative immersion or simulate realistic problem-solving scenarios (Ibanez et al., 2014).

Figure 5. Category Representation of Game Projects

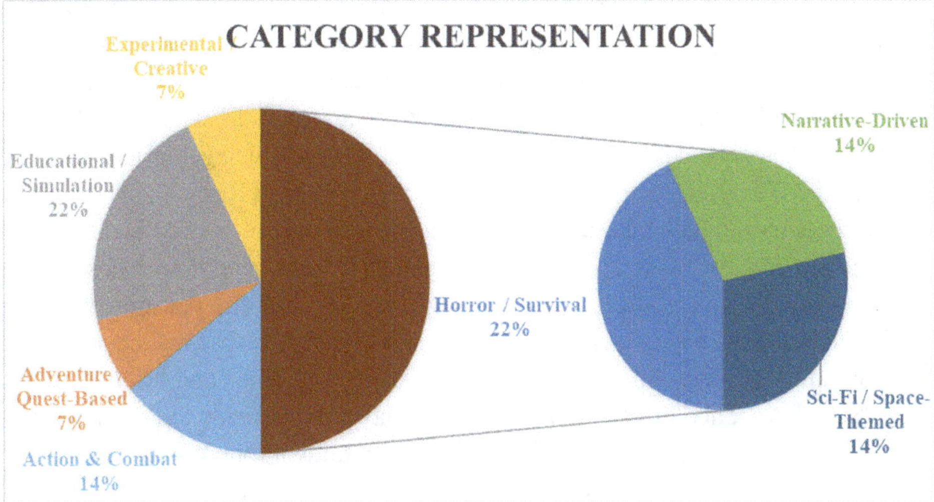

2D vs. 3D Development

A majority (10 out of 14) of the projects are 2D, reflecting students' preferallence for simpler asset creation pipelines, easier debugging, and quicker prototyping cycles. Only 4 projects are planned in 3D (Groups 2, 4, 7, 13, 14), indicating that while some teams are ready to take on the complexity of 3D design, most are focusing on achievable production within resource constraints. The overall distribution shows a healthy mix of educational, entertainment, and narrative-focused concepts, with a tendency toward genres that allow creative freedom and replayability. The predominance of 2D games also aligns with the limited GPU resources available to students, making the projects more feasible within the given semester timeline.

Phase 2: Storyboarding

Storyboarding is an important creative stage during which the conceptual ideas are transformed into systematic visual stories. It is the transition between abstract brainstorming and concrete design and a roadmap of how the game will flow, look, and interact with the user (Laakso et al., 2021). The main purpose of this stage is the visualization of the gameplay experience through the eyes of the player, and the consistency of design and understandability of the goals should be achieved prior to the development stage.

In the case of Rusty Cat as shown in figure 6, the main premise is that of a cyber-enhanced street cat in a post-apocalyptic city that is full of obstacles, traps, and power-ups. The main character aims to get out of a dying industrial area before being covered with toxic gas. In the process, the players need to avoid obstacles, acquire temporary bonuses, and survive the threats of the environment. Difficulties are in the form of high jumps, low slides and precise timing to evade instant-death traps.

The game is organized in the form of constant stages, which get faster and more complicated. This is reflected in the flowchart of the states of Rusty Cat: the cat will go into the Running state once a key is pressed and into the Jumping or Sliding states once the player presses the up or down commands respectively. Power-ups disrupt this flow briefly, as a reward to good navigation. There is the constant threat of death when striking an obstacle-the player has to restart or respawn at checkpoints. The rhythm is set between the heart-pounding running scenes and brief moments of repose (or so-called breathers) allowing the player to get ready to face new challenges. The mood of the game is slightly dramatic, but still playful, as it combines the quick reflexes and action with the moments of tactical choice.

Figure 6. State diagram of game Rustycat

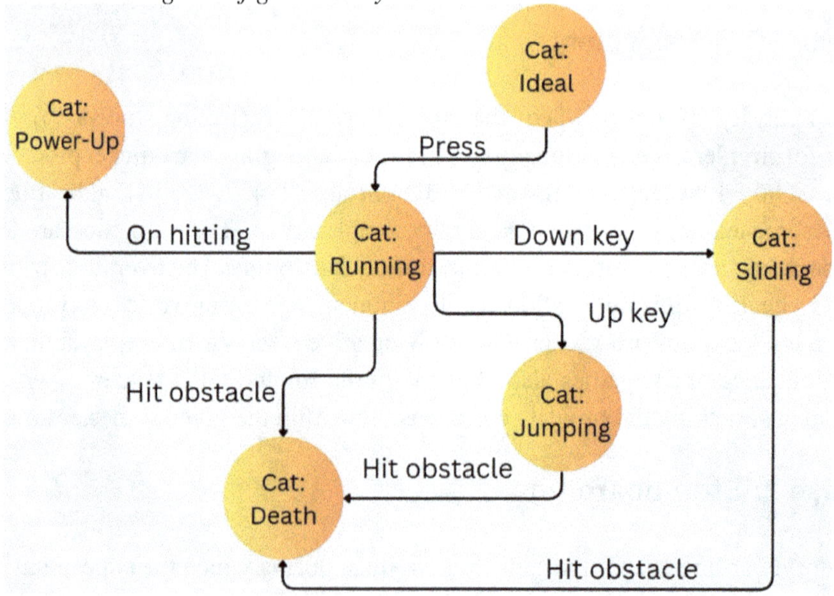

Phase 3: Prototyping

The prototyping phase bridges the gap between concept and playable experience (Roman et al., 2024). It allows the team to validate mechanics, check technical feasibility, and gather early feedback.

- **Core Mechanics Setup**: Implement the most essential actions first (running, jumping, sliding, collecting items) to ensure they feel responsive and having fun.
- **Obstacle & Power-up Placement**: Introduce key obstacles (cars, trash bins, barriers) and power-ups (magnets, shields) in test form. Use placeholder graphics to keep development fast.
- **Basic Level Layout**: Create a short, looped environment to test the pacing and difficulty curve.
- **Scoring & Life System**: Add a preliminary system for tracking collected items and remaining lives.
- **Feedback Collection**: Have a small group of testers try the prototype, focusing on control feel, visual clarity, and pacing.

In Rusty Cat, the prototype featured a simple endless street scene with the cat able to run, jump, and slide to avoid obstacles. Fish bones could be collected for points, and magnets temporarily pulled them closer. Placeholder models represented houses, lampposts, and cars. Testers highlighted that jump timing needed to be more forgiving and obstacle spacing slightly wider, which led to immediate adjustments before moving into full development. The game scene in figure 7 demonstrates obstacle navigation, where the character must dodge barriers and collect items along the path. Such visual cues enhance player engagement and challenge.

Figure 7. In-game obstacle navigation sequence

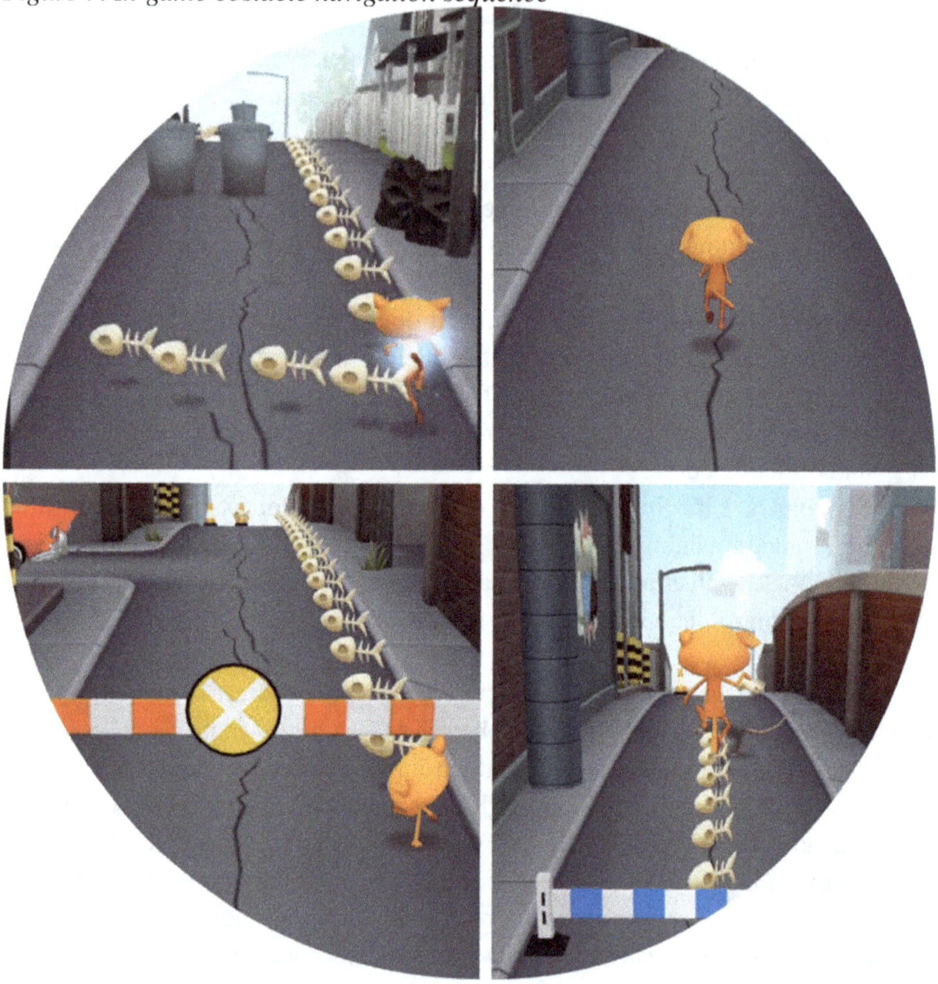

Phase 4: Development

In the development Phase, the project transitions from conceptualization and planning into the actual creation of the game. This stage involves the full-scale implementation of all elements, combining visual assets, core gameplay logic, and interactive environments into a functional product (Sytnyk et al., 2024). The process begins with the creation of detailed visual and audio assets, including 2D or 3D models, textures, animations, background elements, sound effects, and music.

These components are designed to match the intended art style and atmosphere of the game, ensuring consistency across all scenes.

At the same time, the fundamental logic of the gameplay is also coded and the fundamental mechanics of the gameplay, including the movement of the player, controls of interaction, the behavior of enemies or non-player characters, the scoring and health systems, and the rules enforcement are created. The interactive features are coded to react flawlessly to player interaction and in-game occurrences (Kleftodimos, 2024). When the mechanics are established, the work is directed towards level design and integration. The environment is created in a way that is playable by using objects, triggers, and event systems in place to ensure that there is a fluid transition between scenes. This stage also includes testing and optimizing the interaction of visual assets and gameplay systems so that they fit together to create an enjoyable experience.

The products of this stage will consist mainly of the finished game content, integrated into the working build and fully ready to test and, at last, optimize. Rusty is the fast and furious cyber cat that is meant to survive in the concrete jungle. His job is to go through obstacles, and fast reflexes will help him avoid moving and stationary threats. The cybernetic reinforcement that Rusty has enables him to jump higher over parked cars and slide easily under drying clothes lines or street barriers. The assets designed are shown in figure 8.

- **Cars**: These are not mere decorations in the background, as cars can also be used as moving obstacles and as platforms. The vehicles are of a cartoonish nature, and small (like cars), and may be stationery (stationed) or moving across the screen as obstacles Rusty must jump over. They are easily read by the high speed of exaggerated shapes and bright colors.
- **Bins and Trash**: The clusters of environmental hazards include trash bins, garbage bags and dumpsters. The small bins need speedy leaps, whereas the dumpsters can serve as walls which Rusty will have to circumnavigate. Sometimes they conceal collectibles such as temporary speed increases or story lore (e.g. notes on the fall of the city).
- **Houses and Buildings**: They characterize the profile of the city and in some cases, create rooftop running segments. Smaller houses in the suburbs enable the tight jumps between the roofs and the tall industrial buildings provide the vertical area of challenge where Rusty performs the wall jumps or climbs.
- **Street Elements**: Objects such as road barriers, fences and clotheslines compel the players to make certain movement decisions. Barriers encourage leaps, fences prevent slides and clotheslines are converted into low-hanging hazards that demand careful crouching or timing.

Assigning a "role" to every piece of the environment in the gameplay makes the world seem alive and responsive to the player actions. The art style maintains proportions exaggerated and colors vivid in order to ensure that even when the player is moving with high speed, he or she can immediately identify the hazards areas versus safe areas.

Figure 8. Asstes designed for the game Rustycat

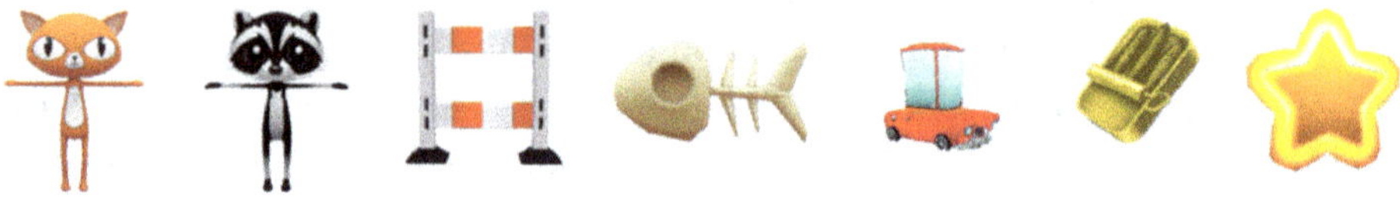

Phase 5: Testing

The testing stage of the Rusty Cat development is aimed at the validation of all the aspects of the game, including the controls of the characters, the level transfer, and so forth. This is done through systematic bug detection, reproduction, and resolution, as well as evaluation of the player experience as a whole as shown in table 4. It starts with a unit testing of each component, e.g. movement mechanics of Rusty Cat, collision detection against obstacles, power-ups functionality. The next step is integration testing to make sure that these components interact well with one another, and this is done to make sure that there is no hitch in the interaction between gameplay logic, animations and sound effects. Playtests enable the testers to play through various levels, engage in combat with the enemies and activate events to ensure that the game reacts accordingly when different circumstances are applied. To ensure that the game does not lag or crash, even in complicated action scenes, performance testing is done to ensure that it is at a steady frame rate. User experience testing is concerned with what the players have to say about the controls, balance of difficulty and whether the game is fun to play to the point that the game is functional and enjoyable. At the conclusion of this stage Rusty Cat becomes a polished, stable experience that is fit to be released to the world.

Table 4. Output for Rusty Cat Testing

Test Area	Description	Status	Issues Found
Movement Controls	Tested Rusty Cat's walking, jumping, crouching	Pass	Controls are responsive and smooth
Collision Detection	Checked interactions with platforms, walls, and enemies	Pass	Minor misalignment fixed in Level 2
Enemy	Tested enemy movement patterns and attack behavior	Pass	One enemy pathing loop corrected in Level 3
Power-Up Functionality	Verified collection and activation of speed and health boosts	Pass	No issues found
Scene Transitions	Moving between levels and cutscenes	Pass	Slight fade delay optimized
Audio-Visual Sync	Checked sound effects and animations for timing accuracy	Pass	Jump sound synced better with animation
Performance	Tested FPS stability in high-action scenes	Pass	Stable at 60 FPS
User Experience	Feedback on difficulty curve and engagement	Pass	Early game made slightly easier for balance

The iterative nature of the prototyping, development, and testing phases aligns closely with rapid instructional design approaches such as Rapid Prototyping and Design Thinking. Students repeatedly cycled through ideation, implementation, feedback, and refinement, enabling early validation of concepts and continuous improvement of gameplay mechanics and visual design. This iterative loop strengthened both technical decision-making and creative problem-solving.

Phase 6: Outcome & Reflection

In order to conclude the course of Computer Graphics and Gaming, we hosted a poster presentation session during which all the student teams presented their finished and tested projects (Hitchner & Sowizral, 2000). Rather than the one demo session, the groups created a poster that would show their concept of the game, story, design process, assets, and technical implementation. In addition to the posters, there were live demonstrations where people could play the games themselves, both interactive 2D platformers and 3D adventure games, as well as more creative simulation games. The sample posters designed by students are shown in figure 9.

The performance was a space of peer-to-peer learning since students had an opportunity to learn more about various ways to render, animate, interact with the user, and tell a story. Faculty members judged projects on the basis of technical accuracy, creativity, quality of presentation, and teamwork. The comments collected in the session provided students with a good idea of how to make the gameplay mechanics more interesting, enhance the visuals and streamline performance.

Figure 9. Sample posters designed for The Rapid Rake and The Rustycat

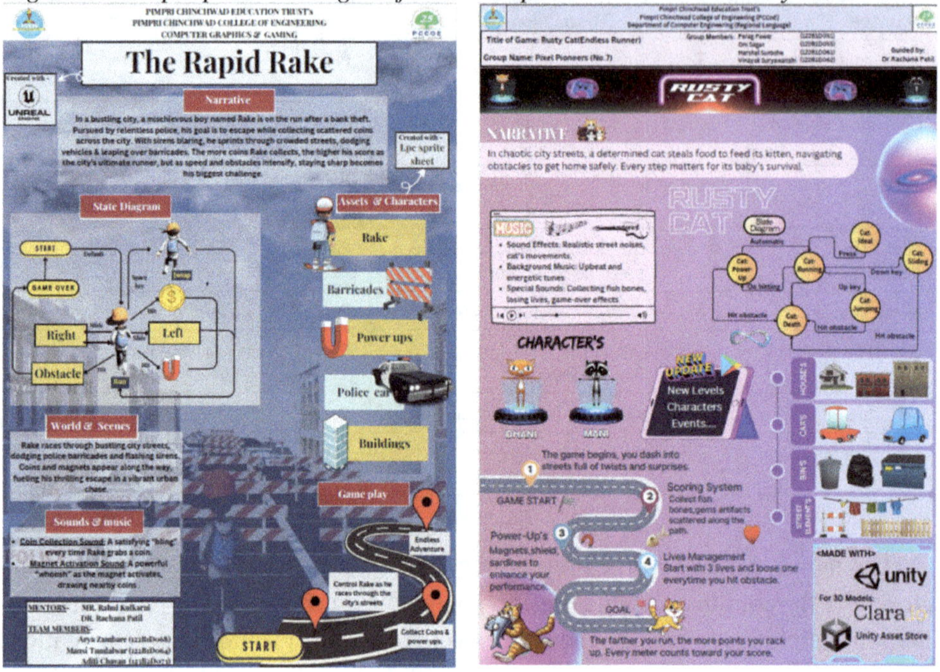

EVALUATION AND ASSESSMENT

The evaluation approach adopted in this chapter is practice-informed rather than experimental. The intent was not to establish causal learning gains through controlled pre–post comparisons, but to document learning patterns emerging from rubric-based assessment, iterative feedback, and reflective observation. Evidence is therefore drawn from structured rubrics, artifact analysis, student reflections, and instructor observations, which together provide indicative rather than statistically generalizable insights into student learning.

Table 5. Evaluation Parameters Used

Sr. No.	Parameter	Description	Marks
1	Rendering / Game Design	Quality of rendering, visual coherence, and design elements, mapped to CO3	5
2	Code Structure	Efficiency, organization, and maintainability of the source code	5
3	Quality (Aesthetics)	Visual appeal, consistency, and user interface polish	5
4	Innovation / Differentiator	Unique features or creative gameplay mechanics	3
5	Working Demo	Functionality, bug-free execution, and completeness	5
6	Poster	Clarity, visual design, and effectiveness in explaining the project	4
7	AI Tools Used	Integration of AI-based assets or features	3
8	Presentation	Verbal and visual communication skills during demonstration	4
9	Sound Effects	Relevance, quality, and integration into gameplay	3
10	Team Collaboration	Coordination, task division, and contribution balance	3

The evaluation of student projects in the CGG course was designed to measure both technical competency and creative expression. A balanced rubric was applied to ensure that programming skills, design choices, innovation, and teamwork were all recognized (Sobota & Pietriková, 2023). Table 5 presents the evaluation parameters employed to assess each project, providing a balanced measure of technical execution, creativity, collaboration, and overall presentation quality. These parameters ensured a fair and comprehensive assessment aligned with the course objectives.

Figure 10. Assessment of students projects

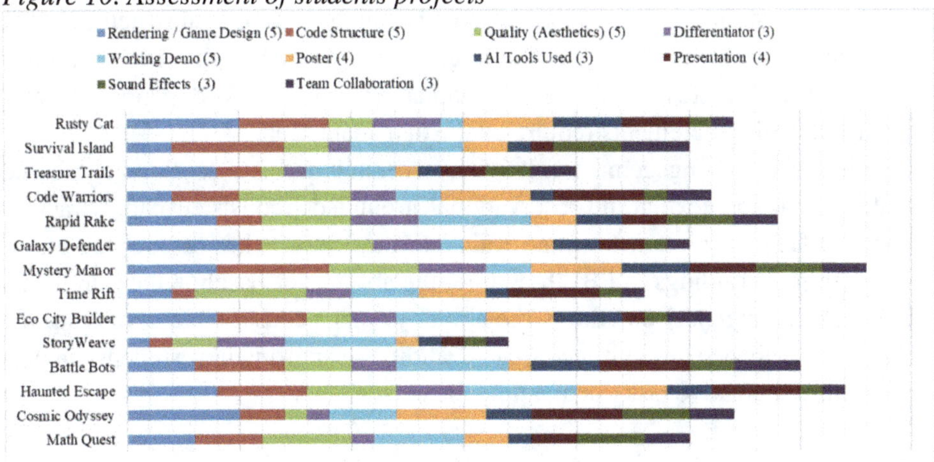

The projects assessment in figure 10 showed that the students have good skills in Rendering/Game Design and presentation of a Working Demo with an average of 3.82 and 3.76 respectively. These findings show that the majority of teams managed to create attractive and playable games. Nevertheless, some gaps can also be noted in the analysis, mainly those related to the use of AI tools (average score 1.58) and introduction of sound effects (average score 1.88), which might have been either ignored or underdeveloped. The top scoring project, Maze Runner (38.0), demonstrated superiority in various parameters, whereas, the lowest scoring project, Pixel Quest (19.0) was poor in terms of design and implementation. In general, the technical implementation and aesthetics are the strong aspects, but it can be improved greatly with a focus on the emerging technologies and the immersive experiences, like audio.

Lower scores in AI tool usage and sound design reflect instructional trade-offs rather than student limitations, including uneven prior exposure and limited curricular emphasis on these components. These outcomes highlight resource and time constraints, offering clear directions for future course refinement.

OUTCOMES AND IMPACT

The Computer Graphics and Gaming course based on the PBL approach produced quantifiable increases in technical skills, levels of engagement and creativity in students (Franco et al., 2006; Wu et al., 2025). In addition to technical knowledge, the method promoted critical professional competence including collaboration, problem-solving, and self-directed learning, which are important in overall development.

While game development provides unique motivational and creative affordances, the transferability of the proposed model lies in its pedagogical structure rather than its domain context. Phased scaffolding, artifact-driven learning, rubric-aligned assessment, and iterative feedback are adaptable across STEM domains, whereas narrative and visual elements require contextual adaptation.

Claims related to engagement, creativity, ownership, and skill development should be interpreted as contextual and observational, grounded in consistent patterns across student artifacts, peer interaction, and evaluation outcomes. While these observations align with prior findings in PBL literature, the absence of baseline measurements and controlled comparisons limits the ability to make causal claims. Instead, the value of the evidence lies in its ecological validity—capturing how students engage with complex, creative tasks in an authentic classroom setting.

Student Learning Outcomes

Students had observable improvements in: Technical Skills on rendering, integrating assets, animation process and optimization solutions. Active involvement with all the phases of the project cycle, ideation to deployment. Creation of original story lines, new game mechanics and a visually unified game world.

Benefits Observed

Team communication and collaboration improved as students divided work tactfully across programming, design, and asset creation roles while regularly updating one another on progress. This structure encouraged peer-to-peer learning, with teams actively supporting and training each other on technical aspects. In terms of problem-solving and debugging, teams were able to resolve complex rendering issues, gameplay logic bugs, and asset compatibility problems. Debugging emerged as a collaborative effort, supported by internal testing and peer review prior to final submission. Ownership and agency in learning were evident as students made independent design and technology choices, selecting tools such as Unreal Engine, Blender, or AI asset generators based on project needs. Responsibility for quality, polish, and presentation rested with the teams, reflecting the development of professional work ethics.

Insights on Feedback

Student feedback indicated that many learners experienced the PBL approach as a studio-like environment that strengthened both technical and soft skills. Faculty observations highlighted increased engagement levels, strong design thinking abilities, and well-organized project documentation. External reviewer feedback emphasized the originality of ideas, the technical depth achieved within short timelines, and the professional quality of final presentations.

CONCLUSION

The computer graphics and gaming activity that was based on PBL was able to combine technical rigor with creativity and provide the students with an opportunity to be able to combine rendering, design, coding, and presentation skills in an integrated way. The organized stages of the conceptualization and asset creation, poster presentation, and the final demonstration promoted intensive involvement, teamwork, and communication among the teams. Evaluation outcomes showed even levels of performance within the technical and creative levels, which is backed by innovative features and the integration of AI. In addition to the learning of skills, the activity fostered problem solving skills, debugging effectiveness and taking ownership of the learning experience. The results of student and faculty surveys highlighted the feeling of greater confidence, enhanced teamwork, and enhanced flexibility to work on real-world projects. With the alignment with NEP 2020 and accreditation standards, the initiative proved that PBL can be an effective pedagogical tool in the development of industry-relevant competencies, as well as an inspirational tool in innovation and lifelong learning in the field of computer engineering education. Beyond reporting a course implementation, this chapter contributes a pedagogically grounded and transferable model for integrating creative digital artifacts into core computing curricula. By explicitly connecting theory, practice, and assessment, the work advances the discourse on how PBL can be structured to move from activity-based engagement to evidence-based learning design in computer science education. Future work may strengthen these findings through pre–post comparisons, learner analytics, and mixed-method evaluation designs.

REFERENCES

Aglen, B. (2016). Pedagogical strategies to teach bachelor students evidence-based practice: A systematic review. *Nurse Education Today, 36*, 255–263. DOI: 10.1016/j.nedt.2015.08.025 PMID: 26375570

Bubenkova, L., & Pietrikova, E. (2024). Game development: Enhancing creativity and independent creation in university course. In Proceedings of the 5th International Computer Programming Education Conference (ICPEC 2024) (pp. 12–1). Schloss Dagstuhl–Leibniz-Zentrum für Informatik. https://doi.org/DOI: 10.4230/OASIcs.ICPEC.2024.12

Caratozzolo, P., Rosas-Melendez, S., & Ortiz-Alvarado, C. (2021). Active learning approaches for sustainable energy engineering education. In *Proceedings of the 2021 IEEE Green Technologies Conference (GreenTech)* (pp. 251–258). IEEE. https://doi.org/DOI: 10.1109/GreenTech48523.2021.00048

Du, B., & Yang, X. (2017). The effect of team-based learning on conventional pathology education to improve students' mastery of pathology. *International Journal of Higher Education, 6*(3), 12–20. DOI: 10.5430/ijhe.v6n3p12

Everwijn, S. E. M., Bomers, G. B. J., & Knubben, J. A. (1993). Ability- or competence-based education: Bridging the gap between knowledge acquisition and ability to apply. *Higher Education, 25*(4), 425–438. DOI: 10.1007/BF01383845

Franco, J. F., da Cruz, S. R., & de Deus Lopes, R. (2006). Computer graphics, interactive technologies and collaborative learning synergy supporting individuals' skills development. In *ACM SIGGRAPH 2006 Educators Program* (pp. 42–es). ACM. https://doi.org/DOI: 10.1145/1179295.1179338

Froyd, J. E., Wankat, P. C., & Smith, K. A. (2012). Five major shifts in 100 years of engineering education. *Proceedings of the IEEE, 100*(Special Centennial Issue), 1344–1360. https://doi.org/DOI: 10.1109/JPROC.2012.2190167

Hatlevik, I. K. R. (2012). The theory–practice relationship: Reflective skills and theoretical knowledge as key factors in bridging the gap between theory and practice in initial nursing education. *Journal of Advanced Nursing, 68*(4), 868–877. DOI: 10.1111/j.1365-2648.2011.05789.x PMID: 21790737

Hitchner, L. E., & Sowizral, H. A. (2000). Adapting computer graphics curricula to changes in graphics. *Computers & Graphics, 24*(2), 283–288. DOI: 10.1016/S0097-8493(99)00162-4

Ibanez, M. B., Di-Serio, A., & Delgado-Kloos, C. (2014). Gamification for engaging computer science students in learning activities: A case study. *IEEE Transactions on Learning Technologies*, *7*(3), 291–301. DOI: 10.1109/TLT.2014.2329293

Jayakanthan, R. (2002). Application of computer games in the field of education. *The Electronic Library*, *20*(2), 98–102. DOI: 10.1108/02640470210697471

Kamp, A. (2023). *Engineering education in the rapidly changing world: Rethinking the vision for higher engineering education*. TU Delft Open Publishing., DOI: 10.59490/mg.71

Kleftodimos, A. (2024). Computer-animated videos in education: A comprehensive review and teacher experiences from animation creation. *Digital*, *4*(3), 613–647. DOI: 10.3390/digital4030031

Kolb, A. Y., & Kolb, D. A. (2017). Experiential learning theory as a guide for experiential educators in higher education. *Experiential Learning & Teaching in Higher Education*, *1*(1), 7–44. DOI: 10.46787/elthe.v1i1.3362

Laakso, N. L., Korhonen, T. S., & Hakkarainen, K. P. (2021). Developing students' digital competences through collaborative game design. *Computers & Education*, *174*, 104308. DOI: 10.1016/j.compedu.2021.104308

Lai, H. Y., & Yap, S. L. (2016). Application of multiple intelligence theory in the assessment for learning. In *Assessment for learning within and beyond the classroom* (pp. 427–436). Springer., DOI: 10.1007/978-981-10-0908-2_36

Lavado-Anguera, S., Velasco-Quintana, P. J., & Terrón-López, M. J. (2024). Project-based learning (PBL) as an experiential pedagogical methodology in engineering education: A review of the literature. *Education Sciences*, *14*(6), 617. Advance online publication. DOI: 10.3390/educsci14060617

Li, H., Öchsner, A., & Hall, W. (2019). Application of experiential learning to improve student engagement and experience in a mechanical engineering course. *European Journal of Engineering Education*, *44*(3), 283–293. DOI: 10.1080/03043797.2017.1402864

Matthews, D. (1988). Gardner's multiple intelligence theory: An evaluation of relevant research literature and a consideration of its application to gifted education. *Roeper Review*, *11*(2), 100–104. DOI: 10.1080/02783198809553176

Patil, R. Y., Patil, Y. H., Bhandari, S., & Bannore, A. (2025). Academic achievement through cooperative learning: The impact of the jigsaw method. *International Journal of Pedagogy & Curriculum*, *32*(1). Advance online publication. DOI: 10.18848/2327-7963/CGP/v32i01/61-79

Patil, R. Y., Vaze, A., Bhandari, S., & Kulkarni, G. (2025). Aligning higher education to NEP by introducing learning in mother tongue. *Journal of Engineering Education Transformations*, 195–209. https://doi.org/DOI: 10.16920/jeet/2024/v38i4/25107

Reddy, S. N., Pathlavath, M., Narsareddygari, S., & Naik, S. M. (2024). Investigating the transformative effects of active learning methodologies in the field of engineering education. *Journal of Engineering Education Transformations, 37*(Special Issue 2). https://doi.org/DOI: 10.34290/jeet.37.2.562

Roman, S., Shatalov, R., & Iryna, S. (2024). Features of using computer graphics under conditions of distance learning in vocational education institutions. In *Proceedings of the 19th International Scientific and Practical Conference: Creative Business Management and Implementation of New Ideas* (pp. 145–149). International Science Group.

Sobota, B., & Pietriková, E. (2023). The role of game engines in game development and teaching. In *Computer science for game development and game development for computer science*. IntechOpen., DOI: 10.5772/intechopen.1002257

Sytnyk, O., Hrozna, O., Filonenko, D., Konoplyannikova, O. S., & Serdiuk, O. (2024). Development of interactive forms of communication through artificial intelligence. *Journal of Theoretical and Applied Information Technology, 102*(21).

Wijnen-Meijer, M., Brandhuber, T., Schneider, A., & Berberat, P. O. (2022). Implementing Kolb's experiential learning cycle by linking real experience, case-based discussion and simulation. *Journal of Medical Education and Curricular Development, 9*, 23821205221091511. DOI: 10.1177/23821205221091511 PMID: 35592131

Wu, C. H., Chien, Y. C., Chou, M. T., & Huang, Y. M. (2025). Integrating computational thinking, game design, and design thinking: A scoping review on trends, applications, and implications for education. *Humanities & Social Sciences Communications, 12*(1), 1–12. DOI: 10.1057/s41599-025-04502-x

KEY TERMS AND DEFINITIONS

Computer Graphics: A computing field focused on creating, transforming, and rendering visual content (2D/3D) using algorithms, modeling, animation, and visualization techniques.

Experiential Learning Theory: A learning model (Kolb) where knowledge is developed through a cycle of experience, reflection, conceptual understanding, and experimentation.

Game Development: The structured process of designing and building a game, including ideation, storyboarding, prototyping, programming, asset creation, testing, and final presentation.

Instructional Scaffolding: A teaching strategy that supports students step-by-step by structuring tasks from simpler to more complex stages to guide learning and project completion.

Multiple Intelligences Theory: Gardner's framework stating that learners possess different forms of intelligence (e.g., visual-spatial, logical, interpersonal), which can be addressed through diverse learning activities.

Project-Based Learning (PBL): A student-centered instructional approach where students learn by actively working over time on authentic projects that result in a real, presentable product.

Rubric-Based Assessment: An evaluation method using predefined criteria (technical quality, creativity, teamwork, presentation, etc.) to assess student outputs consistently and fairly.

Chapter 13
Reimagining Computer Science Education in Remote, Hybrid, and Flipped Classrooms for Future-Ready Learners

Kamlesh Kumar Gautam
https://orcid.org/0009-0004-8731-9539
SDGI Global University, India

Tarun Kumar Vashishth
https://orcid.org/0000-0001-9916-9575
Department of Computer Applications, Vidya University, Meerut, India

Shashiraj Teotia
https://orcid.org/0000-0002-0849-3642
Swami Vivekanand Subharti University, India

Vikas Sharma
https://orcid.org/0000-0001-8173-4548
Department of Computer Applications, SRM Institute of Science and Technology, Ghaziabad, India

Jyotsana Khera
https://orcid.org/0009-0002-9487-0439
IIMT University, India

Anand Kumar
SRM Institute of Science and Technology, India

Shahanawaj Ahamad
University of Hail, Saudi Arabia

ABSTRACT

Advances in Learning Technology are promoting education in Computer Science from models of education utilizing predominantly lectures as forms of education, to innovations in pedagogy and into emerging models of student centered pedagogies. Distance and hybrid education in knowledge delivery and the concepts of the flipped

DOI: 10.4018/979-8-3373-6546-6.ch013

learning environment are changing the learning output in Computer Science, providing more flexible, accessible, and participatory models of education which are synchronous with the evolving demands of the society for skills formation. Challenges to the pedagogical basis, strengths, and weaknesses of these forms of education and how they cope with problem solving and interdisciplinary learning are discussed in the light of the canons of equitable access to education. It examines how distance delivery is increasing access to greater diversity of learner, how hybrid models can help provide a degree of collaborative learning while also affording flexibility, and how flipped learning can enhance levels of active learning and levels of cognitive comprehension.

INTRODUCTION

The increasing advancement of digital technology has had a significant effect on how education is provided and organized, including on the area of computer science education. Inasmuch as computing technology has a presence in almost all areas of modern life, there is a growing need for computer science education to be based on the increased changes taking place, both technologically and societally, if the education of the student at this level is to be meaningful. This section looks at the potential of revamping the computer science curriculum by taking advantage of three models that are being used in developing lecture formats remotely, Hybrid, and Flipped classrooms (where students are taught using videos and materials available online). It also discusses how to transform the way teachers teach by using digital technology, creating a more student-centric instructional model and new technologies such as AI, and learning analytics. Through a critical lens, the authors seek to identify what traditional approaches to teaching do not do effectively and suggest how technology-based pedagogy can improve student participation, skill development in multiple fields of study, inclusion, and adaptability. By combining theoretical principles with practical experiences and real-life examples, this section aims to provide an overall guide to the creation of sustainable and future-focused computer science education environments.

MAIN FOCUS OF THE CHAPTER

This chapter examines how to strategically design and integrate remote, hybrid, and flipped classroom models to transform computer science education for future-ready learners. It discusses how pedagogy has shifted from teacher-centered instructional practices to student-centered technology-enabled learning environments that emphasize active learning and engaging students practically with collaborative ways to practice and develop skills, while also enabling them to grow as self-directed learners. Using established pedagogical theories and supporting empirical evidence, this chapter shows that the utilization of digital technology, learning analytics, and artificial intelligence (AI) will enhance the effectiveness of instruction by personalizing each student's learning experience and optimizing their achievement outcomes. In addition, this chapter addresses issues of Equity, Access, and Inclusion by ensuring that the emerging instructional models support all students, regardless of their background or experiences. This chapter provides a framework for teachers, instructional designers, and policymakers to implement sustainable and scalable computer science education models that can be implemented in the evolving technology-driven society and economy.

This chapter aims to achieve the following objectives:

- To investigate how digital technology, AI, and learning analytic tools can be applied to improve student learning
- To provide evidence of how students engage and perform in various modes of learning
- To create a unified framework, which emphasizes equity and inclusive practices, for creating a future-ready computer science education.

BACKGROUND AND MOTIVATION

The overall impetus for the necessity to re-examine and idea of the nature and design of computer science education, is strictly to enable students to become aware of the necessity of preparing themselves for the eventualities of a technology dominated world environment, (Pentucci & Laici, 2025). Modern industries need graduates who not only have relevant skillsets but also have the ability to work in virtual teams, think critically and creatively solve complex problems. However, the traditional classroom often fails in the cultivation of these skills since they depend upon passive to one-way transmission of knowledge. The modern teaching models of virtual, blended and flipped classrooms promote learner involvement in their learning experiences. They promote independence in their studies, problem solving and application, all things that are necessary in such experientially dynamic disciplines as AI, data science, cyber security, software development.

The COVID pandemic has accelerated the changes which had been coming to the fore revealing the enormous potential of a technology supported education with virtually limitless potential for inclusion, flexibility, and accessibility before students, while previously this was limited due to geographical or personal parameters.

It reaffirmed the necessity for digital pedagogy to be integrated in an educational landscape that we inhabit today, not merely by virtue of necessity, but of far-sighted sustainability (Chiramba et al., 2024). The pace of change will reflect the potential of an education supported by technology as never previously. Students, hitherto inhibited by geographical or personal restrictions have now the potentiality to engage in high quality computer science education from any locus on the globe. It will reveal the educational potency of technology not merely by virtue of necessity, but as a pro – active mode of educational process (Kawane et al., 2025). A strong motive for the introduction of remote, hybrid, and flipped learning processes is as a consequence of the generation of an ecosystem intrinsically related to lifelong learning and adaptability, characteristics of vital import for success in a world whose feature is rapid technological change (Aithal et al. 2024).

Limitations of Traditional Teaching Methods

The traditional pedagogical devices in Computer Science education have for years been dominated by the lecture process which has had the effect of the teacher being the main purveyor of knowledge and the pupils receiving this knowledge passively.

Limited Practical Knowledge

Computer science per se demands a high degree of hands-on application of the ideas of coding, debugging, and implementation of systems. In conventional lectures, for example, students frequently learn about programming ideas in a theoretical manner and have little or no opportunity to apply these ideas through simulations, use of actual data sets or projects in teams. The result is that they are not able to easily move upward and outward from what the students learned in courses to what is demanded of them in industry (Mooney & Williams, 2024).

Rigidity of the Store-Drawing Curriculum-Concept of Learning

Traditional educative techniques generally feature a constant periodicity in the schedule of teaching and place of learning. The rigidity of this method of presenting educational information is such that students' individual learning rates, personal conditions and geographical limitations are frequently not adequately catered to in the teaching.

High Stress on the Memorization of Information and on Examinations

Instead of attempting to measure the learner's efficiency in terms of their ability as thinkers, creative individuals, problem solvers, etc., it is customary to assess the learning efforts of teachers with the written examination or standardized examination reactions which test only memorization and immediate recall. It discourages any educational integration of the use of computer subjects as variables in other subjects (Uzorka & Kalabuki, 2024).

Difficulty in Adjusting to and Implementing Technological Changes

Technological change in computer science is notoriously rapid, but educational training often lags considerably behind in use of new tools, methods, and systems. Large portions of educational materials remain much out of date and teach legacy languages or theoretical models of applications without use of the new technologies of interest, such as data analytics, cybersecurity, AI, machine learning, or cloud computing.

Need for Pedagogical Innovation in Computer Science

The need for pedagogical change in the teaching of computer science comes from the rapid technological changes in the world of computers. Figure 1 shows that computer science technologies like AI, data analysis, security data, and cloud computing obtain rapid change, existing means of teaching are inadequate for their demands (Sharma & Kumar, 2023). The modern student has little need for the old out-of-date theories and techniques. They require, not theory and information, extensive experience, problem solving ability, and means of dealing with new situations presented in real life (Sabrifha et al., 2025).

Figure 1. Pedagogical Innovation in Computer Science

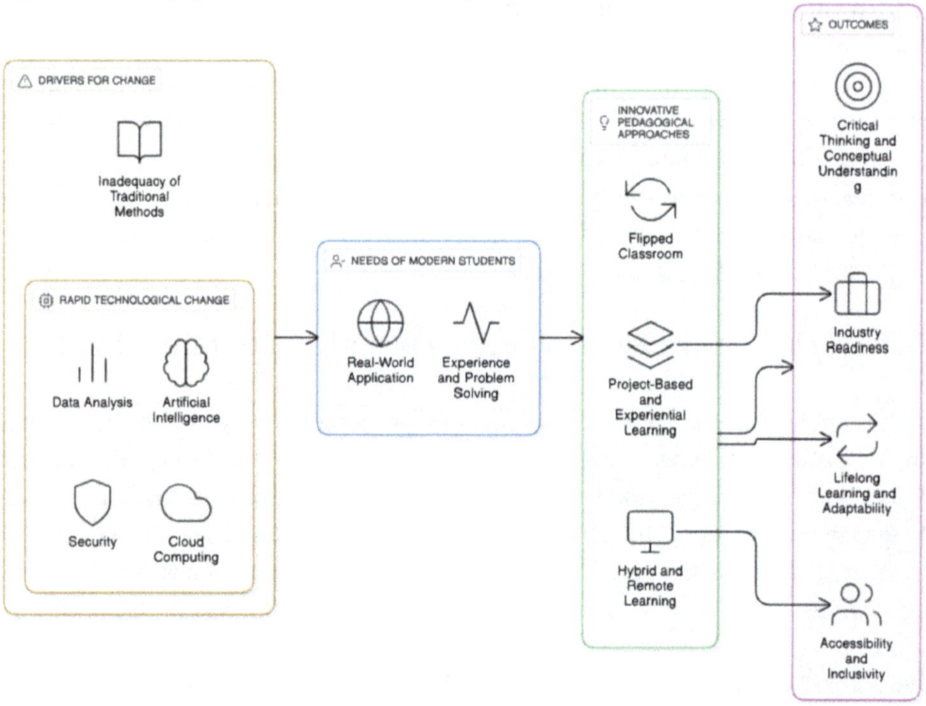

Traditional modes of education tend to emphasize much on theoretical aspects and syntax but do not expose students to applicability, teamwork, or programming environments. Although project learning, case study and experiential business world activities are part of the curriculum, teachers can ensure that students leave university with competencies required and relevant for the current and future take-up conditions (Tsui et al., 2024). Moreover, innovation in pedagogical practice helps to ensure the development of learning for life skills adaptability, which is necessary in a rapidly evolving technological ecosystem. When learners are exposed to environments that are interactive, flexible, and technology based, they gain competence in independent and self-directed learning, and the means of continuous upgrading of their skills. This mindset of curiosity and adaptability pre-indicates competence in people mastering evolving fields, as well as remaining relevant within the workforce (Pandit, 2025).

PEDAGOGICAL FOUNDATIONS AND THEORETICAL FRAMEWORK

Theoretical constructions such as Constructivism, Social Constructivism, experiential learning, and connectivism are all bases for the construction of emergent pedagogies. They emphasize active learning, collaboration and cooperation, reflection, and technology use where technology is used as a medium for constructing and sharing knowledge.

Constructivist and Connectivism Perspectives

The constructivist and connectivism approaches provide the foundational basis for understanding how learning happens within the environment of technologically driven and interactive teaching and learning environments, such as distance education, hybrid, or blended classrooms, and flipped classrooms. These practices provide a different vision of rather than passive learning, which emphasizes active participation and conversation, collaboration, the ceaseless construction and sharing of knowledge. The results of this fat in computer science education are there are great possibilities for teaching students how they can come to develop meaningful and deep conceptual knowledge, critical thinking skills, and effective problem-solving skills in the course of useful and connected learning experiences. As defined by George Siemens and Stephen Downes, connectivism is a theory of learning intended to be appropriate to the modern digital age, where knowledge exists in a network of interconnections rather than within the learner alone (Singh et al., 2023). It states that learning occurs via the capacity to identify and connect with access to various pieces of information across digital environments and communities.

In the area of remote and hybrid computer science education, connectivism is realised through the use of various tools such as learning management systems (LMS), collaborative online coding repositories, discussion forums, and collaboration rooms. Students and their teachers work in an adopted shared digital ecosystem in which they interact. The connectivism learning aims to engender a continuous exploration and self-regulation behaviours and engage with knowledge sharing with peers. In the context of this research where students in computer science participate in various open-source projects online or in a coding community, not only do they learn new programming techniques, but also continue to contribute to shared or collective knowledge creation. Connectivism changes learning from a semistatic process to one which is inter-relation, with knowledge interacting through connections that are made constantly, communication and ongoing engagement with technology (Chasokela & Mangena, 2025).

Principles of Student-Centered Learning

Learner Autonomy and Self-Direction

Significant autonomy is given to students in the student-centered learning process, which learners take charge of their own learning process. This independence develops responsibility skills to be accountable for progress in their learning, thus developing life-long learning skills, which are necessary varieties for students of computer science to remain informed and adaptive to expanding technologies. (Zhu et al., 2024).

Collaboration and Peer Learning

Collaboration is yet another crucial aspect of student-centered means of learning because it reflects the collaborative nature of the work done in computer science jobs and become more inclusive in learning, thus building a greater sense of community. It is here that students learn not only technical aspects of education but also the leadership and social skills which so much in professional life. (Bakri 2025)

Personalization and Differentiation

All students have different interests, abilities, and learning styles, and practice of personalization is one of the great principles of student-centered learning. If students can have their methods, materials, and requirements individualized, there can be a reasonable prospect that all the students will be challenged and be interested in the work that they are doing. Learning technologies, such as adaptive learning systems and learning analytics tools, aid teachers in tracking the progress of the students and providing individualized feedback.

Reflection and Feedback

Reflection and feedback are essential in deeper learning and development (Vikas et al., 2023). Through the encouragement of students in the reflection on their performance, they will discover their strengths, their weaknesses and eventually establish the goals towards improvement. Feedback, ongoing feedback provided by teachers or others such as fellow students or even digital agents, a form of ongoing feedback provides immediate feedback on ongoing events and events in learning. Reflection allows the learning process to become one of ongoing improvement and advancement, instead of a one-off assessment (Ching et al., 2024).

REMOTE LEARNING IN COMPUTER SCIENCE EDUCATION

This remote learning phenomenon is becoming more widespread through improvements in technology, the ever-increasing necessity for flexible education and a global realisation or onset of environments of virtual learning.

Technologies and Platforms Supporting Remote Learning

Remote learning in the discipline of computer science relies heavily on a diverse range of technologies and digital platforms that provide an array of opportunities for teaching, communication, and assessment in the virtual classroom. The success of online education is correlated not only to the curriculum but also the technologies that provide and sustain the interactive and engaging learning experiences (Fitriya et al., 2025).

Learning Management System

LMS tools are able to facilitate both synchronous and asynchronous learning modes, enabling students to learn not only at consistent, but also faster, paces while still accommodating interactive sessions that are scheduled. In this way, communication and course administration are improved to lead to greater organization, participation, and accountability through distance learning environments. (Kot & Nykyporets, 2025)

Collaborative coding platforms

Collaborative coding platforms e.g. GitHub, GitLab, Replit and Google Collab help students write, test, and share code in real time. They help facilitate group assignments, version control and peer review processes closely matching the real life working of software developers. In computer science education these collaborative coding forums help students work together on coding exercises, they trouble shoot together the response of their programs and contribute to established repositories.

Video Conferencing and Communication Tools

Video conferencing programs such as Skype, Microsoft Teams, and Google Meet can play a considerable role in maintaining synchronous remote learning. Such programs allow students and instructors to communicate in real-time discussions, seminars, and lectures. Communication tools included with those programs, such as chat features, breakout group, and poll functions, promote collaboration, quick feedback, and active student participation. These tools also imitate the environment of the traditional classroom by providing the social environment needed for effective learning and promoting the maximization of interaction and engagement.

Cloud-Based Development and Virtual Labs

Cloud-based environments and virtual labs give students access to necessary programming environments, software, and computing resources through the Internet without the necessity for high-end local hardware. Programs such as AWS Educate, Azure Lab Services, and virtual machine environments allow students to run sophisticated programs, check experimentation, and do experimentation safely through the Internet. These tools allow for real-world phones technologies, and practical implementation learning experiences, thus making learning relatively practical and scaled.

Strategies for Enhancing Remote Learner Engagement

In remote education in computer science, the use of inter-active multimedia content is a key avenue to continue motivating students. The use of video, animation, simulation, and coding demonstration, for example, helps present the more subtle concepts which abound in computer science, like algorithms, data structures, or the architecture of software, graphically as well as with easier understanding.

Use of Interactive Multimedia Content

This is another important way of meeting the problem of keeping the students motivated in distance education in science subjects, namely, the use of interactive multimedia content. As far as video, animation is concerned, showing programming in computers, simulate etc., the teacher can give a more concrete and intelligible shape to the more abstract conceptions involved such as algorithms, data structures, methods of programming, etc. But this is the case in all subjects, but there are such wonderful and stimulating results which can come about with the aid of interactive multimedia however, that it is here especially worthwhile considering.

Gamification of the Learning Processes

The use of gamification is one of the best devices for increasing the motivation and the interest of the pupil, and as far as their use in education puts, there are various devices which in themselves may be game like, such as computer programming assignments, leader boards, badges, time short quizzes, and the like. These are some of the devices which have the effect of producing competition and hence rewards for attainment and accomplishment. As far as computer science education is at all involved, these gamified learning processes promote for the pupil regular study, thinking out of problems, critical thinking as to problems.

Synchronous Co-operation and Socialising

This is done by working together in videoconferencing, working in groups in their breakout rooms, by using collaborative continuing on programming, corresponds to processes which are normal in co-operating in work in class, i.e. discussion, peers feedback, group solving of problems, etc. Also, the peer pressure increases under these pandemic circumstances the peer process actually increases their understanding and ability to learn the concepts, inferring, of community and accountability, and social presence, which are the things which are necessary to keep up the motivation to those involved in distance learning.

HYBRID LEARNING: BALANCING FLEXIBILITY AND COLLABORATION

In the teaching of computer science, hybrid learning is playing a transformative role. Faculty can incorporate the advantages present in face-to-face and distance learning homework. Students can access the course materials online or attend ding and discussion periods. The hybrid learning experience exposes students to both instructional experiences while utilizing them differentially through the use of synchronous (real time) and asynchronous methods.

Designing Effective Hybrid Computer Science Courses

The goal is to combine the convenience, flexibility, and accessibility offered by the online medium with the engagement and collaboration available from face-to-face instructing and the experiential aspects of hands-on learning. Effective course design, however, requires a clear lay-out of the course learning objectives, an assessment of the instructional components most effective for meeting those objectives and an organization of activities for learning the technical and cognitive intellections called for in the course content. One important principle of hybrid course design is that the delivery of course content (lectures, readings, media) must be coordinated with the course learning outcomes. Theoretical concepts, algorithms, coding principles, etc., would be learned outside of class through reading and online lectures, while face-to-face time is devoted to application of this knowledge through laboratory exercises, collaborative group projects, or interactive problem-solving exercises.

For example, students may study data structures in a distance learning environment and then, when they meet face-to-face, they would implement these structures through collaborative project work in real-world applications. Such a structure allows for students to be well prepared to engage in the experiential learning activities, while at the same time conserving classroom meeting time, which is limited. The integration of technology and digital media is of such importance. Online assessments of students may be made. Engagement in hybrid courses necessitates the active learning techniques. The methods which are typically employed in hybrid courses are the flipped classroom, problem-based learning, and project-based assessments, which allow students to apply knowledge, use such knowledge to investigate and solve the realities of world existence. Hands on activities, exercises on coding, debugging, algorithmic problems on in class time, validate the theoretical knowledge and allow for cooperative efforts to occur. The online component may supplement class time with tutorials and simulation exercises, where students are called upon to practise their skills and reflect on their efforts independently.

Role of Collaborative Tools and Learning Management Systems

The collaboration tools and LMS can provide the infrastructure and support necessary for the success of the hybrid model. They can help with communication, collaboration, sharing of resources, and assessment procedures that can keep students engaged and learning regardless of the site they may be resident.

Collaborative Tools

Several tools such as GitHub, GitLab, Replit, Slack, and Microsoft Teams provide students with both experience and ability to collaborate on programming projects, share resources, and furnish peer feedback in real time. These tools provide the students with an opportunity to practice versioning, collaborative coding, and project management skills. The use of collaborative repositories, discussion threads, and real-time coding session provides students with the means to share ideas, troubleshoot issues collaboratively, and to learn the tools and techniques as used by their peers.

Learning Management Systems

Centralized pedagogical delivery sites such as Moodle, Canvas, and Blackboard that facilitate access to instructional materials, assignment submission, assessment, and course progression. LMS are designed to house instructional materials, facilitate access to multimedia, and provide a discussion forum for asynchronous instruction. Instructors may track student engagement, assess learning deficiencies, and provide relevant feedback concerning progress. Automated grading, analytical dashboards to monitor progress, and customizable reminders allow instructors to meet individual learning needs while maintaining effectiveness and quality in the course for individual students.

FLIPPED CLASSROOMS: FOSTERING ACTIVE AND COGNITIVE LEARNING

Flipped classrooms offer a learning approach that fundamentally changes the traditional delivery of teaching and instructional method. The delivery of the instructional content takes place outside of the classroom, and the classroom time is used to process and engage in active learning, problem solving and collaborative activities.

Principles and Design of Flipped Learning

First and foremost, the principles and design of flipped learning focus on changing the classroom model from a teacher-centred to an active and student-centred learning experience. In computer science education the concept involves the delivery of the key instructional content outside of the classroom through the use of digital resources such as video lectures, readings, or interactive tutorials. The classroom time is then used for the practice, application, and discussions of that content through collaborative interaction problem solving.

Pre-class Preparation

One of the key principles of flipped learning. as aforementioned is pre-class preparation where students experience subject resources presented in the form of video lectures, readings, and interactive tutorials prior to attendance at class. In computer science education this will enable learners to become accustomed with the theoretical aspects of the subject area, algorithms, data structures, or program frameworks to mention but a few (their full detailed syllabus) at their own pace and leisure. The pre-class preparation allows students in many cases to develop this fundamental knowledge or understanding of the subject area so that when they arrive at class, they have a level of awareness of the subject area, enabling a more effective engagement in the activities, discussions and problem-solving scheduled in that class.

Active In-Class Participation

In flipped learning there is a very high value placed on active participation in the classroom. It is not to listening to a lecture as in the great tradition, but rather lab work, coding exercises, debugging work, group projects, etc. Hence, what these students do in class is to take their theoretical understanding of computer science and apply it in practical situations. In that way they have the immediate feedback of their instructors and peers, rather than at a later date.

Personalisation and Differentiation

Personalisation is a hallmark of flipped learning course design. Each student can learn at their own speed and level dealing with their own areas of deficit. The use of the material available online, (pre-class material), lends itself to different levels of knowledge previously acquired, as well as different learning styles and interests in the class. Differentiation is very easy during class time as into the levels of material required to overcome deficits by finding the right amount of appropriate material or support. They can also be further challenged, if they wish, by some advanced content and encouraged to collaborate, even when they reach the limits of their own knowledge.

Integration of Technology

Technology plays a critical role in the flipped learning environment. The use of LMS, video applications, joint code development areas, and evaluation instruments gives students ease of management in respect to the instructional material, the means of communication and feedback. It is this technology that produces a connected environment of learning wherein students may learn in an asynchronous manner, execute the projects assigned in code and participate in discussions.

Continuous Evaluation and Reflection

Continuous evaluation and self-reflection are factored within the design of flipped learning. The students become involved in formative evaluations, processes in code development, peer evaluations of other students and self-evaluation bids which give each individual the opportunity to determine his or her own progress and the areas needing improvement. The instructor is enabled to provide timely feedback and adapt the teaching-learning strategies to the fluctuating requirements of the students involved.

Pre-Class and In-Class Activity Structures

In flipped classrooms, the organization of pre-class and class activities is fundamental to achieve active learning, motivation, and cognitive development in computer science education. Pre-class activities serve to introduce students to primary concepts and provide basic knowledge to the student before attending class. These activities generally include video lectures, readings, tutorials, and interactive exercises to explain theoretical contents, such as algorithms, data structures, programming paradigms, or principles of software design. By engaging with these materials on their own, students learn at their own pace and can pause or repeat those parts that are most difficult, generating questions they have for discussion in class. For this reason, it is ensured that the students arrive at the class with a basic knowledge that will allow them more meaningful participation in practical and collaborative activities. Class activities focus on the application, analysis and synthesis of knowledge acquired during the preparation in pre-class activities. Time in class is dedicated to interactive and practical exercises, such as coding labs, debugging sessions, algorithm implementations, project work, and solution to problems shown in Figure 2. These activities require collaboration between students as well as discussions about different ways of solving the problems, at the same time the students receive immediate orientation and feedback from the teachers. Opportunities are created for students to learn to connect theoretical concepts and practical situations.

Figure 2. Pre-Class and In- Class Activity

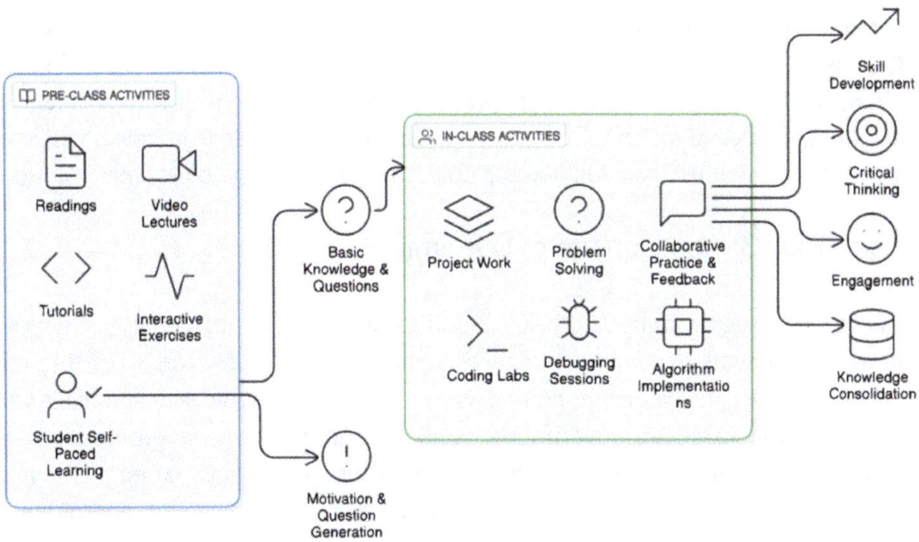

Case Studies in Programming and Algorithm Design

In programming and algorithm design case studies, we demonstrate how flipped classroom models can improve learning outcomes in computer science education. Such case studies illustrate how a learner may apply theoretical knowledge to real life, including the ability to develop problem-solving abilities, computational thinking, and the ability to work with others.

Case Study 1: Implementation of sorting algorithms

In this case study, the students are assigned pre-field material teaching them about the various sorting algorithms however as bubble sort, merge sort and quicksort appear not just above the surface. They view lecture and exercise videos of the various working algorithms in their own time fully understanding the logic of the algorithmic adaptations and the complexity of those algorithms prior to field work. During field hours, the learners in small groups implement these algorithms on large datasets, examine their working efficiency (Vikas, 2025).

Case Study 2: Techniques of Graph Traversal

This case study concerns itself with teaching graph traversal algorithms, specifically breadth-first search (BFS) and depth-first search (DFS). Students interact with the material via tutorials, readings and example problems taken before class, and which concern graph structures and graph traversal techniques. During the class, students work in groups to apply the algorithms to problems taken from practice, e.g. network routing or social network analysis. Students are relatively free to discuss techniques, problems, and ways to make the traversal techniques more efficient in execution. The peer dynamic, the instructor's input and the hands-on aspect will lead towards greater comprehension and the ability to relate theory to problem solution.

Case Study 3: Applications of Dynamic Programming

Dynamic programming (DP) is generally viewed as a difficult topic for the majority of students in computer science. In this case study, students work through some of the concepts via the pre-class material, which also includes the tutorials and sample example exercises covering the concepts and breaking the problem down. Then, during the in-class session, the students solve problems relating to the real world, e.g. allocation of resources in the optimum way, to solve knapsack problems, or design sequence alignment algorithms. The groups look at different techniques available, as well as time and space complexity for them, and improve iteratively on their solutions. The flipped classroom method helps the students to deal with some of the more difficult material while developing critical thought processes, teamwork skills, algorithm design skills etc.

COMPARATIVE AND INTEGRATIVE PERSPECTIVES

Comparative pedagogical models offer educators a way to contrast various pedagogies to determine which are most effective in realizing various learning objectives, for differing populations of students, and for differing course types, in order to create educational encounters that are designed to maximize engagement, skill set development, and cognitive growth.

Comparative Overview of the Pedagogical Models

A comparative overview of pedagogic models employed in the teaching of computing subject's directions attention to the various characteristics, merits, disadvantages, and applications of remote learning (asynchronous and synchronous), of hybrid learning and of flipped learning. Each of these methods provides opportunities for intellectual engagement, skill enhancement, and cognitive growth, at area, and with a clear understanding of their specificity, teachers may prepare alternative educational experiences and approaches to learning.

Remote Learning

The learner learns from any location at any time, has access to learning materials, learning tutorial assistance and skill-building activities (coding practice) Great, therefore, for learners with less flexible time schedules or geographical restrictions. Leaves possibility for independent learning and possible asynchronous experience, thereby enhancing the possibility of autonomous learning and degrees of personalization of study. Lack of social interaction involved in remote learning, lack of opportunities for practical learning experiences, reliance on technology infrastructures.

Hybrid Learning

It combines the best of online and face-to-face instruction and offers a balance between flexibility and collaboration. The online components provide asynchronous access to content, and the face-to-face components provide opportunities for hands-on to the material, peer collaboration, and feedback in real time. This learning environment adds experiential learning and practical applications of the theoretical concepts, and it is usable for computer science courses with laboratory assignments, programming projects, or collaborative assignments where these are provided.

Flipped Classrooms

The traditional lecture structure by emphasizing active cognitive learning through active learning strategies. Students study instructional materials prior to attending class, after which they use their newly acquired knowledge to work on problems, coding exercises, and group projects in class, in so doing requiring engagement in higher-order learning, practical skill development, and the application of their new knowledge to problem situations in their world.

Leveraging AI, Analytics, and Automation in Digital Pedagogies

Using AI and analytics with digital pedagogies will enable the instructor to zone in on each learner and avoid the historical one-size-fits-all attitude toward learning outcomes and objectives. Learning experiences will be more effective and data driven as they adapt learning to the needs of students, preparing them for any eventuality of the future. AI will support individual learning patterns through the analysis of not only student interactions, but performance and engagement patterns. AI based platforms can also, for example, offer students with resources, activities or tutorials based on their learning patterns, needs and so forth. In computer science education AI can provide not only automated code review but can suggest debugging strategies as well as provide learners with adaptive problem sets that can increase in complexity as the student's skills improve. This intelligent platform for support enables student autonomy, independent learning, and more rapid mastery of technical skills.

Learning analytics aid educational institutions to track and report on data regarding student engagement working across e-learning platforms with respect to assessments, performance, participation and so on. It enables educators to establish trends and patterns in learner influx, which will in turn enable them to detect students who are disadvantaged in terms of learning. In addition, they can predict difficulty with respect to trends happening in the past and prescribe remedial support in a timely manner. Analytics additionally provide course teachers with guidance on how effective their pedagogy is, thereby assisting them in improving their course design, course format, and delivery modes and in-class actions. In other words, it provides a more data sensed approach for teachers in assessing their pedagogical frae of choices. As education goes digital, automation combines with AI, analytics, and other automation processes, it allows digital education to produce adaptable, personalized, and scalable experiences for learning. It allows for improved learning output and engagement but also provides students and teachers with exposure to technological investment and data-filled environments which promote digital literacy and the adaptive parts that yield performance of outcome in the computer-based marketplace today.

AI and Learning Analytics (LA) are becoming increasingly crucial to the method of flipped learning for Computer Science students in practical applications. Within a Flipped Classroom, LA tools embedded into LMSs have the ability to track students' interactions with their pre-assigned videos, articles, and coding instruction tools. Thus, LMSs will automatically identify which students have failed to complete their assigned material and remind them or provide additional resources prior to an in-class or synchronous session. In Hybrid Classrooms, AI-powered learning analytics can help monitor students' participation in both online/hybrid and in-person learning opportunities. The use of learning analytics allows for the identification of variances in student participation and achievement between both types of learning environments. The results of this analysis can then be utilized by Adaptive Learning Systems to recommend targeted practice exercises, debugging suggestions, or opportunities for student collaboration to assist these students in obtaining additional assistance. Similarly, in a fully remote learning environment, AI-enabled tutor systems and automated code review platforms can provide instructor-like assistance by providing immediate feedback, identifying errors, and personalizing their learning path.

Framework for Integrating Pedagogical Innovations in Computer Science Education

The chapter will propose an integrative pedagogical innovation framework, which attempts to go beyond a simple description of individual pedagogical models by integrating each type of learning environment (remote, hybrid, and flipped), with an emphasis on AI-supported personalized learning and learning analytics. While previous frameworks have treated these learning environments as separate and distinct from one another, this chapter will treat all three types of models as part of an integrated framework of pedagogical innovation. Remote learning provides access to learning materials and content flexibility; hybrid learning provides the structure for collaborative interactions and opportunities for guided practice; and flipped learning provides opportunities for higher-level cognitive engagement through active participation in the classroom.

AI-enabled personalized learning and learning analytics will provide the mechanisms that enable the continuous and dynamic adaptation of instructional pathways based on learners' individual progress and needs; therefore, instructional decision-making will always be informed by data-driven decision support. The integrative perspective presented in this chapter builds on existing pedagogical models by identifying the relationship between the way in which technology facilitates instructional design and how pedagogical engagement will lead to improved educational outcomes. Unlike earlier studies that have focused on the individual models, this framework is oriented toward the pedagogical orchestration of the three models to improve the educational outcomes related to specific computer science discipline demands, for example, algorithmic thinking, coding proficiency, and collaborative problem-solving.

DATA ANALYSIS AND EMPIRICAL EVIDENCE

This area outlines the empirical aspect of the study providing evidence-based insights which supplement the theoretical discussion. The quantitative and qualitative analyses carried out to access the various methods of remote, hybrid and flipped learning methods in computer science.

Methodology and Source of Data

The theoretical framework was developed through a mixed method research approach that utilized quantitative survey data and qualitative feedback in addition to secondary Learning Analytics data. The research study sample consisted of 120 undergraduate Computer Science students from three different Higher Education Institutions in North India, as well as 15 Faculty members. The Institutions were made up of one private university, One State Funded Public University, and One Autonomous Technical Institute that provide Undergraduate Degrees in Computer Science and related fields. The Student Sample included students from the First Year (38%), Second Year (34%), and Final Year (28%), which allowed for diversity across the different academic years.

Table 1. Comparative Analysis of Student Engagement, Performance, and Satisfaction Across Learning Modes

Learning Mode	Average Engagement (%)	Improvement in Grades (%)	Satisfaction (1–5 scale)
Remote	72	65	4
Hybrid	81	78	4.3
Flipped	89	85	4.6

The results showed clear patterns indicating support for imposter and flipped learning formats with respect to insights regarding engagement and cognitive results. Analysis of LMS data subjects to the individual classes results show that flipped learning discovered the highest level of assignment completion at 92% and peer collaboration level. Hybrid showed the best balance between flexibility and synchronous participation. Remote learning, while being most accessible, produced reduced levels of engagement indicating that enhanced levels of interactivity are needed. A structured survey instrument was developed by the researchers to collect data through structured, closed, and open-ended questions. The quantitative measures collected through this survey included a Likert scale (1 = strongly disagree; 5 = strongly agree), which was used to measure various aspects of student engagement including: perceived learning effectiveness; satisfaction; collaboration. The "average engagement" score was calculated from the survey responses using the following indicators from the LMS: number of logins; time spent on course materials; assignment submission rates; and participation in discussion forums. "Improvement in Grades," was calculated by taking the percentage of the increase in average assessment scores between two semesters of courses taught using lecture-based delivery methods.

Qualitative Findings and Thematic Analysis

The qualitative aspect of the study was obtained through open ended survey responses and instructor reflection, which were examined through thematic analysis. The three most important themes that emerged from both student and faculty feedback are as follows: 1) Increased levels of student engagement and accountability in the flipped learning mode, because both identified being able to review lecture content at their own pace prior to the class and using the class for hands-on coding and problem solving as reasons for increased engagement. One student commented, "The flipped classes helped me to better grasp programming because I had the chance to pause videos and prepare for class with my questions." 2) Instructors believed that the flipped learning mode is effective in encouraging students to actively participate in class and work collaboratively with their peers, most notably during programming labs and in group discussions among classmates. Instructors noted that students appear to be more confident and clearer in their understanding of algorithms when applying them to real time tasks. 3) Both students and instructors valued timely feedback, because it contributes to higher levels of satisfaction with the instructor and with the learning experience. Timely feedback, particularly in combination with automated code evaluation and instructor-led discussion about student submitted code, was commonly noted as important for both groups.

EQUITY, ACCESS, AND INCLUSIVITY IN DIGITAL PEDAGOGIES

Equity, access, and inclusion all are basic considerations in curriculum design in effective digital pedagogy for computer science education. To the extent that the experience of learning is increasingly impact by the digital, hybrid or flipped way of learning, equity and the opportunity for all students to have an equal opportunity to engage the content, participate in the activities, and achieve the learning outcomes becomes a vital need.

The Digital Divide in Computer Science Education

An obstacle to equitable access to and participation in computer science education. It pertains to the unequal access by students with socio-economic, geographical, or institutional differences to technology, the internet, digital skills, and resources for learning. As computer science increasingly moves towards remote, hybrid and flipped learning, the digital divide aggravates inequalities, by denying opportunities to students who lack reliable devices, fast internet access, or experience with digital platforms. This results in an absence of learning, lower levels of engagement, and poorer performance than students who possess full access to the digital tools available. Limited exposure to computational resources results in diminished opportunity for the development of technical skills, problem solving skills, various computing processes. Institutions may provide student lap tops to loan, inexpensive Internet service, and on campus digital laboratories. By addressing the hole created by the effect of the digital divide, each student regardless of background or situation will be able to acquire necessary technical skill, exercise meaningful engagement in activities pertaining to their subject learning and finally taste success in a digital driven technological environment and education world (Shanmugam et al, 2025).

Designing Accessible and Inclusive Digital Courses

The goal of computer science education is to provide flexible and equitable opportunities for all students through accessible and inclusive digital learning experiences for diverse learners. The goal of accessibility is to assure that all learners who have different learning styles, abilities, and access to technology could fully participate in courses, while inclusivity is the goal of offering equitable access to opportunities, cultural understanding, and participation for all students. Together, they provide principles by which digital pedagogies can be constructed that are effective, flexible, and equitable. One of the ways in which they can be accomplished is by using multimodal forms of content delivery because they allow for the kinds of content that is taught to be delivered using multiple kinds of instructional methods. To enhance the accessibility of the materials presented to learners with disabilities of the sensory variety, different learning styles and so forth, accessibility features such as captions, transcripts, read-aloud versions of content, and different speeds of watching video, etc. are included. This kind of delivery is also useful to students because they enter into courses with different amounts of prior knowledge in a subject area and this allows them to choose the means of presentation that best enables them to comprehend the content. Flexible course design is another major area of consideration in respect of access and accommodation of diverse learners and includes such things as but not limited to participation in lectures and assignments asynchronously, modular, as opposed to completed in a specific unit of time, methods of accomplishment of the content, and multiple means of assessment.

Gender and Socioeconomic Considerations

Gender and socio-economic factors play a major role in access, participation, and success in computer science education particularly from a vantage point of access to digital learning environments (Siddiqi & Ahmad, 2025). Students of undefined non represented genders or socio economically difficult situations may have to deal with social structures that put them at a disadvantage in their exposure to programming or the fact that their efforts to establish computing careers may be undermined by a deterioration in opportunity and feelings of self-confidence (Albakri & Wood-Harper, 2025).

Gender considerations

This will involve the recognition of and efforts at eliminating hindrances to participation in computer science. These might relate directly to gender and technology stereotypes, absence of role models, and classroom interpersonal dynamics affecting confidence, engagement, and success in continuing studies on the part of those identifying as women and non-binary persons. Taking inclusive steps in the form of reference to female and persons of variable gender identification interesting models and role models in technology will diminish gender-related differences and create a supportive environment.

Socio-economic Concerns

It is associated with inequalities in access to appliances, broadband, software and learning tools. Students from economically disadvantaged backgrounds may not be able to cope with technology in remote or hybrid learning and not be able to complete homework, collaborate on projects or engage in independent study. Provision of resources in the shape of loaned laptops, subsidised connection, learning materials in offline form, and means of connection which necessitate low bandwidth can reduce these inequalities and help enable equitable participation.

FUTURE-READY ASPECTS FOR LEARNING ENVIRONMENTS

The learning environments are such that they facilitate innovative pedagogies, high technology and flexible structured for the facilitation of learning, problem solving and critical thinking in order that lifelong learning can be facilitated for students. The emphasis in these environments is on preparing learners for the current educational experience for now and to be adaptable to the demands of the workforce and for interdisciplinary learning situations which may arise in the future.

Flexibility and Adaptability

A learning environment that is future-ready will offer the flexibility and adaptability needed to accommodate the needs of numerous learners who will bring differing learning styles, prior knowledge, and individual situations. Distance learning, hybrids, and flipped modalities will give learners the opportunity to gain access to educational materials synchronously for both individual and group projects. This flexibility is important to facilitate learning of learners to enable them to schedule as desired, to concentrate on the mastery of essential and instrumental competencies and technical skills for both educational improvement and personal developments.

Incorporation of Presently Used Technologies

The incorporation of present technologies involving noted growth technologies is essential for environments which are to allow the readiness for the future. These technologies give individualized learning opportunities, formative feedback, and simulation experiences for the view adopted in solving complex problems. In the area of Computer Science Education, this results in improved computational thinking capabilities, ability to perform in the computer coding platform, both verbal and written communication optimizations, effective data processing and decision-making skills through decision making based on data.

Integration and Collaboration

Students will work in teams toward the resolution of authentic problems via projects necessitating the integration of knowledge from areas such as Computer Science, Engineering, Data Science, and other study areas. The collaborative opportunities such projects will afford will contribute to the development of essential skills in evaluation, teamwork and project management while stimulating creativity in the form of imaginative solutions to problems.

Equity, Inclusivity and Accessibility

Pupils irrespective of sex, class and financial position, or their geographical position, must be found in situations affording the largest possible participation. Such factors as accessibility of educational material, mentorship directed toward the child, and culture-dominant modes of instruction will form the bridges across the gaps which fashion disparity, in that they alone can embrace the large individual, whether learners or enrolled in education, by rendering possible conditions for subjectively most useful participation in computer education.

Faculty Readiness, Training and Support

Faculty transitioning to remote, hybrid, and flipped classroom instructional methods, from traditional lecture-based instruction, may experience many challenges related to instructional design, time commitment, and familiarity with the required technology to execute these models. Designing quality pre-class materials hyper video, interactive tutorials and browsing demonstrations may require both pedagogical training and comfort with digital authoring tools. Additionally, creating an active learning environment during in-class sessions requires shifting the role of the instructor from delivering content to mentoring, moderating, and providing real-time feedback to students.

Infrastructure and Affordability Challenges

To effectively implement a collaborative coding platform, virtual laboratories hosted in the cloud, learning analytics software, and AI assessments will generally incur ongoing costs such as cloud service, licensing, and maintenance fees to operate. Institutions will need to invest in the creation of server infrastructures and procure a level of information systems security as well as qualified technical support to maintain system reliability and protect student data privacy. Creating the infrastructure necessary to support the growth of all students is an additional source of operational difficulty related to the financial burden associated with scaling these types of technologies. Strategies that help institutions create affordability while maintaining their ability to innovate include utilising cost-effective solutions such as open source learning platforms, partnering with other institutions, and sharing cloud resources, establishing institutional licensing agreements or phased implementation of technologies, and collaborating with technology providers.

CONCLUSION

Using an integrated, conceptual, technological, and empirical approach, this chapter has examined the remote, hybrid, and flipped learning models in computer science education. The purpose of this research is not to determine which of these learning models provides the highest overall level of effectiveness or success; instead, this analysis illustrates that pedagogically effective learning environments are created through a combination of intentional integration, contextual adaptation, and reflective practices. The empirical findings from this analysis provide evidence for the potential for increased student engagement and student satisfaction associated with hybrid and flipped learning environments. As a result of remote, hybrid, and flipped learning models, computer science education has become a student-centered, flexible, and technology-enhanced method of education. These types of instructional models lead to greater student engagement, improved student support for and transferability of active and conceptual learning experiences and develops necessary technical and professional skills. By using technology, collaborative instructional strategies and addressing equity, access, and inclusivity, instructors at all educational levels can design flexible learning environments that support a broader range of learner needs. Instruction which can be sustained emphasizes flexible instructional strategies, interdisciplinary learning, and lifelong adaptability, so that students will acquire the necessary skills to deal with the rapidly changing technological landscape in both their academic and vocational lives.

REFERENCES

Aithal, P. S., Prabhu, S., & Aithal, S. (2024). Future of higher education through technology prediction and forecasting. Poornaprajna International Journal of Management, Education, and Social Science (PIJMESS), 1(1), 01-50.

Albakri, M., & Wood-Harper, A. T. (2025). Contextualisation of Digital Education. In *Innovation Strategy for the Future of Teaching and Learning: Addressing the Digital Education Paradox* (pp. 35–58). Springer Nature Switzerland.

Bakri, Y. M. (2025). The Role of Digital Leadership in Cultivating a Supportive Ecosystem for Pedagogical Innovation: A Focus on Trainee Teacher Graduates. In *Digital Leadership for Sustainable Higher Education* (pp. 219–254). IGI Global Scientific Publishing., DOI: 10.4018/979-8-3693-9989-7.ch007

Chasokela, D., & Mangena, N. (2025). The Future of Learning in the Digital Age. In *Insights into International Higher Education Leadership and the Skills Gap* (pp. 471–500). IGI Global., DOI: 10.4018/979-8-3693-3443-0.ch018

Ching, G. S., Chao, P. C., del Castillo, F., Gungon, J. L., Trajera, S. M., Roberts, A., & Zuo, Y. (2024, May). Check for updates Teacher Fatigue, Social-Emotional Learning, Online Teaching Engagement and Facilitation: Experiences of Teachers during COVID-19. In Learning Technology for Education Challenges: 12th International Workshop, LTEC 2024, Kaohsiung, Taiwan, July 29–August 1, 2024 []. Springer Nature.]. *Proceedings*, *2082*, 266.

Chiramba, O., & Agbaje, O. (2024). Promoting institutional resilience through blended learning during and post-covid-19 in South African universities. *Journal of Educational Studies*, *2024*(si2), 12–26. DOI: 10.59915/jes.2024.si2.1

Fitriya, R. L., Akbar, M. F., Mukhlisa, A., Putri, D. D., & Gunawan, R. N. (2025). Digital Education and Curriculum Design: A Scientometric Analysis (2005–2025). *Journal of Technological Pedagogy and Educational Development*, *2*(2), 1–11.

Kawane, T., Adu-Gyamfi, B., & Shaw, R. (2025). Exploring the elements of strengthening online higher education in disaster risk reduction: A perspective of sustained strategy in post COVID-19. *International Journal of Disaster Resilience in the Built Environment*, *16*(2), 173–192. DOI: 10.1108/IJDRBE-12-2022-0125

Kot, S. O., & Nykyporets, S. S. (2025). *Activating studentscognitive engagement in technical English learning with AI tools. Science and education in the third millennium: information technology, education, law, psychology, social security and work, management: international collective monograph* (Vol. I). Polska.

Mooney, J. G., & Williams, M. L. (2024). Enabling Technologies of the Fourth Industrial Revolution. In Handbook of Research on Strategic Leadership in the Fourth Industrial Revolution (pp. 35-61). Edward Elgar Publishing. https://doi.org/ DOI: 10.4337/9781802208818.00009

Pandit, R. R. (2025). Hybrid Learning in Global Contexts: A Comparative Analysis of Pedagogical Models across Diverse Education Systems. *IJSAT-International Journal on Science and Technology*, *16*(3). Advance online publication. DOI: 10.71097/IJSAT.v16.i3.7679

Pentucci, M., & Laici, C. (2025). Reimagining learning in the post-digital era: student perceptions of screen-mediated teaching. In *EDULEARN25 Proceedings* (pp. 9494-9502). IATED.

Sabrifha, E., Wasari, R., & Mokoena, T. (2025). Revolutionizing Education: 10 Innovative Teaching Strategies for the 21st-Century Classroom. *Journal of Educational Teaching and Trends*, *1*(1), 56–66. DOI: 10.64840/jett.v1i1.19

Shanmugam, R., Perumal, M. G., & Krishnamoorthy, U. M. (2025, March). Bridging Tradition and Innovation: A Thoughtful Approach to Future-Ready Education. In 2025 ASEE North Central Section (NCS) Annual Conference. DOI: DOI: 10.18260/1-2--54652

Sharma, V., & Kumar, S. (2023). Role of Artificial Intelligence (AI) to Enhance the Security and Privacy of Data in Smart Cities. In *Proceedings of the 3rd International Conference on Advance Computing and Innovative Technologies in Engineering (ICACITE)* (pp. 596–599). IEEE.

Siddiqi, M. M., & Ahmad, D. S. (2025). Innovations in Digital Learning. Shaping the Future: Emerging Trends and Opportunities in Commerce, Management, and Information Technology, 7.

Singh, B., Kumar, V., Gupta, K., Vashishth, T. K., Sharma, S., & Kumar Gupta, V. (2023). Transforming education in the digital age: A comprehensive study on the effectiveness of online learning. [IJSREM]. *International Journal of Scientific Research in Engineering and Management*, *7*(7), 1–11. DOI: 10.55041/IJSREM24405

Tsui, E., Dragicevic, N., Fan, I., & Cheng, M. (2024). Co-creating curriculum with students, teachers, and practitioners in a technology-enhanced environment. *Educational Technology Research and Development*, *72*(2), 869–893. DOI: 10.1007/s11423-023-10301-5

Uzorka, A., & Kalabuki, K. (2024). The transformative impact of technological advancements in educational leadership on student experiences and outcomes. *Education and Information Technologies*, *29*(16), 20883–20904. DOI: 10.1007/s10639-024-12714-y

Vikas, D., R. P., Kumar, D., Charan, P., Ingilela, R. S. K., & Rastogi, R. (2023). Intrusion Detection in Wireless Sensor Networks using Hybrid Deep Belief Networks and Harris Hawks Optimizer. In *Proceedings of the 4th International Conference on Electronics and Sustainable Communication Systems (ICESC)* (pp. 1631–1636). IEEE.

Vikas. (2025). Optimization of Graph Neural Networks for Real-Time Intrusion Detection in Dynamic Mobile Ad-Hoc Networks. *International Journal of Environmental Sciences*, 11(11s), 740–748.

Zhu, Y., Jafari, A., Behzadan, A. H., & Issa, R. R. (2024). A roadmap to the next-generation technology-enabled learning-centered environments in AEC education. *Journal of Civil Engineering Education*, *150*(3), 05024002. DOI: 10.1061/JCEECD.EIENG-1972

KEY TERMS AND DEFINITION

Artificial Intelligence: The use of intelligent digital tools to support instruction through automation, personalization, and adaptive feedback such as code review and customized practice activities.

Equity and Inclusion: Ensuring all students—regardless of gender, socioeconomic status, or location—have fair access to technology, learning opportunities, and supportive digital learning environments.

Flipped Classroom: A learning model where students study lecture materials before class (videos/readings), while class time is used for active learning such as coding labs, collaboration, and problem-solving.

Hybrid Learning: A balanced instructional model combining online learning flexibility with face-to-face sessions for collaboration, labs, and hands-on activities.

Learning Analytics: The collection and analysis of student learning data (engagement, performance, completion) to improve instruction and provide timely targeted support.

Remote Learning: Education delivered virtually using digital platforms, allowing students to learn from any location through synchronous and/or asynchronous formats.

Student-Centered Learning: An approach that prioritizes learner autonomy, collaboration, reflection, and personalized learning paths rather than teacher-dominated instruction.

Chapter 14
A Bibliometric Review of Pedagogical Innovations and Future Directions for Generative Artificial Intelligence in Computer Science Education

Damola Olugbade
https://orcid.org/0000-0003-3938-6273
First Technical University, Nigeria

Samson O. Ajao
https://orcid.org/0009-0003-8758-0908
Bowen University, Nigeria

Hassan Abuhassna
https://orcid.org/0000-0002-5774-3652
Sunway University, Malaysia

Ifedayo Emmanuel Adu
https://orcid.org/0000-0002-7939-4510
Bamidele Olumilua University of Education, Science, and Technology, Nigeria

Owolabi Paul Adelana
https://orcid.org/0000-0002-4829-5106
The Open University, Milton Keynes, UK

DOI: 10.4018/979-8-3373-6546-6.ch014

ABSTRACT

This chapter provides a bibliometric review of research on Generative Artificial Intelligence (GAI) in Computer Science (CS) education over the past decade. A total of 582 documents been catalogued in Scopus for the period of 2014-2024 was used. The publications were analyzed using Biblioshiny for Bibliometrix and the results were used to identify gaps in the literature and guide future research directions on GAI's impact in education. The findings revealed the surge in publications and citations post 2020 can be attributed to large language models and AI coding assistants. Thematic and keyword analyses show that GAI has been applied primarily in programming education, intelligent tutoring, personalized learning, and assessment. These applications yield outcomes such as enhanced efficiency, student engagement, and scalability, yet also raise concerns about academic integrity, over-reliance, and algorithmic bias. GAI research is spearheaded by developed nations which poses fairness concerns, and simultaneously fosters advancement and moral quandaries in computer science pedagogy.

INTRODUCTION

The swift advancement of Generative Artificial Intelligence (GAI) has transformed global educational practices. Within this broader transformation, one of the most active areas of GAI is Computer Science (CS) education. GAI is a type of artificial intelligence that utilizes deep learning architectures, such as Transformers and Generative Adversarial Networks (GANs), to generate new and realistic outputs in text, images, code, and multimedia (Brown et al., 2020; Chen, Balan, & Brown, 2023). Current applications, such as ChatGPT, GitHub Copilot, and DALL·E, demonstrate how they may alter pedagogy, curriculum development, and the way students learn (Franklin, Denny, Gonzalez-Maldonado, & Tran, 2025).

Against this technological backdrop, recent scholarly investigations reveal that the educational incorporation of GAI is advancing across several pivotal dimensions. First, GAI is being used more and more to personalize lessons and create adaptive learning paths that give students feedback, practice opportunities, and real-time scaffolding that are tailored to their requirements (Roll & Wylie, 2016). Second, GAI makes exercises, tutorials, and assignments that automatically produce material. This makes things easier for teachers and allows students access to a greater range of learning materials (Siemens & Baker, 2012). Third, a lot of people need programming and debugging support. Students can use GitHub Copilot and other tools to write code, explain it, and rectify faults. Fourth, GAI is transforming how we evaluate papers, discover plagiarism, and give comments that can be used by a lot of people. Finally, ethical concerns regarding fairness, transparency, and academic integrity are influencing the discourse on the responsible application of GAI in education (Floridi & Cowls, 2019; Jobin, Ienca, & Vayena, 2019; Dawson & Sutherland-Smith, 2018). Taken together, the application of GAI in computer science education reveals both opportunities and challenges. Intelligent teaching systems that use GAI are getting better at giving personalized feedback and allowing students to talk to one another to help them understand concepts better. At the same time, GAI helps make programming exercises and teaching materials, which makes them easier to get to and gives students more interesting ways to learn about difficult ideas (Graesser & Person, 1994; Siemens & Baker, 2012). Getting help with programming can help you work faster, spend less time fixing bugs, and get more done. But there are still concerns that students are using it too much (Zastudil et al., 2023). The capacity of GAI to automate grading and plagiarism detection is widely recognized as a potential solution to scalability challenges in higher education, while simultaneously provoking discourse on academic ethics.

Initial research, from an outcome perspective, suggests that GAI integration enhances engagement, creativity, and productivity; nevertheless, its long-term effects on critical thinking and advanced cognitive development remain inadequately explored (Chan & Hu, 2023; Lee & Song, 2024; Franklin et al., 2025). The tension between efficiency and educational integrity underscores the imperative for a balanced, critically informed approach to adoption. Accordingly, the goal is not just to teach GAI in computer science classes, but also to make sure that it is used in a responsible, ethical, and open way. This necessitates curricula that prepare students for human–AI collaboration (Wing, 2006; Shneiderman, 2020), institutional strategies that promote digital equity (Warschauer, 2004; Olugbade, 2025), and policy frameworks that guarantee transparency, fairness, and accountability in AI utilization (Veale & Binns, 2017; Buolamwini & Gebru, 2018). In summary, GAI is altering computer science education swiftly by making it more customized, automating content creation, helping students practice programming, coming up with new ways to assess them, and starting crucial ethical debates. Teachers need to have various roles, students need to be better at AI, and the setting needs to value honesty, creativity, and inclusion for it to work.

A growing body of review studies has broadly examined artificial intelligence in education. These reviews include systematic and bibliometric syntheses in artificial intelligence in education (AIED), learning analytics, and educational data mining. However, these efforts have typically treated generative technologies as either emergent subthemes or have aggregated them with rule-based and predictive AI systems (Chen et al., 2020; Zawacki-Richter et al., 2019). As a result, the distinctive epistemic, pedagogical, and ethical implications of Generative AI, particularly within the disciplinary context of computer science education, remain insufficiently mapped in literature. Existing reviews in adjacent domains tend to privilege qualitative thematic analysis or narrative synthesis, offering limited insight into the intellectual structure, knowledge diffusion patterns, and thematic evolution of research specific to Generative AI in CS education (Donthu et al., 2021; Zawacki-Richter et al., 2019; Kitchenham et al., 2009). In contrast, bibliometric analysis enables a large-scale, systematic examination of research development by revealing co-citation structures, thematic clusters, and longitudinal shifts in scholarly attention that are not readily observable through traditional review methodologies (Donthu et al., 2021; Aria & Cuccurullo, 2017). This is particularly important in the context of Generative AI due to the rapid emergence of Transformer-based models in educational research (Bommasani, et al., 2021). By focusing explicitly on Generative AI within computer science education, this chapter moves beyond general AI-in-education surveys to provide a foundational mapping of the field's research landscape. The bibliometric synthesis presented here identifies dominant research paradigms, underexplored thematic intersections, and emerging scholarly frontiers. It therefore offers an empirical basis for future pedagogical innovation, curriculum design, and policy development in CS education.

This chapter situates GAI within the pedagogical and disciplinary context of computer science education, employing a bibliometric methodology to identify research trends, evaluate emerging practices, and designate future directions.

MAIN FOCUS OF THE CHAPTER

Research Gap and Rationale

The utilization of Generative Artificial Intelligence (GAI) in education has garnered significant scholarly interest; yet, comprehensive evidence about its specific influence on Computer Science (CS) training remains disjointed. There has been a lot of talk lately about big studies of artificial intelligence in education (Chen, Chen, & Lin, 2020) or about using intelligent tutoring systems and automated assessment in general learning environments. These studies illustrate the revolutionary potential of AI for tailored learning and increased efficiency; nevertheless, they frequently neglect to expressly address the distinct opportunities and problems that GAI presents to computer science education.

Recent contributions have started a direct investigation into the pedagogical possibilities of GAI. Franklin, Denny, Gonzalez-Maldonado, and Tran (2025) discussed the possible pros and cons of using GAI in programming classes. Hazzan and Erez (2024) talked about the changes in how computer science is taught. Chan and Hu (2023) and Lee and Song (2024) also studied how GAI makes students and teachers feel. This helped them see how it could affect society and education. Even still, these studies are still different from each other, and there isn't a bibliometric synthesis that brings together information from different times, places, and themes. Also, most of the present study is on short-term benefits for teaching, including less time spent debugging, more engagement, or more productivity (Pesovski et al., 2024). There isn't much research on long-term educational results, especially those related to critical thinking, creativity, and advanced computer abilities. Ethical considerations, comprising academic integrity, fairness, bias, and data privacy, are often recognized (Floridi & Cowls, 2019; Jobin, Ienca, & Vayena, 2019; Buolamwini & Gebru, 2018; Veale & Binns, 2017), yet are seldom incorporated into systematic assessments of GAI adoption in computer science education.

The lack of a unified bibliometric review on these subjects shows a major flaw. This chapter provides an evidence-based summary of the study, contemplation, and application of GAI in computer science education during the last decade by analyzing trends in publications, citations, and topics. This is because of three things. First, bibliometric mapping indicates how GAI research has changed over time by indicating both the key themes and the areas that haven't been investigated enough (Siemens & Baker, 2012). Second, it offers empirical confirmation for the recognition of innovative practices and pedagogical advancements, essential for informing future curriculum development and educator training (Edwards, Olugbade, & Ojo, 2024; Ariza, Restrepo, & Hernández, 2025). Third, it puts current discussions about justice, morality, and inclusiveness in a wider intellectual setting. This makes sure that people all over the world utilize GAI wisely and well (Warschauer, 2004; Olugbade, 2025). This chapter seeks to transcend mere description of GAI in education by doing a comprehensive bibliometric analysis that enhances both theoretical frameworks and practical applications in computer science education.

Objectives and Research Questions

The primary objective of this chapter is to provide a thorough and evidence-based analysis of the impact of Generative Artificial Intelligence (GAI) on the pedagogy of Computer Science (CS). The chapter aims to consolidate disparate literature, identify trends in knowledge production, and clarify the relationship between technological advancements and instructional practices using bibliometric approaches. This strategy gives researchers, instructors, and policymakers relevant information about GAI that they may use to weigh the merits and cons.

There are four goals for the chapter, and they are all related to each other. The first goal is to look at the publication trends of GAI in computer science education during the past ten years, paying close attention to the speed, places, and locations of research. The second is to look at citation patterns and intellectual structures to determine the authors, sources, and materials that have had the most effect on the field. The third purpose is to uncover new areas of research and theme clusters that highlight how GAI has been applied in CS education for teaching, learning, programming, and testing. The fourth is to critically evaluate the implications of these findings for pedagogy, curriculum creation, and ethical behavior, emphasizing issues of equality, inclusivity, and digital literacy.

Guided by these objectives, the chapter is structured around three central research questions:

RQ1: What are the major trends in GAI research for CS education?

RQ2: How has GAI been applied in CS education, and what outcomes have emerged?

RQ3: What are the implications of GAI for teaching and learning in CS education?

Through these research questions, the bibliometric lens serves not only to document the growth of the field but also to surface the conceptual, methodological, and ethical dimensions that define its current trajectory. In doing so, the chapter positions itself at the intersection of technological innovation and educational transformation, ensuring that the discussion of GAI in CS education is both analytically rigorous and pedagogically grounded

CONCEPTUAL FRAMEWORK FOR BIBLIOMETRIC ANALYSIS

In this chapter, Generative Artificial Intelligence (GAI) is conceptualized using a capability-based and historically grounded definition, rather than being restricted to contemporary large language models. Specifically, GAI is defined as artificial intelligence systems designed to generate novel artifacts, including text, code, or problem solutions, through probabilistic or learned representations (He et al., 2025; Feuerriegel et al., 2024). This includes early neural generative models, intelligent tutoring systems with generative components, and later Transformer-based architectures (He et al., 2025; Feuerriegel et al., 2024). This definition allows for analytical continuity across time while acknowledging substantive technological evolution within the field.

The term "Generative AI" gained prominence following the widespread adoption of Transformer architectures and large-scale foundation models after 2018. However, earlier research in computer science education employed generative mechanisms that align with the functional definition above, including automated content generation, adaptive feedback systems, and code synthesis tools. In this study, such contributions are treated as proto-generative systems, representing foundational strands of generative intelligence rather than modern conversational agents. To mitigate potential conceptual drift, bibliometric classification was guided by explicit inclusion criteria based on system functionality and generative capability, rather than publication date or terminology alone. This approach is consistent with best practices in longitudinal bibliometric research, which emphasize construct stability over time to preserve analytical validity and interpretability of thematic evolution (Donthu et al., 2021; Börner et al., 2003).

To understand how Generative Artificial Intelligence (GAI) is used in Computer Science (CS) education, we need a paradigm that takes into account both the technological capabilities of GAI and the pedagogical settings in which it is used. This chapter organizes the bibliometric framework into four related areas: Generative AI Technologies (GAITs), Pedagogical Innovations (PIs), Computer Science Education Contexts (CSEC), and Outcomes and Future Directions (OFDs). When you look at these dimensions together, you can see how GAI tools are produced, utilized, and tested in schools, and how research on these processes changes over time.

Generative AI Technologies (GAITs) are the fundamental tools and models that enable the creation of novel concepts. Advancements in extensive language models, code-generation platforms, and multimodal systems have enabled educational technology to produce authentic and pertinent learning materials (Brown et al., 2020; Chen, Balan, & Brown, 2023). These technologies are not static; their continuous evolution indicates improvements in model architectures and advances resulting from their instructional utilization (Mittal et al., 2024; Ariza, Restrepo, & Hernández, 2025).

Pedagogical Innovations (PIs) are the new ways of teaching and learning that GAI makes possible. Bibliometric analyses indicate that customization, automated content development, intelligent tutoring, programming support, and innovative assessment are the most crucial domains of pedagogical transformation (Roll & Wylie, 2016). For example, intelligent tutoring systems that use GAI can benefit students in many ways, and programming assistants like GitHub Copilot can help people who are new to coding get started (Hazzan & Erez, 2024). GAI uses scalable systems for feedback and plagiarism detection, but it has to be fair and ethical.

Computer Science Education Contexts (CSEC) act as a middle ground that affects how GAI is used. Computer science education is different from other fields since it includes both hands-on and theoretical work with computers. This means that GAI can be applied in real life and in specific fields (Franklin et al., 2025; Lee & Song, 2024). How GAI is employed in CS classes depends on how ready schools are, how fair access to technology is, and how people feel about AI in general (Warschauer, 2004; Olugbade, 2025). Bibliometric mapping demonstrates that these contextual determinants influence adoption and also determine the trajectory of educational achievements across various regions and institutions (Edwards, Abuhassna, Olugbade, Ojo, & Jaafar, 2025).

Outcomes and Future Directions (OFDs) include the effects of GAI that have been recorded and the possible paths for research and practice. Reported effects encompass heightened efficiency in teaching and learning, as well as improved student involvement, creativity, and productivity (Graesser & Person, 1994; Pesovski et al., 2024). However, bibliometric trends also show that there are still worries about students relying too much on technology, losing their ability to think critically, and facing ethical problems that haven't been solved yet (Zastudil et al., 2023; Floridi & Cowls, 2019). Future-oriented research underscores the necessity for a curriculum that incorporates AI literacy, ethics, and computational thinking to equip learners for collaborative engagement with intelligent systems (Wing, 2006; Shneiderman, 2020; Fullan, 2013). This methodology allows for an organized investigation of the literature by placing these four dimensions inside a bibliometric framework. Methods like citation analysis, keyword co-occurrence, and thematic mapping show how new technologies lead to new ways of teaching, how different fields of study affect their use, and how what we see happen affects future research and policy (Siemens & Baker, 2012; Chen, Chen, & Lin, 2020). The framework illustrates the dynamic interaction between technology and pedagogy, while also establishing a basis for pinpointing research deficiencies and exploring innovative pathways in GAI for computer science education.

The bibliometric analysis presented in this chapter is conceptually anchored in two established frameworks: the Technological Pedagogical Content Knowledge (TPACK) model and a Sociotechnical Systems perspective. TPACK provides a lens through which to interpret the convergence of generative AI technologies, pedagogical innovations, and computer science content that emerges from our keyword and thematic mappings. This framework moves our interpretation beyond surface-level trends to consider how the field is navigating the integration of advanced technological tools into discipline-specific teaching practices. Concurrently, the sociotechnical lens situates these trends within broader institutional, ethical, and geopolitical contexts. It helps explain the observed geographical research imbalances, the foregrounding of certain ethical debates, and the formation of influential scholarly networks as manifestations of systemic forces shaping technology adoption in education. Together, these frameworks ensure our bibliometric findings are analytically grounded, connecting empirical publication patterns to deeper questions of pedagogical integration and social equity in the age of generative AI.

METHODOLOGY

Research Design

This study uses bibliometric research methods to carefully map out the intellectual landscape of Generative Artificial Intelligence (GAI) in the field of Computer Science (CS) education. Bibliometric analysis offers a structured approach for synthesizing varied academic works by evaluating publishing trends, analyzing citation impact, and establishing topic frameworks within a designated body of literature (Chen, Chen, & Lin, 2020). This method is especially useful for new study areas like GAI, where rapid technological progress means that evidence-based summaries are needed to guide both academic research and teaching methods.

Data Collection Methods

The dataset was gathered from the Scopus database, which is known for containing a lot of peer-reviewed publications and conference proceedings in topics including education, computer science, and others that span disciplines. The initial search brought up 1,573 documents. We utilized criteria for inclusion and exclusion to cut them down and make sure they were relevant to the issue. There were 582 documents in the last collection of data that were made between 2014 and 2024. They were all in English and were organized by subject, like the arts and humanities, social sciences, and computer science. The search employed a combination of title, abstract, and keyword words to discover studies on computer science education and artificial intelligence, with a focus on generative applications. Here is the query:

TITLE-ABS-KEY (AI in Computer Science Education) AND PUBYEAR > 2013 AND PUBYEAR < 2025 AND (LIMIT-TO (SUBJAREA, "COMP") OR LIMIT-TO (SUBJAREA, "SOCI") OR LIMIT-TO (SUBJAREA, "ARTS")) AND (LIMIT-TO (EXACTKEYWORD, "Artificial Intelligence") OR LIMIT-TO (EXACTKEYWORD, "Computer Science Education") OR LIMIT-TO (EXACTKEYWORD, "Generative Ai") OR LIMIT-TO (EXACTKEYWORD, "Ai") OR LIMIT-TO (EXACTKEYWORD, "Generative Artificial Intelligence") OR LIMIT-TO (EXACTKEYWORD, "Ai Education") OR LIMIT-TO (EXACTKEYWORD, "Artificial Intelligence Education") OR LIMIT-TO (EXACTKEYWORD, "Computer Science Students") OR LIMIT-TO (EXACTKEYWORD, "Computer Science Course")) AND (LIMIT-TO (LANGUAGE, "English").

The query included controlled terms such as Artificial Intelligence, Computer Science Education, Generative AI, AI Education, and Computer Science Students. This approach ensured a broad yet focused retrieval of literature addressing GAI integration into CS teaching, learning, programming, and assessment.

Data Coding and Analysis

We used the Biblioshiny interface from the Bibliometrix package in R to make bibliometric indicators. The analysis used descriptive statistics to illustrate how much science was produced each year, how many citations there were each year, and how much each country added to the body of work. We looked at authorship trends to discover the most important authors and assess how much work they did. To find out how important a source was, we employed local and worldwide citation metrics. To demonstrate research focus clusters and intellectual linkages between key ideas, we used thematic and co-word mapping approaches.

Figures taken straight from the dataset show that there are unique patterns in publishing activity, citation impact, and scholarly influence across the field. Figure 1 shows how much scientific work is done each year, and Figure 2 demonstrates how the number of citations changes over time. Figure 3 shows the ten countries that have done the most research in this area, and Figure 4 shows the authors that have had the biggest effect on the field's progress.

Figure 1. Annual scientific production in GAI and CS education (2014–2024)

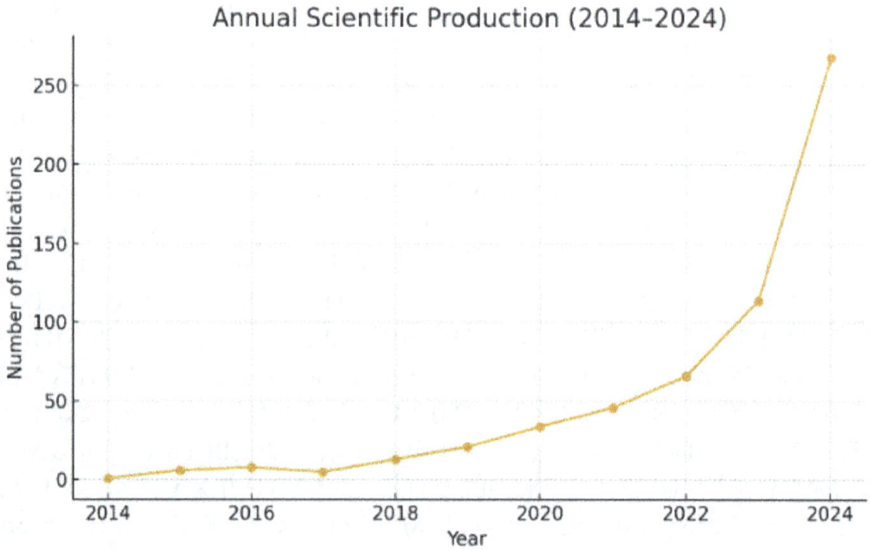

Figure 2. Annual citations of GAI and CS education publications (2014–2024)

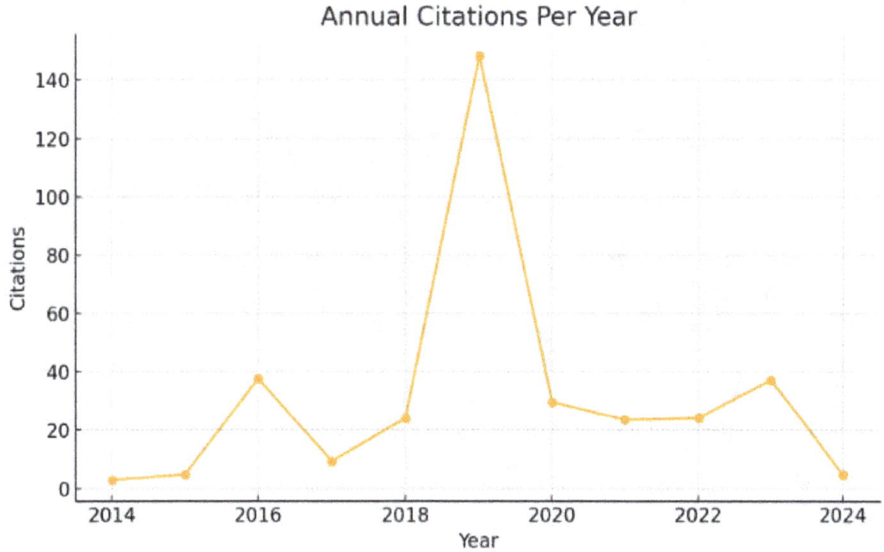

Figure 3. Top 10 most productive countries in GAI and CS education research

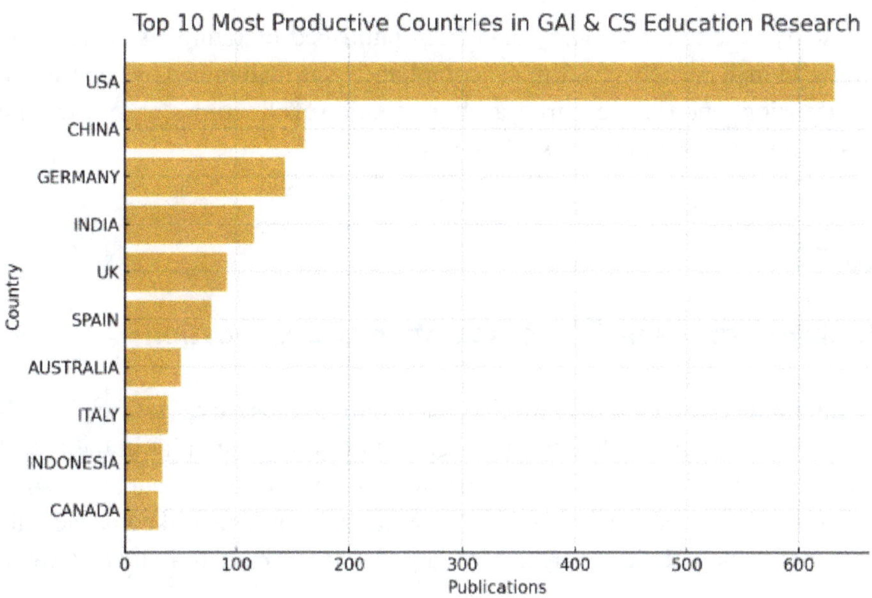

Figure 4. Top 10 most relevant authors in GAI and CS education research

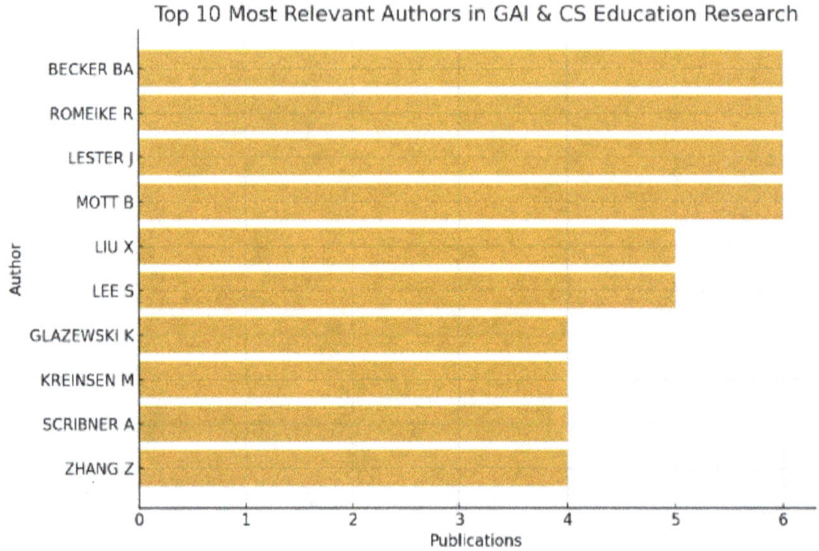

Ethical Considerations

This study relied on secondary data from published literature; as such, it did not involve human participants. Ethical compliance was maintained by adhering to Scopus licensing conditions, ensuring accurate citation of all sources, and presenting aggregated bibliometric indicators without manipulation.

RESULTS

RQ1: Major Trends in GAI Research for CS Education

The bibliometric analysis shows that research on Generative Artificial Intelligence (GAI) in Computer Science (CS) education has grown a lot in the recent ten years. From 2014 to 2024, scientific productivity has been continuously rising, with a substantial increase after 2020, as seen in Figure 1. This spike in academic research correlates with the emergence of large language models and AI-powered programming assistants, which shows that technological breakthroughs directly led to greater research.

In that same time period, the number of citations every year likewise increased a lot (Figure 2). The increase in citations indicates a proliferation of publications and signifies that GAI-related studies are emerging as significant contributions to the domains of education and computer science. All of these tendencies show that GAI is now a big topic of research in current educational technology.

RQ2: Applications of GAI and Emerging Outcomes

Bibliometric mapping identified multiple domains where GAI has been applied in computer science education, resulting in unique outcomes from each application area. Code assistants and other GAI-powered tools make it easier to develop, debug, and explain code when learning how to program. Reported results include shorter debugging times, higher efficiency, and more student confidence in doing programming tasks. However, there were worries in the literature about relying too much on automated help and how it could hurt computational thinking.

GAI has been applied to tools and systems that automatically grade tests and look for plagiarized material. These apps work well with big groups, but the results are not always good. Some schools believe that grading is now more consistent and quicker, but there are still moral arguments concerning privacy, fairness, and openness.

GAI helps make customized and adaptive learning feasible by helping to develop custom learning routes. Figure 5 shows that co-word analysis found that terms like "personalized learning," "adaptive systems," and "intelligent tutoring" were used a lot. This highlights how crucial it is to focus on the learner in this profession. Outcomes include higher engagement, simpler access, and more methods to learn, especially when used to aid new programmers or promote schools that are accessible to everyone.

RQ3: Implications Emerging from the Results

The results give us an early look at how GAI is transforming teaching and learning, even though the discussion goes into greater detail about what this means. Most research is done in countries with advanced technology, as seen in Figure 3. The US, China, and the UK are the top three. There are still not many contributions from the Global South, which makes some worry about digital inequalities and the uneven diffusion of innovative ideas (Warschauer, 2004; Olugbade, 2025).

Authorship analysis (Figure 4) reveals a distinct cohort of researchers with substantial production, signifying the emergence of a specialized research community that is shaping pedagogical discourse, curriculum development, and teacher preparation in computer science education. Figure 6 shows the most cited documents. These suggest that a few major studies are holding the field together and will be the basis for future research. Most of these papers are about intelligent tutoring, AI-powered code help, and moral frameworks. This is a good example of how new ways of teaching and responsible use are coming together.

Finally, source impact analysis (Figure 7) shows that the best sites to publish are journals and conferences that focus on computer science education and educational technology. The most important places for computing education have a big impact on local citations. This suggests that conversations regarding GAI are becoming a part of mainstream CS education research instead of sticking on the outskirts of the field.

Figure 5. Top 20 keywords in GAI and CS education research

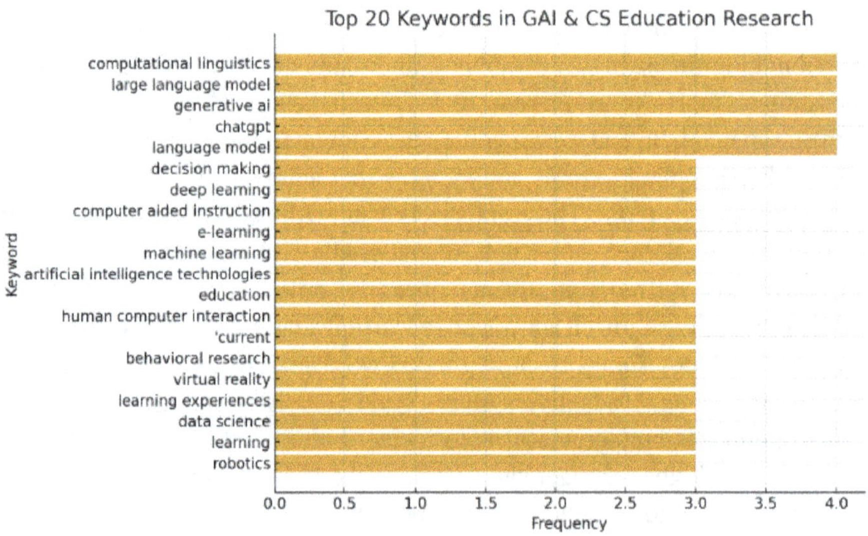

Figure 6. Top 10 most globally cited documents on GAI in CS education

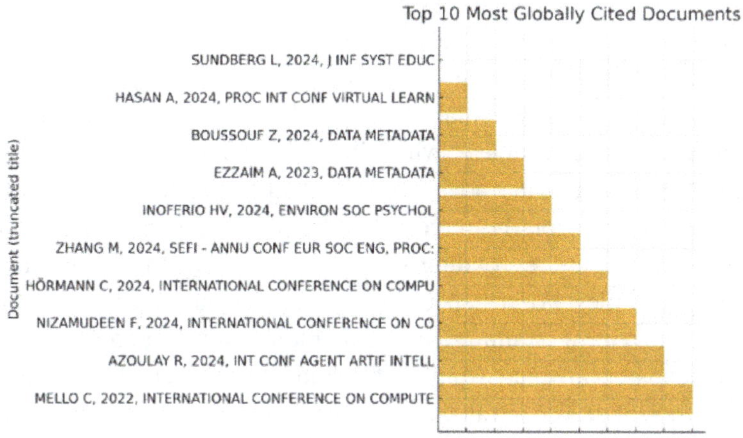

Figure 7. Top 10 publication sources by local citation impact

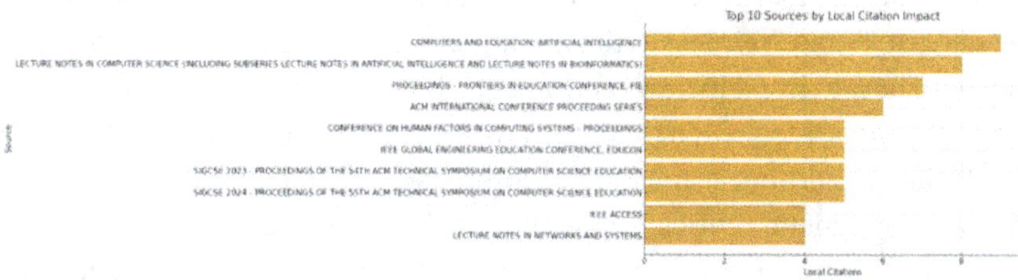

Summary of Findings

The results show that the field is vibrant, diverse, and becoming more important. Trends in research suggest that both the amount and the effect are growing faster. Applications encompass programming teaching, evaluation, and individualized learning, yielding results that vary from enhanced efficiency and engagement to significant ethical and equity concerns. Thematic and keyword studies underscore that the domain is characterized not only by technological advancements but also by pedagogical and institutional considerations. Most referenced works and high-impact sources confirm that the profession is becoming more unified, yet regional inequalities and equality issues show that there are still areas that need immediate attention. These results from the empirical basis for the subsequent part, which examines their wider educational and policy ramifications.

DISCUSSION

While the bibliometric trends presented—such as the exponential growth in publications post-2020 and the clustering of keywords around intelligent tutoring and automated assessment—offer a valuable map of the field's expansion, their pedagogical significance becomes clear when interpreted through the lens of instructional readiness and curricular adaptation. The rapid rise in research output does not merely indicate scholarly interest; it signals a paradigm shift in how computer science educators are responding to generative AI's capacity to alter foundational teaching activities. For instance, the strong co-occurrence of "GitHub Copilot" and "introductory programming" in the literature points to an emerging pedagogical reality: educators are increasingly integrating AI-driven code assistants not as supplemental tools, but as central agents in the learning process. This shift demands concrete changes in instructional design, such as rethinking problem sets to emphasize higher-order debugging and system design over syntax recall, and developing formative assessments that evaluate a student's ability to critique and refine AI-generated code rather than merely produce it from scratch.

Furthermore, the thematic prominence of ethical keywords, such as "bias," "academic integrity," and "fairness", alongside technical terms reflect a field grappling not only with how to implement generative AI, but why and under what constraints. Pedagogically, this means curriculum developers cannot treat AI integration as solely a technical add-on; it must be accompanied by modular ethics instruction, transparent assessment rubrics, and policies that promote responsible use. The geographic imbalance in research production further underscores a practical imperative: instructional models developed in high-resource contexts may not translate to classrooms in the Global South, where access to reliable AI tools and training varies widely. Therefore, these bibliometric patterns do more than describe the research landscape, they highlight urgent needs for differentiated faculty development, locally relevant curricular frameworks, and assessment strategies that prioritize computational thinking and ethical reasoning alongside technical proficiency. By framing these trends as signals of deeper pedagogical renegotiation, this chapter provides a foundation for evidence-based decisions in course design, accreditation, and educational policy.

The findings of this bibliometric review indicate that Generative Artificial Intelligence (GAI) has rapidly emerged as a transformative force in Computer Science (CS) education, despite its effects being complex, varied, and inconsistent. The rise in publications after 2020, which coincided with the development of large language models and AI-driven programming assistants, shows how new technologies can quickly lead to important research (Chen, Chen, & Lin, 2020; Brown et al., 2020). Nonetheless, the identified patterns suggest that while GAI possesses considerable potential for educational and institutional innovation, its implementation is complicated by unresolved contradictions that pose challenges for both educators and policymakers. So, the debate puts the results in three related contexts: pedagogical applications, ethical and equity issues, and institutional contexts. It also looks at the strengths, weaknesses, or lack of evidence in different areas.

Pedagogical Applications: Promise and Ambivalence

Programming assistance, intelligent tutoring, automated assessment, and adaptive learning are the most important areas of innovation in GAI. People have said good things about GAI-powered code assistants like GitHub Copilot because they help beginners write code, cut down on debugging time, and give quick explanations (Prather & Karkare, 2021; Karkare & Prather, 2020). The bibliometric evidence strongly supports the notion that these tools enhance productivity and confidence, empowering students to overcome challenges that might otherwise deter them from pursuing their studies in computer science (Finnie & Pazzani, 2019; Parnin & Gellenbeck, 2019). These apps fit with long-term teaching goals of scaffolding learning and making it more efficient (Roll & Wylie, 2016). However, the same body of literature demonstrates a considerable shortcoming. There is considerable evidence of short-term enhancements in speed and student satisfaction; however, there is a lack of long-term research examining whether reliance on these tools enhances or impairs advanced computational thinking (Zastudil et al., 2023; Franklin et al., 2025). Students who heavily depend on AI-generated ideas might finish their work faster, but it's not clear if they develop the resilience, debugging skills, and advanced reasoning skills that computer science education is supposed to teach (Wing, 2006; Shneiderman, 2020). In this regard, the evidence base is inconsistent: it strongly supports efficiency improvements but falls short of supporting long-term conceptual mastery.

Studies on intelligent tutoring and adaptive learning exhibit a similar ambivalence. Generative models have brought back interest in intelligent tutoring systems by making interactions more responsive and conversational. These technologies promise to make one-on-one tutoring available to everyone by changing in real time to meet the needs of each learner. The bibliometric mapping, particularly the incorporation of keywords such as "personalized learning" and "adaptive systems," indicates that this is a dynamic field of research (Pesovski et al., 2024). Reports of heightened engagement, tailored feedback, and inclusivity suggest that GAI may possess the potential to expand the parameters of learner-centered pedagogy (Graesser & Person, 1994; Ariza, Restrepo, & Hernández, 2025). However, the evidence continues to be limited when evaluated from the standpoint of sustainability. Some evidence suggests that adaptive learning driven by GAI can enhance short-term comprehension and motivation; however, there is limited evidence indicating its efficacy in fostering long-term academic achievement or transferable skills (Chan & Hu, 2023; Lee & Song, 2024). This difference between quick technical testing and slow pedagogical testing shows a long-standing trait of the field: new ideas often outpace real-world evidence (Mittal et al., 2024).

GAI is also changing how people think about tests and honesty in school. Automated grading and AI-driven plagiarism detection have been recognized for improving efficiency, scalability, and consistency in large groups, particularly in programming-heavy classes (Leinonen & Järvelä, 2020). Schools that need to handle more students without lowering the quality of their work will like these results. But they do have some big issues. The conversation is mostly about fairness, openness, and surveillance, as shown by how often words like "plagiarism" and "ethics" come up in the bibliometric clusters. Empirical research confirms the effectiveness of algorithmic grading; however, its fairness remains insufficiently examined. There remain enquiries concerning the capability of generative models to assess creativity, originality, and contextual reasoning, all of which are vital for advanced learning in computer science (Siemens & Baker, 2012). Furthermore, the increasing reliance on automated plagiarism detection methods has raised apprehensions about student trust and the potential for adversarial relationships between learners and educational institutions. In this field, evidence backs up efficiency, but ethical soundness is not as strong.

There is a common theme in all of these uses, GAI has clear short-term benefits, but not enough proof that it will be useful for learning in the long run. The educational trajectory of GAI in computer science education remains indeterminate. Its integration could transform educational environments; however, without scrutiny and intervention, there is a risk that it may inadvertently weaken the skills it seeks to improve (Wing, 2006; Shneiderman, 2020).

Ethical and Equity Dimensions: Foregrounded but Underexplored

Besides pedagogy, moral and fair issues are also very important to the GAI discussion. This current wave of innovation is different from past educational innovations, which sometimes led to ethical debates only after they were widely used (Floridi & Cowls, 2019). In the case of GAI, ethical concerns are prioritized from the beginning, underscoring the lack of transparency and impact of generative models (Jobin, Ienca, & Vayena, 2019). Right now, bias, fairness, openness, academic integrity, and equity are all big problems in academia. This shows that people know that the stakes are not just technological but also social and cultural. Bias and fairness are still big problems. Research in a number of fields has shown that generative models can encode and make worse social biases that are already there. This has led to fears that educational applications might unintentionally keep inequalities in the classroom (Buolamwini & Gebru, 2018; Veale & Binns, 2017). While this issue is extensively acknowledged in the literature, empirical data regarding the manifestation of bias in actual computer science learning environments is scarce. This creates a paradox: even though bias is a well-studied topic, its real-world effects in computer science classrooms have not been studied in a systematic way. There is also the problem of transparency. Students and teachers often don't know how models make outputs, explanations, or evaluations (Floridi & Cowls, 2019). This lack of clarity makes it harder to hold people accountable and question decisions, especially when it comes to tests (Veale & Binns, 2017). While frameworks have been proposed to improve explainability, there is limited evidence of their implementation in classroom settings. Ethical dangers are therefore essential to the discourse, yet remain inadequately scrutinized by empirical research.

Academic integrity has emerged as a paramount and contentious issue. GAI's ability to write essays, code, and solve problems makes it hard to use traditional ways of testing. Many people are worried that it will be easier and harder to catch students who do bad things, which will make academic qualifications less valuable. But the answers are not the same. Some people want stricter rules and more monitoring, while others want teaching methods that include originality, oral defense, or human–AI collaborative problem-solving (Hazzan & Erez, 2024; Franklin et al., 2025). These solutions look like they might work, but they haven't been tried out very much. In theory, the debate makes sense, but in practice, it doesn't. People won't be able to stop using GAI tools because they are so easy to get (Chan & Hu, 2023). The real challenge is to come up with a new way to assess that keeps honesty while also letting in new ideas (Shneiderman, 2020).

Worries about fairness make things even harder. The geographical distribution of publications shows that most research leadership is in countries with advanced technology, and there isn't much coming from the Global South (Warschauer, 2004; Olugbade, 2025). This trend shows that there are big differences in infrastructure, money, and how ready institutions are. If GAI adoption stays uneven, the problem is that differences in CS education around the world will get worse. Students with abundant resources may benefit from personalized and adaptive instruction, whereas those with limited resources may experience further setbacks (Warschauer, 2004). The literature often talks about these problems, but there aren't enough proven ways to solve them (Olugbade, 2025; Edwards, Abuhassna, Olugbade, Ojo, & Jaafar, 2025). There is a lack of research examining low-resource settings or assessing culturally pertinent strategies for GAI integration. Consequently, equity is recognized as a concern but inadequately prioritized as a research focus. Without deliberate efforts, the use of GAI may make global education even more unequal, rather than less so (Warschauer, 2004).

Institutional and Disciplinary Contexts: Opportunities and Constraints

Institutional and disciplinary contexts also affect how GAI is used and understood. The large number of publications in fields with cutting-edge technology demonstrates how infrastructure and policy can influence the subject (Chen, Chen, & Lin, 2020). It is easier for institutions with a lot of money, technology, and supportive governance frameworks to try out GAI than for those that don't. However, empirical studies linking institutional policy to pedagogical outcomes are rare (Edwards, Olugbade, & Ojo, 2024). This shows that more structured research is needed to find out how governance frameworks and institutional readiness affect outcomes.

There are pros and cons to using GAI in computer science classes. Computer science students' study and use the basic ideas of AI in a way that is different from most other fields (Wing, 2006). This dual role suggests that computer science classrooms could serve as laboratories for fostering responsible AI literacy (Fullan, 2013; Edwards, Olugbade, & Ojo, 2024). Nonetheless, bibliometric evidence suggests that many studies perceive computer science education merely as an ancillary application domain, rather than exploring its disciplinary distinctiveness (Franklin et al., 2025; Hazzan & Erez, 2024). There is inadequate research regarding the impact of students' technical understanding on their engagement with GAI, as well as how curricula might integrate AI literacy alongside essential computer skills (Wing, 2006; Shneiderman, 2020). This gap represents a lost opportunity: computer science education could lead the way in developing responsible AI pedagogy, but this role has not yet been fully embraced.

The discipline's intellectual framework also makes important dynamics clear. A few well-known authors and big newspapers are in charge of the conversation. This indicates consolidation and maturation, as the field coalesces around recognized authorities (Chen, Chen, & Lin, 2020). On the other hand, it makes people worry about how limited viewpoints are, especially if they come from a small number of areas and methodological traditions. Interdisciplinary collaboration appears to be deficient, with computer scientists often prevailing in discussions, whereas educational researchers, ethicists, and policy scholars remain underrepresented (Mittal et al., 2024; Ariza, Restrepo, & Hernández, 2025). This imbalance could mean that the social and educational aspects of GAI adoption are not given enough attention, which requires a lot of different points of view to fully understand (Floridi & Cowls, 2019; Jobin, Ienca, & Vayena, 2019).

Implications for Research, Policy, and Practice

When considered collectively, these findings significantly impact research, policy, and practice. From a research point of view, the field needs to go beyond just noting improvements in efficiency and look into the long-term effects on higher-level cognitive processes, creativity, and problem-solving skills (Wing, 2006; Franklin et al., 2025). Long-term studies are needed to find out if relying on GAI makes long-term computing skills better or worse (Zastudil et al., 2023). Furthermore, empirical investigations into prejudice, equity, and transparency within educational contexts are essential (Buolamwini & Gebru, 2018; Veale & Binns, 2017), as are equity-focused research endeavours in resource-constrained and culturally heterogeneous environments (Warschauer, 2004; Olugbade, 2025). In the absence of such evidence, policy and practice may be swayed by speculation rather than definitive conclusions.

Study Limitations and Future Directions

This study has some limitations. Only Scopus and English-language publications are used; contributions from other regions or languages may not be fully represented. Bibliometric methods help discover patterns, but they just look at statistics like citations, which don't demonstrate all the different ways that new teaching methods can be good (Siemens & Baker, 2012). Additionally, because technology changes so quickly, the most recent changes may not yet be clear in citation patterns (Brown et al., 2020; Chen, Balan, & Brown, 2023). These limitations indicate that the findings should be considered indicative rather than exhaustive.

To advance beyond general calls for ethical integration, future research must generate actionable, pedagogically sound frameworks for classroom implementation. The following directions propose specific, researchable pathways grounded in the bibliometric trends identified, designed to produce usable knowledge for instructors and curriculum designers. First, pedagogical research must shift from *whether* to *how* generative AI can be used to develop higher-order cognitive skills. This requires designing and testing scaffolded instructional sequences that strategically integrate tools like GitHub Copilot to transition students from AI-assisted code generation to AI-augmented system design and critical evaluation. Controlled studies should compare learning outcomes in courses where AI is used for debugging support versus those where it is used for generating algorithmic explanations, measuring impacts on problem decomposition and metacognitive awareness. Second, the field urgently needs empirically validated assessment rubrics for AI-collaborative work. Future work should develop and validate scalable methods for evaluating originality, process, and conceptual understanding in assignments where students co-create with generative AI. This includes research into oral defense protocols, reflective portfolio components, and scenario-based assessments that can authentically measure learning in an era of accessible code generation, moving beyond easily automatable tasks. Third, faculty development must become a primary research focus. We need evidence-based models for preparing CS educators, many of whom are not AI specialists, to design prompts, facilitate AI ethics discussions, and troubleshoot model outputs in real time. Research should investigate the efficacy of just-in-time training modules, disciplinary teaching communities of practice, and scaffolded curriculum kits that lower the adoption barrier while maintaining pedagogical integrity. Finally, equity-oriented research must move from identification to intervention. This entails participatory design of lightweight, offline-capable AI tools for low-resource settings and culturally responsive curriculum adaptations that address local educational priorities rather than importing technological solutions from high-income contexts. Studies should document implementation challenges and student outcomes in underrepresented regions to build a truly global evidence base for equitable AI integration.

By pursuing these concrete, instructionally-grounded questions, the field can transition from principled discussion to transformative classroom practice, ensuring that generative AI serves as a lever for pedagogical innovation rather than a generic disruptor.

CONCLUSION

This chapter examines the application of Generative Artificial Intelligence (GAI) in Computer Science (CS) education through the perspective of bibliometrics. It has provided a summary of publication trends, citation patterns, thematic frameworks, and academic impact during the last decade. The study found that research activity has expanded significantly after 2020, thanks to better big language models and AI-powered programming helpers. The increase in citations implies that more and more scholars are paying attention to this topic. In CS education, GAI is usually utilized for four things: teaching programming, testing, customized learning, and keeping an eye on ethics. Outcomes include more efficiency, better engagement, and the potential to scale instructional methods. However, there are also problems, including too much reliance on automated systems, dangers to academic integrity, and continuous worries about fairness and openness. Keyword and topic patterns suggest that instructional innovation and ethical responsibility are evolving simultaneously, positioning equity and integrity as fundamental issues rather than secondary considerations.

The study also found flaws with the structure. Countries that have better technology are more likely to be leaders in research. Countries in the Global South are less likely to be leaders in research. A few highly referenced works and publication venues dominate the conversation. This shows that intellectual consolidation is happening, but it also shows that more people need to get involved. These findings emphasize that the incorporation of GAI in computer science education is both a societal and institutional issue, as well as a technical one. This review addresses the three primary research topics and demonstrates that GAI serves not only as an educational tool but also as a means to reevaluate the objectives and methodologies of computer science education. Its transformational promise lies in fostering personalized, inventive, and flexible learning environments, but its related risks demand a vigilant emphasis on ethics, equity, and digital literacy. Policymakers, educators, and researchers must utilize GAI responsibly, ensuring that innovations enhance rather than compromise the fundamental principles of education.

This chapter's key contribution is that it presents an evidence-based map of the field, demonstrating where progress has been made and where there are still important gaps. It brings together global trends, applications, and consequences to give researchers and practitioners a starting point for their work in the future. As GAI keeps changing, its position in CS education will rely on how effectively it interacts with technology and how schools, instructors, and students choose to use it in ways that are ethical, equitable, and improve the way things are done.

REFERENCES

Aria, M., & Cuccurullo, C. (2017). Bibliometrix: An R-tool for comprehensive science mapping analysis. *Journal of Informetrics*, *11*(4), 959–975. DOI: 10.1016/j.joi.2017.08.007

Ariza, J., Restrepo, M., & Hernández, C. (2025). Generative AI in engineering and computing education: A scoping review of empirical studies and educational practices. *IEEE Access : Practical Innovations, Open Solutions*, *13*, 30789–30810. DOI: 10.1109/ACCESS.2025.3541424

Bommasani, R., Hudson, D. A., Adeli, E., Altman, R., Arora, S., von Arx, S., Bernstein, M. S., ... (2021). On the opportunities and risks of foundation models. *arXiv*. https://doi.org//arXiv.2108.07258DOI: 10.48550

Börner, K., Chen, C., & Boyack, K. W. (2003). Visualizing knowledge domains. *Annual Review of Information Science & Technology*, *37*(1), 179–255. DOI: 10.1002/aris.1440370106

Buolamwini, J., & Gebru, T. (2018). Gender shades: Intersectional accuracy disparities in commercial gender classification. *Proceedings of the 1st Conference on Fairness, Accountability and Transparency (FAT*)* (pp. 77–91). ACM. Available from https://proceedings.mlr.press/v81/buolamwini18a.html

Chan, C., & Hu, W. (2023). Students' voices on generative AI: Perceptions, benefits, and challenges in higher education. *International Journal of Educational Technology in Higher Education*, *20*, 43. Advance online publication. DOI: 10.1186/s41239-023-00411-8

Chen, L., Chen, P., & Lin, Z. (2020). Artificial intelligence in education: A review. *IEEE Access : Practical Innovations, Open Solutions*, *8*, 75264–75278. DOI: 10.1109/ACCESS.2020.2988510

Chen, Z., Balan, M., & Brown, K. (2023). Language models are few-shot learners for prognostic prediction. *arXiv*. https://doi.org//arXiv.2302.12692DOI: 10.48550

Donthu, N., Kumar, S., Mukherjee, D., Pandey, N., & Lim, W. M. (2021). How to conduct a bibliometric analysis: An overview and guidelines. *Journal of Business Research*, *133*, 285–296. DOI: 10.1016/j.jbusres.2021.04.070

Edwards, B. I., Abuhassna, H., Olugbade, D., Ojo, O. A., & Jaafar Wan Yahaya, W. (Eds.). (2025). *Generators, bots, and tutors: Creative approaches to human–AI synergy in classroom instruction*. IGI Global., DOI: 10.4018/979-8-3373-0847-0

Edwards, B. I., Olugbade, D., & Ojo, O. A. (2024). Facilitating cognitive load management and improved learning outcomes and attitudes in middle school technology and vocational education through AI chatbot. *Journal of Technical Education and Training*, *16*(3), 114–131. DOI: 10.30880/jtet.2024.16.03.009

Feuerriegel, S., Hartmann, J., Janiesch, C., & Zschech, P. (2024). Generative AI. *Business & Information Systems Engineering*, *66*, 111–126. DOI: 10.1007/s12599-023-00834-7

Floridi, L., & Cowls, J. (2019). A unified framework of five principles for AI in society. *Harvard Data Science Review*, *1*(1). Advance online publication. DOI: 10.1162/99608f92.8cd550d1

Franklin, D., Denny, P., Gonzalez-Maldonado, D. A., & Tran, M. (2025). *Generative AI in computer science education: Challenges and opportunities*. Cambridge University Press., DOI: 10.1017/9781009581738

Fullan, M. (2013). *Stratosphere: Integrating technology, pedagogy, and change knowledge*. Pearson Education.

Graesser, A. C., & Person, N. K. (1994). Question asking during tutoring. *American Educational Research Journal*, *31*(1), 104–137. DOI: 10.3102/00028312031001104

Hazzan, O., & Erez, Y. (2024). Generative AI in computer science education. *Proceedings of the 55th ACM Technical Symposium on Computer Science Education (SIGCSE)* (Vol. 2). ACM. https://doi.org/DOI: 10.1145/3626253.3633409

He, R., Cao, J., & Tan, T. (2025). Generative artificial intelligence: A historical perspective. *National Science Review*, *12*(5), nwaf050. Advance online publication. DOI: 10.1093/nsr/nwaf050 PMID: 40191253

Jobin, A., Ienca, M., & Vayena, E. (2019). The global landscape of AI ethics guidelines. *Nature Machine Intelligence*, *1*(9), 389–399. DOI: 10.1038/s42256-019-0088-2

Kitchenham, B. A., Brereton, O. P., Budgen, D., Turner, M., Bailey, J., & Linkman, S. (2009). Systematic literature reviews in software engineering – A systematic literature review. *Information and Software Technology*, *51*(1), 7–15. DOI: 10.1016/j.infsof.2008.09.009

Lee, S., & Song, K. (2024). Teachers' and students' perceptions of AI-generated concept explanations: Implications for integrating generative AI in computer science education. *Computers & Education: Artificial Intelligence*, *7*, 100283. Advance online publication. DOI: 10.1016/j.caeai.2024.100283

Mittal, U., Sai, S., Chamola, V., & Sangwan, D. (2024). A comprehensive review on generative AI for education. *IEEE Access : Practical Innovations, Open Solutions*, *12*, 142733–142759. DOI: 10.1109/ACCESS.2024.3468368

Olugbade, D. (2025). Democratizing education in rural Nigeria through AI and mobile technologies as a transformative pathway to inclusive learning. In M. Sanmugam, B. Edwards, N. Mohd Barkhaya, & Z. Khlaif (Eds.), *Fostering inclusive education with AI and emerging technologies* (pp. 233–250). IGI Global. https://doi.org/DOI: 10.4018/979-8-3693-7255-5.ch010

Pesovski, I., Santos, R., Henriques, R., & Trajkovik, V. (2024). Generative AI for customizable learning experiences. *Sustainability*, *16*(7), 3034. Advance online publication. DOI: 10.3390/su16073034

Roll, I., & Wylie, R. (2016). Evolution and revolution in artificial intelligence in education. *International Journal of Artificial Intelligence in Education*, *26*(2), 582–599. DOI: 10.1007/s40593-016-0110-3

Shneiderman, B. (2020). Human-centered artificial intelligence: Reliable, safe, and trustworthy. *International Journal of Human-Computer Interaction*, *36*(10), 887–896. DOI: 10.1080/10447318.2020.1741118

Siemens, G., & Baker, R. S. (2012). Learning analytics and educational data mining: Towards a new learning science. *Journal of Educational Technology & Society*, *15*(3), 1–4.

Veale, M., & Binns, R. (2017). Fairer machine learning in the real world. *Proceedings of the ACM Conference on Fairness, Accountability, and Transparency (FAT*)* (pp. 1–15). ACM. https://doi.org/DOI: 10.1177/2053951717743530

Warschauer, M. (2004). *Technology and social inclusion: Rethinking the digital divide*. MIT Press.

Wing, J. M. (2006). Computational thinking. *Communications of the ACM*, *49*(3), 33–35. DOI: 10.1145/1118178.111821

Zastudil, C., Rogalska, M., Kapp, C., Vaughn, J., & Macneil, S. (2023). Generative AI in computing education: Perspectives of students and instructors. *Proceedings of the IEEE Frontiers in Education Conference (FIE)* (pp. 1–9). IEEE. https://doi.org/DOI: 10.1109/FIE58773.2023.10343467

Zawacki-Richter, O., Marín, V. I., Bond, M., & Gouverneur, F. (2019). Systematic review of research on artificial intelligence applications in higher education: Where are the educators? *International Journal of Educational Technology in Higher Education*, *16*, 39. Advance online publication. DOI: 10.1186/s41239-019-0171-0

KEY TERMS AND DEFINITIONS

Bibliometric Analysis: A quantitative research method that analyzes academic publications to examine research trends, impact, and scholarly relationships.

Computer Science: The academic discipline concerned with the study of computation, algorithms, data structures, and the design of hardware and software systems.

Curriculum Development: The systematic planning, design, implementation, and evaluation of educational content and learning experiences.

Generative Artificial Intelligence: A branch of artificial intelligence that focuses on creating systems capable of generating new content—such as text, images, code, or audio—based on learned patterns from existing data.

Intelligent Tutoring: The use of AI-driven systems to provide adaptive instruction, feedback, and support that simulates one-on-one human tutoring.

Learning Technologies: Digital tools and platforms that support, enhance, or transform teaching and learning processes.

Pedagogical Innovation: The adoption of new teaching methods, strategies, or tools to enhance learning effectiveness, engagement, and educational outcomes.

Personalized Learning: An instructional approach that tailors learning experiences to individual learners' needs, preferences, pace, and prior knowledge.

Programming Instruction: The process of teaching learners how to design, write, test, and debug computer programs using programming languages.

Afterword

Technological innovations lead to a reality in which we increasingly live in a digital world rather than a purely physical one. Technologies evolve at a rapid pace, creating a growing demand for skilled specialists and putting significant pressure on educational institutions. Educators face a fundamental challenge: how to keep up with rapidly changing technological trends while providing students with timely and relevant knowledge and simultaneously embedding ethics and responsibility into the learning process. Without this balance, technological progress risks advancing faster than our ability to manage its societal impact.

Therefore, modern computer science education extends far beyond the transfer of technical knowledge. As illustrated throughout this volume, it involves interdisciplinarity, inclusivity, and sociotechnical pedagogy. Innovations in computing do not emerge in isolation. If technological innovations are meant to respond to societal needs, then the people who design and develop them should reflect the diversity of the societies they serve and share values that support long-term societal well-being. This requires tertiary education institutions to cultivate diverse and inclusive learning environments that prepare a broad, representative body of responsible professionals.

The transition to digital environments has reshaped how younger generations perceive the world and interact with information. Educational institutions must recognize these shifts and adapt pedagogical approaches accordingly. The expansion of remote, hybrid, and online learning, which intensified during the COVID-19 pandemic, has become an established part of higher education. While these formats present challenges such as reduced engagement and depersonalization, they also offer opportunities to rethink how learning environments are designed. Pedagogical innovation is therefore not only about adopting new tools, but about intentionally creating meaningful, engaging, and supportive educational experiences.

One promising direction highlighted across this book is the integration of artificial intelligence into computer science education. Rather than focusing on potential risks and harms, educators are encouraged to explore how AI can support learning and assessment, while remaining critically aware of its ethical implications. When approached responsibly, AI can be a powerful pedagogical ally, helping educators better support diverse learners and prepare students for the realities of a rapidly evolving technological landscape.

Taken together, the contributions in this volume demonstrate that pedagogical innovation in computer science education requires continuous dialogue between technology, pedagogy, ethics, and inclusion. By embracing innovation responsibly and inclusively, educators can help shape a future in which technological progress supports, rather than undermines, sustainable and equitable development.

I would like to congratulate the editor of this book, Dr. Manuel B. Garcia, and all contributing authors for expanding the body of knowledge in computer science education by highlighting pedagogical innovation, inclusivity, social responsibility, and the integration of AI and intelligent systems into the learning process. The collection of works from twelve countries creates an international dialogue that enriches academic discussion and reflects the global nature of the educational and technological challenges addressed in this book.

Yekaterina Kovaleva
LUT University, Finland

Compilation of References

Abdulla, S., Ismail, S., Fawzy, Y., & Elhaj, A. (2024). Using ChatGPT in Teaching Computer Programming and Studying its Impact on Students Performance. *Electronic Journal of e-Learning*, *22*(6), 66–81. DOI: 10.34190/EJEL.22.6.3380

Abelha, M., Fernandes, S., Mesquita, D., Seabra, F., & Ferreira-Oliveira, A. T. (2020). Graduate Employability and Competence Development in Higher Education—A Systematic Literature Review using PRISMA. *Sustainability*, *12*(15), 5900. Advance online publication. DOI: 10.3390/su12155900

Abichandani, P., Sivakumar, V., Lobo, D., Iaboni, C., & Shekhar, P. (2022). Internet-of-things curriculum, pedagogy, and assessment for stem education: A review of literature. *IEEE Access : Practical Innovations, Open Solutions*, *10*, 38351–38369.

Abouelenein, Y. A. M., Ghazala, A. F. A., Mahdy, E. M. M., & Khalaf, M. H. R. (2025). The R5E pattern: Can artificial intelligence enhance programming skills development? *Education and Information Technologies*, *30*(15), 22177–22205. DOI: 10.1007/s10639-025-13616-3

Ackerman, M. K., Armour, V., Najeeb, Z., & Mendoza, N. (2025). Experiential Learning Internship for Teaching Design Research. *Proceedings of the Extended Abstracts of the CHI Conference on Human Factors in Computing Systems*. https://doi.org/DOI: 10.1145/3706599.3707654

Acut, D. P. (2026). Gamification in Computer Science Education: A Systematic Review of Pedagogical Strategies and Learning Outcomes. In *Pedagogical Innovations in Computer Science Education*.

Adams, M., & Morgan, K. (2021). Relational Sensibilities and Women's Participation in Computer Science and Information Technology Degrees: A Cultural-Historical Approach. *Learning, Culture and Social Interaction*, *28*, 100464. DOI: 10.1016/j.lcsi.2020.100464

Adamu, A. (Ed.). R., Okebukola, P., Assistants, E., Gbeleyi, O., Oladejo, A., Agbanimu, D., Onowugbeda, F., Foreword, E., & Jackson-Hammond, C. (2025). *AI and Curriculum Development for the Future Book in honour of.* Retrieved November 11, 2025, from https://eprints.gouni.edu.ng/4428/1/Volume%202-AI%20and%20Quality%20Higher%20Education%20Handbook-January%202025.pdf#page=74

Adler, I., & Shani, Y. (2026). Hybrid Human-GenAI Cognitive Apprenticeship: Encouraging Pre-Service Teachers to Implement Instructional Practices to Support Students' Self-Regulated Learning. *Teaching and Teacher Education*, *169*, 1–19. DOI: 10.1016/j.tate.2025.105268

Aerts, W., Fletcher, G., & Miedema, D. (2024). *A Feasibility Study on Automated SQL Exercise Generation with ChatGPT-3.5.* 13–19. DOI: 10.1145/3663649.3664368

Afzal, A., Khan, S., Daud, S., Ahmad, Z., & Butt, A. (2023). Addressing the Digital Divide: Access and Use of Technology in Education. *Journal of Social Sciences Review*, *3*(2), 883–895. DOI: 10.54183/jssr.v3i2.326

Agbo, F. J., Olivia, C., Oguibe, G., Sanusi, I. T., & Sani, G. (2025). Computing education using generative artificial intelligence tools: A systematic literature review. *Computers and Education Open*, *9*, 100266. 10.1016/j.caeo.2025.100266

Agbo, F. J., Olivia, C., Oguibe, G., Sanusi, I. T., & Sani, G. (2025). Computing Education Using Generative Artificial Intelligence Tools: A Systematic Literature Review. *Computers and Education Open*, *9*, 1–13. DOI: 10.1016/j.caeo.2025.100266

Agbo, F. J., Sanusi, I. T., Oyelere, S. S., & Suhonen, J. (2021). Application of virtual reality in computer science education: A systemic review based on bibliometric and content analysis methods. *Education Sciences*, *11*(3), 142.

Aglen, B. (2016). Pedagogical strategies to teach bachelor students evidence-based practice: A systematic review. *Nurse Education Today*, *36*, 255–263. DOI: 10.1016/j.nedt.2015.08.025 PMID: 26375570

Ahmad, I., Sharma, S., Singh, R., & Gehlot, A., Lovi Raj Gupta, Amit Kumar Thakur, Neeraj Priyadarshi, & Bhekisipho Twala. (2024). Inclusive learning using industry 4.0 technologies: Addressing student diversity in modern education. *Cogent Education*, *11*(1). Advance online publication. DOI: 10.1080/2331186x.2024.2330235

Aithal, P. S., Prabhu, S., & Aithal, S. (2024). Future of higher education through technology prediction and forecasting. Poornaprajna International Journal of Management, Education, and Social Science (PIJMESS), 1(1), 01-50.

Akçapınar, G., & Sidan, E. (2024). AI chatbots in programming education: Guiding success or encouraging plagiarism. *Discover Artificial Intelligence*, *4*(1), 87. DOI: 10.1007/s44163-024-00203-7

Alaboudi, A., & LaToza, T. D. (2023). What constitutes debugging? An exploratory study of debugging episodes. *Empirical Software Engineering*, *28*(5), 117.

Alam, A., & Mohanty, A. (2023b). Design, development, and implementation of software engineering virtual laboratory: A boon to computer science and engineering (CSE) education during Covid-19 pandemic. In *Proceedings of third international conference on sustainable expert systems: ICSES 2022* (pp. 1-20). Singapore: Springer Nature Singapore.

Alam, A. (2022, March). Educational robotics and computer programming in early childhood education: a conceptual framework for assessing elementary school students' computational thinking for designing powerful educational scenarios. In *2022 International Conference on Smart Technologies and Systems for Next Generation Computing (ICSTSN)* (pp. 1-7). IEEE.

Alam, A., & Mohanty, A. (2023a). Discerning the application of virtual laboratory in curriculum transaction of software engineering lab course from the lens of critical pedagogy. In *Sentiment analysis and deep learning* [Singapore: Springer Nature Singapore.]. *Proceedings of ICSADL, 2022*, 53–68.

Alanazi, M., Soh, B., Samra, H., & Li, A. (2025). PyChatAI: Enhancing Python Programming Skills—An Empirical Study of a Smart Learning System. *Computers*, *14*(5). Advance online publication. DOI: 10.3390/computers14050158

Al-Azawei, A., & Alshahrani, S. (2022). The Role of Adaptive Learning Technologies in Enhancing Programming Education. *Education and Information Technologies*, *27*(9), 12451–12468.

Albakri, M., & Wood-Harper, A. T. (2025). Contextualisation of Digital Education. In *Innovation Strategy for the Future of Teaching and Learning: Addressing the Digital Education Paradox* (pp. 35–58). Springer Nature Switzerland.

Alenezi, M., Akour, M., & Alfawzan, L. (2024). Evolving Microcredential Strategies for Enhancing Employability: Employer and Student Perspectives. *Education Sciences*, *14*(12), 1–24. DOI: 10.3390/educsci14121307

Alharthi, M. (2024). Voices in Crisis: High-Salience Stakeholders' Experiences and Perceptions of Communication During Educational Management Crisis. Studies in Educational Management (SEM), 16.

Al-Hunaiyyan, A. A., Bimba, A. T., & Alsharhan, S. (2020). A Cognitive Knowledge-based Model for an Academic Adaptive e-Advising System. *Interdisciplinary Journal of Information, Knowledge, and Management, 15*, 247–263. DOI: 10.28945/4633

Alsmadi, H., Kandasamy, G., Kafri, A. A., & Zahirah, K. F. (2024). Empowering computing students through multidisciplinary project based learning (PBL): Creating meaningful differences in the real world. *Social Sciences & Humanities Open, 10*, 101180. Advance online publication. DOI: 10.1016/j.ssaho.2024.101180

Alvarez, C., Samary, M. M., & Wise, A. F. (2023). Modularization for Mastery Learning in Cs1: A 4-Year Action Research Study. *Journal of Computing in Higher Education*, •••, 1–44. DOI: 10.1007/s12528-023-09366-1 PMID: 37359038

Amiri, S. M. H. (2025). Project-Based Learning Pedagogy: Bridging Theory and Practice for Real-World Impact. Available at *SSRN* 5333995.

Andrei, O., & Nabi, S. W. (2023). On Students' Experiences with Algorithm Tracing using Pair Programming. *Proceedings of the 2023 ACM Conference on International Computing Education Research* - Volume 2. DOI: 10.1145/3568812.3603477

Annuš, N. (2025). Investigation of Generative AI Adoption in IT-Focused Vocational Secondary School Programming Education. *Education Sciences, 15*(9). Advance online publication. DOI: 10.3390/educsci15091152

Anthraper, N., Javiya, P., Iluru, S., Chen, L. K., & Kleinsmith, A. (2024). PeerConnect: Co-Designing a Peer-Mentoring Support System with Computing Transfer Students. *Extended Abstracts of the CHI Conference on Human Factors in Computing Systems*. https://doi.org/DOI: 10.1145/3613905.3650936

Apiola, M., López-Pernas, S., & Saqr, M. (2022). The evolving themes of Computing Education Research: Trends, topic models, and emerging research. SSRN *Electronic Journal*. DOI: 10.2139/ssrn.4190583

Araujo, L., Lopez-Ostenero, F., Plaza, L., & Martinez-Romo, J. (2025). Automated Formative Feedback for Algorithm and Data Structure Self-Assessment. *Electronics (Basel), 14*(5), 1034. DOI: 10.3390/electronics14051034

Arawjo, I., & Mogos, A. (2021). Intercultural Computing Education: Toward Justice Across Difference. *ACM Transactions on Computing Education, 21*(4), 1–33. DOI: 10.1145/3458037

Archambault, S. G., Ramachandran, S., Acosta, E., & Fu, S. (2024). Ethical Dimensions of Algorithmic Literacy for College Students: Case Studies and Cross-Disciplinary Connections. *Journal of Academic Librarianship, 50*(3), 1–20. DOI: 10.1016/j.acalib.2024.102865

Ardito, C. G. (2024). Generative AI Detection in Higher Education Assessments. *New Directions for Teaching and Learning*. Advance online publication. DOI: 10.1002/tl.20624

Aria, M., & Cuccurullo, C. (2017). Bibliometrix: An R-tool for comprehensive science mapping analysis. *Journal of Informetrics*, *11*(4), 959–975. DOI: 10.1016/j.joi.2017.08.007

Arias, E., Barba-Sánchez, V., Carrión, C., & Casado, R. (2018). Enhancing Entrepreneurship education in a Master's Degree in Computer Engineering: A Project-Based Learning approach. *Administrative Sciences*, *8*(4), 58. Advance online publication. DOI: 10.3390/admsci8040058

Ariza, J., Restrepo, M., & Hernández, C. (2025). Generative AI in engineering and computing education: A scoping review of empirical studies and educational practices. *IEEE Access : Practical Innovations, Open Solutions*, *13*, 30789–30810. DOI: 10.1109/ACCESS.2025.3541424

Aruleba, K., Sanusi, I. T., Obaido, G., Ogbuokiri, B., & Mienye, I. D. (2025). *Beyond the Prompt: Student Strategies, Ethical Reflections, and Learning with ChatGPT in Computer Science*. Technology, Knowledge and Learning., DOI: 10.1007/s10758-025-09899-7

Asbell-Clarke, J., Ibrahim Dahlstrom-Hakki, Voiklis, J., Attaway, B., Barchas-Lichtenstein, J., Edwards, T., Bardar, E., Robillard, T., Paulson, K., Grover, S., Israel, M., Ke, F., & Weintrop, D. (2024). Including neurodiversity in computational thinking. *Frontiers in Education*, *9*. Advance online publication. DOI: 10.3389/feduc.2024.1358492

Ashlock, J. M., & Tufekci, Z. (2024). Gender Differences in Computing Interest: The Role of Social Constructs in Early Paths. *Computer Science Education*, •••, 1–33. DOI: 10.1080/08993408.2024.2433354

Ashraf, M., Zaman, M., & Ahmed, M. (2020). An intelligent prediction system for educational data mining based on ensemble and filtering approaches. *Procedia Computer Science*, *167*, 1471–1483.

Association for Computing Machinery (ACM). IEEE-Computer Society. (2023). Computer Science Curricula 2023. https://csed.acm.org/wp-content/uploads/2023/03/Version-Beta-v2.pdf

Atta, A., Esmat, M., Amasha, N., Elayat, E., & Elsaid, W. K. (2025). A Smart ChatGPT Mobile Application for Improving C# Programming Skills for Students in Educational Institutions. *Qubahan Academic Journal*, *5*(2), 49–62. DOI: 10.48161/qaj.v5n2a1772

Avram, A. I. (2024). Developing the interest for learning through interdisciplinariness in primary class students. *Studia Universitatis Moldaviae Seria tiin e Ale Educa iei*, *9*(169), 176–182. DOI: 10.59295/sum9(169)2024_26

Aymen, D. I. F., & Zakarya, B. O. U. S. I. O. U. D. (2024). The Influence of Artificial Intelligence on Students' Critical Thinking (Doctoral dissertation, university center of abdalhafid boussouf-MILA).

Azevedo, L., Robles, P., Best, E., & Mallinson, D. J. (2025). Institutional Policies on Artificial Intelligence in Higher Education: Frameworks and Best Practices for Faculty. *New Directions for Adult and Continuing Education*, *2025*(188), 70–78. DOI: 10.1002/ace.70013

Azoulay-Schwartz, R., Hirst, T., & Reches, S. (2024). Academia and Industry Synergy: Addressing Integrity Challenge in Programming Education. *International Conference on Agents and Artificial Intelligence, 3*, 1135–1143. DOI: 10.5220/0012451000003636

Babu, S., & Anbumozhi, A. S, P., N, V., & Kaliamoorthy, V. (2026). Blockchain for Credentialing and Academic Record-Keeping. In J. Moore, S. Gupta, M. Sharma, A. Garg, & H. Josephine V. L (Eds.), *Transforming Education With Data Science in the AI Era* (pp. 407-448). IGI Global Scientific Publishing. DOI: 10.4018/979-8-3373-2185-1.ch014

Baglieri, S. (2022). *Disability Studies and the Inclusive Classroom*. https://doi.org/DOI: 10.4324/9781003138808

Bakri, Y. M. (2025). The Role of Digital Leadership in Cultivating a Supportive Ecosystem for Pedagogical Innovation: A Focus on Trainee Teacher Graduates. In *Digital Leadership for Sustainable Higher Education* (pp. 219–254). IGI Global Scientific Publishing., DOI: 10.4018/979-8-3693-9989-7.ch007

Baltoski, M. (2024). Counting Connections: Exploring Preschool Numeracy, Early Interventions and Parent-Child Relationships (Doctoral dissertation, University of Wollongong).

Banwo, B. O., Navarrete-Burks, L., McGee, S., & McGee-Tekula, R. (2024). Building Bridges in STEM Education: Minoritized Secondary School Student Computer Science Pathways and Experiences. *Education in Science, 14*(8), 831. DOI: 10.3390/educsci14080831

Barambones, J., Moral-Martos, C., De Antonio, A., Imbert, R., Martínez-Normand, L., & Villalba-Mora, E. (2024). ChatGPT for Learning HCI Techniques: A Case Study on Interviews for Personas. *IEEE Transactions on Learning Technologies, 17*, 1486–1501. DOI: 10.1109/TLT.2024.3386095

Barros, B., Conejo, R., Ruiz-Sepulveda, A., & Triguero-Ruiz, F. (2021). I explain, you collaborate, he cheats: An empirical study with social network analysis of study groups in a computer programming subject. *Applied Sciences (Basel, Switzerland), 11*(19), 9328.

Barus, O. P., Hidayanto, A. N., Handri, E. Y., Sensuse, D. I., & Yaiprasert, C. (2025). Shaping Generative AI Governance in Higher Education: Insights from Student Perception. *International Journal of Educational Research Open, 8*, 1–12. DOI: 10.1016/j.ijedro.2025.100452

Basti, T. (2022). Model pendidikan karakter kewirausahaan terintegrasi di perguruan tinggi [An integrated entrepreneurial character education model in higher education]. *Prosiding Seminar Nasional Fakultas Tarbiyah Dan Ilmu Keguruan IAIM Sinjai, 1*, 7–14. DOI: 10.47435/sentikjar.v1i0.824

Baumer, B. S. (2022). Integrating data science ethics into an undergraduate major. *ACM Inroads, 13*(2), 34–41. DOI: 10.1145/3524188

Beerends, S., & Aydin, C. (2021). Negotiating authenticity in technological environments. *Philosophy & Technology, 34*(4), 1665–1685.

Belitz, C., Lee, H., & Nasiar, N.. (2024). Hierarchical dependencies in classroom settings influence algorithmic bias metrics. In *Proceedings of the 14th International Conference on Learning Analytics and Knowledge (LAK 2024)* (pp. 1–10). Association for Computing Machinery. https://doi.org/DOI: 10.1145/3583780

Belland, B. R., Walker, A. E., Kim, N. J., & Lefler, M. (2017). Synthesizing Results From Empirical Research on Computer-Based Scaffolding in STEM Education: A Meta-Analysis. *Review of Educational Research, 87*(2), 309–344. DOI: 10.3102/0034654316670999 PMID: 28344365

Belmar, H. (2022). Review on the teaching of programming and computational thinking in the world. *Frontiers of Computer Science, 4*, 997222.

Benedicenti, L., Blachford, D., Chan, C. W., East, A. L. L., Gelowitz, C. M., Huang, G., Paranjape, R., Petty, S., Yao, J., & Yao, Y. (2013). Multidisciplinary approaches to computing. *Canadian Conference on Electrical and Computer Engineering*, 1–8. DOI: 10.1109/CCECE.2013.6567668

Bernik, A., Radošević, D., & Čep, A. (2025). A Comparative Study of Large Language Models in Programming Education: Accuracy, Efficiency, and Feedback in Student Assignment Grading. *Applied Sciences (Switzerland)*, *15*(18). Advance online publication. DOI: 10.3390/app151810055

Bertram, L. (2020). Digital learning games for mathematics and computer science education: The need for preregistered RCTs, standardized methodology, and advanced technology. *Frontiers in Psychology*, *11*, 2127. PMID: 33178055

Besic, E. (2020). Intersectionality: A pathway towards inclusive education? *Prospects*, *49*(49), 111–122. DOI: 10.1007/s11125-020-09461-6

Bhatnagar, R., & Singh, P. (2023). AI-Assisted Evaluation Systems for Programming Education: Opportunities and Challenges. *International Journal of Artificial Intelligence in Education*, *33*(2), 288–305.

Bhattacharya, P., Joshi, S., Bandyopadhyay, S., & Mittal, R. (2022). Virtual Computer Science Education in India: Challenges and Opportunities. SSRN *Electronic Journal*. https://doi.org/DOI: 10.2139/ssrn.4026251

Bird, K. A., Castleman, B. L., Denning, J. T., Goodman, J., & Lamberton, C. (2023). Are algorithms biased in education? Exploring racial bias in predictive models. *Educational Researcher*, *52*(2), 1–12. DOI: 10.3102/0013189X231157201

Bisson, L., Grindstaff, L., Brazil-Cruz, L., & Barbu Editors, S. (2022). *Uprooting Bias in the Academy Lessons from the Field*. https://library.oapen.org/bitstream/handle/20.500.12657/51948/1/978-3-030-85668-7.pdf#page=36

Boguslawski, S., Deer, R., & Dawson, M. G. (2025). Programming Education and Learner Motivation in the Age of Generative AI: Student and Educator Perspectives. *Information and Learning Science*, *126*(1/2), 91–109. DOI: 10.1108/ILS-10-2023-0163

Bommasani, R., Hudson, D. A., Adeli, E., Altman, R., Arora, S., von Arx, S., Bernstein, M. S., ... (2021). On the opportunities and risks of foundation models. *arXiv*. https://doi.org//arXiv.2108.07258DOI: 10.48550

Bonnette, R., Abramovich, S., Decker, A., & Fabiano, G. A. (2022). Building Ecosystems of Belonging for Neurodiverse Students. *Proceedings of the 53rd ACM Technical Symposium on Computer Science Education* v. 2, 1192–1192. https://doi.org/DOI: 10.1145/3478432.3499182

Börner, K., Chen, C., & Boyack, K. W. (2003). Visualizing knowledge domains. *Annual Review of Information Science & Technology, 37*(1), 179–255. DOI: 10.1002/aris.1440370106

Borsotti, V., Begel, A., & Bjørn, P. (2024). Neurodiversity and the Accessible University: Exploring Organizational Barriers, Access Labor and Opportunities for Change. *PACM on Human-Computer Interaction, 8*(CSCW1). https://doi.org/DOI: 10.1145/3641011

Boudia, C., & Krismadinata, K. (2024). Early insights into SLA with chatGPT: Navigating CS teachers and student perspectives in an opinion-based exploration. *Edelweiss Applied Science and Technology, 8*(5), 648–661. http://dx.doi.org/10.55214/25768484.v8i5.1729

Bozkurt, A., Xiao, J., Farrow, R., Bai, J. Y. H., Nerantzi, C., Moore, S., & Asino, T. I. (2024). The Manifesto for Teaching and Learning in a Time of Generative AI: A Critical Collective Stance to Better Navigate the Future. *Open Praxis, 16*(4), 487–513. DOI: 10.55982/openpraxis.16.4.777

Braverman, H. (1974). *Labor and monopoly capital*. Monthly Review Press.

Bray, A., Devitt, A., Banks, J., & Sanchez Fuentes, S., Marta Sandoval Mena, Katerina Riviou, Byrne, D., Flood, M., Reale, J., & Terrenzio, S. (2023). What next for universal design for learning? A systematic literature review of technology in UDL implementations at second level. *British Journal of Educational Technology, 55*(1). Advance online publication. DOI: 10.1111/bjet.13328

Bringula, R. (2024). ChatGPT in a Programming Course: Benefits and Limitations. *Frontiers in Education, 9*, 1–6. DOI: 10.3389/feduc.2024.1248705

Brown, N., Xie, B., Sarder, E., Fiesler, C., & Wiese, E. S. (2024). Teaching ethics in computing: A systematic literature review of ACM computer science education publications. *ACM Transactions on Computing Education, 24*(1), 1–29. DOI: 10.1145/3610217

Bubenkova, L., & Pietrikova, E. (2024). Game development: Enhancing creativity and independent creation in university course. In Proceedings of the 5th International Computer Programming Education Conference (ICPEC 2024) (pp. 12–1). Schloss Dagstuhl–Leibniz-Zentrum für Informatik. https://doi.org/DOI: 10.4230/OASIcs.ICPEC.2024.12

Buolamwini, J., & Gebru, T. (2018). Gender shades: Intersectional accuracy disparities in commercial gender classification. *Proceedings of the 1st Conference on Fairness, Accountability and Transparency (FAT*)* (pp. 77–91). ACM. Available from https://proceedings.mlr.press/v81/buolamwini18a.html

Caeli, E. N., & Yadav, A. (2020). Unplugged approaches to computational thinking: A historical perspective. *TechTrends*, *64*(1), 29–36.

Çakiroğlu, Ü., & Er, B. (2023). A Model to Develop Activities for Teaching Programming Through Metacognitive Strategies. *Thinking Skills and Creativity*, *48*, 1–11. DOI: 10.1016/j.tsc.2023.101279

Caratozzolo, P., Rosas-Melendez, S., & Ortiz-Alvarado, C. (2021). Active learning approaches for sustainable energy engineering education. In *Proceedings of the 2021 IEEE Green Technologies Conference (GreenTech)* (pp. 251–258). IEEE. https://doi.org/DOI: 10.1109/GreenTech48523.2021.00048

CAST. (2024). *Universal Design for Learning*. CAST. https://www.cast.org/what-we-do/universal-design-for-learning/

Century, J., & Weisberg, L. (2023). Growing Knowledge about Using Culturally Responsive Pedagogy and Universal Design for Learning in Computer Science Education. *2023 Conference on Research in Equitable and Sustained Participation in Engineering, Computing, and Technology (RESPECT)*. https://doi.org/DOI: 10.1109/RESPECT60069.2023.00013

Chakraborty, T. (2018). Role of interdisciplinarity in computer sciences: Quantification, impact and life trajectory. *Scientometrics*, *114*(3), 1011–1029. DOI: 10.1007/S11192-017-2628-Z

Chan, C., & Hu, W. (2023). Students' voices on generative AI: Perceptions, benefits, and challenges in higher education. *International Journal of Educational Technology in Higher Education, 20*, 43. Advance online publication. DOI: 10.1186/s41239-023-00411-8

Chang, H., Ngunjiri, F., & Hernandez, K. A. C. (2013). *Collaborative Autoethnography*. Left Coast Press. https://books.google.com.ph/books?id=-yLHAGZ3VeAC

Chang, C. S., Chung, C. H., & Chang, J. A. (2020). Influence of problem-based learning games on effective computer programming learning in higher education. *Educational Technology Research and Development*, *68*(5), 2615–2634.

Charteris, J., Anderson, J., & Page, A. (2021). Psychological safety in innovative learning environments: Planning for inclusive spaces. *International Journal of Inclusive Education*, *28*(5), 1–17. DOI: 10.1080/13603116.2021.1974108

Chasokela, D., & Mangena, N. (2025). The Future of Learning in the Digital Age. In *Insights into International Higher Education Leadership and the Skills Gap* (pp. 471–500). IGI Global., DOI: 10.4018/979-8-3693-3443-0.ch018

Chen, H.-M., Nguyen, B.-A., & Dow, C.-R. (2022). Code-Quality Evaluation Scheme for Assessment of Student Contributions to Programming Projects. *Journal of Systems and Software*, *188*, 1–18. DOI: 10.1016/j.jss.2022.111273

Chen, L., Chen, P., & Lin, Z. (2020). Artificial intelligence in education: A review. *IEEE Access : Practical Innovations, Open Solutions*, *8*, 75264–75278. DOI: 10.1109/ACCESS.2020.2988510

Chen, L., Gillan, J., Decker, M., Eteffa, E., Marzan, A., Thai, J., & Jewett, S. (2023). Embedding Digital Data Storytelling in Introductory Data Science Course: An Inter-Institutional Transdisciplinary Pilot Study. *Journal of Problem Based Learning in Higher Education*, *11*(2), 126–152. DOI: 10.54337/ojs.jpblhe.v11i2.7767

Chen, P., Yang, D., Metwally, A. H. S., Lavonen, J., & Wang, X. (2023). Fostering computational thinking through unplugged activities: A systematic literature review and meta-analysis. *International Journal of STEM Education*, *10*(1), 47.

Cheryan, S., Ziegler, S. A., Montoya, A. K., & Jiang, L. (2017). Why Are Some STEM Fields More Gender Balanced Than Others? *Psychological Bulletin*, *143*(1), 1–35. DOI: 10.1037/bul0000052 PMID: 27732018

Chevalier, M., Giang, C., El-Hamamsy, L., Bonnet, E., Papaspyros, V., Pellet, J.-P., & Mondada, F. (2022). The Role of Feedback and Guidance as Intervention Methods to Foster Computational Thinking in Educational Robotics Learning Activities for Primary School. *Computers & Education*, *180*, 1–15. DOI: 10.1016/j.compedu.2022.104431

Ching, G. S., Chao, P. C., del Castillo, F., Gungon, J. L., Trajera, S. M., Roberts, A., & Zuo, Y. (2024, May). Check for updates Teacher Fatigue, Social-Emotional Learning, Online Teaching Engagement and Facilitation: Experiences of Teachers during COVID-19. In Learning Technology for Education Challenges: 12th International Workshop, LTEC 2024, Kaohsiung, Taiwan, July 29–August 1, 2024 [). Springer Nature.]. *Proceedings, 2082*, 266.

Chiramba, O., & Agbaje, O. (2024). Promoting institutional resilience through blended learning during and post-covid-19 in South African universities. *Journal of Educational Studies, 2024*(si2), 12–26. DOI: 10.59915/jes.2024.si2.1

Choi, H., Jovanovic, J., Poquet, O., Brooks, C., Joksimović, S., & Williams, J. J. (2023). The Benefit of Reflection Prompts for Encouraging Learning with Hints in an Online Programming Course. *The Internet and Higher Education*, *58*, 1–10. DOI: 10.1016/j.iheduc.2023.100903

Choi, K. S. (2014). A Comparative Analysis of Different Gender Pair Combinations in Pair Programming. *Behaviour & Information Technology*, *34*(8), 825–837. DOI: 10.1080/0144929x.2014.937460

Choi, S., Jang, Y., & Kim, H. (2023). Influence of pedagogical beliefs and perceived trust on teachers' acceptance of educational artificial intelligence tools. *International Journal of Human-Computer Interaction*, *39*(4), 910–922.

Chrysafiadi, K., & Virvou, M. (2023). Evaluating the User's Experience, Adaptivity and Learning Outcomes of a Fuzzy-Based Intelligent Tutoring System for Computer Programming for Academic Students in Greece. *Education and Information Technologies*, *28*, 6453–6483.

Cochran-Smith, M., & Lytle, S. L. (2009). *Inquiry as Stance: Practitioner Research for the Next Generation*. Teachers College Press. https://eric.ed.gov/?id=ED527594

Conklin, S., Ovarzun, B., Kim, S., & Dikkers, A. G. (2024). Exploring the Relationships of Learners and Instructors in Online Courses. *Online Learning : the Official Journal of the Online Learning Consortium*, *28*(4), 257–281. DOI: 10.24059/olj.v28i4.3934

Córdova-Esparza, D.-M., Romero-González, J.-A., Córdova-Esparza, K.-E., Terven, J., & López-Martínez, R.-E. (2024). Active Learning Strategies in Computer Science Education: A Systematic Review. *Multimodal Technologies and Interaction*, *8*(6), 1–20. DOI: 10.3390/mti8060050

Cowan, B., Watanobe, Y., & Shirafuji, A. (2023). *Enhancing Programming Learning with LLMs: Prompt Engineering and Flipped Interaction*. 10–16. DOI: 10.1145/3634814.3634816

Cri an, E. L., Beleiu, I. N., Salan ă, I., Bordean, O. N., & Bunduchi, R. (2023). Embedding entrepreneurship education in non-business courses: A systematic review and guidelines for practice. *Management Learning*, *55*(4), 553–575. DOI: 10.1177/13505076231169594

Cronin, K. S. (2024). The Intentional Pursuit of Purpose: Nurturing Students' Authentic Motivation for Practicing Law. Legal Writing. *J. Legal Writing Inst.*, *28*, 159.

Crowston, K., & Bolici, F. (2025). Deskilling and upskilling with AI Systems. *nformation Research an International Electronic Journal, 30*(iConf), 1009-1023. https://doi.org/DOI: 10.47989/ir30iconf47143

Crow, T., Luxton-Reilly, A., & Wuensche, B. (2018). Intelligent tutoring systems for programming education: a systematic review. *Proceedings of the 20th Australasian Computing Education Conference*, 53–62. DOI: 10.1145/3160489.3160492

Daby-Seesaram, A., Škardová, K., & Genet, M. (2025). Finite element neural network interpolation: Part II—hybridisation with the proper generalised decomposition for non-linear surrogate modelling. *Computational Mechanics*, •••, 1–26.

Dai, Y., Lin, Z., Liu, A., & Wang, W. (2024). An embodied, analogical and disruptive approach of AI pedagogy in upper elementary education: An experimental study. *British Journal of Educational Technology*, *55*(1), 417–434.

Damaševičius, R. (2024). ChatGPT-Supported Student Assessment – Can we rely on it? *Journal of Research in Innovative Teaching & Learning*, *17*(2), 414–416. DOI: 10.1108/JRIT-09-2024-195

Davis, K., Twarek, B., Becton-Consuegra, D., & Koshy, S. (2022). The Needs of K-12 Computer Science Educators towards Building an Inclusive Classroom. *Proceedings of the 53rd ACM Technical Symposium on Computer Science Education* V. 2. https://doi.org/DOI: 10.1145/3478432.3499229

DeCook, J. R. (2020). A [White] Cyborg's Manifesto: The overwhelmingly Western ideology driving technofeminist theory. *Media, Culture &amp. Society*, *43*(6), 1158–1167. DOI: 10.1177/0163443720957891

DeDecker, S. (2025). The Impact of Instructors' Assessment Design on Undergraduate Student Motivation and Learning Approach within STEM Problem-Solving Learning Environments.

DeMatthews, D. E., Serafini, A., & Watson, T. N. (2021). Leading inclusive schools: Principal perceptions, practices, and challenges to meaningful change. *Educational Administration Quarterly*, *57*(1), 3–48. DOI: 10.1177/0013161x20913897

Detmer, R., Li, C., Dong, Z., & Hankins, J. (2010). Incorporating Real-World Projects in Teaching Computer Science Courses. *Proceedings of the 48th annual ACM Southeast Conference*. https://doi.org/DOI: 10.1145/1900008.1900042

Dewsbury, B. M., Swanson, H. J., Moseman-Valtierra, S., & Caulkins, J. (2022). Inclusive and active pedagogies reduce academic outcome gaps and improve long-term performance. *PLoS One*, *17*(6), e0268620. DOI: 10.1371/journal.pone.0268620 PMID: 35704639

Dickey, E., Bejarano, A., & Garg, C. (2024). AI-Lab: A Framework for Introducing Generative Artificial Intelligence Tools in Computer Programming Courses. *SN Computer Science*, *5*(6), 720. DOI: 10.1007/s42979-024-03074-y

Dirzyte, A., Perminas, A., Kaminskis, L., Žebrauskas, G., Sederevičiūtė-Pačiauskienė, Ž., Šliogerienė, J., Suchanova, J., Rimašiūtė-Knabikienė, R., Patapas, A., & Gajdosikiene, I. (2023). Factors contributing to dropping out of adults' programming e-learning. *Heliyon*, *9*(12), e22113. DOI: 10.1016/j.heliyon.2023.e22113 PMID: 38107286

Doboli, S., Tang, W., Ramnath, R., Impagliazzo, J., VanEpps, T., Agarwal, A., Romero, R., & Currie, E. H. (2010). Models of entrepreneurship education and its role in increasing creativity, innovation and leadership in computer science and engineering students. *2021 IEEE Frontiers in Education Conference (FIE)*, *15*, F1B-4. DOI: 10.1109/fie.2010.5673380

Donisch, L., Schacht, S., & Lanquillon, C. (2024). Inference optimizations for large language models: Effects, challenges, and practical considerations. arXiv preprint arXiv:2408.03130.

Donthu, N., Kumar, S., Mukherjee, D., Pandey, N., & Lim, W. M. (2021). How to conduct a bibliometric analysis: An overview and guidelines. *Journal of Business Research*, *133*, 285–296. DOI: 10.1016/j.jbusres.2021.04.070

Dost, G. (2024). Students' Perspectives on the 'STEM Belonging' Concept at A-Level, Undergraduate, and Postgraduate Levels: An Examination of Gender and Ethnicity in Student Descriptions. *International Journal of STEM Education*, *11*(1), 1–33. DOI: 10.1186/s40594-024-00472-9

Douville, H. (2025). Doing better rather than promising more: A basic principle applicable to both climate modelling and climate policies. *PLOS Climate*, *4*(1), e0000466.

Doyle, T., & Zakrajsek, T. D. (2023). *Learner-Centered Teaching*. https://doi.org/ DOI: 10.4324/9781003445630

Druga, S., Otero, N., & Ko, A. J. (2022, July). The landscape of teaching resources for AI education. In *Proceedings of the 27th ACM Conference on on Innovation and Technology in Computer Science Education* Vol. 1 (pp. 96-102).

Du, B., & Yang, X. (2017). The effect of team-based learning on conventional pathology education to improve students' mastery of pathology. *International Journal of Higher Education*, *6*(3), 12–20. DOI: 10.5430/ijhe.v6n3p12

Dudyrev, F., & Maksimenkova, O. (2020). Training simulators in vocational education: pedagogical and technological aspects. *Voprosy obrazovaniya/Educational Studies Moscow*, (3), 255-276.

Dunder, N., Lundborg, S., Wong, J., & Viberg, O. (2024). Kattis vs ChatGPT: Assessment and Evaluation of Programming Tasks in the Age of Artificial Intelligence. *Proceedings of the 14th Learning Analytics and Knowledge Conference*. DOI: 10.1145/3636555.3636882

Edwards, B. I., Abuhassna, H., Olugbade, D., Ojo, O. A., & Jaafar Wan Yahaya, W. (Eds.). (2025). *Generators, bots, and tutors: Creative approaches to human–AI synergy in classroom instruction*. IGI Global., DOI: 10.4018/979-8-3373-0847-0

Edwards, B. I., Olugbade, D., & Ojo, O. A. (2024). Facilitating cognitive load management and improved learning outcomes and attitudes in middle school technology and vocational education through AI chatbot. *Journal of Technical Education and Training*, *16*(3), 114–131. DOI: 10.30880/jtet.2024.16.03.009

Efendi, F. K. (2021). Efektivitas model pembelajaran terpadu tipe webbed berbantuan media teknologi untuk meningkatkan kualitas pembelajaran IPS tema makanan sehat murid sekolah dasar gugus 29 campaga loe kabupaten bantaeng [The effectiveness of the webbed type integrated learning model assisted by technology media to improve the quality of social studies learning on the theme of healthy food for elementary school students in cluster 29 campaga loe bantaeng district]. *Journal of Teacher Education*, *2*(2), 58–65. DOI: 10.3100/jote.v2i2.1464

El Koshiry, A., Eliwa, E., Abd El-Hafeez, T., & Shams, M. Y. (2023). Unlocking the Power of Blockchain in Education: An Overview of Innovations and Outcomes. *Blockchain: Research and Applications*, *4*(4), 1–19. DOI: 10.1016/j.bcra.2023.100165

Elamin, M. O. I. (2024). AI through the ages: Unlocking key opportunities and navigating challenges in the history and future of artificial intelligence. *International Journal of Religion*, *5*(12), 1152–1166.

El-Hamamsy, L., Bruno, B., Audrin, C., Chevalier, M., Avry, S., Zufferey, J. D., & Mondada, F. (2023). How Are Primary School Computer Science Curricular Reforms Contributing to Equity? Impact on Student Learning, Perception of the Discipline, and Gender Gaps. *International Journal of STEM Education, 10*(1), 1–43. DOI: 10.1186/s40594-023-00438-3

El-Hamamsy, L., Chessel-Lazzarotto, F., Bruno, B., Roy, D., Cahlikova, T., Chevalier, M., & Mondada, F. (2021). A computer science and robotics integration model for primary school: Evaluation of a large-scale in-service K-4 teacher-training program. *Education and Information Technologies, 26*(3), 2445–2475. PMID: 33162777

Ellis, H. J. C., Hislop, G. W., Goldweber, M., Rebelsky, S., Pearce, J., Ordonez, P., & Gordon, N. (2024). Computing for Social Good in Education. *ACM Inroads, 15*(4), 47–57. DOI: 10.1145/3699719

Erwin, J. C. (2024). *The Classroom of Choice: 100+ Strategies to Reach and Teach Every Learner*. ASCD.

Eswaran, U. (2024). Project-based learning: Fostering collaboration, creativity, and critical thinking. In *Enhancing education with intelligent systems and data-driven instruction* (pp. 23–43). IGI Global Scientific Publishing.

European Institute for Gender Equality. (2024). *Gender Equality Index 2024 – Sustaining Momentum on a Fragile Path*. Publications Office of the European Union., DOI: 10.2839/9523460

Eurostat. (2023). *Men Represented 84% of People Employed with an ICT Education*. https://ec.europa.eu/eurostat/web/products-eurostat-news/w/ddn-20231016-1

Eurostat. (2024). *Women Make Up 52% of Science & Technology Employment*. https://ec.europa.eu/eurostat/web/products-eurostat-news/w/ddn-20240613-2

Everwijn, S. E. M., Bomers, G. B. J., & Knubben, J. A. (1993). Ability- or competence-based education: Bridging the gap between knowledge acquisition and ability to apply. *Higher Education, 25*(4), 425–438. DOI: 10.1007/BF01383845

Fagerlund, J., Häkkinen, P., Vesisenaho, M., & Viiri, J. (2021). Computational thinking in programming with Scratch in primary schools: A systematic review. *Computer Applications in Engineering Education, 29*(1), 12–28.

Fan, G., Liu, D., Zhang, R., & Pan, L. (2025). The Impact of AI-Assisted Pair Programming on Student Motivation, Programming Anxiety, Collaborative Learning, and Programming Performance: A Comparative Study with Traditional Pair Programming and Individual Approaches. *International Journal of STEM Education, 12*(1), 1–17. DOI: 10.1186/s40594-025-00537-3

Ferguson, T., & Roofe, C. G. (2020). SDG 4 in higher education: Challenges and opportunities. *International Journal of Sustainability in Higher Education*, *21*(5), 959–975. DOI: 10.1108/ijshe-12-2019-0353

Ferraioli, V., Mondada, F., & Abou-Khalil, V. (2025). Reframing Computational Thinking for AI Education. https://doi.org/DOI: 10.1007/9

Feuerriegel, S., Hartmann, J., Janiesch, C., & Zschech, P. (2024). Generative AI. *Business & Information Systems Engineering*, *66*, 111–126. DOI: 10.1007/s12599-023-00834-7

Fietta, V., Navarin, N., Monaro, M., & Gaggi, O. (2023). Women and Gender Disparities in Computer Science: A Case Study at the University of Padua. *Proceedings of the 2023 ACM Conference on Information Technology for Social Good*. https://doi.org/DOI: 10.1145/3582515.3609521

Fincher, S. A., Blikstein, P., Ko, A. J., Haden, P., Haden, P., Tenenberg, J., Margulieux, L. E., Robins, A. V., Shephard, K., Loui, M. C., Robins, A. V., Krishnamurthi, S., Lancaster, T., Falkner, K., & Lewis, C. M. (2019). *The Cambridge Handbook of Computing Education Research*. Cambridge University Press. DOI: 10.1017/9781108654555

Fincher, S., Jeuring, J., Miller, C. S., Donaldson, P., Du Boulay, B., Hauswirth, M., & Petersen, A. (2020). Notional machines in computing education: The education of attention. In *Proceedings of the working group reports on innovation and technology in computer science education* (pp. 21-50).

Fisher, A., & Margolis, J. (2003). Unlocking the Clubhouse: Women in Computing. *ACM SIGCSE Bulletin*, *35*(1). Advance online publication. DOI: 10.1145/792548.611896

Fitriya, R. L., Akbar, M. F., Mukhlisa, A., Putri, D. D., & Gunawan, R. N. (2025). Digital Education and Curriculum Design: A Scientometric Analysis (2005–2025). *Journal of Technological Pedagogy and Educational Development*, *2*(2), 1–11.

Flechais, I., & Chalhoub, G. (2023). Practical cybersecurity ethics: Mapping CyBOK to ethical concerns. *ACM Computing Surveys*, *56*(4), 1–28. DOI: 10.1145/3595312

Fleming, P. (2021). *Dark academia: How universities die*. Pluto Books.

Floridi, L., & Cowls, J. (2019). A unified framework of five principles for AI in society. *Harvard Data Science Review*, *1*(1). Advance online publication. DOI: 10.1162/99608f92.8cd550d1

Fodouop Kouam, A. W. (2024). The Effectiveness of Intelligent Tutoring Systems (ITS) in Supporting Students with Varying Levels of Programming Experience. *Discover Education*, *3*, 278.

Fogarty, R. J., & Pete, B. M. (2009). How to integrate the curricula. Corwin Press. http://us.corwin.com/en-us/nam/how-to-integratethe-curricula/book229128

Forbes. (2024). *Women in Tech Stats: How the Industry Can Provide Equal Opportunities*. https://www.forbes.com/sites/cherylrobinson/2024/06/18/women-in-tech-stats-how-the-industry-can-provide-equal-opportunities/

Fovet, F. (2020). Universal Design for Learning as a Tool for Inclusion in the Higher Education Classroom: Tips for the Next Decade of Implementation. *Education Journal*, *9*(6), 163. DOI: 10.11648/j.edu.20200906.13

Franco, J. F., da Cruz, S. R., & de Deus Lopes, R. (2006). Computer graphics, interactive technologies and collaborative learning synergy supporting individuals' skills development. In *ACM SIGGRAPH 2006 Educators Program* (pp. 42–es). ACM. https://doi.org/DOI: 10.1145/1179295.1179338

Frankford, E., Sauerwein, C., Bassner, P., Krusche, S., & Breu, R. (2024). AI-Tutoring in Software Engineering Education Experiences with Large Language Models in Programming Assessments. *Proceedings - International Conference on Software Engineering*, 309–319. DOI: 10.1145/3639474.3640061

Franklin, D., Denny, P., Gonzalez-Maldonado, D. A., & Tran, M. (2025). *Generative AI in Computer Science Education: Challenges and Opportunities*. Cambridge University Press., DOI, DOI: 10.1017/9781009581738

Friend, M., Mcgill, M., & Reinking, A. (2022, November). Solve this! K-12 CS education teachers' problems of practice. In Proceedings of the 22nd Koli Calling International Conference on Computing Education Research (pp. 1-13).

Froyd, J. E., Wankat, P. C., & Smith, K. A. (2012). Five major shifts in 100 years of engineering education. *Proceedings of the IEEE, 100*(Special Centennial Issue), 1344–1360. https://doi.org/DOI: 10.1109/JPROC.2012.2190167

Fullan, M. (2013). *Stratosphere: Integrating technology, pedagogy, and change knowledge*. Pearson Education.

Gabela, J. G. F., & Retscher, G. (2023). Interdisciplinary approach to curricula development in geomatics education: erasmus+ lbs2its project. *ISPRS Annals of the Photogrammetry, Remote Sensing and Spatial Information Sciences*, X-5/W1-2023, 19–26. DOI: 10.5194/isprs-annals-x-5-w1-2023-19-2023

Gale, L., Bhushan, P., Eidnani, S., Graham, L., Harrison, M., McKay-Brown, L., Pande, R., Shreeraman, S., & Sivashunmugam, C. (2022). Overcoming barriers to inclusion in education in India: A scoping review. *Social Sciences & Humanities Open*, *5*(1), 100237. DOI: 10.1016/j.ssaho.2021.100237

Galpaya, H., & Zainudeen, A. (2022). Gender and Digital Access Gaps and Barriers in Asia: But What About After Access? *LIRNEasia*. http://hdl.handle.net/10625/61914

Gamage, K. A. A., & Dehideniya, S. C. P. (2025). Unlocking Career Potential: How Micro-Credentials Are Revolutionising Higher Education and Lifelong Learning. *Education Sciences*, *15*(5), 1–18. DOI: 10.3390/educsci15050525

Gambo, I., Abegunde, F.-J., Gambo, O., Ogundokun, R. O., Babatunde, A. N., & Lee, C.-C. (2025). GRAD-AI: An Automated Grading Tool for Code Assessment and Feedback in Programming Course. *Education and Information Technologies*, *30*(7), 9859–9899. DOI: 10.1007/s10639-024-13218-5

Gamusa, E. V., Sim, M. J. C., Medina, J. B., Acut, D. P., Garcia, M. B., & Lahby, M. (2025). From Chalkboards to Chatbots: The Role of Generative AI in Philippine Teacher Education Assessment. In *Innovative Educational Assessment with Generative AI: Opportunities, Challenges, and Practical Case Studies* (Vol. 70, pp. 245-274). Springer Nature. https://doi.org/DOI: 10.1007/978-3-032-05306-0_12

Gandhi, A., & Muldner, K. (2025). Beyond verbal self-explanations: Student annotations of a code-tracing solution produced by ChatGPT. *British Journal of Educational Technology*. Advance online publication. DOI: 10.1111/bjet.13600

Gantalao, L. C., Calzada, J. G. D., Capuyan, D. L., Lumantas, B. C., Acut, D. P., & Garcia, M. B. (2025). Equipping the Next Generation of Technicians: Navigating School Infrastructure and Technical Knowledge in the Age of AI Integration. In *Pitfalls of AI Integration in Education: Skill Obsolescence, Misuse, and Bias*. IGI Global., DOI: 10.4018/979-8-3373-0122-8.ch009

Garcia, M. B., & Revano, T. F., Jr. (2021). Assessing the Role of Python Programming Gamified Course on Students' Knowledge, Skills Performance, Attitude, and Self-Efficacy. *2021 IEEE 13th International Conference on Humanoid, Nanotechnology, Information Technology, Communication and Control, Environment and Management (HNICEM)*. https://doi.org/DOI: 10.1109/HNICEM54116.2021.9731935

Garcia, M. B., Revano, T. F., Jr., Maaliw, R. R., III, Lagrazon, P. G. G., Valderama, A. M. C., Happonen, A., . . . Yilmaz, R. (2023). Exploring Student Preference Between AI-Powered ChatGPT and Human-Curated Stack Overflow in Resolving Programming Problems and Queries. *2023 IEEE 15th International Conference on Humanoid, Nanotechnology, Information Technology, Communication and Control, Environment and Management (HNICEM)*. DOI: 10.1109/HNICEM60674.2023.10589162

García-Holgado, A., Soledad, C., Silveira, I. F., & García-Peñalvo, F. J. (2022). A Case Study in Brazil and Spain about the Students' Perception of the Gender Gap in Computing. *International Journal of Engineering Education*, *38*(3), 663–672. https://www.researchgate.net/publication/360912221_A_Case_Study_in_Brazil_and_Spain_about_the_Students%27_Perception_of_the_Gender_Gap_in_Computing

Garcia, M. B. (2021). Cooperative learning in computer programming: A quasi-experimental evaluation of Jigsaw teaching strategy with novice programmers. *Education and Information Technologies*, *26*(4), 4839–4856.

Garcia, M. B. (2021). Cooperative Learning in Computer Programming: A Quasi-Experimental Evaluation of Jigsaw Teaching Strategy with Novice Programmers. *Education and Information Technologies*, *26*(4), 4839–4856. DOI: 10.1007/s10639-021-10502-6

Garcia, M. B. (2023). Facilitating Group Learning Using an Apprenticeship Model: Which Master is More Effective in Programming Instruction? *Journal of Educational Computing Research*, *61*(6), 1207–1231. DOI: 10.1177/07356331231170382

Garcia, M. B. (2023b). Fostering an Innovation Culture in the Education Sector: A Scoping Review and Bibliometric Analysis of Hackathon Research. *Innovative Higher Education*, *48*(4), 739–762. DOI: 10.1007/s10755-023-09651-y PMID: 37361114

Garcia, M. B. (2024). Profiling the skill mastery of introductory programming students: A cognitive diagnostic modeling approach. *Education and Information Technologies*, *30*, 6455–6481. DOI: 10.1007/s10639-024-13039-6

Garcia, M. B. (2025). Teaching and Learning Computer Programming Using ChatGPT: A Rapid Review of Literature Amid the Rise of Generative AI Technologies. *Education and Information Technologies*, *30*, 16721–16745. DOI: 10.1007/s10639-025-13452-5

Garcia, M. B. (2025a). Self-Coded Digital Portfolios as an Authentic Project-Based Learning Assessment in Computing Education: Evidence from a Web Design and Development Course. *Education Sciences*, *15*(9), 1150. DOI: 10.3390/educsci15091150

Garcia, M. B., Yousef, A. M. F., Pereira de Almeida, R. P., Arif, Y. M., Happonen, A., & Barber, W. (2023). Teaching Physical Fitness and Exercise Using Computer-Assisted Instruction: A School-Based Public Health Intervention. In Garcia, M. B., Lopez Cabrera, M. V., & de Almeida, R. P. P. (Eds.), *Handbook of Research on Instructional Technologies in Health Education and Allied Disciplines* (pp. 177–195). IGI Global Scientific Publishing., DOI: 10.4018/978-1-6684-7164-7.ch008

Garcia, R., Morreale, P., Verdi, G., Garcia, H., Noa, G. J., Madsen, S. P., & Burnett, M. (2024). The Matchmaker Inclusive Design Curriculum: A Faculty-Enabling Curriculum to Teach Inclusive Design Throughout Undergraduate CS. *Proceedings of the CHI Conference on Human Factors in Computing Systems.* https://doi.org/ DOI: 10.1145/3613904.3642475

Gill, S. S., Wu, H., Patros, P., Ottaviani, C., Arora, P., Pujol, V. C., & Buyya, R. (2024). Modern Computing: Vision and Challenges. *Telematics and Informatics Reports*, *13*, 1–38. DOI: 10.1016/j.teler.2024.100116

Gleeson, M. (2024). Exploring the Use of Generative AI in Computer Science Education in a Technological University in Ireland. *European Journal of Open. Distance and E-Learning*, *26*(1), 107–118. DOI: 10.2478/eurodl-2025-0004

Goetze, T. S. (2023). Integrating ethics into computer science education: Multi-, inter-, and transdisciplinary approaches. In *Proceedings of the 54th ACM Technical Symposium on Computer Science Education (SIGCSE '23)* (pp. 645–651). Association for Computing Machinery. https://doi.org/DOI: 10.1145/3545945.3569797

Goetze, T. S. (2023). Integrating Ethics into Computer Science Education: Multi-, Inter-, and Transdisciplinary Approaches. *Proceedings of the 54th ACM Technical Symposium on Computer Science Education* V. 1. https://doi.org/DOI: 10.1145/3545945.3569792

Goldan, J. Hoffmann, L., & Schwab, S. (2021). A Matter of Resources? – Students' Academic Self-Concept, Social Inclusion and School Well-being in Inclusive Education. *Emerald Publishing Limited EBooks*, 89–100. https://doi.org/DOI: 10.1108/s1479-363620210000015008

Goode, J., Skorodinsky, M., Hubbard, J., & Hook, J. (2020). *Article 162 Citation. 4*. https://doi.org/DOI: 10.3389/feduc.2019.00162

Goode, J., Ivey, A., Johnson, S. R., Ryoo, J. J., & Ong, C. (2021). Rac (e) ing to computer science for all: How teachers talk and learn about equity in professional development. *Computer Science Education*, *31*(3), 374–399.

Gopal, B. C. (2025). Cognitive, Motivational, and Pedagogical Factors Influencing Effective Teaching and Learning in Math Education. *Journal of Musikot Campus*, *3*(1), 186–199.

Graél, I., Musliu, X., & Fraser, G. (2025). Programming Art: Does Creative Programming Shift Girls' Stereotypes, Affections, and Comprehension of Programming? *Proceedings of the ACM Global on Computing Education Conference 2025* Vol 1. https://doi.org/DOI: 10.1145/3736181.3747161

Graesser, A. C., & Mcnamara, D. S. (2022). The Evolution of Intelligent Tutoring Systems: From Cognitive Models to AI-Driven Education. *Computers & Education*, *184*, 104497I.

Graesser, A. C., & Person, N. K. (1994). Question asking during tutoring. *American Educational Research Journal*, *31*(1), 104–137. DOI: 10.3102/00028312031001104

Grandel, S., Schmidt, D. C., & Leach, K. (2025). Applying Large Language Models to Enhance the Assessment of Java Programming Assignments. *Proceedings of the ACM SIGSOFT Symposium on the Foundations of Software Engineering*, 789–799. DOI: 10.1145/3696630.3727236

Greenberg, J., & Rague, B. (2022). Computational thinking and the humanities: Interdisciplinary collaboration in computer science and theatre design. *INTED Proceedings*, *1*, 1769. Advance online publication. DOI: 10.21125/inted.2022.0530

Grover, S. (2021). Toward A Framework for Formative Assessment of Conceptual Learning in K-12 Computer Science Classrooms. *Proceedings of the 52nd ACM Technical Symposium on Computer Science Education*. https://doi.org/DOI: 10.1145/3408877.3432460

Gudoniene, D., Staneviciene, E., Huet, I., Dickel, J., Dieng, D., Degroote, J., Rocio, V., Butkiene, R., & Casanova, D. (2025). Hybrid Teaching and Learning in Higher Education: A Systematic Literature review. *Sustainability*, *17*(2), 756. Advance online publication. DOI: 10.3390/su17020756

Güner, H., & Er, E. (2025). AI in the classroom: Exploring students' interaction with ChatGPT in programming learning. *Education and Information Technologies*. Advance online publication. DOI: 10.1007/s10639-025-13337-7

Guo, C., Wu, W., Hu, T., & Gao, T. (2025). Unequal Access, Equal Outcomes? Gender Differences in the Relationship Between University-Led STEM Program Factors and Undergraduates' Career Commitment in STEM. *International Journal of STEM Education*, *12*(1), 1–21. DOI: 10.1186/s40594-025-00569-9

Gupta, V., & Nguyen-Duc, A. (2021). *Real-World Software Projects for Computer Science and Engineering Students.* CRC Press., DOI: 10.1201/9781003119883

Güss, C. D., & Starker, U. (2023). The influence of emotion and emotion regulation on complex problem-solving performance. *Systems, 11*(6), 276.

Gutierrez-Pachas, D. A., Garcia-Zanabria, G., Cuadros-Vargas, A. J., Camara-Chavez, G., Poco, J., & Gomez-Nieto, E. (2022). How do curricular design changes impact computer science programs?: A case study at San Pablo Catholic University in Peru. *Education Sciences, 12*(4), 242. DOI: 10.3390/educsci12040242

Habiballa, H., Kotyrba, M., Volna, E., Bradáč, V., & Dusek, M. (2025). Artificial Intelligence (ChatGPT) and Bloom's Taxonomy in Theoretical Computer Science Education. *Applied Sciences (Switzerland), 15*(2). Advance online publication. DOI: 10.3390/app15020581

Haji Amin Shirazi, S. H. A., Pang, A., Knight, A., Salloum, M., & Vahid, F. (2025). *Midterm Exam Outliers Efficiently Highlight Potential Cheaters on Programming Assignments., 1*, 437–442. DOI: 10.1145/3641554.3701883

Halimah, S. (2018). Integrasi nilai-nilai agama dan karakter dalam kurikulum pendidikan guru mengacu KKNI dan SNPT [Integration of religious values and characters in the teacher education curriculum refers to KKNI and SNPT]. *Jurnal Tarbiyah, 24*(2), 201–225. DOI: 10.30829/tar.v24i2.214

Hall, B., Grantham, S., & Whyte, R. (2024, January). Embedding culturally relevant pedagogy in practice: Considerations for training and resource development. In *Proceedings of the 8th Conference on Computing Education Practice* (pp. 29-32).

Hall, M. E. L. (2021). Teaching students to doubt well: The roles of intellectual humility and uncertainty tolerance. *Christian Scholar's Review, 50*(3), 261–279.

Han, J., Yang, Y., Li, Y., & Ren, B. (2022). Students' Responses to a HyFlex Course: A Case Study in the Educational Technology Setting. *Proceedings of the 5th International Conference on Big Data and Education.* https://doi.org/DOI: 10.1145/3524383.3524394

Hanstedt, P. (2023). *Creating wicked students: Designing courses for a complex world.* Routledge.

Happe, J., & Marquardt, K. (2023). Authentic Interdisciplinary Online Courses for More Diversity in Computer Science. *SSRN.* DOI: 10.2139/ssrn.4632668

Happe, L., Buhnova, B., Koziolek, A., & Wagner, I. (2021). Effective measures to foster girls' interest in secondary computer science education: A literature review. *Education and Information Technologies*, *26*(3), 2811–2829.

Hatlevik, I. K. R. (2012). The theory–practice relationship: Reflective skills and theoretical knowledge as key factors in bridging the gap between theory and practice in initial nursing education. *Journal of Advanced Nursing*, *68*(4), 868–877. DOI: 10.1111/j.1365-2648.2011.05789.x PMID: 21790737

Hazzan, O., & Erez, Y. (2024). Generative AI in computer science education. *Proceedings of the 55th ACM Technical Symposium on Computer Science Education (SIGCSE)* (Vol. 2). ACM. https://doi.org/DOI: 10.1145/3626253.3633409

Hazzan, O., Lapidot, T., & Ragonis, N. (2020). *Guide to teaching computer science*. Springer International Publishing.

Heath, J., Whyte, R., & Sentance, S. (2025). FLARE: A Framework Supporting Code Comprehension and Formative Assessment in Block-Based Programming Education. *Proceedings of the 9th Conference on Computing Education Practice*. https://doi.org/DOI: 10.1145/3702212.3702219

Hedayati-Mehdiabadi, A. (2022). How do Computer Science Students Make Decisions in Ethical Situations? Implications for Teaching Computing Ethics based on a Grounded Theory Study. *ACM Transactions on Computing Education*, *22*(3), 1–24. DOI: 10.1145/3483841

Heikkinen, K.-P., & Räisänen, T. (2018). Role of Multidisciplinary and Interdisciplinary Education in Computer Science: A Literature Review. *Managing Global Transitions*, *16*, 159–172. DOI: 10.26493/1854-6935.16.159-172

Hennessy Elliott, C., Nixon, J., Gendrau Chakarov, A., Bush, J. B., Schneider, M. J., & Recker, M. (2024). Characterizing teacher support of debugging with physical computing: Debugging pedagogies in practice. ACM transactions on computing education, 24(4), 1-28.

He, R., Cao, J., & Tan, T. (2025). Generative artificial intelligence: A historical perspective. *National Science Review*, *12*(5), nwaf050. Advance online publication. DOI: 10.1093/nsr/nwaf050 PMID: 40191253

Herckis, L., & Oden Choi, J. (2025). Portable Pedagogy: Teaching Computer Science Across Institutions. *Proceedings of the 56th ACM Technical Symposium on Computer Science Education* V. 2. https://doi.org/DOI: 10.1145/3641555.3705229

Hickman, H., McKeown, P., & Bell, T. (2023). Beyond Question Shuffling: Randomization Techniques in Programming Assessment. *2023 IEEE Frontiers in Education Conference (FIE)*. DOI: 10.1109/FIE58773.2023.10342976

Hitchner, L. E., & Sowizral, H. A. (2000). Adapting computer graphics curricula to changes in graphics. *Computers & Graphics*, *24*(2), 283–288. DOI: 10.1016/S0097-8493(99)00162-4

Holland-Minkley, A., Barnard, J. E., Barr, V., Braught, G., Davis, J., Reed, D., Schmitt, K., Tartaro, A., & Teresco, J. D. (2025). CS2023: Computer Science Curriculum Guidelines: A New Liberal Arts perspective. *ACM Inroads*, *16*(1), 40–52. DOI: 10.1145/3700773

Holley, K. A. (2024). *Interdisciplinary curricula*. Edward Elgar Publishing., DOI: 10.4337/9781035317967.ch66

Holly, M., Hildebrandt, J., & Pirker, J. (2025). *A Computer-Supported Collaborative Learning Environment for Computer Science Education*. Immersive Learning Research Network., DOI: 10.1007/978-3-031-80475-5_21

Holmes, W., Porayska-Pomsta, K., & Holstein, K.. (2022). *Ethics of AI in education: Towards a community-wide framework*. Springer., DOI: 10.1007/978-3-031-10427-0

Huang, W., & Looi, C. K. (2021). A critical review of literature on "unplugged" pedagogies in K-12 computer science and computational thinking education. *Computer Science Education*, *31*(1), 83–111.

Huang, W., & Looi, C.-K. (2021). A Critical Review of Literature on "Unplugged" Pedagogies in K-12 Computer Science and Computational Thinking Education. *Computer Science Education*, *31*(1), 83–111. DOI: 10.1080/08993408.2020.1789411

Huff, E., Koushik, V., Ladner, R., Ludi, S., Milne, L., College, M., Mountapmbeme, A., Perkoff, M., & Stefik, A. (2020). *Accessible Tools and Curricula for K-12 Computer Science Education*. https://www.microsoft.com/en-us/research/wp-content/uploads/2021/02/Accessible-Tools-and-Curricula-for-K-12-Computer-Science-Education_Group-A.pdf

Hulus, A. (2025). Execute_reboot(): Defining MetaTech feminism as a unified framework for FemTech approaches. *Sustainable Futures : An Applied Journal of Technology, Environment and Society*, *10*, 101172. DOI: 10.1016/j.sftr.2025.101172

Humble, N., Boustedt, J., Holmgren, H., Milutinovic, G., Seipel, S., & Östberg, A.-S. (2024). Cheaters or AI-Enhanced Learners: Consequences of ChatGPT for Programming Education. *Electronic Journal of e-Learning*, *22*(2), 16–29. 10.34190/ejel.21.5.3154

Husain, A. (2024). Potentials of ChatGPT in Computer Programming: Insights from Programming Instructors. *Journal of Information Technology Education*, *23*, 1–25. 10.28945/5240

Hutson, J., Fulcher, B., & Ratican, J. (2024). Enhancing Assessment and Feedback in Game Design Programs: Leveraging Generative AI for Efficient and Meaningful Evaluation. *IJERI: International Journal of Educational Research and Innovation*, (22), 1–20. DOI: 10.46661/ijeri.11038

Ibanez, M. B., Di-Serio, A., & Delgado-Kloos, C. (2014). Gamification for engaging computer science students in learning activities: A case study. *IEEE Transactions on Learning Technologies*, *7*(3), 291–301. DOI: 10.1109/TLT.2014.2329293

Idowu, J. A. (2024). Investigating algorithmic bias in student progress monitoring systems. *Computers & Education: Artificial Intelligence*, *5*, 100156. DOI: 10.1016/j.caeai.2023.100156

Indriasari, T. D., Luxton-Reilly, A., & Denny, P. (2020). A Review of Peer Code Review in Higher Education. *ACM Transactions on Computing Education*, *20*(3), 1–25. DOI: 10.1145/3403935

Israel, M., Kester, B., Williams, J. J., & Ray, M. J. (2022). *Equity and Inclusion through UDL in K-6 Computer Science Education: Perspectives of Teachers and Instructional Coaches*. ACM Transactions on Computing Education., DOI: 10.1145/3513138

Jamal, R., & Renzella, J. (2024). Enhancing Formative Feedback at Scale with the Intelligent Feedback Assistant. *Proceedings of the 55th ACM Technical Symposium on Computer Science Education* V. 2. https://doi.org/DOI: 10.1145/3626253.3635482

Jarzemsky, J., Paup, J., & Fiesler, C. (2023). "This Applies to the Real World": Student Perspectives on Integrating Ethics into a Computer Science Assignment. *Proceedings of the 54th ACM Technical Symposium on Computer Science Education* V. 1. https://doi.org/DOI: 10.1145/3545945.3569846

Jarzemsky, P., Fiesler, C., & Payne, B. (2023). Student perspectives on integrating ethics into a computer science course. *Proceedings of the ACM on Human-Computer Interaction, 7*(CSCW2), 1–27. https://doi.org/DOI: 10.1145/3610105

Jayakanthan, R. (2002). Application of computer games in the field of education. *The Electronic Library*, *20*(2), 98–102. DOI: 10.1108/02640470210697471

Jiang, C., & Pang, Y. (2023). Enhancing design thinking in engineering students with project-based learning. *Computer Applications in Engineering Education*, *31*(4), 814–830.

Jobin, A., Ienca, M., & Vayena, E. (2019). The global landscape of AI ethics guidelines. *Nature Machine Intelligence*, *1*(9), 389–399. DOI: 10.1038/s42256-019-0088-2

Johnson, A., & Elliott, S. (2020). Culturally relevant pedagogy: A model to guide cultural transformation in STEM departments. *Journal of Microbiology & Biology Education*, *21*(1), 10–1128. PMID: 32431767

Jubi, R. (2024). *Business analytics-unleashing data driven decision making*. NEHAS PUBLICATIONS.

Julien, G. (2024). How Artificial Intelligence (AI) impacts inclusive education. *Educational Research Review*, *19*(6), 95–103. DOI: 10.5897/ERR2024.4404

Juriyah, N. (2021). Profil implementasi model shared pada pembelajaran ipa terpadu di indonesia: Kajian literatur (2012-2021) [Implementation profile of shared model in integrated science learning in indonesia: A literature review (2012-2021)]. *Jurnal Inovasi Penelitian Dan Pengabdian Masyarakat*, *1*(1), 32–46. DOI: 10.53621/jippmas.v1i1.6

Kadirbergenovna, B. L. (2022). Teaching computer graphics as a pedagogical problem on the basis of massive open online courses in information conditions. *World Bulletin of Social Sciences*, *8*, 71–74.

Kakharov, R., Khusanov, K., & Jamolov, O. (2023). Some Aspects of Development of E-Learning Evaluation System Based on LMS in Uzbekistan. *The 17th IEEE International Conference on Application of Information and Communication Technologies (AICT2023) to be held on 18-20 October 2023 in Baku, Azerbaijan.* https://doi.org/DOI: 10.1109/AICT59525.2023.10313202

Kallia, M., & Cutts, Q. (2021). Re-Examining Inequalities in Computer Science Participation from a Bourdieusian Sociological Perspective. *Proceedings of the 17th ACM Conference on International Computing Education Research.* https://doi.org/DOI: 10.1145/3446871.3469763

Kamp, A. (2023). *Engineering education in the rapidly changing world: Rethinking the vision for higher engineering education.* TU Delft Open Publishing., DOI: 10.59490/mg.71

Kanika, Chakraverty, S., & Chakraborty, P. (2020). Tools and techniques for teaching computer programming: A review. *Journal of Educational Technology Systems*, *49*(2), 170–198.

Karnalim, O. (2023). Maintaining Academic Integrity in Programming: Locality-Sensitive Hashing and Recommendations. *Education Sciences*, *13*(1), 1–23. DOI: 10.3390/educsci13010054

Kawane, T., Adu-Gyamfi, B., & Shaw, R. (2025). Exploring the elements of strengthening online higher education in disaster risk reduction: A perspective of sustained strategy in post COVID-19. *International Journal of Disaster Resilience in the Built Environment*, *16*(2), 173–192. DOI: 10.1108/IJDRBE-12-2022-0125

Kayyali, M. (2026). The Rationales Behind the Creation of Applied Models for Problem Solving. In Building Applied Models for Problem Solving (pp. 123-152). IGI Global Scientific Publishing.

Keith, P. K., Sullivan, F. R., & Pham, D. (2019). Roles, Collaboration, and the Development of Computational Thinking in a Robotics Learning Environment. In Kong, S.-C., & Abelson, H. (Eds.), *Computational Thinking Education* (pp. 223–245). Springer Singapore., DOI: 10.1007/978-981-13-6528-7_13

Kendon, T., Wu, L., & Aycock, J. (2023). AI-Generated Code Not Considered Harmful. *Proceedings of the 25th Western Canadian Conference on Computing Education*. DOI: 10.1145/3593342.3593349

Kesler, A., Shamir-Inbal, T., & Blau, I. (2021). Active Learning by Visual Programming: Pedagogical Perspectives of Instructivist and Constructivist Code Teachers and Their Implications on Actual Teaching Strategies and Students' Programming Artifacts. *Journal of Educational Computing Research*, *60*(1), 073563312110177. DOI: 10.1177/07356331211017793

Khan, A. A., Badshah, S., & Liang, P.. (2021). Ethics of artificial intelligence: A systematic literature review of principles and challenges. *AI and Ethics*, *1*(4), 351–366. DOI: 10.1007/s43681-021-00081-7

Khozin, K., Haris, A., & Asrori, A. (2021). Pengembangan integrasi kurikulum [Development of curriculum integration]. *TADARUS*, *10*(1), 84–94. DOI: 10.30651/td.v10i1.9090

Khusanov, K., & Kakharov, R. (2023). Development of Electronic Course as the Element of Adaptive Training System. *The 17th IEEE International Conference on Application of Information and Communication Technologies (AICT 2023)*, 1–5. https:// DOI: <ALIGNMENT.qj></ALIGNMENT>10.1109/AICT59525.2023.10313159

Kieran, L., & Anderson, C. (2019). Connecting universal design for learning with culturally responsive teaching. *Education and Urban Society*, *51*(9), 1202–1216. DOI: 10.1177/0013124518785012

Kitchenham, B. A., Brereton, O. P., Budgen, D., Turner, M., Bailey, J., & Linkman, S. (2009). Systematic literature reviews in software engineering – A systematic literature review. *Information and Software Technology*, *51*(1), 7–15. DOI: 10.1016/j.infsof.2008.09.009

Klamen, D., Suh, B., & Tischkau, S. (2022). Problem-based learning. In *An introduction to medical teaching: The foundations of curriculum design, delivery, and assessment* (pp. 115–131). Springer International Publishing.

Kleftodimos, A. (2024). Computer-animated videos in education: A comprehensive review and teacher experiences from animation creation. *Digital*, *4*(3), 613–647. DOI: 10.3390/digital4030031

Klein, J. T. (2010). A Taxonomy of Interdisciplinarity. In Frodeman, R., Klein, J. T., & Mitcham, C. (Eds.), *The Oxford Handbook of Interdisciplinarity* (pp. 15–30). Oxford University Press.

Kolb, A. Y., & Kolb, D. A. (2017). Experiential learning theory as a guide for experiential educators in higher education. *Experiential Learning & Teaching in Higher Education*, *1*(1), 7–44. DOI: 10.46787/elthe.v1i1.3362

Kolosnjaji, B., Xiao, H., Xu, P., & Zarras, A. (2024). *Artificial Intelligence for Cybersecurity: Develop AI approaches to solve cybersecurity problems in your organization*. Packt Publishing Ltd.

Kong, S. C., Lai, M., & Sun, D. (2020). Teacher development in computational thinking: Design and learning outcomes of programming concepts, practices and pedagogy. *Computers & Education*, *151*, 103872.

Kopcha, T. J., & Ocak, C. (2023). Children's Computational Thinking as the Development of a Possibility Space. *Computers and Education Open*, *5*, 1–14. DOI: 10.1016/j.caeo.2023.100156

Ko, S.-H., & Stephens-Martinez, K. (2024). The Trees in the Forest: Characterizing Computing Students' Individual Help-Seeking Approaches. *Proceedings of the 2024 ACM Conference on International Computing Education Research* - Volume 1. https://doi.org/DOI: 10.1145/3632620.3671099

Kosar, T., Ostojič, D., Liu, Y. D., & Mernik, M. (2024). Computer Science Education in ChatGPT Era: Experiences from an Experiment in a Programming Course for Novice Programmers. *Mathematics*, *12*(5). Advance online publication. DOI: 10.3390/math12050629

Kot, S. O., & Nykyporets, S. S. (2025). *Activating studentscognitive engagement in technical English learning with AI tools. Science and education in the third millennium: information technology, education, law, psychology, social security and work, management: international collective monograph* (Vol. I). Polska.

Kouam, F., & William, A. (2024). The effectiveness of intelligent tutoring systems in supporting students with varying levels of programming experience. *Discover Education, 3*(1), 278. DOI: 10.1007/s44217-024-00385-3

Kovaleva, Y., Happonen, A., & Kindsiko, E. (2022b). Designing Gender-Neutral Software Engineering Program. Stereotypes, Social Pressure, and Current Attitudes Based on Recent Studies. *Proceedings of the Third Workshop on Gender Equality, Diversity, and Inclusion in Software Engineering*. https://doi.org/DOI: 10.1145/3524501.3527600

Kovaleva, Y., Happonen, A., Garcia, M. B., & Kasurinen, J. (2024a). Female-Inclusive Practices for Software Engineering and Computer Science Higher Education: A Literature Review. *Proceedings of the Annual Doctoral Symposium of Computer Science 2024*. https://ceur-ws.org/Vol-3776/paper08.pdf

Kovaleva, Y., Happonen, A., & Hasheela-Mufeti, V. (2022a). Pros and Cons of Running Educational Hackathons in a Gender-Neutral Fashion. *Proceedings of the Third Workshop on Gender Equality, Diversity, and Inclusion in Software Engineering*. https://doi.org/DOI: 10.1145/3524501.3527603

Kovaleva, Y., Happonen, A., & Kindsiko, E. (2024b). *Literature-Based Practices for Designing Female-Inclusive Software Engineering and Computer Science Programs*. Intelligent Sustainable Systems., DOI: 10.1007/978-981-99-8111-3_23

Kovaleva, Y., Happonen, A., & Mbogho, A. (2022c). Towards Gender Balance in Modern Hackathons: Literature-Based Approaches for Female Inclusiveness. *Proceedings of the Third Workshop on Gender Equality, Diversity, and Inclusion in Software Engineering*. https://doi.org/DOI: 10.1145/3524501.3527594

Kovaleva, Y., Hyrynsalmi, S., Saltan, A., Happonen, A., & Kasurinen, J. (2023). Becoming an Entrepreneur: A Study of Factors with Women from the Tech Sector. *Information and Software Technology, 155*, 107110. DOI: 10.1016/j.infsof.2022.107110

Kovaleva, Y., Kasurinen, J., Kindsiko, E., & Happonen, A. (2024c). State-of-the-Art Review on Current Approaches to Female Inclusiveness in Software Engineering and Computer Science in Higher Education. *IEEE Access : Practical Innovations, Open Solutions, 12*, 1360–1373. DOI: 10.1109/ACCESS.2023.3346767

Kozhuharova, D., Kirov, A., & Al-Shargabi, Z. (2022). *Ethics in cybersecurity: Challenges and approaches*. Springer., DOI: 10.1007/978-3-030-93699-5

Krathwohl, D. R. (2002). A Revision of Bloom's Taxonomy: An Overview. *Theory into Practice*, *41*(4), 212–218.

Krüger, F. A., Queen, Z., Radelva, O., & Lawrence, N. D. (2024). Comparative Analysis of Scientific Approaches in Computer Science: A Quantitative Study. *International Transactions on Education Technology*, *2*(2), 120–128. DOI: 10.33050/itee.v2i2.567

Kubincová, Z., Dropcová, V., & Homola, M. (2016). Students' Acceptance of Peer Review in Computer Science Course. *EAI Endorsed Transactions on e-Learning*, *16*(10), 1-8. https://doi.org/DOI: 10.4108/eai.11-4-2016.151153

Kumar, A. N. (2012). A Study of Stereotype Threat in Computer Science. *Proceedings of the 17th ACM Annual Conference on Innovation and Technology in Computer Science Education*. https://doi.org/DOI: 10.1145/2325296.2325361

Kumar, A. N., Becker, B. A., Pias, M., Oudshoorn, M., Jalote, P., Servin, C., Aly, S. G., Blumenthal, R. L., Epstein, S. L., & Anderson, M. D. (2023). A Combined Knowledge and Competency (CKC) model for computer science curricula. *ACM Inroads*, *14*(3), 22–29. DOI: 10.1145/3605215

Kurti, E., Ferati, M., & Kalonaityte, V. (2024). Closing the Gender Gap in ICT Higher Education: Exploring Women's Motivations in Pursuing ICT Education. *Frontiers in Education*, *9*, 1–13. DOI: 10.3389/feduc.2024.1352029

Kuzmenko, O., Tomchuk, M., & Kysiuk, D. (2024). The importance of interdisciplinary integration in training specialists to work in modern conditions. *Педагогіка Безпеки*, *9*(1), 8–13. DOI: 10.31649/2524-1079-2024-9-1-008-013

Laakso, N. L., Korhonen, T. S., & Hakkarainen, K. P. (2021). Developing students' digital competences through collaborative game design. *Computers & Education*, *174*, 104308. DOI: 10.1016/j.compedu.2021.104308

Lagesen, V. A., Pettersen, I., & Berg, L. (2021). Inclusion of Women to ICT Engineering – Lessons Learned. *European Journal of Engineering Education*, *47*(3), 467–482. DOI: 10.1080/03043797.2021.1983774

Lai, H. Y., & Yap, S. L. (2016). Application of multiple intelligence theory in the assessment for learning. In *Assessment for learning within and beyond the classroom* (pp. 427–436). Springer., DOI: 10.1007/978-981-10-0908-2_36

Lallie, H. S., Sinclair, J., & Joy, M.. (2022). Pedagogic challenges in teaching cybersecurity: A UK perspective. *Education and Information Technologies*, *27*(5), 6657–6680. DOI: 10.1007/s10639-021-10834-3

Lamrani, R., & Abdelwahed, E. H. (2020). Game-based learning and gamification to improve skills in early years education. *Computer Science and Information Systems*, *17*(1), 339–356.

Landorf, H., & Wadley, C. (2022). The importance of John Dewey's philosophy for global learning theory and practice. *Social Studies Research & Practice*, *17*(1), 6–18.

Lapidot-Lefler, N. (2025). Teacher Responsiveness in Inclusive Education: A Participatory Study of Pedagogical Practice, Well-Being, and Sustainability. *Sustainability*, *17*(7), 2919. DOI: 10.3390/su17072919

Latulipe, C., & Jaeger, A. D. (2022). Comparing Student Experiences of Collaborative Learning in Synchronous CS1 Classes in Gather.Town vs. Zoom. *Proceedings of the 53rd ACM Technical Symposium on Computer Science Education* - Volume 1. https://doi.org/DOI: 10.1145/3478431.3499383

Lau, S., & Guo, P. (2023). From "Ban It Till We Understand It" to "Resistance is Futile": How University Programming Instructors Plan to Adapt as More Students Use AI Code Generation and Explanation Tools such as ChatGPT and GitHub Copilot. 106–121. DOI: 10.1145/3568813.3600138

Lavado-Anguera, S., Velasco-Quintana, P. J., & Terrón-López, M. J. (2024). Project-based learning (PBL) as an experiential pedagogical methodology in engineering education: A review of the literature. *Education Sciences*, *14*(6), 617. Advance online publication. DOI: 10.3390/educsci14060617

Lee, A. (2015). Determining the Effects of Computer Science Education at the Secondary Level on STEM Major Choices in Postsecondary Institutions in the United States. *Computers & Education*, *88*, 241–255. DOI: 10.1016/j.compedu.2015.04.019

Lee, D.-K., & Joe, I. (2025). A GPT-Based Code Review System With Accurate Feedback for Programming Education. *IEEE Access : Practical Innovations, Open Solutions*, *13*, 105724–105737. DOI: 10.1109/ACCESS.2025.3581139

Lee, S., & Song, K.-S. (2024). Teachers' and students' perceptions of AI-generated concept explanations: Implications for integrating generative AI in computer science education. *Computers and Education: Artificial Intelligence*, *7*. Advance online publication. DOI: 10.1016/j.caeai.2024.100283

Leinonen, J., Denny, P., MacNeil, S., Sarsa, S., Bernstein, S., Kim, J., Tran, A., & Hellas, A. (2023). Comparing Code Explanations Created by Students and Large Language Models. *Annual Conference on Innovation and Technology in Computer Science Education, ITiCSE, 1*, 124–130. DOI: 10.1145/3587102.3588785

Leonard, H. C., & Sentance, S. (2021). Culturally-relevant and responsive pedagogy in computing: A Quick Scoping Review. *International Journal of Computer Science Education in Schools*, *5*(2), 3–13. DOI: 10.21585/ijcses.v5i2.130

Lepp, M., & Kaimre, J. (2025). Does Generative AI Help in Learning Programming: Students' Perceptions, Reported Use and Relation to Performance. *Computers in Human Behavior Reports*, *18*, 1–12. DOI: 10.1016/j.chbr.2025.100642

Lharoui, M. (2025). Role-specific AI use cases for enhancing daily operations in energy upgrades projects.

Liao, J., Zhong, L., Zhe, L., Xu, H., Liu, M., & Xie, T. (2024). Scaffolding Computational Thinking With ChatGPT. *IEEE Transactions on Learning Technologies*, *17*, 1668–1682. DOI: 10.1109/TLT.2024.3392896

Lić, J., Ivanović, M., & Klašnja-Milićević, A. (2024). The Impact of Intelligent Tutoring Systems and Artificial Intelligence on Students' Motivation and Achievement in STEM Education: A Systematic Literature Review. *Journal of Educational Studies in Mathematics and Computer Science*, *1*(2), 5–18.

Li, H., Öchsner, A., & Hall, W. (2019). Application of experiential learning to improve student engagement and experience in a mechanical engineering course. *European Journal of Engineering Education*, *44*(3), 283–293. DOI: 10.1080/03043797.2017.1402864

Lim, W. K. (2023). Problem based learning in medical education: Handling objections and sustainable implementation. *Advances in Medical Education and Practice*, •••, 1453–1460. PMID: 38164409

Liu, Z., Gearty, Z., Richard, E., Orrill, C. H., Kayumova, S., & Balasubramanian, R. (2024). Bringing Computational Thinking into Classrooms: A Systematic Review on Supporting Teachers in Integrating Computational Thinking into K-12 Classrooms. *International Journal of STEM Education*, *11*(1), 1–18. DOI: 10.1186/s40594-024-00510-6

Li, Y., & Chen, J. (2023). Gamified Intelligent Tutoring for Python Programming: Motivating Students Through Adaptive Challenges. *Journal of Interactive Learning Research*, *34*(1), 12–29.

Li, Y., & Singh, C. (2022). Inclusive learning environments can improve student learning and motivational beliefs. *Physical Review. Physics Education Research, 18*(2). Advance online publication. DOI: 10.1103/physrevphyseducres.18.020147

Loksa, D., Margulieux, L., Becker, B. A., Craig, M., Denny, P., Pettit, R., & Prather, J. (2022). Metacognition and Self-Regulation in Programming Education: Theories and Exemplars of Use. *ACM Transactions on Computing Education, 22*(4), 1–31. DOI: 10.1145/3487050

Lopatecki, D. (2022). The Body Navigated Through Moments of Abstraction.

Lopes, A. G. (2022). Women in Computing: Attitudes and Experiences. *International Journal of Technology and Human Interaction, 18*, 1–11. DOI: 10.4018/IJTHI.302663

Lopez-Fernandez, D., Gordillo, A., Alarcon, P. P., & Tovar, E. (2021). Comparing Traditional Teaching and Game-Based Learning Using Teacher-Authored Games on Computer Science Education. *IEEE Transactions on Education, 64*(4), 1–7. DOI: 10.1109/te.2021.3057849

López-Fernández, D., & Vergaz, R. (2025). ChatGPT in Computer Science Education: A Case Study on a Database Administration Course. *Applied Sciences (Switzerland), 15*(2). Advance online publication. DOI: 10.3390/app15020985

Lorenzo, M. G. (2020). Abordaje interdisciplinar para la enseñanza de las ciencias y la actualización de profesores. Lorenzo, M. G. (2020). Abordaje interdisciplinar para la enseñanza de las ciencias y la actualización de profesores. *Revista Educación En Ciencias Biológicas, 5*(1), 1–9. DOI: 10.36861/recb.5.1.2

Louder, J. R. (2025). Alternative Educational Pathways: Stackable and Micro-Credentials to Bridge Education and Employment. In *The Emerald Handbook on International Higher Education: Navigating Workforce and Leadership Changes in a Digital Age*. Emerald Publishing Limited., DOI: 10.1108/978-1-83549-788-320251007

Lovellette, E., Bouvier, D. J., & Matta, J. (2024). Contextualization, authenticity, and the problem description effect. *ACM Transactions on Computing Education, 24*(2), 1–32.

Lubin, I. A. (2016). *Intentional ICT: Curriculum, Education and Development.* UNESCO International Bureau of Education. https://unesdoc.unesco.org/ark:/48223/pf0000244081

Lunn, S., Ross, M., Hazari, Z., Weiss, M. A., Georgiopoulos, M., & Christensen, K. (2021). How Do Educational Experiences Predict Computing Identity? *ACM Transactions on Computing Education, 22*(2), 1–28. DOI: 10.1145/3470653

Luo, J. (2024). A Critical Review of GenAI Policies in Higher Education Assessment: A Call to Reconsider the "Originality" of Students' Work. *Assessment & Evaluation in Higher Education, 49*(5), 651–664. DOI: 10.1080/02602938.2024.2309963

Lynch, M., Sage, T., Hitchcock, L. I., & Sage, M. (2021). A Heutagogical Approach for the Assessment of Internet Communication Technology (ICT) Assignments in Higher Education. *International Journal of Educational Technology in Higher Education, 18*(1), 1–16. DOI: 10.1186/s41239-021-00290-x PMID: 34778541

Lyon, J. A., & Magana, J., A. (2020). Computational thinking in higher education: A review of the literature. *Computer Applications in Engineering Education, 28*(5), 1174–1189.

Madkins, T. C., Howard, N. R., & Freed, N. (2020). Engaging Equity Pedagogies in Computer Science Learning Environments. *Journal of Computer Science Integration*, •••, 1–27. DOI: 10.26716/jcsi.2020.03.2.1 PMID: 37547748

Madkins, T. C., Howard, N. R., & Freed, N. (2020). Engaging equity pedagogies in computer science learning environments. *Journal of Computer Science Integration, 3*(2), 1. PMID: 37547748

Maesschalck, S. (2024). Critical Thinking: The Code to Crack Computer Science Education. *Journal of Information Technology Education: Innovations in Practice, 23*, 1–20. DOI: 10.28945/5387

Mahdiyin, K. A., Zamzami, M. J., Silaban, M. R., & Suyudi, M. (2025). Pengembangan Kurikulum Integratif: Al-Qur'an, Faraidh, dan Ilmu Sains/Teknologi [Integrative Curriculum Development: Qur'an, Faraidh, and Science/Technology]. *Instructional Development Journal, 8*(1), 114. DOI: 10.24014/idj.v8i1.36340

Mahon, J., Namee, B. M., & Becker, B. A. (2024). Guidelines for the Evolving Role of Generative AI in Introductory Programming Based on Emerging Practice. *Proceedings of the 2024 on Innovation and Technology in Computer Science Education* V. 1. DOI: 10.1145/3649217.3653602

Malik, S. I., & Coldwell-Neilson, J. (2017). Comparison of Traditional and ADRI Based Teaching Approaches in an Introductory Programming Course. *Journal of Information Technology Education, 16*, 267–283. 10.28945/3793

Mangubat, R., Calasang, V., Espina, R. C., Capuyan, D. L., Gamusa, E. V., Pernaa, J., & Garcia, M. B. (2025). Understanding the Role of Technological Self-Efficacy in Fostering Creative Problem-Solving and Curiosity in Teacher Education: A Structural Equation Modeling Approach. *Journal of Technology and Science Education, 15*(2), 456–478. DOI: 10.3926/jotse.3233

Mansilla, V. B., & Duraisingh, E. D. (2007). Targeted assessment of students' interdisciplinary work: An empirically grounded framework proposed. *The Journal of Higher Education*, *78*(2), 215–237. DOI: 10.1353/jhe.2007.0008

Mansour, K. H., Jackson, D. K., Bievenue, L., Voight, A., & Sridhar, N. (2023). Understanding the Impact of Peer Instruction in CS Principles Teacher Professional Development. *ACM Transactions on Computing Education*, *23*(2), 1–21. DOI: 10.1145/3585077

Margolis, J., & Fisher, A. (2002). *Unlocking the clubhouse: Women in Computing*. MIT Press.

Margulieux, L. E., Morrison, B. B., & Decker, A. (2020). Reducing withdrawal and failure rates in introductory programming with subgoal labeled worked examples. *International Journal of STEM Education*, *7*(1), 19. DOI: 10.1186/s40594-020-00222-7

Marifah, S. N. (2022). Systematic literatur review: Integrasi computational thinking dalam kurikulum sekolah dasar di indonesia [Systematic literature review: Integration of computational thinking in the Indonesian primary school curriculum] [Creative of Learning Students Elementary Education]. *COLLASE*, *5*(5), 928–938. DOI: 10.22460/collase.v5i5.12148

Martin, F., Chen, Y., Moore, R. L., & Westine, C. D. (2020). Systematic review of adaptive learning research designs, context, strategies, and technologies from 2009 to 2018. *Educational Technology Research and Development*, *68*(4), 1903–1929. DOI: 10.1007/s11423-020-09793-2 PMID: 32837122

Matei, S. A., & Bertino, E. (2023). Educating for AI cybersecurity work and research: Ethics, systems thinking, and communication requirements. *IEEE Security and Privacy*, *21*(2), 75–83. DOI: 10.1109/MSEC.2022.3226902

Matejić, J., & Milenković, A. (2025). Impact of Peer Feedback in a Web Programming Course on Students' Achievement. *International Journal of Cognitive Research in Science* [IJCRSEE]. *Engineering and Education*, *13*(1), 33–49. DOI: 10.23947/2334-8496-2025-13-1-33-49

Mathrani, A., Sarvesh, T., & Umer, R. (2021). Digital Divide framework: Online Learning in Developing Countries during the COVID-19 Lockdown. *Globalisation, Societies and Education*, *20*(5), 1–16. DOI: 10.1080/14767724.2021.1981253

Matthews, D. (1988). Gardner's multiple intelligence theory: An evaluation of relevant research literature and a consideration of its application to gifted education. *Roeper Review*, *11*(2), 100–104. DOI: 10.1080/02783198809553176

May, H., & Bridger, K. (2010). *Developing and embedding inclusive policy and practice in higher education Developing and embedding inlcusive policy and practice in higher education*. https://www.aau.org/wp-content/uploads/sites/9/2018/04/Developing-Embedding-Inclusive-Policy-Practice-Report-final.pdf

McLaughlin, G., Ahmadi, S., Novak, E., & Borgerding, L. (2025). Mentoring in K-12 Computer Science Classrooms: Exploring Mentors' and Mentees' Experiences. *ACM Transactions on Computing Education*, *26*(1), 1–20. DOI: 10.1145/3772073

Meihami, H., & Alexander, C. (2024). Adopting Gartner's hype cycles to investigate the lifespan of computer assisted language learning from EFL learners' perspectives. *Asian-Pacific Journal of Second and Foreign Language Education*, *9*(1), 31.

Memon, F. N., & Memon, S. N. (2024). Digital Divide and Equity in Education. *Advances in Educational Technologies and Instructional Design Book Series*, 107–130. https://doi.org/DOI: 10.4018/979-8-3693-1854-6.ch004

Messer, M., Brown, N. C. C., Kölling, M., & Shi, M. (2023). Automated Grading and Feedback Tools for Programming Education: A Systematic Review. *ACM Transactions on Computing Education*, *23*(4), 45–67.

Mezzaro, S., Gambi, A., & Fraser, G. (2024). *An Empirical Study on How Large Language Models Impact Software Testing Learning*. 555–564. DOI: 10.1145/3661167.3661273

Michela, E. (2022). This Uncertain Space of Teaching": How Design Studio Instructors Talk about Design Critiques along with Themselves When Giving Critiques. *The Journal of Scholarship of Teaching and Learning*, *22*(1), 48–66.

Mills, K. A., Cope, J., Scholes, L., & Rowe, L. (2024). Coding and Computational Thinking Across the Curriculum: A Review of Educational Outcomes. *Review of Educational Research*, *95*(3), 581–618. DOI: 10.3102/00346543241241327

Miranda, J., Navarrete, C., Noguez, J., Molina-Espinosa, J., Ramírez-Montoya, M., Navarro-Tuch, S. A., Bustamante-Bello, M., Rosas-Fernández, J., & Molina, A. (2021). The core components of education 4.0 in higher education: Three case studies in engineering education. *Computers & Electrical Engineering*, *93*, 107278. Advance online publication. DOI: 10.1016/j.compeleceng.2021.107278

Mishra, A., & Siy, H. (2020). An Interdisciplinary Approach for Teaching Artificial Intelligence to Computer Science Students. *Proceedings of the 21st Annual Conference on Information Technology Education (SIGITE '20)*. Association for Computing Machinery, New York, NY, USA. DOI: 10.1145/3368308.3415440

Mittal, U., Sai, S., Chamola, V., & Sangwan, D. (2024). A comprehensive review on generative AI for education. *IEEE Access : Practical Innovations, Open Solutions, 12*, 142733–142759. DOI: 10.1109/ACCESS.2024.3468368

Moghaddam, R. Z., Bailey, B., & Fu, W.-T. (2012). Consensus Building in Open Source User Interface Design Discussions. *Proceedings of the SIGCHI Conference on Human Factors in Computing Systems*. https://doi.org/DOI: 10.1145/2207676.2208611

Mohammed, F. S., & Ozdamli, F. (2024). A Systematic Literature review of Soft skills in Information Technology education. *Behavioral Sciences (Basel, Switzerland), 14*(10), 894. Advance online publication. DOI: 10.3390/bs14100894 PMID: 39457766

Monib, W. K., Qazi, A., Apong, R. A., Azizan, M. T., De Silva, L., & Yassin, H. (2024). Generative AI and future education: A review, theoretical validation, and authors' perspective on challenges and solutions. *PeerJ. Computer Science, 10*, e2105. DOI: 10.7717/peerj-cs.2105 PMID: 39650462

Mooney, J. G., & Williams, M. L. (2024). Enabling Technologies of the Fourth Industrial Revolution. In Handbook of Research on Strategic Leadership in the Fourth Industrial Revolution (pp. 35-61). Edward Elgar Publishing. https://doi.org/ DOI: 10.4337/9781802208818.00009

Moore, D. J. (2025). Motivating Students Through Problem-Based and Project-Based Learning.

Moore, M., & Urness, T. (2024). Inclusive Practices and Universal Design in the Computer Science Classroom. *Journal of Computing Sciences in Colleges, 39*(6), 93–102.

Moriña, A. (2020). Faculty members who engage in inclusive pedagogy: Methodological and affective strategies for teaching. *Teaching in Higher Education, 27*(3), 1–16. DOI: 10.1080/13562517.2020.1724938

Moura, W., Delbem, E., França, J., & Dias, A. (2025). Exploring Cooperation and Competition in Computer Science Education: An Investigation Based on Game Theory. *Proceedings of the 17th International Conference on Computer Supported Education*. https://doi.org/DOI: 10.5220/0013216700003932

Muringa, T. P. (2025). Exploring ethical dilemmas and institutional challenges in AI adoption: a study of South African universities. *Frontiers in Education, Volume 10-2025*. https://www.frontiersin.org/journals/education/articles/10.3389/feduc.2025.1628019

Muslimin, J., Reksiana, R., & Munawar, W. (2022). Constructivism and Teaching Design: In search of an appropriate learning Process of Sharia Entrepreneurship for Pesantren-Based University. *MIQOT Jurnal Ilmu-ilmu Keislaman*, *46*(2). Advance online publication. DOI: 10.30821/miqot.v46i2.969

Nadir, H. M. (2021). *Investigating a Teacher's Scaffolding for Design Problem Solving in Project-Based Learning*. Indiana University.

Nancy, W., Parimala, A., & Livingston, L. M. (2020). Advanced teaching pedagogy as innovative approach in modern education system. *Procedia Computer Science*, *172*, 382–388.

Nan, J. (2025). In-Depth Practice and Strategic Exploration of Project-Based Learning in Primary and Secondary School Music Teaching. *OAlib*, *12*(6), 1–9.

Napier, N. P., & Bourgeois, A. G. (2024). RISE in Computing Scholars: A Cohort-Based Community for Black Women. *Proceedings of the 2024 on RESPECT Annual Conference*. https://doi.org/DOI: 10.1145/3653666.3656100

Nathaniel, J., Oyelere, S. S., Suhonen, J., & Tedre, M. (2025). Investigating the Impact of Generative AI Integration on the Sustenance of Higher-Order Thinking Skills and Understanding of Programming Logic. *Computers and Education: Artificial Intelligence*, *9*, 1–19. DOI: 10.1016/j.caeai.2025.100460

Nazarova, N. M. (2020). Comparative analysis of the inclusive education paradigm implementation in Russia and abroad. *Perspectives of Science and Education*, *44*(2), 354–365. DOI: 10.32744/pse.2020.2.28

Neagu, S., Vasile, S., & Costache, R. (2025). Digital and psychological well-being among technical students: Implications for ethics education. *Education Sciences*, *15*(2), 112. DOI: 10.3390/educsci15020112

Nemadziva, B. (2023). Using science communication strategies to close the resource gap in under-resourced schools: A focus on rural schools in South Africa (Doctoral dissertation, University of Otago).

Neves, R. (2024). The Engineering Leadership Playbook: Strategies for Team Success and Business Growth. Apress.

Ni, L., Bausch, G., & Benjamin, R. (2023). Computer science teacher professional development and professional learning communities: A review of the research literature. *Computer Science Education*, *33*(1), 29–60.

Nouri, J., Zhang, L., & Mannila, L. (2022). Personalized Feedback in Programming Education Using Intelligent Systems: A Design-Based Study. *Computers in Human Behavior, 134*, 107324.

Novak, M., Joy, M., & Kermek, D. (2019). Source-Code Similarity Detection and Detection Tools Used in Academia: A Systematic Review. *ACM Transactions on Computing Education, 19*(3), 1–37. DOI: 10.1145/3313290

Nugraha, M. G., Kidman, G., & Tan, H. (2024). Interdisciplinary STEM education foundational concepts: Implementation for knowledge creation. *Eurasia Journal of Mathematics, Science and Technology Education, 20*(10), em2523. Advance online publication. DOI: 10.29333/ejmste/15471

O'Brien, L., Kanij, T., & Grundy, J. (2025). Assessing Gender Bias in the Software Used in Computer Science and Software Engineering Education. *Journal of Systems and Software, 219*, 112225. DOI: 10.1016/j.jss.2024.112225

O'Leary, T. K., Batti, V., Dhindsa, S., Krishnan, V. H., Wilcox, L., Woods-Giscombe, C. L., . . . McCall, T. (2025). "It was Empowering": Care Pathways a Novel Culturally Informed Inspiration Card Game for Community-Engaged Co-Design with Black American Women and Clinicians. *Proceedings of the Extended Abstracts of the CHI Conference on Human Factors in Computing Systems*. https://doi.org/DOI: 10.1145/3706599.3720056

O'Reilly, C. A.III, & Tushman, M. L. (2021). *Lead and disrupt: How to solve the innovator's dilemma*. Stanford University Press.

Obaidellah, U., Blascheck, T., Guarnera, D. T., & Maletic, J. (2020). A Fine-Grained Assessment on Novice Programmers' Gaze Patterns on Pseudocode Problems. *ACM Symposium on Eye Tracking Research and Applications*. DOI: 10.1145/3379156.3391982

Obiakor, F. E., Aluka, I. J., Obiakor, G. C., & Obi, S. O. (2022). Educating culturally and linguistically diverse students with disabilities in inclusive settings: Beyond debates. *Multicultural Learning and Teaching, 0*(0). Advance online publication. DOI: 10.1515/mlt-2022-

Ogegbo, A. A., & Ramnarain, U. (2022). A systematic review of computational thinking in science classrooms. *Studies in Science Education, 58*(2), 203–230.

Olugbade, D. (2025). Democratizing education in rural Nigeria through AI and mobile technologies as a transformative pathway to inclusive learning. In M. Sanmugam, B. Edwards, N. Mohd Barkhaya, & Z. Khlaif (Eds.), *Fostering inclusive education with AI and emerging technologies* (pp. 233–250). IGI Global. https://doi.org/DOI: 10.4018/979-8-3693-7255-5.ch010

Öqvist, M., & Nouri, J. (2018). Coding by Hand or on the Computer? Evaluating the Effect of Assessment Mode on Performance of Students Learning Programming. *Journal of Computers in Education*, *5*(2), 199–219. DOI: 10.1007/s40692-018-0103-3

Organisation for Economic Co-operation and Development. (2023). *Algorithmic bias and education: Policy considerations*. OECD Publishing., DOI: 10.1787/7c9c7c8a-

Organisation for Economic Co-operation and Development. (2024). *Ethical AI in education and workforce development*. OECD Publishing., DOI: 10.1787/4c7e4f8f-

Ortiz, I. (2023). Integrating advanced data handling approaches in modern architectural designs to optimize efficiency and scalability. Journal of Sustainable Technologies and Materials.

Otoyo, L., Russell, A., Silver, K., & Unger, A. (2022). *Legal Education Meets Computer Science: An interdisciplinary Approach to teaching LawTech*. Routledge. DOI: 10.4324/9780429351082-11

Otterborn, A., Schönborn, K. J., & Hultén, M. (2020). Investigating preschool educators' implementation of computer programming in their teaching practice. *Early Childhood Education Journal*, *48*(3), 253–262.

Ouyang, X., & Spitzer, M. (2025). *Adaptive Intelligent Tutoring Systems for STEM Education: Analysis of Design and Evaluation*. Smart Learning Environments.

Page, M. J., McKenzie, J. E., Bossuyt, P. M., Boutron, I., Hoffmann, T. C., Mulrow, C. D., & Moher, D. (2021). The PRISMA 2020 Statement: An Updated Guideline for Reporting Systematic Reviews. *BMJ (Clinical Research Ed.)*. Advance online publication. DOI: 10.1136/bmj.n71 PMID: 33782057

Pagliara, S. M., Gianmarco Bonavolontà, Pia, M., Falchi, S., Antioco Luigi Zurru, Gianni Fenu, & Mura, A. (2024). The Integration of Artificial Intelligence in Inclusive Education: A Scoping Review. *Information (Basel)*, *15*(12), 774–774. DOI: 10.3390/info15120774

Paiva, J. C., Leal, J. P., & Figueira, Á. (2022). Automated assessment in computer science education: A state-of-the-art review. [TOCE]. *ACM Transactions on Computing Education*, *22*(3), 1–40.

Paju, B., Kajamaa, A., Pirttimaa, R., & Kontu, E. (2021). Collaboration for Inclusive Practices: Teaching Staff Perspectives from Finland. *Scandinavian Journal of Educational Research*, *66*(3), 1–14. DOI: 10.1080/00313831.2020.1869087

Palvia, P., Cooper, V., & Kakhki, M. D. (2026). The Flight of Women from the Information Technology Profession: Nuances and Global Perspectives. *Information &amp. Management*, *63*(3), 104299. DOI: 10.1016/j.im.2025.104299

Pandit, R. R. (2025). Hybrid Learning in Global Contexts: A Comparative Analysis of Pedagogical Models across Diverse Education Systems. *IJSAT-International Journal on Science and Technology*, *16*(3). Advance online publication. DOI: 10.71097/IJSAT.v16.i3.7679

Pan, W. H., Chok, M. J., Wong, J. L. S., Shin, Y. X., Poon, Y. S., Yang, Z., & Lim, M. K. (2024). Assessing AI Detectors in Identifying AI-Generated Code: Implications for Education. *Proceedings of the 46th International Conference on Software Engineering: Software Engineering Education and Training*. DOI: 10.1145/3639474.3640068

Pan, Z., Cui, Y., Leighton, J. P., & Cutumisu, M. (2023). Insights into Computational Thinking from Think-Aloud Interviews: A Systematic Review. *Applied Cognitive Psychology*, *37*(1), 71–95. DOI: 10.1002/acp.4029

Papadakis, S. (2022). Apps to promote computational thinking and coding skills to young age children: A pedagogical challenge for the 21st century learners. [EDUPIJ]. *Educational Process: International Journal*, *11*(1), 7–13.

Parshyna, O. A., Parshyna, M., & Chumak, T. V. (2022). Conceptual aspects of the interdisciplinary approach to regional studies in the global economy system. *Êvropejs kij Vektor Ekonomičnogo Rozvitku*, *1*(32), 80–90. DOI: 10.32342/2074-5362-2022-1-32-8

Patel, P., Chu, J., Kumar, Y., Kwak, D., Morreale, P., Garcia, R., & Burnett, M. (2023). Implementing Inclusive Software Design in the CS Curriculum. *Proceedings of the 54th ACM Technical Symposium on Computer Science Education*. https://doi.org/DOI: 10.1145/3545947.3573254

Patil, R. Y., Vaze, A., Bhandari, S., & Kulkarni, G. (2025). Aligning higher education to NEP by introducing learning in mother tongue. *Journal of Engineering Education Transformations*, 195–209. https://doi.org/DOI: 10.16920/jeet/2024/v38i4/25107

Patil, R. Y., Patil, Y. H., Bhandari, S., & Bannore, A. (2025). Academic achievement through cooperative learning: The impact of the jigsaw method. *International Journal of Pedagogy & Curriculum, 32*(1). Advance online publication. DOI: 10.18848/2327-7963/CGP/v32i01/61-79

Peel, A., Sadler, T. D., & Friedrichsen, P. (2022). Algorithmic explanations: An unplugged instructional approach to integrate science and computational thinking. *Journal of Science Education and Technology, 31*(4), 428–441. PMID: 35535350

Penney, J., Acharya, P., Hilbert, P., Parekh, P., Sarma, A., Steinmacher, I., & Gerosa, M. A. (2025). *Outcomes, Perceptions, and Interaction Strategies of Novice Programmers Studying with ChatGPT*. DOI: 10.1145/3719160.3736625

Pentucci, M., & Laici, C. (2025). Reimagining learning in the post-digital era: student perceptions of screen-mediated teaching. In *EDULEARN25 Proceedings* (pp. 9494-9502). IATED.

Perez-Felkner, L., Erichsen, K., Li, Y., Chen, J., Hu, S., Ramirez Surmeier, L., & Shore, C. (2024). Computing Education Interventions to Increase Gender Equity from 2000 to 2020: A Systematic Literature Review. *Review of Educational Research, 95*(3), 536–580. DOI: 10.3102/00346543241241536

Pesovski, I., Santos, R., Henriques, R., & Trajkovik, V. (2024). Generative AI for customizable learning experiences. *Sustainability, 16*(7), 3034. Advance online publication. DOI: 10.3390/su16073034

Peters, A.-K., Capilla, R., Coroamă, V. C., Heldal, R., Lago, P., Leifler, O., & Venters, C. C. (2024). Sustainability in Computing Education: A Systematic Literature Review. *ACM Transactions on Computing Education, 24*(1), 1–53. DOI: 10.1145/3639060

Petropoulos, F., Laporte, G., Aktas, E., Alumur, S. A., Archetti, C., Ayhan, H., & Zhao, X. (2024). Operational Research: Methods and applications. *The Journal of the Operational Research Society, 75*(3), 423–617.

Petrova, J., & Vasichkina, O. (2021). Computer aspect of interdisciplinary research in philosophy of education and computer science. *SHS Web of Conferences, 109*, Article 01029. DOI: 10.1051/shsconf/202110901029

Phung, T., P\uadurean, V.-A., Cambronero, J., Gulwani, S., Kohn, T., Majumdar, R., Singla, A., & Soares, G. (2023). Generative AI for Programming Education: Benchmarking ChatGPT, GPT-4, and Human Tutors. *Proceedings of the 2023 ACM Conference on International Computing Education Research* - Volume 2, 41–42. DOI: 10.1145/3568812.3603476

Phung, T., P durean, V.-A., Singh, A., Brooks, C., Cambronero, J., Gulwani, S., Singla, A., & Soares, G. (2024). Automating Human Tutor-Style Programming Feedback: Leveraging GPT-4 Tutor Model for Hint Generation and GPT-3.5 Student Model for Hint Validation. 12–23. DOI: 10.1145/3636555.3636846

Pomelov, V. B. (2021). The William Heard Kilpatrick's Project Method: on the 150th anniversary of the American educator. Перспективы науки и образования, (4), 436-447.

Pournaghshband, V., & Medel, P. (2020). Promoting Diversity-Inclusive Computer Science Pedagogies: A Multidimensional Perspective. *Proceedings of the 2020 ACM Conference on Innovation and Technology in Computer Science Education*. https://doi.org/DOI: 10.1145/3341525.3387360

Pouso, S., Borja, Á., & Uyarra, M. C. (2020). An Interdisciplinary Approach for Valuing Changes After Ecological Restoration in Marine Cultural Ecosystem Services. *Frontiers in Marine Science*, *7*, 1–16. DOI: 10.3389/FMARS.2020.00715

Prather, J., Denny, P., Leinonen, J., Becker, B. A., Albluwi, I., Craig, M., & Savelka, J. (2023). The robots are here: Navigating the generative ai revolution in computing education. In *Proceedings of the 2023 working group reports on innovation and technology in computer science education* (pp. 108-159).

Prather, J., Reeves, B. N., Leinonen, J., MacNeil, S., Randrianasolo, A. S., Becker, B. A., & Briggs, B. (2024). The Widening Gap: The Benefits and Harms of Generative AI for Novice Programmers. *Proceedings of the 2024 ACM Conference on International Computing Education Research*. DOI: 10.1145/3632620.3671116

Price, E., Lau, A. C., Goldberg, F., Turpen, C., Smith, P. S., Dancy, M., & Robinson, S. (2021). Analyzing a faculty online learning community as a mechanism for supporting faculty implementation of a guided-inquiry curriculum. *International Journal of STEM Education*, *8*(1), 17. Advance online publication. DOI: 10.1186/s40594-020-00268-7 PMID: 33643775

Prihantoro, C. R. (2021). Examining the use of Wheeler-Model based curriculum development in a learning management system for vocational study program. *International Journal of Education and Practice*, *9*(3), 507–519. DOI: 10.18488/journal.61.2021.93.507.519

Qureshi, B. (2023). Exploring the use of chatgpt as a tool for learning and assessment in undergraduate computer science curriculum: Opportunities and challenges. *arXiv preprint arXiv:2304.11214*.

Raihan, N., Goswami, D., Puspo, S. S. C., Siddiq, M. L., Newman, C., Ranasinghe, T., Santos, J. C. S., & Zampieri, M. (2025). On the performance of large language models on introductory programming assignments. *Journal of Intelligent Information Systems*. Advance online publication. DOI: 10.1007/s10844-025-00968-y

Raji, I. D., Scheuerman, M. K., & Amironesei, R. (2021, March). You can't sit with us: Exclusionary pedagogy in ai ethics education. In *Proceedings of the 2021 ACM conference on fairness, accountability, and transparency* (pp. 515-525).

Ralston, S. J. (2021). Higher Education's Microcredentialing Craze: A Postdigital-Deweyan Critique. *Postdigital Science and Education, 3*(1), 83–101. DOI: 10.1007/s42438-020-00121-8 PMID: 40476912

Ravet, J., & Mtika, P. (2021). Educational inclusion in resource-constrained contexts: A study of rural primary schools in Cambodia. *International Journal of Inclusive Education, 28*(1), 1–22. DOI: 10.1080/13603116.2021.1916104

Reddy, S. N., Pathlavath, M., Narsareddygari, S., & Naik, S. M. (2024). Investigating the transformative effects of active learning methodologies in the field of engineering education. *Journal of Engineering Education Transformations, 37*(Special Issue 2). https://doi.org/DOI: 10.34290/jeet.37.2.562

Reid, J., Ahmadian, M., & Jennings, D., Anathea Abad Pepperl, Adkins, A., Anthony, K. C., Volkan Aytar, Basu, M., Bosworth, K., Bristow, A. S., Cannon, L., Cario, C., Carpenter, E., Coston, E., Crenshaw, J., Davis, J. L., Durfee, R., Gandhi, P., Ghahramani, Z. N., & Gibson, R. (2025). Saying It Aloud: Inclusive Teaching Statements Impact on Sense of Belonging and Engagement. *Journal of College Science Teaching*, •••, 1–14. DOI: 10.1080/0047231x.2025.2487437

Reihanian, I., Hou, Y., Chen, Y., & Zheng, Y. (2025). A Review of Generative AI in Computer Science Education: Challenges and Opportunities in Accuracy, Authenticity, and Assessment. In Arabnia, H. R., Deligiannidis, L., Shenavarmasouleh, F., Amirian, S., & Ghareh Mohammadi, F. (Eds.), *Computational Science and Computational Intelligence* (pp. 144–158). Springer Nature Switzerland.

Retscher, G., Gabela, J., & Gikas, V. (2024). Lessons Learned from the LBS2ITS Project—An Interdisciplinary Approach for Curricula Development in Geomatics Education. *Geomatics, 5*(1), 2. Advance online publication. DOI: 10.3390/geomatics5010002

Revano, T. F., Jr., & Garcia, M. B. (2020). Manufacturing Design Thinkers in Higher Education Institutions: The Use of Design Thinking Curriculum in the Education Landscape. *2020 IEEE 12th International Conference on Humanoid, Nanotechnology, Information Technology, Communication and Control, Environment and Management (HNICEM).* https://doi.org/DOI: 10.1109/HNICEM51456.2020.9400034

Rinta-Kahila, T., Penttinen, E., Salovaara, A., Soliman, W., & Ruissalo, J. (2023). The vicious circles of skill erosion: A case study of cognitive automation. *Journal of the Association for Information Systems, 24*(5), 1378–1412. DOI: 10.17705/1jais.00829

Robinson, R. (2025). Investigating the Impact of a Mentoring Program for Computer Science Students with Disabilities. *Proceedings of the 30th ACM Conference on Innovation and Technology in Computer Science Education* V. 2. https://doi.org/DOI: 10.1145/3724389.3730808

Roehrig, G. H., Dare, E. A., Ring-Whalen, E., & Wieselmann, J. R. (2021). Understanding Coherence and Integration in Integrated STEM Curriculum. *International Journal of STEM Education, 8*(1), 1–21. DOI: 10.1186/s40594-020-00259-8

Roll, I., & Wylie, R. (2016). Evolution and revolution in artificial intelligence in education. *International Journal of Artificial Intelligence in Education, 26*(2), 582–599. DOI: 10.1007/s40593-016-0110-3

Roman, S., Shatalov, R., & Iryna, S. (2024). Features of using computer graphics under conditions of distance learning in vocational education institutions. In *Proceedings of the 19th International Scientific and Practical Conference: Creative Business Management and Implementation of New Ideas* (pp. 145–149). International Science Group.

Rychly, L. (Ed.). (2024). *What Do We Mean by That?: Interrogating Familiar Expressions in Education.* Stylus Publishing, LLC.

Ryoo, J. J. (2019). Pedagogy that Supports Computer Science for All. *ACM Trans. Comput. Educ., 19*(4). Advance online publication. DOI: 10.1145/3322210

Ryoo, J. J., Tanksley, T., Estrada, C., & Margolis, J. (2020). Take space, make space: How students use computer science to disrupt and resist marginalization in schools. *Computer Science Education, 30*(3), 337–361.

Sabrifha, E., Wasari, R., & Mokoena, T. (2025). Revolutionizing Education: 10 Innovative Teaching Strategies for the 21st-Century Classroom. *Journal of Educational Teaching and Trends, 1*(1), 56–66. DOI: 10.64840/jett.v1i1.19

Salas-Pilco, S. Z., Xiao, K., & Oshima, J. (2022). Artificial Intelligence and New Technologies in Inclusive Education for Minority Students: A Systematic Review. *Sustainability, 14*(20), 13572. DOI: 10.3390/su142013572

Salguero, A., Griswold, W. G., Alvarado, C., & Porter, L. (2021). Understanding Sources of Student Struggle in Early Computer Science Courses. *Proceedings of the 17th ACM Conference on International Computing Education Research*. https://doi.org/DOI: 10.1145/3446871.3469755

Sánchez-García, R., & Reyes-de-Cózar, S. (2025). Enhancing Project-Based Learning: A Framework for Optimizing Structural Design and Implementation—A Systematic Review with a Sustainable Focus. Sustainability (2071-1050), 17(11).

Sanusi, I. T., Oyelere, S. S., & Omidiora, J. O. (2022). Exploring teachers' preconceptions of teaching machine learning in high school: A preliminary insight from Africa. *Computers and Education Open, 3*, 100072.

Saputra, I., Astuti, M., Sayuti, M., & Kusumastuti, D. (2023). Integration of Artificial Intelligence in Education: Opportunities, Challenges, Threats and Obstacles. A Literature Review. *The Indonesian journal of computer science, 12*(4).

Saripudin, S., Djohar, A., Rohendi, D., & Abdullah, A. G. (2020). Developing Information Technology in OpenCourseWare: From movements to opportunities in Asia. *Indonesian Journal of Science and Technology, 5*(3), 308–320. DOI: 10.17509/ijost.v5i3.24886

Schreffler, J., Vasquez, E.III, Chini, J., & James, W. (2019). Universal Design for Learning in postsecondary STEM education for students with disabilities: A systematic literature review. *International Journal of STEM Education, 6*(1). Advance online publication. DOI: 10.1186/s40594-019-0161-8

Selvaraj, A., Zhang, E., Porter, L., & Raj, A. G. S. (2021). Live Coding: A Review of the Literature. *Proceedings of the 26th ACM Conference on Innovation and Technology in Computer Science Education* V. 1. DOI: 10.1145/3430665.3456382

Semenov, S., Kolomiitsev, O., Hulevych, M., Mazurek, P., & Chernyk, O. (2025). An Intelligent Method for C++ Test Case Synthesis Based on a Q-Learning Agent. *Applied Sciences (Basel, Switzerland), 15*(15), 1–31. DOI: 10.3390/app15158596

Shaffer, D., & Resnick, M. (2021). Developing Computational Thinking Through Interactive Feedback Systems in Programming Courses. *Journal of Educational Computing Research, 59*(3), 495–518.

Shafii, R. A., & Berger, J.-L. (2025). Teacher assessment literacy, formative assessment practices, and their perceived efficacy in Tanzania: A scoping review. *Studies in Educational Evaluation*, *86*, 101496. 10.1016/j.stueduc.2025.101496

Shafik, W. (2024). Artificial intelligence and machine learning with cyber ethics for the future world. In *Future communication systems using artificial intelligence, internet of things and data science* (pp. 110–130). CRC Press.

Shanmugam, R., Perumal, M. G., & Krishnamoorthy, U. M. (2025, March). Bridging Tradition and Innovation: A Thoughtful Approach to Future-Ready Education. In 2025 ASEE North Central Section (NCS) Annual Conference. DOI: DOI: 10.18260/1-2--54652

Shanto, S. S., Ahmed, Z., & Jony, A. I. (2025). Generative AI for Programming Education: Can ChatGPT Facilitate the Acquisition of Fundamental Programming Skills for Novices? *Proceedings of the 3rd International Conference on Computing Advancements*, 685–692. DOI: 10.1145/3723178.3723268

Sharma, B. K., & Shukla, V. K. (2023). Interdisciplinary Approach to Education with Special Reference to Social Science at Secondary Schools. *BSSS Journal of Education*, *12*(01), 41–51. DOI: 10.51767/je1203

Sharma, K., Torrado, J. C., Gómez, J., & Jaccheri, L. (2021). Improving Girls' Perception of Computer Science as a Viable Career Option Through Game Playing and Design: Lessons from a Systematic Literature Review. *Entertainment Computing*, *36*, 100387. DOI: 10.1016/j.entcom.2020.100387

Sharma, V., & Kumar, S. (2023). Role of Artificial Intelligence (AI) to Enhance the Security and Privacy of Data in Smart Cities. In *Proceedings of the 3rd International Conference on Advance Computing and Innovative Technologies in Engineering (ICACITE)* (pp. 596–599). IEEE.

Shepitko, V. I., Sherstyuk, O. O., Boruta, N., Tykhonova, O., Tarasenko, Y. A., Skotarenko, T. A., & Levchenko, O. A. (2023). Interdisciplinary Integration as a Main Factor in the Development of Clinical and Professional Thinking of Students of Medical Higher Education Institutions of Ukraine. *Ukraïns kij Žurnal Medicini. Bìologìï Ta Sportu*, *8*(1), 268–272. DOI: 10.26693/jmbs08.01.268

Shi, Y. R., Sin, K. F. K., & Wang, Y. Q. (2025). Teacher professional development of digital pedagogy for inclusive education in post-pandemic era: Effects on teacher competence, self-efficacy, and work well-being. *Teaching and Teacher Education*, *168*, 105230. DOI: 10.1016/j.tate.2025.105230

Shneiderman, B. (2020). Human-centered artificial intelligence: Reliable, safe, and trustworthy. *International Journal of Human-Computer Interaction*, *36*(10), 887–896. DOI: 10.1080/10447318.2020.1741118

Siddiqi, M. M., & Ahmad, D. S. (2025). Innovations in Digital Learning. Shaping the Future: Emerging Trends and Opportunities in Commerce, Management, and Information Technology, 7.

Siemens, G., & Baker, R. S. (2012). Learning analytics and educational data mining: Towards a new learning science. *Journal of Educational Technology & Society*, *15*(3), 1–4.

Silma, N., Maulida, I., Wulan, A. P., Merawati, J., & Hasan, M. K. (2024). A comprehensive review of Project-Based Learning (PBL): Unravelling its aims, methodologies, and implications. Journal of Education, Social &. *Communication Studies*, *1*(1), 10–19.

Silva, C. A., Ramos, F. N., de Moraes, R. V., & Santos, E. L. (2024). ChatGPT: Challenges and Benefits in Software Programming for Higher Education. *Sustainability*, *16*(3), 1–23. DOI: 10.3390/su16031245 PMID: 38756353

Simms, L., Baker, S., & Clark, M. D. (2013). The Standardized Visual Communication and Sign Language Checklist for Signing Children. *Sign Language Studies*, *14*(1), 101–124. DOI: 10.1353/sls.2013.0029

Simon, L.-R. A., Ajanovski, V. V, Fouh, E., Gonsalvez, C., Leinonen, J., Parkinson, J., Poole, M., & Thota, N. (2019). Pass Rates in Introductory Programming and in other STEM Disciplines. *Proceedings of the Working Group Reports on Innovation and Technology in Computer Science Education*, 53–71. DOI: 10.1145/3344429.3372502

Singh, B., Kumar, V., Gupta, K., Vashishth, T. K., Sharma, S., & Kumar Gupta, V. (2023). Transforming education in the digital age: A comprehensive study on the effectiveness of online learning. [IJSREM]. *International Journal of Scientific Research in Engineering and Management*, *7*(7), 1–11. DOI: 10.55041/IJSREM24405

Smith, J. M., & McGill, M. M. (2025). How Should We Measure Race, Ethnicity, and Gender Equity in Undergraduate CS Programs? *Proceedings of the 56th ACM Technical Symposium on Computer Science Education* v. 2, 1625–1626. https://doi .org/DOI: 10.1145/3641555.3705196

Smith, R., Liggett, W., Niewola, J., & Hegarty, K. (2024, March). From Dimes to Deadlines: What Project Management Techniques Are Right for You? In *2024 IEEE Aerospace Conference* (pp. 1-17). IEEE.

Sobota, B., & Pietriková, E. (2023). The role of game engines in game development and teaching. In *Computer science for game development and game development for computer science*. IntechOpen., DOI: 10.5772/intechopen.1002257

Soomro, S. A., Nanjappan, V., Casakin, H., & Georgiev, G. V. (2024). Fostering Technical Skills and Creativity in the Digital Fabrication Spaces: An Open-Ended Prototyping Approach. *International Journal of Technology and Design Education*. Advance online publication. DOI: 10.1007/s10798-024-09940-3

Spieler, B., & Girvan, C. (2025). The PECC Framework: Promoting Gender Sensitivity and Gender Equality in Computer Science Education. *Computers*, *14*(7), 249. DOI: 10.3390/computers14070249

Spieler, B., Hummel, D., Herbertz, S., & Mädche, A. (2018). Reinforcing Gender Equality by Analysing Female Teenagers' Performances in Coding Activities. *Proceedings of the 4th Conference on Gender & IT - GenderIT '18*. https://doi.org/ DOI: 10.1145/3196839.3196871

Stefaniak, J., & Moore, S. (2024). The Use of Generative AI to Support Inclusivity and Design Deliberation for Online Instruction. *Online and Blended Learning in the Age of Generative AI*, *28*(3), 181–205. DOI: 10.24059/olj.v28i3.4458

Stoeger, H., Duan, X., Schirner, S., Greindl, T., & Ziegler, A. (2013). The Effectiveness of a One-Year Online Mentoring Program for Girls in STEM. *Computers & Education*, *69*, 408–418. DOI: 10.1016/j.compedu.2013.07.032

Stoyanova, D., Stoyanova-Petrova, S., & Mileva, N. (2025). Exploring Students' and Teachers' Perceptions about Using ChatGPT in Programming Education. *International Journal of Engineering Pedagogy*, *15*(2), 15–41. DOI: 10.3991/ijep.v15i2.50607

Suleiman, A. D., Hou, D., Liu, Y., DeWaters, J., Shepherd, D. C., & Souza, J. G. D. (2025). Systematic Literature Review on Project-Based Learning in Computing Education. *ACM Transactions on Computing Education*, *25*(4), 1–53. DOI: 10.1145/3743684

Sulla, F., Agueli, B., Lavanga, A., Logrieco, M. G. M., Fantinelli, S., & Esposito, C. (2025). Analysis of the Development of Gender Stereotypes and Sexist Attitudes Within a Group of Italian High School Students and Teachers: A Grounded Theory Investigation. *Behavioral Sciences (Basel, Switzerland)*, *15*(2), 230. DOI: 10.3390/bs15020230 PMID: 40001861

Sun, D., Boudouaia, A., Zhu, C., & Li, Y. (2024). Would ChatGPT-facilitated programming mode impact college students' programming behaviors, performances, and perceptions? An empirical study. *International Journal of Educational Technology in Higher Education, 21*(1), 14. DOI: 10.1186/s41239-024-00446-5

Sunday, A. O., Agbo, F. J., & Suhonen, J. (2025). Co-Design Pedagogy for Computational Thinking Education in K-12: A Systematic Literature Review. *Technology. Knowledge and Learning, 30*(1), 63–118. DOI: 10.1007/s10758-024-09765-y

Susanto, R., Rachmadtullah, R., & Rachbini, W. (2020). Technological and Pedagogical models. *Journal of Ethnic and Cultural Studies, 7*(2), 1–14.

Swiecki, Z., Khosravi, H., Chen, G., Martinez-Maldonado, R., Lodge, J. M., Milligan, S., Selwyn, N., & Gašević, D. (2022). Assessment in the age of artificial intelligence. *Computers and Education: Artificial Intelligence, 3*, 100075. 10.1016/j.caeai.2022.100075

Sytnyk, O., Hrozna, O., Filonenko, D., Konoplyannikova, O. S., & Serdiuk, O. (2024). Development of interactive forms of communication through artificial intelligence. *Journal of Theoretical and Applied Information Technology, 102*(21).

Taeb, M., Chi, H., & Bernadin, S. (2024). Assessing the Effectiveness and Security Implications of AI Code Generators. *Journal of The Colloquium for Information Systems Security Education, 11*(1), 1–6. DOI: 10.53735/cisse.v11i1.180

Taheri, R., Nazemi, N., Pennington, S. E., Clark, J. A., & Dadgostari, F. (2025). Factors influencing educators' AI adoption: A grounded meta-analysis review. *Computers and Education: Artificial Intelligence, 9*, 100464. 10.1016/j.caeai.2025.100464

Tang, K. Y., Chou, T. L., & Tsai, C. C. (2020). A content analysis of computational thinking research: An international publication trends and research typology. *The Asia-Pacific Education Researcher, 29*(1), 9–19.

Tariq, R., Aponte Babines, B. M., Ramirez, J., Alvarez-Icaza, I., & Naseer, F. (2025). Computational Thinking in STEM Education: Current State-of-the-Art and Future Research Directions. *Frontiers of Computer Science, 6*, 1–19. DOI: 10.3389/fcomp.2024.1480404

Tegegn, D. A. (2024). The Role of Science and Technology in Reconstructing Human Social History: Effect of Technology Change on Society. *Cogent Social Sciences, 10*(1), 1–10. DOI: 10.1080/23311886.2024.2356916

Thangaraj, J., Ward, M., & O'Riordan, F. (2023). A Systematic Review of Formative Assessment to Support Students Learning Computer Programming. *4th International Computer Programming Education Conference (ICPEC 2023)*. https://doi.org/DOI: 10.4230/OASIcs.ICPEC.2023.7

Thomsen, K. (2024). A heuristic sketch how it could fit all together with time. arXiv preprint arXiv:2405.10335.

Tkachuk, V., Yechkalo, Y., & Khotskina, S. (2020). Selection of mobile ICT for learning informatics of future professionals in engineering pedagogy.

Tokuhama-Espinosa, T. (2021). *Bringing the neuroscience of learning to online teaching: an educator's handbook*. Teachers College Press.

Tong, A. (2024). OpenAI launches free AI training course for teachers. *Reuters*. https://www.reuters.com/technology/artificial-intelligence/openai-launches-free-ai-training-course-teachers-2024-11-20/

Tromp, C., & Baer, J. (2022). Creativity from Constraints: Theory and Applications to Education. *Thinking Skills and Creativity*, *46*, 1–11. DOI: 10.1016/j.tsc.2022.101184

Troussas, C., Krouska, A., Mylonas, P., Sgouropoulou, C., & Voyiatzis, I. (2025). Fuzzy Memory Networks and Contextual Schemas: Enhancing ChatGPT Responses in a Personalized Educational System. *Computers*, *14*(3). Advance online publication. DOI: 10.3390/computers14030089

Troussas, C., Krouska, A., & Sgouropoulou, C. (2020). A novel teaching strategy through adaptive learning activities for computer programming. *IEEE Transactions on Education*, *64*(2), 103–109.

Troussas, C., Krouska, A., & Sgouropoulou, C. (2020). Collaboration and fuzzy-modeled personalization for mobile game-based learning in higher education. *Computers & Education*, *144*, 103698.

Tsai, C.-W., Lee, L., Yu-Ching Lin, M., Cheng, Y.-P., Lin, C.-H., & Tsai, M.-C. (2025). Effects of Integrating Self-Regulation Scaffolding Supported by Chatbot and Online Collaborative Reflection on Students' Learning in an Artificial Intelligence Course. *Computers & Education*, *232*, 1–19. DOI: 10.1016/j.compedu.2025.105305

Tsai, Y.-C. (2023). Empowering Learner-Centered Instruction: Integrating ChatGPT Python API and Tinker Learning for Enhanced Creativity and Problem-Solving Skills. *Lecture Notes in Computer Science*, •••, 531–541. DOI: 10.1007/978-3-031-40113-8_52

Tsui, E., Dragicevic, N., Fan, I., & Cheng, M. (2024). Co-creating curriculum with students, teachers, and practitioners in a technology-enhanced environment. *Educational Technology Research and Development*, *72*(2), 869–893. DOI: 10.1007/s11423-023-10301-5

Tubino, L., Cain, A., Schneider, J.-G., Thiruvady, D., & Fernando, N. (2020). Authentic Individual Assessment for Team-Based Software Engineering Projects. *Proceedings of the ACM/IEEE 42nd International Conference on Software Engineering: Software Engineering Education and Training*. https://doi.org/DOI: 10.1145/3377814.3381702

Tucker, M. C., Wang, X., Son, J. Y., & Stigler, J. W. (2024). Prediction Versus Production for Teaching Computer Programming. *Learning and Instruction*, *91*, 1–13. DOI: 10.1016/j.learninstruc.2023.101871

Tuitt, F. (2023). Conclusion. *Race, Equity, and the Learning Environment*, 205–221. https://doi.org/DOI: 10.4324/9781003446637-16

Twarek, B., Koressel, J., Smith, J. M., & McGill, M. M. (2024). Reimagining CS Pathways Interim Report# 2: Defining Pathways Beyond a Foundational High School CS Course.

Tweeten, J., & Hung, W. (2023). Design-Based Research Method in PBL/PjBL: A Case in Nursing Education. *The Interdisciplinary Journal of Problem-Based Learning*, *17*(2), n2.

Tzafilkou, K., Perifanou, M., & Economides, A. A. (2023). Assessing teachers' digital competence in primary and secondary education: Applying a new instrument to integrate pedagogical and professional elements for digital education. *Education and Information Technologies*, *28*(12), 16017–16040. PMID: 37361819

Ullrich, C., & Gütl, C. (2024). AI-Enhanced Assessment and Feedback in Computer Science Education: A Comprehensive Review. *Computers & Education: Artificial Intelligence*, *5*, 100146.

UNESCO. (2017). *Cracking the Code: Girls' and Women's Education in Science, Technology, Engineering and Mathematics*. STEM., DOI: 10.54675/QYHK2407

United Nations Children's Fund. (2023). *Bridging the Gender Digital Divide: Challenges and an Urgent Call for Action for Equitable Digital Skills Development*. UNICEF. https://data.unicef.org/wp-content/uploads/2023/05/Bridging-the-Gender-Digital-Divide-1.pdf

United Nations Economic and Social Commission for Asia and the Pacific. (2023). *Bridging the Digital Gender Divide: How Girls and Women Can Lead the Way.* UNESCAP. https://www.unescap.org/story/bridging-digital-gender-divide-how-girls-and-women-can-lead-way

United Nations Economic Commission for Europe. (2025). *Moving Forward in Gender Statistics in the EU*. UNECE. https://unece.org/sites/default/files/2025-03/WP3%20Eur%20GenderstatsEU.pdf

United Nations. (2025). Goal 4 | Ensure Inclusive and Equitable Quality Education and Promote Lifelong Learning Opportunities for All. United Nations. https://sdgs.un.org/goals/goal4

Uzorka, A., & Kalabuki, K. (2024). The transformative impact of technological advancements in educational leadership on student experiences and outcomes. *Education and Information Technologies*, *29*(16), 20883–20904. DOI: 10.1007/s10639-024-12714-y

Vakil, S. (2020). "I've always been scared that someday I'm going to sell out": Exploring the relationship between political identity and learning in computer science education. *Cognition and Instruction*, *38*(2), 87–115.

Valderama, A. M. C., Tuazon, J. B. D., & Garcia, M. B. (2022). Promoting Student Thinking and Engagement Through Question-Based and Gamified Learning. *2022 IEEE 14th International Conference on Humanoid, Nanotechnology, Information Technology, Communication and Control, Environment and Management (HNICEM)*. https://doi.org/DOI: 10.1109/HNICEM57413.2022.10109470

Van Petegem, C., & Maertens, R.. (2022). Dodona: Learn to Code with a Virtual Co-Teacher that Supports Active Learning. *Computers & Education*, *190*, 104610.

Vartiainen, H., Kahila, J., Tedre, M., López-Pernas, S., & Pope, N. (2024). Enhancing children's understanding of algorithmic biases with generative AI. *Learning, Media and Technology*, *49*(1), 1–16. DOI: 10.1080/17439884.2023.2283475

Veale, M., & Binns, R. (2017). Fairer machine learning in the real world. *Proceedings of the ACM Conference on Fairness, Accountability, and Transparency (FAT*)* (pp. 1–15). ACM. https://doi.org/DOI: 10.1177/2053951717743530

Velicea, F. P., Ghimbă an, A. E., Filip, R. C., Danciu, G. M., & Kertész, C. Z. (2025). *Programming Examination Platform: Generative AI-Driven Evaluation Tool for Computer Programming Classes*. Futureproofing Engineering Education for Global Responsibility., DOI: 10.1007/978-3-031-83520-9_33

Videnovik, M., Vold, T., Kiønig, L., Madevska Bogdanova, A., & Trajkovik, V. (2023). Game-based learning in computer science education: A scoping literature review. *International Journal of STEM Education*, *10*(1), 54.

Vikas, D., R. P., Kumar, D., Charan, P., Ingilela, R. S. K., & Rastogi, R. (2023). Intrusion Detection in Wireless Sensor Networks using Hybrid Deep Belief Networks and Harris Hawks Optimizer. In *Proceedings of the 4th International Conference on Electronics and Sustainable Communication Systems (ICESC)* (pp. 1631–1636). IEEE.

Vikas. (2025). Optimization of Graph Neural Networks for Real-Time Intrusion Detection in Dynamic Mobile Ad-Hoc Networks. *International Journal of Environmental Sciences*, 11(11s), 740–748.

Villegas-Ch, W., Buenano-Fernandez, D., Navarro, A. M., & Mera-Navarrete, A. (2025). Adaptive intelligent tutoring systems for STEM education: Analysis of the learning impact and effectiveness of personalized feedback. *Smart Learning Environments*, *12*(1), 41. DOI: 10.1186/s40561-025-00389-y

Visual Language and Visual Learning (VL2). (n.d.). Gallaudet University. https://gallaudet.edu/visual-language-visual-learning/

Vitaliy, K., Nataliia, V., Ievgen, B., Volodymyr, S., & Anna, K. (2022). Innovative educational technologies in management training: Experience of EU countries. *International Journal of Computer Science & Network Security*, *22*(6), 45–50.

Vitores, A., & Gil-Juárez, A. (2016). The Trouble with 'Women in Computing': A Critical Examination of the Deployment of Research on the Gender Gap in Computer Science. *Journal of Gender Studies*, *25*(6), 666–680. DOI: 10.1080/09589236.2015.1087309

Vogel, S., Hoadley, C., Castillo, A. R., & Ascenzi-Moreno, L. (2020). Languages, literacies and literate programming: Can we use the latest theories on how bilingual people learn to help us teach computational literacies? *Computer Science Education*, *30*(4), 420–443.

von Briesen, E., Dutton, R., Duvall, S., Hutchings, D., Mattfeld, R., & Spurlock, S. (2025). Interventions for Increasing Belonging and Inclusion in Undergraduate Computer Science Classrooms. *Proceedings of the 56th ACM Technical Symposium on Computer Science Education* V. 1. https://doi.org/DOI: 10.1145/3641554.3701941

Vrieler, T., & Salminen-Karlsson, M. (2022). *A Sociocultural Perspective on Computer Science Capital and its Pedagogical Implications in Computer Science Education*. ACM Transactions on Computing Education., DOI: 10.1145/3487052

Vygotsky, L. S. (1978). *Mind in Society: Development of Higher Psychological Processes*. Harvard University Press., DOI: 10.2307/j.ctvjf9vz4

Wahyuni, D. S., Rozimela, Y., Ardi, H., Mukhaiyar, M., & Darmansyah, D. (2022). PROSPER (Project, Sustainability, and Perseverance) learning model in English for computer science. *Sustainability, 14*(24), 16749. DOI: 10.3390/su142416749

Wajcman, J. (2004). *TechnoFeminism*. Polity. https://www.wiley.com/en-sg/TechnoFeminism-p-9780745630434

Wajcman, J. (2009). Feminist Theories of Technology. *Cambridge Journal of Economics, 34*(1), 143–152. DOI: 10.1093/cje/ben057

Wali, N., & Hooshangi, S. (2025). Transfer Students in Computer Science: Examining Barriers, Success Metrics, and Research Gaps. *Proceedings of the 30th ACM Conference on Innovation and Technology in Computer Science Education* V. 1. https://doi.org/DOI: 10.1145/3724363.3729118

Walker, H. M. (2017). Classroom Vignettes Connecting computing with other disciplines and the wider community. *ACM Inroads, 8*(2), 29–32. DOI: 10.1145/3078315

Wang, A. Y., Chen, Y., Chung, J. J. Y., Brooks, C., & Oney, S. (2021). PuzzleMe: Leveraging Peer Assessment for In-Class Programming Exercises. *Proceedings of the ACM on Human-Computer Interaction*. DOI: 10.1145/3479559

Wang, H., & Flory, J. (2024). Room for Breathing: Mindfulness, Currere, and Contemplative Practices in Teacher Education. *Journal of Contemplative and Holistic Education, 2*(1), 3.

Wang, J., & Fan, W. (2025). The effect of ChatGPT on students' learning performance, learning perception, and higher-order thinking: Insights from a meta-analysis. *Humanities & Social Sciences Communications, 12*(1), 621. DOI: 10.1057/s41599-025-04787-y

Wang, L., & Zhao, T. (2023). Data-Driven Feedback Mechanisms in Online Programming Environments. *Journal of Learning Analytics, 10*(1), 45–63.

Warner, J. R., Childs, J., Fletcher, C. L., Martin, N. D., & Kennedy, M. (2021). *Quantifying Disparities in Computing Education: Access*. Participation, and Intersectionality., DOI: 10.1145/3408877.3432392

Warschauer, M. (2004). *Technology and social inclusion: Rethinking the digital divide*. MIT Press.

Werder, C., & Otis, M. M. (Eds.). (2023). *Engaging student voices in the study of teaching and learning*. Taylor & Francis.

Wijnen-Meijer, M., Brandhuber, T., Schneider, A., & Berberat, P. O. (2022). Implementing Kolb's experiential learning cycle by linking real experience, case-based discussion and simulation. *Journal of Medical Education and Curricular Development, 9*, 23821205221091511. DOI: 10.1177/23821205221091511 PMID: 35592131

Wille, S., Century, J., & Pike, M. (2017). Exploratory Research to Expand Opportunities in Computer Science for Students with Learning Differences. *Computing in Science & Engineering, 19*(3), 40–50. DOI: 10.1109/mcse.2017.43

Williams, R., Ali, S., & Devasia, N.. (2023). AI + ethics curricula for middle school youth: Lessons learned from project-based curricula. *Computer Science Education, 33*(3), 257–281. DOI: 10.1080/08993408.2023.2193942

Wilson, S., & Nishomoto, M. (2023). Assessing Learning of Computer Programing Skills in the Age of Generative Artificial Intelligence. *Journal of Biomechanical Engineering, 146*(5), 1–6. DOI: 10.1115/1.4064364 PMID: 38140801

Winarno, N., Rusdiana, D., Riandi, R., Susilowati, E., & Afifah, R. M. A. (2020). Implementation of Integrated Science Curriculum: A Critical Review of the Literature. *Journal for the Education of Gifted Young Scientists, 8*(2), 795–817. DOI: 10.17478/jegys.675722

Wing, J. M. (2006). Computational thinking. *Communications of the ACM, 49*(3), 33–35. DOI: 10.1145/1118178.111821

Wolz, U., & Taylor, S. R. (2019). Towards a More Inclusive Tech Culture. *Proceedings of the 50th ACM Technical Symposium on Computer Science Education.* https://doi.org/DOI: 10.1145/3287324.3293742

Woolard, T. (2022). No Teacher Left Behind: The Science (and Psychology) of Sustaining PBL PD (Doctoral dissertation, Morgan State University).

World Economic Forum. (2023). *Global Gender Gap Report 2023.* WEF. https://www3.weforum.org/docs/WEF_GGGR_2023.pdf

Wu, C. H., Chien, Y. C., Chou, M. T., & Huang, Y. M. (2025). Integrating computational thinking, game design, and design thinking: A scoping review on trends, applications, and implications for education. *Humanities & Social Sciences Communications, 12*(1), 1–12. DOI: 10.1057/s41599-025-04502-x

Wu, J., & Uttal, D. H. (2024). Diversifying Computer Science: An Examination of the Potential Influences of Women-in-Computing Groups. *Science Education, 108*(3), 957–980. DOI: 10.1002/sce.21861

Xia, L., Wang, L., & Huang, C. (2024). Implementing a Social Presence-Based Teaching Strategy in Online Lecture Learning. *European Journal of Investigation in Health, Psychology and Education, 14*(9), 2580–2597. DOI: 10.3390/ejihpe14090170 PMID: 39329838

Xiao, J., Bozkurt, A., Nichols, M., Pazurek, A., Stracke, C. M., Bai, J. Y. H., & Themeli, C. (2025). Venturing into the Unknown: Critical Insights into Grey Areas and Pioneering Future Directions in Educational Generative AI Research. *TechTrends, 69*, 582–597. DOI: 10.1007/s11528-025-01060-6

Xue, Y., Chen, H., Bai, G. R., Tairas, R., & Huang, Y. (2024). Does ChatGPT Help With Introductory Programming?An Experiment of Students Using ChatGPT in CS1. *Proceedings of the 46th International Conference on Software Engineering: Software Engineering Education and Training*. DOI: 10.1145/3639474.3640076

Xu, Z., & Sheng, V. S. (2024). Detecting AI-Generated Code Assignments Using Perplexity of Large Language Models. *Proceedings of the AAAI Conference on Artificial Intelligence, 38*(21), 23155–23162. DOI: 10.1609/aaai.v38i21.30361

Xu, Z., Zhao, Y., Liew, J., Zhou, X., & Kogut, A. (2023). Synthesizing Research Evidence on Self-Regulated Learning and Academic Achievement in Online and Blended Learning Environments: A Scoping Review. *Educational Research Review, 39*, 1–17. DOI: 10.1016/j.edurev.2023.100510

Yang, S., Zhao, H., Xu, Y., Brennan, K., & Schneider, B. (2024). Debugging with an AI Tutor: Investigating Novice Help-seeking Behaviors and Perceived Learning. *Proceedings of the 2024 ACM Conference on International Computing Education Research*. DOI: 10.1145/3632620.3671092

Yang, T.-C., Hsu, Y.-C., & Wu, J.-Y. (2025). The effectiveness of ChatGPT in assisting high school students in programming learning: Evidence from a quasi-experimental research. *Interactive Learning Environments, 33*(6), 3726–3743. DOI: 10.1080/10494820.2025.2450659

Yang, X., Zhao, G., Yan, X., Chao, Q., Zhao, X., Lu, T., & Dong, Y. (2022). Pre-setting stances for students during collaborative argumentation: Parallel thinking versus adversarial thinking. *Research in Science Education, 52*(6), 1829–1850.

Yates, J., & Plagnol, A. C. (2021). Female Computer Science Students: A Qualitative Exploration of Women's Experiences Studying Computer Science at University in the UK. *Education and Information Technologies, 27*(3), 3079–3105. DOI: 10.1007/s10639-021-10743-5

Yau, C. B. (2021). Interaction of Scientist-Teacher-Students in Problem-Project Based Learning (Master's thesis, University of Malaya (Malaysia)).

Yeni, S., Grgurina, N., Saeli, M., Hermans, F., Tolboom, J., & Barendsen, E. (2024). Interdisciplinary Integration of Computational Thinking in K-12 Education: A Systematic Review. *Informatics in Education, 23*(1), 223–278. DOI: 10.15388/infedu.2024.08

Yeom, S., Herbert, N., & Ryu, R. (2025). Exploring Gender Disparities and Collaborative Learning in IT Education. *Proceedings of the 27th Australasian Computing Education Conference*. https://doi.org/DOI: 10.1145/3716640.3716645

Yilmaz Ince, E., & Koc, M. (2021). The consequences of robotics programming education on computational thinking skills: An intervention of the Young Engineer's Workshop (YEW). *Computer Applications in Engineering Education, 29*(1), 191–208.

Yilmaz, R., & Karaoglan Yilmaz, F. G. (2023). The effect of generative artificial intelligence (AI)-based tool use on students' computational thinking skills, programming self-efficacy and motivation. *Computers and Education: Artificial Intelligence, 4*, 100147. 10.1016/j.caeai.2023.100147

Yilmaz, R., & Karaoglan Yilmaz, F. G. (2023). Augmented Intelligence in Programming Learning: Examining Student Views on the Use of ChatGPT for Programming Learning. *Computers in Human Behavior: Artificial Humans, 1*(2), 1–7. DOI: 10.1016/j.chbah.2023.100005

Yu, E. (2018). The Impact of Culturally Inclusive Pedagogy on Student Achievement in a Multicultural Urban School Setting. *Urban Education, 57*(1), 004208591880401. DOI: 10.1177/0042085918804013

Yue, M., Jong, M. S. Y., & Dai, Y. (2022). Pedagogical design of K-12 artificial intelligence education: A systematic review. *Sustainability, 14*(23), 15620.

Zarestky, J., Bigler, M., Brazile, M., Lopes, T., & Bangerth, W. (2022). Reflective Writing Supports Metacognition and Self-regulation in Graduate Computational Science and Engineering. *Computers and Education Open, 3*, 1–12. DOI: 10.1016/j.caeo.2022.100085

Zastudil, C., Rogalska, M., Kapp, C., Vaughn, J., & Macneil, S. (2023). Generative AI in computing education: Perspectives of students and instructors. *Proceedings of the IEEE Frontiers in Education Conference (FIE)* (pp. 1–9). IEEE. https://doi.org/DOI: 10.1109/FIE58773.2023.10343467

Zawacki-Richter, O., Marín, V. I., Bond, M., & Gouverneur, F. (2019). Systematic review of research on artificial intelligence applications in higher education: Where are the educators? *International Journal of Educational Technology in Higher Education*, *16*, 39. Advance online publication. DOI: 10.1186/s41239-019-0171-0

Zhang, A., Olelewe, C. J., Orji, C. T., Ibezim, N. E., Sunday, N. H., Obichukwu, P. U., & Okanazu, O. O. (2020). Effects of innovative and traditional teaching methods on technical college students' achievement in computer craft practices. *SAGE Open*, *10*(4), 2158244020982986.

Zhang, W., Guan, Y., & Hu, Z. (2024). The Efficacy of Project-Based Learning in Enhancing Computational Thinking Among Students: A Meta-Analysis of 31 Experiments and Quasi-Experiments. *Education and Information Technologies*, *29*(11), 14513–14545. DOI: 10.1007/s10639-023-12392-2

Zhan, Z., He, L., Tong, Y., Liang, X., Guo, S., & Lan, X. (2022). The effectiveness of gamification in programming education: Evidence from a meta-analysis. *Computers and Education: Artificial Intelligence*, *3*, 100096.

Zheng, Q., Li, Y., Yin, Q., Zhang, N., Wang, Y., Li, G., & Sun, Z. (2023). The effectiveness of problem-based learning compared with lecture-based learning in surgical education: A systematic review and meta-analysis. *BMC Medical Education*, *23*(1). Advance online publication. DOI: 10.1186/s12909-023-04531-7 PMID: 37528406

Zhou, C., & Zhang, W. (2024). Computational Thinking (CT) towards Creative Action: Developing a Project-Based Instructional Taxonomy (PBIT) in AI Education. *Education Sciences*, *14*(2), 1–14. DOI: 10.3390/educsci14020134

Zhu, Y., Jafari, A., Behzadan, A. H., & Issa, R. R. (2024). A roadmap to the next-generation technology-enabled learning-centered environments in AEC education. *Journal of Civil Engineering Education*, *150*(3), 05024002. DOI: 10.1061/JCEECD.EIENG-1972

About the Contributors

Manuel B. Garcia is the Senior Director for Educational Technology and Digital Learning and the Founding Director (concurrent) of the Educational Innovation and Technology Hub (EdITH) at FEU Institute of Technology, Manila, Philippines. He is also an Adjunct Professor at the Graduate School of Education, Korea University, Seoul, South Korea. He earned his Doctor of Information Technology degree from the University of the East and is presently pursuing a Doctor of Philosophy in Education at the University of the Philippines Diliman. His interdisciplinary research interest includes topics that, individually or collectively, cover the disciplines of education and information technology. He is a Licensed Professional Teacher and a member of the National Research Council of the Philippines. Dr. Garcia is the first-ever recipient of the Ramon Dimacali Award for Information Technology, conferred by the Philippine Association for the Advancement of Science and Technology, and has been recognized as one of the World's Top 2% Scientists by Elsevier for the last three consecutive years (2023–2025).

***

Akhrorbek Abdullayev is a lecturer in the Department of Digital Learning Technologies at Namangan State University, Uzbekistan. Since 2024, he has been conducting research in the field of Theory and Methodology of Electronic Education. His research work is titled "Development of an Intelligent System for Assessing Students' Knowledge and Skills in Artificial Intelligence and Neural Network Technologies."

Hassan Abuhassna is an Associate Professor and Deputy Dean for Employability and Alumni at Sunway University. His work is at the forefront of advanced, technology-enhanced approaches to teaching and learning. His perspective adds significant value to the ongoing conversation about how postgraduate supervision is evolving in an AI-enabled world.

Dharel P. Acut is a licensed professional teacher and Science Education Instructor at Cebu Technological University, Cebu City, Philippines. He holds a Bachelor's degree in Secondary Education, major in General Science, from MSU–Iligan Institute of Technology, and is currently completing his Master's degree in Science Education at Cebu Normal University. An Associate Member of the National Research Council of the Philippines (DOST–NRCP), his research interests include science and STEM education, gender-inclusive and equity-oriented pedagogies, systematic literature reviews, education for sustainable development, and educational technology. His ongoing research examines inclusive teaching practices, scientific creativity, and learners' identity formation in STEM contexts, with the aim of advancing equitable, reflective, and socially responsive approaches to computing and science education.

Michael Agyemang Adarkwah is a Research Associate at Friedrich Schiller University Jena, Germany. He was a Postdoctoral Researcher at Beijing Normal University, China. He is an Editor of the book series Assessment of Educational Technology (AET) at Routledge. He is a Senior Editor for Frontiers of Digital Education. He is also an Associate Editor for SN Social Sciences, the Journal of Applied Learning and Teaching (JALT), and the Journal of University Teaching and Learning Practice (JUTLP). He is part of the editorial board of multiple journals including Discover Education.

Owolabi Paul Adelana is affiliated with the Institute of Educational Technology (IET), Faculty of Wellbeing, Education and Language Studies (WELS), The Open University, Milton Keynes, UK. His research interests lie at the intersection of AI-enabled STEM/STEAM education, Artificial Intelligence in Education (AIED), AI ethics, policy and governance, and educational technology.

Adu Emmanuel Ifedayo is an educational technology expert and currently a Lecturer in Educational Technology at Bamidele Olumilua University of Education, Science and Technology, Ikere. His areas of expertise include artificial intelligence, podcasting, instructional design, and distance learning.

Fred Agbo is an Assistant Professor of Computer Science at the School of Computing and Information Science, Willamette University. He completed his PhD in Computer Science from the School of Computing, University of Eastern Finland (UEF) in Joensuu, Finland, specializing in computing education and educational technology. Fred teaches computer science and data science courses, supervises undergraduate and graduate students, and lives in Salem Oregon, USA. Fred's research interests include computer science education, Human-computer interaction (HCI), software engineering, game-based learning, virtual and augmented reality technology, and persuasive technology for teaching and learning.

Shahanawaj Ahamad is affiliated with the College of Computer Science and Engineering, University of Hail, Saudi Arabia. His academic interests include computer science education, emerging computing technologies, and innovative teaching–learning methodologies. He is actively involved in academic and research activities aimed at advancing technology-driven education and interdisciplinary research.

Qurrotul Aini is an Assistant Professor and Head of the Department of Information Systems in the Faculty of Science and Technology at the State Islamic University (UIN) Syarif Hidayatullah Jakarta. Her interdisciplinary research interests include text mining, artificial intelligence, social computing, and business intelligence.

Samson O. Ajao is a System Analyst at Bowen University, Nigeria, and the Co-Founder and Chief Operating Officer of Datum Africa. He works at the intersection of information technology and education, with research interests spanning artificial intelligence, human–computer interaction, immersive technologies (AR/VR/XR), digital literacy, and educational innovation. His interdisciplinary work focuses on designing and applying technology-driven solutions to enhance teaching, learning, and inclusion, particularly in resource-constrained contexts.

Ashraf Alam is currently a Research Faculty member at the Centre of Excellence in Public Policy, Sustainability and ESG Research under the Faculty of Law and Policy Studies at Alliance University, Bengaluru. He is widely recognized for his transdisciplinary expertise across education, technology, and policy studies, and has been listed among the World's Top 2% Scientists by Stanford University and Elsevier. His scholarly contributions include over fifty SCOPUS-indexed publications and more than one hundred presentations at national and international academic forums. He holds a Ph.D. in Education from the Indian Institute of Technology (IIT) Kharagpur, an M.Ed. specializing in Mathematics Education, and a B.S. in Computer Science from the University of Delhi, along with postgraduate degrees in Public Administration (M.A.) and Mathematics (M.Sc.), and multiple postgraduate diplomas in areas such as Higher Education, Educational Technology, Guidance and Counselling, and Value Education. Dr. Ashraf actively contributes to global scholarly discourse as an Associate Editor of Frontiers in Education and also serves as Founder and Director of Academic Chronicles Private Limited, where he supports the development of strategic frameworks for peer-reviewed publishing in the social and human sciences. His work has been published by leading academic outlets including Elsevier, Springer, Taylor & Francis, Wiley, Routledge, Sage, Emerald, and IEEE, and spans diverse themes such as pedagogy, educational administration and psychology, educational sociology and policy, technology-integrated learning, mathematics education, teacher education, and AI/ML-enabled learning environments. He has qualified several prestigious examinations, including UGC-NET-JRF in Education and Adult and Continuing Education, UGC-NET in Public Administration, and GATE in Humanities and Social Sciences.

Joel D. Canlas is a faculty member at Pampanga State University specializing in Information Technology and Computer Science. His research focuses on predictive modelling and data-driven approaches to student success. He is committed to innovation in teaching, professional development, and advancing quality education through technology and community engagement.

Mark Anthony A. Castro is a licensed Electronics Engineer with expertise in electronics engineering, engineering management, mathematics, and audio engineering. He currently serves as an Assistant Professor at Pampanga State University and as Officer-in-Charge (OIC) Campus Director of the Apalit Campus. He holds advanced degrees in Engineering Management and is currently pursuing a PhD in Business Administration. With prior industry experience as a preventive maintenance engineer, he has authored multiple research publications in engineering, energy systems, and technology innovation.

Thomas Chiu is a researcher of AI and STEM education at the Department of Curriculum and Instruction at The Chinese University of Hong Kong. He has a strong academic background in software development and mathematics. He is an associate director of the Centre for University and School Partnership and Centre for Learning Sciences and Technologies.

Robertas Damaševičius received a Ph.D. in Informatics Engineering from Kaunas University of Technology, Lithuania, in 2005. He is currently the Director of the Centre of Real Time Computer Systems at Kaunas University of Technology, and professor in the Department of Applied Informatics at Vytautas Magnus University, Lithuania. He lectures software maintenance, human-computer interface, and robot programming courses. He is the author of more than 500 articles and two books. His research interests include sustainable software engineering, human-computer interfaces, and smart healthcare. He is the editor-in-chief of Information Technology and Control. He has served as a guest editor of several invited issues of international journals, such as BioMed Research International, Computational

Intelligence and Neuroscience, Journal of Healthcare Engineering, IEEE Access, Sensors, and Electronics.

Aileen P. De Leon is a researcher with interests in education, computing, and information technology. She is an Associate Professor I at Pampanga State University and a member of the College of Computing Studies.

Fitroh Fitroh is a Lecturer in the Department of Information Systems in the Faculty of Science and Technology at the State Islamic University (UIN) Syarif Hidayatullah Jakarta. Her interdisciplinary research interests include enterprise architecture, information systems audit, information technology governance, and knowledge management.

Narcisan S. Galamiton is a Professor of Information Technology at Cebu Technological University Main Campus. Her research spans pedagogy, AI, and digital literacy, with a focus on creating inclusive and equitable learning environments in computing education. She leads initiatives that integrate community engagement, mentorship, and technology innovation, including the BarangayConnect Training project, and guides students in national IT competitions. Dr. Galamiton is particularly committed to fostering participation and success among underrepresented learners in technology, emphasizing gender-inclusive practices, collaborative learning, and curriculum strategies that support equity and belonging in computer science education.

Kamlesh Kumar Gautam is a Senior Member of IEEE and a member of CSI Ghaziabad, CEGR, and ACM. He specializes in Artificial Intelligence and Machine Learning and has authored numerous research papers published in prestigious Scopus-, SCI-, WoS-, and UGC CARE-indexed journals. He has also authored books covering a wide range of computer science topics, including Python for Beginners, Digital Electronics & Computer Organization, Software Engineering, and Basics of Artificial Intelligence & Machine Learning, among others.

Juvy C. Grume is an Associate Professor in the Department of Computer Engineering at Pampanga State University, Philippines. She holds a bachelor's degree in computer engineering and a master's degree in information technology and is a certified professional computer engineer. She is a lifetime member of the Institute of Computer Engineers of the Philippines and the Mechatronics and Robotics Society of the Philippines. Her research interests include automation, autonomous systems, embedded systems, the Internet of Things (IoT), artificial intelligence, and technology-based educational systems. She has served as a research adviser and paper reviewer and has actively participated in academic conferences and scholarly forums in engineering and information technology.

Ari Happonen is an Associate Professor, project manager/principal investigator, and university–industry collaborator at LUT School of Engineering Science, Lappeenranta University of Technology, Finland. Prof. Happonen also holds an Adjunct Professor position at Taylor's University, where he works closely with Taylor's Impact Lab and contributes to intensive education, sustainability, and technology development research and educational efforts. His research interests include AI/LLMs, digitalization and digital twins, augmented/virtual reality and metaverses, ICT and digitalization for sustainability, hackathons for digital transformation, and modern circular economy and sustainability-enhancing strategies and methodologies. His research focuses mainly on practical and efficient industry-related, nationally and internationally funded applied research collaboration activities in both B2B and B2C contexts. He contributes to the future of software engineering and digitalization, Createch utilization, ICT and sustainability, AI solutions, and hackathon- and education-related research areas. He actively contributes to education development, with more than 20 years of experience, including experience as the Head of a bachelor's program. He works as a university–industry intermediary in multiple research projects with innovative front-line companies. He is a well-established IEEE Senior Member and has supervised over 200 theses and published over 200 academic publications in books, journals, conferences, and other outlets.

Hilene E. Hernandez serves as an Assistant Professor at Pampanga State University – Bacolor Campus and holds a Master of Information Technology degree from Systems Plus College Foundation. In addition to teaching, she serves as the adviser to the University Student Council, Internship Coordinator, and Gender and Development Focal Person for the College of Computing Studies. Her commitment to student development and promoting diversity in technology education is evident in her multifaceted responsibilities. Her academic interests include educational technology, information technology, and computer science education, and she has contributed to these areas through scholarly publications.

Asegul Hulus is an Assistant Professor in Computer Science and a Fellow of the Higher Education Academy (FHEA). She is a distinguished researcher and published author with expertise across multiple Computer Science disciplines, including but not limited to Artificial Intelligence, blockchain, cybersecurity, human–computer interaction, and educational technology. She serves on the ACM Council on Women in Computing (ACM-W), where she is an investigative journalist, (co) social media manager, and one of the leaders in the global committee members for the ACM-W Chapters.

Ravshanjon Kakharov is a lecturer in the Department of Digital Educational Technologies at Namangan State University, Uzbekistan. Since 2021, he has been conducting research on the topic "Improving the e-learning process in interfaculty specialties (using computer science and related disciplines as an example)" within the field of Theory and Methodology of Electronic Education.

Mustafa Kayyali is an ardent advocate for excellence in higher education, driven by a relentless pursuit of quality, recognition, and innovation. His academic journey began with a Master's degree in Quality Management and Evaluation in Higher Education, followed by a Ph.D. in Quality Management. These academic achievements have laid a strong foundation for his expertise in accreditation, quality assurance, and higher education rankings. As an entrepreneur, researcher, translator, and publisher, he is deeply engaged in multiple facets of the academic world. His diverse interests span management, translation, interpretation, and academic consulting, contributing to a well-rounded and comprehensive understanding of the industry. Throughout his career, he has made significant contributions to academic literature, with more than 40 published papers and 30 book chapters to his name. In addition, he has translated six books, helping bridge language gaps and promote global knowledge exchange. He remains committed to fostering positive change in higher education and contributing to its continuous improvement.

Ioannis Kazanidis is an Assistant Professor (Educational Technology and Databases) at the Computer Science Department of the International Hellenic University, Director of the international MSc in Immersive Technologies - Innovation in Education, Training and Game Design, Vice Director at the Advanced Educational Technologies & Mobile Applications Lab of the same University, and founding member of the International Association for Blended Learning (IABL). He has BSc from the Dept. of Mechanical Engineering Educators from School of Pedagogical & Technological Education (ASPAITE), BSc from the Dept. of Informatics from the Hellenic Open University, MSc in Computing from Coventry University and PhD in Educational Technology from the Dept. of Informatics of University of Macedonia. He has participated in several international funded research projects related to immersive technologies in education and educational technology. He has published more than 130 papers in international journals and conferences. His research interests mainly focus on Educational Technology and on the adoption of innovations in different fields of study such as educational technology, e-learning,

AR/VR in education, mixed reality environments, learning analytics and tangible user interfaces.

Bright Keswani is a Research Professor in the Faculty of Computer Science and Engineering at Poornima University, Jaipur, where he has been serving since June 2023 and is actively associated with the University's Research & Development Cell. He is an accomplished academic and researcher with a strong interdisciplinary orientation, having published numerous book chapters and research papers in reputed Scopus- and Web of Science–indexed journals. Dr. Keswani completed his post-doctoral research in the Department of Creative Technologies and Product Design at the National Taipei University of Business (NTUB), Taiwan, where he conducted advanced research in mobile ad-hoc networks. His research portfolio is further strengthened by the award of multiple patents, including utility and design patents, reflecting his commitment to innovation and applied research. Known for his academic rigor, professional integrity, and global outlook, Dr. Keswani actively contributes to curriculum design, research mentorship, and the advancement of emerging technologies in higher education.

Jyotsana Khera is affiliated with the School of Computer Science and Applications at IIMT University. With a strong academic foundation and 8 years of work experience, she is deeply committed to teaching and has contributed significantly to the academic community through research and scholarly work. Her areas of interest include emerging technologies and innovative teaching methodologies. She is recognized for her dedication to student development and academic excellence.

Kasim Khusanov is a professor in the Department of Natural and Mathematical Sciences at Turin Polytechnic University in Tashkent, Uzbekistan. His interdisciplinary research interests include ICT in engineering and education.

Lawrence Kujur is an Assistant Professor of Computer Science at Christ (Deemed to be University), Delhi NCR Campus, India. He teaches and mentors undergraduate and postgraduate students, delivering courses in programming, data structures, algorithms, and artificial intelligence. His academic and professional interests lie in computer science education and emerging computational technologies, with a focus on developing strong analytical and problem-solving skills among students.

Anand Kumar is a prominent academic and researcher with extensive experience in teaching and administration. He holds a postgraduate degree in Computer Science and is currently a faculty member at SRM University,

Lucknow. With a strong interest in emerging technologies, he has published in various national and international journals. He is dedicated to mentoring students and advancing research in areas such as data science, artificial intelligence, and software engineering. His commitment to education and innovation is reflected in his continuous efforts to bridge the gap between academia and industry.

Hanh Le is a passionate researcher and accomplished Full Stack Software Developer with deep expertise in software development, data analytics, data science, and cloud computing. She holds a Ph.D. in Information Technology and a master's degree in computer science, bringing both academic rigor and a solution-driven mindset to her work. With extensive experience in both front-end and back-end development, she specializes in scalable, database-driven applications that support evidence-based decision-making. Dr. Le has led transformative technology initiatives across healthcare, law enforcement, and retail, translating complex needs into high-performing systems. She values interdisciplinary collaboration, believing that impactful innovation often emerges at the intersection of fields. Her blend of technical skills, research excellence, and collaborative spirit continues to drive progress in both academia and industry.

Vernon Grace M. Maniago is an Assistant Professor at Don Honorio Ventura State University (DHVSU), College of Computing Studies, Bacolor, Pampanga, Philippines. He holds a master's degree in information technology and is a Licensed Professional Teacher. He currently serves as the Program Chairperson for the Bachelor of Science in Information Technology at DHVSU Sto. Tomas Campus. With a decade of experience in academia and freelance industry work, he has specialized in software development, computer security, and educational technology. Mr. Maniago is also a member of several professional organizations, including the Philippine Society of Information Technology Educators, the Center for Scholarly Research Educators in the Philippines, and the Professional Organization of Researchers and Educators of the Philippines.

John Paul P. Miranda is an Associate Professor at Pampanga State University, Philippines. He also serves as the International Linkages and Partnerships Project Head under the Office for International Partnerships and Programs of the same institution.

Damola Olugbade is a scholar in educational technology, serving as a Research Fellow at Abiola Ajimobi Technical University, Nigeria, and as a Professor Extraordinarius at the University of South Africa. His interdisciplinary research centers on the convergence of emerging technologies and education, with a focus on creating sustainable and equitable technology-enhanced solutions for resource-limited environments. He has authored scientific books and more than 30 peer-reviewed publications, and his work directly advances the aims of Sustainable Development Goal 4.

Rachana Yogesh Patil is an Associate Professor and Head of the Department of Computer Engineering (Regional Language) at Pimpri Chinchwad College of Engineering, Pune, India. She received her PhD in Computer Engineering from the University of Mumbai in 2020. Her research expertise spans cryptography, network security, cybersecurity, and digital forensics, with a particular focus on network forensics. She has authored and co-authored more than sixty research papers in reputed international journals and conferences. She is featured in the Top 2% Scientist List (2024) published by Stanford University and Elsevier, recognizing her global research impact and scholarly excellence. She actively contributes to academic and professional communities through memberships in IEEE, ACM, and IETE. She has guided several student projects and continues to mentor young researchers in areas aligned with her expertise. Her academic and research contributions reflect a strong commitment to advancing secure communication systems and promoting innovative approaches in cybersecurity.

Yogesh Patil is an Associate Professor at D. Y. Patil College of Engineering, Akurdi, Pune, India. He holds a PhD in Optical Fiber Communication and has more than twenty-four years of academic and research experience in engineering education. His expertise includes computer engineering and optical communication, with a strong focus on applying emerging technologies to solve practical challenges. Over the course of his career, Dr. Patil has mentored numerous undergraduate and postgraduate students, guiding projects that integrate both theoretical depth and practical applications.

Joel B. Quiambao is an Instructor at the College of Computing Studies, Pampanga State University, Main Campus, Bacolor, Pampanga, Philippines.

Jordan L. Salenga is an Assistant Professor at Pampanga State University under the College of Computing Studies. He is an active coach in academic conferences, particularly in IT education. He served as a panelist during the International Research Conference on Information Technology Education 2024, hosted by the Philippine Society of Information Technology Educators (PSITE), where he evaluated research contributions in computing. As a PSITE member, he actively engages in research-driven discussions and collaborations. He also coaches participants in the Regional Assembly on Information Technology Education and the International Research Conference on Information Technology Education, guiding students and faculty in research and technical competitions. His research interests include data analytics, IoT, and mobile applications, with a focus on innovative solutions in computing.

Serhiy O. Semerikov is a full professor in the Department of Computer Science and Applied Mathematics at Kryvyi Rih State Pedagogical University in Ukraine.

Ramesh Sharma, Ph.D., is currently working as Director of Human Resource Development Centre at Dr B R Ambedkar University Delhi, India. Previously he has served as an Associate Professor of Educational Technology and Learning Resources in the Educational Technology Unit at Wawasan Open University, Malaysia; Visiting Professor at University of Fiji, Fiji; Commonwealth of Learning as Director of the Commonwealth Educational Media Centre for Asia, New Delhi; Indira Gandhi National Open University, India; and University of Guyana, Guyana, South America. He is the co-Editor of the 'Asian Journal of Distance Education'. In addition, he has been associated with peer reviewed journals as Reviewer, Editor and Editorial Advisory Board member in the field of Open and Distance Learning such as "Distance Education", " International Review of Research in Open and Distributed Learning (IRRODL)", "International Journal of Distance Education Technologies (IJDET)", and "Indian Journal of Open Learning (IJOL)". He is also on the Editorial Advisory Board and an author for the "Encyclopedia of Distance Learning (4 volumes), 2005"

Vikas Sharma is an academician and researcher in the field of Computer Science with 10 years of experience. He earned an MTech degree in Computer Science and is currently pursuing a PhD in Computer Applications. He is actively involved in academic development and scholarly activities and is a member of the International Association of Engineers, the Society of Digital Information and Wireless Communications, the Global Professors Welfare Association, the International Association of Academic plus Corporate (IAAC), the Computer Science Teachers Association, and the Internet Society. His research interests include Cloud Computing, Artificial Intelligence, and Machine Learning. He has published more than 55 research articles and has contributed to 4 books and 107 book chapters in edited volumes. He also serves as a member of editorial and reviewer boards for conferences and various computer science journals and edited books published by Elsevier, CRC Press, Taylor & Francis, Springer, IGI Global, Wiley, IET, De Gruyter, River Publishers, and others.

Akshara Singh is a third-year undergraduate student at Christ University, pursuing a degree in Data Science and Artificial Intelligence. Her academic interests include data analytics, machine learning, and intelligent systems, with a growing focus on applying data-driven techniques to solve real-world problems. She actively engages in coursework and projects that integrate statistical methods, programming, and AI concepts.

Shashiraj Teotia is the Head of the Department of Computer Applications at Swami Vivekanand Subharti University, Meerut. He has 18 years of experience in teaching and research and is an active member of IAENG and IJMRA. He has published approximately 40 papers in national and international journals and has authored four books.

Tarun Kumar Vashishth is an academician and researcher in the field of Computer Science with 22 years of experience. He earned a PhD in Mathematics with a specialization in Operations Research and has held several academic positions, including Deputy Director, Head of Department, NAAC Coordinator, Academic Coordinator, Member Secretary of the Department Research Committee, Assistant Centre Superintendent, and Head Examiner for University Examinations. He is actively involved in academic development and scholarly activities. He is a member of the International Association of Engineers, the Society of Digital Information and Wireless Communications, the Global Professors Welfare Association, the International Association of Academic plus Corporate (IAAC), the Computer Science Teachers Association, and the Internet Society. His research interests include Cloud Computing, Artificial Intelligence, Machine Learning, and Operations Research. He has published more than 50 research articles and conference papers and has contributed to 2 books and 80 book chapters. He also serves on editorial and reviewer boards for conferences and various computer science journals and edited books published by Elsevier, CRC Press, Taylor & Francis, Springer, IGI Global, Wiley, IET, De Gruyter, River Publishers, and others.

Xoshimjon Erkinjonovich Xolmirzayev is a Senior Lecturer in the Department of Digital Learning Technologies at Namangan State University, Uzbekistan. Since 2024, he has been conducting research in the field of Theory and Methodology of Education and Training. His research work is titled "Methodology for Developing Students' Programming Competencies in Python Through Intelligent Systems."

Ramazan Yılmaz is an Associate Professor in the Department of Computer Education and Instructional Technology (CEIT) at Bartın University, Türkiye. He earned his B.S. degree from Hacettepe University, Faculty of Education, Department of CEIT in 2007. He completed his M.A. in CEIT at Gazi University in 2010 and obtained his Ph.D. in CEIT from Ankara University in 2014. His research interests include educational technology, human-computer interaction, smart learning environments, learning analytics, educational data mining, eye tracking, multimedia design, adaptive learning, and augmented and virtual reality (AR and VR).

Ahmed Mohamed Fahmy Yousef is a Faculty Member at Fayoum University, Egypt. Responsibilities of this position include teaching undergraduate, master's and PhD level courses in Educational Technology along with courses in learning theory, distributed learning, educational research, web design technologies, learning management systems, online assessment strategies, and curriculum theory and development, which are offered across the department's programs. He designs and evaluates new learning technologies that aim at combining cognitive science, learning analytics, and interactive media to enhance students' learning outcomes in connected learning environments. Dr. Ahmed received his undergraduate B.Sc. degree in Education Technology (Excellent with Honors degree, 2002) from Cairo University, Egypt. He acquired his two diploma and master's degree in in Education Technology, with specialization in online learning environments, with grade “Excellent” from Ain Shams University, Egypt. He holds a Ph.D. in Computer Science (Learning Technologies) Highest Distinction with grade “Magna Cum Laude” from RWTH Aachen University, Germany.

Index

D

E

F

G

H

I

L

M

N

P

R

S

T

U